MINNESOTA
BOOK STORE
Ave. S.E., Minneapolis

AN INTRODUCTION TO
EDUCATIONAL PSYCHOLOGY

AN INTRODUCTION TO EDUCATIONAL PSYCHOLOGY

By
COLEMAN R. GRIFFITH
ASSOCIATE PROFESSOR OF EDUCATIONAL PSYCHOLOGY
DIRECTOR, BUREAU OF INSTITUTIONAL RESEARCH
UNIVERSITY OF ILLINOIS

New York
FARRAR AND RINEHART, INC.
1935

COPYRIGHT, 1935, BY COLEMAN R. GRIFFITH
PRINTED IN THE UNITED STATES OF AMERICA
BY QUINN & BODEN COMPANY, INC., RAHWAY, N. J.
ALL RIGHTS RESERVED

PREFACE

There are at least four reasons why teachers do not get the practical help they have a right to expect from books on educational psychology. The same four reasons explain why it is that these books are read by undergraduate students simply as another one of the academic and, more often than not, uninteresting tasks required of them by a curriculum. In the first place, there are too many persons, mostly indolent in disposition, who suppose that the psychologist is a magician who has already discovered, or who will discover in the near future, a "fool-proof" formula that can be applied to students in the schoolroom with as much assurance as the engineer applies his formulae to bridge-building or to the fabrication of an automobile. These persons suppose that a little knowledge of psychology will make a task easy which, by nature, is full of perplexities, which requires many hours of devoted personal tutelage, and which demands a feeling for, rather than a knowledge of, human nature. There are, however, no standardized formulae for teaching and neither are there any easy processes of promoting growth which have been registered in the Patent Office.

In the second place, the teacher is an integral part of a whole configuration of events which does not admit of division into parts. The experimenter, on the contrary, must deal with parts. He must take one thing at a time, while assuming that other things have remained equal. It is a wonder, then, that the teacher and the experimenter ever get together. It is still more of a wonder that a book on educational psychology should be phrased both for the teacher and the experimenter. If this book is not so phrased, it is no better than some of the others. The author has earnestly sought, however, to keep both persons in mind, the one in order that the student may see what the experimenter is doing and the other in order that he may catch a glimpse of the very real problems which a teacher has to solve.

In the third place, there are too many people who suppose that the main facts about psychology are already known or that the particular brand of psychology to which they have been exposed is the final judgment of the science. In other words, it is commonly felt that the major concepts of educational psychology which were prevalent a score of years ago (or even ten years ago) cannot be seriously questioned at the present time. When, therefore, a prodigiously active science offers evidence of change in its points of view, they draw the conclusion that psychologists are so instable that nothing serious can be expected of them.

It is not too much to say, perhaps, that the last ten years have seen more substantial progress in the experimental study of human nature than any preceding period of twice or thrice that length. In any case, the author has tried to create a distinct impression of the way in which educational problems must be reinterpreted if teachers are to do their work most effectively. He chooses this path even though it means that the book contains more psychology than education. If justification for this procedure is required, it lies in the simple fact that the first educational psychologies were similarly balanced. In other words, the books which laid out the foundations of educational psychology almost assumed that the psychological basis of education had been laid out once and for all. It was easy to suppose, therefore, that future books should be more "practical" in the sense that they should simply apply the fundamental principles already known. We shall try to show that a part of the "practical" side of education is to be found in a different psychological basis for teaching methods and in the constant discovery of new facts.

In the fourth place, many teachers, and especially those at the high school and university levels, work with a growth pattern that is nearing functional completion. That is, they work with persons who have already achieved considerable measures of stability or of fixity in the degrees of excellence with which they can use their several psychological functions. This fact holds true because learning processes quickly bring the average child to a practical limit of efficiency. When, therefore, teachers see the discrepancy between the maxims of an educational psychology, on the one hand, and the results of their attempt to use these maxims, on the other, they incline to the belief that the fault lies with educational psychology rather than with the character of the problems that must be solved.

Just as we have sought to phrase this book both in the language of practical teaching situations and in the language of educational and psychological experimentation, so we have sought to break down the discrepancy between maxims and actual teaching methods. We have felt that the chief way to do this was to establish our whole introduction to the study of educational psychology upon the facts and principles of genetic psychology. The growth of a human being is an essentially continuous process, and it takes, under the influence of education, a particular form or pattern which must be viewed from end to end as well as from side to side. This means that one of the faults commonly found in surveys of educational psychology is derived from the failure to gain a sufficient measure of perspective over a field of forward-moving events.

Since teachers at the higher levels of schooling deal with persons the quality of whose psychological functions is already nearing maturity, and since many of these functions have behind them no recognizable educative process, one may leap easily to the conclusion that these functions and some of the services they render, as well, are hereditary or instinctive. In any case, various doctrines of original nature have played a very large part in methods of teaching and in educational philosophy. We shall discover in the following pages that the rapid development of a genetic psychology based wholly on experimentation has almost, if not quite, upset the balance that had been struck a few years ago between original nature and learning. We have considered it imperative, therefore, that the problems of teaching that may occur at any given level of schooling shall be met, in part, at least, with a perspective on the developmental events out of which the problems have emerged. Hence the genetic point of view.

Every author of a textbook on educational psychology is faced with the choice of emphasizing a systematic arrangement of facts or of emphasizing instances drawn from the daily life of teachers in the schoolroom. In the one case, there is too much space devoted to laboratory research and to the formal presentation of facts independently of their practical and social values. In the other case, there is plenty of practical material but no coherent view of the one concept that is essential to the teacher, viz., the whole pattern of growth as it is promoted and guided by formal and informal schooling. If this book has come anywhere near a steady course between these extremes, it will have served a very useful purpose; for the experimental facts upon which education must be based have increased so rapidly during the last decade that practical instances of teaching problems lose meaning and importance where there is no appreciation of scientific progress or of systematic arrangements of new discoveries.

A note is in order, perhaps, concerning the use of this book in the classroom. In his teaching and writing, the author has experimented with several different sequences of presentation. The sequence actually followed in the book has proven useful; but it must be admitted that Chapters II-VIII are probably the most difficult in the book.

Some teachers, therefore, may find it wiser to begin with Chapter I and then proceed through Part Two and even through Part Three, before returning to the remainder of Part One. This can be done without prejudice to the continuity either of reading or discussion.

COLEMAN R. GRIFFITH.

Urbana, Illinois
January, 1935.

CONTENTS

PART ONE

METHODS OF PROMOTING GROWTH

	PAGE
Chapter I: THE BEGINNINGS OF THE EDUCATIVE PROCESS	3

The Infant and the Adult: Introduction—Psychological Growth—Psychology and Education—The Purpose of the Chapter

The New-Born Child: The "Zero Point" of Development—Prenatal Development—The Neonate

Characteristics of the Preschool Child: Functions and Services—Psychological Equipment—Plasticity—Fixity

Summary

Chapter II: THE DEVELOPMENT OF ACTIONS AND ATTITUDES	44

The Method of Sectioning: Introduction—Mind and Behavior—Major Features of Behavior—Summary

Properties of Behavior: Introduction—Speed—Coördination—Speed and Accuracy

Types of Behavior: Introduction—Manual Skills—Verbal Skills

Speech Disorders: Introduction—The Mechanisms of Speech—Speech and Handedness—Theories of Stammering—Methods of Cure

Reading: Introduction—Reading and Eye Movement—Oral and Silent Reading—Reading and Comprehension—Summary

Writing: Introduction—Origin of Writing Movements—Methods of Teaching—Speed and Style

Sources of Training: Introduction—Play—Physical Education

Chapter III: TRAINING THE PERCEPTUAL FUNCTIONS	94

Stimuli and Situations: Introduction—Relevant and Irrelevant Environments—Stimulus-Patterns

The Major Types of Perception: Introduction—Visual Perception—Hearing

The Development of Meanings: Introduction—Stimulus and Object—Comments on Introspective Psychology—Figure and Ground—The Development of Concepts—Sign Learning—Summary

Sources of Training: Introduction—The Natural Sciences—The Experimental Sciences

Chapter IV: THE DEVELOPMENT OF ATTENTION AND INTEREST	125

Sources of Action: Introduction—The Stimulus-Response Theory—Stimulus-Response Relations—The Phenomena of Selection—Attention and Interest—Purpose of Chapter

The Problems of Attention: Introduction—Attention as a Faculty—The Concept of Prepotency—Varieties of Attention

CONTENTS

The Conditions of Attention: Introduction—External Determinants of Attention—Training—Attitude and Set—Biological Importance

The Nature of Interest: Introduction—Interest and Feeling—Acquired Interests

Measures of Interest: Introduction—Vocational Interests—Permanence of Interests—Interests and Abilities—Summary

Chapter V: THE PROBLEMS OF MOTIVATION 157

The "Why" of Human Action: Commonsense—Differences Between "What" and "How"—Purpose and Intention—Purpose of the Chapter

Theories of Motivation: Will Power—Motivation and Selection—Examples of Motivation

The Primary Desires: Introduction—Tissue Needs

The Development of Motives: Introduction—Initial Processes of Conditioning—Dependence of Motives on Previous Learning—Emotion and Motivation

Complex Motives: Introduction—The Nature of Purpose—Ideals—Sentiments

Sources of Training: Introduction—The Function of the Teacher—Biographies

Chapter VI: THE DEVELOPMENT OF EMOTIONALIZED ACTIONS 188

Introduction: Illustrations—The Teaching Problem—Purpose of the Chapter

The Bodily Basis of Emotionalized Actions: Introduction—The Autonomic System—Glandular Mechanisms—Emotion and Its Expression

The Nature of Mood and Emotion: Introduction—Physical Analogies—Sources of Energy—Genetic Views of Emotion—The Nature of Emotionalized Action

The Education of the Emotions: Introduction—Maturation—Conditioned Emotions

The Rôle of Emotion in Tutored Behavior: Introduction—Emotion and Reason—The "Higher" Feelings—Aesthetic Feelings

Chapter VII: THE DEVELOPMENT OF PROBLEM-SOLVING . . 221

Commonsense Views of Thinking: Introduction—Thinking and Remembering—Thinking and Sign Learning—Thinking and Imagination—Thinking and the Syllogism—Thinking and the Mind

The Nature of Problem-Solving: Introduction—Tools—The Delayed Reaction—The Field of Thinking

The Bases of Problem-Solving: Introduction—Freedom from a Temporal Order—Teaching Problem-Solving

Sources of Training: Introduction—Preschool Training—Progressive Schools—School Subjects

Chapter VIII: THE DEVELOPMENT OF PERSONALITY AND CHARACTER 258

Short-Time and Long-Time Views of Human Nature: Introduction—Personality—Animal Personalities—Infant Personality—The Genetic View

CONTENTS

Contemporary Definitions of Personality: Traditional View of Personality—Personality and Instinct—Personality and the Nervous System—Personality and Behavior—Summary

Specificity and Configurationism in Personal Development: Introduction—Experimental Studies

Personality Types and Traits: Introduction—Differences in Imagery—Physical Types—Chemical Composition

The Development of Personality Traits: Introduction—Introversion-Extroversion—Jealousy—Obstinacy—Leadership—Ethical Traits

The Influence of Special Factors on the Development of Character Traits: Hereditary Factors—Physical Condition—Intelligence—Family Relationships—Social Factors

PART TWO

ORIGINAL NATURE AND LEARNING

Chapter IX: THE PROBLEMS OF ORIGINAL NATURE . . . 291

Directed Growth Patterns: Introduction—The Directedness of the Pattern—Hereditary Factors—Learning Situations—The Purpose of this Chapter

The Evidence for Psychological Inheritance: The Commonsense View of Heredity—The Doctrine of Innate Ideas—Human and Animal Instincts—Family Resemblances—Constancy of the I.Q.—Individual Differences and Training

The Problems of Original Nature: Introduction—The Reaction Against Instincts—Criticisms of Studies on Family Resemblances—The Interpretation of the Constancy of the I.Q.—Individual Differences and Acquired Fixity

The Logic of Research on Hereditary Factors: Introduction—The Importance of Chromosomes—The First Principle of Genetic Research—The Second Principle of Genetic Research—The First Assumption of Genetic Research—The Second Assumption of Genetic Research—Summary

Chromosomes and Their Environments: The "Part" vs. the "Whole"—The Inertia of Parts—Field Relationships—The Origin of Intrinsic Properties—The Inertia of Germ Plasm—The Principle of Buffering—Summary

Some Major Features of Development: Temporal Sequences—Types of Environment—Environmental Control, Physical Methods—Environmental Control, Psychological Methods—Summary

Chapter X: THE ORIGINAL NATURE OF MAN 344

Psychological Inheritance: Introduction—What is Psychological Inheritance?

The Minima of Original Nature: Introduction—Examples of Original Nature

Hereditary Neural Connections: Introduction—The Meaning of "Organism"—The Maturation Factor—Plasticity—Intelligence

General Principles of Development: Maturation—Causative Principles of Development—Descriptive Principles

Original Nature and the Art of Teaching: Introduction—Logic and Practice—Particular and General Environments

CONTENTS

Chapter XI: MAJOR VARIETIES AND THEORIES OF LEARNING . 380
   The Significance of Learning: Introduction—Environmental Influences—Learning and Growing—The Importance of Teaching
   Types of Learning: Introduction—Rote Learning—Trial-and-Error Learning—Associative Learning—Conditioning—Sign Learning—Learning by Insight
   The Laws of Learning: Introduction—The Law of Exercise—Criticisms of the Law of Exercise—The Law of Effect—Criticisms of the Law of Effect
   A Theory of Learning: Introduction—Points of Similarity—Points of Dissimilarity—Conclusion

Chapter XII: ENGINEERING THE LEARNING PROCESS . . 426
   Theory and Practice: Introduction—Purpose of the Chapter
   Whole vs. Part Learning: Introduction—Historical Note—Meaning—Intelligence—Practical Conclusions—Conclusion
   The Distribution of Practice and Rest Periods: Introduction—Experimental Results—Explanations of Distributed Effort—Conclusions
   Types of Inhibition: Introduction—Experimental Results—Practical Consequences—Associative Inhibition
   Learning and Recitation: Introduction—Experimental Studies—Learning and Understanding—Summary
   Motivation and Learning: Introduction—Incidental Learning—Incentives
   Order of Presentation: Introduction
   Retention and Recall: Introduction—Measuring of Retention—Recall

Chapter XIII: THE TRANSFER OF TRAINING 469
   Specialization and General Training: Introduction—Identities in Training—Differences in Training—Formal Discipline—Particular Discipline—The Nature of the Controversy—Purpose of the Chapter
   Experimental Studies on Transfer: Introduction—Relationships Between Learning Periods—Cross-Education—Laboratory Studies on Transfer—Transfer in School Situations
   Explanation of Transfer: Introduction—The Theory of Identical Elements—Generalized Habits and Attitudes—Experimental Methods—Growth and Transfer—Conclusion

Chapter XIV: THE ART OF TEACHING 502
   Science and Practice: Introduction—The Genetic Point of View—The Teacher's Point of View
   The Functions of the Teacher: Introduction—The Rôle of the Teacher—Psychological Growth—Types of Teaching Effort—Summary
   The Qualities of a Teacher: Introduction—Ratings—Causes of Success and Failure
   Types of Teaching Procedure: Introduction—Recitation Method—Project Methods—Laboratory Methods
   Classroom Management: Introduction—The Warming-up Effect—Class Size
   Measuring the Results of Teaching: The Examination—Objective Examinations—Achievement Tests—Nonmeasurable Factors

CONTENTS

PART THREE

CONCEPTUAL AND METHODOLOGICAL TOOLS OF EDUCATION

Chapter XV: THE NATURE OF INTELLIGENCE 533

    The Nature of Conceptual Tools: Introduction—Facts and Concepts—Purpose of the Chapter

    Current Definitions of Intelligence: Varieties of Intelligence—Motor and Mechanical Intelligence—Perceptual Intelligence—Intelligence and Attention—Intelligence and Learning—Intelligence and Problem-Solving—Intelligence and Adjustment—Intelligence and Character

    Manufacturing an Intelligence Test: The Basis of Intelligence—Empirical Measures of Intelligence—Experimental Measures of Intelligence—The Stanford Revision—The Meaning of Test-Intelligence—Summary

    Practical Uses of Intelligence Tests: Intelligence and Achievement—Individual Differences—Homogeneous Grouping—Achievement and Ability—Elimination—Individual Instruction

Chapter XVI: PROBLEMS OF TEACHING CREATED BY INDIVIDUAL DIFFERENCES 565

    The Part and the Whole: Introduction—An Illustration from Physics—Statistical Averages—Individual Differences

    The Problem of Psychological Differences: Individual and Social Psychology—Normative Psychology—Types of Individual Differences

    Age, Sex and Race Differences: Introduction—Age Differences—Sex Differences—Race Differences

    The Problem of Exceptional Talent: Introduction—Qualities of Gifted Children

    Deficient Children: Introduction—Feeblemindedness—Special Deficiencies

    The Nature of Individual Differences: Introduction—Range—Qualitative and Quantitative Differences—Effects of Practice on Individual Differences

    The Origin of Individual Differences: Introduction—Environmental Constancy

    Application of Individual Differences to Education: Introduction

    Summary

Chapter XVII: THE SOCIALIZED PERSON 604

    The Concept of the "Self": Introduction—The Origin of Socialized Action—Purpose of the Chapter

    The Development of Social Behavior: Things and Persons—Early Social Behavior—Types of Social Behavior—Sources of Socialized Behavior

    Normal Social Behavior: Norms and Values—Reaction Patterns—Information and Knowledge—Emotionalized Actions—Character Traits—Conclusion

    Antisocial Conduct and Delinquency: Introduction—The Causes of Delinquency

Special Social Problems: Introduction—Only Children—Birth Order

Chapter XVIII: ADJUSTMENT AND MENTAL HYGIENE . . 628

Physical and Mental Hygiene: Introduction—Psychological Excellence—Mental Hygiene and Education—Purpose of the Chapter

Types of Adjustment: Hygiene and Adjustment—Adjustment and and Adaptation—Adjustment and Efficiency

Conflict: Introduction—Sources of Conflict—Tissue Needs and Conflict—Summary

Methods of Resolving Conflicts: Introduction—Trial-and-Error—Non-Adjustive Reactions—Regressive Reactions—Repression—Compensatory Actions

Mental Hygiene: Introduction—Environmental Changes—Conclusion

Chapter XIX: THE CONCEPT OF EFFICIENCY IN THE SCHOOLROOM 656

Adjustment and Efficiency: Ratios and Values—Efficiency—Purpose of the Chapter

Psychological Work: Introduction—Mental and Physical Work—Measures of Work

The Effect of Physical Conditions on Efficiency: Organic Conditions—Environmental Conditions

Sources of Loss in Efficiency: Introduction—The Typical Work Period—Fatigue and Efficiency—Causes of the Work Decrement—Monotony—Rest and Relaxation

The Effect of Drugs on Efficiency: Introduction—Alcohol—Nicotine—Caffeine—Conclusion

Chapter XX: POINTS OF VIEW IN PSYCHOLOGY . . . 690

The Genetic Point of View: Introduction—Points of View—Purpose of the Chapter

The Psychological Background of Education: Introduction—Primitive Psychology—The Origin of the "Soul"—Rational Psychology—Experimental Psychology

The Rational View of Education: Introduction—Primitive Education—Scholastic Education

Mind and Behavior in Education: Introduction—Empirical Behaviorism—Behaviorism

A Psychological Way of Describing Behavior: Introduction—The Nature of Psychological Experimentation—Animal Experimentation—Reactions and Mental Processes

Definitions of Educational Psychology: Introduction—Education as Applied General Psychology—Educational Sociology—Education and Animal Psychology

The Genetic Approach to Education: Introduction—Recapitulation—The Genetic View—Conclusion

INDEX 737

PART ONE

METHODS OF PROMOTING GROWTH

CHAPTER ONE

THE BEGINNINGS OF THE EDUCATIVE PROCESS

I. THE INFANT AND THE ADULT

1. *Introduction:* Were we to come upon it for the first time, the passage of a human being from a state of helpless infancy to a state of competent maturity would strike us as one of the most amazing events to be found anywhere in nature. Our amazement would, no doubt, be all the greater in proportion as we were able to summarize or condense the first twenty years of a person's life and thus get a short-time view of what is, so far as our own immediate human experience goes, a fairly lengthy process. Even our memories of the process, especially those drawn from the first three or four years, would be sufficiently exciting, if only, by taking thought about the matter, we could revive some of the major episodes for further inspection.

That the growth or development of a human being does not strike us with amazement is due, in part, to the fact that we have seen it take place so many times as to let familiarity breed indifference and, in part, to the fact that, until fairly recent times, neither parents nor teachers have really pretended to take an objective (that is, a scientific) interest in what happens to an educable child. From at least one point of view, society has been more concerned about the stars, about bridges and dams, about automobiles and other symbols of our technical culture than it has about the more immediate environmental factors which are known to transmute an infant into an efficient workman or a cultured gentleman. In other words, the technical spirit which has refashioned the physical world in which we live has not penetrated very far into the domain of social and personal becoming.[1] This is, no doubt, one reason why the claim is made that education should stand out as a major social enterprise.

There is, in human development, a size factor which is not without considerable interest. The weight of the human ovum from

---

[1] The student will find great value in reading Mumford, L., *Technics and Civilization.* New York: Harcourt, Brace and Co., 1934. The author writes a story of the technical attitude and cites some of the pressing social problems created by our devotion to the machine.

4   INTRODUCTION TO EDUCATIONAL PSYCHOLOGY

which a child grows amounts to about $\frac{1}{100}$ thousandth of a gram. The weight of an average man or woman, on the contrary, is about 100,000 grams, and a very stout man may weigh as much as 1,000,000 grams. The male germ cell is even smaller than the female cell, its weight probably amounting to less than one-billionth of a gram. In other words, it weighs about as much as a red corpuscle.[2]

Even more striking are some of the facts concerning complexity. At the time of fertilization, both the male and the female cells are single units of protoplasmic material. From one point of view they may be described as relatively simple. By way of comparison, an adult human body is composed of upwards of twenty-six trillion cells, twenty-two and one-half trillion of which float around in the blood stream as corpuscles. It is estimated that there are about thirteen billion nerve cells in a human brain and more than two-thirds of these—as a matter of fact, about nine billion—lie in the outer rind or cortex of the cerebrum. It is hardly necessary to argue that any object which passes within a relatively short period of time (say, twenty years) from a stage so simple as a germ cell to the size and complexity of a normal adult might well be regarded as the seat of an amazing series of changes.[3]

2. *Psychological Growth:* From the point of view of education, however, these physical aspects of human growth are not the most important that can be named. Still more amazing is the story of how the seven or eight pounds of an "animated vegetable" grows toward or acquires what are commonly recognized as the psychological and social traits of a normal adult.

A. ACTION SYSTEMS: For purposes of general orientation, let us take several typical examples from the psychological growth pattern. A more nearly complete picture of the principal features of this pattern will appear in due time. In the first place, many of the movements of a new-born infant are about as awkward and as devoid of social value as could be imagined and yet, within a few years, they will have become so highly specialized and coördinated that a Liszt concerto may be played on a piano, an oration delivered from a platform, or a gracious entrance made into a social group. The contrast between these two extremes would stand out even more clearly were it possible easily to observe the types of movement which an infant

[2] For an illuminating table of comparative sizes, see Haldane, J. B. S., and Huxley, J., *Animal Biology.* Oxford: The Clarendon Press, 1927, pp. 276-280.
[3] Some of the main stages in the growth of the individual will be described later on. In the meantime, refer to Jennings, H. S., *The Biological Basis of Human Nature.* New York: W. W. Norton and Co., 1930, Chapters III and IV. Also Herrick, C. J., *Brains of Rats and Men.* Chicago: Univ. of Chicago Press, 1926.

can make some weeks before it is born. We shall describe some of these movements in the next section, for they stand near the beginning of the educative process which is the topic of this book.

B. PERCEPTUAL SKILLS: Contrasts of equal significance may be discerned among the range of objects and events to which an infant, on the one hand, and an adult, on the other, can react in an effective or adequate manner. The word "adequate," when used in this manner, means either that actions should resemble those of a competent, mature person, or that they are generally approved by society. There is, of course, no final or absolute definition of adequacy.

It is only with difficulty that a new-born infant can be stirred into action by the events which are taking place around it. As an example, no one of the words spoken to it will have any psychological or social significance.[4] Before many months have passed, however, the growing infant will be taking note of and reacting to words and to a variety of objects and situations which is almost beyond calculation. Most of its first movements will be made in response to stimulus-situations which are produced within its own body; but by the time it has attained the age of twenty it will be able to respond "intelligently" and in an immense variety of other ways to thousands of forms and figures printed upon pieces of paper, to an equal number of sounds spoken by the human voice, and to a host of other objects and events as well.[5]

C. LEARNING PROCESSES: It is sometimes said by the poetically minded that new-born infants act as though they cherished memories of the celestial home they have just left; but there is no evidence to support this assertion. It does not seem possible to say that the new-born infant remembers anything and the number of "skills" it has acquired during the period of gestation may be counted almost on the fingers of one hand. Beginning with birth, however, and continuing with great speed during childhood, a series of psychological changes will take place within the infant for the description of which language is not yet sufficiently exact.

[4] Many of the principal facts about language development have been summarized by McCarthy, D., "Language Development," in Murchison, C. (Ed.), *Handbook of Child Psychology*. Worcester, Mass.: Clark Univ. Press, 1933, Chapter VIII. See also De Laguna, G., *Speech, Its Function and Development*. New Haven: Yale Univ. Press, 1927, *passim*.

[5] The student of educational psychology should always make use of some of the important books on child psychology. See, for example, Curti, M. W., *Child Psychology*. New York: Longmans, Green and Co., 1931; Johnson, B. J., *Child Psychology*. Springfield, Ill.: C. C. Thomas, 1932; Murchison, C. (Ed.), *Handbook of Child Psychology* (2nd ed.). Worcester, Mass.: Clark Univ. Press, 1933; Goodenough, F. L., *Developmental Psychology*. New York: D. Appleton-Century Co., 1934; Morgan, J. J. B., *Child Psychology* (2nd ed.). New York: Farrar and Rinehart, 1934.

Among the terms which have been used to describe the sources of these changes are "instinct," "heredity," "chromosomes," "conditioning," "learning," "skill," "habit," "maturation," "development," "memory," "recall," "recognition," "ideation," "imagination," "association," and "memory images." The very fact that there are so many of these words raises a problem about education which will give us deep thought as we proceed with our study. Most of them refer to the fact that people can be trained or educated. That is, human nature can be altered; the pattern of growth can be guided; and this is another one of the reasons why the art of teaching ought to stand high among the major interests of any social group.[6]

D. ATTENTION: Fortunately, no human being has to try to make all of the movements of which he is capable at any single moment. Similarly, he is never called upon to sense and to feel, at one and the same time, everything that can be sensed or felt. On the contrary, it usually happens that only one object or a single pattern of objects is the dominant one from moment to moment. Subject to changes in the circumstances under which they take place, human beings respond selectively to the events around them by the exercise of "voluntary attention," of "involuntary attention," of a major "interest," of a "motive," or of a "purpose." The extent to which "voluntary attention" or "purposes" are used by a person has been set down as one of the signs of his intellectual quality; but there are only vague symptoms of either of these features of conduct in the new-born infant. The process of acquiring the "faculty of attention" or of creating "interests" and "purposes" is one of the things that makes human becoming a picture of such amazing complexity.[7]

E. PROBLEM-SOLVING: The most striking difference between early infancy and adulthood, perhaps, is created by the fact that a person at the former level of development does not solve problems or evade difficulties in a clever way, and neither does he recognize or know anything about such situations. A mature person, on the contrary, is to be distinguished from all of the lower animals and from every other object in nature in direct proportion to his skill in finding a new or "reasonable" method of escape from complex situations and difficulties.

[6] Cf. Allport, F. H., *Institutional Behavior*. Chapel Hill: Univ. of North Carolina Press, 1933, Chapter XIX.
[7] Cf. Pillsbury, W. B., *Attention*. New York: The Macmillan Co., 1908, *passim*. See also, below, Chapter Four, where the development of attention will be considered, and Chapter Five, where we shall try to solve some of the problems of motivation and purpose.

THE BEGINNINGS OF THE EDUCATIVE PROCESS

Clear evidence that the growing child can solve problems does not appear before the second or third year; and yet, between this time and full maturity, the one talent that has led to almost everything that we can call science, philosophy, art, culture, or civilization makes its appearance and comes to full fruition.[8] Truly, this is an amazing type of change to take place in human nature. The contrast between the physico-chemical processes under way in a human ovum just as it is about to divide into two daughter cells and those that go on in the brain of a philosopher when he is trying to resolve a difficult problem is so great as to stand nearly beyond all possibility of exaggeration. We may say again, then, that from every point of view the passage of a human being from infancy to adulthood is one of the most amazing series of events that can occur anywhere in nature.

3. *Psychology and Education:* It is natural that a variety of sciences should have directed their attention to the series of events described by the word "growth." Among these we may name the sciences of anatomy, embryology, physiology, dietetics, sociology, and psychology.[9] Parents and teachers are particularly interested, however, in the work of the psychologist, for it is upon the science of psychology that a large part of education must be based. It has been one of the primary functions of educators, that is, of all persons who exert an influence on the growth of a child, to try to promote and to direct, at the psychological level, the amazing processes of which we have just given a sample. In other words, education is the only means society has of seeing to it that its oncoming members shall acquire some of the same types of equipment, on the one hand, and a serviceable share of the general fund of information, on the other, that its mature members have already found useful in the business of living.

To be sure, there are some persons who would say that society has found two means instead of one for improving the mental and physical quality of its members. In addition to the art of education, there is the science of eugenics, which aims at better mating and hence, at better physical and psychological quality; but it is a plain fact that the returns that are now in from the science of eugenics are pitifully small. In view of the complex factors which surround human mating, and in view of the social mores which are

[8] Cf. Dewey, J., *How We Think* (2nd ed.). Boston: D. C. Heath and Co., 1933, *passim*.
[9] For an appraisal of the many-sided attack that is being made on the development of the child, see the proceedings of the White House Conference on Child Welfare, published by D. Appleton-Century Co., as a series of special monographs.

adverse to the elimination or sterilization of the unfit, it will be a long time before significant measures of social improvement can be produced in this way. Society must, therefore, base most of its hopes for immediate self-improvement, to say nothing of self-maintenance, upon education.[10]

The processes of teaching begin, of course, as soon as the infant is born. It is even possible that some of them, in the form of special growth-promoting situations, begin before birth, for the unborn child is not hermetically sealed from the external environment. Still less is it shielded from environmental influences created by the mother who carries it. This means that neither the psychologist nor the teacher can afford to emphasize a distinction which is sometimes drawn between formal and informal education; for this distinction implies that the only training which really counts is that which takes place in the schoolroom after the child has reached the age of five or six years.

4. *The Purpose of the Chapter:* It is the purpose of this first chapter, then, to review some of the main facts about the first stages of the educative process. Many students are beginning to realize more clearly than ever before that an educational psychology ought properly to start with the story of how a new-born infant comes by those traits, talents, and dispositions that it will use when first it enters the formal school system. This story should be based upon a direct study of the whole growth pattern and not, as some students of educational psychology would have it, upon anecdotes and general traditions about original nature.

As soon as "formal" education begins, that is, during the fifth or the sixth year of a person's life, the growth of many of these traits and talents will be further promoted by teachers who will make use of systematically organized curricula. In other words, the teacher will lay before the child a vast number of those learning-situations (as, for example, daily lessons based upon the three R's) which are commonly recognized by society as an adequate point of departure in education and for the use of which society is willing to pay immense sums of money. Long before the child makes its formal entrance into the school system, however, educational processes of the most significant type will have been brought to bear upon it. This means, among other things, that the problems of teaching at a higher

---

[10] Cf. Hogben, L., *The Nature of Living Matter.* New York: A. A. Knopf, 1931, Chapter VIII; Cowdry, E. V. (Ed.), *Human Biology and Racial Welfare.* New York: Paul Hoeber, 1930, Part V; Holmes, C. J., *The Eugenics Predicament.* New York: Harcourt, Brace and Co., 1933.

level can neither be understood nor properly interpreted unless we find out something about lower level processes.[11]

II. THE NEW-BORN CHILD

1. *The "Zero Point" of Development:* There have been several occasions in the history of education when it has been easy to suppose that the psychological and educational study of children should properly begin at birth. Since the act of leaving the mother's body brings the child for the first time into open observation and since, also, it is introduced for the first time to the sort of world in which adults live, it has been natural to suppose that birth should mark a "zero point" of departure not only for physical and mental growth curves but also for teaching effort.

There is another reason, however, why birth has been taken as an important point of reference in the whole growth pattern. Either in the act or by implication, teachers, parents, and even serious students of genetic psychology have sometimes assumed that a new-born child possesses little or no psychological life. The most casual onlooker, however, will report that every infant carries out a good many actions which it cannot owe to the promoting and guiding influence of the type of environment in which adults live. The inference is plain. It must be that a new-born child possesses a variety of modes of action for which it is indebted to its heredity or to its original nature rather than to its training. Given a "zero point" for the growth curve behind which an environment, in the form of particular learning situations, could not have been effective, all modes of action and all temperaments or dispositions which become observable at or immediately after birth must be attributed to forces which reside within the child itself. In other words, it will be argued that the child has already reached a considerable measure of maturity in some of its psychological traits on the day it is born.[12] To be sure, every child is phylogenetically or racially old because it has the entire story of evolution behind it; but some of the more extreme views of heredity give the appearance of arguing for an advanced ontogenetic age, as well.

[11] See, for example, Gesell, A., *The Guidance of Mental Growth in Infant and Child.* New York: The Macmillan Co., 1930. For some phases of the history of the genetic point of view in education, see Eby, F., and Arrowood, C. F., *The Development of Modern Education.* New York: Prentice-Hall, Inc., 1934, Chapters XVII, XX, XXI, and *passim.*

[12] The assertion that a new-born child is already very old was an essential feature of the theory of recapitulation. See Hall, G. S., *Adolescence* (2 vols.). New York: D. Appleton-Century Co., 1904, *passim.*

With original nature of this type as a starting point, it has been easy to say that the function of education is to find out how many varieties of innate or instinctive actions there are and how this original nature can be amended by the processes of training.[13] By way of comparison with this point of view, we shall lay before the reader a series of facts which show that the original nature of which so many educators have spoken is not really original nature at all but a first observable nature.[14] There are many features of human behavior which can be called original only because it has been assumed that birth really marks a "zero point" in the growth pattern and because it has been assumed that no education or training of any consequence can take place between birth and the first year of schooling. In any case, the initial step in our study of the problems of educational psychology requires a brief glimpse of some of the psychological events that take place before birth.[15]

2. *Prenatal Development:* If it is at all possible, we intend to leave no doubt in the mind of the student that there is, perhaps, no branch of psychology that can throw more light upon the problems of education and upon the possible successes of teaching methods than the study of the prenatal development of human beings, for it is during this period that some of the essential qualities of the mature person are being fashioned. This study is richly supplemented by a vast amount of information drawn from the prenatal development of the lower animals.

Because of disease, injury, and other unavoidable circumstances, it is often necessary to take the human foetus from the mother long before the end of a normal term. Such foetuses can be kept alive for variable periods of time by placing them in a physiological saline solution. Experiments upon the behavior of such subjects, supplemented by appropriate knowledge concerning the general physiology of growth, on the one hand, and the development of the nervous system, of sense organs, and of muscle groups, on the other, are beginning to suggest some of the main outlines of prenatal development. It will not be possible for us to mention more than two or

[13] An immense number of "instincts" has been attributed to human nature and many social, economic, and political problems have been solved by appealing to these instincts. See Bernard, L. L., *Instinct, A Study in Social Psychology.* New York: Henry Holt and Co., 1924, *passim;* Wilm, E. C., *The Theories of Instinct.* New Haven: Yale Univ. Press, 1925, *passim.*

[14] The standard list of instincts for educators has been furnished by Thorndike, E. L., *Educational Psychology* (3 vols.). New York: Columbia Univ. Press, 1913. See Vol. I, *The Original Nature of Man.*

[15] A large literature on the prenatal development of the lower animals and of the human foetus has been reviewed and summarized by Carmichael, L., "Origin and Prenatal Growth of Behavior," in Murchison, C. (Ed.), *op. cit.,* Chapter II.

THE BEGINNINGS OF THE EDUCATIVE PROCESS 11

three general features of this phase of the growth pattern; but, as we have said above, there is no group of facts which throws more light upon the scope and upon the possible attainments of education than this group.

A. INITIAL MOVEMENTS: It seems to be fairly clear that developmental processes in the forward end of an animal keep a full step ahead of processes of the same type in the rear end. The first movements made by many living creatures, therefore, are slow, pendular movements of the upper portions of the body or of the head. During the earlier stages of development, these and other movements can be excited only by direct stimulation of muscle tissue. Shortly, however, as nerve connections are established between the surface layers (sense organs) and the lower muscle tissues (motor organs), contact at the surface will bring about movement.

These movements mark the beginning of true sensori-motor actions. In other words, they mark the beginning of psychological problems, for it looks as though sensori-motor patterns form the framework within which the whole pattern of behavior will be built.[16] Even in a new-born child, the maturity of the upper part of the body runs so far in advance of the lower part that moderately painful stimuli which will excite a violent response when applied to the cheek will scarcely arouse a response when applied to the sole of the foot.[17]

As a rule, most of the initial movements of a growing organism are masslike in character.[18] That is, they involve large segments of the body and much diffuse action. It is out of these larger patterns of movement that the more specific types emerge—a course of events which lies just contrary to common opinion; for it has usually been assumed that the first movements are simple reflexes which, when brought together in simultaneous and successive units, yield the larger patterns. The emergence of more specialized types of behavior out of larger patterns can be seen in the origin and development of limb movements. The arm, for example, first moves as a single unit, not only in the human infant but in many of the lower animals as well. Shortly, the forearm acquires competence independently of the whole arm, and finally the hand and the fingers

---

[16] We shall meet this problem in Chapter Twenty. As the student already knows, there are many different ways of defining the subject matter of psychology. Cf. Murchison, C. (Ed.), *Psychologies of 1930*. Worcester, Mass: Clark Univ. Press, 1930.
[17] Sherman, M., and Sherman, I. C., *The Process of Human Behavior*. New York: W. W. Norton and Co., 1929, Chapter I.
[18] Cf. Pratt, K. C., Nelson, A. K., and Sun, K. H., "The Behavior of the Newborn Infant." *Ohio State Univ. Contrib. to Psychol.*, 1930 (No. 10), *passim*.

become equally independent.[19] To be sure, a finger movement always implies a posture of the hand and of the arm, but this fact does not contradict the increasing specialization of movement in all parts of the body during the earlier phases of development. The student already knows that this course of events holds true of his own attempts to acquire a new skill.

B. ORGANIZATION: The full significance of these facts will not appear until we learn that every growing individual follows a pattern of development which is an intrinsic feature of the fertilized ovum. There is abundant experimental evidence to show that living cells are polarized or patterned in such a way that there will be a functional head end and a functional rear end, even though there may be no parallel structures for these functional differences. If, for example, we assume that the amount of carbon dioxide given off from different areas on the surface of a cell is indicative of the rate of metabolism within different portions of the cell itself, then it appears that the rate normally stands at a higher level at one end of the cell than at the other.[20]

This fact means that every cell is a dynamic system of processes, a system which is patterned from the very first in such a way that it must be viewed as a single and highly integrated unit. No cell is a simple accumulation of identical parts where one piece has been added to another. If the rate of metabolism (sometimes called the physiological or the metabolic gradient) stands at a higher level at one end than at the other, we can see why it is that development takes place more rapidly at the one end.

These same considerations appear to hold true of collections of cells or of organisms. It would follow, therefore, that the development of the whole individual is subject to a mode of patterning which makes the events going on in any particular part of the organism contingent upon events taking place elsewhere in it. In other words, the other parts of a growing system may serve as effective "environmental" agents in regulating the growth of any one part.

[19] Some of the main facts about prenatal development can be gained from three major papers, viz., Coghill, G. E., *Anatomy and the Problem of Behavior*. New York: The Macmillan Co., 1929; Avery, G. T., "Responses of Foetal Guinea Pigs Prematurely Delivered." *Genet. Psychol. Monog.*, 1928, III, 245-331; Minkowski, M., "Uber Bewegungen und Reflexe des menschlichen Fötus während der ersten Hälfte seiner Entwicklung." *Schweiz. Arch. f. Neur. u. Psychiat.*, 1921, VIII, 148-151; Minkowski, M., "Uber frühzeitige Bewegungen, Reflexe und muskuläre Reaktionen beim menschlichen Fötus und ihre Beziehungen zur fötalen Nerven- und Muskel-system." *Schweiz. med. Woch.*, 1922, LII, 721-724, 751-755.
[20] Cf. Child, C. M., *Physiological Foundations of Behavior*. New York: Henry Holt and Co., 1924, Chapter I-IX. Also, Child, C. M., *Origin and Development of the Nervous System*. Chicago: Univ. of Chicago Press, 1921, Chapters II and IV.

THE BEGINNINGS OF THE EDUCATIVE PROCESS 13

We shall find this fact of great value as we proceed with our study of educational psychology, for it has been easy to suppose that all complex things are a simple accumulation of parts instead of highly integrated patterns. It now looks as though greater emphasis must be laid upon the factors of organization and of relationship.

C. PRENATAL SOURCES OF STIMULATION: This fact will become of great importance to us when, in a later chapter, we say more about the problems of original nature. Moreover, it is a fact in which we may begin to catch the significance for education of the full course of prenatal development, for a description of the dynamics of growth (that is, a description of the actual origins of behavior-patterns in their natural context) is one thing, and the argument that the new-born child is fairly well equipped with innate tendencies and instinctive urges toward specialized modes of action is quite another.

Let us think, first, of some of the simpler phases of this contrast. As the foetus grows, the weights of various parts of the body change. Since alterations of this type are taking place constantly, those tissues which must support changing weights will receive a functionally important stimulus to further growth. The very fact that some of the parts of a developing foetus can move or be moved means that proper nerve connections between the stimuli created by movement and the organs to be moved will be excited to further growth.[21]

In addition to these circumstances which arise out of a very complex set of physiological events, there is that whole problem of the possible effect of stimuli from the outside. The human foetus is, of course, pretty well shielded from such stimuli, save in the case where bodily movements are made by the mother. It is not impossible, however, that light, and even sound, may occasionally find their way to the foetus. Certainly, there are variable sources of contact, especially during the later months of pregnancy, occasioned by the movements of the foetus itself. That is, the foetus must often stimulate itself to further action. The chances are that the movements made by the mother cannot help but become effective sources of stimulus to the child she bears, and it is quite clear that even stimuli of this sort may play a significant rôle in promoting certain types of growth. It has been observed, for example, that

[21] Very important matters of research are suggested by this statement. See Lashley, K. S., "Nervous Mechanisms in Learning," in Murchison, C. (Ed.), *Foundations of Experimental Psychology*. Worcester, Mass.: Clark Univ. Press, 1929, Chapter XIV. See especially, pp. 526 ff.

excitations in the organs of balance may have wide effects in the development of coördination among muscles and even in promoting the functional organization of the cerebellum.[22]

As we shall see in a later chapter, these possible sources of stimulation, not only to the general growth of the nervous system but to growth in particular directions or for carrying out particular functions, have an important bearing upon the whole question as to what is original or native in human nature and what is acquired. We may say again that it is one thing to describe reflexes and instincts which owe their origin to immutable factors in the germ plasm, and quite another to describe the inevitable properties of a forward-moving but highly integrated pattern of vital energies.

In the meantime, let us remember that the actions of a new-born infant are not manufactured simply by putting a number of partial actions or simple actions together.[23] Instead, they appear as the result of two major circumstances, the one being the patterning of the whole living system from the very first, and the other being the progressive individuation of single structures and functions out of, but nevertheless under the influence of, the whole.

D. MASS MOVEMENTS: It may be worth while to emphasize even more than we have this second feature of the early history of human behavior. As was said above, the first observable movements of a new-born infant, like some of the first movements of an embryo, are diffuse and uncoördinated with respect to particular stimuli. It has often been argued, however, that the infant begins its psychological life with a large number of specific reflex movements which, since they commonly appear at birth in functional order, must be called innate. Growth meant that these movements were gradually integrated into larger and more complex patterns. As the studies mentioned above show, however, some of the first movements of the foetus may take the form of mass movements involving the entire action system. To be sure, an inspection of foetal behavior reveals many local movements, and some of these are related to specific stimulus-patterns; but this fact cannot be accepted as proof of the existence of nerve connections which have been ordained by special hereditary factors. We propose, however, to look more earnestly into this question in Part II.

[22] Consult Freeman, G. L., *Introduction to Physiological Psychology.* New York: The Ronald Press, 1934, Chapters I and II.
[23] The reflex theory of human behavior has had a long history. See Fearing, F. S., *Reflex Action.* Baltimore: The Williams and Wilkins Co., 1930, *passim.* Compare this theory with the gestal theory as described by Wheeler, R. H., and Perkins, F. T., *Principles of Mental Development.* New York: T. Y. Crowell Co., 1932, *passim.*

THE BEGINNINGS OF THE EDUCATIVE PROCESS

If we say that a specific movement involves (i) a single segment of the body and (ii) fairly low speed, then mass movements may be described (i) as the result of stimuli acting on widely distributed sense organs, (ii) as non-segmental or organismic in the sense that all parts of the body are involved, (iii) as fairly rapid and continuous, (iv) as excessive in amount, (v) as uncoördinated, and (vi) as almost wholly unmodified by the environment.[24]

We have already remarked the fact that movement often begins in some of the lower animals with a slow and pendular movement of the head region. Gradually, as other parts of the body develop, and as an adequate supply of nerve connections are established between surface organs and underlying muscles, specific types of action will be individuated out of the total complex of action. It looks as though these more local and specialized movements conform at first to the general dynamic pattern mentioned above. In other words, it has become fruitful to think that behavior is, from the very first, a roughly integrated unit out of which special or partial patterns may emerge and pass on their way toward a large measure of independence.[25]

As we shall see in a moment, this feature of prenatal development is full of significance for the problems of education. Among other things, it throws new light upon the question of original nature and it emphasizes in no uncertain manner the importance of patterning or of configuration in all phases of human development.

3. *The Neonate:* For a good many reasons it is useful, in genetic psychology, to designate in a special way the new-born child. The word "neonate" serves this purpose. In general, the word refers to the first seven to twenty days of the infant's post-natal life, for it is during this time that the original birth weight is regained and the umbilical cord disappears. In other words, the term "neonate" describes the infant during that period when it is laying aside the structures and functions which made it physiologically dependent upon the mother and when it is beginning to use some of the structures and functions which will permanently identify it as a new individuality.[26]

We do not intend to say that there is anything about the neonate which breaks up the essential continuity of the whole growth pat-

---

[24] Irwin, O. C., and Weiss, A. P., "A Note on Mass Activity in Newborn Infants." *J. Genet. Psychol.*, 1930, XXXVIII, 20-30.
[25] Coghill, G. E., "The Early Development of Behavior in the Amblystoma and in Man." *Arch. Neur. and Psychiat.*, 1929, XXI, 989-1009.
[26] Cf. Gesell, A., *The Mental Growth of the Pre-school Child.* New York: The Macmillan Co., 1925, Chapter I and *passim.*

tern. On the contrary, the actions of a new-born infant stand in direct sequence to the actions of the unborn infant. To be sure, certain well-defined reflexes have appeared; but most bodily movement is of the mass type.[27] Since, however, the infant is now open to direct inspection, more exact studies can be made of its various modes of action. Essential continuity is illustrated by the fact that much of the behavior of the infant during the first few weeks still calls for description in terms of mass activity. Even adults will sometimes behave in this manner when they have to meet a new situation. The first movements of a golfer are more diffuse and more highly generalized than are his later skilful movements.

A. INDIVIDUATION: In the case of a child, the first reaching movements are also diffuse in character in the sense that they involve activity in almost the whole body. The arms are moved as though they were a single unit. A moving picture analysis of the changes that take place in this pattern from the twelfth to the sixtieth weeks shows that partial movements of the forearm, the wrist, and the fingers gradually emerge out of the larger pattern in a definite series of steps. This phase of development proceeds so rapidly that, at the sixtieth week, most children can oppose the thumb and the first finger in grasping a small object without bringing so many other groups of muscles into play.[28]

It seems to be fairly clear that the individuation of specific types of behavior out of an original matrix of mass movement, and the parallel individuation of various types of sensitivity have gone on apace during the late months of foetal development. This means that the neonate can be stimulated to action by a great many different agents and that it can respond in a great many different ways to these agents. It is known, for example, that new-born infants are sensitive to variations in the intensity of light, although it has not been shown that they can distinguish between light drawn from different parts of the spectrum.

Among the more stable responses to specific stimulus-patterns are the pupillary reflex, blinking, the grasping reflex, sucking, and other sensori-motor patterns of the same order. It appears that some new-born infants cannot coördinate the two eyes with any great degree

---

[27] For a plausible theory of the origin of the grasping reflex, see Holt, E. B., *Animal Drive and the Learning Process.* New York: Henry Holt and Co., 1931, Chapter II.

[28] Halverson, H. M., "An Experimental Study of Prehension in Infants by Means of Systematic Cinema Records." *Genet. Psychol. Monog.*, 1931, X, 107-286. Also, "A Further Study of Grasping." *J. Gen. Psychol.*, 1932, VII, 34-64. A magnificent study of development is to be found in Gesell, A., *An Atlas of Infant Behavior* (2 vols.). New Haven: Yale Univ. Press, 1934.

THE BEGINNINGS OF THE EDUCATIVE PROCESS 17

of success, though skill in this respect is acquired with great speed.[29] There are certain mechanical obstacles in the way of sensitivity to tones and sounds during the first few days of life, high pitched notes and quick sharp sounds of considerable intensity being reacted to first. The usual response to sounds of this character is variously described as a shock or a fear reaction. That is, the first response resembles to some extent a mass movement out of which the more typical fear reaction will develop.[30]

Some of the initial responses to odors (ammonia, acetic acid, and other more intense forms of chemical stimuli) are avoiding or defense reactions, diffuse squirming, crying, and sneezing. It seems to be fairly certain that these movements appear in response to the pain-exciting properties of stimuli rather than to a developed sensitivity to the milder odors.[31] Sensitivity to tastes is certainly more highly developed at birth than sensitivity to odors. This fact can be determined by measuring differences in the vigor of sucking responses and by changes in facial expression.[32] Sugar, salt, quinine, and citric acids are substances used most frequently by the experimenters.

Not a great deal is known about sensitivity to changes in temperature where the stimulus is applied to a limited area. It seems to be clear, however, that marked changes in temperature will produce vigorous movement near the areas stimulated and increased vigor in the sucking response. General changes in temperature will induce shivering. Crying, together with some movements of avoidance, are the common responses to painful stimuli. These responses appear even before the moment of birth.[33]

B. MATURATION: We have said above that the movements that are most clearly individuated out of the original behavior matrix are the so-called reflexes, such as sucking, the palmar or grasping reflex, the plantar response, various types of postural responses, smiling, crying, and the iris reflex. Since all of these movements are so specific at birth, it is easy to argue that they must have an origin which is different from the origin of other patterns of action. It is clear, however, that none of them makes its appearance until several weeks after conception. They must, therefore, have a pre-

[29] Cf. Pratt, K. C., Nelson, A. K., and Sun, K. H., "The Behavior of the Newborn Infant." *Ohio State Univ. Stud., Contrib. to Psychol.,* 1930 (No. 10), *passim.*
[30] Cf. Sherman, M., and Sherman, I. C., *op. cit.,* Chapters I and II.
[31] Pratt, K. C., et al., *op. cit., passim.*
[32] Jensen, K., "Differential Reactions to Taste and Temperature Stimuli in Newborn Infants." *Genet. Psychol. Monog.,* 1932, XII, 361-479.
[33] Pratt, K. C., in Murchison, C. (Ed.), *Handbook of Child Psychology.* Worcester, Mass.: Clark Univ. Press, 1933, pp. 185 ff.

natal history which ought to be described before it can be said of them that they are original or innate in the older sense of these words.

It is now popular to describe the first reactions of the neonate as the fruit of maturation.[34] This term includes all of the dynamic factors which were mentioned in the preceding section on prenatal development. In other words, experimental psychology has seen fit to avoid some of the older contrasts between heredity and training by giving close attention to the entire history of any action pattern and to the matrix of events of which all action patterns are a part. As we have seen, this history can be traced only with the greatest difficulty. Since the prenatal career of a human individual is a natural product of a complex system of interacting structures and functions, it may be a long time before the so-called reflexes will be traced to their origin. There is every reason to believe, however, that when the origins have been discovered, much more emphasis will be placed upon the dynamic processes of growth than upon native or original traits that are to be set in sharp opposition against acquired traits.[35]

C. EMOTIONALIZED ACTIONS: A most important question about the neonate arises in conjunction with the range and variety of its emotionalized types of action. For a long time it has been taken for granted that every human being is born with a fairly elaborate equipment in this respect, but this part of the picture of original nature shows, as a result of recent experimentation, as much change as do the other parts.

In one series of studies carried out by Watson, it appeared that the emotional reactions of a group of infants could be placed in three classes, viz., (i) fear reactions induced by sudden loud sounds and by the removal of support, (ii) anger induced by confining the movements of the infant, and (iii) "love" (including smiling, gurgling, and cooing) induced by rocking, petting, and tickling certain zones on the body.[36] More recently, it has been decided that the initial emotional reactions of an infant are not even as specific as the studies of Watson made it appear. When a group of judges

---

[34] Cf. Witty, P. A., and Lehman, H. C., "The Instinct Hypothesis versus the Maturation Hypothesis." *Psychol. Rev.*, 1933, XL, 33-59. See also Stone, C. P., Learning: I. "The Factor of Maturation," in Murchison, C. (Ed.). *A Handbook of General Experimental Psychology*. Worcester, Mass.: Clark Univ. Press, 1934, Chapter VIII.

[35] Some of the important literature bearing upon the topics now under discussion can be found in Pratt, K. C., "The Neonate," in Murchison, C. (Ed.), *Handbook of Child Psychology*. Worcester, Mass.: Clark Univ. Press, 1933, Chapter III.

[36] Watson, J. B., and Rayner, R., "Conditioned Emotional Reactions." *J. Exper. Psychol.*, 1920, III, 1-14. Also Watson, J. B., and Watson, R. R., "Studies in Infant Psychology." *Scient. Mo.*, 1921, XIII, 493-515.

THE BEGINNINGS OF THE EDUCATIVE PROCESS

were asked to name the emotion expressed by a number of infants, they were unable to do so with any great degree of success unless they knew the character of the stimulus-situation which had produced the responses.[37]

It looks very much as though the one feature of stimulus-situations which is essential for the production of emotional reactions is unexpectedness. That is, if an infant is excited by an intense and suddenly applied stimulus-situation, it will respond with a mass movement in which kicking, pushing movements of the hands, and crying are dominant features.[38] The largest share of the behavior of new-born infants is not excited, however, by situations external to it, that is, external to its own body. Instead, the events that are taking place within its alimentary canal are the most important. Among these we may mention hunger contractions of the stomach and pressures and pains in the digestive system.[39]

D. LEARNING: Even a most casual inspection of the first few days of life will show that processes of learning bring about quick changes in behavior.[40] This fact holds true, in particular, of feeding and of all of the other situations created by the daily care of the infant.[41] It is not to be supposed, however, that the moment of birth marks the beginning of the learning process, for there is nothing to be gained, apparently, in drawing too sharp a distinction between growth processes which are "intrinsic" to the developing individual and those which are dependent upon external learning situations. The point is that no developing animal can ever escape from either a context or an environment.

Although it remains to be found out in detail just how and when environmental factors operate before birth we may, nevertheless, make due allowance for these factors and proceed intensively to a study of their effects on growth whenever and wherever they can be controlled. This means that a learning situation is to be distinguished from general environmental situations and from prenatal contexts only in the sense that, after birth, a teacher or a parent tries to guide and promote growth by defining and repeating stable

---

[37] Sherman, M., "The Differentiation of Emotional Responses in Infants." *J. Comp. Psychol.*, 1927, VII, 265-284, 335-351.

[38] Jones, H. E., and Jones, M. C., "A Study of Fear." *Childhood Educ.*, 1928, V, 136-143.

[39] Irwin, O. C., "The Amount and Nature of Activities of Newborn Infants under Constant Stimulation During the First Ten Days of Life." *Genet. Psychol. Monog.*, 1930, VIII, 1-92.

[40] Cf. Wagoner, L. C., *The Development of Learning in Young Children*. New York: The McGraw-Hill Book Co., 1933, *passim*.

[41] Cf. Watson, J. B., *Psychological Care of Infant and Child*. New York: W. W. Norton and Co., 1928, *passim*.

units of stimulus-connection-response patterns until the child has acquired maturity, that is, adequate modes of action, with respect to them.

In general, the first few hours after birth, and all subsequent hours as well, stand in direct continuity with prenatal development. The student may feel that this fact is too obvious to mention; but so many teachers forget it so often in their methods of handling schoolroom problems that it cannot be mentioned too frequently. Some attempt will be made in a later chapter to distinguish more clearly between the native and the environmental components of the growth continuum. In the meantime, however, it is necessary to remark the fact again that this continuum is a very complex affair, only a few of the main features of which have been established by experiment. As we have said, the new-born infant acts very largely under the impetus of excitations from its own alimentary canal. When the hunger contractions of the stomach begin, the child displays an increased measure of irritability. During this period other stimulus-situations, and principally those outside of the child's own body, are relatively ineffective. After the child is fed, mass movements tend to disappear, and the infant either falls asleep or becomes increasingly sensitive, for a short time, to external sources of stimulation. Every movement that it makes, however, must lead to some change in its modes of reaction, for the infant can do nothing that does not immediately become a part of its history. In other words, the infant learns or in some other way becomes an embodiment of previous experience. As time passes, the previous history of the infant will become more and more powerful in determining the character of its responses to new situations, and it is for this reason that the beginnings of the educative process stand out so significantly in all later attempts to guide and to promote growth.

III. CHARACTERISTICS OF THE PRESCHOOL CHILD

1. *Functions and Services:* Even though we shall continue to draw heavily upon the experimental study of the developing child, it will not be possible, either here or in the pages which follow, to give the reader a complete picture of all that is being done in this field.[42] As we have noted above, however, no student of education,

---

[42] The best available summary of the principal facts of child development is to be found in Murchison, C. (Ed.), *op. cit., passim.* See also Stoddard, G. D., and Wellman, B. L., *Child Psychology.* New York: The Macmillan Co., 1934. Gesell, A., Thompson, H., and Armatruda, C. S., *Infant Behavior: Its Genesis and Growth.* New York: McGraw-Hill Book Co., 1934.

THE BEGINNINGS OF THE EDUCATIVE PROCESS

and especially no student of the processes of elementary education, should feel that he is really competent for his work until he has put himself in touch with this domain of research. This fact holds true not only of the earlier stages of the growth pattern which were outlined above but also of the general psychological equipment of the preschool child as well.

In preparation for a brief recital of this equipment, let us draw a distinction between equipment which is truly psychological in character, on the one hand, and the various services that are rendered to the individual and to society by the use of this equipment, on the other.[43] As a single example, we may take the development of the arm, hand, and finger movements which finally make it possible for a person to grasp a small object between the thumb and the forefinger. As we have intimated, this motor skill has a long and highly characteristic history. Even a three-year-old child can use the skill rather well; but it is one thing to describe the origin and the general nature of the skill and quite another to list all of the personal and social functions that may be served by the proper use of it.[44] Somewhat the same type of movement, for example, would be used in picking up a pencil, holding a pencil while writing, handling a sheet of paper, using a knife, fork, or spoon, buttoning a jacket or coat, or in holding out an object to another person.

Let us agree, then, that a fruitful distinction can be drawn between skills or modes of operation which are more or less fundamental in character and all of the services that are rendered by the daily use of these skills and modes of operation.[45] This distinction becomes of importance in the school system, where it is often said that it is the primary function of the early years of schooling to give children a high degree of skill in the use of their psychological equipment, whereas the later years of schooling emphasize the content subjects, that is, the subjects which will be mastered for better or for worse, depending upon the quality of the psychological instrument that a person has become because of his earlier training.

---

[43] Cf. Ruckmick, C. A., "The Use of the Term 'Function' in English Textbooks of Psychology." *Amer. J. Psychol.*, 1913, XXIV, 99-123.

[44] Those readers who have studied psychology will see at once that we have here touched upon a very difficult psychological problem. See, for example, Carr, H. A., "Functionalism," in Murchison, C. (Ed.), *Psychologies of 1930*. Worcester, Mass.: Clark Univ. Press, 1930, Chapter III; Angell, J. R., "The Province of Functional Psychology." *Psychol. Rev.*, 1907, XIV, 61-91; Heidbreder, E. F., *Seven Psychologies*. New York: The D. Appleton-Century Co., 1933, *passim*, and especially the section on functionalism.

[45] The distinction here drawn between primary modes of psychological operation and services rendered will play an important part in our study of the nature of intelligence. See below, Chapter Fifteen.

22 INTRODUCTION TO EDUCATIONAL PSYCHOLOGY

The distinction is important, also, because those types of training which lead to an actual change in the psychological equipment of the child differ in many important respects from types of training which simply take a given level of maturity for granted. As we have said above, many of the problems to be met by the school teacher arise out of the fact that the children under his care possess inadequate levels of psychological skill. We may take reading as an instance. Reading depends, among other things, on a given degree of skill in the use of the eyes.[46] Since this skill serves a great many different purposes, these purposes will be achieved in direct proportion to the measure of excellence attained. If, then, a teacher is absorbed with the services to be rendered by a skill rather than with the art of improving the skill itself, he is going to be perplexed by some of the inadequacies of his pupils.

In addition to a general picture of the psychological equipment of the preschool child, we shall find it helpful to say something about the concepts of plasticity, on the one hand, and of fixity, on the other. Both of these concepts, and especially the second, have been badly misused in educational theory and practice. The immediate experimental study of the development of children has now given them a wholly new meaning, and if the student can see what this new meaning is, he will be able to appreciate the general significance of child research in so far as it concerns the educative process.

2. *Psychological Equipment:* The student already knows that there are a great many ways of defining the nature of psychology. For this reason, the phrase "psychological equipment" carries a different meaning to different persons. Some of these meanings will be described at the beginning of the next chapter and others in the final chapter. In the meantime, without prejudice to these difficult matters, let us consider the equipment of the child in a very simple way.

A. ACTION: We have already caught a partial glimpse of the prenatal and neonate trends of events which lead to the appearance of special motor skills. We have found that many of the earliest movements of an infant are highly generalized in character. Out of this matrix of action and under the influence of particular situations, partial movements are individuated from the whole mass and finally raised to the level of specialized skills. During the preschool years, this process of individuation or of specialization takes place with great speed. The student has, perhaps, watched a small infant reach-

[46] Some of the main facts about the nature of reading will be included in Chapter Two.

ing for an object. He knows that the reaching movements include not only action in the two arms but a considerable amount of action in the legs, in the head, in the face, and even in the torso itself. After a few weeks of practice, the number of leg movements is markedly decreased, leaving only the arm movements, and, perhaps, a general posture in the body which furnishes a point of departure for the arm movements.[47]

This is a pattern of events which lies behind almost all of the skills the child acquires. By the time the infant is two or three years of age, it will have learned to use its leg muscles for maintaining an erect posture, for walking, for running, and for the early and more awkward stages of kicking and jumping. The movements of its arms will have become sufficiently specialized to admit of holding a great many different objects, of scribbling in a crude way upon sheets of papers, of handling blocks and other playthings, and of throwing. The muscles around the mouth parts and in the throat, together with all of the supplementary structures that are used in speech, will have become sufficiently integrated so that the child can make a variety of sounds.[48] These sounds furnish the essential skills out of which verbal language can be manufactured.

Even though the growth of these motor skills has followed a course marked by the progressive individuation or specialization of movements, all of the part movements, nevertheless, will have retained more than their original measure of membership within an integrated whole. We have appeared, of course, to lay emphasis upon individuation as a primary feature of every developmental schedule, but the student should remember that patterning and organization supply a continuous supplement to individuation. In addition to particular movements, therefore, the child will take an immense variety of postures in response to the situations within which it finds itself.

Much is to be accomplished before the child will have reached those high levels of special skill and of adequate posture which are characteristic of the adult; but it is significant to note that a great many of the fundamental features of the actions that will be useful to it in later life have begun to take form in the early part of the preschool period.[49] This fact holds true, in particular, of some of

[47] Cf. Curti, M. W., *Child Psychology*. New York: Longmans, Green and Co., 1931, pp. 169 ff.
[48] Cf. Watson, J. B., *Psychology from the Standpoint of a Behaviorist* (3rd ed.). Philadelphia: J. B. Lippincott, 1929, Chapters VII, VIII.
[49] Cf. Shirley, M. M., "Locomotor and Visual-manual Functions in the First Two Years," in Murchison, C. (Ed.), *op. cit.*, Chapter V.

the fundamental features of all motor performance, viz., speed, patterns of coördination, and accuracy of movement.

B. PERCEPTION: The same general course of events has been found to hold true of what is commonly called the development of perception. This development involves two processes, viz., (i) the gradual perfection of those organs and structures by means of which stimulus-patterns can become effective in regulating the behavior of the child, and (ii) the progressive translation of the general environment of the child into a large number of definite stimulus-objects.

Within two or three years after birth, the visual apparatus will have acquired all of those fundamental skills which will be prophetic of its future competence. It is believed, for example, that a new-born child is not much more than barely sensitive to differences in brightness and perhaps to rough differences in areas and distances. Within a few months, however, most infants will have learned to distinguish a multitude of particular shapes and sizes, and certainly by the end of the first year they can distinguish near objects from far objects and many other spatial and temporal features of the environment with a fair measure of accuracy.[50]

The rapid development of perception is revealed in the fact that, by the end of the first year, most children are able to distinguish between, and sometimes to name the difference between, letters of the alphabet, even though they are printed in small type. Long before this, of course, all children can identify a large variety of the more common objects about the household. The magnitude of this achievement will be realized only if the student can think of himself as devoid of all skill in distinguishing shapes from distances and rates of movement. If it were possible to imagine oneself at this low level of perceptual skill and then to set oneself at the task of acquiring proficiency in all these respects, one could get a partial glimpse of the amount of training which has been assimilated, often prior to the end of the first year.[51] The teacher, even in the first grade, takes many of these skills for granted. Sometimes, they are so much taken for granted that further improvement in them is more a by-product of training than a direct product.

The same considerations hold true of auditory, tactual, and other forms of perception. Within a few days after birth an infant prob-

---

[50] Cf. Koffka, K., *The Growth of the Mind*. New York: Harcourt, Brace and Co., 1924, Chapter III.
[51] Cf. Shirley, M. M., "Locomotor and Visual-manual Functions in the First Two Years," in Murchison, C. (Ed.), *op. cit.,* Chapter V.

THE BEGINNINGS OF THE EDUCATIVE PROCESS

ably hears most of the sounds that occur around him, but it is not known that he can distinguish them accurately from one another or identify the position of the sounding object. Certainly by the end of the first year he has made an immense amount of progress in these two respects, and by the time he is three years old he will have acquired a fairly large vocabulary in the sense that he can react adequately to words spoken to him and to the sounds made by a variety of objects around him.[52]

Just as specialized types of action emerge out of a larger pattern of action, so specialized and discrete stimulus-patterns emerge out of a more generalized pattern.[53] This fact used to be described in the saying that the infant is probably surrounded by a "big, blooming, buzzing confusion." The point is that, from the very first, the physiological and nervous apparatus necessary to perception is no doubt available, but preschool training must point the way toward differential types of response to specific parts of the whole pattern of events in which the child is placed.

C. ATTENTION: A further piece of psychological equipment has already been implied in the facts just mentioned. By the time a child has reached the age of three, it can respond differentially to a great many words spoken to it by the persons around it. It can also respond differentially to a large number of objects perceived through other sensory channels. Now, it happens that no child ever attempts to respond to all of these objects and events at one and the same moment. Neither does it make an effort to respond to any single object or event by using all of the skills that have been acquired. In other words, the whole range of events described by stimulus-situations, response-patterns, and paths of conduction in the nervous system displays a high degree of selectivity. A definite object calls out a definite response, and a moment later some other object has called out another response.

This feature of human and animal behavior has often been described by the word "attention."[54] It used to be thought that attention named a special faculty of the mind, but it is now argued that it names a special property of the relation between objects and the behaving animal.[55] This property has been acquired, in part,

---

[52] The experimental literature on the development of language has been summarized by McCarthy, D., "Language Development," in Murchison, C. (Ed.) *op. cit.,* Chapter VIII.

[53] Cf. Koffka, K., *op. cit.,* Chapter III.

[54] Cf. Washburn, M. F., *The Animal Mind* (3rd. ed.). New York: The Macmillan Co., 1926, Chapter XII.

[55] Some of the essential facts about the history of the concept of attention can be found in Titchener, E. B., *The Psychology of Feeling and Attention.* New York: The Macmillan Co., 1924, *passim.*

because of the events mentioned above, viz., the progressive individuation of discrete stimulus-patterns out of the total context of events within which the child is placed, and in part, because of the fact that the nervous system of the child is characterized by a unique mode of functioning described by the words "facilitation" and "inhibition." [56] That is, whenever an adequate set of connections has been established between a given stimulus-pattern and a specific mode of action, there will be a tendency for these connections to assert themselves over other connections and a parallel tendency for other connections to be weakened or inhibited. We shall return to this phase of development in a later chapter. We propose here only to point out the fact that the word "attention" does describe one of the important modes of psychological operation which has its beginnings in the nature of nervous function and which may, if properly tutored, come to a fairly efficient level of serviceability during the preschool years.

As every teacher knows, this equipment stands out as a major feature of schoolroom procedure, for, by precept and by example, teachers are told to gain and to hold the attention of their students. The art of gaining and holding the attention does not depend, however, so much on further perfection of the processes of facilitation and inhibition, that is, on one of the modes of nervous operation that makes attention possible, as on the services rendered by these modes of operation in different classroom situations.

D. MOTIVES: There is another set of factors which makes it possible for particular stimulus-situations to act in a selective manner. These factors are sometimes overlooked by teachers of preschool youngsters even though it is obvious that three- or four-year-olds are immensely interested in the objects and events which are happening around them rather than simply attending to them. As we have seen, the neonate is moved to action mostly by events that occur within its own body and, especially, within its alimentary canal. It is now known that these events in the alimentary canal make up a single group within a whole class of events which can be described as urges, desires, drives, or motives.[57]

Among the desires most frequently described are the desire for food and for liquids, the desire for activity, and the desire for rest. As we shall see later on, there are some persons who hold that,

[56] Cf. Freeman, G. L., *op. cit.,* Chapter XXI.
[57] A good description of desires has been given by Dorcus, R. M., and Schaffer, G. W., *Textbook of Abnormal Psychology.* Baltimore: The Williams and Wilkins Co., 1934, Chapter V. See also Tolman, E. C., "The Nature of the Fundamental Drives." *J. Abnorm. and Soc. Psychol.,* 1926, XX, 349-358.

THE BEGINNINGS OF THE EDUCATIVE PROCESS

among preschool children and even at still earlier ages, the desire for sex expression is of first-rate importance.[58] In any case, every normal child displays physiological hungers or bodily needs which serve as highly important sources of action. It is now supposed that these hungers and needs are the primitive sources out of which all motives and purposes may be derived.

It will be the function of a later chapter to describe in more detail the machinery by which this transition is effected.[59] In the meantime, it is only necessary to assert that the psychological equipment of the preschool child does include a considerable variety of incentives to action other than those which issue from the "attention value" of stimulus-patterns in the environment of the child. The student knows, for example, that every preschool child is almost incessantly at play. As a matter of fact, playful activities are so incessant that it is supposed to be necessary to attribute them to some native driving force or agent. Students of education often speak, therefore, of the play instinct.[60] Then, too, most preschool children have a great variety of special interests, derived partly from urges or desires and partly from training. Pending a further description of these matters, we leave them for the moment with the comment that the word "interest" and the phrase "the play instinct" mark only two ways of giving witness to a very important type of psychological equipment, viz., selectivity between possible stimulus-connection-response patterns.

E. EMOTIONALIZED ACTION: Closely related to the desires just mentioned, there is that whole domain of human nature which can be identified by the words "feeling," "mood," and "emotion." The preschool child, like his elders, and like a good many of the lower animals, is happy or unhappy, satisfied or displeased, angry or calm, and frightened or placid. He differs, however, from the neonate by the notable variety of his feelings and moods or, more accurately, in the tremendous variety of objects and events which will excite moody or emotionalized action—indeed, it is not possible to use any of the above expressions with reference to a new-born infant. That is, it is not possible to use them unless one already knows the char-

---

[58] Cf. Freud, S., *New Introductory Lectures on Psychoanalysis.* New York: W. W. Norton and Co., 1934, *passim.*
[59] See below, Chapter Five. Consult, also, Dashiell, J. F., *Fundamentals of Objective Psychology.* Boston: Houghton Mifflin Co., 1928, Chapter VIII.
[60] Many current beliefs about the nature and functions of play date from Groos, K., *The Play of Animals* (trans. by E. L. Baldwin). New York: D. Appleton-Century Co., 1898; Groos, K., *The Play of Man* (trans. by E. L. Baldwin). New York: D. Appleton-Century Co., 1901. For a more recent appraisal, see Curti, M. W., *op. cit.,* Chapter XI.

acter of the stimulus-situations which excite the infant or which make him more placid.[61]

A major fraction of a day in the life of a new-born infant is spent in sleeping. A small amount of waking time is spent in activity, most of which is initiated within its own body. Some of this activity may be emotionalized in the sense that it is highly intensified and restless or even energetic, on the one hand, or highly becalmed and placid, on the other. Situations which will bring about emotionalized forms of action in the preschool child have no such effect at all upon the neonate. Apparently, then, a considerable amount of learning has taken place between the first day of birth and the third or fourth years, for there is immense variability in the emotionalized actions of the preschool child, especially when it is making social contacts.[62]

In order to realize the profound significance of this change, we may ask the student to do for himself again that which was asked above, viz., to try to fancy himself devoid of all fears, angers, jealousies, rivalries, discontents, and satisfactions in the presence of the objects with which he is most familiar. If the student's fancy can go this far, then he may try to imagine what it would mean to learn how to fear the dark, a loud noise, or a dominant person, how to feel jealous of another person, or to try to emulate him, how to be unhappy because of a low grade in a course, or because of an insult, how to be satisfied when certain words are spoken to him by a friend, or how to secure some of the pleasures from an aesthetic object.

The point is that the preschool child, even though he has lived for only three or four years, has acquired, as a part of his psychological equipment, a rich variety of feelings or of emotionalized levels of response with respect to the objects and events around him. The most disturbing feature of this phase of early training lies in the fact that many forms of emotionalized action become highly stabilized long before the child enters the schoolroom. Moreover, many of them mark the source of some of the most difficult problems the teacher will have to solve.[63] These problems are known as the problems of "mental hygiene" and we shall give them the attention they deserve in Chapter Eighteen.

[61] Sherman, M., and Sherman, I. C., *op. cit.,* Chapter II.
[62] Cf. Jones, M. C., "Emotional Development," in Murchison, C. (Ed.), *op. cit.,* Chapter VI.
[63] Cf. Sherman, M., *Mental Hygiene and Education.* New York: Longmans, Green and Co., 1934, *passim.* Also Symonds, P. M., *Mental Hygiene of the School Child.* New York: The Macmillan Co., 1934.

THE BEGINNINGS OF THE EDUCATIVE PROCESS

F. PROBLEM-SOLVING: When asked about it, a mature person will usually say that he takes most pride in his ability to get himself out of a difficult situation by hitting upon some new tool or upon some new combination of skills, or by making some new arrangement of the situation itself. In other words, we all like to congratulate ourselves on our status as rational animals or upon our ability to solve problems. A new-born infant, however, is almost, if not quite, wholly devoid of this piece of psychological equipment. It has no past experience upon which it may draw for guidance in meeting a new situation, and neither does it display any ability to reconstruct the situations which surround it so as to achieve ends that could not be achieved without such reconstruction. It does not even enjoy the ability to discern similarity among objects which, in most respects, are dissimilar to one another. In other words, it has no concepts, it draws no comparisons, it passes no judgments on objects, and it makes no abstractions.[64]

By the end of the third year, a great many of these things will have been done over and over again. Even a two-year-old child can sometimes discern and react adequately to those respects in which dissimilar objects may be similar to one another. It is possible for some two-year-old children to invent a tool or devise a method for solving a problem. It may have learned that out of one box, one chair, and one table, the concept of unity or of singleness may be derived. It is frequently able to overcome difficulties by reconstructing the stimulus-situation so as to avoid the difficulty, as in taking a roundabout path to an objective. Moreover, it can sometimes bring about quick changes in previously acquired modes of action, changes that are suggestive, not so much of previous learning or of habit, as of genuine problem-solving.

The ability to solve problems, then, must be counted as a part of the psychological equipment of the preschool child. It is equipment which, although dependent upon special types of nervous function, has been acquired subsequent to birth and owes its origin and its state of development to the educative influences that have been brought to bear upon the child during the preschool years.[65]

G. SOCIALIZED BEHAVIOR: There is one further characteristic of the preschool child which should be brought into this preliminary appraisal of early stages of development. The new-born infant is,

[64] Cf. Dewey, J., *How We Think* (2nd. ed.). Boston: D. C. Heath and Co., 1933, *passim*.
[65] Cf. Peterson, J., "Learning in Children," in Murchison, C. (Ed.), *op. cit.*, Chapter X.

for all practical purposes, wholly unaware of the presence or the social significance of other persons. It remains unaware of these persons as persons for several months. This fact means that another child or an adult can be nothing more than an additional object in the whole environment of the child. Even when the infant begins its social recognition of other persons it can concern itself with only one such person. By the end of the first year, however, the distinction between persons and things has been drawn with a considerable degree of accuracy, and from that time forward almost everything that it does will bear social meaning.[66]

Here again we find evidence that a large variety of psychological changes have been taking place in it; but of these changes we shall speak of only one group at the moment, viz., that which has led to the child's identification of itself as an entity or a person distinct from other objects and events. In short, we may say that the concept of "selfhood" constitutes one of the many pieces of equipment which will emerge during the preschool years. To be sure, there are some who would argue that the child has recognized himself as an independent personality from the very first; but there is no experimental evidence to show that this is the case. On the contrary, the origin and the early development of the self and of most of the traits which may be characterized as personality traits is one of the products of the preschool educational program.[67]

As an example, we may take those attitudes or dispositions which are often known as introversion and extroversion. The former describes the fact that some children are bashful, diffident, uncertain in the presence of other children, and disposed to find their chief interests within themselves. The latter refers to the fact that some children are aggressive, forward, full of initiative, and mightily interested in the objects and events around them. It used to be supposed that differences of this type must be innate or hereditary, but it has now been shown abundantly that they are mostly a product of the daily contacts which children make with one another.[68] The same facts hold true of selfishness, jealousy, honesty, friendliness, and all other dispositions or attitudes associated with the concept of personality. In short, then, a living being which, on the day of its birth, is impersonal and asocial in all of its attitudes, will have be-

---

[66] Cf. Bühler, C., "The Social Behavior of Children," in Murchison, C. (Ed.), *op. cit.*, Chapter IX.
[67] Curti, M. W., *op. cit.*, Chapter XIV.
[68] Marston, L. R., "The Emotions of Young Children: An Experimental Study in Introversion and Extroversion." *Univ. of Iowa Stud. in Child Welfare*, 1925, III (No. 3), 7-99.

THE BEGINNINGS OF THE EDUCATIVE PROCESS

come, by the third and fourth years, highly personalized and highly socialized.[69]

3. *Plasticity:* All of the suggestions and intimations that have just been made about the psychological equipment of the preschool child will be stated more concisely and put into practical teaching situations in the following chapters. In the meantime, we propose to give the student an impression of the general character of the changes which may occur between infancy and the first years of schooling under the influence of educative processes which are not often called educative and which are certainly not formal. If we have become keenly aware of the great difference between the neonate and the three- or four-year-old, we shall see almost at once that the possibility of making such a difference suggests a very important fact about human nature, viz., its extraordinary plasticity, flexibility, or fluidity.

The highly plastic character of the human infant has, as a matter of fact, been recognized for a long time, and it is often used as an explanation of the large difference between the human species and the lower animals.[70] The human infant is of such a character that it can learn with great speed, and this is the fact which makes human nature so highly educable. Many of the lower animals are not only more mature at birth but more highly individuated in their actions. This is to say that post-natal environmental situations are much less effective in determining the final character of the adult animal than is the case with the human species. Moreover, most of the lower animals can hardly compare with the human animal in that rich supply of physical and nervous instruments in terms of which behavior of a psychological type is made possible.[71]

The plasticity of the human infant has been abundantly revealed, perhaps, in the above description of the psychological equipment of the preschool child. If we review this equipment briefly, we may say that the preschool child has learned how to use most of the members of its body in fairly skilful ways without interference from other members. This condition is to be compared with that of a new-born infant which, in making its responses, must move practically every member of its body at one and the same moment. The preschool child has learned how to react in these various ways to multiplied hundreds of specific stimulus-situations.

[69] Cf. Murphy, G., and Murphy, L. B., *Experimental Social Psychology*. New York: Harper and Bros., 1931, Chapter VI and *passim*.
[70] Cf. Fiske, J., *The Meaning of Infancy*. Boston: Houghton Mifflin Co., 1909, *passim*.
[71] Cf. Herrick, C. J., *op. cit., passim*.

There are, perhaps, no such specific stimulus-patterns for a new-born infant. Certainly, there are none which have social value. As we have said, most of its actions are the result of bodily needs, and if external events have any effect at all in regulating its behavior, they must do so only in a highly generalized manner. Gradually, however, the total context of the infant is broken down into an immense number of more local stimulus-patterns with which specified modes of response, including verbal actions, become associated. Moreover, the preschool child has been changed by its experiences with objects and events so that some of them can become and remain, for at least a short period of time, prepotent over others. The objects and events that will be selected, that is, that will direct attention or arouse an interest, differ greatly from those that are most potent for the new-born infant. In the latter case, the events in the alimentary canal are almost always the most important.[72] In the former, a color, a plaything, a spoken word, a moving object, a sentence on the board, a word to be spelled, or a sum to be added can become, for short periods of time, more important than hunger or thirst.

This change in the relative importance of the objects that lead to action, together with rapid fluctuations of attention from one to another, may be described as a shifting of attention or as a shifting of interest, or as a shifting of desires, incentives, motives, and purposes. In every one of these respects, however, the preschool child has passed far beyond the vegetative level of existence on which the infant lives. This passage is certainly a witness to the extraordinary plasticity of human nature.

The most that one can do with the new-born infant, so far as emotionalized types of action are concerned, is to soothe or excite it. When it is soothed, it remains more or less at rest, smiling slightly, cooing and gurgling on occasion, or gently moving various parts of its body. When it is excited, it may cry, jerk restlessly from side to side, or otherwise wriggle and struggle. Its remarkable degree of plasticity is revealed in the fact that these two extremes in behavior will have become, within three or four years, differentiated into an immense number of more localized types of mood and of emotionalized action and attitude, and almost inevitably associated with an equally immense variety of stimulus-patterns. The same impression about human nature is gained from the above description of the development of ability in problem-solving and

---

[72] Cf. Blatz, W. E., "The Physiological Appetites," in Murchison, C. (Ed.), *op. cit.*, Chapter XVIII.

THE BEGINNINGS OF THE EDUCATIVE PROCESS

from the development of personality traits. In other words, there is more truth than jest in the statement that a major share of the educative processes can become effective long before the child has ever entered a formal school system.

If once more we may let our imaginations run freely, let us suppose that, at the age of four years, we have suddenly been deprived of the ability to utter some three or four thousand words, to walk, run, and jump, to throw or handle any kind of an object, to balance ourselves on a bicycle or on one foot, to hold our heads erect, to distinguish between five or six thousand words uttered by some other person, to distinguish near sounds from remote sounds, to distinguish between large objects and small, to distinguish between the shapes of objects or the shapes of letters, to locate accurately the point of contact made by an object on the skin, to remain wholly indifferent to most of the events that are happening around us, to be afraid of some objects and aggressive toward others, to distinguish one person from another, to detect similarities amid differences and draw comparisons between unlike objects, to solve simple problems, to remember the events of yesterday or of yesteryear and to use them in moderating our reactions to the same objects today, to be kind, envious, angry, friendly, respectful, and jealous.

If we may read ourselves into this measure of psychological poverty, and if, having done so, we propose to acquire all of these possessions anew, we shall see clearly enough, first, that we must presuppose an extraordinary amount of plasticity in human nature and, second, that the psychological equipment of the preschool child has been remarkably improved over the equipment of the new-born child.[73] One might almost be tempted to say that the teaching tasks which begin when the child formally enters the school system are, by all odds, the simplest which have to be faced.

The pupil who comes to the first grade already knows how to grasp a pencil, sit in a chair, posture his body, and make all of the other movements that are necessary to school conduct. He already knows how to see and discriminate between the objects in the room even to the extent of knowing, in some cases, the difference in the stimulus value of the letters and numbers which are printed in his books or which are placed on the blackboard. He has acquired some facility in paying attention to some objects rather than to others, and he has developed a wide range of interests and preferences. Long before the teacher first brings his influence to bear upon a growing child, the child's primary tissue needs have been converted

[73] Cf. Goodenough, F. L., *op. cit.*, Chapters XII and XIII.

into intentions and motives which he may use to good advantage in his daily schoolroom procedure. The child has already acquired a good many essential concepts, he is able to see the relation between objects which may be almost wholly different from one another, and he can solve a variety of simple problems. He has a personality in the sense that he is timid, bashful, alert, eager, conscientious, patient, friendly, loyal, selfish, jealous, envious, suspicious, honest, or egotistical.

Let us conclude, then, that the problems of educational psychology that arise during the preschool years are as important, if not more so, than any that may arise during the later years. They are important because common methods of drawing curves of growth show greater degrees of acceleration in growth in the years immediately following birth than at any other time. This fact will become abundantly clear as we pass on from chapter to chapter.[74]

4. *Fixity:* The word "fixity" is often thrown into contrast against the word "plasticity." It is important that the student have in mind the significance of the word, partly because it is easy to let the flexibility of human nature blind one to those features of human nature which are not flexible, and partly because the word "fixity" itself has often been badly misused.

A. FIXITY AND ORIGINAL NATURE: As an example of its misuse, we may think for a moment of that whole group of problems named by the words "original nature," "instinct," "innate tendencies," "innate ideas," and even "human nature" itself. All of these terms imply that there are some things about a person that may be called inevitable because they are a result of his heredity. If, however, the student will run over again the preceding sections of this chapter, he ought to get the impression that the concept of original nature and even the concept of instinct must be changed.

As a single example, we may refer to our comments on the differences between the introvert and the extrovert. Most persons would say that dispositions of this type are original or innate, but we have seemed to argue that they are acquired. In a later chapter it will become still clearer that they must be acquired. Moreover, it will be seen that, because of the studies that have been made on the origin and development of a vast number of other traits and dis-

[74] Cf. Gesell, A., *The Mental Growth of the Pre-school Child.* New York: The Macmillan Co., 1926; *Infancy and Human Growth.* New York: The Macmillan Co., 1929. Also Baldwin, B. T., "Physical Growth and School Progress: A Study in Experimental Education." *Bull. U. S. Bur. Educ.,* 1914 (No. 10); "The Relation between Mental and Physical Growth." *J. Educ. Psychol.,* 1922, XIII, 193-203.

THE BEGINNINGS OF THE EDUCATIVE PROCESS

positions, the teacher must get an entirely new idea of the influence of the educative process in giving direction to the growth pattern.

In brief, it begins to look as though the word "instinct" should be dropped out of educational theory and practice altogether.[75] Moreover, the terms "original nature" and "innate ideas" can now be placed in an entirely new setting. Instead of saying that any attitude or action whose history is not known must, on that account alone, be instinctive or original, the teacher ought now to confess that no aspect of human nature should be called native or original until it has been definitely shown to be almost, if not quite, wholly independent of the processes of training during the preschool years. When we draw a contrast, therefore, between fixity and plasticity, it should not be supposed that we are drawing a contrast between instinct and learning. Subject to the facts which are to be mentioned in a later chapter, we shall not even say that a contrast can be drawn between original nature and learning.

B. ACQUIRED FIXITY: There is, however, another way to describe the meanings in the word "fixity." This way is suggested by the fact that the preschool child does have all of the pieces of psychological equipment described above and a good many others besides. Moreover, it is fairly certain that a great many of these pieces of equipment, that is, a great many of his attitudes, dispositions, habits and skills, emotionalized forms of action, and other traits will be with him when he becomes a mature person.

We may infer from this fact that the word "fixity" still has an important descriptive value both for psychology and for education. It is important to note, however, that its descriptive value is now gained for another reason than that which has been commonly held by educators. As we have just said, the older reason for the descriptive value of the word "fixity" was found in traditional concepts about the impelling power of original nature and instinct. Now it must be found in the great speed of preschool training, and in the fact that the results of this training will have become more or less permanent even before the child enters the schoolroom.[76]

There are several useful illustrations of this conclusion. For example, we have said above that a new-born infant displays practically no original or native fears. A three- or four-year-old child does

---

[75] Cf. Dunlap, K., "Are There Any Instincts?" *J. Abnorm. Psychol.*, 1919, XIV, 307-311; "The Identity of Instinct and Habit." *J. of Phil.*, 1922, XIX, 85-99; *Habits, Their Making and Unmaking.* New York: Liveright Publishing Corp., 1932, Chapters I and II.

[76] In a later chapter, we shall find still another view of the nature of fixity which results from early experience. This is a view which has come from Freudian Psychology. See below, Chapter Eighteen.

express such fears.[77] He may have a pronounced fear of the dark, of fire, of certain species of animals, or of his fellow human beings. If there are no pronounced fears, he is almost certain to have a variety of feelings of shyness in the presence of other people or in the presence of a good many objects and situations. He may be shy of the water, shy of high places, shy of bodily contact, or shy of falling. We may say again that a new-born infant knows nothing about either these fears or these feelings of shyness unless it be of falling, for if the support under an infant is suddenly removed, it will make somewhat the same types of movement that it will make when it is angered. As everyone knows, one or more of these fears or feelings of shyness may persist throughout the life history of a person, once they have become established. They are not only apt to persist, but they will often place a definite handicap upon a person. Undue shyness in the presence of other people, for example, is a trait which accompanies many people as long as they live.

As another illustration of the fixity which may issue from preschool training, let us take the so-called competitive instinct. That competition is truly an instinct has been so plain to some people that they have established whole systems of social organization, of economics, and of politics upon it.[78] There is, however, a good deal of experimental data available regarding this attitude, and it now seems possible to say that the more extreme forms of competition, at least, must certainly be a result of teaching attitudes which have prevailed during the preschool years.[79]

Competition is, of course, an easy and effective method of securing higher degrees of motivation, both among preschool children and among adults, and it may be, therefore, that a sound philosophy of education should accept those modes of early training which initiate this trait and strengthen it. This is, however, a matter of educational philosophy. The point we wish to make is that, even though the infant and the preschool child may be highly plastic, this very plasticity lends itself to the quick freezing of traits and attitudes long before a child enters the formal school system.

C. PLASTICITY AND FIXITY: We may conclude, then, that the first-grader is a curious combination of plasticity and fixity. He will be plastic in the sense that he can still learn quickly how to read, how to write, how to do simple sums, how to draw, and how

---

[77] Cf. Hagman, E. R., "A Study of Fear of Children of Preschool Age." *J. Exper. Educ.*, 1932, I, 110-130.

[78] For an appraisal of instinct theories in social psychology, see Dunlap, K., *Civilized Life*. Baltimore: The Williams and Wilkins Co., 1934, *passim*.

[79] Murphy, G., and Murphy, L. B., *op. cit.*, Part II.

THE BEGINNINGS OF THE EDUCATIVE PROCESS

to sing. Having learned these and other essential skills, he will be able to pass on to the content subjects, and thus become acquainted with a considerable proportion of the information which ought to be the property of a well-educated and cultured person. That is, the equipment he gains can be used for a great many different purposes. The formal school system, then, has, as one of its large tasks, the completion of a process which has been initiated and which has gone on apace long before the child is ready for the more formal modes of training. The teacher must always recognize, however, that the plasticity upon which he can depend has already resulted in large measures of fixity.

This conclusion becomes of extreme importance when we remember that fixity will be characteristic of many of the methods of working, and especially of personal and social traits and dispositions which will be far more significant than sheer information in giving a person his proper place in the social group. In order to illustrate this point, we may look ahead for a moment to our discussion of the sources of delinquency among young people, and to the inadequacy of reëducation at this level. It is now abundantly clear that those traits which will make a child delinquent are traits which have reached a considerable measure of fixity very early in life.[80] It has also become clear that not much can be done to help a delinquent child to escape from its previous training unless the processes of reëducation include a new and highly favorable environment which can be brought to bear upon the delinquent over a long period of time.[81] In other words, the plasticity of which we have spoken decreases rapidly as a person grows older. This means that reëducation during the adolescent and post-adolescent periods is a slow process. It is almost, if not quite, as slow as are some of the processes of adult education.

These facts present a very interesting situation. They argue that the formal school system must spend a considerable amount of time and energy in the attempt to modify traits and dispositions which have already been acquired by a child before he has entered the formal system. It is not helpful to try to excuse this situation by saying that the parents of a child must be held wholly responsible for those measures of fixity which he will display when he enters the kindergarten or the first grade. The parents are, of course, responsible, but this shifting of responsibility does not alter, in any way whatsoever, the scope of educational psychology.

[80] Cf. Curti, M. W., *op. cit.,* Chapters XII and XIII.
[81] Cf. Healy, W., and Bronner, A. F., *Delinquents and Criminals, Their Making and Unmaking.* New York: The Macmillan Co., 1926, *passim.*

38 INTRODUCTION TO EDUCATIONAL PSYCHOLOGY

In brief, then, we have tried to point out during this entire chapter that a sound educational psychology can be based only upon child psychology or upon the genetic point of view. Even though the teacher in the formal school system does not get acquainted with children until they are six or seven years of age, the things he will attempt to do with them must be modified by the information that he can assemble concerning the processes of training that have already taken place.[82]

IV. SUMMARY

It has been the purpose of this chapter to help the student to get an impression of the general character of the earlier sections of the growth pattern rather than to give him a list of facts to be remembered.[83] The impression for which we have been seeking concerns the essential continuity of growth, the curious mixture of plasticity and fixity, the relation between the growth pattern and all of the formal and informal agents which give a precise direction to the pattern, and the relation which earlier parts of the pattern must sustain to later parts.

In order to make the impression complete, we ought, perhaps, to follow our brief study of the preschool child with a similar study of later childhood, with a study of the adolescent, and with a study of the earlier stages of maturity.[84] Since, however, most of these phases of development will be taken account of in later chapters, we shall omit them for the time being. Instead, let us try to crystallize the purpose of this first chapter by drawing certain comparisons between the new-born infant or the preschool child and a mature person.

At a good many points during this chapter we have directly said, and at a good many other points we have implied, that the essential psychological modes of function which will be characteristic of the adult reach fairly stable levels of excellence before the first years of schooling.[85] The student will not be convinced of this fact, perhaps, unless he sees clearly the distinction we have drawn between

---

[82] For example, one of the recent books on educational psychology carries the title "Principles of Mental Development." Cf. Wheeler, R. H., and Perkins, F. T., *Principles of Mental Development*. New York: T. Y. Crowell Co., 1932, *passim*.
[83] Cf. Goodenough, F. L., *Developmental Psychology*. New York: D. Appleton-Century Co., 1934, *passim*.
[84] As, for example, Brooks, F. D., *Psychology of Adolescence*. Boston: Houghton Mifflin Co., 1929, *passim*.
[85] Cf. Hollingworth, H. L., *Mental Growth and Decline*. New York: D. Appleton-Century Co., 1927, *passim*. This book divides growth into successive periods and gives, therefore, cross-sections rather than a timewise sequence of the growth pattern.

THE BEGINNINGS OF THE EDUCATIVE PROCESS

the major modes of psychological function and the various services rendered to a person by the use of these functions.

We may illustrate this difference once more by looking at some of the habits and skills that a child acquires fairly early in his career. The child who is just ready to enter the school system has learned how to stand, walk, balance himself, kick, run, throw, manipulate objects, in some cases use his eye muscles in the art of reading, write or, at least, scribble, use his vocal machinery in uttering a fairly large number of words, and otherwise adapt himself, so far as his motor equipment is concerned, to many of the more common objects and events around him. He has not, of course, reached the highest levels of skill in all of these respects, and neither has he acquired all of the different skills he will possess when he becomes a mature person. It is important to note, however, that, barring sheer range of information, the ground that has been covered before the sixth year is probably more extensive than the ground that will be covered after the sixth year.

In other words, from the sixth year onward, the child is not increasing so much the number of his skills or the quality of the skills already acquired as he is increasing the serviceability of these skills in variable situations. This fact appears to hold true, in particular, of what we shall describe later on as some of the essential properties of habits and skills, viz., their speed, their coördination or rhythm, and their accuracy. As we shall see in the next chapter, most children acquire, at a fairly early age, preferred rates of movement for most of their habits. As a single instance, let us take rate of movement in the eye muscles during the act of reading. The chances are that the average child, by the time he has reached the fourth or fifth grade, will have acquired a definite pace habit in this respect. This pace habit does not represent the highest skill the child might reach, but only an average skill or a favored level of excellence which is a by-product of his training in the art of reading. An adult will be able to read a great many things a child cannot read, and he will be able, also, to use the motor phase of his visual functions in a great many situations and for a great many purposes which still remain unknown to the child. The adult, however, will not differ greatly from the child in the absolute maturity of the perceptual skills that he uses.[86]

[86] For summaries of experimental work on eye movements during reading, see Tinker, M. A., "Eye Movement Duration, Pause Duration, and Reading Time." *Psychol. Rev.,* 1928, XXXV, 385-397; "Physiological Psychology of Reading," *Psychol. Bull.,* 1931, XXVIII, 81-98.

A further illustration of this phase of the difference between childhood and adulthood can be found in other types of perceptual skill. The child learns fairly early to distinguish one geometrical form from another, discriminate between different intensities of light and between color qualities, distinguish variable distances and sizes, distinguish between tones, note the relative positions of sounding objects, and otherwise use his sensory apparatus with a passable measure of excellence.[87] The adult will differ from the child in all of these respects, not by his greater skill, but by the greater variety of circumstances under which an attained level of excellence may be used. If we may refer again to the visual operations involved in reading, we may say that these operations do not have to be fundamentally changed or even increased in quality before the more mature person can learn a new language. If a person has acquired a given facility in the use of the visual apparatus for comprehending letters, words, and phrases, he will use approximately this same facility when he comes to study a foreign language.

In other words, as we have said above, the difference between the child and the adult is not so much a difference in actual skill as it is a difference in the variable services rendered to the person by the use of the skill. The child is using his visual adeptness in order to learn the English language at a given rate. The adult is using adeptness of the same type and of approximately the same degree of excellence for learning French, German, or Italian. We may say again, then, that the difference between the child and the adult is a difference which lies, for the most part, in the services rendered.[88] It must not be assumed, however, that such differences are insignificant. On the contrary, the distance between a small child and an adult is all but immeasurable.

One of the best illustrations, perhaps, of the distinction that can be drawn between fundamental modes of psychological operation, on the one hand, and the services rendered by these modes of operation, on the other, is to be found in problem-solving. Although the newborn infant does not display this trait, even small children show some signs of it. In other words, there is revealed in their intercourse with their environments those unique relations between stimuli and responses which are of the problem-solving type.[89] They can, for example, take note of, and react adequately to, the existence of similarity amid differences (abstraction or conception), they have

---

[87] Cf. Shirley, M. M., *op. cit.,* Chapter V.
[88] Cf. Wagoner, L. C., *op. cit.,* Chapter XX.
[89] Cf. Peterson, J., *Learning in Children,* in Murchison, C. (Ed.), *op. cit.,* Chapter X.

THE BEGINNINGS OF THE EDUCATIVE PROCESS 41

acquired a considerable variety of verbal substitutes for objects and for the relations between objects (ideas), and they are observed quickly to readjust their attitudes and actions to complex or puzzling situations.[90]

The chances are that these fundamental modes of operation are fairly well developed long before maturity is reached. The adult, however, having reached a given level of competence in these respects somewhere during his earlier periods of training, can use his competence in a larger number of situations or with more different types of material than is the case with the child. In other words, his problem-solving functions enable him to be more serviceable to himself and to society in a larger variety of situations.

The distinction we are drawing between the child and the adult is one that has long been drawn by teachers, but they have not, perhaps, fully realized its significance. In education, the distinction we are making has concerned the so-called tool subjects as opposed to the content subjects. Reading, writing, and arithmetic, for example, are called tool subjects. They are distinguished from the content subjects simply because, after a child has learned to read, his reading may be taken as a fundamental skill which can be used for the purpose of reading history, literature, civics, or philosophy. In the same way, arithmetic is called a tool subject because, after the child has learned some of the principles of arithmetical procedure, he can use these principles in a grocery store, in the bank, or in casting up his own accounts.[91]

It seems, however, that the distinction between tool subjects and content subjects fails to throw the emphasis, in preschool as opposed to high school and college education, where it should be thrown. It is convenient, of course, to speak of reading as a tool subject, for the word "reading" includes a number of different types of psychological operation. It avoids, therefore, the fallacy that writers in educational psychology often make, viz., of trying to study a growing child part by part. We mean to argue, however, that the full significance of the educative process, in so far as it affects the growth of a person, will be missed if the student does not see that even so complex an act as reading depends upon processes of development that may already have come to a practical limit fairly early in the growth pattern.

[90] It is now known that animals also possess considerable ability in these respects. Cf. Moss, F. A. (Ed.), *Comparative Psychology.* New York: Prentice-Hall, Inc., 1934, Chapter XI.
[91] Cf. Judd, C. H., *The Psychology of High School Subjects.* Boston: Ginn and Co., 1915, *passim.* Also Cole, L., *Psychology of the Elementary School Subjects.* New York: Farrar and Rinehart, Inc., 1934.

This fact may be illustrated clearly in the case of problem-solving. Partly because problem-solving has been attributed to the innate or intrinsic nature of the *mind,* and partly because very few persons have known how to go about the task of increasing facility in problem-solving, it is usually taken for granted that this type of psychological operation marks an uneducable phase of human nature. If the points of view expressed above have been convincing, it would seem that we ought to say that skill in problem-solving has come almost as a by-product from training periods which emphasize other types of psychological function. In short, the average teacher does not try to teach problem-solving during those years when teaching methods would be most effective. The child enters maturity, then, with a degree of competence in problem-solving which is not much more than a precipitate from teaching methods which have really aimed at other results.

We may, of course, dismiss this whole question by saying that arithmetic is a tool subject and geometry is a content subject which ought, because of their own nature, to develop problem-solving. It seems to be clear, however, that increased measures of problem-solving do not come in this way. We shall, therefore, in a later chapter, give this phase of the growth pattern the full attention that it deserves. As a matter of fact, it will be the function of all of the remaining chapters in this part of our study of educational psychology to survey some of the facts that are now known about the various phases of the growth pattern, in so far as the teacher has a part in it. For the present, we are interested primarily in the proposition that most of the essential psychological operations pass through a major part of their total history before the formal processes of education begin. This means that the function of the teacher in the schoolroom has not been so much to increase competency in the psychological functions as it has been to try to widen the horizon on which such competency as has already been acquired may be used. This is one of the facts which makes preschool education so significant a part of the whole domain of educational psychology.

READINGS

The main purpose of this chapter has been to give the student an impression of the beginnings of the educative process. Since the chapter rests upon experimental materials which may be unfamiliar, the student should, perhaps, supplement his study by making reference to other books in this field. The standard work in child psychology is Murchison, C. (Ed.), *Handbook of Child Psychology* (2nd ed.). Worcester, Mass.: Clark Univ.

THE BEGINNINGS OF THE EDUCATIVE PROCESS

Press, 1933. One or more of the following texts may be available: Stoddard, G. D., and Wellman, B. L., *Child Psychology*. New York: The Macmillan Co., 1934; Gesell, A., Thompson, H., and Armatruda, C. S., *Infant Behavior: Its Genesis and Growth*. New York: McGraw-Hill Book Co., 1934; Morgan, J. J. B., *Child Psychology* (Rev. ed.). New York: Farrar and Rinehart, Inc., 1934; Curti, M. W., *Child Psychology*. New York: Longmans, Green and Co., 1931; Johnson, B. J., *Child Psychology*. Springfield, Ill.: C. C. Thomas, 1932; Gesell, A., *The Mental Growth of the Pre-School Child*. New York: The Macmillan Co., 1925.

Later stages of the developmental pattern have been described by Brooks, F. D., *Psychology of Adolescence*. Boston: Houghton Mifflin Co., 1929; Garrison, K. C., *The Psychology of Adolescence*. New York: Prentice-Hall, Inc., 1934. A sweeping picture of the whole process of development from infancy to old age can be found in Goodenough, F. L., *Developmental Psychology*. New York: D. Appleton-Century Co., 1934. A division of the earlier part of the growth pattern into cross-sections, each of which is discussed as a unit, can be found in Hollingworth, H. L., *Mental Growth and Decline*. New York: D. Appleton-Century Co., 1927. A more general survey of genetic psychology has been supplied by Gilliland, A. R., *Genetic Psychology*. New York: The Ronald Press, 1933.

Since educational psychology cannot help but be modified by the various modes of approach to experimental psychology itself, the student should be prepared to acquaint himself with the different varieties of psychology. For this purpose, he may turn to Heidbreder, E. F., *Seven Psychologies*. New York: D. Appleton-Century Co., 1933, or to Woodworth, R. S., *Contemporary Schools of Psychology*. New York: The Ronald Press, 1931.

The student will find it helpful if, early in his study of educational psychology, he will plunge seriously into the vexing problems of heredity and environment. A good point of entrance will be found in Jennings, H. S., *The Biological Basis of Human Nature*. New York: W. W. Norton and Co., 1930. Another valuable book is Schwesinger, G. C., *Heredity and Environment: Studies in the Genesis of the Psychological Characteristics*. New York: The Macmillan Co., 1933.

A standard reference for factual material in the field of experimental psychology has been compiled by Murchison, C. (Ed.), *Handbook of General Experimental Psychology*. Worcester, Mass.: Clark Univ. Press, 1934.

CHAPTER TWO

THE DEVELOPMENT OF ACTIONS AND ATTITUDES

I. The Method of Sectioning

1. *Introduction:* The last chapter has given us a very general sketch of the early part of a typical growth pattern. We have, of course, barely touched the surface of a large field of research, but the most of our space must be given to more general problems in educational psychology than could come out of a study of the beginnings of the educative process alone.

The ideal way to go about our task, from this point forward, would require that we take real children in real teaching situations. Moreover, it would require that we keep the learner intact from the beginning of his education to the end. The intact person, however, is a very complex set of operations in an equally complex environment. No teacher ever deals now with one bodily movement, then with the perception of a single line or figure upon the blackboard, or yet again with an isolated act of discourtesy to a stranger. He must deal with an actual person in an actual situation. Both the person and the situation involve so many factors that it takes whole books to describe only a part of them. It will take the whole of this book to describe only that fraction of them that appear to be the most important to the teacher.

Obviously, however, a whole book cannot be written in a single sentence or in a single paragraph. This means that successive sentences and successive paragraphs must take up particulars which have been drawn for the moment from the complete pattern.[1] It means, also, that each of the chapters that are to follow must pay particular attention to one facet only of the whole person. As we move on, then, from our very general picture of the beginnings of the educative process to the topics which now lie before us, the student must constantly remind himself that each topic is but a single instance or one phase of growth which has been selected

[1] For a practical illustration of the difficult problems created by the study of particulars as opposed to the study of a total situation, see Link, H. C., *The New Psychology of Selling and Advertising*. New York: The Macmillan Co., 1932, Chapter IV and *passim*.

THE DEVELOPMENT OF ACTIONS AND ATTITUDES 45

from a whole configuration. That is, he must study educational psychology in the same way that he would study a series of sections drawn from the spinal cord. The student of physiology knows well enough that, when one section of the spinal cord is placed under the microscope, the instrument does not miraculously give him a picture of nerve tracts which run from one end of the whole system to the other. On the contrary, he gets single sections from which he can construct the whole. It is only necessary that he take enough sections to give him a true picture of those parts of the spinal cord which are not actually placed under observation. Eventually, of course, so many sections will have been studied as to make it almost fruitless to take further samples.

2. *Mind and Behavior:* It is our purpose, therefore, to take several sections out of the whole course of development. We could do this in two ways. On the one hand, we might divide the growth pattern crosswise and thus get a picture of the child at one year, at two years, at three years, and so on. On the other hand, we can divide growth longitudinally or from the timewise point of view. That is, we can assume that the whole developmental schedule is made up of part-schedules, each of which can be described on its own account but which represents, nevertheless, only a single phase of a configured whole. This method, which is the one we shall use, requires of us some statement as to what features of the whole growth pattern lend themselves to separation from the rest. This, then, is the first task of the present chapter.

We know whereof we speak when we say that we can take sections of a spinal cord. This part of the nervous system is a physical object like all other vital objects, but the situation is different when we speak of sections of human nature, for human nature appears to be partly physical and partly mental. In short, it is required of us that we speak briefly of mental events, on the one hand, and of the events known as stimulus-patterns, response-patterns, and types of connection and of relatedness between stimuli and responses, on the other.[2] During the actual course of any display of human nature, as, for example, in playing tennis, there are all types of stimulus-patterns operating on the player and as many types of response-patterns directed toward or in some other way related to, the stimulus-patterns. The whole sequence of behavior and of experience involved in playing a game of tennis is so complex that we simply cannot deal with it as a configured whole. It must be, like every

[2] Cf. Heidbreder, E. F., *Seven Psychologies.* New York: D. Appleton-Century Co., 1933, *passim.*

other segment of human action, divided into parts, if for no other reason than to promote ease of discussion.

Since we are not quite ready to discuss the different points of view which have been held concerning the nature of psychology, we shall simply make a few comments about a psychology which is defined as the science of the mind, as opposed to a psychology defined as the science of behavior.[3] In the first place, neither minds nor mental processes are observable except, perhaps, by the person who is at one and the same time the experimenter and the observer.[4] In the second place, all information concerning the minds of small children and of the lower animals must come by way of inference or analogy; that is, it must come by the method of extrapolation, and this is a hazardous method. In the third place, many of the terms used by students of the *mind* are wrapped up so completely in systems of philosophy and theology as to make them almost useless to a science. In the fourth place, the teacher is not so much interested in what pupils think about as in what they do and how they grow and in the devices that can be used to gain some measure of control over action and growth. In other words, if the reader will allow the author to lay aside, for the moment, the difficult question of the relation between thought and action, we may say that modern psychology leans heavily toward the study of conduct or behavior.

3. *Major Features of Behavior:* In addition to these matters, there are a number of other reasons why modern psychology is more behavioristic than the older psychologies. The student has already sensed these reasons from the general tone of the first chapter. In any case, before we perplex ourselves with difficult questions drawn from psychology proper, let us list and describe, as straightforwardly as we can, some of the major features of human behavior as they actually appear in the schoolroom and on the playground. Several suggestions pointing in this direction have already been presented.

A. ACTION PATTERNS: In the first place, it is clear that all persons attempt to adjust themselves to their environments by making a variety of bodily movements. These movements may simply maintain a posture, or they may get things done. The same movement may get a large number of different things done, and it may have all types of social significance. In any case, an educated person has

[3] Cf. Murchison, C. (Ed.), *Psychologies of 1930*. Worcester, Mass.: Clark Univ. Press, 1930.
[4] Cf. Washburn, M. F., "Introspection as an Objective Method." *Psychol. Rev.*, 1922, XXIX, 89-112. Also Titchener, E. B., "Prolegomena to a Study of Introspection." *Amer. J. Psychol.*, 1912, XXIII, 427-448; Lashley, K. S., "The Behavioristic Interpretation of Consciousness." *Psychol. Rev.*, 1923, XXX, 237-272, 329-353.

THE DEVELOPMENT OF ACTIONS AND ATTITUDES 47

learned to use his muscles in appropriate ways, and the present chapter will attempt to show how maturity in this phase of the whole growth pattern may be gained.[5]

Movement, of course, is made possible because contractile tissue operates on a bony framework which not only provides resistance, but also creates a great many levers throughout the body. There are, however, other features of movement which are dependent upon the properties of nerve tissue as well as upon the properties of muscles. There is, for example, a wide difference among various persons in the quickness with which they may react to a stimulus.[6] We commonly say that these differences are hereditary, and there are times when we speak of the instinctive quickness of a certain athlete. It is clear, of course, that quickness in reaction must depend, first, upon the total length of the path that has to be traced between a receptor and an effector and, second, upon the readiness with which the physico-chemical events can take place that have to do with the propagation of the nerve impulses.[7]

Chemistry has made us familiar with the fact that the speed of the reaction in a test tube depends upon the temperature at which the reaction takes place and upon the presence or absence of what are called catalyzers. This latter means of contolling the speed of chemical reactions is highly characteristic of a great many types of physiological activity. It would seem to follow, therefore, that speed of reaction might be determined by the presence or absence of catalytic agents rather than by the possession of some mythical force or agent that can be called an instinct.

Moreover, living tissue appears to be made up of an enormous variety of protoplasms. These, in turn, are based upon at least a score of amino acids which differ from one another in certain essential respects. It is not only conceivable but highly probable that the nerve tissues of various individuals must vary slightly in their molecular constitution so as to favor a given rate of metabolic process.[8] A further factor bearing upon rate of reaction is known as chronaxie. This word has been applied to differences in the sensitivity of muscle to the intensity and duration of a stimulus.[9] Various types of muscle in the body have different chronaxies.

[5] Cf. Watson, J. B., *Psychology from the Standpoint of a Behaviorist.* Philadelphia: J. B. Lippincott, 1924, *passim.*
[6] Cf. Garrett, H. E., *Great Experiments in Psychology.* New York: D. Appleton-Century Co., 1930, Chapter IX.
[7] Gould, A. G., and Dye, J. A., *Exercise and Its Physiology.* New York: A. S. Barnes and Co., 1932, Chapter V.
[8] Cf. Lillie, R. S., *Protoplasmic Action and Nervous Action.* Chicago: Univ. of Chicago Press, 1923, *passim.*
[9] Cf. Gould, A. G., and Dye, J. A., *op. cit.,* pp. 62 ff.

One of the theories of nerve function has it that the neurones, that is, the structural elements of which the nervous system is composed, are separated from one another by some sort of a functional resistance, but practically nothing is known of the events which cause this change in resistance or of the circumstances under which the resistance may be modified.[10] In any case, however, it is easier to think of differences in reaction time as bearing some analogy to the differences of the conductivity of various metals than it is to suppose that quickness is a function of an instinct or the product of a gene bearing various amounts of quickness. The genes, as we shall see, are chemical substances, and they would, therefore, determine the molecular constitution of the organs and tissues whose growth depends upon them. Quickness, then, would become one of the properties of nerve tissue in the same sense that conductivity is one of the distinguishing properties of certain metals.

Considerations of the same general type hold for that behavior trait called coördination.[11] It seems fairly clear that great athletes are characterized by extraordinary measures of flexibility or of muscular adaptability. It is also clear that the types of integration which makes adaptability possible depend upon the properties or functions of nerve tissue.[12] The balance that is struck between antagonists and synergists, together with the factors that determine rate of learning, would contribute, then, to an understanding of versatility in athletic and other motor performances. It is one thing, however, to say that great athletes appear because of these and other properties of organic tissue and quite another to say that some individuals are born with a set of athletic instincts.

Let us assume, then, that one of the part-schedules to be drawn from the whole pattern of growth is made up of motor equipment—of habits, skills, postures and other resources leading to action or conduct. For the moment, we shall assume that this equipment can be studied apart from the various personal and social services rendered by it.

B. STIMULUS-PATTERNS AND SENSATION: In the second place, the movements that a person makes always rise in response to a stimulus-situation. Most of these stimulus-situations occur within the body itself during the prenatal period of growth and for variable

---

[10] Cf. Herrick, C. J., *Neurological Foundations of Animal Behavior*. New York: Henry Holt and Co., 1924, *passim*.

[11] The classical work in this field is Sherrington, C. S., *The Integrative Action of the Nervous System*. New Haven: Yale Univ. Press, 1906, *passim*.

[12] Cf. Freeman, G. L., *Introduction to Physiological Psychology*. New York: The Ronald Press, 1934, Part III.

THE DEVELOPMENT OF ACTIONS AND ATTITUDES

periods after growth, but subject to the major principles of learning, it does not take long for a great variety of external situations to acquire the same function. To be sure, internal sources of stimulation continue their effectiveness throughout life, and many stimuli achieve rather stable relations to these internal conditions, but the development of the sense organs creates a wide variety of new sources of ingress to the reaction mechanisms of the body. A second group of essential psychological problems is created, therefore, by the development of the sensory apparatus and by the development of what are commonly called the powers of observation and discrimination. Training does make it possible to "open the windows of the soul" farther and farther.[13]

A more detailed picture of the development of the perceptual functions will reveal at least four part-processes. In the first place, the sense organs of the body and the various structures related to them increase gradually in maturity. This feature of development has already received some notice in the previous chapter. It requires a suitable measure of maturation in the eyes, the ears, and all of the other sense organs. As we shall see, however, even maturation of this type depends upon motor development and upon the creation of paths of conduction between the sense organs and the motor organs.

In the second place, the development of perception requires that large portions of the environment which surrounds a child, and which is at first wholly irrelevant or ineffective so far as its influence in initiating and regulating action is concerned, shall be changed into what we may call a relevant or an effective environment. These terms simply mean that objects and patterns of objects which at first have no influence upon the child acquire such an influence. The teacher commonly speaks of this phase of the development of perception in terms of an increase in the amount of knowledge or an increase in the range of information possessed by a child. A part of this phase of perceptual development calls for an increasing ability to draw minor distinctions between different objects. The student who knows something of the history of psychology will remember that many of the first experimental studies were related to this problem, for several different investigators tried to find out the least possible discriminations that a subject might make in intensities, qualities, or other properties of stimulus-patterns. These problems are known as the problems of psycho-physics.

In the third place, it looks as though the translation of an irrele-

[13] Cf. Murchison, C. (Ed.), *A Handbook of General Experimental Psychology*. Worcester, Mass.: Clark Univ. Press, 1934, Chapters XIII-XX.

vant environment into relevant or effective objects and patterns of objects comes by way of specialization and differentiation out of larger configurations of events rather than by way of adding one simple object to another. This is not to say, however, that if individuation has taken place there may not be further, subsequent processes of patterning or organization. After all, the world of objects that we know is not a world made up of items which are sharply separated from one another. On the contrary, a great many patterns are formed out of them. This book, for example, is made up of a very large number of words, but the words have been brought together into a new pattern which is of greater significance than any dictionary list of them could furnish.

In the fourth place, subsequent to both of the types of development just described, perceptual skill depends upon the discovery of relationships, comparisons, the detection of identities amid similarities, and the classification of objects into groups. In other words, some of the objects which initiate and regulate the course of behavior make up the class known as concepts.

Altogether, then, perceptual development is a highly complex matter. In the one direction, it looks toward the sense organs themselves and, in the other direction, it looks toward the gradual transformation of an undifferentiated environment into all of the discrete objects and patterns of objects which make up the domain of everyday experience. The entire process runs parallel with, and is reciprocally dependent upon, the development of particular modes of response. It is by no accident, then, that we speak of sensori-motor development. The most difficult phase of this problem, that is, the circumstances under which light waves, sound waves, and other types of "physical" events are transformed into the objects we directly experience, can well be left to the final chapter.

C. SELECTION: A description of the mechanisms of response, on the one hand, and of the mechanisms of stimulation, on the other, marks only the first step in the study of human nature. It marks, however, that step which enters into much of the educational psychology of the day, viz., an educational psychology based upon the stimulus-response formula for human conduct.[14] That is, there are a great many persons who hold that all of the problems of psychology and of education can be exhausted, first, by describing all possible modes of action, second, by describing all possible modes of stimu-

---

[14] Cf. Rexroad, C. N., *General Psychology for College Students*. New York: The Macmillan Co., 1929, *passim*. Also Gates, A. I., *Psychology for Students of Education*. New York: The Macmillan Co., 1930, *passim*.

THE DEVELOPMENT OF ACTIONS AND ATTITUDES 51

lus, and third, by describing or assuming the presence of connections between stimulus and response.[15]

In general outlines, the S-R formula does seem to state the general framework of conduct and experience, but the details of this framework can be seen only after several important types of relation between stimulus and response have been taken into account. The facts appear to be as follows. When a child in the schoolroom follows the instruction of his teacher to write down and work out the arithmetical sums placed on the blackboard, the instruction, the sums, and the general schoolroom environment can be taken as the stimulus-situation and the copying, together with the subsequent solution of the problems, can be taken as samples from the response-pattern. As we have said, however, the questions the psychologist would ask are hardly more than begun at this point. He will desire to know why the pupil reacts to the teacher rather than to any other feature of the whole situation, what the qualities of the response are that permit them to be called solutions to the problems, how the problems presented maintain their dominance over other types of action, and so on. In short, within the general range of events named by the words "stimulus" and "response," certain unique relationships are set up, and it is in these relationships that we shall discover the most important tasks of the teacher.

We shall return to this matter on another occasion. For the present, let us state briefly five features of the growth pattern that spring out of the situation just described. In the first place, even the most casual observation of human behavior will make it plain that no person uses all of the responses of which he is capable at one and the same moment. Moreover, no person responds to the whole range of effective objects and events at a single effort. On the contrary, selection is the rule. It is now one thing and then another which dominates in the initiation and regulation of behavior, and it is now one movement and then another which satisfies the flow of stimulus events.

There are two words which describe one phase of these facts, viz., "attention" and "interest." [16] Among other things, the word "attention" points to the fact that there are times when a moving object will be more apt to excite a response in a small child than a colored object will. The word "interest" implies that the moving

[15] Cf. Thorndike, E. L., *Educational Psychology."* New York: Columbia Univ. Press, 1913 (3 vols.). See Vol. I, *The Original Nature of Man.*
[16] The problems named by the word "attention" have had a confused history. See Titchener, E. B., *The Psychology of Feeling and Attention.* New York: The Macmillan Co., 1924, *passim.*

object will sometimes take precedence over the colored object because of some favorable disposition within the child itself.[17] In other words, interest and attention refer to sets of internal and external conditions which makes some objects prepotent over, or selected in preference to, others in the initiation and regulation of behavior. Obviously, no teacher can be really effective in his work until he knows what these conditions are, where they have had their origin, and how they may be controlled. The development of attention and interest, then, is the third major section we shall take of the whole child.

D. EMOTIONALIZED ACTION: The second feature of the unique relations that may obtain between stimuli and responses arises out of such facts as the following. There are some places in nature where the violence of an action stands in direct proportion to the violence of a "cause." Other things being equal, the distance covered by a golf ball is directly proportional to the weight and speed of the club at the moment of impact. There are other places, however, where the violence of action has no relation at all to the initiating "cause." When the trigger of a gun is released, the impact of the hammer has no points in common with the energy with which the shell leaves the chamber.

Almost all human action is more like this second instance than it is like the first. A very slight stimulus applied to the eye will sometimes cause a tremendously violent and long-continued series of movements. A part of this discrepancy between the energies of stimulus and the energies of response is due to the way in which the nervous system works, a way which will be described more fully in another chapter. A more significant part is due to the fact that human beings have special resources of energy which can be tapped for use in emergencies. When these resources are tapped, conduct and experience reveal that mode of behavior which is commonly described as emotional.[18]

It used to be thought that there were many objects and events which would call out an emotional response simply because it was a part of original nature to act in this way. As we have seen, however, the only type of situation which will normally excite an emotionalized form of action is a sudden or unexpected situation. It does not take long, however, for other situations to acquire this

[17] Cf. Pillsbury, W. B., *Attention*. New York: The Macmillan Co., 1908, Chapter IV.
[18] Cf. Cannon, W. B., *Bodily Changes in Pain, Hunger, Fear, and Rage*. New York: D. Appleton-Century Co., 1929, *passim*.

THE DEVELOPMENT OF ACTIONS AND ATTITUDES 53

function. In short, the emotional behavior of an adult is almost completely a product of the way in which it has been trained. Clearly, the origin and development of stimulus-response patterns of this type is of extreme importance to the individual and to society.[19]

E. MOTIVES: In the third place, in spite of the complexity and richness of the world into which a new-born child is introduced, and in spite of variations in attention and interest which lead to rapid fluctuations both in the stream of behavior and in the stream of initiating events, there are some objects and events which exercise a steady influence on conduct throughout the life of a person. A new-born infant, for example, does at least two things with persistence. It eats and it sleeps. If food is not forthcoming at regular intervals, it becomes more and more restless, it cries and, when older, it makes a variety of searching movements which will not cease until food has been found. In short, the infant is motivated. It is driven into action by the persistence of the hunger contractions in the walls of the stomach.[20] After food has been secured and after a period of gurgling comfort, it will usually fall asleep. The act of falling asleep is not a cessation of behavior but a response to another type of bodily need or drive, viz., the desire for rest.

As we shall see in a later chapter, these two needs must be supplemented by other needs. For the present, we wish only to point out that the principal needs of the body furnish the starting point for the study both of motives and of purposes. As the child grows older, other objects and events will acquire the same persistence in regulating the flow of behavior as is possessed by tissue needs. In other words, motives and incentives may be either primary or derived, the first class being made up of the direct operation of tissue needs and the second of those objects which have been associated with the tissue needs.[21]

At first sight, it may appear that a long road must be covered before one can pass from tissue needs to purposes, intentions, ambitions and other types of impelling motive to action; but if the road is long, the demand on the teacher that it be travelled is all the greater, for an educative process that cannot furnish some sort of

[19] Jones, M. C., "Emotional Development," in Murchison, C. (Ed.), *Handbook of Child Psychology* (2nd ed.). Worcester, Mass.: Clark Univ. Press, 1933, Chapter VI.
[20] Cf. Murchison, C. (Ed.), *A Handbook of General Experimental Psychology.* Worcester, Mass.: Clark Univ. Press, 1934, Chapter V.
[21] Young, P. T., *Motivation of Human and Animal Behavior.* Ann Arbor: Edwards Bros., 1933, *passim.*

guidance here and there along the way must certainly confess its weakness with respect to a group of traits that have more to do with comfort and success in living than almost any other traits that might be named.

F. PROBLEM-SOLVING: A fourth feature of the relations between stimuli and responses is usually described as problem-solving, thinking, or reasoning.[22] Problem-solving has its origin in the following circumstances. A new-born child has two general devices for meeting situations. In answering normal or familiar stimulus-patterns, it makes trial-and-error movements which are intensified and still further diversified by tapping its reserve supplies of energy. A year later, the normal trial-and-error responses and some of its emotionalized forms of action will have been reduced to the level of habits. There will be, then, three general types of behavior, viz., trial-and-error responses to new situations, habit-responses to older and more familiar situations, and emotionalized responses to unexpected situations and to those situations which have acquired the faculty of arousing emotion.

Shortly after the first year, however, a fourth type of response will appear. In the face of a new situation which is not too complex and not too unexpected, a child will quickly reorganize the stimulus-situation or reconstruct its previously acquired modes of response so that a new stimulus-response pattern will appear.[23] This is, perhaps, the one thing about the behavior of the child that distinguishes him most significantly from the lower animals. To be sure, chimpanzees and some of the other higher animals can behave in the same way,[24] but quick reorganizations of response in the face of new situations is the one type of psychological operation which makes human beings higher than the animals. For this reason, if for no other, the origin and development of problem-solving should stand high among the interests of the teacher.[25]

G. THE ORGANIZATION OF BEHAVIOR: Finally, every normal child and every normal adult exists as a coherent, integrated unit. That is, a single person's whole stream of behavior will give the impression of essential unity, if a long time view is taken of it. For short periods of time, to be sure, the stream of behavior displays a vast amount of variability, but the very emphasis which we have placed

[22] Cf. Tolman, E. C., *Purposive Behavior in Animals and Men.* New York: D. Appleton-Century Co., 1931, Chapters XVIII-XXIII.
[23] Cf. Peterson, J., "Learning in Children," in Murchison, C., *op. cit.,* Chapter X, especially pp. 442 ff.
[24] Cf. Köhler, W., *The Mentality of Apes.* New York: Harcourt, Brace and Co., 1925, *passim.*
[25] Dewey, J., *How We Think* (Rev. ed.). Boston: D. C. Heath and Co., 1933.

THE DEVELOPMENT OF ACTIONS AND ATTITUDES

upon the phrase, the "growth pattern," seems to suggest that the timewise picture of each person is really a pattern and not a chaos. This patterning of the whole stream of behavior is known as personality or self or character.[26]

Then again, each individual possesses his own preferred actions and attitudes. Thus we speak of personality traits or of character traits. When we use these phrases we mean to testify to the fact that each person can be *characterized*. Were there nothing stable and persistent and enduring about the growth pattern or about the course of daily action, such descriptions would not be possible. To be sure, character and personality change, but after we have become acquainted with a friend we have some confidence in our ability to predict what this friend will do, even in wholly new situations. The personality of a growing child, then, marks the seventh general feature of behavior which we shall inspect.[27]

4. *Summary:* For each of these major features of psychological growth there are many subdivisions, but their description is a task for psychology proper. Our main point is that the teacher must never forget the fact that a whole child is undergoing growth under her direction and guidance. No child is a bundle of separate acts and attitudes. He is not even a bundle of the several features of behavior just listed. Growth does not take place by adding, so to speak, one stone after another to the whole building. On the contrary, the whole child represents a broad sweep of forward-moving events, all of which belong to a single pattern. Obviously, however, language is not devised to describe everything at once. The sciences get nowhere by attempting to put into a single paragraph the whole universe and all it contains. To be sure, we speak of the cosmos, and we all know that this word refers to everything that is, but the word is meaningless unless "everything that is" has been broken down in our thinking and in our observation into a *this* and a *that*. In the same way, the phrase "human development" or "education of a child" tells the whole story only when immense numbers of the parts of the story have preceded the generalization. In this and the next six chapters we shall proceed, therefore, to tell about *this* and *that* feature of human nature. As we do so, the student should remember that it is the whole child from which *this* and *that* have been abstracted, for otherwise he will not get the general per-

[26] Cf. Titchener, E. B., *A Textbook of Psychology*. New York: The Macmillan Co., 1910, pp. 544 ff.
[27] Hartshorne, H., *Character in Human Relations*. New York: Charles Scribner's Sons, 1932, *passim*.

spective of the unity of human nature that is essential to successful control over growth pattern.[28]

II. Properties of Behavior

1. *Introduction:* It is the purpose of this chapter to consider the first of the sections of the whole child taken above, viz., the origin and development, under schoolroom guidance, of modes of action. As we go about this task, the student should remember that there is a difference between an action-pattern or a response, on the one hand, and the services rendered by this pattern, on the other. Let us take, for instance, the origin and development of skill in grasping. This is a skill which may be studied apart from the services rendered to the individual by it and apart, also, from the social significances of the skill. The skill itself has certain properties or characteristics which can be described. Moreover, different persons will vary widely from one another in these properties or characteristics.

Let us think, for example, of the speed of the skill, of the types of coördination involved, and of its accuracy. Each of these characteristics is sharply distinguished from the various uses to which the skill may be put. A child may grasp a pencil, a spoon, a marble, a piece of chalk, a button, or a dog's tail. These are only a few of the services rendered to the child by the use of this skill. Moreover, each of these services may have a variable social significance. There are times when grasping a dog's tail would have approvable social significance, for it might keep the dog from biting another child. On another occasion, the same skill would have doubtful social value, for it might imply a desire to be abusive and cruel. We propose, then, to consider behavior-patterns, first as behavior-patterns and in terms of the properties or characteristics they possess apart from the services rendered and apart from the social implications of these services. The properties have already been named. They are speed of reaction, coördination, and accuracy.[29]

2. *Speed:* The child which comes out of the schoolroom today and passes into even the most usual channels of living, has to move more rapidly and more deftly than has ever been the case before. We call our present culture a technical culture, and one of the features of this culture is the existence of all types of machines and de-

[28] For a criticism and a recital of the dangers of the method of analysis, see Köhler, W., *Gestalt Psychology.* New York: Liveright Publishing Corp., 1929, *passim.*

[29] For a review of papers on definition, see McGeoch, J. A., "The Acquisition of Skill." *Psychol. Bull.,* 1931, XXVIII, pp. 436 ff.

THE DEVELOPMENT OF ACTIONS AND ATTITUDES 57

vices, some of which have been geared to a high rate of speed.[30] Although the schoolroom does not specifically attempt to teach a child how to drive a car or how to handle a great many other symbols of an industrial civilization, except when it enters an engineering or manual arts curriculum, nevertheless a high premium is now being placed on all phases of speed in thought and conduct.

The word "speed" may be used to name the relative quickness of a person in all types of tasks.[31] This means that speed depends upon a number of different factors. One of these factors is known as reaction time. As a rule the phrase "reaction time" refers to the interval that elapses between the moment a stimulus is presented to a person and the moment some small measurable movement can be made in response to it, say the slight movement of the fingers necessary to press a key. This interval exists, first, because it takes a measurable amount of time for nerve currents to pass from one part of the body to another and, secondly, because muscle tissue possesses a property known as viscosity, that is, relative quickness or thinness.[32]

Other things being equal, the more complex the type of movement to be made, the longer the reaction time, for complex movements require a considerable amount of activity throughout the central nervous system. Few persons, however, ever act in response to a stimulus as quickly as they can. On the contrary, it begins to look as though most people have acquired preferred rates of acting or of working, and it is this fact about speed that brings it into the field of teaching, for some timing or pace habits are obviously not adequate to the tasks that have to be accomplished by an educated person.[33]

One of the simplest illustrations of time or pace habits is to be found on the athletic field.[34] Let us take, for example, the skill a punter acquires in getting the ball away for good height and good distance. Skill in punting requires not only a bodily form but a rate of movement which is nicely geared to the time available. The opposing team will, of course, charge as rapidly as possible in order to block the punt. The punter has, therefore, only a limited amount

[30] Cf. Mumford, L., *Technics and Civilization*. New York: Harcourt, Brace and Co., 1934, *passim*.
[31] Hill, A. V., *Muscular Movement in Man*. New York: McGraw-Hill Book Co., 1927, Chapter VI, and *passim*.
[32] Hill, A. V., *op cit.*, Chapter VII.
[33] Some of the principal facts about reaction time can be found in Ladd, G. T., and Woodworth, R. S., *Elements of Physiological Psychology*. New York: Charles Scribner's Sons, 1911, Chapter VI.
[34] Cf. Griffith, C. R., "Timing as a Phase of Skill." *J. Educ. Psychol.*, 1932, XXIII, 204-213.

of time in which to receive the ball and kick it away. This time usually amounts to about one second. During practice periods, however, it can be shown that punters develop pace or timing habits in punting which require a longer interval than one second. If they have practiced a great deal outside of game conditions, their pace or time habits in punting will become just as stabilized as their style or form. When they get into a game, therefore, and are compelled to hasten the punt, the effect on their skill is just as great as it would be were they to change the form of the punt at the last moment.[35]

When we consider that there are a great many skills which possess not only a form or coördination factor, but a speed factor as well, this phase of the training of behavior-patterns becomes important indeed. Rates of walking, speaking, writing, using the eyes during the act of reading, applying the brakes to an automobile, and handling a power machine in a factory are all subject, perhaps, to the timing or pace factor mentioned above.[36]

As we shall see later on in this chapter, rates of reading vary widely from one person to another. These variations are not so much dependent upon intelligence or upon rate of comprehension as they are upon the speed and accuracy with which the eyes may be moved. Those factors of speed which are dependent upon rate of nerve conduction and upon the viscosity of the muscles are probably native, and hence not highly subject to modification through training. But all features of speed that do not call for a maximal rate of working are subject to training. Since human beings rarely move as fast as they can, they will have a tendency to move at rates which are optimal for them. An optimal rate of moving is obviously a product of training.

3. *Coördination:* A person would gain no advantage simply from moving rapidly, if quickness implied a lack of coördination and rhythm. The problems of rhythm are important, both to the pupil and to the teacher, partly because no human action can ever take place without some measure of balance between different muscle groups, and partly because every posture that we take and every skill we exercise has a given measure of coördination as one of its principal properties.[37]

As a very simple illustration of these facts, we may take so local a movement as extending the arm. This movement requires simul-

---

[35] Unpublished data from the University of Illinois Laboratories for Research in Athletics.
[36] Cf. Viteles, M. S., *Industrial Psychology.* New York: W. W. Norton and Co., 1932, *passim.*
[37] Cf. Freeman, G. L., *op. cit.,* Part III.

THE DEVELOPMENT OF ACTIONS AND ATTITUDES 59

taneous activity in a group of muscles known as the extensors and in another group known as the flexors. The movement is actually made, of course, by the activity of one group, but this activity is always smoothed out and balanced by simultaneous activity on the part of the other group.[38]

The practical significance of measures of coördination in action can be illustrated by some of the studies that have been made on motor performance at a lathe, or at some other type of industrial machine. If the movements a workman makes under these conditions are photographed by a moving picture camera and then analyzed, it can be shown that most workmen not only make a large number of unnecessary movements, but that these and some of the other essential movements are poorly coördinated or poorly patterned with respect to the task that has to be done.[39] All forms of industrial education might be asked, therefore, to include methods of training that might lead to proper types of coördination and hence, to a minimal expenditure of the bodily energies.

The movements made by a small infant can be described as wholly uncoördinated, if we assume that movement should be made for the purpose of adjusting the body quickly, easily, and accurately to some external situation. An adult does not find it necessary to move the entire body with considerable vehemence in order to escape a pin prick. An infant, however, has no choice in the matter. Somewhere between infancy and adulthood, muscles acquire the capacity to get things done for the organism with a minimal or at least with an optimal or favored amount of effort.

Coördinations fall naturally into two types. The first type is made up of all of those measures of balance between different muscle groups which lead to postures or bodily attitudes. We may speak, then, of postural coördination or of static movement systems, that is to say, of movement systems which maintain a member of the body or the whole body in a given posture.[40] Examples can be found in the standing posture, the sitting posture, and even the sleeping posture, for, obviously, during a period of sleep, some parts of the body must be held in a definite position with respect to other parts.

A second type of coördination may be called phasic, for a person who is writing at a typewriter, running along a race track, or throw-

[38] Cf. Sherrington, C. S., *The Integrative Action of the Nervous System.* New Haven: Yale Univ. Press, 1906, *passim.*
[39] Cf. Gilbreth, F. B., *Motion Study.* New York: D. Van Nostrand Co., 1911, *passim.*
[40] Cf. Washburn, M. F., *Movement and Mental Imagery.* Boston: Houghton Mifflin, 1916, Chapter I and *passim.*

ing an object at a target is carrying out a series of coördinations which fall into a timewise pattern. Some of these phasic coördinations may be described by the word "rhythm." An expert runner, for example, moves his limbs and his arms back and forth in a way that makes each member of the body support every other member in the best possible fashion. No track man would undertake to move the right arm forward while the right foot was taking a forward stride.

Other examples of phasic or rhythmic coördination are the swing of the golfer, the sequence of finger and arm movements used in piano playing, the particular pattern of movement which places an automobile in high gear and at a reasonable speed on the highway, and most of the actions that workmen use in the factory or on the farm.

For a long time it has been supposed that the phasic forms of coördination were of no particular importance to the average teacher, because grace and flexibility of movement were required only of those who wished to make a graceful entrance into a social group or to dance easily and lightly with a partner. It now appears, however, that failure in coördination is one of the major factors behind labor turnover in industry and behind proneness to accident in the factory and on the highway.

For these reasons, the whole problem of coördination in muscular movement has undergone multiplied examination both in the experimental laboratory and in the field of practical operations.[41] It has been shown that persons with low measures of coördination can be kept out of certain types of occupations. Moreover, a number of special methods of training are in common use for the purpose of giving workmen and technicians a higher measure of facility in using their motor apparatus.[42]

We have left out of the above account of coördination some of the most important experimental work, viz., that which has to do with postures or attitudes, because it will be more convenient to discuss this problem in greater detail in connection with another topic. When a person takes a posture, he may do so either because it is the foundation upon which some special skill must be built, or he may do so because postures are ways of preparing the body for new stimulus-situations.[43]

[41] Cf. Perrin, F. A. C., "An Experimental Study of Motor Ability." *J. Exper. Psychol.*, 1921, IV, 24-56; Seashore, R. H., "Stanford Motor Skills Unit." *Psychol. Monog.*, 1928, XXXIX (No. 178), 51-66.
[42] Cf. Viteles, M. S., *op. cit.*, Chapters XI, XII, and XX.
[43] Cf. Young, P. T., *Motivation of Human and Animal Behavior*. Ann Arbor: Edwards Bros., 1933, Chapter V.

THE DEVELOPMENT OF ACTIONS AND ATTITUDES 61

As an example of the first use, we may take the posture of a track man who is just preparing to run a hundred-yard dash. This particular posture acts as the background for the phasic skills involved in starting quickly from the marks. Another illustration is found in the posture of a child at his desk in the schoolroom. Much has been said and written about the particular posture which should furnish the background for the specific skill of writing or of studying.[44] An illustration of the second use of posture is to be found in the instructions which always form a preface to an intelligence test. The examiner not only reads the few sentences which indicate the nature of the test but he may frequently give such preparatory signals as "ready" or "now" just before the test is begun. These instructions and the preparatory signals result in an attitude or set which makes the person more open to the stimulus-situation created by the test than to any other stimulus-situation.

4. *Speed and Accuracy:* If a person had learned how to be highly coördinated in all of his movements, the chances are that he could move accurately with respect to any particular situation. In throwing a ball at a target, for example, perfect coördination ought to mean perfect accuracy. The ball should always hit the bull's eye. Likewise, a child which had acquired complete control over its finger and arm movements should be able to write with perfect accuracy where accuracy would be defined in terms of a style of writing laid down by the teacher.

Clearly, there are frequent and wide departures from accuracy of this type. Some of these departures are the result of an inadequate training and hence of poor coördination. As we have pointed out above, however, some of them are due to the fact that the timing or pace phase of movement may be exceedingly variable. Under experimental conditions a learner may throw at a target just as quickly or just as slowly as he pleases. It looks as though most persons acquire a speed of action in such skills, which is an optimal speed for them. This means that the speed factor would become a component part of the coördination factor in skill.

There are times when human beings are called upon to react with some new and unfamiliar degree of speed. Let us say, for example, that a student is asked to write the letter "a" over and over again at a speed of his own choosing. In another trial, we may ask this student to write the letter "a" just as rapidly as he can. It will take no fine measuring instrument to show that the second per-

[44] Cf. Bennett, H. E., "A Study of School Posture and Seating." *Element. School J.,* 1925, XXVI, 50-57.

formance is much less coördinated than the first. In other words, the addition of a new level of speed to a fairly stabilized skill brings about a serious modification of the skill.

A number of experiments have been done on the relation between speed and accuracy, partly in order to find out what effect emphasis upon the one rather than upon the other will have upon skill.[45] Let us suppose, for example, that some teachers, in teaching a child how to write, emphasize speed, whereas others emphasize accuracy. We may wish to know what the ultimate outcome of these two different types of emphasis in teaching method will be. In general, it appears that, when a training program aims first at accuracy, high levels of accuracy will be attained, together with a gradual improvement in speed. On the other hand, when the primary aim of the training period is speed, there will not be a great amount of improvement in accuracy.[46]

These facts seem to hold true of such tasks as typesetting, cancelling letters out of closely printed material, adding figures, copying figures, cutting out patterns, arranging cards, and constructing patterns out of colored cubes. There is some evidence, also, which shows that occasions which demand an unfamiliar speed in the use of the language mechanisms will result in pseudo speech defects.[47]

It is not yet clear as to why emphasis upon speed should interfere more seriously with the acquisition of accuracy than emphasis upon accuracy interferes with speed. One suggestion, however, is offered by the facts mentioned above. If speed or tempo of movement is a matter of training, it might be that it is a factor which is acquired more slowly than sheer accuracy. Since the whole rhythm of our modern life depends so heavily upon tempo or speed, it might be fruitful to experiment with the speed factor in learning more intensely than has been the case up to the present time. Some suggestions of the results that might be attained are already offered by new methods of training people to increase their speed in reading. Since speed in reading is dependent, in part, upon rate and accuracy of eye movement, such training programs would have to be directed

---

[45] Hahn, H. H., and Thorndike, E. L., "Some Results of Practice in Addition under School Conditions." *J. Educ. Psychol*, 1914, V, 65-84; Sturt, M., "A Comparison of Speed with Accuracy in the Learning Process." *Brit. J. Psychol.*, 1921, XII, 289-300.

[46] Much of the literature in this field has been summarized by McFarland, R. A., "The Rôle of Speed in Mental Ability." *Psychol. Bull.*, 1928, XXV, 595-612.

[47] Cf. Travis, L. E., "Speech Pathology," in Murchison, C. (Ed.), *op. cit.*, pp. 654 ff.

THE DEVELOPMENT OF ACTIONS AND ATTITUDES 63

toward improved skill in the use of the eyes.[48] We shall consider this matter in a moment.

III. TYPES OF BEHAVIOR

1. *Introduction:* The student will recall the distinction that has been drawn between (i) the common traits or properties of all behavior patterns, (ii) the several varieties of behavior patterns, and (iii) the various personal and social services which may be rendered by the use of habits and skills. The first group of problems have just been considered. We may now bring together some of the major facts about various types of behavior. No good purpose will be served, however, by taking the division of habits and skills into various types too seriously. If we speak of manual skills, verbal skills, skill in reading, and skill in writing, we do so only because these are skills which require a large amount of training in the schoolroom and about which a considerable amount of information is available.

The new-born child, of course, possesses none of these skills. He comes into the world with sense organs, with nerve connections, and with muscles, all of which are in fairly advanced stages of anatomical development. As we have seen, however, most of the movements the child makes are highly general in character. Almost any intense stimulus will excite a mass-reaction in a major portion of the body. It is out of this matrix of generalized action that such fine movements as grasping, speaking, reading, and writing emerge.

2. *Manual Skills:* Physical education is a part of most teaching programs because it serves two very important functions. On the one hand, it furnishes a way of correcting and guiding the spontaneous expression of energy, as in play.[49] It serves, therefore, to increase the strength of the various muscle groups and to promote normal health and growth in the child. On the other hand, it renders a tremendous service in training children in the use of hands, arms, limbs, and other bodily members.

The actual emergence of a single skill, viz., grasping, out of a previous stage of more generalized action, can be illustrated by a special experiment in this field.[50] The study was made on a group

---

[48] Cf. Tinker, M. A., "Legibility and Eye Movement in Reading." *Psychol. Bull.*, 1927, XXIV, 621-639.
[49] Cf. Curti, M. W., *Child Psychology.* New York: Longmans, Green and Co., 1931, Chapter XI.
[50] Halverson, H. M., "An Experimental Study of Prehension in Infants by Means of Systematic Cinema Records." *Genet. Psychol. Monog.*, 1931, X, 107-286.

of small infants with the aid of the moving picture camera. The first movements made by the subjects were described as palming movements, for a small object such as a cube was seized simply by placing the fingers in opposition to the palm. During this stage the thumb plays a very minor rôle. Gradually the fingers were observed to increase in refinement of movement and the thumb to play a more important part, in the sense that it was gradually substituted for the fingers and opposed to the first finger rather than to the palm of the hand. By the end of the thirty-sixth week, it was found that the thumb had definitely acquired the ability to stand in opposition to the forefinger, and, save for large objects, grasping by palming quite disappeared. The experimenter in this case was able to distinguish seven different types of grasping, and if the number of instances of each type is plotted against a time curve from the twelfth to the sixtieth week, it appears that the first or more primitive types become less and less frequent, while the latter or more skilful types become more and more frequent.[51]

This process is, of course, only a sample drawn from an immense number of studies not only on grasping but on all other types of manual and bodily performance. In general, the varieties of learning to be described in a later chapter, when used advisedly, lead not only to gradual increases in the strength of manual movements but to finer and finer degrees of coördination at higher and higher levels of speed.

One of the essential features of this entire process is the gradual elimination of useless movements. There is, however, another phase of the problem that ought to have high significance, at least for grade school teachers. Many of the playthings which are given to small children and many of the types of exercise which are used in schoolroom practice serve more to increase the strength of muscle groups than to increase flexibility of movement and coördination. For example, children who are asked to get a major part of their exercise by making set types of movement over and over again certainly increase the strength of the muscles used in making these movements, but they acquire, also, the habit of making these movements rather than any other movements.

It would appear, therefore, that types of exercise which require a large amount of flexibility in response would be more favorable to phasic types of coördination than the so-called setting-up exercises. In other words, games and pieces of apparatus which require much

[51] For similar studies, see Shirley, M. M., in Murchison, C., *op. cit.*, Chapter V.

THE DEVELOPMENT OF ACTIONS AND ATTITUDES 65

turning, twisting, starting, stopping, and variation in action would not only promote health and increase strength, but they would also require children constantly to use their motor apparatus in new and varied ways.

It is possible, of course, to set up some standard form of bodily movement for each of the major situations in which a person may be placed. The effect of this, however, would be to freeze the motor apparatus in a set series of habits and skills. It looks as though modern industry, on the one hand, and even the ordinary skills required by social intercourse, on the other, require more than this. They require motor equipment which is not only stabilized in some of its parts, but which is highly flexible and adaptable and subject, therefore, to continual modification.[52]

3. *Verbal Skills:* The proper development of manual and bodily skills seems important, of course, to the coach, to taxicab companies, and to industries which employ men because of their motor adeptness. It would not be worth while to minimize, therefore, the educative processes that lead to proper levels of motor adeptness, but no one would seriously argue against the fact that verbal skills are, perhaps, the most important skills which human beings can acquire, for it is these skills which lay the foundation not only of all communication, but of a large part of cultural attainment as well. This proposition is supported by the fact that spoken words are said to be our chief means of communicating our thoughts to one another. It is said that the lower animals do not have a culture because they cannot speak.[53]

The phases of speech which will concern us most in the present chapter are the origin and development of the speech functions and the disorders to which these functions are subject. Before we consider these matters, however, we ought to see why it is that speech and language can be described as verbal skills.[54] This will not be an easy thing to do, for, as we have said just above, we all think of speech, not as a skill, but as a bodily device which the mind uses in order to express itself. When two persons converse with each other or when a teacher tells her students the fundamental facts of civics or of history, we do not at all suppose that contact is being made through the use of habits which are, in some respects, like manual and bodily habits. On the contrary, we believe that one mind is

[52] Viteles, M. S., *The Science of Work.* New York: W. W. Norton and Co., 1934, Chapter VIII and *passim.*
[53] Cf. De Laguna, G., *Speech, Its Function and Development.* New Haven: Yale Univ. Press, 1927, Chapter I and *passim.*
[54] Cf. Watson, J. B., *op. cit.,* Chapter IX.

meeting another, the function of speech acting only as a necessary but wholly physical medium between the two.

As a simple illustration, let the reader ask one of his friends how he feels when he has a toothache. The friend will proceed to recite a story of his pain. When the recital is finished, the reader will suppose that the words he has heard are not so much a product of an intricate combination of muscular movements as a direct view of another person's toothache. In short, most of us have learned to think of words as though they were actually sensations, feelings, thoughts, or other parts of the private view which each person has of his own experience.[55] We acquire words, therefore, to express our thoughts and do not suppose that the having of thoughts may be intimately dependent upon the acquisition of words. It is easy to imagine, for example, that new-born infants have thoughts which they cannot express simply because they have not learned how to express them. The contrary argument would be that infants do not have thoughts and will not have them until they have acquired the ability to speak or to make some other type of "symbolic" movement.

What, then, is the place of language in psychology and in the schoolroom? Do we teach grammar for the sake of providing further outlets for thoughts that are already present, or is an increase in vocabulary a means of increasing one's intellectual stature? Since we cannot choose between these two options in advance of a study of the origin and development of verbal skill, we must proceed to ask where words have their beginning and how they acquire the psychological and social significance they are known to possess.[56]

A. ORIGINS OF VERBAL SKILL: Let us say that a small infant is under observation in its crib. As a result of stimulus-situations which are partly intra-organic and partly extra-organic, it will, unless it is sleeping, respond to these sources of stimulation by making a variety of movements. These movements include the normal processes of breathing, the movements around the mouth parts which open and close the mouth and change the position of the tongue, and movements of other organs in the throat region. Now it happens that normal processes of breathing, when taken together with a proper patterning of events in the throat and mouth regions, will ordinarily result in the creation of sounds. We commonly think

[55] Cf. Hunter, W. S., "Anthroponomy and Psychology," in Murchison, C. (Ed.), *Psychologies of 1930*. Worcester, Mass.: Clark Univ. Press, 1930, Chapter XIV.
[56] McCarthy, D., "Language Development," in Murchison, C. (Ed.), *Handbook of Child Psychology*. Worcester, Mass.: Clark Univ. Press, 1933, Chapter VIII.

THE DEVELOPMENT OF ACTIONS AND ATTITUDES 67

of sounds as having their origin primarily in the vocal cords, but, as we shall see, a great many other structures are involved in this whole process.

There is a stage in the development of an infant when the sounds that it makes can have no other meaning or significance than any of its other movements. That is, the movements which lead to sound are a part of the random and masslike character of much of its initial behavior. We have already tried to show, however, that the psychological growth of the child is displayed, in part, by the gradual emergence of specific stimulus-situations, on the one hand, and of equally specific response-patterns, on the other.

The emergence of stimulus-response patterns which have been individuated out of a total configuration of events can be variously described as due to trial-and-error learning, to conditioning, or even to learning by insight. When the infant actually reaches for and gets hold of an object, the movements actually necessary to reaching and seizing will have a tendency to persist, whereas fruitless movements will drop out. The very fact that some movements can be described as fruitful while others are described as fruitless seems to imply some insight into the significant relation between an object reached for and the types of movement actually necessary for success.

If, now, the student will keep this situation firmly in mind, that is, if he will realize that the sounds made by an infant are, during the early stages of growth, incidental accompaniments of patterns of movement in the chest and throat regions, he ought to be able to see that the making of these movements can come to be associated with stimulus-objects in the same way that other types of movement are made in response to such objects.[57] From one point of view, the first sounds an infant utters are simple, that is, they are such sounds as would occur were the infant to open its mouth and allow its breath to pass over its vocal cords. It has no skill whatsoever in raising and lowering the tongue or otherwise shaping the mouth parts into a resonance chamber which will give to vocal sound all of the variety necessary to adult speech. The process of acquiring variety is a process of coördinating and individuating all of the mechanisms of speech in the same fashion as arm and finger movements are individuated and patterned before digital grasping can take place.

The inference to be drawn from these facts is simply this. Chil-

[57] Curti, M. W., *op. cit.*, Chapter VII. The student may expect, of course, an extended discussion of types of learning in later chapters.

dren do not pass through a period of trial-and-error learning in their use of the vocal apparatus in order to find socially approvable ways of giving expression to their thoughts.[58] This inference seems almost too obvious to state, and yet, as we have said above, adult persons commonly think of language and of its functions without any reference to the circumstances under which it has had its origin.

B. SYMBOLIC FUNCTIONS: Now let us suppose that a stage is reached in the process of random babblings where some particular sound, that is to say, some particular pattern of vocal movement has come to a successful termination. By successful termination we may mean just exactly what we mean when we say that some movement in the arms or in the body has come to successful termination. In other words, an object is grasped. To be sure, the making of movements in the vocal apparatus does not enable a child to grasp an object or in any other way to manipulate it, but it happens that every child is surrounded by friends and parents who are anxious to discern its every wish. It may happen, therefore, that the making of a particular sound will secure results, in the sense that the adults around the child will see a relation between the sound and some object at which the child may be looking.[59] The adults will infer that the child desires the object, whereupon the object is placed within reach.

By one or more of the processes of learning which are to be described in a later chapter, the vocal movements which have thus led to satisfaction will be stabilized, whereas other vocal movements will become attached to other objects or drop out of use. If these learning processes proceed for any length of time, the growing infant will be in possession of a series of words (or a series of coördinations in the vocal apparatus) which will serve as supplements to coördinations elsewhere in the body in the presence of objects and events around it. In other words, the child will have reached that stage in its language development which is sometimes called the naming stage.[60]

It is important for the student to remember that this naming stage in the development of language stands on exactly the same psychological foundations as do the other movements made by the child. It is, of course, a very fortunate thing that certain types of movements in the vocal apparatus will lead to the production of sound,

---

[58] Cf. Hunter, W. S., *Human Behavior*. Chicago: Univ. of Chicago Press, 1928, p. 67 and *passim*.
[59] Watson, J. B., *op. cit.*, pp. 340 ff.
[60] Cf. Allport, F. H., *Social Psychology*. Boston: Houghton Mifflin Co., 1924, Chapter VII.

THE DEVELOPMENT OF ACTIONS AND ATTITUDES 69

for, even during the processes which have been described up to this point, the fact that the child hears itself speak does much to hasten the associations that can be established between objects and words or speech movements. Moreover, all of the persons around the child are using words. This means that there are a number of agencies at work in hastening the process of developing a vocabulary. If coördinations of movement in other parts of the body could create sounds, there is no reason why a language could not be produced in terms of these other coördinations.

The relations that may be established between the sounds which the child hears itself speak and the actual act of speaking are very much like the relations that are established between a verbal response to an object and the object. Moreover, the relations that are established between words spoken by others and the words heard by the child, or the words spoken by the child, are of the same order. There is, as yet, no question of words becoming expressive of thoughts or of any attempt on the part of the child to create for itself a vehicle of communication between itself and other people.[61] Among adults, however, words do offer a means of communication. In our common language we say that words stand for or represent either objects or events within our own private experience.[62] We must, therefore, try to see how the naming functions of language are expanded into what is commonly known as the symbolic function of language.

For this purpose, let us again take the child which we have placed under observation. The child is now somewhat older. We find that there are times when words are spoken in the absence of objects. This means that the child has discovered a way of using a mode of response independently of the presentation of an immediate stimulus-pattern. It is difficult to know just when the transition from naming habits to symbolizing habits is effected, and it is also difficult to describe all of the circumstances which surround the transition. Some suggestion, however, is offered by the following considerations. Let us say that the child has learned to respond to a bright box or to its rattle by saying "da." The box and the rattle never are, of course, isolated objects. They are objects which are always placed in a context which includes other objects. This is to say that the word "da" is not only a specific response to a specific

[61] McCarthy, D., *The Language Development of the Preschool Child*. Minneapolis: Univ. of Minn. Press, 1930, *passim*.
[62] The relation between ideas and words has been a difficult problem. Some light is thrown upon it by the study of "imagery" in animals. Cf. Munn, N. L., *Animal Psychology*. Boston: Houghton Mifflin Co., 1933, Chapter VII.

object but a specific response to a specific object *in* its setting.

That method of learning known as conditioning argues that when two stimulus-situations are presented to a human being almost, if not quite, simultaneously, the one of them may acquire the capacity to call out a response which previously has been called out only by the other. If, then, a child has learned how to say "da" in the presence of a situation which includes a box among other objects, it may happen that this same situation minus the box will acquire the capacity also to excite the "da" response.[63] In other words, a naming habit has been transformed into a demanding habit. The child is in the process of learning how to ask for objects which are not present. We may say, then, that the use of the word "da" has become a symbol or a substitute for an object.

It is clear that if a child has acquired a large number of symbols for an equally large number of objects and if, at the same time, it has acquired a variety of symbols for a variety of relations between objects and for the respects in which dissimilar objects resemble one another, it has gained a piece of behavioral equipment which the lower animals cannot secure. Human beings would be scarcely "higher" than the animals if, like the animals, they had to make all of their responses, both to objects and to their properties, in terms of manual movements and bodily postures. It is the symbolic use of words, therefore, that contributes so largely to the difference between men and even the highest of the lower animals.

There is, however, one other factor to be considered. The chances are that even the development of naming habits would not carry the human child to a very high level of development were it not for the fact that the very act of speaking a word may, in its turn, become a stimulus-situation which will arouse a further verbal response.[64] The child not only hears itself speak, but it hears the sounds made by other persons around it. If these other persons are adults, the sounds they make will have acquired a symbolic function exactly comparable to that acquired by the child.

C. WORDS AND IDEAS: There is one thing about this account of the transition of language from random babblings to words which

[63] Watson, J. B., *op. cit.*, pp. 340 ff. A systematic survey of all of the problems of psychology and of teaching in terms of the above facts has been made by Hollingworth, H. L., *Psychology: Its Facts and Its Principles.* New York: D. Appleton-Century Co., 1928. See also, *Educational Psychology.* New York: D. Appleton-Century Co., 1933.

[64] This process can be illustrated neatly in animal learning. See Fulton, B. B., "Sound Perception by Insects." *Scient. Mo.*, 1928, XXVII, 552-556.

THE DEVELOPMENT OF ACTIONS AND ATTITUDES 71

are symbols or substitutes for objects that may confuse the student. Nothing has been said in our account of the presence or absence of ideas. The student will be inclined to say of the infant who has spoken the word "da" in the absence of the "da" object, "Doesn't the infant have an idea of the object which is not now present?" In other words, what reason is there to believe that, having once seen a "da" object, the infant will not remember this object with the aid of its memory images and then ask for the object.[65]

We may, for the moment, assume that this is a better description of the transition of which we have been speaking than is the one given above. It is clear, however, that the processes behind the transition can still be of the same order as those we have described. For example, on one occasion the child faces a situation where the "da" object is present. A moment later, the "da" object is absent. Clearly, the other objects in the total situation which have become associated with the "da" object could call forth a memory of the absent object as easily as they could call forth a verbal response to it. This is a type of learning which has long been described as associative learning. If a memory image of the absent "da" object is revived, associative learning would also explain the revival of other memory images, for such other memory images would be revived as had been associated in time or in place with the one image.[66] Many methods of teaching have used this principle.

We cannot push our inquiry into these matters to a satisfactory conclusion in the present chapter, for obviously we are beginning to move toward the problems of creative imagination and of thinking. We shall, therefore, say much more about the relation between ideas and words in another place. In the meantime, we may simply ask this question: Does a human being ever have a memory image or an idea of an absent object without, at the same time, making some verbal or other response to it? In other words, when a child is thinking, is the process one that goes on in the mind alone, or is it a process that is intimately tied up with the verbal machinery?

As a preliminary consideration in any answer to these questions, it must be said that the use of the verbal machinery does not always require audible speech.[67] In other words, a distinction can be drawn

[65] Cf. Hunter, W. S., "The Symbolic Process." *Psychol. Rev.*, 1924, XXXI, 478-497; "The Subject's Report." *Psychol. Rev.*, 1925, XXXII, 153-170.
[66] This is a very difficult psychological problem, and the literature on it is large. Cf. Titchener, E. B., *Elementary Psychology of the Thought Processes.* New York: The Macmillan Co., 1909.
[67] Cf. Watson, J. B., *op. cit.,* Chapter VI.

between overt verbal habits and implicit verbal habits. Overt verbal habits pertain to those uses of the verbal machinery which actually lead to audible sounds. Implicit verbal habits refer to those uses of the verbal machinery which play so large a part in silent reading. One of the questions we have to answer, therefore, is whether silent reading is actually silent, in the sense that neither the vocal apparatus nor any other type of motor organ is in operation, or whether silent reading implies the use of implicit types of verbal action.

D. THE EXPRESSION OF IDEAS: We shall be able to answer this question much more effectively in the chapter on the nature of problem-solving. In the meantime, it will be worth while to point out one very important educational inference to be drawn from the above facts. If the development of language follows a pattern anything like that which has been described, we must conclude that the ideas a child has will be just as numerous as the means that it has acquired for the expression of ideas. That is, its ideas will be just as numerous as its verbal habits.

When we say that a man is a good all-around athlete, we mean that he has trained the muscles of his body in such a variety of ways that he can respond quickly and effectively to an astonishing variety of the objects and events that are to be found on the playground or on the athletic field. Likewise, when we say of a man that he is well educated or that he is intelligent or that he displays large measures of learning, we may mean that he is a person who has acquired a large variety of verbal habits, especially verbal habits of the symbolic sort which can be used in his intercourse with his environment and with his friends. Such a man ought to be able to use immediate stimulus-situations as a starting point for a series of reflections, that is, verbal comments both of the explicit and of the implicit type, which will keep him active for a considerable period of time.

To take an extreme case, the philosopher in his chair appears relatively inactive. We say of him that he appears to be paying no attention to the objects and events around him. On the sheet of paper in front of him, however, we may discover a half-completed sentence. It may be that the sentence will not be completed for an hour, a day, or a month. Its completion will depend, perhaps, upon the completion of a period of implicit action in his vocal apparatus or, as some of the older psychologies would prefer to put it, upon a period of deep reflection which will come to an end only if some

THE DEVELOPMENT OF ACTIONS AND ATTITUDES 73

sequence of words has been formulated which will serve as an adequate completion to a half-begun sentence.[68]

Obviously, however, we have now left the development of language and have entered into another group of problems. We shall leave the subject at this point with the comment that one of the chief functions of early education is to equip every child with a large vocabulary—that is, a series of verbal skills, both of the explicit and of the implicit type, which shall make its contribution to the child in its attempts to get along in its physical and social environment.

IV. SPEECH DISORDERS

1. *Introduction:* The development of verbal skills in the schoolroom is associated with so many other teaching operations that it is hardly worth while to separate them from other acts of learning. Every time a child reads new material, learns a new spelling list, or engages in a conversation with a more mature person, he may add a few words to his vocabulary. It is clear that these additions may be more or less fruitless unless he finds out, at the same time, what the meaning of each word is and how it may be used as a substitute for some definable one of the objects and events around him or of some definable property of or relation between these objects and events.

In other words, there may be some justification for an older method of teaching which required constant search through the dictionary, for a dictionary is, among other things, a list of all of the distinctions which human beings have been able to make in dealing with environments. The teaching situation is a little different, however, with respect to disorders of the speech functions. When a person stammers or has any other type of hesitancy in his speech, he is not only unprepared to express himself well, but his deficiency may become an important factor in his inability to adjust himself to his social context.[69]

2. *The Mechanisms of Speech:* There is, perhaps, no phase of motor development which offers more perplexities to psychology and to education than the explanation of stammering, together with proper remedies. Some suggestions, however, are to be gained from

---

[68] Cf. Dashiell, J. F., *Fundamentals of Objective Psychology.* Boston: Houghton Mifflin Co., 1928, Chapter XV; Watson, J. B., "Is Thinking Merely the Action of Language Mechanisms?" *Brit. J. Psychol.*, 1920, XI, 87-104.

[69] Much of the experimental literature on stammering has been summarized by Travis, L. E., "Speech Pathology," in Murchison, C. (Ed.), *op. cit.*, Chapter XVI.

the fact that speech is the one major type of motor skill for which there is no special organ.[70] In the case of grasping, the fingers act as a special agent. The muscles around the eyes are special agents for focusing the eyes upon an object and for turning the eyeballs from one point to another. There is, however, no single set of muscles upon which the speech functions can rest. On the contrary, in order that a word may be spoken precisely or in order that a sentence may be uttered without hesitation, the muscles in the diaphragm and the walls of the chest, in the mouth parts, and in the tongue must all coöperate together in a finely balanced way. The student may realize this fact if he will, while trying to utter the word "stammer," take note of all of the events that transpire in the upper part of his body while the word is being said.

Now it happens that nerve fibres from wholly different centers are the fibres which control the movements of the various organs involved in speaking. This means that, before there can be integration among all of these organs, some higher center in the brain shall have acquired facility in balancing one lower center against another. It is usually assumed that this higher center is to be found in the right cerebrum, at least among those persons who are right-handed.[71] Since the control of finger, hand, and arm muscles among right-handed persons is effected through the coördination centers in the left hemisphere, and since these centers have about the same location on the left side that the speech centers do on the other side, it might be argued that speech difficulties would arise whenever an attempt is made to force both types of coördination into a single part of the cerebrum. Some cases are known, for example, where attempts to change a left-handed person to a right-handed have resulted in interference with the normal flow of language responses. It is for this reason that the origin and development of right-handedness has become so important a problem in child psychology.[72]

3. *Speech and Handedness:* There is, at the present time, no satisfactory explanation of right-handedness. As an example of the theories that can be devised, we shall take only one. This theory says that the presence of right- or left-handedness will depend upon the position of the unborn child and of the relation of the aorta to this position.[73] If, for example, the child lies upon its left side, the left arm would be less free to move than the right arm. As we have

[70] Travis, L. E., *op. cit.,* pp. 650-651.
[71] Cf. Freeman, G. L., *op. cit.,* Chapter XIV.
[72] Travis, L. E., *op. cit.,* pp. 689 ff.
[73] Cf. Travis, L. E., *Speech Pathology.* New York: D. Appleton-Century Co., 1931, pp. 96 ff.

THE DEVELOPMENT OF ACTIONS AND ATTITUDES 75

seen, prenatal growth is very sensitive to the movements that are possible to the foetus. The left hemisphere, then, might quickly acquire a dominance over the right hemisphere so far as manual movement is concerned. In any case, our common observation assures us that most persons are right-handed, and studies upon the localization of functions in the cortex indicates clearly enough that for most persons the control of the speech functions is centered in the opposite hemisphere.[74]

4. *Theories of Stammering:* In view of the fact that so many different structures which have their own particular functions are involved in the act of speech, it would be natural to suppose that any circumstances that would disturb the equilibrium of a person would reflect itself rather quickly in speech. It is generally believed that drugs, for example, affect more complex types of action and more recently acquired types of action more quickly than they do older types of action. So, too, it is believed that emotional disturbances operate in the same way. Speech is, of course, one of the most recently acquired functions in the animal series.

By analogy with the situation that obtains in the use of drugs and in emotional excitement, it might be inferred that any tendency to instability on the part of a child would quickly reflect itself in speech coördination. There are, therefore, several theories which emphasize this fact. Since speech is used most frequently in social situations, it might be argued that any circumstances which would affect a child's social adjustments would also affect its facility in speech. In any case, it has been shown that, when improper levels of social adjustment have been removed so that a child can feel himself at ease among his fellows, both speech hesitancies and stuttering may disappear.[75]

Another theory argues that speech difficulties are due to temporary forgetfulness for the proper sound of a word. Still another theory relates speech in the same way to visual imagery.[76] The evidence for these theories lies in the fact that persons who suffer from speech defects are weak in auditory imagery and in visual imagery, but in view of the difficulties which lie in the way of determining the amount and quality of imagery, these theories must remain open to question.

[74] A good discussion of several theories of handedness can be found in Dorcus, R. M., and Shaffer, G. W., *Textbook of Abnormal Psychology.* Baltimore: The Williams and Wilkins Co., 1934, pp. 70 ff.
[75] Cf. Fletcher, J. M. *The Problem of Stuttering.* New York: Longmans, Green and Co., 1928, p. 223 and *passim.*
[76] Cf. Swift, W. B., "A Psychological Analysis of Stuttering." *J. Abnorm. Psychol.,* 1915, X, 225-235.

A number of attempts have been made to relate the phenomena of stammering to conflicts of different types. For example, stuttering is more common among boys than it is among girls. In view of this fact, it may be argued that since boys are apt to pick up an unsocial, if not an obscene, vocabulary much more frequently than girls, they will find difficulty in expressing themselves normally because of the interference between a vocabulary they know will not be approved by their parents and a vocabulary that would be approved.[77]

Other types of conflict are known to reveal themselves, as we shall see, in anxiety and in deeply running emotional complexes.[78] Every child, for example, has a good many desires or native urges which will not receive social approval until they have been modified or sublimated into socially approvable form. It has been argued that the sex desires stand high in importance in this situation. Since there are so many social taboos about sex matters among the adults who supervise the child, many of the words which the child might normally use would be repressed. Repression, of course, means interference with the normal types of coördination that would be necessary to facility in the use of language, and stammering or some form of speech hesitancy would be the result.

These assumptions about the driving power of native urges and desires will come in for further discussion at a later point. We refer to them now only in order to point out the fact that the causes for stuttering may be just as complex as is the mechanism which makes speech possible.

5. *Methods of Cure:* In view of the protean character of speech defects, it would be strange indeed if any one method of cure could be discovered. This means that the teacher who attempts to handle speech difficulties must take each case as an individual case and try to apply to it the particular treatment which the case itself seems to suggest.[79] Among the methods of treatment that have been found most effective, we may name the method of distraction first. This is a very old method. It implies that the speaker can be drawn away from his fears or anxieties about speaking or about his social contacts by directing his attention to some other matter. Demosthenes, for example, placed pebbles in his mouth.

---

[77] Cf. Dunlap, K., "The Stuttering Boy." *J. Abnorm. Psychol.,* 1917, XII, 44-48.
[78] Cf. Adler, A., *Practice and Theory of Individual Psychology.* London: Kegan Paul, 1927, *passim.* Also Coriat, J. H., *Abnormal Psychology.* New York: Moffat, Yard and Co., 1923, *passim.*
[79] Cf. Travis, L. E., "Speech Pathology," in Murchison, C. (Ed.), *op. cit.,* Chapter XVI.

This method leads naturally to what is, perhaps, the most important method of all, viz., correcting speech defects by correcting more fundamental types of maladjustment. It seems to be fairly clear that speech defects occur most frequently among children who are nervously unstable. Their nervousness is most certainly a product of repression or of conflict. Before the speech difficulties can be corrected, some attempt must be made to get at and remove the sources of conflict. As we shall see in the chapter on the development of personality traits and in the chapter on the socialized person, there are a great many sources of conflict in children, many of them created by the school situation itself or by a contrast between the school situation and the home life of the children. The student should expect, then, to place these few facts about the causes and cure of stammering in a perspective furnished by a discussion of these other matters.[80]

V. Reading

1. *Introduction:* It is a pity that words cannot be used in such a way that they will describe in a single sentence all of the various facets of growth. This fact appears nowhere to better advantage than in the study of reading. If we could say that, during the reading of this very material, for example, the mind or the soul of the student simply looks out of the windows of the body (that is, through the eyes) in order to see and to understand the words that are here written, the problem would be easy. It is now known, however, that reading is a psychological performance which depends upon a great many different factors. It depends, for example, upon the skill which has been acquired in distinguishing one form from another. It depends, also, upon the meanings which have become attached to all of these forms.

Although we have not yet taken account of the origin and development of meaning, we may say that objects, and especially such objects as make up each of the letters in the words that are now being read, acquire meaning in somewhat the same way that words acquire their symbolizing functions. Reading also depends, however, upon the way in which the eyes are used, and it is this fact which makes it possible to say that reading, like speaking, is in part a motor skill which can be acquired through practice.[81]

[80] Cf. Dunlap, K., *Habits: Their Making and Unmaking.* New York: Liveright Publishing Corp., 1932, pp. 197 ff.
[81] Judd, C. H., "Reading, Its Nature and Development." *Suppl. Educ. Monog.,* 1918, II (No. 10).

2. *Reading and Eye Movement:* It has long been known that, during the process of reading, the eyes do not move smoothly and continuously over the material being read.[82] The student can prove this fact to himself if he will make a pinhole in this page, and then look through the pinhole at the eyes of a person on the other side of the page who is reading the lines near the pinhole. In this experiment, the student will observe that the eyes of the reader jump from one point of fixation to another. These jumps are frequently called flights. The flights are interrupted, a half-dozen or more times per line, depending upon the length of the line, by momentary periods of fixation called perches. Both the rate of reading and the degree of comprehension of what is read depend, in a very intimate way, upon the number of flights and the number of perches that are made per line. They depend, also, upon the number of return movements which the eyes make. In the experiment described above, for example, the student may discover that the eyes of his subject will jump back on occasion in order to pick up some letter or word that has not been observed. In any case, it is known that vision of printed material occurs only during the moments when the eye is perched. Practically nothing is seen when the eye is in movement.[83]

There are two important inferences to be drawn from these facts. In the first place, it is clear that reading is not the purely psychological matter it is often alleged to be. On the contrary, it is closely related to the skill which a person has acquired in using the muscles in and around the eye. In the second place, since reading is dependent upon ocular skill, it must follow that these ocular skills have been brought to whatever level of competence they possess by previous periods of practice. It is known, for example, that fast and slow readers differ from one another in the number of perches they make per line of printed material, in the duration of the perches, and in the number of return movements which are made.[84] If, then, a slow reader could learn how to move his eyes more rapidly and more accurately, that is, if he could reduce the number of perches and the number of return movements per line, he ought to be able to increase in a proportionate amount both his rate of reading and his rate of comprehension.

[82] Tinker, M. A., "The Physiological Psychology of Reading." *Psychol. Bull.*, 1931, XV, 241-247.
[83] Dodge, R., "Visual Perception During Eye Movement." *Psychol. Rev.*, 1900, VII, 454-465.
[84] Buswell, G. T., "Fundamental Reading Habits: A Study of Their Development." *Suppl. Educ. Monog.*, 1922 (No. 23).

THE DEVELOPMENT OF ACTIONS AND ATTITUDES

It now looks as though a major part of the skill which the average person uses in reading is acquired by the time he has finished the fourth or fifth grades. This means, apparently, that teachers have been more interested in teaching their pupils how to enunciate clearly during reading than they have in teaching them how to read rapidly. This fact is revealed, in part, by the discovery that the best readers in an average classroom may be at least twice as good as the poor readers.[85]

Under proper circumstances, most persons can learn how to effect large increases in their rate of reading. These increases are dependent primarily upon speed drills given to pupils in direct connection with the reading work in the schoolroom. It is true, of course, that when a person attempts to increase his skill beyond an older habit level, the first results will be disappointing for, as we have seen, accuracy of bodily movement usually decreases with an increase in the speed of movement. A typist, however, who wishes to increase her speed in operating her machine would not be unduly discouraged by an increase in errors during the first part of the practice period. Obviously, the muscles and nervous system have to adjust themselves to a new tempo of movement. The same thing holds true of learning how to read at a faster pace.[86]

3. *Oral and Silent Reading:* There are certain important facts concerning the relation between oral and silent reading. As a rule, silent reading can be done at a faster rate than oral reading. This speed factor holds true not only of the actual material covered but of degrees of comprehension as well.[87] A part of the difference between oral and silent reading is to be explained by the time consumed in actually enunciating words. This time is decreased in silent reading because of certain essential differences between overt speech and implicit speech.

The student will recall that, in the distinction drawn above between these two types of speech, it was said that implicit speech may involve only tentative movements in the vocal apparatus. There is some evidence to show that these tentative movements may become abbreviated in form, and consequently will be highly symbolical in character, just as certain bodily gestures are abbreviated.

---

[85] Cf. Book, W. F., "How Well College Students Can Read." *School and Soc.*, 1927, XXVI, 242-248.
[86] Averill, L. A., and Mueller, A. D., "The Effect of Practice on the Improvement of Silent Reading Habits in Adults." *J. Educ. Res.*, 1928, XVII, 125-129; Book, W. F., "The Development of Higher Orders of Perceptual Habits in Reading." *J. Educ. Res.*, 1930, XXI, 161-176.
[87] Cf. O'Brien, J. A., *Silent Reading with Special Reference to Methods for Developing Speed.* New York: The Macmillan Co., 1921, *passim.*

In tipping one's hat to a lady, for example, it sometimes happens that a partial movement will be just as acceptable, so far as courtesy is concerned, as a completed movement.

One of the primary inferences to be drawn from these considerations is as follows. While the transition from oral to silent reading cannot, apparently, be pushed down into the grades much further than is the case at present, teachers may, nevertheless, expend considerable time to good advantage on speed drills in silent reading. As we have said, the effect of these drills is to decrease the number of perches per line, to eliminate a large number of unnecessary return movements, and to increase the relative amount of comprehension. These changes in skill depend, of course, upon a number of factors which have to do with the reading material itself. It has been found, for example, that rate of reading may depend upon the size of the type, the length of the printed line, and the amount of leading placed between the lines.[88] Return movements, for example, occur most frequently when a reader has finished one line and is trying to find the start of the next. If we may assume, then, a proper size of type, the most favorable length of line, and a proper amount of leading between lines, speed of reading can be markedly increased by speed drills. Moreover, increase in speed in reading can be gained with an almost negligible loss, in relative terms, in degrees of comprehension. Let us, however, look at this phase of the situation at a little closer range.

4. *Reading and Comprehension:* It is almost too obvious to say that a student may read for a good many other purposes than comprehension. When, for example, he is preparing for participation in a play, he reads not so much in order to understand the text as in order to commit it to memory. Then, too, the student may simply scan over a number of pages in search of facts, the general location of which he may already know. The proofreader presents a special case in the art of reading, for at least in one phase of his work he is interested not so much in the meaning of the printed material as he is in the detection of errors. Finally, one may read solely for enjoyment. This will require, to be sure, a certain amount of comprehension, but words often serve the purpose of painting pictures rather than of promoting knowledge. Of these several functions of reading, we are interested mostly in degree of comprehension.

Teachers often take it for granted that students who read rapidly

[88] Cf. Bentley, M., "Leading and Legibility." *Psychol. Monog.,* 1921, XXX (No. 136).

THE DEVELOPMENT OF ACTIONS AND ATTITUDES

must, therefore, read superficially. There are, of course, individual differences in this field just as there are elsewhere, but, on the whole, the rapid reader also comprehends well.[89] To be sure, slow and careful reading of difficult material may yield more ideas per page than more rapid reading, but it is also true that rapid reading will yield a greater number of ideas per unit of time spent.

These facts need to be supplemented by a number of other considerations. It has been pointed out, for example, that reading bears some similarity to problem-solving. Each of the words that appears on this page, for example, has a primary meaning, and some of them have secondary meanings. In order for the student to understand what the author is trying to say, it is necessary for him to catch these meanings, relate them to one another, balance some against others, emphasize those that should be emphasized, and especially correlate and organize a whole paragraph or page so that it will strike the student somewhere near the meaning the author intended to put into it.[90]

It follows from these considerations that degree of comprehension will depend largely upon the equipment a student possesses for using words. It has been pointed out, for example, that even mature readers, when they come to an unfamiliar or difficult word, will revert to an earlier level of reading before they can pass on.[91] This, however, is only a minor feature of the delay that will occur in reading, for unfamiliar words signify that the student cannot carry out the problemlike features of reading described above. The same fact is suggested by studies on the relation of rate of reading and intelligence. Although the correlations at this point are not exceptionally high, there is fairly good evidence that achievement in silent reading may be taken as a rough index of test intelligence. In any case, one of the essential preconditions to comprehension in reading is familiarity with words gained through previous experience.

5. *Summary:* We may summarize this section by naming briefly some of the circumstances which surround the diagnosis and treatment of inadequate types of reading skill.[92] In the first place, the

---

[89] Cf. Gray, W. S., "Summary of Investigations Relating to Reading." *Suppl. Educ. Monog.*, 1925 (No. 28).
[90] Cf. Thorndike, E. L., "Reading as Reasoning: A Study of Mistakes in Paragraph Reading." *J. Educ. Psychol.*, 1917, VIII, 323-332. Also, "The Understanding of Sentences: A Study of Errors in Reading." *Element. School J.*, 1917, XVIII, 98-114.
[91] Buswell, G. T., "An Experimental Study of Eye-Voice Span in Reading." *Suppl. Educ. Monog.*, 1920, XVII, pp. 101 ff.
[92] Gray, W. S., "Remedial Cases in Reading: Their Diagnosis and Treatment." *Suppl. Educ. Monog.*, 1922 (No. 22). See also Gates, A. I., *The Improvement of Reading*. New York: The Macmillan Co., 1929.

teacher must make certain that reading difficulties are not created by defects in the visual and in the auditory apparatus. These defects include memory for vision and for sound as well as the initial perception. It is known, for example, that some children have real difficulty in reading because of congenital word blindness.[93]

In the second place, there is the whole matter of the nature of eye movements, including the duration of the pauses and the use which the reader may make of portions of the retina lying near to the points of clearest vision. Obviously, the eye-span must reach beyond a single letter or word. As a matter of fact, rapid reading almost always depends upon the ability to "see" whole phrases and even whole sentences in one single act of fixation. Practice in increasing the eye-span and in decreasing the number of pauses per line is about the only remedy for this source of reading defect.

In the third place, failures in reading due to a limited vocabulary obviously require an increase in the size of the vocabulary. To be sure, there are those who would say that the number of words in common use is altogether too large in view of the more ordinary services rendered by conversation. Words represent, however, the accumulated distinctions which men have been able to draw, and it is difficult to see how clear and critical thinking can be carried on unless a sufficient vocabulary is available. The study of foreign languages and of the ancient languages contributes, no doubt, to this end.

In the fourth place, dullness in reading is often associated with lack of interest. Lack of interest may have its origin, in part, in the attempt to force students to read material that is too difficult for them and, in part, in choosing material which is unrelated to previously acquired interests. The chances are that the development of a new interest cannot take place by reading alone. If, however, the interest is attacked from some other source, the reading process will take care of itself.

VI. Writing

1. *Introduction:* Just as it is a mistake to think of the origin of verbal skills without reference to the random play of vocal activities out of which skill emerges, so it is a mistake to think of the origins of handwriting apart from the first random arm and finger movements which lead to scribbling and to drawing. The chances are that a small child writes and draws for the same reason that it makes any other movements. Writing and drawing possess a certain advantage over other movements, however, because they produce re-

[93] Gray, W. S., *op. cit.,* pp. 13-14.

THE DEVELOPMENT OF ACTIONS AND ATTITUDES 83

sults which may include, in their turn, a further source of stimulus to activity for the child. Just as he may, after making one sound, repeat the sound largely as a response to hearing himself speak, so he may continue to move a pencil in a random way over the page in response to lines and figures that have already been produced.[94]

2. *Origin of Writing Movements:* As a rule, writing and drawing appear after a considerable degree of perfection has been reached in grasping objects. We may say, then, that the original matrix of behavior out of which the finer movements which lead to true drawing emerge is just as highly generalized as is the case with other skills. Under the influence of learning situations, a child gradually acquires the ability to localize and specify its finger and arm movements for the sake of producing forms and diagrams which will have the same symbolical value to it and to the persons around it that spoken words have acquired. Testimony in favor of the extreme refinement of writing movements comes from the fact that supplementary movements, such as facial grimaces, tenseness in bodily posture, and even excessive arm movements continue for a longer time in the process of learning how to write than they do in a good many other processes.

All of the movements which children make in learning how to write have been described with considerable fidelity.[95] Unskilled and immature writers show a high degree of tension in the hand and in the arm while the fingers produce three or four letters. Then the position of the hand and arm is changed so that three or more letters may be added. The hand and arm positions, in their turn, are taken with respect to a bodily posture which keeps the child in a fairly cramped position. The art of teaching writing, then, requires the discovery of a bodily posture which will be favorable not only to good postural habits but to ease and flexibility in the writing movements themselves. Moreover, proper degrees of correlation between finger movements and wrist and arm movements must be discovered.[96]

It is usually assumed that methods of writing which force the hand to roll over to the left are faulty. It is also said that writing movements which are limited to the fingers alone are faulty, the assumption being that finger movements should be an intimate part

[94] Cf. Goodenough, F. L., "Children's Drawings," in Murchison, C. (Ed.), *Handbook of Child Psychology* (1st ed.). Worcester, Mass.: Clark Univ. Press, 1931, Chapter XIV, *passim.*
[95] Gates, A. I., "The Acquisition of Motor Control in Writing by Preschool Children." *Teachers Coll. Rec.,* 1923, XXIV, 459-469.
[96] Gates, A. I., and Brown, H., "Experimental Comparisons of Print-script and Cursive Writing." *J. Educ. Res.,* 1929, XX, 3-16.

84 INTRODUCTION TO EDUCATIONAL PSYCHOLOGY

of the smoothly coördinated pattern in the whole forearm. In other words, the fingers serve only the primary function of grasping the writing instrument. Some measure of coördination can be secured by allowing the mass of the arm to flow over the surface layers that are in contact with the desk. This is a feature of coördination, however, which is dependent upon the viscosity of muscle tissue rather than upon the integration of different groups of muscles. Since finger movements represent a genetically later type of action, it would seem to follow that writing should depend upon coördination in the forearm, only to the extent necessary to create a proper background for the finer finger movements.[97]

3. *Methods of Teaching:* There is one feature of the art of teaching handwriting which differs from older methods. As an illustration, we may take the following experiment. A group of subjects was asked to learn to write while tracing letters through a groove, while tracing on transparent paper a model of the letters placed below the paper, while trying to imitate a model copy near at hand, and while using a combination of these three methods.[98] There are, however, only two essentially different conditions in this experiment, viz., learning to write with the aid of some type of objective guidance versus learning to write through the making of trial-and-error movements during which the correct movements will emerge out of the total behavior complex.

The results of this experiment indicated that the development of skill in writing proceeds most quickly when there is no objective guidance.[99] This conclusion fits in well with the conclusions that have been drawn from a great many other experiments of the same general type making use of other skills. These experiments seem to suggest that the attempt to follow a model places the learner in too passive a condition for effective progress. As we have seen, learning does not take place to good advantage when the learner is more or less witless about his actions. If he is to increase his skills rapidly, he must do so under conditions that require of him a maximal amount of intention to learn and a maximal opportunity to sense the relation between success and failure.[100]

Since writing is a skill which is individuated out of a series of

---

[97] Studies on the development of grasping and other manual movements are important in this connection. Cf. Halverson, H. M., *op. cit., passim.*
[98] Hertzberg, O. E. "A Comparative Study of Different Methods Used in Teaching Beginners to Write." *Teachers Coll. Contrib. to Educ.*, 1926 (No. 214).
[99] Cf. Gates, A. I., *op. cit.*, p. 467.
[100] Carr, H. A., and Koch, H., "The Influence of Extraneous Controls in the Learning Process." *Psychol. Rev.*, 1919, XXVI, 287-293. Also Carr, H. A., "The Influence of Visual Guidance in Image Learning." *J. Exper. Psychol.*, 1921, IV, 399-417.

THE DEVELOPMENT OF ACTIONS AND ATTITUDES 85

movements which are more generalized or masslike in character, it would seem to follow that the first steps in learning how to write should require large-scale writing.[101] A blackboard offers, then, a simple way of meeting this requirement, although the act of writing while standing before a blackboard involves other postures and skills than those required while sitting at a desk. In any case, we may infer that desk writing should allow the child to make letters which are as large as practicable. In other words, the paper used by the child should be ruled so as to make generous allowance for large letters.

Progress, both in form and speed of writing, comes with the application of the general features of efficient learning to be described in a later chapter. In other words, the teacher must supplement the trial-and-error practice periods with cautions, special instructions, continuous reference to favorable postures and favorable types of movement, and, where copy is used, with remarks about the details of the copy that may lie behind the perceptual skills of the learner.

4. *Speed and Style:* There is one additional feature of learning to write about which there is much disagreement. This feature has to do with the proper relations between form of writing and speed of writing. Some of the older methods of teaching were based upon the premise that writing should be an end in itself. In other words, it was assumed that no person was properly skilled until his style of writing conformed to a standard which could be judged by its aesthetic qualities or by some artificial measure of legibility. A minimal amount of attention was paid to speed in writing.[102]

More recently it has been held that writing is merely a means to an end. It is a type of skill which is to be judged in terms of the services it renders to the person rather than in terms of its aesthetic qualities. If a way out of this difference in attitude toward writing is to be found, it will probably lie in some of the facts we have already considered concerning timing or pace habits. When emphasis is placed upon form of writing, the very form that is acquired will imply a pace or a tempo. Any attempt to change this pace will result, as we have seen, in large amounts of inaccuracy.

It might be urged, therefore, that children should be taught to write with a form that just passes a given level of legibility but

[101] Cf. Freeman, F. N., and Dougherty, M. L., *How to Teach Handwriting.* Boston: Houghton Mifflin Co., 1923, *passim.*
[102] Scales for measuring handwriting sometimes make this assumption. Cf., for example, Freeman, F. N., *The Teaching of Handwriting.* Boston: Houghton Mifflin Co., 1914, *passim.*

86 INTRODUCTION TO EDUCATIONAL PSYCHOLOGY

which emphasizes the speed factor, for modern methods of teaching require speed in taking notes which cannot be attained by those who have emphasized a style. Since speed habits can be established, speed drills in writing ought to have the same effect as speed drills in reading.

If one may be permitted to carry this notion to its logical completion, one ought to say that the complete abandonment of handwriting as a part of formal school training would be a desirable thing. In its place it would be a simple matter to substitute one or more of the common systems of shorthand. The significance of writing, of course, is to be found not in its aesthetic qualities, but in its symbolic and social functions. Words, whether written or spoken, have meanings which are their primary source of value to an educated person. The lines and curves usually employed by systems of shorthand become just as definite symbols to a stenographer as written words become to a person untrained in stenography.

VII. Sources of Training

1. *Introduction:* It goes almost without saying that every situation in which the child is placed will be a situation that must lead to some modification in its skill. We shall see the full significance of this fact in the next chapter, for it is clear that no child ever escapes altogether from the objects and events which surround it. These objects and events offer a continuous appeal to action, with the result that the child must grow older in the quality of its reactions. This fact holds true, in particular, of coördination and of timing or pace habits.

There is, of course, no place in the school program where the teacher has as his main purpose the creation of pace habits of a given type; but the very existence of these pace habits implies that they have been acquired as a result of rates of response to everyday situations. Even if a child were left to itself it would develop a considerable variety of skills with variable properties, simply because the phrase "left by itself" cannot mean that the child is ever left without an environment.[103] We wish to inquire, therefore, about the resources that are available for training behavior-patterns aside from those that make up the unorganized portions of the environment. Of these sources we shall discuss two, in particular, viz., play and formal systems of physical education.

[103] A splendid example of this fact is to be found in Itard, J., *The Wild Boy of Aveyron.* (Trans. by G. and M. Humphrey.) New York: D. Appleton-Century Co., 1932.

THE DEVELOPMENT OF ACTIONS AND ATTITUDES 87

2. *Play:* It is a curious fact that, even though all children and most of the lower animals expend considerable amounts of time in activity that may be called playful, there is as yet no adequate explanation of the source of this activity, nor is there a complete appraisal of the results that may come from it.[104] We must, however, review briefly such facts as are now known about it.

In the first place, we ought to find out why it is that play activities have been and should be distinguished from other types of action. It has become a custom to compare playful activities with work. When this is done, it is discovered that play is a type of action which does not have to be supported by some end or goal beyond sheer action.[105] Work is usually defined as a type of action which must be so supported. This means, then, that playful activity is done "just for fun."

There is, in the second place, a kind of spontaneity about playful action which is rarely found in gainful action. In other words, playful activity is often random in character. It is not organized, except at a later stage, around some definite objective. To be sure, a game may be defined as playful activity which has been caught up in a series of rules; but these rules are not usually of such a character as to take away from play its initial spontaneity and inherent pleasure.

Finally, it may be said that playful activity implies a minimal amount of conflict. When the student reads this book, he will often get a sense of effort and of strain owing to the fact that the obligation upon him to study the book is opposed by desires and impulses that would attract him elsewhere. The person who is at play, however, does not choose to be anywhere else. There is, then, a considerable freedom from conflict.[106]

The theories that have been invented to explain the nature of play are even more variable than the attempts that have been made to characterize it. The student is already familiar, perhaps, with the excess energy theory which suggests that some types of play occur out of sheer exuberance of spirit. Although this theory is more largely a product of critics who have tried to make more out of the theory than was actually put into it by its authors, the argument that children play because they are concentrated bundles of energy appears plausible.[107] The chief objection to the theory lies in the fact

---

[104] Cf. Curti, M. W., *op. cit.*, Chapter VI.
[105] Cf. Lehman, H. C., and Witty, P. A., *The Psychology of Play Activities.* New York: A. S. Barnes and Co., 1927, *passim.*
[106] Curti, M. W., *op. cit.*, pp. 333 ff.,
[107] Cf. Schiller, F., *Essays, Aesthetical and Philosophical.* London: Bell, 1875, pp. 112 ff. Also Spencer, H., *Principles of Psychology.* New York: D. Appleton-Century Co., 1896, pp. 627-648.

88 INTRODUCTION TO EDUCATIONAL PSYCHOLOGY

that weak children and elderly people get as much satisfaction out of play as normal children.

A second theory asserts that playful activities are attempts on the part of children to duplicate adult activity, the attempts being largely a result of an instinctive awareness of what these activities will be.[108] A great many games are, to be sure, reminiscent of more mature modes of living, but the student will see later on in our study of the nature of instinct that serious attention cannot be paid to this theory. For a time, the theory was strongly supported by the argument that playful activity must be an echo of actions which were common to our ancestors.[109] In other words, the child in its play activities is attempting to live over again in terms of motor performance the major occupations of the generations that have preceded him. This theory, too, can be discarded. It would not even be worth while to mention it were it not for the fact that it did have a tremendous vogue for a time and were it not for the fact that a great many teachers have allowed its vogue to influence them in handling problems created by the play life of school children.[110]

A fourth theory comes out of the following facts. As we have seen in the first chapter, the adult acquires a good many types of psychological operation that the child does not possess. Some of these operations require high levels of sustained attention, concentration, and integration. It may be argued, therefore, that they represent levels of effort and strain which cannot be sustained. Since they are functions which have been acquired recently in the history of the race and which are the most recent to be acquired in the history of the individual, there will be a tendency during periods of fatigue for them to drop out, leaving in their places some of the more stable and practical types of activity. Since these actions are much older, that is, much more habitualized, they will not involve the strain brought about by other actions. They may, therefore, be called playful activities.

3. *Physical Education:* The real value of research after the origin of play lies not so much in the theories that are formulated as in the fact that playful activity lies at the foundation of all forms of athletic competition and of a good many types of physical education as well. The theories, then, may not be so important, but the

---

[108] Cf. Groos, K., *The Play of Animals.* New York: D. Appleton and Co., 1898 (Trans. by E. L. Baldwin). Also *The Play of Man.* New York: D. Appleton-Century Co., 1901 (Trans. by E. L. Baldwin).
[109] Cf. Hall, G. S., *Adolescence.* New York: D. Appleton and Co., 1904. Vol. I, pp. 202-203 and *passim.*
[110] Cf. Patrick, G. T. W., *The Psychology of Relaxation.* Boston: Houghton Mifflin Co., 1916, *passim.*

values of physical education are to be searched for and judged in their own terms.

On this matter, there is a great deal of confusion and much more of wishful thinking than there is of solid fact. Athletic games and contests, for example, have a large popular appeal, for it has been easy for programs of physical education to be converted into great spectacles. These spectacles almost inevitably give rise to a variety of abuses and as a defense, therefore, physical educators have all been exhausting their imaginations in trying to describe not only favorable healthy outcomes of athletic competition but psychological, social, and aesthetic outcomes as well.[111]

The claim that the desire for physical activity, as it is expressed in different forms of competition, leads to increased measures of health is pretty well supported by the facts. Save where training programs become too severe and where injuries are inflicted during the more rugged games, such as football, wrestling, and boxing, both physical education and participation in athletic contests appear to increase muscular strength, tone all of the processes of metabolism, and increase the resistance of the body to various types of diseases. To be sure, exactly the same products could be secured from gainful occupations which would require the same amount of actual physical exercise and which would keep workers in the open as much as they are kept in the open by physical training programs. Athletic participation and physical education have the advantage, however, of being able to draw upon the pleasures that seem to attend playful activity, on the one hand, and upon competition or rivalry, on the other.[112]

There can be still less doubt about the contribution which athletic competition and physical education make to the development of habits, skills, and postures. Even the casual observer knows that the athlete and the gymnast are often to be admired because of the extremely clever and graceful way in which they can use their bodies. Not only do they reach a high level of accuracy in movement but there are many types of physical training which make their contribution to fine muscular coördination. It is not known that any significant change can be wrought in the simpler phases of reaction time by practice, but speed of movement can be materially

[111] A large amount of the literature on school and college athletics has been abstracted by Ryan, W. C., *The Literature of American School and College Athletics.* New York: The Carnegie Foundation for the Advancement of Teaching, 1929 (No. 24).
[112] Cf. McCurdy, J. H., *The Physiology of Exercise.* Philadelphia: Lea and Febeiger, 1924, *passim.*

increased, partly by using all those muscles necessary to carry out a given act, and partly by increasing the general tone of muscle tissue.

These advantages are to be qualified in the following way. It seems to be true that playground activities make their contribution to the various features of skill at a time when general profit may be gained from increased measures of competence. During the high school, however, and certainly at the college level, the measures of skill which are attained by athletes and gymnasts appear to serve only one purpose, viz., the winning of a particular game. There is no reason to suppose that a football player who has developed high accuracy in throwing forward passes will have thereby acquired a skill which will be of any service to him at any other place save the professional football field.

In other words, the special skills demanded by the various competitive sports probably do not make as much of a contribution to the general fitness of a person as the time spent on them would justify. It is to be taken for granted, of course, that programs of physical education which are essentially corrective in nature have everything in their favor, but much of the adverse comment passed upon athletic competition in general springs from the fact that no good purpose is served by the development of habits and skills which are so technical as those required of distinguished athletes.

Education may, therefore, use the athletic field and the gymnasium as a fruitful source of training so far as health and bodily competence are concerned, especially during the earlier stages of the growth pattern. In addition to these values, it is often remarked that athletic competition, in particular, serves a good many other functions. Among these we may name the development of a social sense, the development of principles of fairness and of honesty, the development of the problem-solving functions, and the development of essential character traits.

A social sense is said to be a product of athletic competition because many games require high degrees of teamwork and constant contact with opponents who must be recognized as distinctive personalities. A sense of fairness or of sportsmanship is said to be developed because many coaches require strict adherence to the rules of the game and favor those types of generosity which will recognize superior ability on the part of an opponent. The problem-solving functions are said to be developed because many group games require the quick readjustment of previously learned habits and skills to new situations. The typical instance of a problem-solver on the athletic field is usually found in the quarterback of a

THE DEVELOPMENT OF ACTIONS AND ATTITUDES 91

football team. The development of character and personality traits is described as a product of athletic competition mostly because athletes have to rid themselves of all forms of cowardice and shyness in the presence of difficult situations.

With respect to all of these by-products of physical education, it may be said that there is nothing about the playing of games which, in and of itself, will increase them. The game of football is, of course, an extreme example, but the reader needs hardly to be reminded of the fact that there is nothing soft or easy about this game. If it is played as the rules allow, every participant must expect to take a considerable amount of punishment. If, therefore, any of the by-products mentioned above are to come from such a game as football, they will come only because the coach—that is to say, the teacher—takes the initiative in allowing them to come. In other words, a game of football does furnish the opportunity for an astonishing amount of training of a fundamental character. The coach is in a particularly fortunate position with respect to these types of training; but he is not often able to take advantage of his position simply because the people in the bleachers require that he be a "showman" rather than a teacher. We may draw the conclusion, then, that the educational values of the competitive sports are a function of the attitude and disposition of the coach rather than of the contests themselves.

READINGS

The student should not expect to know and to understand, after a single reading, all that has been said and implied in the first section of this chapter unless he has done a good deal of work in experimental psychology. Lack of understanding, therefore, should be no occasion for dismay. As he proceeds with his reading and his study of educational psychology, the matters that have been discussed in the first part of this chapter, together with other similar material from other parts of the book, will gradually fall into a much more satisfactory picture. This picture belongs, however, to the background of education rather than to the foreground. As we have noted in the readings suggested for the last chapter, one of the best places to fill out this background material is in Heidbreder, E. F., *Seven Psychologies*. New York: D. Appleton-Century Co., 1933. See also Woodworth, R. S., *Contemporary Schools of Psychology*. New York: The Ronald Press, 1931. Because of its more direct relation to education, the student will find it helpful to refer frequently to Ragsdale, C. E., *Modern Psychologies and Education*. New York: The Macmillan Co., 1932.

The second section of this chapter has considered some of the typical forms and properties of movement systems. Both the student and the teacher will have missed, no doubt, a discussion of the various instruments and devices by means of which movements can be produced. This information is to be found in almost any one of the standard textbooks in elementary psychology. A very good treatment has been given by Dashiell, J. F., *Fundamentals of Objective Psychology*. Boston: Houghton Mifflin Co., 1928, Chapters II, III, and IV. A useful book in this field, written from the point of view of physiology, is Gould, A. G., and Dye, J. A., *Exercise and Its Physiology*. New York: A. S. Barnes and Co., 1932, *passim*. See also Watson, J. B., *Psychology from the Standpoint of a Behaviorist*. Philadelphia: J. B. Lippincott, 1924, *passim*.

Much of the material of this chapter concerns a type of education which is much more useful in the trades and in industry than it is in the professions. A standard reference for the psychological facts considered is Murchison, C. (Ed.), *Handbook of General Experimental Psychology*. Worcester, Mass.: Clark Univ. Press, 1934. See especially, Chapter III, "The Mechanism of Reaction" (by A. Forbes), and Chapter XII, "Work of the Integrated Organism" (by E. S. Robinson). A good study of the nature of motor aptitude and of a variety of motor tests can be found in Hull, C. L., *Aptitude Testing*. Yonkers, New York: World Book Co., 1928. The practical side of motor skills is discussed either directly or by implication and at great length by Viteles, M. S., *Industrial Psychology*. New York: W. W. Norton and Co., 1932. See also, Viteles, M. S., *The Science of Work*. New York: W. W. Norton and Co., 1934.

The most important feature, perhaps, of this chapter, a feature which is still full of difficulties and which should gain more extended study, is described by the phrase "the development of verbal skills," or "the functions of speech." The student can consult with considerable profit Watson, J. B., *Psychology from the Standpoint of a Behaviorist*. Philadelphia: J. B. Lippincott, 1924, Chapter IX. See also, Hunter, W. S., *Human Behavior*. Chicago: University of Chicago Press, 1928, Chapter IX, and *passim*. A very good description somewhat similar to the point of view taken by the present author can be found in Curti, M. W., *Child Psychology*. New York: Longmans, Green and Co., 1931, Chapters VII, VIII, and IX. See also Morgan, J. J. B., *Child Psychology* (Rev. ed.). New York: Farrar and Rinehart, Inc., 1934, Chapter IX.

A major source of information concerning speech defects is Travis, L. E., *Speech Pathology*. New York: D. Appleton-Century Co., 1931, *passim*. See also Fletcher, J. M., *The Problem of Stuttering*. New York: Longmans, Green and Co., 1928. A splendid survey of the general function of language, together with theories of the racial and individual origin and development of speech, has been supplied by De Laguna, G., *Speech, Its Function and Development*. New Haven: Yale Univ. Press, 1927.

The schoolroom side of reading, writing, and other elementary school subjects is admirably presented in Cole, L., *Psychology of the Elementary School Subjects*. New York: Farrar and Rinehart, Inc., Chapters II, III, and V. See also, O'Brien, J. A., *Silent Reading with Special Reference to Methods for Developing Speed*. New York: The Macmillan Co., 1921.

The brief reference made at the end of the chapter to certain problems in physical education ought to be followed up by some students, at least, with a further examination of the whole field. The best place to enter this field is through Ryan, W. C., *The Literature of American School and College Athletics*. New York: The Carnegie Foundation for the Advance-

THE DEVELOPMENT OF ACTIONS AND ATTITUDES 93

ment of Teaching, 1929, Bulletin No. 24. For special topics, see Berry, E., *The Philosophy of Athletics*. New York: A. S. Barnes and Co., 1927. Griffith, C. R., *Psychology and Athletics*. New York: Charles Scribner's Sons, 1928. Hetherington, C. W., *School Progress and Physical Education*. Yonkers, New York: World Book Co., 1926. The student will realize, of course, that athletics form only one branch of the so-called extracurricular activities. For appraisals of these activities, see Fretwell, E. K., *Extracurricular Activities in Secondary Schools*. Boston: Houghton Mifflin Co., 1931. Roberts, A. C., and Draper, E. M., *Extra-Class and Intra-mural Activities in High Schools*. Boston: D. C. Heath and Co., 1928.

CHAPTER THREE

TRAINING THE PERCEPTUAL FUNCTIONS

I. Stimuli and Situations

1. *Introduction:* We shall use again, in this chapter, the same method that was used in the last. That is, we shall take a single feature of the whole pattern of growth as it moves on its way under the influence of education, because the words which are in common use for describing the processes of human becoming simply do not enable us to tell all that happens in one or two sentences. The growing child must, for practical purposes, be taken part by part, even though we try to keep always in view the complete pattern out of which each part is momentarily abstracted.

It is the purpose of this chapter to supplement the facts that were described in the last by taking up what is, after all, another phase of a single series of events. We have tried, in the facts already presented, to see how children change in their habits, skills, and postures, that is, in their modes of reaction to situations. Now we must try to find out how they change with respect to the variety of objects and events which can excite them to action.

These two phases of growth are often put together by the use of such phrases as perceptual-motor growth, stimulus-response patterns, the reflex arc, and sensation and movement.[1] Clearly, no child can grow older in its modes of reaction to objects and events unless it grows older also in its devices for the reception of objects and events. Likewise, no child can grow older in the reception of objects and events unless it grows older in its ways of reacting to them.

2. *Relevant and Irrelevant Environments:* The general nature of the problems of education to be studied in the following pages can be illustrated by drawing a simple distinction between the meaning that might be given to the phrase "relevant environment" as compared with the meaning that might be given to the phrase "irrelevant environment." Every event which takes place is always in a con-

---

[1] Cf. Shirley, M. M., "Locomotor and Visual-Manual Functions in the First Two Years," in Murchison, C. (Ed.), *Handbook of Child Psychology* (2nd ed.). Worcester, Mass.: Clark Univ. Press, 1933, Chapter V.

text of other events. That is, it is surrounded by events which are not itself. As examples, let us think of a molecule of water surrounded by other molecules and by fields of force, of an amoeba surrounded by water, by chemicals, and by light, of a foetus surrounded by the body of the mother, of the new-born infant surrounded by its clothing and by all of the objects and events which make up the room in which it lies, or of an adult surrounded by other adults, by lighted and sounding objects, by laws and institutions, and other features which are more commonly called environmental.[2]

Now let us compare the environment of a new-born infant with that of an adult person. Obviously, the new-born infant is surrounded by the same environment as is an adult. That is, all of the events described by physics and chemistry, by psychology, and by the social sciences continue to exist as a part of the environment of an infant even though an infant "knows" nothing about them. In the case of the adult, however, a considerable portion of the total environment has been translated into what we may call a "relevant environment." In other words, the difference between relevant and irrelevant environments is simply this. A relevant environment is that part of the total surroundings of a person which can become effective in initiating action on the part of that person and of regulating his actions through a period of time. Irrelevant portions of the environment, on the contrary, exercise no such functions.

There are, to be sure, some types of the environment which can never become relevant. The person who is reading these lines, for example, is surrounded by radio waves and by other types of vibration in the ether. There is no method, however, of training a person so that these waves can become effective in exciting him to action unless they have been transformed by a radio receiver into another form of energy. Radio waves differ, then, from the sound waves that surround a new-born infant, for these latter hold promise of sometime becoming relevant. The chances are that a new-born infant cannot react to sounds of low intensity. In other words, he does not hear them. After a few days, however, it is clear that sound waves have become a part of its effective environment. They have not become effective, however, in the same way that they have for the adult, because a parent or a nurse may talk to an infant hour after hour without the infant making any differential response to different patterns of sounds. That is, the sounds have not acquired

[2] Cf. Bentley, M., "Environment and Context." *Amer. J. Psychol.*, 1927, XXXIX, 54-61.

meaning. If the same things were to be said to an adult person, however, the adult would react to each of the words or to each combination of words in a differential way. He would understand what was being said.

We may say again, then, that an environment or an effective environment is that part of the total context of a human being (or of any other living creature) which can become effective in initiating and regulating behavior. This distinction holds very great importance for education for the following reason. Since the infant differs from the adult, in part, in the size or in the range of its relevant environment, while differing not at all in the size of its irrelevant environment, it must follow that education and training are, in part, processes which favor the gradual transformation of the context of an infant into the relevant environment of the adult. If the adult can respond in verbal or manual ways to a range and variety of objects and events which are wholly irrelevant or ineffective so far as the infant is concerned, he must do so because he has been trained in that respect. Moreover, if some persons can react in an effective way to a larger variety of objects than other persons can, the difference must have been created by differences in education.

This fact may be simply illustrated by any one of the tests of intelligence which are now in common use. As a rule, these tests include a test of the range of the child's vocabulary.[3] A vocabulary is made up of words which are symbols of objects, of relations between objects, and of events. If one child can tell the meaning of more words than another, it is clear that there must have been a difference in the rate of growth of these two children. The one has grown faster in the sense that more words have been changed from the status of irrelevant to the status of relevant environmental events. We may infer, then, that the development of an effective environment, that is, the gradual transformation of a context into an environment, is a highly important feature of the whole growth pattern.

3. *Stimulus-Patterns:* It is customary to think of the environment as made up of an enormous number of objects and events. The list includes all lighted objects, all sounding objects, and a great variety of relationships between these and other objects. As a rule, no single object is sufficient in and of itself to excite an appropriate response. On the contrary, objects usually stand in clusters or in patterns; and it is for this reason that we may speak of them as

[3] Cf. Freeman, F. N., *Mental Tests.* Boston: Houghton Mifflin Co., 1926, *passim.*

TRAINING THE PERCEPTUAL FUNCTIONS

situations. When, for example, we say that a child has been presented with a learning-situation, we mean that it has been presented with a group or cluster of objects or events which have gained, for the time being, the capacity to excite a definite mode of response in the child. These responses may be any one of the several types described in the last chapter.

The distinction, then, between an object and a situation is fairly simple. It is not so easy, however, to distinguish between either an object, or a situation, on the one hand, and a stimulus, on the other. For a long time it was supposed that the psychologist and the educator could use the word "stimulus" in the same way as it is used by the physiologist, for the physiologist thinks only of some unit of energy rather than of an object or a cluster of objects.[4] When, for example, the student looks at this page, it may be said that light waves are being reflected from the page in variable patterns. A minimal amount of light is being reflected from the black lines and dots which make up the letters. A larger amount is being reflected from the sheet of paper.

It is clear, however, that the student is not reacting to a pattern of light waves of different intensity. On the contrary, he is actually reacting to a pattern of light waves which has been converted into a series of objects, viz., the printed words on the page. If, then, we may draw a distinction between patterns of light waves, on the one hand, and objects or situations, on the other, we shall have laid the basis for the distinction between a stimulus and an object.

We shall wish to inquire, therefore, how it happens that patterns of stimulus can be converted into objects. This we shall do in a later portion of the chapter. In the meantime, let us confess that it is not easy to be consistent in the use of the words "stimulus" and "object" or "situation." We shall speak frequently, for example, of a stimulus-situation. This phrase simply refers to the fact that, whenever emphasis is being laid upon the events which start a reaction, those events can be called stimuli. They are not stimuli, however, in the physiological sense. They can be called stimuli only because they do start off a train of action.[5]

[4] For a discussion of this matter, see Tolman, E. C., *Purposive Behavior in Animals and Men.* New York: D. Appleton-Century Co., 1932, Chapter I.
[5] Cf. Hunter, W. S., "Anthroponomy and Psychology," in Murchison, C. (Ed.), *Psychologies of 1930.* Worcester, Mass.: Clark Univ. Press, 1930, Chapter XIV.

II. The Major Types of Perception

1. *Introduction:* The gradual transformation of the environment of a person into an effective environment is made possible, in part, by the possession of special structures which are called sense organs and, in part, by the development of adequate modes of response. The sense organs of the body—the eyes, the ears, the nose, the mouth, the organs of balance, and the contact organs imbedded in the skin—furnish pathways of entrance into the nervous system. All of them have been developed out of much more primitive structures and these, in turn, have grown out of a still more primitive property of all living tissue, the property of sensitivity.[6] The conversion of this original property into sense organs has served two very useful purposes. In the first place, it has enormously increased the amount of the environment that can be converted into an effective or relevant environment. In the second place, it has increased the extent to which fine discriminations may be drawn between stimulus-patterns.

A study of the instruments which the body possesses for giving external objects and events a means of access to the nervous system is of importance to education for several different reasons. In the first place, the child who is in any way deficient in these instruments furnishes the opportunity for specialized instruction. Consider, for example, a blind child. Blindness means that the whole domain of lighted objects must remain a part of the irrelevant environment of that child. It is necessary, then, that he be taught how to use his other sensory devices to the best advantage.

In the second place, since the sense organs are highly important members of the body, it has become essential that they should receive the same care as is given to the other members. Nowadays, a teacher is not said to be fully qualified for his work unless he helps students in such personal matters as care of the teeth, proper posture, proper exercise, and proper diet. We may add, then, the hygiene of the sense organs as one of the qualifications of a good teacher.

In the third place, a study of the sensory apparatus has become important because it is this apparatus which the teacher must use in presenting learning situations to children. We might wish to know, for example, whether it is better to present learning situations in visual terms or in auditory terms, or whether a combina-

---

[6] Cf. Freeman, G. L., *Introduction to Physiological Psychology.* New York: The Ronald Press, 1934, Chapters IV and V.

TRAINING THE PERCEPTUAL FUNCTIONS

tion of the two methods would be the most effective. As we shall see during this chapter, a large number of other problems of this same type must be considered.

2. *Visual Perception:* A number of different ways have been used in order to classify the perceptual functions. There has been, for example, a tendency to divide the senses into the higher and the lower senses, the inference being that vision and audition serve nobler purposes than touch, taste, and smell. Clearly, this is a classification of perception based upon other considerations than the essential psychological differences between them.[7]

A second type of classification sets the distance receptors off from the contact receptors. The primary contact receptors are, of course, those lodged in the skin, for perception mediated through these receptors cannot take place until they have actually been touched by the stimulus-object. Taste and smell are also spoken of as contact receptors, since gaseous particles, emanating from an odorous object, must actually come in contact either with the taste buds on the tongue or with the olfactory areas in the nasal passages. Vision is the primary distance receptor because it enables a person to make adjustments to objects which stand remote from the body. The same fact holds true of audition. Clearly, however, it is neither the lighted object nor the sounding object which actually stimulates the ear or the eye. On the contrary, energy waves are transmitted to these sense organs and it is not until they actually make contact with the sense organs that visual and auditory perceptions are made possible. The difference between contact receptors and distance receptors, then, is a difference created by the fact that, in the one case, the object itself must be in contact with the body whereas, in the other case, the distance between the object and the body can be covered by energies which travel freely through the air and through the ether.

For all practical purposes, the best way of classifying the perceptual functions is based upon differences in the types of energy involved and upon differences in the types of sense organs involved. Visual perceptions, then, would include all of those perceptions which are dependent upon the eyes or upon the retina and upon related structures. In the same way we may speak of auditory perceptions and of tactual, gustatory, olfactory, and perhaps vestibular perceptions. The last group is rarely counted as a true type of perceptual function because the excitation of the organs of balance in the inner

---

[7] Titchener, E. B., *A Textbook of Psychology.* New York: The Macmillan Co., 1910, pp. 46 ff.

ear leads to postures which do not involve either concepts of space or of position.

Of these several types of perceptual function the educator is interested primarily in vision and hearing because practically every stimulus-pattern which he uses in learning situations is made up of lighted or sounding objects. For a number of reasons, the visual functions are even more important than the auditory functions. The most vital of these is that the visual functions furnish the basis for judging most of the other functions. In short, there appears to be a primacy about vision. This primacy has even affected the various sciences; the physicist and the chemist, for instance, do not feel satisfied with their experimental work until they have been able to reduce a given set of phenomena to visual form. Somewhat the same sort of primacy is found in our commonsense opinion. As we commonly express it, "seeing is believing."

A. THE VISUAL APPARATUS: This is not the place to give a detailed description of the instruments which make it possible for lighted objects to exercise an initiating and regulating influence upon human action.[8] In normal conditions the visual apparatus consists of two structures which are very similar in principle to an ordinary camera. Light penetrating the outer layers of the eyeball passes through lenses which focus it upon a highly sensitive area at the back of the eyeball known as the retina. The retina is made up of nerve endings which are extremely sensitive to light energy. It appears that light energy is transformed in the retina into nerve energy, which, in turn, is propagated along well-defined pathways to the so-called visual area at the back of the cerebrum.[9] The rest of the details of the anatomy and physiology of vision can be found in any of the texts devoted to this particular topic.

B. DISTANCE, SIZE AND MOVEMENT: There are a number of aspects of visual perception which have an important bearing upon the work of the teacher. These aspects are described by such phrases as the "perception of form," "the perception of distance," and "the perception of movement." It is often supposed that these different types of visual perception are something which the teacher can simply take for granted, because they must be the result of intrinsic properties of the visual apparatus and not subject, therefore, to training.

[8] Cf. Troland, L. T., "Visual Phenomena and Their Stimulus Correlations," in Murchison, C. (Ed.), *A Handbook of General Experimental Psychology*. Worcester, Mass.: Clark Univ. Press, 1934, Chapter XIII.

[9] Cf. Hecht, S., "The Nature of the Photoreceptor Process," in Murchison, C. (Ed.), *op. cit.*, Chapter XIV.

Within limits this is true, perhaps, of the perception of form or of shape. Since the retina is an area, and since the images focused upon the retina often differ from one another in spatial extent, it seems fair to say that discriminations between forms and shapes must depend in part upon those mechanical features of the visual apparatus which give rise to a spatial pattern of nerve energy in the retina.[10] This fact marks, however, only the beginning of skill in differential but, at the same time, adequate types of response to differences in forms and shapes. For, as every teacher knows, children differ widely from one another in these skills. Some children appear to be highly competent in judging not only forms but extent or area as well.

These differences appear to best advantage, perhaps, in drawing and in other phases of art where a premium is place upon the adequate perception of the lengths of lines and proportions, and of the ratios of areas to one another. It is now known that skill in drawing and in painting does not depend so much upon the manual or motor aspects of the whole performance as it does upon a high level of ability to discriminate the form or shape of one object from another. There is, to be sure, no place in the grades where children are given definite practice in judgments of length, area, shape, or size, and it seems fair to say, therefore, that any skill that is acquired in these respects must be a by-product of training rather than the outcome of direct effort. In any case, we know that children differ widely from one another in what is sometimes called their artistic ability.

Both parents and teachers are very apt to dismiss these differences with the comment that they must owe their origin to hereditary factors. As we shall see, an appeal to heredity in cases of this sort adds nothing in particular either to the description of the case or to the competence of the teacher. On the contrary, it should be recognized that at least a part of the differences between children in artistic ability may depend upon the informal training which they have received in the discrimination of forms and shapes. Something might be done to increase the relative levels of skill reached by the majority of pupils if this phase of perception were made a more direct part of formal instruction.[11]

[10] Cf. Spearman, C., "The New Psychology of Shape." *Brit. J. Psychol.*, 1924, XV, 211-225.
[11] Cf. Peterson, J., "Learning in Children," in Murchison, C. (Ed.), *Handbook of Child Psychology*. Worcester, Mass.: Clark Univ. Press, 1933, Chapter X, *passim*.

C. PRACTICAL APPLICATIONS: A number of factors have brought about a new interest in the conditions under which judgments of distance and of movement become possible. For example, so long as men were moving slowly, as in a horse and carriage, it was not necessary precisely to judge on the spur of the moment how far away an approaching automobile might be and neither was it necessary to estimate with a high degree of accuracy its rate of movement. To be sure, educators have not been unmindful of this feature of training, especially during the periods when so many of the finer tools and instruments which are in common use had to come from the hands of skilled artisans. Now, however, with the introduction of high speed machinery, there has been a new emphasis upon skill in judgments of both distances and rates of movement.[12] A workman simply must adjust himself to rapidly moving machinery. It can be said, of course, that some persons are endowed by nature to judge distances in movement more quickly and more accurately than others, but the facts do not warrant any such assumption. On the contrary, it is now known that both of these types of perception are highly subject to training. Lack of skill is more a product of an educative process that has led to a barely acceptable measure of skill than to levels of skill that are actually necessary to safety on the highway or in the factory.

Judgments of distance appear to depend upon a number of different factors, the most important of which is the spatial separation of the two eyes.[13] The student already knows, perhaps, that, as he looks at a near-by object with both eyes, the one eye gets an image which differs in certain respects from the image reflected to the other eye. If these images differ too greatly from each other, the subject will report that he sees two overlapping objects rather than one. Under optimal conditions, however, a single object will be seen, not as a flat object, but as an object extending in three dimensions. This fusion of the impressions upon the two retinas and the conversion of this fusion into a judgment about the relative distance of an object is a learning process which takes place very early. It is supplemented, of course, by a number of accessory facts such as the relative size of distant objects, the extent to which the portions of an object are cut away by nearer-lying objects, and by the relative clearness or distinctness of objects.

[12] Cf. Viteles, M. S., *Industrial Psychology*. New York: W. W. Norton and Co., 1932, Section Three, *passim*.
[13] Cf. Koffka, K., "Some Problems of Space Perception," in Murchison, C. (Ed.), *op. cit.*, Chapter IX.

There is plenty of evidence to show that judgments of distance, and especially of the distance of objects which are beyond arm's reach, can be greatly increased by practice. It is only necessary that a child shall be put in learning situations which lay special emphasis upon increased skill in the distance factor. As we have implied above, the chances are that the normal processes of training give to every person sufficient measures of skill in this respect to enable him to get along in an ordinary environment. On the athletic field, on the highway, in the artist's salon, and in the factory, however, average levels of skill are simply not sufficient. Personnel managers for industries and for taxicab companies have found it necessary, therefore, to make special studies of these and of related types of skill, looking toward training periods that will considerably increase the competence in the persons employed.

All of these considerations hold true of skill in judgments of rates of movement.[14] Judgments of this type appear to depend, in part, upon the rate at which the image which is focused upon the retina moves across the retina and, in part, upon the rate at which the eyes themselves are moved from point to point. Of these two factors, the first is perhaps the most important. It is known that images cannot travel too slowly over the retina if a judgment about movement is to be made. As the student knows, he cannot actually see that the minute hand on his watch is moving even though he will report that it has moved. Since clearest vision occurs only when the eyes are at rest, judgments about rates of movement drawn from actual movements of the eyes must be secondary in their contribution to this skill.

More recently it has been discovered that judgments of movement will sometimes be made when one object is presented immediately after another in the same general visual field.[15] The student has, no doubt, noticed that, as he waits for traffic lights to change, the red light will appear to hop down to the position of the green light. Clearly, there has been no objective movement. Through a proper device, the red light is simply extinguished and the green light turned on. Most persons will report, however, that there has been an actual movement.

This feature of movement has led to the development of a special theory of the way in which the nervous system may act, a theory

[14] Troland, L. T., *op. cit., passim.*
[15] Cf. Dimmick, F. L., "An Experimental Study of Visual Movement and of the Phi Phenomena." *Amer. J. Psychol.*, 1920, XXXI, 317-332.

which throws considerable light upon some of the factors that may be operative during problem-solving.[16] We shall return to it, therefore, in our study of the nature of problem-solving. In the meantime, let us draw the inference that skill in judging different rates of movement is a skill that comes to an average level of efficiency largely as a by-product of the educative process. For certain special types of education, as in preparation for driving a taxi and as in preparation for certain occupations in industry, it is necessary that some people achieve far higher levels of skill than are necessary to the rest of us.

D. DEFECTS IN PERCEPTION: All that has been said up to this point about the visual functions takes it for granted that the eyes and all of their related structures are anatomically normal. There are, however, a good many children in whom this is not the case, and the teacher is frequently faced, therefore, with a variety of special educational problems. As an example, we may take faulty lenses.[17] Lenses may be faulty either because they are structurally inadequate or because the muscles which control them vary from one another in strength. The clear perception of objects can occur only when the lens adjusts itself to the lighted object in such a way that a clear image is thrown upon the retina. If the image comes to a focus in front of the retina, the child is said to be shortsighted. On the contrary, if the image comes to a focus behind the retina, the child is said to be farsighted.

In either case, the child will have difficulty in vision, and it has been shown that a substantial amount of retardation in schoolwork can be attributed to these factors. In consequence, it is now considered a regular part of the teacher's obligations that he shall be sensitive to those symptoms in behavior which point toward visual difficulties.[18] The most frequent symptoms are lack of attention, squinting, errors in reading letters that are somewhat similar to one another, and general slowness in rate of reading. There is another feature of faulty functioning which is probably even more important than nearsightedness and farsightedness. It has been suspected for a long time that people might be right- or left-eyed, just as they

---

[16] Cf. Köhler, W., "Some Tasks of Gestalt Psychology," in Murchison, C. (Ed.) *Psychologies of 1930*. Worcester, Mass.: Clark Univ. Press, 1930, Chapter VIII.

[17] Cf. Whipple, G. M., *Manual of Mental and Physical Tests* (rev. ed.). Baltimore: Warwick and York, 1914-15, Vol. I, *passim*.

[18] Cf. Pressey, S. L., *Psychology and the New Education*. New York: Harper and Bros., 1933, Chapter III. See especially the references at the end of the chapter.

are right- or left-handed. This suspicion has now been confirmed. In some cases, the dominance of the one eye over the other is rather intense. Where there is dominance, all of the visual functions will be carried out with the dominant eye taking the constant lead. In some cases, this may mean ocular strain and consequently faulty visual perception which would not be discovered by a simple test for near- and far-sightedness.[19]

The problems of education created by persons who, because of hereditary blindness or because of injury to the eyes, cannot depend upon vision, constitute a series of special problems to which much serious attention has been given. It is clear that, in all of these cases, the victim must learn how to use his other perceptual devices as a substitute for the visual functions.[20] It has sometimes been argued that these other functions will actually become more acute as a compensation for blindness. There is, however, no substantial evidence to support this point of view. Under normal circumstances, the visual functions do occupy a dominant place in the contacts which we make with the objects and events around us, and where vision is lacking some other perceptual function must take the lead.

In brief, then, the education of the blind is simply a process of giving more direct attention to higher levels of skill in other perceptual functions than would be achieved were the pupil left to his own devices.[21] It is interesting to note that some of the very people who argue that differences in perceptual skills must owe their origin to hereditary factors are the people who also argue that blind children must be subjected to those special types of training which will bring larger measures of skill to other perceptual functions.

3. *Hearing:* It will be necessary for us to give the same short shrift to the anatomical features of hearing as was given to the anatomical features of vision. The student already knows that sounding objects can become effective sources of action, because sound waves are transmitted through the air to a sort of funnel which leads toward the acoustic organs. The acoustic organs themselves appear to consist of a band of fibres in the cochlea of the inner ear. There is still a great amount of disagreement as to just

[19] Miles, W. R., "Ocular Dominance in Adults." *J. Gen. Psychol.,* 1930, III, 412-430.
[20] Cf. Cutsworth, T. D., *The Blind in School and Society.* New York: D. Appleton-Century Co., 1933.
[21] Cf. Gault, R. H., "Progress in Experiments on Interpretation of Speech by Touch." *J. Abnorm. and Soc. Psychol.,* 1925, XX, 118-127.

how this band of fibres is affected by the vibrations transmitted to it. There is also disagreement as to how the acoustic fibres influence the auditory nerve. These are, however, matters that concern the specialist in audition and only indirectly the teacher in the schoolroom.[22]

A. DEAFNESS: The features of hearing which concern the teacher are the degree of sensitivity to tones of low intensity, the degree of sensitivity to slight differences in the pitch of tones, the skill of the child in judging tonal complexes (that is, chords and melodies), and skill in judging the spatial location of sounding objects. The ability to discriminate tones of low intensity is not a very serious problem save in those cases where children are partially or totally deaf. In normal cases, everything that transpires in a schoolroom is sufficiently intense to meet all of the requirements for adequate hearing. In partial and in total deafness, however, special problems of education arise.

These problems are of the same type as are created by the blind child except that many modes of training can take place more easily with a deaf child than with a blind child.[23] It usually happens that deaf children are slow to pick up the speech functions. As we have seen, this slowness can be explained, in part, by the fact that the hearing of the words which the child himself speaks is almost essential to the development of words which symbolize objects that are not actually present. In short, deafness offers quite a barrier to the rapid and easy development of ideas.[24]

B. MUSICAL ABILITY: Considerable skill in distinguishing between differences in pitch of sounds is of interest primarily to the music teacher, for singing and the development of skill in the playing of a musical instrument often depend upon a good sense of pitch. There is a great amount of disagreement among psychologists as to the extent to which discriminations of pitch difference are dependent upon hereditary factors as opposed to training. One of the most serious students of this group of problems and of a special skill, known as memory for absolute pitch, is convinced that fine sensitivity to pitch differences is wholly a matter of heredity.[25]

[22] Cf. Banister, H., "Hearing, I," in Murchison, C., *op. cit.,* Chapter XVI. Also Banister, H., and Hartridge, H., "Hearing, II," *ibid.,* Chapter XVII.
[23] Cf. Pintner, R., and Paterson, D. G., "Learning Tests with Deaf Children." *Psychol. Monog.,* 1916, XX (No. 88).
[24] Bond, N. J., and Dearborn, W. F., "The Auditory Memory and Factual Sensibility of the Blind." *J. Educ. Psychol.,* 1917, VIII, 21-26.
[25] Cf. Seashore, C. E., *The Psychology of Musical Talent.* Newark: Silver, Burdett and Co., 1919, *passim.*

TRAINING THE PERCEPTUAL FUNCTIONS 107

There are, however, a good many experiments which show that many children can gain a considerable amount of skill as a result of special practice. It is even possible for children who do not have a memory for absolute pitch, that is, who, upon hearing a sound, cannot identify the actual pitch of the sound, to acquire the ability to do so under suitable practice.[26]

It is barely possible that the conflicting results which have come from the experiments in this field can be explained by the fact that a good many children acquire stabilized levels of pitch discrimination during the first few years of development and that much practice is required to modify the levels of skill already attained. In any case, the music teacher is called upon to do whatever she can to increase levels of skill in these several respects. For this purpose she uses the tonal scales, singing exercises, and other special methods of training.

Skill in response to chords and melodies has been the subject of an astonishing number of experiments. It looks as though this skill must be related in some way to the ratios that obtain between different pitches. In the chord represented by the symbol c, e, g, for example, the vibration numbers of c, e, g sustain a definite proportion to one another. This proportion would hold even though the three notes were struck one after the other rather than simultaneously. The creation of melodies, however, together with a satisfactory ending for a melody, is subject to a great many other conditions which lie outside the scope of our own study.[27]

The general inference which ought to be drawn from the researches in this field is that both chords and melodies, in addition to being subject to harmonic relations of various types, are also largely subject to training. Not the least important factor in such training periods is the creation of rhythms.[28] As we have seen in the last chapter, rhythm is more frequently a muscular or motor skill than it is a skill directly related to perceptual operations; but even though we have described the motor phase of sensori-motor development in one chapter and the sensory phase in another, the reader has already been warned that we have done so only for pur-

[26] Mull, H. K., "The Acquisition of Absolute Pitch." *Amer. J. Psychol.,* 1925, XXXVI, 469-493; Gough, E., "The Effects of Practice on Judgments of Absolute Pitch." *Arch. Psychol.,* 1922 (No. 47).
[27] Cf. Seashore, C. E., *op. cit., passim.*
[28] Cf. Ruckmick, C. A., "The Rôle of Kinaesthesis in the Perception of Rhythm." *Amer. J. Psychol.,* 1913, XXIV, 305-359; Entwisle, B. S., "An Experiment with Rhythm on Teaching Typewriting." *Univ. Iowa Monog. Educ.,* 1928, 1st Series (No. 8).

poses of exposition and not because a defensible line of division between them can be drawn.

If we say that judgments about chords and melodies are subject to practice, it would seem to follow that the teachers of music have a group of educational problems which are entirely their own. These problems are centered upon the use of chords and melodies as learning situations and upon a variety of tests of musical ability.[29] As we shall discover in a later chapter, a great many of these tests are now available, and they have introduced a large measure of increased competence in handling the problems of musical education where heretofore there has been confusion and much haphazard procedure.[30]

C. SOUND LOCALIZATION: There are not very many places in normal living where special skill in judging the spatial location of sounding objects is of any great import.[31] As primary instances, we may take certain types of athletic games where signals from one player to another would, if accurately judged, greatly increase the competence of a man. We may mention also the greater dependence which blind people place upon the spatial location of sounding objects. It is known, for example, that echoes from a cane, from a building, or even from an approaching person may help a blind person immensely in his arduous task of moving safely from one point to another. These problems are not lacking in significance simply because we do not have the space to devote to them. They concern, however, special problems of education rather than the general principles of educational psychology.

III. The Development of Meanings

1. *Introduction:* There is no phase of the growth pattern which offers more difficulty to teachers and to psychologists than the phrase "the development of meanings." This phrase refers to the fact that we do not see light waves, hear sound waves, or taste chemicals. On the contrary, we react to lighted objects, to sounding objects, and to odorous objects. We may think of these and of all other objects as somehow being in existence outside of the body and as making themselves known to us in perception, or we may think of

---

[29] Mursell, J. L., "Psychology of Music." *Psychol. Bull.*, 1932, XXIX, 218-241.
[30] Cf. Seashore, C. E., *op. cit.*
[31] Ruckmick, C. A., "Experiments in Sound Localization." *Psychol. Monog.*, 1921, XXXIX (No. 136), 77-83.

them as sources of stimuli which, when they enter through the sense organs into the nervous system, are somehow miraculously transformed into sensations or conscious processes or states of mind.

This difference in ways of thinking about objects appears in an even more difficult form when we talk of ideas, for ideas which are commonly alleged to be purely mental in character are often set in opposition to objects which are physical in character. And yet, objects are not wholly physical, because we know that they may appear different on different occasions.[32] For a time in the history of philosophy, it was supposed that an object must *really* be that which it was felt to be by the contact senses, whereas those visual qualities which it possessed must be secondary and hence dependent upon the character of our sensations.[33]

Education, too, has had its difficulties with the nature of meaning. There has been, for example, a very famous theory in the history of education which argued that one of the chief methods of training required the presentation of new schoolroom situations to children in such a way that they would arouse what was called the "apperception mass." The apperception mass was alleged to be made up of mental processes which were duplicates of older experiences, the inference being that the meanings which might be attached to a new object or situation would depend upon the richness of previous experiences. Whenever a teacher was able to equip a child with rich apperceptions or with rich meanings the child was said to be well on its way toward a good education.[34]

From these several suggestions about the nature of meaning we may draw two fundamental problems. In the first place, we shall wish to inquire how it is that the patterns of energy which make up a stimulus-situation can be converted into an object and, in the second place, we shall wish to inquire how an object that has once thus become converted can acquire further meanings. Of these two questions the first holds far more importance for the psychologist than for the educator. The second is much more important to the educator, although it is not without considerable interest to the psychologist.

[32] For this reason, the existence of illusions has always constituted a part of the discussion of perception, both in books on psychology and in books on educational psychology.
[33] Cf. Höffding, H., *A History of Modern Philosophy* (Trans. by B. E. Meyer). New York: The Macmillan Co., 1920, Vol. I, pp. 384 ff., and *passim*.
[34] Cf. Bronner, A. F., "Apperceptive Abilities." *Psychol. Rev.*, 1921, XXVIII, 270-279.

2. *Stimulus and Object:* It would not be worth while to include a study of the relation between stimuli and objects in a book on educational psychology were it not for the fact that so much confusion has been wrought in this field by a failure to see just what the problem involves. As the student knows, the physicist pretends to deal with a world which lies beyond or back of the actual objects which make up the environment. Instead of speaking of a lighted object he speaks of light waves, some of which may be absorbed by the object while others are being reflected from the object to a human eye. The object itself is described in terms of clusters of atoms which, in their turn, are made up of still more elementary units called electrons and protons.[35]

There is, of course, nothing about a pattern of light energy which is, in and of itself, white or colored. On the contrary, the whiteness or the color is something that appears to be added to ether vibrations after these vibrations have been transformed into nervous energy and after the nervous energy has been propagated to appropriate regions of the brain and to the muscles. Since the physicist insists that color is not a property of light waves, but since the objects with which he deals are actually colored, it has been customary to suppose that color is an addition which the mind makes to the constitution of objects.

A. SIMPLE SENSATIONS: A great many attempts have been made to explain this type of construction, one of the most common of which runs somewhat as follows. It has been said that if an experimenter takes a sufficiently narrow band of light waves, that is, light waves that come from a very restricted section of the spectrum, the normal effect would be the creation of a simple mental process called a sensation. Every other restricted region in the spectrum would lead to some other simple mental or sensory process. Thus one might proceed through the whole range of light stimuli, of sound stimuli, and of stimulus-patterns for each of the other sense organs and thus arrive at a whole list of mental processes which could be called elementary or unitary in character.[36]

This procedure was hailed as a great achievement in psychology, for it seemed to furnish the elementary materials out of which the whole domain of mind might be constructed. Since the physical sciences had made so much progress by breaking down a complex world of objects into its least common denominators, it seemed rea-

[35] Cf. Eddington, A. S., *The Nature of the Physical World.* New York: The Macmillan Co., 1928, Introduction and *passim.*
[36] Cf. Titchener, E. B., *The Psychology of Feeling and Attention.* New York: The Macmillan Co., 1924, *passim.*

TRAINING THE PERCEPTUAL FUNCTIONS

sonable to suppose that the psychologist would reach equal levels of achievement if he used the same methods.[37]

We do not mean to say, of course, that the simple or unitary sensations exhausted all of the elements that went into the manufacture of a mind. On the contrary, these sensory elements were supplemented by two primary feelings called pleasantness and unpleasantness and by a whole array of secondary or centrally aroused sensations more frequently called simple images. The argument in support of the existence of simple images was as follows. Once a subject had experienced a simple sensation—say, a sensation of redness—it was possible that this particular mental quality might be revived in memory as a copy or image of the original sensory process.[38]

B. ORGANIZATION OF SENSATIONS: The student will see at once that the psychologist might take any object, not as an object, but as an experienced object, and break down the whole experience into as many elementary processes as were necessary to account for the existence of the object.[39] When this had once been done, it would then become necessary to see how a number of elementary processes, when put back together into a configured whole, would become the object with which the investigation had started. As an example, let us take our perception of a glass of lemonade. It can quickly be discovered that a glass of lemonade, from the point of view of immediate experience, is made up of the sensation of coolness, the sensation of sweetness, a mild acid taste, and, perhaps, a fragrant odor.

If one takes each of these elementary experiences by itself, there is nothing about any one of them that would suggest the object with which the investigation began. In other words, the object has disappeared. The psychological problem is to discover how adding these elements could create the object we call a glass of lemonade, when, as a matter of fact, "lemonadeness" is not in any of the parts.

One answer to this question may be phrased in the following way. The stimulus-object itself creates a central cluster or core of sensations which, because of previous experience, will call forth a surrounding fringe of simple images. These simple images might include either direct memory traces of previous visual sensations or

---

[37] Cf. Boring, E. G., *A History of Experimental Psychology*. New York: D. Appleton-Century Co., 1929, Chapter XV.
[38] Titchener, E. B., *A Textbook of Psychology*. New York: The Macmillan Co., 1910, pp. 396 ff.
[39] Boring, E. G., *op. cit.*, Chapter XVII.

they might include memory images of movements previously made in response to such an object. In other words, meaning is a function of the fringe or of the context in which a core of sensations has been placed.[40]

We may now look at this theory of the nature of meaning from the point of view of the origin of meanings. It would be necessary to assume that the new-born infant is not introduced into a world of objects but into a confused world of separate sensations. Every time it opened its eyes, its mind would be made up of such patterns of visual sensation as would be required by the nature of the stimulus-pattern. Gradually, as its dealings with sensations increased in number, it would begin to fuse them into more definite and localizable patterns and to attract memory images resulting from previous experience. Where there had been chaos, order would appear, an order brought about by the number of times specific patterns of stimulus had been supplied and by the rate at which these patterns could be given meaning through marginal or context processes.[41]

3. *Comments on Introspective Psychology:* The theory of the origin of meanings which has just been outlined is a product of a type of psychology known as introspective psychology. This is not the place to review the nature of introspectionism. Neither can we enter into all of the difficult problems created by this as opposed to other views of the nature of perception. There are, however, one or two comments about the emergence of meanings out of simple sensations that are of importance to the teacher.

A. SENSATION AND ENERGY: In the first place, we may well wonder whether it is worth while to ask how it is that light waves, sound waves, and other forms of physical energy can be transformed into psychological processes. As we have said above, no person can see light waves or hear sound waves. On the contrary, he reacts to lighted objects and sounding objects.[42] To say the same thing in another way, the sciences of physics and chemistry are said to be sciences of real objects and events, the inference being that light waves, sound waves, and other sources of energy are *more real* than the objects and events with which we actually deal in the laboratory.

This is a point of view which is open to question. The only real objects which we know anything about are those objects which ac-

---

[40] Cf. Titchener, E. B., *op. cit.*, pp. 367 ff., 517 ff.
[41] Bentley, M., *The Field of Psychology.* New York: D. Appleton-Century Co., 1924, Chapter XIX. Cf., however, Bentley, M., *The New Field of Psychology.* New York: D. Appleton-Century Co., 1934, *passim.*
[42] Cf. Hunter, W. S., "The Psychological Study of Behavior." *Psychol. Rev.*, 1932, XXXIX, 1-24.

tually surround a person and which can, under certain circumstances, become relevant or effective in the sense that they initiate and guide a course of action. If we were to assume that such objects make up the real world, then the world with which the physicist and the chemist deal is an abstract world. It is a world which is assumed to be in existence "behind" the world to which men of science actually respond.[43]

In any case, let us assume for our own purposes that every living creature is surrounded by an immense variety of objects and situations which do, as a matter of fact, become effective in initiating and regulating courses of action. If we make this assumption, it is required of the teacher that he find out how such objects can become sources of action. That is, he must find out how environmental objects which are irrelevant or ineffective during early infancy become increasingly effective after the child grows older.

B. CONFIGURATIONS: The second comment to be made about the introspective theory of the development of meaning has given rise to a branch of psychological research known as Gestalt psychology, or as configurationism.[44] Here again, we cannot enter into the difficult problems of systematic psychology, but the student ought to know at least the simpler meanings that may be attached to the terms "Gestalt" and "configuration."

Reverting to the illustration used above, let us ask where the property known as "lemonadeness" comes from. An introspective psychologist would attempt to break the total perception of a glass of lemonade into its simplest parts. No one of these parts, however, is the glass of lemonade. The Gestalt psychologist would argue that the "lemonadeness" cannot be discovered through the method of analysis. On the contrary, he would assert that the sciences must deal with wholes rather than with parts, and that "lemonadeness" is a property or characteristic of a whole pattern of events rather than a product of its component parts.[45]

As another example of the meaning of the configurational point of view, let us take the experiment on the perception of movement referred to above. As one approaches a signal light just as a traffic change is being indicated, one observes that the red light does not simply disappear as the green light appears. Instead, when the two lights are timed properly with respect to each other, the one appears

---

[43] Eddington, A. S., *op. cit., passim*.
[44] Peterman, B., *The Gestalt Theory and the Problem of Configuration*. New York: Harcourt, Brace and Co., 1932.
[45] Cf. Köhler, W., *Gestalt Psychology*. New York: Liveright Publishing Corp., 1929, *passim*.

to flow into the other. There has been, of course, no actual movement. The observer, however, has gained the very distinct impression that something has moved. The inference is that the observed movement, since it is not occasioned by an actual movement in either of the lights, must be a product of the total configuration of events.[46]

From the point of view of Gestalt psychology, then, meanings cannot be produced simply by adding one elementary process to another. For certain purposes, it may be useful to draw fine discriminations in the intensity or the duration or the sense qualities of the objects around us; but if these discriminations are drawn, they do not lead to elementary processes which, on that account alone, are the units out of which the whole of experience can be fashioned. In other words, the Gestalt psychologist, instead of working from the finest discriminations that can be drawn toward larger patterns of stimulus-situations, works from the larger patterns to smaller patterns. At every stage in this process, the Gestalt psychologist is interested in the essential properties or characteristics of the configured wholes actually under observation.[47]

4. *Figure and Ground:* The nature of the Gestalt method of interpreting the development of perception can be illustrated in the following way. In the first place, let us take it for granted that the new-born infant is surrounded by objects and events which are already psychological in character. In other words, when a living creature equipped with certain types of sensory apparatus is placed in an environment, this environment has already acquired psychological value. It is not made up of light waves, sound waves, and other forms of physical energy. It is made up of lighted objects, sounding objects, odorous objects, and contact objects in all sorts of spatial and temporal relationships. In addition to these objects, there is, so far as the child is concerned, a whole set of states or conditions created by the events going on in the body of the child itself.

A. THE BACKGROUND: All of these objects and conditions can be called the background. This background is not uniform in character; subject to the conditions which obtain at the moment, certain parts of it appear to emerge into what the Gestalt psychologist would

[46] Cf. Wertheimer, M., "Experimentelle Studien über das Sehen von Bewegungens." *Zsch. P. Psychol.,* 1912, LXI, 161-265. Also Helson, H., "The Psychology of Gestalt." *Amer. J. Psychol.,* 1925, XXXVI, 342-370, 494-526; 1926, XXXVII, 25-62, 189-223.
[47] For an application of these principles to education, see Wheeler, R. H., and Perkins, F. T., *Principles of Mental Development.* New York: T. Y. Crowell Co., 1932, *passim.*

call a figure.[48] As an example, let an experimenter bring bright light into the field of vision of a new-born infant. The introspective psychologist might attempt to describe the experience of the infant by saying that the bright light is a simple sensory experience or a very simple cluster of simple sensations, which is almost, if not quite, devoid of meaning. Meaning cannot accrue to the sensory process until the infant has had sufficient experience with lighted objects to know that one cluster of visual sensations means a candle, another means a match, and still another means a lighted bulb. It is important to note, however, that the light presented to the infant must be a light rather than a train of light waves. In other words, so far as the infant is concerned, the world of physics has already been transformed into a psychological world.

B. THE EMERGENCE OF FIGURES: The Gestalt psychologist, however, proposes that the lighted object is not a simple sensory experience or a cluster of such experiences. He claims it is a figure on a ground. The figure itself gains part of its properties from the fact that it is set into a background. To quote from Koffka on this point, we may say that "from an unlimited and ill-defined background, there has arisen a limited and somewhat definite phenomenon, a quality." [49]

A great many experiments have been carried out on this feature of the origin and development of objects. The general import of these experiments is about as follows. If we may assume that the new-born infant is actually surrounded by an environment, a major portion of which is irrelevant or ineffective so far as its power of initiating and regulating a course of action is concerned, the growth or the development of perception would require the progressive emergence of figures out of the whole environment. In other words, the growth of perception would require the gradual transformation of irrelevant portions of the environment into relevant or effective portions.

It is not possible, within the scope of this book, to review the entire course of the changes which transform an irrelevant environment into all of the objects and events to which an adult can make some sort of response.[50] The student has only to compare himself with the presumable ability of a new-born infant, however, to sense

---

[48] Cf. Koffka, K., "Some Problems of Space Perception," in Murchison, C. (Ed.), *op. cit.*, Chapter IX.
[49] Koffka, K., *The Growth of the Mind.* New York: Harcourt, Brace and Co., 1924, p. 131.
[50] This would require a close study of all of the materials included in such books on child psychology as were listed on p. 92.

the magnitude of this transformation. In the case of visual perceptions, the number of objects and events which can excite adequate modes of response in an adult is almost beyond counting. Whereas the new-born infant can take note of only major changes in the stimulus-situations around it, the adult can identify not only a wide range of brightnesses of colors but an enormous variety of patterns of brightnesses and colors such as constitute the printed words on this page, the persons whom he meets on the street, the houses along the street, the objects in a museum, or in a zoölogical garden, and so on. The same course of events can be described with respect to each of the other sensory departments.

C. THE PRINCIPLE OF DIFFERENTIATION: If the development of perception can be characterized by a general principle, this principle should probably be called the principle of increasing differentiation and specialization.[51] As examples, we may take our commonsense observations of the way in which children will, at first, call all men "daddy" or all moving objects "autos." Then, too, it does not seem to make much difference to younger children as to a spatial position of printed pages or of pictures. A picture may just as well be upside down as right-side up. Furthermore, the temporal judgments of children are exceedingly imperfect. Sometimes it looks as though everything that has happened is contemporaneous with the present moment, and even where events are recognized as having occurred at some previous time, the time interval is grossly misjudged.

Some of these features of the development of perception and many others in addition have come from studies on the nature of children's drawings. As a rule, many drawings conform to a single pattern or type, irrespective of variations in detail in the objects copied. Then, too, where there is some one feature of an object which attracts attention over all others, this one feature will be emphasized in the drawing even if the drawing itself becomes a sheer caricature of the object depicted.[52] As a further feature of the development of perception it has been pointed out that most of the objects which are first differentiated from the whole perceptual back-

[51] This is a principle which has had a long history in the biological sciences where it is remarked that different animal forms change most rapidly when they are generalized in type. The changes look toward an increased number of specialized structures and functions which will carry out operations previously carried out by the organism as a whole. The development of the sensory apparatus is a case in point. Cf. Parker, G. H., *The Elementary Nervous System*. Philadelphia: J. B. Lippincott Co., 1919.

[52] Cf. Goodenough, F. L., "Children's Drawings," in Murchison, C. (Ed.), *Handbook of Child Psychology* (1st edition). Worcester, Mass.: Clark Univ. Press, 1930, Chapter XIV.

ground take on an intimate personal quality for children. Children are, to be sure, asocial in their character, but it is certainly true that their own needs and their own experiences play a very large part in giving quality to their responses to outside objects.[53]

Some light has been thrown upon the processes of perceptual development by those experiments which undertake to destroy previously acquired perceptual habits and build them anew. Let us suppose, for example, that a group of subjects is equipped with lenses which invert the position of the images on the retina. A method of this type almost, if not quite, destroys some features of the spatial patterning of objects which has already been acquired. The subjects find it necessary, therefore, to rediscover the spatial configuration of objects and refashion their modes of response to these new spatial configurations. The fact that a new order of perceptual habits can be built up out of these circumstances throws a good deal of light upon the nature of perceptual development.[54] Experiments of the same type have been carried out in the field of auditory localization. The subjects were equipped with a device which would transpose, so to speak, the right ear to the left side and the left ear to the right side. New habits of auditory localization were quickly established.[55]

5. *The Development of Concepts:* Up to this point we have touched only that phase of the development of an effective environment which concerns the gradual emergence of particular objects and events out of the total perceptual field which surrounds the child. As the student knows, however, teachers and psychologists often speak of two worlds rather than of one. The first is the physical world which stands, so to speak, outside of us or outside of direct experience, and the other is the inner world or the world of mental objects. This inner world is said to be composed of ideas, some of which are "copies" of the objects and situations outside of us while the remainder are made up of concepts, abstractions, comparisons, and other factors which do not appear to have an objective counterpart.

With respect to this inner world, it is often said that it must be more intimately mental than is the outer world. In the development

---

[53] Piaget, J., *Judgment and Reasoning in the Child.* New York: Harcourt, Brace and Co., 1928, pp. 58 ff. and *passim.*
[54] Stratton, G. M., "Vision without Inversion of the Retinal Image." *Psychol. Rev.,* 1897, IV, 341-360, 463-481. See also Wooster, M., "Certain Factors in the Development of a New Spatial Coördination." *Psychol. Monog.,* 1923, XXXII (No. 4).
[55] Young, P. T., "Auditory Localization with Acoustical Transposition of the Ears." *J. Exper. Psychol.,* 1928, XI, 399-429.

of concepts, for example, we may easily grant that there is nothing in the outer world which is an exact duplicate of the generalized ideas which we sometimes entertain. As a very simple case, let us take all of the human beings we have met as compared with our concept of humanity. The human beings we have met are actually persons outside of us or memories of such persons. There is in the world outside of us no composite object which summarizes, suggests, or in any other way typifies those respects in which all human beings resemble one another as contrasted with the respects in which they are dissimilar from one another. When, however, we say we have a concept of humanity, we appear to say that there is in the mind some generalized idea which is neither one human being nor another but all human beings put together.

Some of the experiments that have been performed in this field give a general indication of the conditions under which abstractions, concepts, discriminations, comparisons, and generalizations are made possible. As an example, let us take an experiment in which the experimenter laid before a group of children a large panel upon which had been painted in different colors three circles. Each circle was two and one-half inches in diameter. Five disks differing from one another in diameter but all smaller than the circles painted upon the board were placed upon one of the circles in the order from smallest to largest. The task assigned to the subjects was to transpose the disks from circle number one to circle number three, using circle number two as a relay. The subjects were told that they could not place a larger disk on a smaller disk, that only one disk at a time could be moved and that the disks should be placed on circle number three in the same relative position as was the case at the beginning of the experiment. In order to solve this problem it was necessary that the subjects see certain relationships between the disks and the circles. The problem could be made simpler or more difficult by changing the number of disks. The results of this experiment showed that there were marked differences between different subjects in the quickness with which they could see the general principle involved. At first, of course, there was much trial-and-error movement, but as soon as essential types of relatedness between the disks and the circles were discovered, the solution to the problem came quickly.[56]

[56] Peterson, J. C., "The Higher Mental Processes in Learning." *Psychol. Monog.*, 1920, XXVIII (No. 129). Also Peterson, J., and Lanier, L. H., "Studies in the Comparative Abilities of Whites and Negroes." *Ment. Meas. Monog.*, 1929 (No. 5).

6. *Sign Learning:* Most of the facts which have been presented up to this point on the development of meaning have to do with what we may call for short "primary meanings." To be sure, a small child may not be able to say the word "light" when a light is presented to it, but the lighted object is nevertheless a distinct figure upon the total perceptual ground before the child. As soon as language responses are attained, primary meanings can be attached to lights in general and to different varieties of lighted objects. There will be not only differences in the size and the intensity of these lighted objects but differences in their color and in their spatial location. At a very early age, however, another variety of meanings will be acquired. These meanings may, for short, be called secondary meanings.

As an illustration of the distinction we wish to draw, let us take a black object which has seemed to be afloat some distance from a ship. At first glance, it may be that we cannot tell what the object is. One phase of primary meaning is expressed, however, in the fact that an object is actually present; another is expressed in the phrase that the object is a black object. Secondary meanings begin to appear when we try to find out just what sort of a black object lies on the horizon. It may be a whale, a bunch of seaweed, a rowboat, logs from a stranded ship, or a floating casket. In other words, a black object floating on the water signifies or points in these several different directions. This feature of meaning owes its origin apparently to a type of learning known as sign learning.

As an example of sign learning, let us suppose that we have seen such an object on the water some time prior to the year 1914. Let us suppose also that we have seen such an object on the water during the year 1917. The chances are that during the year 1914 a black object did not signify or point to a German submarine. In 1917, however, such an object could signify a German submarine. In other words, the signifying value of a primary meaning has been increased through experience.

The student will see at once that a very large part of the stream of conduct has its origin in signifying functions of this type. If it were not possible for every particular object which has emerged out of the total environment to acquire signifying or pointing functions of this type, human beings would more nearly resemble the lower animals in their modes of reaction than they do, for most of our cleverness and our adeptness in getting out of difficulties or in reacting to objects and situations that are not now present depends upon meanings of this type. As we shall see in our discussion of the nature of problem-solving as compared with learning of the simple trial-and-error or rote-memory type, new ways out of difficult and perplexing situations depend upon the extent to which the various parts of such situations point to or signify other facts and events.

7. *Summary:* As the student reads over this material, he should keep constantly before him the things that have already been said in the previous chapter about the development of language responses, together with the relation between these responses and the symbolic functions of the words. Moreover, let him remember that the development of ideas and abstractions and the use which children may make of comparisons, discriminations, and generalizations stand in close relation to the nature and functions of problem-solving. We shall, therefore, consider some of these matters again. In the meantime, the student should keep in mind the general character of the situation named by the phrase "the development of meanings." Most of the objects and events which surround a new-born child are irrelevant so far as their power of initiating and regulating a course of action is concerned. We have described two theories of the way in which more specialized objects can emerge out of the background. The one theory says that the child must experience simple sensations which, during the course of experience, are gradually fused into perceptual patterns, the perceptual patterns, in turn, referring to, or signifying, the existence of special objects. The other theory would assert that objects, as objects, rise as figures which are always on a ground. To be sure, these figures acquire a good many further significations. This fact has been illustrated by our reference to sign learning. In any case, the range of the effective environment of the more mature person is enormously increased over the range of the effective environment of the child under the influence of the educative process. Were we to describe an educated person only in terms of this one feature of the whole growth pattern, we would have to say that that person is most educated who is most versatile in his reactions to a wide variety of objects and situations.

IV. Sources of Training

1. *Introduction:* In our study of the development of habits and skills it was fairly easy to draw a distinction between movements as such and the various services rendered by the movements. It is not so easy, however, to draw a distinction between the development of the perceptual functions and the services rendered by these func-

tions, for the two types of change move forward almost hand in hand. The student can see for himself that every situation in which a person is placed may serve as a source of training, not only for the sensory apparatus and for all of the other structures associated with it, but for an increase in the range and variety of objects and situations which may become thenceforth effective in initiating and regulating a course of action. This fact holds true, in particular, of the preschool years because these years mark the period of greatest progress in the improvement of the eye, the ear, and the other sense organs and they mark, too, a very great improvement in the knowledge which we get of the world in which we live. Every plaything which is given to a child, every book that he reads, and every trip that he makes away from home provides an opportunity for increasing the range and variety of the relevant portions of his environment.

The chances are that by the time a student has passed through the first few years of formal schooling the actual amount of skill he possesses in the use of his eyes and other sensory apparatus has reached as high a level of excellence as it will ever reach, unless the choice of a particular vocation has required some special sort of training. The child will have learned how to distinguish an astonishing number of shapes and forms, make fairly good judgments of rates of movement, and of variable distances, and otherwise be able to pick out many details in the complex situations which surround it. It is easy to see, however, that all of these skills will continue to be used at whatever level of excellence they have already attained, in helping a person to widen the range and the variety of his effective environment. For example, after he has developed a given measure of skill in what is commonly called the power of observation, the child will proceed to use this particular level of skill in reading about and in observing a large number of other and hitherto unfamiliar situations. A part of his gain is made possible by those subjects in the grade school and in the high school curriculum which are called content subjects. That is, after the child has learned how to read and to write, its skill in these respects can be used in order to become acquainted with the facts of history, of geology, of arithmetic, of literature, of civics, of some of the physical and social sciences, and of all other classes of information.

Some of these content subjects are said to be particularly valuable in promoting perceptual skill and in strengthening the so-called "powers of observation." We may conclude this chapter, therefore, with brief reference to some of these matters.

2. *The Natural Sciences:* The natural sciences are said to furnish a fine opportunity for the development of perceptual skill, leading to an increase in the range and variety of the effective environment, simply because they require students to search out and inspect a very large number of objects. Most of these sciences, and especially the sciences of biology and geology, require field trips with constant opportunity for the observation of small differences in the flora, fauna, and geological formations of regions adjacent to the school. Field trips may, if they are properly handled, lead to an actual increase in the functional excellence of the sensory apparatus, but the greatest gain comes, perhaps, from increased knowledge about natural objects and events and in a marked increase in the number of useful primary and secondary meanings. To be sure, teachers who require close attention to details can make these field trips and even laboratory studies of typical specimens of more educational value than they would be if students were left to their own devices.

In addition to their effect upon the powers of observation, all of the natural sciences are said to possess a good many other educational advantages. It is asserted, for example, that no child ought to be without an intimate knowledge of the scientific attitude or without that impersonal or objective type of logic which leads to conclusions that are reached almost, if not quite, independently of personal wishes and desires.

In more detail, it has been said that the sciences, both the empirical and the experimental, equip a person (i) to have some confidence in the general principles of cause and effect and in all of those other features of scientific method which have to do with the collection and interpretation of data and with the validation of tentative conclusions, (ii) to put under proper control whatever curiosity he has about natural events and their consequences, (iii) to develop habits of patience and care in the search for data and an equal amount of patience in the suspension of judgment until proper evidence has been assembled, and (iv) to be duly cautious in accepting suggestions, anecdotes, prejudices, and other types of departure from proper scientific method. These fruits of the natural sciences, however, fall more naturally within a discussion of the nature and value of problem-solving.

3. *The Experimental Sciences:* The experimental sciences are, in many respects, similar to the natural or empirical sciences, save that they may emphasize more strongly attention to detail. It must not be supposed, however, that the use of laboratory techniques will, in

TRAINING THE PERCEPTUAL FUNCTIONS

and of itself, secure this result. Let us admit that a student in a laboratory may be just as superficial in his observations as is the student in the field. If, however, the teacher lays emphasis upon the search for and the discovery of small differences in laboratory materials and if he requires adequate descriptions of objects which superficially resemble one another, he may actually make his teaching of the sciences contribute to perceptual development.

The real essence of experimental procedure is to be found, in part, in the patient search for minor differences among things and, in part, in the processes of comparison, abstraction, and generalization. No one has ever seriously questioned the excellence of mature research men in these several functions, for discoveries in a scientific laboratory would not be possible without them. The student himself will readily see, however, from his own laboratory experiences, that not much emphasis is placed upon these functions. On the contrary, his laboratory work is usually done by close adherence to a series of laboratory manuals which outline for him every step in the work to be done. Once more, then, we may say that there is nothing about the laboratory sciences which, in and of themselves, will contribute to excellence in drawing comparisons, making abstractions, or reaching a defensible generalization. If these results are secured, they must be secured because the teacher formulates his laboratory instruction with these purposes in mind.

READINGS

It was necessary to begin this chapter, as we did the last, with a brief reference to psychological matters that lie in the background of any study of education. The student should, therefore, continue his inspection of the Heidbreder, the Woodworth, or the Ragsdale. If this seems to be too great a task, he should not feel discouraged, for he will find as he proceeds with his study that our picture of the nature of psychology will grow upon him from chapter to chapter.

The second section of the chapter gives a short description of the various types of perception. Both the student and the teacher will miss an extended treatment of the anatomy of the sense organs and of the way in which these organs contribute to the perceptual functions. Authoritative information in this field can be gained from Murchison, C. (Ed.), *A Handbook of General Experimental Psychology*. Worcester, Mass.: Clark Univ. Press, 1934. See especially Chapter XIII. Vision: I. Visual Phenomena and their Stimulus Correlations (by L. T. Troland), Chapter XIV. Vision: II. The Nature of the Photoreceptor Process (by S. Hecht), Chapter XV. Vision: III. Some Neural Correlations (by C. H. Graham), Chapter XVI. Audition: I. Auditory Phenomena and Their Stimulus Correlations (by H. Banister), Chapter XVII. Audition: II. Theories of Hearing (by H. Hartridge), and Chapter XVIII. Audition: III. The Physiological Phenomena of Audition (by H. Davis). Shorter accounts of material of this sort can be found in almost any one of the standard texts in elementary psychology.

It may be that both the teacher and the student will wish to begin at this time on a more detailed study of the connections between the sense organs and the muscles. As we have pointed out, both in this chapter and in the last, motor development or perceptual development are not two different processes. They belong to a single pattern of events, a pattern which is made possible by the connection system. One of the most useful books for the student of educational psychology in the field of nervous structures and functions is Freeman, G. L., *Introduction to Physiological Psychology*. New York: The Ronald Press, 1934. See also Herrick, C. J., *The Brains of Rats and Men*. Chicago: Univ. of Chicago Press, 1926; Lashley, K. S., *Brain Mechanisms and Intelligence*. Chicago: Univ. of Chicago Press, 1929. An extremely readable and interesting book on the functions of the brain has been written by Tilney, F., *The Master of Destiny*. New York: Doubleday, Doran and Co., 1930. There are some good things about Herrick, C. J., *The Thinking Machine*. Chicago: Univ. of Chicago Press, 1929.

Important material on the development of meaning can be found in Curti, M. W., *Child Psychology*. New York: Longmans, Green and Co., Chapter VIII. See also Koffka, K., *The Growth of the Mind*. New York: Harcourt, Brace and Co., Chapters IV and V.

Most of the educational psychologies contain several chapters on the value of different grade school and high school subjects in promoting psychological growth. See, for example, Starch, D., *Educational Psychology*. New York: The Macmillan Co., 1927, Part III; Pressey, S. L., *Psychology and the New Education*. New York: Harper and Bros., 1933; Cole, L., *Psychology of the Elementary School Subjects*. New York: Farrar and Rinehart, Inc., 1934; Judd, C. H., *Psychology of High School Subjects*. Boston: Ginn and Co., 1915; Judd, C. H., *Psychology of Secondary Education*. Boston: Ginn and Co., 1927; Freeman, F. N., *The Psychology of the Common Branches*. Boston: Houghton Mifflin Co., 1916.

CHAPTER FOUR

THE DEVELOPMENT OF ATTENTION AND INTEREST

I. Sources of Action

1. *Introduction:* Before we pass on to a more detailed study of another facet of the whole growth pattern, we ought to spend just a moment in looking at the last two chapters as a single unit. The student has realized, of course, that we have been considering that whole phase of growth which is often described as sensori-motor development. In other words, we have been considering a group of problems which lie at the root of everything else that can be said about human growth.

Every mature person is surrounded by an exceedingly complex and variable environment. This environment is made up of clusters of objects and events which offer a never-ending series of invitations to action. Every mature person is likewise equipped with a great variety of movement systems in all stages of efficiency or in variable degrees adequate to the situations that may be presented. Even though we have described some of the general features of these movement-systems in one chapter and of stimulus-situations in another, we have not meant to imply for a single moment that they can be taken apart from one another. On the contrary, they belong to a single and highly integrated pattern of events.

A part of the unity or patterning of which we speak is dependent upon the fact that every particular stimulus-situation is related to many particular responses by a nervous system.[1] It is the function of the nervous system to furnish connections between the events that take place in the sense organs of the body, on the one hand, and the events that translate nerve energy into muscular contractions, on the other.

2. *The Stimulus-Response Theory:* There are several features of this sensori-motor or stimulus-response series of events that should, perhaps, receive a brief comment. In the first place, there are a good many facts which suggest that all human action comes as a response

[1] The serious student will be interested in a famous argument by Dewey, J., "The Reflex-Arc Concept in Psychology." *Psychol. Rev.,* 1896, III, 357-370.

to a stimulus-situation. In advance of more complete information about the sources of human action, we shall take this proposition for granted, for this is the basis upon which most experimental work in psychology is made possible.[2] In other words, we must set ourselves in opposition to all of those psychologies which have assumed that human action is a result of special mental forces which reside within the body or the brain. The reader knows, of course, both from his own commonsense opinions and, perhaps, from his study of philosophy, that the mind has often been thought of as a source of energy or as an effective agent which is resident within the body and which, by virtue of its own innate powers, can use the body as an instrument or device for converting its thoughts and desires into performance.

Because of a great many facts and inferences which we cannot consider in a book of this type, this older idea of the nature of the mind has been abandoned.[3] Psychologists are forced to infer that action can take place only in response to some source of stimulus. The student must not suppose, however, that the relations between stimulus and response at the human level are by any means as simple and straightforward as they sometimes appear to be among the lower animals. In the lower animals, for example, responses follow almost immediately upon the presentation of a stimulus. In the case of human action, on the contrary, the final or the consummatory response, that is, the response that actually "satisfies" the stimulus-situation, may be delayed for long periods of time. The interval will be filled with tentative or partial responses which themselves furnish stimuli to further tentative action and which are preparatory to the final response. That is, most of the muscles in the human body are equipped with sense organs which stand in the same relation to response mechanisms as do the eye, the ear, and other special senses. This fact holds true, in particular, of the vocal apparatus where the making of one sound may serve as an adequate stimulus for the making of another.[4]

It is for this reason that many of the actions carried out by human beings convey the impression that they are not really related to

---

[2] Cf. Rexroad, C. N., "A Formulation of Practical Assumptions Underlying Psychology." *Psychol. Rev.*, 1927, XXXIV, 116-119.

[3] The student will gain much profit from a study of the shifting scenes in psychology. See Heidbreder, E. F., *Seven Psychologies*. New York: D. Appleton-Century Co., 1933.

[4] These facts enter, however, into a complex picture. For a discussion of the problem at the level of animal learning, see Munn, N. L., *Animal Psychology*. Boston: Houghton Mifflin Co., 1933, Chapter IV.

a source of stimulus. Then, too, it is not necessary that all of the stimuli to which human beings respond shall occur outside of the body. When we come to our study of the nature of problem-solving in a later chapter, we shall see that an outside stimulus-situation may act simply as the starting point for a long series of stimulus-response patterns, most of which will be confined to the body itself. The philosopher, for example, who sits in his chair through his long period of reflection appears to be doing nothing. Certainly he is not making any responses to outside situations save those that give him his posture with respect to the chair in which he sits. There is every reason to suppose, however, that the book which lies open before him, to take only one of the possible starting points, has acted as an initial stimulus-situation for a long series of stimulus-response patterns, mostly verbal in character, which are all directed toward a final or consummatory verbal or manual response which will satisfy the initiating situation.[5]

3. *Stimulus-Response Relations:* In the second place, the student will realize that, in accepting the stimulus-connection-response formula as a working hypothesis for the explanation of all human behavior, we are not supposing for a moment that this formula marks the end of the matter, even though there are some teachers and some psychologists who seem to take this point of view. That is, there are some views of human nature which argue that psychological description will be finished whenever a complete list is made, first of all, of the stimulus-patterns or clusters of stimulus-situations which can become effective in initiating and regulating behavior and, second, whenever a complete list has been made of all of the postures, attitudes, habits, and skills that are used in responding to situations.

If we were to assume that the completion of these two lists could mark the end of psychological effort, the educator could then argue that his only task would involve a study of the connections between stimulus-situations and responses that are present at birth and a study of the conditions under which these connections can be modified and new connections made. The last two chapters have tried to show us that a very small portion of the environment of a new-born infant is truly environmental in the sense that it can become effective in initiating and regulating action patterns. They have shown us, also, that the action-patterns of a new-born infant are extremely

[5] Cf. Watson, J. B., "The Place of Kinaesthetic, Visceral and Laryngeal Organization in Thinking." *Psychol. Rev.*, 1924, XXXI, 339-348.

limited in character and that both action-patterns and the translation of a context into an environment comprise a large part of the difference between a new-born infant and the adult.

There are, however, a good many other differences. These differences have often been explained by saying that there is a *mind* between the environment, on the one hand, and action, on the other, which selects those particular parts of the environment which shall be reacted to and which selects, also, the type of reaction that will be suitable for the occasion.

It is not possible, however, either for the psychologist or the educator to see a mind in action. Even though we may say that psychology is the science of the mind and even though the educator will argue that he is training a mind, it must be clear to the student that the use of the word "mind" in this connection is simply an inference drawn from facts which have been actually observed.[6] To be sure, every person will say that he is aware of his own mind or that he is conscious of his own mental processes, but he cannot take either his mind or his mental processes out of himself and lay them before another person for inspection. As we have already shown, he does not do this even when he tries to describe the quality and the course of his own mental life, for his description must be stated in words. Since words, like other sounds, must be sources of stimulus to another person, the other person must react to such sounds as he has learned how to react. He has not seen the mind of the first person but only inferred the existence of a mind because he knows that he also will speak certain words in connection with mental processes which are a part of his own private view of himself.[7]

The beginning student will find difficulty, no doubt, in reading himself into this situation and we do not wish to require too much of him at the moment, especially in view of the fact that later chapters will consider these matters in more detail. For the present, let us simply assume that it is possible to describe all of the situations which can become really effective in initiating and regulating the behavior of another person. Let us assume also that it is possible to describe all of the possible modes of action which a person possesses for the purpose of meeting situations. When we make these two assumptions, it becomes clear at once that stimulus-situations and

[6] Cf. Johnson, H. M., "Did Fechner Measure Introspectional Sensations?" *Psychol. Rev.*, 1929, XXXVI, 257-284.
[7] Cf. Rosenzweig, S., "The Experimental Situation as a Psychological Problem." *Psychol. Rev.*, 1933, XL, 337-354.

DEVELOPMENT OF ATTENTION AND INTEREST   129

modes of response may stand in all sorts of relations with one another.[8]

4. *The Phenomena of Selection:* As a first example of these relations, we may take the following. It is hardly necessary to argue that no person is ever required to make a response to everything in his environment at one and the same moment. On the contrary, it is the plainest of facts that it is now one object and then another in the total environment of a person which is initiating and regulating behavior. Likewise, no person is ever called upon to respond either to a single object or to a whole cluster of objects by making every posture and every movement of which he is capable. With respect both to environmental situations and to behavior-patterns, there is always a selective factor at work. The student in the schoolroom, to be sure, takes a general posture and follows out a general pattern of conduct suitable to the whole schoolroom situation, but this attitude or posture forms only a background upon which specific objects in the room excite specific modes of response.

The teacher, for example, may have placed some words on the board with the request that these words be written in the notebooks on the desks of each of the pupils. The words written on the blackboard constitute but one of the many patterns of objects present in the room. There are objects to be seen through the window, there are paintings on the walls, there are other pupils in the room, and there are noises in the hall. Under certain conditions, however, there is only one of these several possible sources of action which can actually become effective in initiating action. Likewise, the pupil may react to this single pattern of objects in a great many different ways. He may stand, or continue sitting, or respond by word of mouth, or explore in his desk, or nudge the person in front of him, or write out the words as he has been asked to do. For reasons that are to be named in a moment, he actually does only one of these things, viz., he writes out the words.

5. *Attention and Interest:* Our first observation, then, about the variable relations between stimulus-patterns and behavior-patterns is simply this. Any inspection of human behavior with respect to an environmental situation displays the fact that there must be certain circumstances under which selection can be brought about. This fact has long been noted by students of human nature, and two words have been used to describe it, viz., the words "attention"

[8] Cf. Tolman, E. C., *Purposive Behavior in Animals and Men.* New York: D. Appleton-Century Co., 1932, Chapter I and *passim.*

and "interest." [9] If the student actually responds in a definite or adequate way to the words that have been written on the blackboard rather than to any of the other objects in the room, he will do so, so it is said, either because he is attending to the words, or because he is interested in them.

Obviously, this is a feature of stimulus-connection-response patterns which is of tremendous importance to the whole task of teaching, for the teacher would be hopelessly lost if, in writing down a series of words or in presenting any other situation to his pupils, he knew that the pupils would be just as apt to respond to some other set of objects as they are to respond to the situation actually presented. By tradition and by repeated teaching maxims, every teacher understands that he must secure the attention of his pupils or command their interest. The whole educative process would become a futile process if there were not some way of guaranteeing attention and interest. As a matter of fact, there are times when education actually does become futile simply because, as the teacher says, the pupil is inattentive. This word does not mean at all that pupils can fall into situations where nothing is initiating and regulating their behavior. On the contrary, the word "inattention" simply describes the fact that some other object or event than the one presented by the teacher himself has become dominant.

6. *Purpose of Chapter:* The major topic of discussion in this chapter, then, is plain enough. It is required of us that we name the conditions under which some objects and events can become more important than others in exciting and sustaining action. Moreover, it is required of us that we name the conditions under which actions that are suitable to the exciting and sustaining situations rather than irrelevant actions will occur.

II. The Problems of Attention

Introduction: There is, perhaps, no feature of human behavior which has offered more difficulties both to the psychologist and to the teacher than the problems we are now to discuss. These difficulties have been so great that the term "attention" has even been dropped from a great many books on teaching method.[10]

Some help in clearing up the situation will be gained, however, if we see how these problems have been handled by some of the older

---

[9] Cf. Pillsbury, W. B., *Attention.* New York: The Macmillan Co., 1908, *passim.*
[10] For example, Wheeler, R. H., and Perkins, F. T., *Principles of Mental Development.* New York: T. Y. Crowell and Co., 1932, *passim.*

DEVELOPMENT OF ATTENTION AND INTEREST 131

psychologies. When an older person is asked about it, he will usually say that there is nothing quite so obvious as his ability to "direct" his attention to that object or task to which he wishes to attend. To be sure, there are times when mature persons are drawn away from the thing being attended to by some sudden or alarming cry, but, as a rule, most persons would be willing to argue with considerable fervor that they can set themselves to a task and keep at work until the task is done. It has even been said that the ability to attend strictly to the task in hand is one of the surest signs of the intelligence or general competence of a man, for it is only the weak-willed and the chuckleheaded that allow their attention to drift rapidly from one thing to another. Moreover, it is only the weak-willed who allow themselves to spend a considerable amount of their time in aimless daydreaming or in the shifting luxury of fantasy.

2. *Attention as a Faculty:* From these observations, it would be fair to assume that attention has been used as a name for some faculty or power which we can exercise in directing ourselves to a task. The person who is inattentive or whose attention is consistently shifting from one thing to another, therefore, has less of this faculty than the person who can concentrate himself steadily in one direction.

This is exactly the theory which has prevailed for a great many centuries.[11] Attention is a power. It is the ability to look over a whole configuration of events, select that particular feature of the situation which needs special treatment, and devote oneself to the particular feature until it has been successfully handled. Interest, too, has been conceived in the same way. There are, of course, a good many interests which have been attributed to heredity and to our native desires, but interests of this type are alleged to appear most frequently in small children and in untutored adults. That person who really has command of himself, so the argument runs, can use his faculty of interest to support his devotion to a piece of work just as long as he pleases.[12]

This theory of the nature of attention and interest has an important bearing upon the attitude which a teacher may take toward the student in the classroom. It implies that the teacher is not under any obligation to create favorable conditions either for attention or interest. On the contrary, she can simply ask the students to use

---

[11] For a good perspective on these problems, see James, W., *Principles of Psychology*. New York: Henry Holt and Co., 1890.
[12] Cf. Whitehead, A. N., *The Aims of Education*. New York: The Macmillan Co., 1932, *passim*.

whatever faculties they have with the hope that the sheer use of these faculties will, in the course of time, strengthen them so that they will become adequate to the work that has to be done by serious adults.

As a typical instance, this older theory of attention would enable a teacher to begin an hour of instruction with the remark, "Now, children, give me your attention while I tell you how two two-digit numbers may be multiplied by each other." From this point on, the teacher could assume that the pupils in the classroom ought to exercise their attentive powers, and that skill in multiplying numbers would come as an inevitable consequence. The same procedure might be followed where attention was to take the longer or more enduring form known as interest. It is sufficient not only that attention be given at the beginning of the hour, but that the various tricks of multiplication remain more important than anything else during the entire period of instruction. When, therefore, the attention of the pupils began to lag, the teacher could draw upon the innate power of interest. If there was nothing intrinsically interesting about multiplication, he could at least make a game of the process and thus secure interest by borrowing from some other source.

3. *The Concept of Prepotency:* In this illustration we have, of course, chosen a rather extreme case; but sometimes it is necessary to use extremes in order to bring out the essential features of a theory and of the faults that may go along with the theory. Some of these faults are suggested by the devices used by every teacher in order to support the flagging powers of a child. These devices have usually implied that a child does not really have a faculty of attention at all. On the contrary, they suggest that attention and interest describe either features or properties of stimulus-patterns or sets, postures, or dispositions of the person himself. In other words, they suggest that there are certain circumstances under which some objects and events can be made more important in initiating and sustaining behavior than other objects and events.

In order to get quickly into this situation, let us introduce a word which is not commonly used in connection with the problems here being discussed.[13] This is the word "prepotency." Its opposite would be "impotency." These two words are to be used in the following setting. As we have said above, every person is always in the presence of an environment, that is, in the presence of objects

---

[13] Cf. Thorndike, E. L., *Educational Psychology*. New York: Columbia Univ. Press, 1913, Vol. II, pp. 271 f.

DEVELOPMENT OF ATTENTION AND INTEREST

and events which can become effective in initiating and sustaining behavior. It is a plain fact of observation that not all of these objects and events can become effective at one and the same moment. There is always selection among them. The problems created by the words "attention" and "interest" are simply these. What are the conditions under which some objects and events can become prepotent over others in initiating and sustaining behavior? Likewise, what are the conditions under which some objects and events will remain impotent in initiating and especially in sustaining behavior?[14]

When questions about attention and interest are asked in this form, it is neither said nor implied that variations in prepotency are caused by some mental agent or power, and neither is it implied that objects have any power. On the contrary, the questions in the form in which we have stated them simply raise a query about the relations between stimulus-situations and response-patterns which ought to be and can be answered in terms of proper experimental procedure. It is clear that if there are describable conditions which will favor the prepotency of some situations over others, a knowledge of these conditions would stand among the first prerequisites of a good teacher, for he could, with the aid of his knowledge, lay learning situations before children in such a manner that they would become and remain prepotent for the children.

There is, however, another respect in which the above method of asking about the nature of attention and interest becomes important in teaching. As we have said above, the older theory implied that pupils had a power or faculty which they were duty-bound to use. In other words, the teacher could not be held responsible for a faculty or power which might owe its origin to heredity or to original nature. Our own point of view, however, suggests that if the conditions under which prepotencies are established can be described, the development of attention and interest is not so much an inevitable product of original nature as it is a product of the cleverness of teachers in arranging schoolroom situations.

Of the two possibilities before us, we propose definitely to accept the second. In other words, we shall assume that no teacher is fully prepared to do his work well unless he is able to handle learning

[14] Cf. Washburn, M. F., *The Animal Mind* (rev. ed.). New York: The Macmillan Co., 1926, Chapter XII. There is now renewed interest in the development of attention in children. Cf. Schlacter, H. S., "A Method of Measuring the Sustained Attention of Preschool Children." *J. Genet. Psychol.*, 1933, XLII, 339-371. Also, "Intelligence as a Causal Factor Determining Differences in Sustained Attention." *J. Appl. Psychol.*, 1933, XVII, 478-488.

situations in such a way that some of them will actually become prepotent over others in initiating and sustaining the responses of his students.

4. *Varieties of Attention:* The choice which we have now made can be illustrated, perhaps, if we relate our discussion to some of the other terms that have been used most frequently in discussing these problems. Among these terms, we may mention primary or involuntary attention, secondary or nonvoluntary attention, and active or voluntary attention.[15] The terms "primary attention" or "involuntary attention" have been used as a witness to the fact that there are times when a stimulus-situation, because of its varied intensity or because of its suddenness, overpowers the organism, so to speak, and gains command of the action system, in spite of anything else that may be happening in the whole stream of conduct and experience. Both our commonsense experience and laboratory experimentation show that some stimulus-situations do gain their effectiveness in initiating and regulating behavior for just this reason. We must, then, in a moment, take this phase of attention into consideration.

The terms "secondary" or "nonvoluntary attention" have been used to describe the fact that some situations become prepotent over others in initiating and regulating behavior because of previous experience. That is, with respect to three or four situations presented simultaneously, one of which has been presented before, it will be the one rather than the others, that will be more apt to become predominant in initiating a response. Here again, both our commonsense and the results of suitable experiments offer support. We shall, therefore, try to see how the learning process can be used in order to promote this phase of attention.

The terms "active" or "voluntary attention" have been used hitherto to describe attention and interest which appear to be a direct consequence of the active powers of the mind. In this case, there is a difference between our commonsense views and the results of experimental study. As we have said above, our commonsense views furnish strong support in favor of voluntary attention as the reflection of an active mind. The experimental evidence, however, throws considerable doubt upon our commonsense views, and since belief in the existence of volition as a feature of attention has played so large a part in educational practice, it will be necessary for us to pre-

[15] Cf. Pillsbury, W. B., *The Fundamentals of Psychology* (3rd ed.). New York: The Macmillan Co., 1934, Chapter XII.

DEVELOPMENT OF ATTENTION AND INTEREST

sent some of the experimental material and survey the results with the care that they demand.

III. THE CONDITIONS OF ATTENTION

1. *Introduction:* From some points of view it is possible to say that attention and interest are conditioned by events outside of the organism, on the one hand, and by events inside of the organism, on the other. In general, we shall hold to this distinction, but the student will see clearly enough as we go along that it is no more possible to separate the two in fact than it was to separate stimulus-situations from modes of reaction. In speaking of the distinction at all, we propose only to say that there are times when it is worth while to lay greater emphasis upon one set of conditions than it is upon the other.

In addition to possible differences between inside and outside conditions of attention, the second group, at least, can be broken up into a number of still smaller sets of conditions. We shall give the most of our space to the following, viz., (i) the effect of previous training on the likelihood that any particular stimulus-situation will become more potent than others, (ii) the general concept of biological importance, (iii) the influence of general postures and attitudes, and (iv) the influence both of the primary urges and desires and of the interests which seem to emerge quickly out of these desires on priority.

2. *External Determinants of Attention:* Let us suppose that, while the student has been sitting in his room quietly reading this chapter on the nature of attention, he is suddenly interrupted by the screech of grinding brakes, a loud crash, and a series of cries both from fright and pain. The chances are that the student will jump immediately from his chair and rush either to the window or out of the front door in order to see what has happened. In a situation of this type the sources of stimulus to action have been so intense as literally to assail the organism and demand some sort of action. He hears the sounds without any effort on his part, and certainly without any preliminary tuning. The sheer intensity of the stimulus-situation has thrust away all other stimulus-patterns that may have been predominant during the study period, and the actions that result are just those actions which would normally be associated with the thought of an accident and of possible assistance.

A. INTENSITY AND MOVEMENT: It is in this extreme instance of what commonly goes by the name of passive or involuntary attention that we may find the general features of an external determinant of attention. As an earlier chapter has shown us, this is probably the type of attention which occurs most frequently in very small infants and even in children.[16] It is very difficult to name the time when it is supplanted by other forms of attention, but the chances are that involuntary attention is one of the first examples of prepotency to be found not only in children but in most of the lower animals.[17]

In addition to the sheer intensity of a stimulus-situation, it is usually assumed that objects which are in motion or which are repeated over and over again will have the same effect. To be sure, we may become accustomed both to motion and certainly to repetition, but any person who has observed a small child has noted that objects which are motionless will become prepotent in exciting response much less frequently than objects which are in motion. Most of the playthings of small children, for example, depend for their attractiveness upon movement. The repetition factor is sometimes observed when an attempt is made to distract a child from some occupation in which it is already engaged. The first word spoken to it will not be effective, but further words, especially after they are increased in intensity, will become effective. They do so, apparently, because they are repeated.[18]

These ways of bringing some objects or events to attention have been explained by the assertion that a quickly appearing object or an object that is in motion must have had important meaning to the lower animals. In any case, it is known that most animals hunt one another, not by dashing quickly and powerfully upon them at first, but by approaching with extreme caution and by remaining motionless for long periods of time. As we have promised, we shall look at this biological feature of the determinants of attention below.

In the meantime, it is important to recognize the function which special sense organs play in determining attention. It has been pointed out by a good many writers that the sense organs are really devices for lowering what is called the threshold of sensitivity to stimulus-situations.[19]

[16] The student will see at once that this phase of attention is closely related to the Gestalt theory of *figure* and *ground*. The emergence of *figures* from *grounds* is one reason why Gestalt psychology has abandoned the concept of attention. That is, if the development of perception means the emergence of figures, a further concept of attention is not needed.
[17] Cf. Washburn, M. F., *op cit., passim.*
[18] For a review of some of the literature, see Dallenbach, K. M., "Attention." *Psychol. Bull.*, 1930, XXVII, 497-513.
[19] Cf. Sherrington, C. S., *The Integrative Action of the Nervous System.* New Haven: Yale Univ. Press, 1906, Chapter I and *passim.*

B. MODE OF PRESENTATION: It is clear that any animal which possessed a sense organ which would make it more quickly sensitive to slight changes in a stimulus-situation would have an immense advantage over other animals. We are not so much interested, however, in the lowering of thresholds of sensitivity as we are in the question as to whether some of the senses offer a quicker means of access to organs of response than others. For example, are lighted objects more apt to become prepotent in the regulation of behavior than sounding objects, objects which make contact with the skin, or odorous objects? This question is recognized in the schoolroom whenever teachers ask whether it is better to present material to be learned by way of the eyes or by way of the ear.

The evidence upon this point is rather conflicting. Moreover, it is not possible to carry out experiments which shall actually touch the problem in exactly the same way for different sense organs, for vision furnishes the opportunity for movement and for spatial arrangements of objects, whereas no such arrangements can be effected when sounds are involved. The best place to discover actual differences would be in relative rates of learning a series of words which are presented visually in the one case and by word of mouth in the other.

In this case, it is quite clear that presentation through both sense channels offers many advantages over the use of a single channel alone. For a good many subjects and for a good many types of material, words presented visually are learned more readily than words presented through the ear. We might draw the inference, then, that repetitions of semilearned material or attempts to learn printed material would be promoted when the material is recited aloud. This would be one method of making use both of vision and of audition during the learning process. Since stimulus-situations, acting through the other sense channels, occur infrequently in normal processes of education, we may leave these topics to a later discussion of special problems in teaching.[20]

In the literature on methods of teaching a great deal is written about this phase of attention, but it seems fair to say that the teacher is by no means so skilful in handling stimulus-situations as is the advertiser. In the case of advertising, of course, a manufacturer is intensely interested in securing the best results for his money. He

---

[20] Cf. Henmon, V. A. C., "The Relation between Mode of Presentation and Retention." *Psychol. Rev.*, 1912, XIX, 79-96; Koch, H. L., "Some Factors Affecting the Relative Efficiency of Certain Modes of Presenting Material for Memorizing." *Amer. J. Psychol.*, 1930, XLII, 370-388; Worcester, D. A., "Memory by Visual and Aural Presentation." *J. Educ. Psychol.*, 1925, XVI, 18-27.

has, therefore, given considerable time to a study of the external determinants of attention. He wishes his displays in the newspaper or on the billboard to stand out from the rest of the environmental pattern. He does this by taking advantage of just such factors as we have mentioned, viz., intensity either of sound or of illumination, movement, special regard to what he calls the drawing power of different colors and different combinations of colors, and by making frequent use of bizarre, unusual, new, or strange objects or of familiar objects in new and strange positions.[21]

It is at this point that the external conditions of attention begin to merge more definitely with some of the internal conditions, for obviously nothing could be called new or strange or bizarre unless it has been thrown into contrast against a situation that already obtains. The situation that obtains in these cases must obtain within the individual himself. That is, he must be set for some other situation whenever the one appears strange or bizarre. We may turn, then, to the several phases of internal determinants of attention.

3. *Training:* The first time a person meets a new situation he may not be wholly prepared to react in a way that will be adequate to the situation. As we have seen, he passes through a period of training during which connections will be established between the situation and a series of responses such that further presentations of the situation will almost automatically call forth the proper response. It used to be supposed that these connections were somewhat like a series of telephone connections except that, during use, they offered less resistance to the passage of the nerve current than they did at first. This view of the nature of nerve conduction must certainly be modified.[22] We may, however, infer that changes of some sort do occur, changes that will make a given response follow more easily from a given situation than they did before the training period began. It would seem to follow from these considerations that stimulus-situations for which some adequate mode of response had been already achieved would be likely to predominate over new stimulus-situations. We may offer this, then, as a statement of the way in which one set of internal determinants of attention can be established.[23]

[21] Cf. Griffith, C. R., *Introduction to Applied Psychology.* New York: The Macmillan Co., 1934, Chapter XXI.
[22] Cf. Freeman, G. L., *Introduction to Physiological Psychology.* New York: The Ronald Press, 1934, Chapter I and *passim.*
[23] Cf. Lashley, K. S., "Learning, III. Nervous Mechanisms in Learning," in Murchison, C. (Ed.), *A Handbook of General Experimental Psychology.* Worcester, Mass.: Clark Univ. Press, 1934, Chapter X.

DEVELOPMENT OF ATTENTION AND INTEREST   139

It is hardly necessary to argue that this conclusion places the responsibility for the so-called development of attention squarely upon the teacher and upon any other persons who have anything to do with promoting and guiding the growth of children. If students have a preference to attend to those things which they have attended to before, it is obvious that an appeal to some inherent faculty or power of attention falls quite beside the mark. We have already implied that involuntary attention is probably the first type of attention to appear in the growth pattern, but as soon as learning situations have begun to have an effect upon it, habitualized forms of attention would increase rapidly in number and variety.

The conclusion to be drawn from this fact is plain and straightforward. The preferences which children show for certain types of objects must certainly be a product of training. To be sure, these preferences get their start under circumstances in which the external conditions of attention are more powerful than other conditions. Once a start has been made, however, habitualized forms of attention grow apace and they will be just as variable and as widespread as the earlier conditions of training warrant.[24]

We may now look at these facts from the point of view of a child who finds it difficult to attend to schoolroom matters. The above discussion would seem to say clearly enough that failure in attention cannot be explained by supposing that some essential ingredient has been left out of a child's disposition. On the contrary, we are in position to argue that lack of attention with respect to any particular subject matter may be explained, in part, by the fact that the subject matter has not in times past been associated in a proper way with external determinants. A better illustration of this proposition is to be found, perhaps, in the development of interests. It is commonly recognized, of course, that most children will not attend to those things that are uninteresting. We may say, of course, that a lack of interest is proof of a lack in some part of our original nature. It is not in line with the facts, however, to come to this conclusion. On the contrary, lack of interest is to be explained by a lack of sufficient experience with certain types of subject matter to make the development either of interest or of attention possible.

The counterpart to this fact can be stated as follows. If a child remains inattentive to some particular object, attention might be se-

[24] This course of events has to be gained by implication from studies on the development of perception. The student can, for example, translate many parts of the last chapter into comments about the development of attention.

cured by placing the object with objects for which an interest has already been developed. At this point, we arrive at a principle of good teaching which has been stated over and over again in books on teaching method. The principle says either that those objects will be attended to or will be found interesting which are placed within a framework of previous acts of attention and previous interests, or we may say that those objects will be attended to which are congruent with the immediate attitude and disposition of the person concerned. Both of these ways of stating a venerable principle of teaching method appear to be justified by the facts. They lead, however, to a further class of internal conditions favorable to attention, viz., set, attitude, or posture.

4. *Attitude and Set:* The reader will recall that, in an earlier chapter, where the origin and development of skills and postures was under discussion, the promise was made to return to a special group of problems raised by the term "posture." It was pointed out that we take postures for a good many different purposes, but one purpose was left for later discussion, viz., the effect of posture in preparing a person for the reception of certain stimulus-situations rather than others. The time has now come to fulfil our promise and to see just what can be meant by the postures which create a favorable attitude or a favorable set toward a particular stimulus-situation and toward responses that will be adequate to such a situation.[25]

First, let us say that there is no group of problems in the whole field of psychology which touch so many phases of development and which look in so many directions as do the problems of set and attitude. Our daily experiences have made us familiar with one meaning in these terms, for we have seen many of our common household pets assume a characteristic posture whenever an object has excited attentive regard. A dog, for example, upon hearing a sound, will cock up its ears, point its nose, and otherwise adjust its body apparently for the purpose of getting a firmer hold on the source of stimulation. We may take this common observation as a starting point; but the student will quickly see that the problems of set or posture are much more extensive than can be described in motor terms. Obviously, the dog is not only set, so far as the major muscles of the body are concerned, but it must be set also in its nervous system. As a matter of fact, all of its psychological

---

[25] Cf. Young, P. T., *Motivation of Human and Animal Behavior.* Ann Arbor: Edwards Bros., 1933, Chapter V.

DEVELOPMENT OF ATTENTION AND INTEREST 141

operations must be bending themselves in some way or other to a particular situation.[26]

A. EXPERIMENTAL RESULTS: The relation between posture and set, on the one hand, and the problems of attention, on the other, will appear most quickly, perhaps, if we relate a few of the experiments that have been performed in this field. In one of the earliest experiments a group of subjects was placed in a piece of apparatus which provided several possible sources of food.[27] The animal subjects were kept in their compartment until the experimenter was ready for a trial. In one phase of the experiment, and after they had learned that food was always to be found in a lighted compartment rather than in unlighted compartments, the subjects were detained for a short period of time after the light had been extinguished. It was found that if the subjects were orientated toward the compartment which had been lighted and which contained food, they could still find food. Some of the higher animals found it necessary only to orientate the head rather than the entire body toward the food compartment.

One of the inferences to be drawn from these experiments is that there is something about a posture or an attitude which preserves, so to speak, a stimulus which has been presented and which has subsequently been withdrawn. It is as though the nervous system of the animal had been prepared for a line of action and that this preparation could endure for at least a short time, even after the stimulus itself has been removed. Similar experiments carried out with children as subjects have shown that it is not necessary that either the body or the head shall be orientated toward the object, but it has not been possible to interpret these experiments without assuming that similar preparations have been made somewhere in the body. When, for example, a plaything is hidden from a child who is then distracted toward some other occupation for a short period of time, it will still be able to find the hidden plaything. The inference is that the nervous system can be postured in such a way that a given type of action will result, even though the original stimulus which led to the posture has been removed.[28]

A great many different terms have been used to describe or to explain these nervous and bodily postures or sets. In the case of habit

---

[26] Cf. Freeman, G. L., *op. cit.*, Chapter XXIII. Also Langworthy, O. R., "The Control of Posture by the Central Nervous System." *Physiol. Rev.*, 1928, VIII, 218-231.
[27] Hunter, W. S., "The Delayed Reaction in Animals and Children." *Behav. Monog.*, 1913, II (No. 6).
[28] Cf. Munn, N. L., *op. cit.*, Chapter VII.

formation, for example, it is quite clear that the patterns of conduction necessary to bring about the properly acquired response to a given situation must be disposed to act in a certain way, even though they have not been used for some time. One may speak, therefore, of habituational tendencies. It would follow that every mature person must be in constant possession of an immense number of these habitualized tendencies or of specific determinations to act whenever the appropriate stimulus-situation pulls, so to speak, the trigger.

A further example of the nature of set or posture is revealed in the following simple experiment. Let us say that another person has just laid before the student a sheet of paper upon which is written the two numbers

$$\begin{array}{r}495\\362\\\hline\end{array}$$

No further addition is made to the stimulus-situation. It is clear that the student can do any one of several different things with these two numbers. He may add them, subtract the one from the other, or multiply them, the one by the other. The very fact that a line is drawn under the two numbers induces a set to begin with. This set or posture might be strong enough to prompt the student immediately to some sort of action. It is not yet clear, however, whether he will add, subtract, or multiply. It is almost certain that he will do one of them. The choice that he makes will almost always be determined by the set or attitude of the student at the moment. The chances are that, if the second number is larger than the first, he will add rather than subtract. The chances are, also, that the average person will either add or subtract rather than multiply. The point is that there must be some preliminary tuning or disposition of the subject which makes a preference for one operation rather than another possible.[29]

As a final illustration we may take a common experience of practically every student. Let us suppose, for example, that he has picked up this book and opened it to this particular paragraph. If he begins to read, he will undoubtedly have the experience of beginning at no place in particular. By the time several pages have been covered he will probably begin to recall certain other facts about psychology, and shortly he will, as most persons commonly express it, have warmed up to his task. That is, he warms up to

---

[29] Cf. Gundlach, R. H., et al., "A Test and Analysis of 'Set.'" *J. Exper. Psychol.*, 1927, X, 247-280.

DEVELOPMENT OF ATTENTION AND INTEREST

the act of reading or to a comprehension of what has been read in much the same way as an athlete warms up to his particular skill. Here again, then, we seem to be talking about a tuning or posturing of our psychological apparatus which favors the reception of some stimulus-situations and which disfavors the reception of others.[30]

B. IMPORTANCE IN TEACHING: The importance of these facts for the daily tasks of teaching can scarcely be overemphasized. If the teacher has not been warned in advance, he will certainly discover from his daily efforts that neither learning nor comprehension take place most readily unless a person has been conducted into new subject matter from a point of departure furnished by old and familiar subject matter. The point is that the older subject matter furnishes a predisposition or a specific set which, in their turn, will favor attention to and interest in the material. One cannot, of course, attempt to increase the prepotency value of new material by taking advantage of the external determinants of attention, but these external determinants are often short-lived in their effect. More permanent types of attention and certainly sustained levels of attention can be secured to better advantage when the proper postures or attitudes lie behind the presentation of new material.[31]

5. *Biological Importance:* It is necessary to say only a word about biological importance as a factor in determining attention, partly because most of the learning situations in which human beings are placed do not have an immediate biological value, and partly because the whole problem can be discussed much more adequately in terms of desires or urges. As a single instance, let us take the advertising value of a display which includes an article of food or a picture of a young girl. It will be argued that a display containing either of these objects will have a greater pulling power than other types of display, because the getting of food and the sex impulses are biologically important to all living creatures. There is no doubt but that the biological value of stimulus-situations among the lower animals is a very important factor in determining the direction of attention. Just how important it is in the schoolroom where the three R's are being studied will be a topic that can be discussed to better advantage in our study of motivation.[32]

[30] Griffith, C. R., *op. cit.,* Chapter XXX.
[31] Pillsbury, W. B., *Attention.* New York: The Macmillan Co., 1908, Chapter XVI.
[32] Cf. Washburn, M. F., *op. cit.,* Chapter XII.

IV. The Nature of Interest

1. *Introduction:* There is, perhaps, no phase of education which has offered so many difficulties to successful psychological analysis, or which has lent itself so easily both to praise and to abuse, as the attitudes and circumstances included under the term "interest." In one thing only, perhaps, have the students of education been agreed, viz., that interests are a reflection of, or in some way closely related to, feelings and preferences. That is, a person's interests seem somehow to be a reflection of the bodily desires, or, as some of the older types of psychology would put it, desires of the flesh rather than of the spirit.

This fact is revealed by the movement in education known as education for discipline. This movement was based upon the premise that the native interests of a person are not to be trusted as guides in the educative process. If interests are a true reflection of bodily desires or appetites and if human nature is to be distrusted, obviously the higher forms of education should not be based upon native interests. On the contrary, they should look toward that sort of discipline and training which would lift a man above his more lowly desires.[33]

One of the first contributions to education made by Froebel, Pestalozzi, and Rousseau came at just this point of conflict between a distrust of human nature and the existence of native interests. These and other men pointed out that the processes of education should normally begin with the initial or native interests of a child. The doctrine of native interests was then one important feature of the so-called psychological movement in education, a feature which has not slackened in its intensity since the early part of the last century.[34]

The student will see at once that there are at least two things to be said about this movement. In the first place, the movement is based upon the doctrine that the child does have initial or native interests. There is, however, a difference between the words "initial" and "native." The word "initial" may simply refer to the first observable interests of a child. As we have seen, however, a mistake has often been made by supposing that the first observed actions of

[33] Cf. Morrison, H. C., *Basic Principles in Education.* Boston: Houghton Mifflin Co., 1934, *passim.*
[34] Cf. Kilpatrick, W. H., et al., *The Educational Frontier.* New York: D. Appleton-Century Co., 1933, Chapter VI and *passim.*

DEVELOPMENT OF ATTENTION AND INTEREST

the child are, on that account alone, to be called original.[35] If teachers were to take it for granted that an initial interest is nothing more or less than a first observed interest, it would be profitable to list all such interests and use them to the best of one's ability in the classroom and in other places where training goes forward. The preceding pages have shown us, however, that the obligations placed upon the teacher cannot stop at this point. It may be highly important to know not only that certain interests do appear at certain times but to know as well what the factors were which led to the development of these interests. We shall return to this situation in a moment.

The second observation about the older doctrine of interests is this. If we assume that there are interests, either of the first observable type or of the native type, we may take it for granted that such interests mark almost, if not quite, the limits of the educability of a child. From this point forward, a teacher may seek to make use of interests to the best of his ability. For some time after the beginning of the psychological movement in education, and at periodic intervals since then, teachers have gone to almost any extreme in order to make the subject matter presented in a schoolroom as easy and as interesting as possible.[36] If the serious task of learning could be reduced to the level of a game or if the educative process could be made more of a spectacle than a period of intelligently controlled growth, teachers were more than pleased with themselves, because they felt that they had at last discovered the real key to adequate training.

2. *Interest and Feeling:* We have already pointed out that interests are closely related, on the one hand, to the circumstances under which acts of attention may arise and, on the other hand, to the topic of desires, urges, and motives. There are certain circumstances under which some objects will be selected in preference to others for short periods of time. Except in the case of voluntary attention, most of the psychological events described by selection are more or less fleeting in character. Those modes of selection which are supported by the primary tissue needs, however, are more enduring.

This phase of the phenomena of selection will be considered in the next chapter. In the meantime, the student should remind himself of a very plain fact about any one of his interests, viz., the feeling of satisfaction or of pleasure which he has when he is doing the

---

[35] This whole problem will be considered in greater detail in Chapter Nine.
[36] Cf. Flexner, A., *Universities, American, English, German.* New York: Oxford Univ. Press, 1930, *passim.*

thing he desires to do.[37] Clearly, the desire is not something added to the feeling of satisfaction or pleasure. On the contrary, such an interest as athletics will be pursued simply because it is inherently satisfying to be engaged in that type of activity.

The new-born infant, however, does not have interest in athletic activity. Nevertheless, it seems to prefer to do some things rather than others. Shortly before the proper time for feeding arrives, we might say that it prefers to increase the number and range of its activities until food is secured. The moment food is brought to it, its preference for wriggling and squirming declines, and a pronounced preference for suckling takes their places. When hunger has been satisfied, the act of suckling, in its turn, loses its preferred position in the whole stream of behavior in favor of cooing, gurgling, a variety of gentle bodily movements, and, finally, sleeping.

A great many attempts have been made to explain shifting preferences of these types, but at the present time it does not seem possible to go beyond the following argument. Since infants are actually found to favor those situations or modes of action which can be defined as satisfying or pleasurable or which lead to satisfaction and pleasure, and to avoid as often as possible those situations and modes of behavior which lead to annoyance or pain, it might as well be assumed that pleasure and annoyance or unpleasantness are the basic factors in all preferences.[38] If one searches for further conditions or explanations, one must resort to the conviction that those situations and actions which promote the welfare of the individual will be, on that account, pleasurable, whereas those which hinder welfare or furnish obstructions and create conflicts will be avoided, because they are annoying.[39]

In our study of desires and motives, we shall find that no type of action can take place without calling upon structures which are living. Every connection, for example, that is made between a sense organ and a muscle is a connection supplied by living nerve tissue. Since processes of living go on at different levels, it is almost certain that the pattern of events described by stimulus-situations, nerve connections, and responses will reflect, at some point or other, the rate of living which obtains at the moment. This is at least one of the

[37] Cf. Watson, J., *Hedonistic Theories from Aristotle to Spencer.* New York: The Macmillan Co., 1895, *passim.*
[38] Cf. Beebe-Center, J. G., *The Psychology of Pleasantness and Unpleasantness.* New York: D. Van Nostrand Co., 1932, *passim.* Young, P. T., *op. cit.,* Chapter III.
[39] Cf. Titchener, E. B., *Lectures on the Elementary Psychology of Feeling and Attention.* New York: The Macmillan Co., 1908, *passim.*

ways in which the origin of feelings may be accounted for. In any case, it must be taken for granted that any responses that are made to stimulus-situations usually display a feeling component.[40] The teaching problem, then, is to find out why this feeling component, as it manifests itself in the behavior of the new-born child, can be shifted from one stimulus-pattern to another or from one mode of action to another.

3. *Acquired Interests:* Let us say that an infant has just been supplied with food. It is not possible, of course, for the food to stand alone as a source of stimulus. On the contrary, the food is always an object or a figure which has emerged out of a ground. The ground may be made up of the vessel in which the food is contained, the nurse or the mother, the bed upon which the infant is lying, and all of the other objects which make up the room. Of all of these objects, the chances are that only one, viz., the food itself, will be markedly preferred to the others. This is the one, for example, which brings about the distinctive change in the pattern of behavior represented by the passage of a hungry child to a satisfied child. As we shall see, however, there are certain conditions under which other objects may acquire the same stimulus-value for the child as is possessed by the food itself. This means that other objects can be placed upon the preferred list. This step marks, apparently, one of the first stages in the transition from "original" interest to a "derived" interest.

From this point forward, the processes of learning are so complex and so variable as to resist successful experimental analysis. It is generally believed, however, that the method of transition is the same. Given one type of preference, other objects or clusters of objects will acquire a preference simply through being associated with the original stimulus-pattern. To be sure, this process of progressive change is supported at every step by the other processes of development described in previous chapters and also, perhaps, by changes in the child itself which are dependent upon maturation. In any case, within a few months after birth and certainly long before the child enters the first grade, a fairly well-defined list of preferences for objects and for types of behavior will have been developed.

These preferences are, no doubt, the preferences commonly listed as initial or native interests. Since the environments of children contain a great many "identical" factors, it is natural to find that a great

---

[40] Cf. Young, P. T., "Pleasantness and Unpleasantness in Relation to Organic Response." *Amer. J. Psychol.,* 1921, XXXII, 38-53.

many children display "identical" preferences. In spite of environmental identities, however, there are a large number of variations. These variations may consist either of differences in objects themselves or differences in the order in which stimulus-situations have been presented. In any case, in addition to the interests which are common to large numbers of children, there will be interests which are differential in character.[41]

The other side of the development of interests is furnished apparently by the factor of repetition. Other things being equal, it looks as though any stimulus-situation which has been presented once will be preferred to a stimulus-situation which has not hitherto been presented, unless, perhaps, the second stimulus-situation satisfies the requirement stated above. Most persons would consider, then, that interests can be acquired simply by developing habits of response to oft-repeated environmental situations. In order to illustrate this point, we may use an example described above. As a rule, small boys have a distinct preference for playing baseball as compared with practicing at the piano. A teacher or a parent may, however, create a learning situation in which piano practice is forced to take precedence over ball playing. This precedence will be a result, of course, of other factors than the boy's own interest, but it frequently happens that an interest in piano playing will be acquired if the training periods follow a regular schedule.

One of the standard maxims in books on the art of teaching suggests that, in order to develop a new interest, the teacher should associate new types of subject matter or new modes of action with a previous interest. If the description given above of the first steps in the development of interest is correct, this measurement is based upon a defensible foundation. The feelings of satisfaction and of pleasure which come to be associated with some objects can, under appropriate conditions, be transferred from these objects to others. This is a level of control over the growth pattern which appears most frequently in the grade school and in the high school. One may, of course, dismiss this phase of teaching by saying that older children have native preferences for different high school subjects, but neither the teacher nor the student can gain much from this belief.[42]

[41] Cf. Symonds, P. M., *Diagnosing Personality and Conduct.* New York: D. Appleton-Century Co., 1931, Chapters VI and VII.
[42] Cf. Kilpatrick, W. H. (Ed.), *The Educational Frontier.* New York: D. Appleton-Century Co., 1933, Chapter V. Strong, E. K., *Change of Interests with Age.* Palo Alto: Stanford Univ. Press, 1931, *passim.*

V. Measures of Interest

1. *Introduction:* One of the simplest ways to measure the interests of very young children is to cast up a list of the playthings they use most frequently, or to describe the various games they seem to prefer. As a rule, the preschool child spends its days with a minor amount of direction and control from other persons, especially from the various agents connected with a formal school program, and it will, therefore, turn to those objects and activities which have already acquired for it a preferential value. In the case of play, for example, lists have been made of the most preferred games, lists which include such items as playing with a ball, with blocks, with a wagon, playing house, hide-and-seek, and the like. Any game or activity which involves movement, making a sound, or movement at a fairly rapid rate is highly attractive.[43] This same method has been used with older children, and one may now say with considerable assurance just where, with respect to play activities, the interests of children will be directed at almost any given age level. There are, of course, fairly marked sex differences in interests, in so far as interests can be judged by preferred activities.[44]

A. READING INTERESTS: During the first years of schooling, some of the major interests of children can be detected in their preferences for books and moving pictures and for vocational choices. A number of studies have been made upon the reading interests of children who are just beginning to read. Typical preferences at this age are the *Peter Rabbit* books and the Thornton Burgess stories. A considerable proportion of the books read at a slightly older age have to do with war and scouting. Later on, the Henty books and such stories as *Little Women, Peggy,* and *Alice's Adventures in Wonderland* stand in high favor. Books and magazines having to do with mechanics and with simple fiction interest both boys and girls just before and during the adolescent period.[45]

B. MOVING PICTURES: Preferences of a similar type are expressed for moving pictures. Younger boys, for example, like adventure

---

[43] Lehman, H. C., and Witty, P. A., *The Psychology of Play Activities.* New York: A. S. Barnes and Co., 1927, *passim.*
[44] *Ibid.*, pp. 242 ff.
[45] Jordan, A. M., *Children's Interests in Reading.* Chapel Hill: Univ. of North Carolina Press, 1926, *passim.* Also Grant, E. B., and White, M. L., "A Study of Children's Choices of Reading Materials." *Teachers Coll. Rec.*, 1925, XXVI, 671-678; Terman, L. M., and Lima, M., *Children's Reading: A Guide for Parents and Teachers.* New York: D. Appleton-Century Co., 1931 (2nd ed.).

stories, stories of the Western plains, and comedies. Any picture which requires large amounts of action is almost certain to secure approval not only at earlier but at later age levels as well.[46] It is hardly necessary to argue that the moving picture has come to occupy a very large place in the educational influence it exercises upon young children. Both school administrators and psychologists have been interested, therefore, in finding out just how large a part the moving picture may play and what some of the major results of continued attendance at moving picture theatres may be.

Among the many references and conclusions that have been drawn from these studies, we may mention (i) the repeated emotional stresses to which children are subjected by stirring scenes of action, (ii) the effect of shooting and other forms of "criminal" action upon the moral and ethical judgments of children, (iii) the perverse attitude which many older children develop toward sex and family matters as a result of bedroom scenes and other direct suggestions of sex behavior, and (iv) the development of unprofitable types of compensation or fantasy. In connection with this last point, it has often been remarked that the moving picture furnishes a substitutional means for the solving of problems and the realization of ambitions which can hardly make either children or adults more effective in their intercourse with reality.[47]

C. EARLY VOCATIONAL CHOICES: In addition to these particular types of interest, most children are, upon being questioned, ready to express a preference for some particular vocation or calling. The usual procedure is to ask a group of subjects what they would like to do when they grow up or to check an interest blank, that is, a sheet upon which has been listed a large number of possible occupations. The results of empirical studies of this type reveal much the same picture as is revealed by preferences for activities, preferences for books, and preferences for moving pictures. Boys, for example, usually express a desire to become firemen, policemen, soldiers, or athletes. In later childhood some of these interests continue, but others are replaced by an interest in mechanics and in inventions. During the adolescent period these earlier interests are

---

[46] Seagoe, M. V., "The Child's Reaction to the Movies." *J. Juvenile Res.*, 1931, XV, 169-180. See also Jones, H. E., and Conrad, H. S., "Rural Preferences in Motion Pictures." *J. Soc. Psychol.*, 1930, I, 419-423.

[47] Cf. the series of monographs by Charters, W. W., Holladay, P. W., Stoddard, G. D., Dysinger, W. S., Ruckmick, C. A., and Peters, C. C., published by The Macmillan Co., 1933. A summary has been prepared by Charters, W. W., *Motion Pictures and Youth: A Summary.* New York: The Macmillan Co., 1933.

DEVELOPMENT OF ATTENTION AND INTEREST

crystallized in more definite form and are related to the more serious occupations of adult life.[48]

2. *Vocational Interests:* A more detailed picture of the way in which variations in interest may be measured can be gleaned from a description of a typical vocational interest test.[49] This test is made up of 420 items. The subject is asked to check each one of the items by the letter "L" if he has a preference for the item, by the letter "I" if he is indifferent to it, or by the letter "D" if he dislikes it. The items refer to one hundred different occupations, to 54 amusements, to 39 school subjects, to 82 practical and mechanical activities, to 63 common characteristics of people, to 42 miscellaneous items, and to forty estimates of subjects on present ability and chief characteristics. The subject is asked to fill out the blank as rapidly as possible, although no time limit is set.

The test was standardized by finding out how successful men in the various professions listed in the test differed from the average man. The same procedure was used with respect to all of the other parts of the tests. When appropriate comparisons were drawn between the data secured in this way, answers to each of the items in the test were weighted, the subject receiving a certain number of points on each of the preferences named. In other words, any particular subject could be compared with the scores obtained by persons known to be successful in any particular cluster of traits.

The student will see at once that the value of a test of this sort would depend upon a number of different factors. He may think, for example, of the questions as to whether interests are permanent or not, or whether likes and dislikes change with age or experience. He may wonder, too, whether the relation between a set of preferences for objects and occupations, on the one hand, and actual success in a given vocation, on the other, might not depend upon the way in which a very large number of factors are configured with respect to one another. Some of these features of tests of preferences have been studied in more detail, and it will be fruitful to consider them at least briefly.[50]

3. *Permanence of Interests:* A number of studies have sought an answer to the question as to whether an interest which has been expressed early in life will have a tendency to persist through later

[48] Cf. Fryer, D., *The Measurement of Interests in Relation to Human Achievement.* New York: Henry Holt and Co., 1931, *passim.*
[49] Cf. Strong, E. K., *Manual for Vocational Interest.* Palo Alto: Stanford Univ. Press, 1931.
[50] Other measuring instruments in this field have been described by Symonds, P. M., *op. cit.,* pp. 245 ff.

152 INTRODUCTION TO EDUCATIONAL PSYCHOLOGY

years of schooling. One of the first studies of this type required college juniors to recall their order of preference during elementary school training for mathematics, history, literature, science, music, drawing, and other handwork. The subjects were also asked to recall order of interest for the same subjects during the high school period, and finally to arrange these subjects in order of interest at the time the experiment was conducted. The correlations between these several ratings were, on the average, over .60. The results of this experiment are subject to some question, because they depended upon the recalling of earlier interests, but the indication was that earlier interests had tended to remain fairly constant.[51]

These results have been confirmed by a much more thorough and extensive study. In this study, the same subjects were asked to express vocational preferences on a number of different occasions during a period of three years.[52] The author concluded from his study that, after three years, three children out of every four still prefer their original type of vocational interest. The subjects used in the experiment were junior high school people.

Other experiments have not shown quite such high measures of permanence in interest. In one case, for example, a group of subjects was asked on three successive occasions at one-year intervals to express their choice of school subjects and of future occupations. Among the 488 junior high school pupils in the group there were 121 changes from first to second choice on successive ratings. Other changes in preference led the author to conclude that there was a decided lack of permanency in interest in the majority of the subjects.[53]

One explanation for this conflicting evidence is to be found in the method of classifying different occupations. If a general interest is divided into a great many minor occupations, there will be a good deal of fluctuation from one phase of the general interest to another. Moreover, the readiness with which interests and preferences for vocational choices fluctuate depends, apparently, upon the age of the subjects.[54] The younger the subject, the greater the like-

---

[51] Thorndike, E. L., "The Permanence of Interests and Their Relation to Abilities." *Pop. Sci. Mo.*, 1912, LXXXI, 449-456. See also *School and Soc.*, 1917, V, 178-179.
[52] Franklin, E. E., "The Permanence of Vocational Interests after Three Years." *School and Soc.*, 1926, XXIII, 438-440.
[53] Willet, G. W., "Permanence of Pupil Interests." *School and Soc.*, 1918, VII, 325-330; 1919, IX, 334-338, 365-368.
[54] Fryer, D., "The Significance of Interests for Vocational Success." *Ment. Hyg.*, 1924, VIII, 466-505.

DEVELOPMENT OF ATTENTION AND INTEREST

lihood of change. By the time a student has reached the college level, his major interests have become so firmly established that interest questionnaires may serve as fairly reliable indices for vocational guidance purposes.[55]

4. *Interests and Abilities:* It is obvious that any set of factors which would lead to the early fixation of an interest or a preference for a vocation might be related in some way or another to those features of a person's training which would increase his ability with respect to his interest or vocational choice. The experiments that have been made seem to bear out this proposition, especially where correlations between ability and interests have been computed.[56] The relationship between interests and ability would appear, perhaps, much more clearly where interests were being expressed toward school subjects, and where ability was measured by the grades secured in these subjects.[57]

The measurements that are made on interests and abilities are subject to the same genetic factors as are the measures upon permanency of interests. A very small infant, of course, has neither a large number of interests nor a high level of ability. It would be fair to conclude, then, that the correlation between these two factors during early infancy would stand at or near zero. As the child grows older and as its abilities reach a practical limit, the relation between its abilities and its interests ought to be fairly high. Between these two extremes, one might find a gradually increasing measure of correlation, depending upon the age level of the groups studied.

5. *Summary:* It may be helpful to conclude this section, and the whole of the chapter, as well, with a brief note on the dominant place of interest in education. There are several sections in the chapters yet to come where we shall find that education is placing a major amount of emphasis on learning and hence on knowing, where knowing is defined as being informed. Then, too, there is great respect nowadays for all of the fruits of doing. The persons who graduate from a high school or a college are expected to possess a wide range of information in the sense described in the last chapter and a wide variety of skills in the sense described in Chapter

---

[55] Cf. Cowdery, K. M., "The Interest Inventory in College Vocational Guidance." *Psychol. Clin.*, 1930, XIX, 59-62. See also Husband, R. W., *Applied Psychology*. New York: Harper and Bros., 1934, Chapter XII.

[56] Thorndike, E. L., *op. cit., passim.;* Langlie, T. A., "Interests and Scholastic Proficiency." *Person. J.*, 1930, IX, 246-250.

[57] Thorndike, E. L., "The Correlation between Interests and Abilities in College Courses." *Psychol. Rev.*, 1921, XXVIII, 374-376.

Two. Moreover, there has been so much emphasis on doing that there are some who would say that even knowing must be a kind of doing.

We may draw the inference, then, that education is heavily loaded with both knowing and doing. The topic of interest, however, and all of the attitudes and processes denoted by it refer to something else. It refers to the choices that are made both in the type of information that is secured and in the modes of response that can be associated with information. The word "interest" includes not only a set of conditions under which objects and situations can become prepotent in initiating and controlling behavior but it implies liking and disliking, as well. We are interested in those things we like and we like those things in which we are interested.

Liking and disliking, in their turn, refer to a set of values. That is, learning processes never run along in complete indifference to preferences. Thus we discover that the topic of interest cannot be completed until we have had something to say about the nature of feeling, mood and emotion. In the meantime, however, it is pertinent to remark that education cannot be satisfied with recitals of interests that are wholly inevitable, simply because they are assumed to be innate. This means that education cannot be satisfied with values that are embodied in expressed interests, for this would make values a product of hereditary processes. If the account that has been given above of the origin and development of interests stands upon a sure foundation, it would seem to follow that the teacher not only can but must do something about interests during those years when they are taking shape. To be sure, the interests of a college student are highly stabilized; but those of a preschool child are still in a flexible condition. There is, during this period, a measure of plasticity that should not be left to its own devices. Where interests are profound and dominant, values are sure to be expressed; and it is scarcely conceivable that either interests or values should be left wholly to processes of informal training.

READINGS

The student will recall that he was asked to think of Chapters Two and Three as a single unit, for these chapters have considered those features of development that were formerly known as sensori-motor development and which are now more commonly described in terms of the S-R formula.

The S-R formula, however, has always been somewhat confusing because it has not distinguished a recital of modes of responses and of sources of stimulus, on the one hand, from those unique types of relationship between

DEVELOPMENT OF ATTENTION AND INTEREST

stimulus and response which make the difference between a human machine and a psychological organism. The present chapter has considered the first of these relationships, viz., that expressed by the statement that selection is always at work in making some stimulus-connection-response patterns dominant over others. Dominance of this sort may be described by the words "attention" and "interest." Four more unique types of relationship between stimulus and response will be described in the next four chapters.

The general problems of this chapter have been described nowhere to better advantage than by James, W., *Principles of Psychology*. New York: Henry Holt and Co., 1890, Vol. I, Chapter IX.

Since the time of James, the problems suggested by the word "attention" have had a diversified and difficult history. Those who wish to pursue this history further should consult Titchener, E. B., *Textbook of Psychology*. New York: The Macmillan Co., 1910, pp. 265-302. Titchener, E. B., *Lectures on the Elementary Psychology of Feeling and Attention*. New York: The Macmillan Co., 1908. See also, Bentley, M., *The Field of Psychology*. New York: D. Appleton-Century Co., 1924, *passim*.

A general picture of the nature of attention up to recent years can be gained from Colvin, S. S., *The Learning Process*. New York: The Macmillan Co., 1921, Chapters XVII-XIX. See also, Pillsbury, W. B., *The Fundamentals of Psychology*. New York: The Macmillan Co., 1934, Chapter XII.

A general survey of the varieties of attention and of the conditions under which selection is made possible can be found in Pillsbury, W. B., *Attention*. New York: The Macmillan Co., 1908, *passim*. Shorter statements can be found in the book by Pillsbury mentioned above, or in Murphy, G., *General Psychology*. New York: Harper and Bros., 1933, Chapter XIV.

Some of the important physiological facts underlying the phenomena of selection are to be found in Freeman, G. L., *Introduction to Physiological Psychology*. New York: The Ronald Press, Chapters XVIII, XXI, and *passim*. The general psychological setting for the view of attention and interest outlined above can be found in Hunter, W. S., *Human Behavior*. Chicago: Univ. of Chicago Press, 1928, *passim*, and in Dashiell, J. F., *Fundamentals of Objective Psychology*. Boston: Houghton Mifflin Co., 1928, *passim*.

Studies on the nature of attitude, posture, and set have had a long history in psychology. For a summary of some of the earlier points of view, see Bentley, M., *op. cit.*, Chapter XVI. See also pp. 273 ff. More recently this group of problems has achieved new importance both for psychology and for teaching methods. See Young, P. T., *Motivation of Human and Animal Behavior*. Ann Arbor: Edwards Bros., Inc., 1933, Chapter V. Also, Dashiell, J. F., *op. cit.*, Chapter X. This chapter by Dashiell is astonishingly suggestive. The physiological background for these problems can be found in Freeman, G. L., *op. cit.*, Chapter XXIII.

The topic of interest has earned a large literature but none of it save that which has to do with empirical measurement is experimental. Profit can be gained, however, from James, W., *op. cit.*, Vol. I, pp. 402 ff.; James, W., *Talks to Teachers*. New York: Henry Holt and Co., 1915, pp. 93-99. Charters, W. W., *Methods of Teaching*. Chicago: Row Peterson Co., 1912, pp. 148-199; Arnold, F., "The Psychology of Interest." *Psychol. Rev.*, 1906, XXIII, 221-238; 291-315; Adams, H. F., "An Extension of Pillsbury's Theory of Attention and Interest." *Psychol. Rev.*, 1923, XXX, 20-35.

A major study of interest and effort can be found in Dewey, J., *Interest and Effort*. Boston: Houghton Mifflin Co., 1913. A more recent study has been made by Fryer, D., *The Measurement of Interests in Relation to Human Achievement*. New York: Henry Holt and Co., 1931. A short but useful account of more recent experimental studies can be found in Husband, R. W., *Applied Psychology*. New York: Harper and Bros., 1934, Chapter IV.

CHAPTER FIVE

THE PROBLEMS OF MOTIVATION

I. THE "WHY" OF HUMAN ACTION

1. *Commonsense:* The task of introducing a student even to the elements of experimental psychology and of educational psychology is always much more difficult than the parallel task of introducing him to the elements of physics and of chemistry. This difficulty is due, in part, to the fact that most persons gain their first information about their "minds" from a vast accumulation of commonsense observations and inferences. Some of this information has behind it the authority of religion or of theology and it is taken, therefore, as essentially correct; but much of it is simply an array of casual judgments derived for the most part from comments which men make about their own experiences and about the experiences which other men and the lower animals are supposed to enjoy. It rarely happens that human beings can become strictly impersonal either toward the ways in which they themselves behave or toward the causes of their actions. In short, then, much of our commonsense information about our own conduct and experience may stand in direct conflict with the results of more recent experimental studies.[1]

The teachings of commonsense, however, do not stand at such wide divergence from the first facts learned in the physical sciences. Even though they do not know very much about the nature of the mind or about the sources of human action, most people have used their psychological operations in much the same way in order to get knowledge about the world in which they live. This means that the physical objects which we use in our daily commerce are the objects of which the physicist and the chemist often speak. To be sure, modern physics is full of mathematical formulae and of comments about objects and events that cannot be seen with the naked eye, but even in these cases it is easy to conceive of this unseen world in the same way that we think of the seen world. The beginner in the

[1] Good illustrations are to be found in Titchener, E. B., *A Textbook of Psychology.* New York: The Macmillan Co., 1910, pp. 1 ff. See, also, Bentley, M., *The Field of Psychology.* New York: D. Appleton-Century Co., 1924, Chapter I.

physical sciences, therefore, does not have to "unlearn" a large amount of material before he can understand what is being said.

The situation is really different, however, in the psychological sciences. As psychology and education have conducted their respective investigations of human nature and of the ways in which it may be changed, it has become more and more certain that casual observations about the mind and its functions, even though some of them may be strongly supported by religion and theology, must be changed before they can serve even so practical a purpose as education. In some cases, of course, the experimental psychologist himself does not know exactly where to turn after he has discarded opinions which are so old as to have become venerable, but there can be no doubt about the essential correctness of some of the discoveries that are being made. As the reader has already found in some of the previous chapters, these studies have created a new vocabulary and many new ways of stating questions about human nature.[2]

2. *Differences Between "What" and "How":* This is the situation, for example, with respect to that whole group of problems created by our judgments about the "Why" of human action as compared to our judgments of the "What" or "How" of human action. As we have seen, it is easy enough to know the fact that people do actually behave in different ways. As a single example, we know that each person has developed a large number of special skills which he uses in conjunction with certain types of stimulus-situations. With the aid of proper instruments, most of the general features of these skills may be described. We may study them in terms of their speed, of the types of coördination involved, and of their accuracy with respect to the stimulus-situation, but results of this type simply tell us in more detail what a skill is as a type of movement system. Even though we discover that actions always arise in conjunction with some particular stimulus-pattern, we shall have said nothing as yet as to *why* a person will use one skill or one posture in the presence of an object rather than another.[3] There is, however, no feature of human conduct which is more important than this, both for psychology and for the art of education. No good

[2] If the student has any doubt about this, let him page through such a book as Porter, N., *The Elements of Intellectual Science,* 1871, and then compare it with Murchison, C. (Ed.), *Foundations of Experimental Psychology.* Worcester, Mass.: Clark Univ. Press, 1929.

[3] The teacher may find it helpful to study in more detail the meaning of "description" and "explanation" in science. Cf. Campbell, N. R., *Physics, the Elements.* Cambridge: Cambridge Univ. Press, 1920, Part I.

purpose would be served by making ever so complete a record of the different ways in which people behave, if nothing could be said about the sources of their action or about the reasons why they behave just as they do in a particular case.

3. *Purpose and Intention:* This phase of human action is so important that we can well afford to give several illustrations of it. At a more adult level, we take the distinction between work and play rather seriously. Work is defined as any bodily activity in which one is engaged not for its own sake but for the attainment of some ultimate goal or for the satisfaction of a purpose. If we ask a laborer along the highway why he labors as he does, he may tell us either that he is in need of money in order to buy the ordinary necessities of life, or that he is saving up his money in order to complete his education, or in order to establish a home, or in order to travel, and so on. Play, on the contrary, is often described as a type of activity in which we engage simply because the activity is immediately and inherently satisfying. In other words, then, work seems to be a type of action leading toward the attainment of some future goal or the satisfaction of an intention or purpose. To be sure, there are men who find so much interest in their work that they count it more as play than real work; but even in these cases, their actions seem to be guided by purposes.

There is so much intention or purpose in human action that some people have been inclined to say that no feature of human nature can possibly compare in importance with a proper description of the sources of action.[4] Even when a child starts out in the morning for school, each step that it takes has more meaning than could be found in a description of the types of coördination required in order to walk. The child is *on its way to* school, and this means that a goal or an intention not within the field of vision is somehow exercising a controlling influence over the course of its actions. The whole system of movement required to get from its home to the schoolroom is a system which appears to be directed. It is directed because the child may be pushed from behind by the command of the parents who have told it to go to school or because it is being pulled from ahead by some of the pleasures that it expects to enjoy after the schoolroom has been reached.[5]

[4] Cf., for example, McDougall, W., *Outline of Psychology.* New York: Charles Scribner's Sons, 1923, Chapter II. A useful survey of these more "dynamic" features of human behavior can be found in Woodworth, R. S., *Dynamic Psychology.* New York: Columbia Univ. Press, 1918.
[5] Cf. Tolman, E. C., *Purposive Behavior in Animals and Men.* New York: D. Appleton-Century Co., 1932, Chapter XVIII.

The teacher in the schoolroom is always interested in the causes of action, for he must make constant use of them in his daily work. He can, to be sure, command the student to learn the lesson assigned, but he knows very well that the command will not be wholly effective unless it is supported by some motive or incentive or drive within the child itself. If the child should have some other desire leading it away from the schoolroom or away from the particular task assigned, the sheer command to learn will hardly be sufficient to bring about the right sort of response.

We shall deal with a number of facts of this type in a later chapter. In our study of some of the conditions under which learning may be made most effective, for example, we shall discover that a student must have what is commonly known as the "will" or the "desire" to learn before good progress can be made. Moreover, granted a desire, learning will take place more rapidly if a sufficiently large incentive has been placed before the child. One of the strongest of these incentives is known as competition or rivalry. If a teacher can say to a student that a reward will be offered to that person who makes the best record in any given task, an urge to work with increased speed will be placed upon all of the students in the class.

Rewards may be of almost any type, as, for example, special recognition before the group, a higher grade than is achieved by some other person, relief from special examinations, gold stars pasted near one's name on a chart in the schoolroom, or the promise of an interesting story toward the close of the day. At the time these rewards are mentioned, they stand, so to speak, in front of the learner, and they offer, as we commonly say, an invitation to increased effort, or they serve as a magnet with considerable drawing power.[6]

The "Why" of human action is of particular interest to teachers and parents when students have misbehaved or have seriously failed in the performance of duties which, because of their training, might normally have been expected of them. When, for example, a child is caught in a lie or when it is known to have cheated on an examination, we are not so much interested in the types of muscular movements involved as we are in the causes of the action. Our first question to such a person is, "Why did you do that?" The inference is that there must have been some special agent or some impelling force behind the action which, if it could be discovered, would somehow explain the action or give us a leverage in helping the person to be-

---

[6] Cf. Diserens, C. M., and Vaughn, J., "The Experimental Psychology of Motivation." *Psychol. Bull.*, 1931, XXVIII, 15-65.

THE PROBLEMS OF MOTIVATION 161

have more correctly on another occasion. Just as we wish to know why the sun rises or why water runs downhill, so we wish to know why nations go to war, why some men will murder one of their fellows, why an athlete becomes crowd-shy during a game, why some boys pick on smaller boys, why gangs develop, why adolescents show many difficulties in adjusting themselves to one another, and so on.[7]

4. *Purpose of the Chapter:* These questions, together with hundreds of others like them, set the general problems of this chapter. We must try to find out where the causes of human action are to be discovered. We must search out the sources of motives, desires, urges, purposes, intentions, and ambitions. We must try to describe the conditions under which the urges or factors described by these words can become effective in giving order and direction to human conduct, and we must also see what the teacher can do in order to change these urges and other driving forces for the good of the person himself and for the sake of his value as a member of the social group.

As we have pointed out at the beginning of this introductory section, this may be a rather difficult task, because most of our ways of thinking about the sources of human action have come from our long experience with one another rather than from any experimental study of human nature. The very words which we have used, viz., purpose or intention or desire, reflect this long commonsense story. In any case, we must now look at this whole group of problems in more detail in order to see how the "causes" of human behavior may be described and in order to discover the methods that may be used in order to gain control over these "causes."

II. Theories of Motivation

1. *Will Power:* There are, as we have intimated above, two theories about the sources of human purpose or intention, the one being drawn from an array of more or less casual judgments about the matter, and the other drawn from a group of experimental attacks on the problem. According to the first theory, the "Why" of human conduct is to be found in such words as "will power," "determination," or "volition." Each of these words seems to imply that human beings are, in some manner or other, effective agents in handling themselves and in adjusting themselves to the objects and

[7] Cf. Young, P. T., *Motivation of Human and Animal Behavior.* Ann Arbor: Edwards Bros., 1933, Chapter I.

events around them.[8] To say the same thing in another way, each of these words asserts that human beings are not the passive agents of an environment which can, in and of itself, excite action or regulate or direct the course of action.

The belief that human beings have a power of will or a faculty of volition which gives them mastery over the objects around them has gained most of its authority from the fact that it comprises so essential a part of some of the older points of view about human nature. For example, if we assume at the outset that man is or possesses a living soul or a mind which is endowed, by definition, with the power of free will or of self-determination, the question as to why we act in one way rather than another is answered just as soon as it is stated. A man who is really an agent can use his reason in order to outline a course of action, and then he can use his will power to keep himself to this course of action until the goal has been reached.[9] Even where action is obviously started by some one of the bodily appetites, the reason, so it is said, can illuminate or give direction to the bodily appetites, modify them, or even deny them altogether.

This way of looking at the sources of human action has secured approval because it seems so obvious and so necessary to the dignity of human beings as compared with the lower animals. The latter, of course, can be admitted to be much more passive in response to stimulus-situations and much less capable of guiding present action in the light of future consequences.[10] Moreover, there is nothing so characteristic about human action in the face of a difficult or complex problem as the feeling of freedom or of choice in selecting one course of action in preference to another. When, therefore, some of the newer psychologies took quite a contrary point of view, that is to say, when some of the newer psychologies began to lay more emphasis upon the value of stimuli for initiating and controlling the course of action, they were looked at not only with suspicion but, in some cases, with actual scorn.

As we shall see, some of the more extreme types of behaviorism assert that a human being represents not much more than the me-

---

[8] For a fruitful discussion of this whole problem, see Fullerton, G. S., *A System of Metaphysics*. New York: The Macmillan Co., 1914, Chapter XXXIII.
[9] Experimental psychology of the introspective type has translated these facts into a variety of determining tendencies. Cf. Bentley, M., *The Field of Psychology*. New York: D. Appleton-Century Co., 1924, Chapters VII and XII.
[10] That is, they could be until the development of the experimental study of motivation. Cf. Stone, C. P., "Motivation: Incentives and Drives," in Moss, F. A., *Comparative Psychology*. New York: Prentice-Hall, Inc., 1934, Chapter IV.

THE PROBLEMS OF MOTIVATION

dium in which certain types of events, viz., reactions of a muscular or a glandular sort, may take place in response to the energies embodied in a stimulus-pattern. If it could be shown that all human action is made in response to sources of stimulation outside of the body, there would be, of course, no further use for such words as will power, determination, freedom, or choice.[11]

2. *Motivation and Selection:* In spite of the marked difference between these two points of view toward human nature, a difference which we shall study in more detail later on in the chapter, there is one feature which both theories hold in common. Whether we speak of a special faculty of will, on the one hand, or of the initiating and guiding influence of stimulus-patterns, on the other, it is clear that there are times when human conduct is highly selective in the sense that it is directed for long periods of time toward a single objective. It is in the word "selected," then, that we find a common element between the older and the newer points of view.

The student will recall, however, that the whole of the last chapter was likewise concerned with selection. It was discovered that the term "attention" is a term which we may use to describe some of the conditions under which the action-patterns of a person are momentarily directed toward some single part or phase of a total situation. We found, also, that the word "interest" names a set of conditions which favor this same outcome.[12] When a person is attending to a particular object or when he is deeply interested in it, we may say of him that he is attending *from* all other objects or that he is not interested—that is, for the time being—in a great many of the things in which he might on some other occasion be interested.

It looks, then, as though the topic of this chapter, viz., the nature of motivation or of free will, displays a certain similarity to the problems discussed in the last chapter. For the time being, we shall say that this is really the case. In general, the problem of motivation is the problem of finding out what conditions make it possible for a course of action to be directed toward some single goal. If we say this, then, it becomes necessary to distinguish motivated action from both attention and interest. One possible basis for this distinction lies in the fact that motivated action is more enduring or more persistent than either attentive or interested action. It is certainly more enduring than attentive action.

[11] Cf. Rexroad, C. N., *General Psychology for College Students.* New York: The Macmillan Co., 1929, *passim.*
[12] Considerable light is thrown upon this question by Holt, E. B., *The Freudian Wish and Its Place in Ethics.* New York: Henry Holt and Co., 1915, *passim.*

Interests, as we have seen, differ from attention in part because they, too, are more enduring in their control over a course of action.[13] Motives, however, appear to be made up of those sets of conditions or of those circumstances which may exert almost, if not quite, a life-time control over thought and conduct. To be sure, motives, like interests, may change, and the former more frequently than the latter. But, as we shall see, there are some motives which are really life-long in character.

3. *Examples of Motivation:* In order to make some of these statements appear more real, let us take a fairly simple instance of attentional and motivated behavior in one of the lower animals. Let us say that we have just placed a white rat at the entrance to a maze. If the subject has never been placed in this particular situation before, it will respond to the situation by making all of those movements that are required fully to explore the maze from one end to another.[14] As the subject moves along the various pathways, it will be quite clear that now one feature of the total stimulus-situation and then another has become prepotent in initiating and regulating response.

This is a phase of the whole pattern of reaction which we have already described as attention. Furthermore, we may, if we wish, say that the exploratory movements of the white rat can be taken as evidence of its interest in a new situation. Eventually the white rat will find its way to an inner compartment where food is to be found. As we shall see in a later chapter, a maze of this type is in no sense of the word a problem for a white rat, since it cannot possibly know in advance of an actual reaction to the whole situation that food is to be found in it. Two or three trials later, however, it does appear that the maze situation has been transformed into a problem.[15] Moreover, it appears that a new type of relation between the whole stimulus-situation and the behavior of the rat has developed, for now its behavior is obviously directed or motivated. The animal acts as though it were being driven toward a goal, viz., the satisfaction of hunger or thirst. If this experiment is repeated a sufficient number of times, the rat will learn the correct path to the food and use its skill with a high degree of efficiency whenever it is placed in the same situation.

[13] Cf. Leuba, C. J., "A Preliminary Analysis of the Nature and Effects of Incentives." *Psychol. Rev.*, 1930, XXXVII, 429-440.
[14] Cf. Small, W. S., "Notes on the Psychic Development of the Young White Rat." *Amer. J. Psychol.*, 1899, XI, 80-100.
[15] Cf. Munn, N. L., *Animal Psychology.* Boston: Houghton Mifflin Co., 1933, pp. 307 ff.

Still another illustration, this time from the field of human action, will help to furnish a setting for the matters that are to be discussed in the following pages. Let us say that we have just come upon a young person who is steadily at work in the wheat field. Upon our question as to why this person is working so steadily in the hot sun, we get the answer, "Because I want to go back to school in the fall." The actual action of pitching a sheaf of wheat into a wagon is, of course, an act which involves attention. The sheaf of wheat occupies for a moment a primary position among all of the objects surrounding the worker. This action, however, together with a great many others throughout the entire summer, appear to be related to one another, not because of temporary displays of attention or even because of changing interests, but because the goal named by the words "getting back to college" is a goal which has, somehow, acquired the power to direct action toward itself.

We may say, of course, that the young man in the wheat field is bending all of his energies to the work immediately at hand because he has deliberately formed a plan of completing his education and has settled on this particular means for attaining a complete realization of this plan. We may also search more diligently, however, for some of the other factors that may enter into this whole picture for, after all, nothing in particular is said about human nature if we simply invent a word, viz., will power or ambition, to cover our ignorance of the real factors involved. To be sure, will power has been given meaning by asserting that it refers to some special type of mental energy or to some special faculty of the soul, but neither the energy nor the faculty can be studied. This means, of course, that no real addition has been made either to our knowledge of motivation or to our ability to help people acquire motives during the educative process.

III. The Primary Desires

1. *Introduction:* It would be almost impossible to disentangle all of the factors involved in the sources of human action at the level of maturity. As we know, an adult man may sometimes justify his actions because he is moved by what he calls an ideal, or because he wishes to satisfy an ambition, or because he wishes to gratify some bodily desire, or because he seems to be impelled by some agent, the exact nature of which he cannot describe. If we were to take the normal adult as a standard of comparison, we might be inclined to say that small children and even new-born infants must

also have ideals, ambitions, purposes, or intentions as well as bodily appetites, and that they must be vaguely aware of some impelling urge to action.

As we have seen, infants do have bodily appetites, but nothing is to be gained, apparently, by attributing ideals or intentions to them simply because adults are known to respond to their ideals and intentions. In other words, the real source of information about the beginnings of motivated behavior lies in a direct experimental study of infants and of the lower animals. It is a study of this type which has led almost to a complete abandonment of older notions about will power and determination and to the development of a new vocabulary and a new way of asking questions about the motivated character of human behavior.

As we have seen in one of the earlier chapters, a new-born infant is moved to action almost completely by events that are happening within its own body or within its own alimentary canal. To be sure, there are a few occasions when some external stimulus may become sufficiently prepotent over these other sources of action to initiate a reaction. But, on the whole, the infant seems to be a self-generating agent.

This fact has led students of human nature to hold that the beginnings of motivation are to be found in these internal sources of stimulus.[16] Only a fiction writer could describe the behavior of a new-born infant or even of a young child in such a way as to show that it had any ideals, ambitions, or even conscious purposes. The inference is that conduct which is guided by ideals, ambitions, or purposes, must be a result of training which has become effective some time after birth and before the child has become fully mature. We must then inquire about the primary urges to action, for if they really constitute the beginnings of motivated or purposeful behavior, it is highly important not only that we find out everything we can about these beginnings, but that we discover also the educative changes that take place in them.

2. *Tissue Needs:* As a sample case, let us consider the possible sources to action which particularly arouse an infant from its sleep and which make it become increasingly restless until food has been given to it. We may make a long story short by saying that a sleeping period or a period of quiet cooing is normally interrupted by excitations from the walls of the infant's stomach. As the student knows from his physiology, hunger is an attitude which is induced

[16] Cf. Dashiell, J. F., *Fundamentals of Objective Psychology.* Boston: Houghton Mifflin Co., 1928, Chapter IX.

THE PROBLEMS OF MOTIVATION

by periodic contractions in the walls of the stomach which serve as sources of stimuli to sense organs in the muscle tissue.[17] The movements in the walls of the stomach are induced apparently at regular intervals after the contents of the stomach have passed on to lower parts of the alimentary system.

In other words, we may say that at regular intervals after feeding, a tissue change takes place which serves as the signal for muscular movement in the stomach. The relation between those parts of the nervous system having to do with digestion and other phases of the alimentary system, on the one hand, and the central nervous system, on the other, are of such a character that when the hunger contractions begin, an incentive to movement will be carried over to most of the muscles of the body. Even our common observations will tell us that when a new-born infant has been left unfed for two or more hours, it will become increasingly restless, make squirming and kicking movements with its body and its feet, reaching and waving movements with its arms, and movements leading to crying in its vocal apparatus.[18] Our common observation tells us also that if, during this period of restlessness, the infant is given food, the restlessness will disappear and after the food has been taken, the infant will lie for variable periods of time in a semi-vegetative state. In short, then, the word "hunger" may be used either to describe a general tissue need of the body which recurs at periodic intervals or it may describe a special source of internal stimulation leading to action in a good many of the large muscle groups.

A. HUNGER AND THIRST: As a first class of tissue need or of primary urges to action, we may name, then, such factors as hunger, thirst, the desire for continuous supplies of oxygen, and the desire to get rid of waste products.[19] It has been shown that in each of these cases the lack of food, the lack of water, the lack of oxygen, or the presence of waste products in the organs of excretion can and do serve as sources of stimulus to the larger reaction systems. As we shall see in a moment, however, our main problems concern

---

[17] Cf. Cannon, W. B., "Hunger and Thirst," in Murchison, C. (Ed.), *A Handbook of General Experimental Psychology*. Worcester, Mass.: Clark Univ. Press, 1934, Chapter V.

[18] Cf. Irwin, O. C., "The Amount and Nature of Activities of Newborn Infants Under Constant External Stimulating Conditions During the First Ten Days of Life." *Genet. Psychol. Monog.*, 1930, VIII, 1-92.

[19] Cf. Dunlap, K., *Civilized Life*. Baltimore: The Williams and Wilkins Co., 1934, Chapter III. Also Tolman, E. C., "The Nature of the Fundamental Drives." *J. Abnorm. and Soc. Psychol.*, 1926, XX, 349-358. Watson, G. B., and Spence, R. B., *Educational Problems for Psychological Study*. New York: The Macmillan Co., 1930, pp. 326 ff.

not so much the actual existence of these tissue needs as the conditions and circumstances under which they may be converted into secondary or derived sources of motivation. Before we pass on to this study, it is necessary to inquire whether there are other general bodily conditions which may serve as sources of stimulus to action and to suitable postures in support of action.

B. ACTIVITY: At the present time, there are at least three other bodily conditions which are almost certainly equivalent to the tissue needs just described. The first of these is commonly spoken of as the desire for activity. The desire for activity is based, in part, on the obvious fact that every human being is a living system. It is a total pattern of systems of energy which are always in a state of semiequilibrium with one another, the equilibrium being constantly disturbed by the addition of food, by the amount of activity, by the amount of energy that has just been expended, by the inevitable conduction of nerve impulses to muscles, and by dynamic conditions which may obtain even in the muscles themselves.[20]

In view of all of these circumstances, we can hardly expect that a human being could ever remain for any long period of time in a semivegetative condition. Even after the small infant has been fed, it does not usually drop off immediately into a period of sleep. It may remain for a considerable period of time in a state of activity, waving its arms, wriggling its body, and pulling up or pushing out its feet. To be sure, there are sources of external stimulation which may initiate some of these movements, but any inspection of the first thirty days of an infant's life will certainly give a clear impression to the effect that much of the random activity of a small child must be induced by the simple fact that it is a living, and therefore an active, system. Pending the course of further research in this field, we shall say, then, that the desire for activity describes a complex set of vital or chemical conditions which make it inevitable that human beings will engage in movement simply because of the chemical or vital conditions themselves.

C. REST: The student already knows that, during a period of activity, work is done. Even when the arm is raised, the weight of the arm itself means the expenditure of energy even though no object is moved. The energy for muscular action is gained in part from a bodily sugar known as glycogen. This sugar is burned in the muscle cells, leaving, among other products, a toxin known as

---

[20] The desire for activity has been elevated into a major source of human action by some of the psychoanalysts. Cf. Adler, A., *Understanding Human Nature.* New York: Greenberg, 1927, *passim.*

lactic acid.[21] When the amount of lactic acid in the system passes beyond a certain value, it appears to place certain obstacles in the way of the easy conduction of nervous impulses. In other words, there is induced in the whole living system a state known as fatigue.

The body is equipped, of course, with certain organs of excretion which attempt to take care of most of these waste products of muscular action, but when action is violent or long-continued, the excretory organs are not adequate for the task. Now it appears from the conduct of human beings that the presence of these fatigue-induced substances may serve as a basis for what is commonly described as the desire for rest. It looks as though fatigue products in the nervous system may be even more effective in inducing this desire than is the case with muscle tissues. At any rate, given a sufficiently long period of work, most persons will seek for a set of conditions which will bring an end to further muscular activity.[22] These conditions are usually furnished by complete muscular relaxation as in resting in a prone position or by a period of sleep. Even a new-born infant which does not exercise itself violently falls asleep rather quickly after the feeding period, providing sources of stimulus from its alimentary canal induced by colic and other digestive difficulties are not too dominant.

D. SEX: The primary tissue conditions which we have described up to this point are periodic in character. They would, of course, remain continuous for longer periods of time if proper satisfaction could not be attained. There is, however, one type of tissue condition which is not only recurring but is essentially continuous as well. This tissue condition is furnished by the glands of internal secretion. Among these glands the gonads, that is to say, the glands directly connected with the sex organs, are not only the most typical, but the most important.

It is not known as yet how the glands of internal secretion may become sources of stimulus to action. It may be that instead of becoming actual sources to action, they simply prepare the organism or tune it to the reception of some stimuli rather than others. The substances secreted by the various glands are sometimes called hormones. These hormones are carried throughout the body in the blood stream and it is entirely reasonable to suppose that they may affect the various structures in the body just as the products of exercise may do. At any rate, it is almost certain that the sex glands,

---

[21] Cf. Gould, A. G., and Dye, J. A., *Exercise and Its Physiology*. New York: A. S. Barnes and Co., 1932, Chapters VII and VIII.
[22] Dunlap, K., *op. cit.*, pp. 76 f.

and some of the other glands as well, give rise to a set of conditions which merit the name "desire." We may speak, therefore, of the sex desire.[23]

Opinions as to the date when sex desire as a source of human action really becomes effective differ greatly. As we shall see in a later chapter, there are some persons who suppose that this desire is just as common to new-born infants, if not more so, than the other desires mentioned above.[24] On the other hand, the evidence is pretty clear that the sex organs do not reach maturity until the child enters that point in its growth pattern known as puberty or adolescence.[25] In the former case, then, it could be inferred that a considerable amount of the behavior of new-born infants and small children finds its adequate source in the sex impulses. It is even urged that no one of the other tissue conditions can equal the sex desire in its influence on the course of action.

Those who maintain that the sex desire does not really manifest itself until puberty would simply have to find the major sources of action in other tissue needs. This is, however, a question that does not have to be settled at the present moment. It is a plain fact that general processes of living do furnish conditions under which action can be initiated or motivated. This means that the beginnings of all of those modes of action described as responses to ideals, to ambitions, to intentions, or to purposes may be related by educational processes to primary desires.[26]

E. OTHER DESIRES: In addition to these general bodily conditions certain other desires of equal primacy have been described. There is, for example, an alleged desire for preëminence.[27] Those who urge this desire will argue that not only human beings but some of the lower animals as well behave as though they wanted to be conspicuous. People choose a great many different ways of manifesting this desire, but this is not the question to be settled. If it is in the nature of human nature to shun lack of distinction or lack of recognition, it is necessary either to find some primary tissue condition which underlies the desire or to show how such a desire may emerge out of such a combination of other tissue conditions.

The same thing holds true of an alleged desire to conform to the

[23] Dunlap, K., *op. cit.,* pp. 78-99.
[24] Cf. Freud, S., *New Introductory Lectures on Psychoanalysis.* New York: W. W. Norton and Co., 1933, *passim.*
[25] Cf. Brooks, F. D., *The Psychology of Adolescence.* Boston: Houghton Mifflin Co., 1929, *passim.*
[26] Dashiell, J. F., *op. cit.,* Chapter IX.
[27] Dunlap, K., *op. cit.,* pp. 99-103.

group.[28] Likewise the desire for activity is sometimes translated into a desire for power. In this case, however, it is quite clear that one has stepped over the bounds of experimental information, for the domination which one person may exert over another is related so intimately to socialized conditions of living as to make it almost certain that the will to power refers either to an intrinsic instinct of the soul or to a product of training.

As we have said, however, our main quest is not for a complete list of the primary desires but only for a sample of those desires that are almost certainly primary sources of human action. Even if only one such primary source of action could be discovered, it would be highly important to the teacher to know how this source could be modified or changed by the processes of training. Our next task, then, is to see how the primary tissue needs, viz., hunger and thirst and related desires, the desire for activity, the desire for rest, and the sex desires, may be redirected or changed so that they can be used in the schoolroom, in the form of motives, incentives, urges, intentions, and purposes.[29]

IV. THE DEVELOPMENT OF MOTIVES

1. *Introduction:* The student has felt, no doubt, during this brief study of some of the physiological appetites, that he has not been even within visible distance of the real problems of motivation as he understands them. There is, of course, abundant justification for this feeling. Let us take, for example, the conduct of a person who leaves his home and his friends in order to travel in some of the more backward parts of the earth. He calls himself an explorer. He gives up a great many comforts and a high measure of safety in order to subject himself to privation, thirst, a burning sun, to become the prey of vicious insects, and even to place his life in danger at the hands of hostile tribesmen.

When we ask about the sources or causes of this behavior, we will be told either that the fine ideals of science and of discovery are being served, or that it would be a great satisfaction to be able to write a book about some hitherto unexplored region, or that there is only a desire to get away from a deep sorrow or a great disappointment, or that there is nothing present other than a sheer *Wanderlust*. All of these reasons for such a trip as we have described

---
[28] *Ibid.*, p. 103.
[29] Cf. Wheeler, R. H., and Perkins, F. T., *Principles of Mental Development*. New York: T. Y. Crowell Co., 1932, Chapter XXII.

seem to stand as remote as possible from hunger, the desire for rest, the sex desire, and even from the desire for activity. It hardly seems possible, for example, that a scientific ideal could be in any way related to an original physical appetite.

During the late war, a great many men served their respective countries, not because of some tissue condition, but because of the ideals that are often described by the words patriotism or love of one's country. In one of the most venerable pieces of literature which we possess, it is said that for this cause, viz., religion, a man will leave his home and his friends and go through situations which will obstruct and irritate rather than satisfy any of his primary tissue needs. Or, to make the gap we have to cover still more real, let us try to interpret the childish affection expressed by a pupil who brings a flower to his teacher in terms of one of the primary tissue needs.

In spite of the difficulties implied in the above statements, we must do what we can to see whether motives, purposes, and desires can actually be developed out of the primary tissue needs, and what the teacher may do in order to effect a greater degree of control over these processes.

2. *Initial Processes of Conditioning:* In view of the complexity of the situation, let us take one of the simplest of the possible cases. As the student already knows who has spent any time at all in watching a small infant, the responses which the infant makes to the stimulus-situations in its own alimentary system do not long remain attached to these alimentary conditions alone. He will have noted that, within a few weeks at the most, the mere sight of any person who has been connected with the act of feeding will lead to behavior of a type very much like that originally appearing in response to conditions in the alimentary tract. In other words, it appears that the mother, the nurse, or even the bottle can become a sign or a substitute for an initial tissue condition.[30]

To be sure, small infants will not express the hunger desire just after being fed, and neither will the presence of the mother or the nurse become a source of searching activity under these conditions. As children grow older, however, the stimuli which have become signals or signs of the original stimulus-situation are sufficiently powerful to induce the hunger desire and especially to induce eating reactions even though the child has just been fed.

In view of these simple observations, we seem justified in saying

[30] Cf. Woolley, H. T., "Eating, Sleeping, and Elimination," in Murchison, C., *op. cit.*, Chapter II.

that the hunger desire at least may be quickly changed, even during the first few weeks. It is almost too obvious to say that the sight of the mother or of a bottle during the first day after birth has no stimulus value whatsovever so far as the child is concerned. Within a short time, however, it has achieved a stimulus value. Moreover, this stimulus value is derived, apparently, out of the fact that external objects and situations can be substituted for certain types of internal sources of stimulus.

Our first conclusion about the primary desires, then, is simply this. The primary desires are stimulus-response patterns which are just as amenable to change through learning as are any of the stimulus-response patterns that have been described in previous chapters. It is in this conclusion that we can prepare the way for further studies of the changes that may take place in our primary tissue needs.

3. *Dependence of Motives on Previous Learning:* These changes call for considerable measures of growth in some of the phases of human nature which have been considered in the previous chapters. We may remind ourselves, first of all, of the emergence of a vast number of particular habits, skills, and postures out of the generalized responses of a new-born infant. This is the story that was told in Chapter Two. It is clear that, even when human beings respond directly to primary tissue needs, the character of their responses would change greatly with the number of skills, habits, and postures that have already been acquired.

As a very simple example, let us take the initial eating reactions of an infant. That part of the total reaction which is most specific or most mature at the time of birth is known as the suckling response. Even though many infants have to learn how to suckle after they are born, they acquire this skill within a few practice periods. The act of suckling, however, is quickly supplemented by a large variety of other skills such as learning how to handle a spoon, a knife, a fork, how to hold a glass, how to cut pieces of food on the plate, how to move the hand to the mouth, and so on, with all of the skills which make up what we commonly call good manners at the table. These skills imply, of course, a great many postures and attitudes which form the general background to good manners.[31]

A similar instance is to be found in the responses to the desire for activity. At first the actions of the new-born infant are awkward in the sense that they are too generalized in extent. By the time a child has reached the age of twelve or fifteen, however, it has

[31] Cf. Young, P. T., *op. cit.,* Chapter V.

acquired a tremendous number of special skills any one of which may be used in direct answer to a desire for activity. We have only to think of the skills that are used by an athlete in order to realize how variable they may be and how many different purposes they may serve.

Similar processes of growth are implied with respect to what we have called the increase in the range of the effective environment or the gradual transformation of the irrelevant environment into a relevant environment. The relevant environment of a new-born infant, as we have seen, is greatly limited; that is, only a few objects and events have emerged out of the total perceptual field before the infant. If, then, other situations aside from those which obtain in the body itself are to acquire the persistent and enduring stimulus values which reside in the tissue needs, it is necessary that perceptual development shall have gone on apace.

An illustration of this fact has already been given just above where we tried to point out some of the simpler phases of the relation between motivation and the development of skills. Before a child can acquire any skills with reference to the objects it will use at a table, it is implied that these objects have become differentiated from the whole perceptual field so clearly that they really are objects having a spatial location, a given size and a proper function.

4. *Emotion and Motivation:* It is a little difficult, as yet, to name all of the relations that may obtain between the primary motives and the simpler forms of derived motives, on the one hand, and different varieties of emotionalized action, on the other. It is easy to see, however, that the responses which an infant may make to an unsatisfied desire quickly pass the stage of mere restlessness into a stage which is certainly emotional in character. If the infant does not get its food at the proper time, it will begin to cry, and before many weeks have passed its cry will have taken on that particular form or quality known as an angry cry. Later on, words will take the place of crying, but the emotional levels behind these more specific types of reaction to a tissue need will not become any less intense. We may, therefore, give witness to the fact that the relations between motivation and emotionalized action are probably of a highly intimate character, but since it will be the purpose of the next chapter to consider in more detail the several varieties of emotionalized action, we shall now postpone further comment.

V. Complex Motives

1. *Introduction:* We have tried to keep our discussion of the transition from the primary tissue needs or urges to the secondary motives at as simple a level as possible for two reasons. In the first place, it is important that the student should know that the primary bodily tissue needs actually can be converted into secondary or derived motives. Whenever any object or situation becomes a substitute for the stimulus-patterns that originally give rise to the primary urges or desires, a secondary motive has been developed. If the student has really learned to appreciate this fact, he will have made his first step in a new understanding of how it is that so much of human action can appear to be directed toward or concentrated upon a single object or situation for a long period of time.

In the second place, we have kept the discussion at as simple a level as possible because it is much easier to show how the primary tissue needs can be converted into simple forms of secondary or derived motives than it is to show how these simpler motives can be converted or elaborated into such complex sources of action as are named by the words "purposes," "ideals," and "sentiments." The difficulty here is a product, in part, of a lack of appropriate experimental studies and, in part, a consequence of the tremendous complexity of the changes that take place in this feature of human conduct.

We shall get some glimpse of this complexity in our study of the meaning of adjustment and of mental hygiene, for, during this chapter, we shall try to untangle some of the many ways in which purposes and intentions may go wrong. In spite of these difficulties, however, let us try to see just what the transition from the simpler forms of derived motives to the more complex forms involves.[32]

2. *The Nature of Purpose:* We may turn, first, to the question of purposes. As this word is commonly used, it may include either the volition to act in a given way or the setting up of a goal toward which action shall lead. The chances are that no profit is to be gained at the present time from a study of volition. As has been indicated earlier in the chapter, experimental psychology is probably leading to a marked change in point of view about the nature

---

[32] One of the best approaches to this group of problems is furnished by Tolman, E. C., *op. cit., passim.* See also, Murphy, G., *General Psychology.* New York: Harper and Bros., 1933, pp. 563-575. McDougall, W., *Outline of Psychology.* New York: Charles Scribner's Sons, 1923, Chapter XVII.

of volition, but the experimental work is still inadequate to the immense complexity of the problem.

It may prove of value, however, to cite an instance of the sort of experiment that can be done. The student already knows that there is a marked difference between what is commonly described as voluntary as opposed to involuntary action. A typical instance of voluntary action would be the resolve of a person to reach out toward an object, together with the actual reaching movement. A typical instance of involuntary action is the iris reflex. In other words, if we desire to move an arm, we can do so, but our desire appears to have no effect at all upon closing or opening the iris.[33] This reflex takes place automatically and in more or less direct relation to the intensity of the light thrown into the eye.

Now let us suppose that a subject is placed in the following situation. Just as a bright light is thrown into his eyes, a sound is made. According to the principle of learning known as conditioning, the sound may acquire the ability to induce the original response, viz., the iris reflex. After this stage has been reached, let us suppose that the sound which has been conditioned to the reflex is the sound that the experimenter would make when he speaks the word "close." The iris reflex can, apparently, be conditioned to this sound. The subject himself, however, is also able to say "close." That is, he can hear the sound "close" when it is spoken by himself just as readily as when it is spoken by someone else.

The next step in the experiment is reached, therefore, when the subject himself can bring about a decrease in the size of the iris by saying the word "sound." Still another step is taken when, instead of saying the word aloud, he whispers it to himself. The last stage is reached when instead of whispering, the subject merely thinks the word "sound." [34]

As we have tried to show in an earlier chapter, thinking sustains exceedingly intimate relations with implicit verbal habits. It is not necessary that the vocal apparatus actually move in order that thinking may occur. On the contrary, it may be necessary only that the verbal apparatus be postured or set in order that thinking may go on. In any case, the experimental situation we have just described would give evidence that a subject could, by reducing actual speech to a mere suggestion of speech, acquire some measure of control over

[33] For a characterization of voluntary action, see Hull, C. L., *Hypnosis and Suggestibility.* New York: D. Appleton-Century Co., 1933, *passim.*
[34] Cf. Hunter, W. S., and Hudgins, C. V., "Voluntary Activity from the Standpoint of Behaviorism." *J. Gen. Psychol.*, 1934, X, 198-204.

the iris reflex. One cannot be certain, of course, that control of this type is, on that account, voluntary in character, and further experimental work will have to be done. However, the implication is plain. If such a purely automatic type of movement as change in the size of the pupil can, by a process of training, be brought under the control of internal speech mechanisms, a long step has been taken toward solving the very difficult problems created by volitional action.

Pending further work in this field, let us say that there is a possibility that the volitional side of a purpose may owe its origin to some such process of training as has been outlined above. The student already knows, of course, that words or "thoughts" can become symbols for objects, situations, and relations. If, in the process of becoming symbols, they also become sources of stimulation to further action, it is easy to see how a person might, by taking note about the matter, both outline a projected course of action and give himself a steady source of stimulus toward completing the action.[35]

This second phase of such an action would become still more significant if some of the words which are used to initiate action, even though they may be subvocal or implicit in character, have been substituted in times past for one of the major tissue needs. To say the same thing in another way, if words, both of the explicit and of the implicit type, can be substituted for stimulus-situations that originally were associated with the primary tissue needs, motives will be developed which stand a long way from the vegetative level out of which they may have emerged.

Even though this volitional side of purpose must not be minimized, the student should be ever mindful of the fact that a great many purposes are a consequence of habit. Let us say, for example, that one student has said to another, "I cannot go to the movies with you because I must study." The inference is that the student has the intention to study and that he may even be required to use some volitional power in choosing between a study hour and an hour of pleasure. As a matter of fact, however, study habits may be made to resemble almost any other type of overlearned performance. That is, a room, a desk, an open notebook, or a variety of texts in the bookshelves might, under the right kind of practice, furnish just as much of an incentive to all of the attitudes and skills involved

[35] Cf. Hull, C. L., "Knowledge and Purpose as Habit Mechanisms." *Psychol. Rev.*, 1930, XXXVII, 511-525.

in a study hour as the sight of a cool lake on a hot day might furnish in exciting swimming movements.

In other words, after a person has lived in the same general environment for any length of time, the pattern of his daily course of action will be pretty well determined by the pattern of the events that occur around him. There will be a time to get up, a time to go to breakfast, a time to attend classes, a time to play games, and so on, throughout the day. It is difficult, of course, to know just how prepotent a daily schedule may actually become in regulating the course of action, especially when there are such distractions as an invitation to go, at an odd time, to a movie or to the corner drug store. The chances are, however, that the denial of a pleasure can be strongly supported by habit systems that have been developed by a regular sequence in the events that make up a normal day's living. On any given occasion, then, a student might display a certain amount of purpose or intention in carrying out his work when, as a matter of fact, his apparent purposes have already been caught up in a system of habits, attitudes, and dispositions.[36]

When the word "purpose" is used to name the objective toward which a course of action shall be directed, we may have in mind either some object which exists outside of the body or some object or plan which has been formulated in verbal terms alone. It is in this second type of objective or goal that the most difficulties arise. Let us take, for example, a common but nevertheless very complex case. Months, or even years, in advance of the actual possibility, a person says to himself that he proposes to get an education. This is, then, his general purpose. His actual ambition may be to get an education because it will help him to become a doctor, a lawyer, or an engineer. There are, of course, actual objects which will support an ambition, viz., the bodies and actions of other persons which stand for or represent the goal toward which the intentions of the student are directed, but the student himself may not be thinking of a particular person when he says that it is his intention to enter one of the professions. On the contrary, the goal has been stated entirely in terms of implicit verbal speech, or, as the older psychologies would have it, in terms of a cluster of ideas. In his more contemplative moments, the student will see himself with the "eye of the mind" rather than with the eye of the body, actually engaged in some profession, or he may try to construct for himself a picture of the life that he will be able to live after his ambition has been partially satisfied.

[36] Cf. Young, P. T., *op. cit.*, Chapter III.

The student will see at once that further progress in our discussion of purposes must rest upon all of the things that we have had to say about the function of language as a symbol or substitute for external objects and relations. We do not mean to repeat, of course, all of the facts that have already been presented, but a single instance will help, perhaps, to recall our earlier argument. A few years ago a new meaning was attached to the word "flapper." For reasons which we do not need to ask about, this word originally referred to any object with which one might flap or clap. Swift used it in his account of one of the Laputans whose duty it was to flap or strike another in order to remind him of something he might otherwise forget.

More recently, however, this word has come to refer to a particular type of social and personal attitude, primarily among the female sex. Now the general behavior which came ultimately to be known as "flapperish" was a type of behavior actually observed with the eyes of the body rather than with the eyes of the mind. Moreover, the whole pattern of behavior was of such a character as to require some adequate descriptive term. A man of science who comes, for the first time, upon something hitherto undescribed and who can find no word available, simply resorts to some such means of identification as is furnished by the letter "x." He will continue to use such a symbol until the proper word has been found or until he can invent a word by drawing upon the roots of an older language.

In the case we have in mind, the behavior of certain females might just as well have been "x" behavior, but the word "flapper" quickly acquired all of the meanings necessary for description and comment. Once a verbal expression had acquired this meaning, it could be used, along with other verbal expressions, as a substitute or symbol for a series of events otherwise open only to direct observation.[37] To be sure, the word "flapper" has now almost disappeared, and a student of language in the remote future would, if no dictionary were available, have considerable difficulty in trying to find out just what the symbol meant. He would remain in difficulty until he was able to discover some moving picture or some other verbal description which would restore for him the actions for which the term "flapper" had become a substitute.

3. *Ideals:* If, then, words can become substitutes for objects and for all of the relations that may obtain between them, they readily offer themselves as instruments for the projection of plans and de-

[37] Cf. Hall, G. S., "Flapper Americana Novissima." *Atlantic Mo.*, June, 1922.

sires into almost any type of timeless future. This is, perhaps, the meaning that must be attached to the term "ideal." In other words, an ideal can be described as a thought-of thing. We may, however, think of physical things as well as of social and personal things. It would be better, then, to say that an ideal is a thought or a cluster of thoughts pertaining to some mode of action which may have moral or ethical implications but which, in any case, must refer to the common good.

To be sure, we speak of bad ideals or of unsocial ideals, but this is, perhaps, merely an instance of faulty language. The point is that one may symbolize, with the aid of words, those features of conduct which can actually merit the approval of a cultured person and then describe all of his symbolizations as ideals. In any case, we do speak of an ideal human life or of an ideal society or of an ideal scientific experiment.

These ideals are not something made out of thin air simply because they are constructed in terms of verbal symbols rather than in terms of mortar and brick. They are none the less effective in initiating and sustaining action. Just as a child after a sufficient amount of experience with one chair, one apple, one pencil, and one book may arrive at a concept of oneness which is more than any one of the objects perceived, so we may, in looking at types of human action in a natural social setting, acquire a feeling for those respects in which different actions may contribute to a single goal. Where these goals are acceptable and where they contribute to the common good, we may speak of them as ideals. Where they are related primarily to our appreciation of the beautiful, we speak of artistic or aesthetic ideals. Where they are related to the types of contact that arise between one person and another, we may speak of ethical or moral ideals. Where they are related to the place of man in the universe or to the possible existence of a supernatural being, we may speak of religious ideals. Where they are related to accuracy in observation and in experiment, we may speak of the scientific ideal or of the ideal of truth.

4. *Sentiments:* Sentiments, apparently, have their origin in the same way as do purposes and ideals. That is, a sentiment is also a thought-of object, a thought-of thing, or a thought-of line of action.[38] Sentiments differ, however, from purposes and ideals, partly because they are usually clothed with some measure of feeling. We may take, for example, the sentiment of affection or the sentiment

[38] Cf. McDougall, W., *An Introduction to Social Psychology.* Boston: J. W. Luce, 1931 (rev. ed.), *passim.*

THE PROBLEMS OF MOTIVATION 181

of patriotism. The basis of affection, of course, is to be found in the primary sex impulses.[39] By the time a child has reached the age of accountability, all direct expressions of its sex desires have been pretty well sublimated, that is, transformed into modes of conduct, attitudes, and dispositions which will gain not only the approval of the parents but the general approval of society. At the same time, they may go a long way toward satisfying the energies which are bound up with the primary sex urges.

During adulthood, the initial sex urges may have been transformed so completely as to give almost, if not quite, no suggestion of anything pertaining to sex. In other words, the sex urge will have been completely transformed into an affection. If the affection can be expressed with verbal symbols of sufficient variety, the affection has become not only a sentiment but an ideal as well. As a rule, however, it is more convenient to think of affection as a sentiment rather than as an ideal, because the ideals embodied in a sentiment are richly clothed with feelings and attitudes which have become associated with the object of affection.

This same sort of affection may be expressed toward the flag, toward a battleship, or toward any other object which in any way symbolizes or expresses the power or the dignity of one's own country. Moreover, there are numerous human actions which, when taken together, give rise to a concept about behavior which must have a suitable verbal symbol. If, in the defense of their country, large numbers of men give up their lives, their purpose in so doing can often be expressed by saying that they were patriotic. They felt favorably inclined toward their country and toward the opportunities which their country made possible for them and for the members of their families.

It is at this point, more definitely than at any other point in the above discussion, that we come close to the relationship between the primary urges and the higher purposes, ideals, and sentiments. As we have said before, it looks as though a great gap must exist between tissue needs and such a concept as the ideal home or such a sentiment as patriotism.[40] Anyone who would try to cover this gap would have to write almost a minute-to-minute biography of the development of a human being. He would have to see how external objects and events can become attached to the primary tissue needs and then he would have to describe the long process of acquiring verbal substitutes for all of these objects and situations. He

[39] Dunlap, K., *op. cit.*, pp. 78-99.
[40] Cf. Dashiell, J. F., *op. cit.*, Chapter IX.

would have to take account of the persistent attempts which teachers and parents make to clothe the actions and verbal comments of children with the meanings that already reside in a great many of the words in common use. He would have to say how such a sentiment as patriotism might secure a part of its origin and a part of its motivating power from the desire of a person to protect himself and his family from enemies. This desire, in its turn, would have to be traced back to its origins in the affection which different members of a family have for one another. The affection, in its turn, would have to be traced back to the various ways in which the primary sex impulses can be satisfied with the full approval, and even the religious sanction, of the social group in which the person lives. In short, the faithful biographer of a purpose, ideal, or a sentiment would simply have to live over again in the words of a book the entire course of individual human development.

VI. Sources of Training

1. *Introduction:* It must be clear to the student, from what has been said up to this point, that any training in volitional forms of action or in the development of motives which the child gets in the schoolroom will come more as a by-product of other training exercises than from direct methods of formal education. This fact is revealed, for example, in the use which teachers freely make of motives and incentives which have already been acquired by children.

As an example, we may take the motive furnished by competition. As we shall see in a later chapter on the conditions which favor learning, competition may act as a very powerful incentive in getting work done and in directing long-time courses of action. The same thing holds true of other incentives such as praise, the direct getting of rewards for superior ability or for good conduct, and of affections which students develop toward their instructors.

In other words, teachers have looked at the problems of motivation not so much from the point of view of development as from the point of view of the uses to which they can be put. Since we have already taken as full an account as we can of these various uses, the rest of this chapter must be given over to a statement of some of the resources which the teacher may draw upon for the further development of motives.

2. *The Function of the Teacher:* It is clear at once that there are no books on this subject, and neither are there any curricula which have purposes, ideals, and sentiments as their main content. This

means that the development of motives must be promoted almost wholly in connection with other phases of the teaching program. Among the sources which appear to be the most important, we may name the teacher himself and the study of biographies. The teacher may act as an important guide in the development of motives simply through the revelations that will inevitably come of his own motives or of his own purposes, ideals, and sentiments.

We must, at this point, depart a little from the realm of strict experimental procedure, but the departure is justified by the fact that a great many men, in commenting upon the sources of their own motives, have remarked not the content that was given to them by their teachers, but their personal quality and their intense zeal. One of the classical comments of this type is to be found in the case of Alcibiades, who remarked of Socrates that, although he could not remember a great many of the precise things that Socrates had said, he did have a vivid recollection of the sort of person Socrates was. The inference is that, by word of mouth and by action, Socrates gave expression to purposes, ideals, and sentiments which could not be taught as such, but which could be conveyed by more direct means from one person to another.

Teaching of this type is one of the things to which Socrates returned over and over again and largely because of the concern of the parents of Athenian youth.[41] It was easy enough, so Socrates found, to teach a young man how to throw a spear or play the lyre, and it was also possible to give him some instruction in what it meant to be a good governor of a city; but when it came to the teaching of virtue, and to such other concepts as temperance, justice, and affection, Socrates was just as much troubled as are the teachers and parents of today.

The point is that Socrates gave, perhaps, the solution to the problem, although it was a solution that could not be put down in books. While discussing different virtues, Socrates must have given expression to more of his character than was actually conveyed by the words he used. In the famous death scene of Socrates, for example, it must have been plain to those who saw him take the cup of hemlock that there was a solidity of purpose and a confidence in ideals which became more convincing as a result of Socrates' own conduct than could have ever been the case were such conduct to be translated into formal exercises and taught in a classroom.

Let us infer, then, that one of the primary sources for the de-

[41] Cf. Woodbridge, F. J. E., *The Son of Apollo*. Boston: Houghton Mifflin Co., 1929, *passim*.

velopment of proper motives lies within the purposes, ideals, and sentiments of the teacher himself. This means that the teacher is an inevitable part of the total learning situation in which pupils are placed. By intent, pupils are supposed to learn only those things printed in the textbook or given by word of mouth. As we have tried to say in a great many places, however, this is only to recognize a possible difference between formal education and informal education. Even though this distinction is drawn all too frequently, it cannot be drawn because formal education has been shown to have a greater effect upon students than informal education. As a matter of fact, there is every reason to suppose that the products of formal education have less to do with the final competence of a person than anything else that he learns.

This fact has been revealed in almost every treatise upon the nature and functions of education. Whenever a person tries to point out some of the qualities of an educated man, he does not inquire at all after the amount of technical information that has been acquired nor does he ask primarily about skill.[42] On the contrary, he will come pretty close to saying that an educated man is "a man with certain subtle, spiritual qualities which make him calm in adversity, happy when alone, just in his dealings, rational and sane in the fullest meaning of that word in all of the affairs of life." Not a single one of the virtues mentioned in this quotation is in any direct way related to the formal subjects of a curriculum, but every one is related in an intimate way to the qualities of the teacher.[43]

3. *Biographies:* There is at the present time no indication that psychologists are really more capable as parents or in the conduct of their own lives or in their methods of handling other people than are a good many persons who know nothing about the experimental side of human nature. Likewise, there is no evidence that teachers who have acquainted themselves thoroughly with facts and principles such as are included in this book or who have devoted themselves intensively to the study of experimental psychology are, on that account alone, better than some of their less informed colleagues. One may go even further than this in working out the discrepancy between knowledge about psychology, on the one hand, and the arts of practical control, on the other, for books in the field of applied psychology speak of the domain of human nature

---

[42] Cf. Martin, E. D., *The Meaning of a Liberal Education.* New York: W. W. Norton and Co., 1926. See also, Edman, I., *Human Traits.* Boston: Houghton Mifflin Co., 1920, *passim.*

[43] Cf. Morrison, H. C., *Basic Principles in Education.* Boston: Houghton Mifflin Co., 1934, *passim.*

much as a traveler might speak of distant countries. The persons who hear the "travelogue" know and understand what is being said to them, but they do not suppose for an instant that their "cold" knowledge about a country can be confused with an intimate familiarity with it.[44]

There is, of course, one very obvious reason why knowledge about psychology cannot and should not be confused with an intimate feeling for the nature of human nature. The experimenter in his laboratory must study one thing at a time while assuming that other things have remained equal. He gets, therefore, partial views of a very complex and rapidly shifting train of events. The information which he secures is often highly accurate in the particular setting and under the particular circumstances under which it was gained, but no amount of such information could give a faithful picture of human beings in an actual living situation. We may say again that success in the use of psychological facts depends not so much upon information concerning the details as it does upon a sensitive appreciation of the whole order of human life and of other factors that are operative in regulating and controlling it.

We have referred to this phase of the study of psychology at this point because we wish to let the student know that a considerable amount of exceedingly useful information is to be found outside of technical journals and textbooks. The chief source of this information lies in biographies and autobiographies. One might, of course, get still more direct information through actual acquaintance with great persons, but this is a privilege which is denied to most of us. Intimate records of the way in which these persons have lived, however, are not denied. Let us say, therefore, that biographies and autobiographies furnish one of the most important sources of information we have concerning total patterns of life.[45]

Obviously, we are not making reference here to some of the more objective data regarding great personages. On the contrary, whenever a man tries to write a fairly complete story of the life of another or of his own life, he is really reciting the general features of the educational history of a human being. He is attempting to untangle the many factors that contributed to the whole pattern of living of the person being studied, and he is trying also to see how personal qualities, including motives, intentions, and ideals, have

---

[44] Cf. James' distinction between "knowledge about" and "acquaintance with." James, W., *Principles of Psychology*. New York: Henry Holt and Co., 1890, Vol. I, p. 221.

[45] Outside of biographies and dramas, only one major attempt has been made to draw discriminating pictures of complete life patterns, viz., by Plutarch.

actually been brought into play in concrete situations. It is not possible, of course, to experiment upon a life that has been lived, for no amount of laboratory technique could unravel the full complexity of that intricate and distinctive picture of events which sometimes takes form under the direction of a skilful biographer.

The appeal which we are making to the use of biographies as a source of information about human nature and as a source of instruction regarding the factors that operate in human affairs takes on particular importance in the field which we have studied in this chapter, for ambitions, ideals, and purposes are revealed more clearly in the lives of great men than almost any other feature of their total character. In a great many cases, a reader of biographies will not know how these ambitions, ideals, and purposes have been secured, but if he will leave this part of the story to the child research laboratory, he will still secure useful information concerning the ways in which motives and purposes have been used in concrete situations. By way of conclusion, therefore, to this chapter, let us say that intimate and discerning recitals of the life patterns of other people lend themselves to an educational use far beyond the imaginations of many teachers.

READINGS

If the student has not already done so, he should assure himself that he has been considering in this chapter one of the most important features of human behavior that can be named. Irrespective of the terms that are used in describing it, we all know that one of our chief sources of action appears to lie in the possession of a will. All other things may be ever so favorable to high levels of sustained effort, but these other things will come almost to naught if they are not backed up by the circumstances that have been described in this chapter.

Psychology and education in their attitudes toward the problems of will power have been moving in the direction outlined in this chapter because they are convinced that the educative process can be used to augment the will and exert greater measures of control over it. Some people suppose that any statement of the nature of an object or of a set of events which traces their origin to sources less worthy than the events themselves is, on that account alone, to be discarded. At the present time, however, it looks as though all of the higher forms of self-direction do come out of or are in some way supported by the primary tissue needs, and this is the feature of motivation which has brought it into so many current treatments of educational psychology.

A considerable part of the background for a study of motivation can be found in Tolman, E. C., *Purposive Behavior in Animals and Men.* New York: D. Appleton-Century Co., 1932; and Woodworth, R. S., *Dynamic Psychology.* New York: Columbia Univ. Press, 1918. A splendid survey of the general field of motivation has been written by Young, P. T., *Motiva-*

tion of Human and Animal Behavior. Ann Arbor: Edwards Bros., 1933. A briefer summary of the experimental work in this field can be found in Diserens, C. M., and Vaughn, J., "The Experimental Psychology of Motivation." *Psychol. Bull.,* 1931, XXVIII, 15-65. A study of the nature of motivation based upon a modified form of the classical theory of hedonism can be found in Troland, L. T., *The Fundamentals of Human Motivation.* New York: D. Van Nostrand Co., 1928.

A considerable part of the source material out of which current theories of motivation have sprung has been furnished by studies on the lower animals. These studies have been admirably summarized by Stone, C. P., "Motivation: Incentives and Drives," in Moss, F. A. (Ed.), *Comparative Psychology.* New York: Prentice-Hall, Inc., 1934, Chapter IV. See also, Young, P. T., *op. cit.,* Chapter II.

There is still a great amount of confusion as to the number and the exact character of the primary desires or of the primary tissue needs. Suggestive descriptions of these needs are to be found in Dashiell, J. F., *Fundamentals of Objective Psychology.* Boston: Houghton Mifflin Co., 1928, Chapter IX, and Dunlap, K., *Civilized Life.* Baltimore: The Williams and Wilkins Co., 1934, Chapter III. See also, Cannon, W. B., *Hunger and Thirst,* in Murchison, C. (Ed.), *op. cit.,* Chapter V.

A special theory of the fundamental driving forces in human behavior has come from the Freudian school. This theory will be considered in a later chapter. The student may refer, however, at this time, to Freud, S., *New Introductory Lectures on Psychoanalysis.* New York: W. W. Norton and Co., 1933, *passim.*

A very good account of the development of motives has been written by Curti, M. W., *Child Psychology.* New York: Longmans, Green and Co., 1931, Chapter X. See also, Morgan, J. J. B., *Child Psychology* (Rev. ed.). New York: Farrar and Rinehart, Inc., 1934, Chapter VI.

An extremely suggestive book on the nature of voluntary and involuntary action, together with a survey of many experiments in the field, is Hull, C. L., *Hypnosis and Suggestibility.* New York: D. Appleton-Century Co., 1933, *passim.* The student will find the chapter written by Dashiell and mentioned above also of great help.

In keeping with the suggestion made toward the end of the chapter concerning the usefulness of biography, both in understanding human nature and in discovering the practical value of motives, incentives, purposes, and ambitions in the conduct of life, the teacher can well afford to base at least one of his special exercises upon assigned readings on notable biographies. These assigned readings should request the student to study a biography, not with the eyes of a historian, but with the eyes of a psychologist and a teacher.

CHAPTER SIX

THE DEVELOPMENT OF EMOTIONALIZED ACTIONS

I. Introduction

1. *Introduction:* A quick way to get a picture of one of the most distinctive features of the growth pattern comes out of an effort to imagine such a pattern devoid of this feature. In a general sense, the student already knows what is meant by the words "mood," "emotion," "passion," and "feeling," but if he were pressed to be more exact in his description of this phase of his psychological equipment, he would run into all sorts of difficulties.[1] We shall, therefore, in order to help him identify the particular problems of education that are now to be considered, try to imagine a human being who is unable to react to the objects and situations around him in any of the ways implied by the above words.

2. *Illustrations:* Let us suppose that the members of a football team and all of the people in the bleachers were to carry on without any moods, feelings, or emotions. None of the players on the field, for example, would feel anxious about the next play, and there would be no shouts of excitement from the crowd. Hopes would neither rise nor fall, and the successful completion of a difficult forward pass could be taken as just another one of the colorless events of the afternoon. The coach would have made no appeal to the anger or the resentment or the sense of loyalty of his players before the game began, and there would be no eager discussion of what might be done during the second half to win the game. Were they without the general attitudes or dispositions known as feelings, moods, or emotions, all of the people at the football game would take the events of the afternoon with an extreme degree of nonchalance. Even the word "phlegmatic," which might be used in this connection, implies extreme dullness or listlessness, in other words, moodiness.

As a second illustration, let us suppose that the teacher in the grade school has never had to settle a violent quarrel between two

---

[1] The experimenter has found himself in the same difficulty. See Reymert, M. L. (Ed.), *Wittenberg Symposium on Feelings and Emotions*. Worcester, Mass.: Clark Univ. Press, 1928, *passim*.

boys, or to deal with a bashful child who could not recite because of his timidity, or to put a controlling hand upon too much exuberance or happiness toward the end of the day or toward the end of the year, or to handle any of the difficult problems which arise when some of the students become too affectionate toward other students or toward the teacher himself, or to estimate the presumable value of rewards or punishments in terms of the respective degree of delight or of sorrow expressed.

For a third illustration, let us suppose that no one could find any pleasure or satisfaction in a sunset, any deep sense of yearning induced by a melody, or in any other way enjoy that unique experience known as aesthetic appreciation. There would never be any occasion for going into ecstasies over a beautiful painting, for trying to protect oneself from the fury of others during a panic caused by fear, or for paying much attention to the finer personal contacts that may be established as a result of an intimate friendship.

Were we actually able to create a life wholly devoid of feeling, mood, and emotion, we would take away a considerable part of the compelling power of incentives, urges, desires, motives, and even of purposes, for the student has already seen in our previous discussions that all of these words refer not only to enduring sources of stimulus but to types of preference among stimuli as well.[2]

It is difficult, of course, to imagine the exact character of a mode of living from which fears, hopes, pleasures, states of joy, preferences, anxieties, doubts, shyness, jealousy, states of anger, and aesthetic pleasures have been extracted. We cannot even go to a new-born infant for an approximation to such a state of affairs, simply because most of the performances of the infant are also emotionalized. Even though it enjoys no aesthetic experiences or any of the other attitudes which were just mentioned, we may still say that, on occasion, it must experience an emotionalized phase of hunger, and it also may be startled or frightened by an unexpected event.[3]

The behavior of a new-born infant does help us a little, however, in getting a full perspective upon that feature of the stream of behavior described by moods, feelings, and emotions, because the

[2] The extreme apathy which we are here imagining is sometimes found in psychopathic hospitals. Cf. Dorcus, R. M., and Shaffer, G. W., *A Textbook of Abnormal Psychology*. Baltimore: The Williams and Wilkins Co., 1934, pp. 255 ff.
[3] Cf. Goodenough, F. L., "The Expression of the Emotions in Infancy." *Child Develop.*, 1931, II, 96-101; Bridges, K. M., "Emotional Development in Early Infancy," *Child Develop.*, 1932, III, 324-341.

range of objects which will excite these attitudes is limited indeed.[4] This means that one of the major differences between the neonate and the adult person is a difference created by a rapid spread of whatever resources the individual has for emotionalized forms of action to a wide variety of objects and situations.

Most of the objects or situations in adult life imply the presence of some other person.[5] We may, to be sure, become frightened by an unexpected noise during the night or by some major natural event such as a storm, a fire, or an earthquake, but most of our moods and emotions have a distinct and very important social reference. We learn how to be shy of other people, how to fear solitude or a crowd, how to be jealous of another person, how to have a deep affection for him, how to appreciate a symphony, and how to place some of our deepest hopes upon success in a given occupation.

The transition from a mass-movement of the emotionalized sort in infancy to all of the preferential attitudes and dispositions of an adult is a transition that is made, for the most part, during the preschool period and the grade period. This is certainly true of many fundamental attitudes and dispositions. There is some evidence to show that the richness and variety of emotionalized actions and attitudes may be enormously increased during the early period of adolescence, but even were we to discover that this is not the case, it is almost certain that the twenty-year-old will have acquired almost all of the emotionalized forms of action that he will ever possess.[6]

Moreover, he will have acquired these actions so firmly that there is little likelihood of bringing about major changes in them. If, for example, he has learned how to be timid in the presence of other people, the chances are that he will remain timid throughout his life. Only the severest type of retraining can save him from fear of the water or other natural phenomena, from given levels of dependency upon other people, and from dullness in his aesthetic attitudes toward objects of art or from any of the major temperaments.[7]

3. *The Teaching Problem:* In view of these several considerations, it is hardly necessary to assert that the development of emo-

---

[4] Cf. Jones, M. C., "Emotional Development," in Murchison, C. (Ed.), *Handbook of Child Psychology*. Worcester, Mass.: Clark Univ. Press, 1933, Chapter VI.

[5] *Ibid.*, pp. 289 ff.

[6] Cf. Brooks, F. D., *The Psychology of Adolescence*. Boston: Houghton Mifflin Co., 1929, *passim*.

[7] This fact is revealed in the field of mental hygiene where attempts are made to refashion emotionalized and other forms of action. Cf. Dunlap, K., *Habits, Their Making and Unmaking*. New York: Liveright Publishing Corp., 1932, Chapters X, XI.

tionalized forms of action is one of the most important problems which the teacher has to face. With respect to this phase of education, we have already said that most persons acquire their emotionalized forms of action as a by-product of training rather than as a direct result of special teaching methods. Neither parents nor teachers try to make their children helpless or independent, fearful or courageous, jealous or friendly, and so on. To be sure, church schools have sought to bend some of the major emotional attitudes toward the support of moral and ethical traits. That is, students are sometimes taught to hold that honesty is a good policy, not merely because honesty is a reasonable way to act but because it is, in the long run, a pleasant or comfortable way to act. By and large, however, the development of emotionalized habits and attitudes has been left almost completely to the domain of informal education.[8]

4. *Purpose of the Chapter:* It is the purpose of this chapter, then, to find out where emotionalized forms of action have their origin and how changes may be made in these forms under proper methods of teaching. This will not be an easy task, because there is no group of problems in psychology which has offered more difficulties to the experimenter than these.

It used to be thought that men might possess a special type of soul (the vegetative soul) which was responsible for the emotions and the passions. It has been argued, also, that the moods and emotions represent a type of psychological function which, though closely related to action, must, nevertheless, have an independent status. The reader will recall that all of those processes by means of which information is gained can be called cognitive, while all of those modes of operation which get things done through the use of the muscles can be called conative. The third major group of faculties of the soul included the feelings, moods, emotions, passions, and sentiments. That is, these words referred to a separate class of essential psychological traits.

In spite of the perplexities that surround the topic, we must try to see where psychology is going in its study of emotionalized forms of action. Since this study has by no means been brought to an end, we shall, perhaps, be able to draw no significant conclusions. Of one thing, however, we may be pretty certain. Emotionalized forms of action can be transferred from one situation to another. They can be changed in their character to such a degree that the

[8] Cf. Watson, J. B., *Psychological Care of the Infant and Child.* New York: W. W. Norton Co., 1928, *passim.*

deep yearning of a lover appears to have no relation whatsoever to the keen sentiment of a religious mystic. If, then, emotionalized forms of action can be modified through training, and if the teacher is one of the chief instruments for bringing about modification in human nature, the responsibility for these modifications must be taken over in part, at least, by the teacher.

II. The Bodily Basis of Emotionalized Actions

1. *Introduction:* It will not be possible for the student to get a clear picture of the nature of emotionalized and moody actions, and neither will he be able to see how the experiences which are dependent upon these actions can express themselves in such widely divergent forms unless he knows something about the physiological conditions which underlie them. Since the main facts can be found so easily in other places, we shall attempt to do no more than to suggest the main outlines of the physiology of emotional expression.[9]

2. *The Autonomic System:* A part of the physiological basis of emotionalized actions is to be found in that part of the nervous system which is known as the autonomic nervous system. This system supplies most of the organs of digestion, the heart, the lungs, a great many of the organs in the skin, and the glands of internal secretion. The central portions of the system are made up of ganglia lying alongside of the spinal cord and in three other parts of the body, viz., near the head region, near the stomach and the liver, and near the lower part of the viscera.

There are a good many different connections between the autonomic system and the central nervous system. It looks as though one of the important functions of the autonomic system is to keep the central nervous system "informed" of the events that are taking place throughout the body. Since the body is a living organism and since all types of energy changes are taking place in it, these energy changes must be controlled and integrated. A part of this control arises from within the autonomic system itself, but the central nervous system also sustains intimate relations with all of the events taking place in the body.

There are three major divisions of the autonomic system, viz., the

---

[9] Cf. Bard, P., "The Neuro-humoral Basis of Emotional Reactions," in Murchison, C. (Ed.), *A Handbook of General Experimental Psychology.* Worcester, Mass.: Clark Univ. Press, 1934, Chapter VI.

THE DEVELOPMENT OF EMOTIONALIZED ACTIONS

cranial, the thoraco-lumbar or the sympathetic, and the sacral. There is a certain amount of antagonism between these three divisions and especially between the thoraco-lumbar division and the other two divisions. The fibres of the sympathetic division pass to the ciliary muscles in the eye, the arteries and arterioles, the viscera, the sweat glands, the liver, and other similar structures. The fibres of the cranial ganglia pass to the smooth muscles in the eyes, and one large nerve, viz., the vagus nerve, passes to the lungs, the heart, the stomach, and the small intestines. The fibres from the sacral divisions lead to the colon, the bladder, and the genitals.[10]

In view of all of these facts, it is easy to see how the physiological operations of the body can be controlled and how marked changes in any one part of the body could quickly reflect themselves in other parts of the body. It is easy to see, too, what might happen were the organism placed in an emergency. During a fight, intense pain, extreme hunger, or any other exceptional conditions, heart action may be changed, respiration increased or decreased, the processes of digestion halted, blood pressure modified, and other preparations made to mobilize the energy resources of the body or modify them as the occasion demanded.

3. *Glandular Mechanisms:* These features of the action of the autonomic nervous system can be seen to better advantage if we consider for a moment some of the ways in which the glands of internal secretion affect action. Of these glands, one of the most important, for our purpose, are the adrenal glands or, to speak more correctly, the secretions which come from that portion of these glands known as the cortex. It has been shown that, when a person is angered or frightened, the functional activity of the adrenal glands will be increased in such a way as to pour into the blood stream the substance that is peculiar to these glands.

This substance is one of the most remarkable in the body because it has such pronounced effects upon a great many other physiological processes. It has been shown, for example, that during emotional excitement, that is, after certain amounts of adrenalin have been poured into the blood stream, heart action will be increased, the capacity of the red corpuscles to absorb oxygen will be enlarged, appropriate changes in the rate of respiration will be brought about, the intricate events that take place when glycogen is transformed into useful energy with the by-product of lactic acid will be pro-

---

[10] Cf. Young, P. T., *Motivation of Human and Animal Behavior.* Ann Arbor: Edwards Bros., 1933, Chapter VI.

moted, and the rate at which the blood can be coagulated will be increased.[11]

The student will see at once that effects of this sort might play a very important part in helping an enraged or frightened animal to adapt itself more adequately to its environment. If an animal has been enraged, the chances are that the rage is either an outcome of, or a preface to, a period of combat. In any case, during an actual fight, that animal which could tap its resources in the ways mentioned above, would have a notable advantage over animals possessing no such mechanism. If glycogen can be used to better advantage, muscular strength is increased, and the effects of fatigue will be diminished. The expenditure of greater energy, of course, will call for compensatory adjustments of heart and lung action. Furthermore, if the animal were wounded, increased rate of coagulation would serve as a defense mechanism.[12]

All of these circumstances are known to hold true of other emotionalized forms of action such as extreme pain, hunger, and, perhaps, of fatigue. The common point in all of these conditions is the extent to which an animal can make use of reserve supplies of energy. It is for this reason, in part, that fear and anger, to take only typical instances, are called emergency emotions.

4. *Emotion and Its Expression:* Obviously, the person who is angered or frightened is quite unaware of the existence of the several devices for tapping reserve energies that have just been outlined. On the contrary, he will report that an emotionalized action is for him a type of experience. When he says that he is "beside himself with rage" he is not referring so much to what his body is doing as he is to his consciousness of anger. The same considerations hold true not only of all of the other forms of emotionalized action, but of the moods and even of the vague feelings of pleasantness and unpleasantness that always accompany any train of action. We are led to ask, therefore, what relations obtain between an experienced emotion, on the one hand, and the expression of the emotions, on the other.[13]

Two major theories have been formulated in answer to this question. The first asserts that emotional experiences precede the expression of the emotions. For example, let us say that a student

---

[11] Cannon, W. B., *Bodily Changes in Pain, Hunger, Fear and Rage.* New York: D. Appleton-Century Co., 1929, *passim.*

[12] Cf. Crile, G. W., *Man—An Adaptive Mechanism.* New York: The Macmillan Co., 1916, *passim.*

[13] Cf. Landis, C., "The Expression of Emotion," in Murchison, C. (Ed.), *op. cit.,* Chapter VII.

THE DEVELOPMENT OF EMOTIONALIZED ACTIONS 195

has just been startled by an unexpected sound outside of the room in which he has been resting. It might be said of this unexpected sound that it excites the appropriate sense organs but that, because of its intensity and, perhaps, because of previous experiences, it sets up excitations which would occasion the experience described as a startle. The excitations would also flow out of the central nervous system into the autonomic system and thus give rise to appropriate changes of the sort described above. The initial perception of the sudden noise would, therefore, be set into an emotional background and thus constitute a type of experience which ought, under proper conditions, to be describable.[14]

It is a noteworthy fact, however, about all forms of mood and emotion that they do not lend themselves readily to description according to the principles of introspective psychology. That is, whenever experimenters have tried to examine the moods and the emotions in the same way that they examine perceptions, memories, and processes of reasoning, they have discovered that the moods and the emotions somehow evaporate just before they can be inspected. They appear to behave for an experimenter in the same way that they behave for the small boy on the playground who has been told by his father that before he begins to fight he should count to ten. Somewhere during the period of counting a major part of the emotional experience has disappeared. The boy knows that he was angry but that after a moment or two of delay the emotional reason for the fight has suddenly disappeared.[15]

The second theory of the relation between an experienced emotion and the expression of the emotion states that all of the devices for response must be considered as a unit, both because they are dependent upon the central nervous system and because they are dependent upon the autonomic nervous system. In other words, it is inferred that pathways of conduction, wherever they are found in the body, are pathways which are imbedded in a living system. Some of these pathways, to be sure, coördinate, in particular, the metabolic and other devices of the body, including the glands of internal secretion. It would follow, therefore, that every stimulus-pattern must lead to nervous excitations which radiate freely through many portions of the body.

[14] For a discussion of the older theory of emotional experience, see Titchener, E. B., *A Textbook of Psychology*. New York: The Macmillan Co., 1910, pp. 471 ff.
[15] The fact is explained by saying that feelings do not possess a property known as clearness. See Dallenbach, K. M., "Attributive vs. Cognitive Clearness." *J. Exper. Psychol.*, 1920, III, 183-230.

At a fairly early age, sudden or unexpected stimuli will be conducted more freely to some of the emergency mechanisms of the body than will less intensive forms of stimulus, unless, by previous training, they have already been conditioned to the resources for emotionalized action. It seems to be clear, however, that no patterns of excitation can pass through any portion of the nervous system without in some way being modified by the fact that this system and all of the organs and structures associated with it exercise some influence on the pattern simply because living structures are involved.

In any case, let us suppose again that the student has been startled by a sudden sound. The excitations set up by this source of stimulus pass into the autonomic system where glandular and other changes may be brought about, subject to the conditions described above. In short, the student will make a reaction to the sound not only by using his normal muscle tissue but by using all of the glandular, respiratory, and other organs upon which muscles are dependent for their energy. If this were indeed the course of events, it might be said that the emotion of fright which the student experiences would be his way of experiencing the changes that are taking place in his body in response to a startling situation. As one of the exponents of this theory of the emotions has expressed it, a person does not weep because he is sorry, but he is sorrowful because he is weeping. Similarly, a person does not run because he is afraid, but he is afraid because he is running.[16]

The student of education is not so much interested in the question as to which precedes the other, the felt emotional experience or the bodily expression of the emotions, as he is in the methods that may be used in order to study emotionalized forms of action.[17] Then, too, there is the question as to how emotionalized forms of action may be modified by training. We have already indicated why it is that the introspective psychologies have not been very effective in their treatment of these problems. If moods and emotions seem to dissipate as they are placed under self-observation, one must report not how he feels at the moment but how he felt a moment ago. To be sure, a considerable amount of information can be gained in this way, but more objective studies of the emo-

---

[16] Cf. James, W., *Principles of Psychology*. New York: Henry Holt and Co., 1890, Vol. II, Chapter XXV. See, however, Cannon, W. B., "The James-Lange Theory of the Emotions." *Amer. J. Psychol.*, 1927, XXXIX, 106-124; also Bard, P., *op. cit., passim*.

[17] Cf. Landis, C., *op. cit., passim*. Also Symonds, P. M., *Diagnosing Personality and Conduct*. New York: The Century Co., 1931, Chapter XI.

tions have been much more fruitful. This fact will become clear as we now pass to a more detailed statement as to the nature of emotionalized actions.

III. THE NATURE OF MOOD AND EMOTION

1. *Introduction:* Let us say again that the most fruitful way of experimenting upon the affective life of human beings and of animals is by way of their behavior. We must find out, therefore, what there is about a stimulus-response situation which will give that situation an affective or emotional quality.

The initial step is taken when we remember that one large group of psychological problems is made up of the situations which may become effective in initiating and regulating the behavior of a person. A second group of problems is made up of the various types of reaction, including postures or attitudes, which any individual is able to make to the situations around him. Most of the other features of the growth pattern arise out of the unique types of relationship that obtain between stimulus-situations, on the one hand, and behavior-patterns, on the other. Chapter Four, for example, considered one such set of relationships. The facts of attention and of interest become psychological problems because single portions of a total stimulus-situation sometimes achieve a unique functional value over all other parts in initiating and regulating the behavior of an individual. This unique functional value is secured, in part, because of factors external to the person himself and, in part, because of factors that are internal to him. The main point, however, is that the phenomena of attention arise out of observed correlations between stimulus-situations and responses.

The events which we describe as moods and emotions secure their psychological value for the same reason. In any particular stimulus-response situation, it can be shown that the energy with which a response is carried out has all sorts of values with respect to "constant" stimulus-situations. We remark this fact when we say that an individual is "beside himself with anger." On one occasion, an object, say something black that is in movement, may excite only a momentary readjustment of the visual apparatus. On another occasion, this same object may excite a widespread reaction on the part of the whole body, a reaction which will culminate in running quickly away from the scene. The inference is that living creatures must have some device whereby the energies of response can be quickly intensified or otherwise adjusted with respect to certain properties of the stimulus-situation.

From the evidence that is now in, it appears that the energy reserves of the body will be poured into a response most frequently when the situation to be met is new or unexpected.[18] As we shall see later on in the chapter, all living creatures develop three modes of reacting to a situation. In the first place, they may appeal to past experience, in general, and to habit and skill, in particular. In the second place, they may use their problem-solving functions. In both of these cases the inference is that the situations to be met are well within the range of the competence of the individual, a competence which is secured from previous training. Other situations, however, may be too much for him. In the absence of an habitualized or rationalized action, the organism will come to the aid of a person by tapping its reserve energies.

There is, however, another feature of emotional behavior to which we must call attention. It has been shown, in studies on the emotional behavior of small infants, that all of its modes of emotional expression are very similar to one another. In other words, it is not possible to say what type of an emotion the infant is experiencing, unless something is already known about the character of the stimulus-situation.[19] Given a knowledge of the stimulus-situation, together with a description of the nature of the response, and almost any observer will be able to describe the emotional character of the response. As the individual grows older, emotional modes of reaction acquire unique properties of their own, so that fear or rage, depression or exultation, and all other patterns of emotional expression can be recognized in posture and in action even though nothing is known about the stimulus-situation. At every point, then, the isolation of that type of event which we call an emotion or mood is dependent upon a particular class of relations that obtain between stimulus-situations and behavior-patterns.

2. *Physical Analogies:* There are a great many places in the physical sciences where the energy value of a reaction is directly correlated with the energy value of the agents which occasion the reaction. This is true, in particular, of most types of mechanical reaction. Just as many, if not more, cases can be found, however, where the energy expressed in a "stimulus" acts as a sort of trigger

---

[18] Sherman, M., and Sherman, I. C., *The Process of Human Behavior*, 1929, Chapter II; Jones, M. C., "The Development of Early Behavior Patterns in Young Children." *Ped. Sem.*, 1926, XXXIII, 537-585.

[19] Sherman, M., and Sherman, I. C., *op. cit., passim.*

THE DEVELOPMENT OF EMOTIONALIZED ACTIONS

for the release of multiplied volumes of energy in the system acted upon.

This "trigger-effect" is one of the most characteristic features of human and animal behavior. Every living organism is an elaborate system of energies embodied in a great variety of structures. The physiological processes of metabolism are a case in point. The individual must live and this means that an infinite variety of events are taking place throughout the entire system, including even that part of the system most concerned in activities of the psychological sort.[20] Animal behavior can never be divorced, therefore, from variable energy factors created by its own unstable equilibrium.

We say that the process of boiling a liter of water is a constant process simply because the energy conditions within each molecule are fairly stable with respect to the type of event brought to pass during boiling. The energy values of different parts of a living system, however, cannot thus be described. On the contrary, they manifest themselves through continuous changes in the tonus of the organs of response, in the sensitivity of the organs of reception, and in the types of integration that become possible in the central nervous system. All of these factors make it forever impossible that any precise relation shall be established between the intensity values of a stimulus and the intensity values of a response.

3. *Sources of Energy:* In addition to these factors, the behavior of all of the higher animals is modified by the fact that they possess definite mechanisms for controlling the energy values of response. A part of this mechanism is to be found in the muscles themselves. If any given muscle fibre is to respond at all, it will respond with its total available energy. Increases in the intensity of response are made possible, therefore, only by an increase in the number of elements participating.[21] Moreover, a certain amount of energy is stored within the muscles themselves so that they are, for short times at least, self-sustaining. The most elaborate provision for tapping reserves of energy is to be found in the glands of internal secretion.[22] One set of these glands, viz., the adrenal glands and the adrenal cortex has been much studied in their relations to the energy levels of response. Some of these facts are yet to be studied. We touch upon them now merely to show that they put into genetic psychology that whole group of perplexing problems

---

[20] Cf. Lillie, R. S., *Protoplasmic Action and Nervous Action.* Chicago: Univ. of Chicago Press, 1923, *passim.*
[21] Cf. Gould, A. G., and Dye, J. A., *Exercise and Its Physiology.* New York: A. S. Barnes and Co., 1932, Chapter III.
[22] Cannon, W. B., *op. cit., passim.*

subsumed under the words emotion, mood, passion, feeling, and the like.

4. *Genetic Views of Emotion:* In the lowest animals, say, amoeba, the energy value of response is much more nearly correlated with the energy value of stimulus than is the case with the higher animals. But even in amoeba there are certain physiological conditions which seriously modify the character of behavior even though the intensity of the stimulus remains constant. In other words, it becomes possible to say, even of amoeba, that states of pleasantness and of unpleasantness may be reflected by the general character of behavior.[23] Any experimenter who has worked with the higher animals knows that these creatures certainly react to various situations in what may be called an emotional way.

The thyroid gland is one of the most ancient of the structures which may have something to do with emotional modes of response. It is found in all vertebrates, sometimes in the throat, sometimes near the heart but generally somewhere in the neck region. The suprarenals are also found in most vertebrates. In man they stand near the kidneys, but in birds and reptiles near the reproductive organs. It is these and other structures such as the pituitary bodies and the corpus luteum which appear to be involved in that aspect of behavior now under consideration.

We have, then, two phases of emotional behavior which may be subjected to genetic treatment. On the one hand, there is that total aspect of behavior and of posture or attitude which is sometimes described by such words as melancholic, lethargic, happy, morose, sullen, energetic, and the like. These words refer, so far as objective observation is concerned, to the first set of conditions described above, viz., to the general state of the reacting individual. In a sense, they become a reflection in behavior of the way in which the vital processes are going on. On the other hand, we have such words as anger, rage, frenzy, fear, and, perhaps, love. These words refer to the fact that certain energies of the body may become effective in increasing the vigor of response during emergencies.

A. ANIMAL EMOTIONS: Neither of these phases of behavior has received much treatment from the genetic point of view, especially with respect to phylogenetic development. Regen has studied variations in the rate of breathing among insects during emotional stimulation.[24] A vast amount of empirical observation on the expression

---

[23] Jennings, H. S., *Behavior of the Lower Organisms.* New York: Columbia Univ. Press, 1906, *passim.*

[24] Regen, J., "Untersuchungen über die Atmung von Insekten unter Anwendung der graphischen Methode." *Pflüg. Arch. f. d. ges. Physiol.,* 1911, CXXXVIII.

THE DEVELOPMENT OF EMOTIONALIZED ACTIONS 201

of the emotions among men and animals was included by Darwin in his study of this problem.[25] One of the best studies of this problem among the lower animals comes from Köhler:

"The chimpanzee's register of emotional expression is so much greater than that of average human beings, because his whole body is agitated and not merely his facial muscles. He jumps up and down both in joyful anticipation and in impatient annoyance and anger; and in extreme despair—which develops under very slight provocation—flings himself on his back and rolls wildly to and fro. He also swings and waves his arms about above his head in a fantastic manner, which may not be unknown among non-European races, as a sign of disappointment and dejection.—I have never seen anthropoids *weep,* nor laugh in quite the human sense of the term. There is a certain resemblance to our laughter in their rhythmic gasping and grunting when they are tickled, and probably this manifestation is, physiologically, remotely akin to *laughter.* And, during the leisurely contemplation of any objects which give particular pleasure (for example, little human children), the whole face, and especially the outer corners of the mouth, are formed into an expression that resembles our 'smile.'" [26]

B. EMOTIONS IN CHILDREN: Serious questions directed toward the concepts of instinct and heredity have produced much more information regarding emotional behavior in infants and small children than is available for the lower animals. As we have seen, one of the first studies in this field reduced the number of identifiable situations that would be reacted to by infants in an emotional way to three. These were (i) a loud sound, or sudden dropping which led to a behavior-pattern called fear, (ii) tightly confining the movements of an infant which led to a kind of reaction called anger, and (iii) stroking, petting, tickling erogenous zones, and the like, which led to a pattern called love. It is now known that behavior-patterns elicited in this way cannot be so easily distinguished from one another as the original study made it appear; but in any case some sort of response which could be called emotional was found to be correlated with specified situations.[27]

It has not been possible as yet to identify such responses prior to birth. There are, to be sure, periodic outbursts of activity on the part of the foetus before birth and it may be that these periods of activity are associated with internal stimuli which may be of such

---
[25] Darwin, C., *The Expression of the Emotions among Men and Animals.* New York: D. Appleton-Century Co., 1873.
[26] Köhler, W., *The Mentality of Apes.* New York: Harcourt, Brace and Co., 1925, pp. 318-319.
[27] Watson, J. B., and Morgan, J. J. B., *op. cit.*

a character as to denote emotional responses. Regardless of their origin and development before birth, however, it is now known that this entire aspect of behavior is mightily subject to the processes of maturation and learning. A spreading of emotional behavior is thought to take place through the processes of conditioning. Watson and Rayner, for example, were able to build up such reactions in response to objects and events associated with loud sounds, sudden falling, and stroking and petting. A more recent study, however, has thrown some doubt upon the adequacy of conditioning to account for all types of emotionalized learning, but we may well leave this matter to our treatment of the major theories and varieties of learning.[28]

5. *The Nature of Emotionalized Action:* We are now in a position, perhaps, to describe more accurately the true nature of an emotionalized action. For this purpose, let us remember that the general framework for all studies of human nature is furnished by the relations between stimulus-patterns, on the one hand, and action-patterns, on the other. These relations are made possible because of the existence of types of connection between sense organs and the motor apparatus. These connections are living systems of events. They are supported by a good many other living systems. Our first inference, therefore, is that no type of response to a stimulus-pattern can be wholly devoid of that form of experience known as feeling or of that quality of action described by moodiness at the one extreme and emotion or passion at the other.

This is to say that all action-patterns must reflect, in some manner or other, the vital processes in which they are placed or by virtue of which they are made possible. If the nervous system acted like an electric wire which, within limits, is always the same wire, there would be no variations in the tone or in the intensity of human action worthy of the names "mood" and "emotion." Nervous tissue is, however, living tissue. Moreover, it is connected with and supported by organs and structures which are the sources of all of the bodily energies. We ought to find, therefore, in any suitable study of stimulus-connection-reaction patterns a variable quality or pattern of action which is related not only to the precise character of the stimulus-situation itself but to the organic or energy condition of the body.

The difference, then, between an "unemotionalized" action and an

---

[28] Watson, J. B., and Rayner, R., "Conditioned Emotional Reactions." *J. Exper. Psychol.*, 1920, III, 1-14; Bregman, E. O., "An Attempt to Modify the Emotional Attitudes of Infants by the Conditioned Response Technique." *J. Genet. Psychol.*, 1934, XLV, 169-198.

THE DEVELOPMENT OF EMOTIONALIZED ACTIONS

emotionalized action is not so much a difference in kind as it is a difference marked by the variable display of the energy resources behind action. These energy resources might, of course, modify the general pattern of response as, indeed, they do when a man reacts to an object in a fearful way; but on the whole the words "mood," "emotion," and "passion" are qualifying terms used in connection with the term "action." They are not the names of a separate kind of mental faculty and neither is it certain that they refer to a special class of psychological operations. In other words, if we were to think of all actions as ranged along a single line, that is to say, if we were to think of a continuum of action, then some of the actions in this continuum could be called relatively unemotionalized, others could be called mildly emotionalized, and the remainder could be called intensely emotionalized.[29]

This is not, however, quite the whole story, for it looks as though emotions and moods, like other features of human nature, are intimately related to services rendered. At the simpler level represented by feelings of pleasantness and unpleasantness, for example, the organism may take a definite attitude either toward or away from an object or situation. Those things that we like we tend to accept, and those things that we do not like we tend to reject. It is exceedingly difficult to know just how acceptance and rejection are related to the well-being of the body, but it is usually thought that those circumstances which promote the welfare of the organism are pleasurable and hence acceptable, whereas those things that are inimical to the welfare of the organism are unpleasant and hence rejected. We shall, however, leave these conjectures to the psychologist. Our main concern is with the fact that emotions and moods are accompanied by attitudes, postures, or sets and it is in the readiness with which such modes of action are transferred from one situation to another through the processes of learning that education finds one of its major problems.[30]

IV. The Education of the Emotions

1. *Introduction:* So far as education is concerned, there is one important fact that follows from the method we have chosen for considering the problems of emotion. If such words as mood, feel-

---

[29] Duffy, E., "Emotion: An Example of the Need for Reorientation in Psychology." *Psychol. Rev.*, 1934, XLI, 184-198. See also Dashiell, J. F., "Are There Any Native Emotions?" *Psychol. Rev.*, 1928, XXXV, 319-327.

[30] Cf. Judd, C. H., *Psychology* (Rev. ed.). Boston: Ginn and Co., 1917, Chapter VII and *passim*.

ing, and emotion refer more or less directly to the energy values of response, on the one hand, and to the general euphoria of the body, on the other, no type of human action is possible without being characterized by an affective tone.

It is theoretically possible, perhaps, to say that neutrality in feeling tone does occur at rare intervals. As a matter of fact, it has been suggested that there are midway points between pleasantness and unpleasantness which are psychologically or affectively neutral in character. Even where the zero point of bodily tonus is psychologically attainable, however, it would still follow that a vast majority of human reactions display, in some manner or other, the general metabolic condition of the body. This is to say that all of the various types of psychological operation, behavioral, perceptual, attentive, motivational, rational, and characterlike, are placed in an affective setting. It does not follow, however, either from the point of view of personal efficiency or from the point of view of society, that affective dispositions are always the inevitable outcome of an original nature. On the contrary, it will become quite obvious before we are through with this topic that few of them are innately determined. During the normal course of maturation they become much worked over, modified, changed, reorganized, and otherwise refashioned in such a way as to give the impression that many of them must have been instinctive or original. As we have seen, this is the position taken by McDougall and others. It is one thing to say, however, that all types of psychological function are related to that energy system known as the body and quite another to say that a great many special patterns of energy expenditure and, consequently, a great many patterns of emotional and moody experience, are hereditary.

To say all of this in another way, we may begin with the general formula upon which all psychological and educational work depends, viz., a stimulus-pattern which has been put into a significant and describable relation to a response-pattern. This relationship involves the machinery of a living body, including processes of metabolism in every one of the special organs of reception and action, and including the glands of internal secretion which make reserve energies available on demand. No action can take place independently of these background processes. It ought to follow, then, that if learning becomes effective with respect to relatively unemotionalized forms of action, it ought to be equally effective with respect to modes of action that really belong to the same continuum. As a matter of fact, we shall discover that learning is even more effective with

THE DEVELOPMENT OF EMOTIONALIZED ACTIONS 205

respect to emotionalized actions than it is with respect to some of the less intensive forms. It is this discovery—it may well rank among the great discoveries of the present century—that brings new hope and new responsibility to education.

2. *Maturation:* We may consider, first, the evidence which seems to suggest that emotional behavior may be subject to a certain amount of maturation contingent upon the maturation of other psychological functions. Gesell, for example, writes of emotional behavior as follows: "The primary emotions have been discussed as though they were elementary, stable phenomena subject only to the changes of social conditioning. . . . Fear is not a simple entity. It waxes and alters with growth. It is shaped by intrinsic maturation as well as by experience, certainly during the period of infancy. . . . This pattern (the fear pattern) is as much the pattern of organic growth as the various stages in the elaborated and perfect prehension." [31]

Some of the experimental evidence on this feature of emotional behavior runs as follows. In one study, for example, children of the preschool age were placed in a small pen within which a number of blocks and toys were placed.[32] The pen also contained two black suitcases, both of which could easily be opened by a child. The one contained a familiar toy and the other a snake of a harmless variety. The snake was some six feet in length, slightly less than four inches in girth at the middle of the body. The movements of the snake in the pen when released from the suitcase were powerful and quick. Children of the age of two years showed no fear of the snake. At the age of three or three and a half, however, a certain amount of caution was manifest, the children paying closer attention to the snake's movements and approaching it and touching it in a tentative way only. Definite fear behavior appeared rather frequently, however, at the age of four years, and this behavior was much more pronounced in adults than in children.

It is clear that these results can be interpreted in several different ways. In the first place, it may be said that the development of the fear reaction is the result of conditioning, but the circumstances surrounding the earlier history of children make this explanation seem rather unlikely. In the second place, it is possible to say that

---

[31] Gesell, A., "The Individual in Infancy," in Murchison, C. (Ed.), *Foundations of Experimental Psychology.* Worcester, Mass.: Clark Univ. Press, 1929, pp. 628-660. See also Peiper, A., "Untersuchung über den galvanischen Hautreflex (Psychogalvanischen Reflex) im Kindesalter." *Jahrbuch f. Kinderhk.*, 1924, CVII, 139-150.

[32] Jones, H. E., and Jones, M. C., "A Study of Fear." *Childhood Educ.*, 1928, V, 136-143.

a distinct fear instinct had ripened during the ages from two to four and a half years. The instinct theory implies, of course, that the nervous systems of children must be organized or patterned in such a way as to lead to a specific response directly on the presentation of an adequate stimulus-pattern. Some of the experimental work seems to suggest that this situation can prevail in the present case. In the third place, it is possible to say that a fear reaction had been precipitated out of a general process of maturation, the most important phases of which are a consequence of greater perceptual and discriminative sensitivity.

Of this third mode of explanation, the experimenters write:

"Fear may be regarded as a response to certain changes in a total situation: changes requiring a sudden new adjustment which the individual is unprepared to make. The arousal of fear depends not only upon situational changes, but also upon the individual's *general* level of development. With the young infant, perhaps the only changes which are fear-producing are those which substitute loud sounds for quiet, pain for comfort, or loss of support for a previous state of bodily balance. As a child develops, his intelligence innately matures, and his perceptions become enriched through experience. New things startle him because of his keener perception of the fact that they *are* new and unusual. . . . Fear arises when we know enough to recognize the potential danger in a situation but have not advanced to the point of a complete comprehension and control of the change in situation." [33]

Similar conclusions are to be drawn from the studies of Washburn and of Bayley on the development of negative responses of various types. Washburn, for example, reports that smiling is almost predominant among infants from eight to twenty weeks of age. During the period from twenty to forty weeks, however, the number of negative responses increases after which time the smile appears more readily. Washburn explains the development of negative responses to the maturation of the perceptual functions which enable the child to become increasingly aware of strangers.[34]

Bayley recorded the crying behavior of sixty infants under a series of standard situations set up each month from birth to twelve months of age. A number of negative reactions, including crying, occurred when the children were brought into a strange room and when they were taken from their mothers by a strange person. The behavior

---

[33] Jones, H. E., and Jones, M. C., *op. cit.*, 136-143. See also Jones, H. E., and Jones, M. C., "Genetic Studies of Emotions." *Psychol. Bull.*, 1930, XXVII, 40-64.

[34] Washburn, R. W., "A Study of Smiling and Laughing in Infants in the First Year of Life." *Genet. Psychol. Monog.*, 1929, VI, 397-537.

THE DEVELOPMENT OF EMOTIONALIZED ACTIONS 207

involved bodily movements of turning to and clinging to the mother. Such behavior, including crying, was inhibited when the child was held by the mother while becoming accustomed to strange places and persons.[35]

It seems to be clear, then, that emotional behavior may be modified in character under the same circumstances as other types of psychological function are modified. The experiments which have just been cited emphasize, among other things, the factor of suddenness or unexpectedness in the fear-exciting situation. This factor is obviously dependent upon sufficient maturation with respect to the perceptual functions as to make some sort of discriminatory reaction between familiar and unfamiliar objects possible. In Jones' study of fear responses, for example, seventy children between the ages of three months and seven years were tested in such situations as the following, viz., flashlights, mechanical toys, stuffed animals, false-faces, darkness, slimy animals, and furry objects in various configurations.

The conditions observed in the experiment included (i) preparing the child for the appearance of the stimulus, (ii) arranging the situation so that the child might come upon the stimulus unexpectedly, (iii) having the stimulus offered by a friendly adult, (iv) having the stimulus presented by a stranger, (v) presenting the stimulus in the presence of other emotionally adjusted children, (vi) presenting the stimulus in the presence of unadjusted children. The results showed clearly enough that there was one factor common to all of the fear-exciting situations, viz., the suddenness or unexpectedness of the stimulus. Under these circumstances the subject was obliged to make a quick adjustment to a strange situation, the result being a more or less chaotic type of behavior which might be called fear. A frog, for example, was more startling than any of the other animals, apparently because it jumped unexpectedly during attempts to touch it.[36]

3. *Conditioned Emotions:* It is now believed that the major changes that take place in the emotional behavior of human beings are more subject to the processes defined by learning than to the processes defined by maturation, where maturation means the expression of native factors.[37] One of the first direct experimental verifications of this fact comes from the so-called "case of Albert." At

---

[35] Bayley, N., "A Study of Crying of Infants during Mental and Physical Tests." *J. Genet. Psychol.*, 1932, XL, 306-329.
[36] Jones, M. C., "The Elimination of Children's Fears." *J. Exper. Psychol.*, 1924, VII, 382-390.
[37] See above, p. 205.

the time the experiment began, Albert had shown fear reactions to only two types of stimulus-situations, viz., loud sounds and loss of support. With respect to such small furry animals as rabbits, dogs, and white rats, and with respect to some of the larger animals at the zoo, he displayed a lively and in some cases even an inquisitive interest.

The experimental situation was arranged in such a way that, at the moment when his hand touched the fur of a white rat, a steel bar just behind his head was struck heavily. The subject immediately reacted by withdrawing from the white rat. Shortly, his curiosity manifested itself in another tentative effort to touch the white rat. The loud sound was again produced, and the withdrawing reaction appeared to be more intense. After seven such coincidences between curiosity and the withdrawing reaction, the attitude of the subject toward the white rat was markedly changed. The mere presentation of the white rat was now sufficient to induce shrinking and avoiding movements.[38] It goes almost without saying that this modification of behavior bears a good many resemblances to the sort of modification described by Pavlov as conditioned behavior.

About a week after the initial experiment, a white rat was again presented, suddenly and without the attending sound stimulus. The subject fixated the white rat steadily, but there was no tendency to reach for it. When, however, a white rat was brought anywhere near the subject, tentative reaching movement began. Just before touching the animal with the forefinger of the left hand, the hand was suddenly withdrawn. It is clear that the modification of behavior induced by conditioning had persisted to some extent at least through the week. After further presentations of the white rat and of the loud sound, the negative reaction to the white rat was further strengthened. Not only was this so, but the child appeared to be negatively disposed toward other types of furry objects.

Similar modifications of behavior have been reported by Jones. The subject of the experiment was placed upon a platform in the midst of a group of toys. The platform was inlaid with thin brass strips through which a mildly irritant tickle could be induced with the aid of proper electric connections. This furnished one of the stimulus-situations. The original reaction of the subject to an electric bell is described by the experimenters as one of mild interest. Repetition, however, led to adaptation, the subject preferring to play

[38] Watson, J. B., and Rayner, R., "Conditioned Emotional Reactions." *J. Exper. Psychol.*, 1920, III, 1-14.

with the toys on the platform. At this juncture the bell and the irritating tickle were administered almost simultaneously. The characteristic reaction induced by the electrical stimulation was quickly transferred to the bell.

One of the results as described by the author runs as follows: "After 72 hours the first application of the bell resulted in momentary crying; on the second he cried and withdrew his hand slowly; on the third he started and cried. . . . It should be noted that the conditioning was distinctly to the bell and not to the platform, as in the intervals between stimulation he played about freely in contact with the brass strips and showed no hesitation in touching them. There was no conditioning against the total situation (of handling and playing in the room), and no indication that the experiment produced any harmful carry-over in the child's normal play activities." [39]

Experiments such as these are, of course, highly formal in character, and they are subject to variable interpretations. A distinct effort has been made, however, to make them more accurate by using a variety of physiological symptoms of emotionalized activity.[40] The psychogalvanic technique cannot be used as a method for describing various kinds of emotional response, but only for noting the presence or absence of such response. It is clear, then, that the variations in a galvanometer created by a situation which, prior to conditioning, did not arouse such variations, could be taken as an index of the transfer of the emotional factors in response to a new situation. Jones, for example, adapted his subjects to the sounds made by a bell and by a buzzer. The process of conditioning was effected by sounding the bell for a period of twenty seconds during the last half of which the sound was accompanied by an electro-tactual stimulus. A response to the bell was reestablished in from four to fourteen associations to the irritating stimulus, whereas the subject remained negatively adapted to the buzzer. In further experiments stimuli were used which were neutral at the outset. The same results appeared. Seven weeks after the experiment there was still evidence that the conditioned response had been retained.[41]

In at least one case it has been shown that a previously condi-

[39] Jones, H. E., "The Conditioning of Overt Emotional Responses." *J. Educ. Psychol.*, 1931, XXXII, 127-130.
[40] Cf. Jones, H. E., and Jones, M. C., "Genetic Studies of Emotions." *Psychol. Bull.*, 1930, XXVII, 40-64.
[41] Jones, H. E., "The Retention of Conditioned Emotional Response in Infancy." *J. Genet. Psychol.*, 1930, XXXVII, 485-498.

tioned fear reaction can be unconditioned by associating a pleasurable stimulus with the fear stimulus. The subject of the experiment reacted in a distinctly fearful way to a rabbit. In one attempt at unconditioning this fear several children who reacted in a favorable manner to animals were allowed to play with the rabbit in the presence of the subject. The subject gradually reacted to the rabbit in the same manner as did his playmates. At this point an unavoidable encounter with a dog made it necessary to retrain the subject. In this part of the experiment, food was used as the positive stimulus. During the act of eating the rabbit was brought nearer and nearer to the child until finally it could be placed on his lap during the eating period. Not only had the subject been unconditioned with respect to the rabbit, but with respect to white rats and to other furry objects as well.[42]

All of these experiments seem to suggest that learning through conditioning is most effective in the modification of emotional behavior. It still remains true, however, that the use of conditioning in this field must remain subject to all that will be said in a later chapter about the adequacy of conditioning as an associative type of learning.[43] Among the several comments that must be made about this type of learning, we may remark the fact that some of the emotional responses thought to be due to conditioning are acquired after a single traumatic experience of great intensity. This fact is to be compared with the relative instability of the ordinary conditioned reflex. It may be true, of course, that a single experience may become effective simply because of its intensity for intensity might well focalize all of the processes involved. This fact has seemed to be true even in the case of Pavlov's original experiments, where it seemed to be clear that speed of learning through conditioning varied directly with an increase in the control of the total stimulus-situation. As we shall have occasion to point out, a more adequate control of the situation means a more definite specification of the two aspects of a total environment between which association is to be expected. The moment a subject recognizes the relevant aspects of the total situation, learning takes place no matter whether the process is described as conditioning or as learning through insight.

There are, of course, a great many other things to say about learn-

---

[42] Jones, M. C., "A Laboratory Study of Fear: The Case of Peter." *Ped. Sem.*, 1924, XXXI, 308-315.

[43] Cf. Guthrie, E. R., "Conditioning as a Principle of Learning." *Psychol. Rev.*, 1930, XXXVII, 412-428.

ing, both with respect to emotionalized reactions and with respect to more general psychological problems. One thing, however, seems to be quite clear. All those factors and situations which have to do with emotionalized or energized response can be shifted with great readiness from situation to situation and from response to response. It is this fact which makes the phrase, "the education of the emotions," have unusual significance in education.

V. The Rôle of Emotion in Tutored Behavior

1. *Introduction:* It is frequently said that human beings possess three different ways of reacting to situations. In the first place, with respect to situations that have been faced before, a person may respond either with a specific habit or with whatever cluster of organized habits that may be necessary to meet the situation efficiently and adequately. There are times, of course, when special habits or clusters of habits will be fully adequate to normal situations with no more training than has already taken place. On other occasions, however, an attempt will be made to use habits that are not of such long standing, and before these habits can be truly effective, they must pass through the process described as learning. These acquired modes of reacting to a situation hold true both in the case of manual skills and in the case of verbal skills, either implicit or overt.

In the second place, there are times when previously acquired skills are not adequate to a situation if they are used just as they stand. In the case of implicit verbal reactions, for example, habitualized types of response may shift over easily and quickly to that type of activity called problem-solving. As a rule, a problematic situation is made up of components for each of which there may be some previously established reaction, but such situations gain their problematic character out of the fact that they are now configured in a manner different from all previous configurations. In the absence of appropriately coördinated movements, either at the manual or verbal level, most educated persons will attempt to respond to such situations by making a quick and constructive repatterning of the whole situation so that the problem can be solved. There are, then, two normal provisions for meeting average situations, viz., through habits and skills which have been learned for that particular purpose and through problem-solving, a function which is more or less unique to the human animal.

Both of these modes of meeting various situations are to be distinguished from the emotionalized response. This does not mean that habits and solutions are necessarily emotionless, for, as we have seen, all behavior-patterns fall in the same continuum; but some types of action become highly energized when the conditions are just right. Situations which are presented suddenly and unexpectedly, for example, frequently lead to an emotional reaction rather than to an habitual or to a problem-solving reaction. It is as though the organism were attempting to make up, by its very vehemence and frenzy, that which it cannot do in terms of habit or thinking. This means, of course, that emotions are essentially maladjusted or inappropriate types of behavior, and the inference is frequently drawn, therefore, that emotional types of reaction should be eliminated as fast as possible from the psychological inventory of an educated man.[44]

2. *Emotion and Reason:* There are certain other facts which look in this same direction. We have in mind the relationship between primitive and more natural modes of response, on one side, and so-called cultural or civilized responses, on the other. It is sometimes argued that emotional types of reaction represent a more primitive mode of response to the environment, whereas high skill, on the one hand, and problem-solving activities, on the other, especially at the level described by rational thinking, represent the most recently acquired talents of the race. When, therefore, in the face of difficult, perplexing, or confusing situations, a person reacts emotionally rather than intelligently, we say of him that he is reverting to type. The inference is that a complete education would almost, if not quite, eliminate emotionalized behavior from a well-ordered society.

It is often argued that, if human affairs could be settled in terms of an objective consideration of verifiable facts rather than in terms of prejudice, emotion, sympathy, devotion, and other sublimations of emotional behavior, human society would find itself in a highly respectable condition. The same sort of contrast is found in descriptions of mob action versus individual action, in justifying wartime propaganda in favor of hate and peace-time propaganda in favor of patriotism, in reactions of the adolescent as opposed to reactions of the adult, and in some of the sharpened contrasts between the religious mind and the scientific mind. In all of these cases it is argued that great advantage is to be sought by an almost, if not complete, elimination of emotional types of reaction and of all of their relatives, both near and remote.

[44] There is, however, much controversy concerning the adaptive value of emotionalized action. Cf. Darwin, C., *op. cit.*, pp. 46 ff., and *passim,* and Watson, J. B., *op. cit.,* pp. 192 ff.

THE DEVELOPMENT OF EMOTIONALIZED ACTIONS 213

Further justification for this point of view is found in the occasional contrasts that are drawn between the prevailing culture of Eastern Europe as opposed to the prevailing culture of the Orient. It is often remarked, for example, that the Westerner is continually active, in the sense that he can readily interpret the problems of knowing in terms of the functions of doing. It is even said that his religion must somewhere acquire a conative rather than a feeling content. Certain religious sects have proceeded as though religion must mean for them much preaching and testifying, much dancing about the altar, and other objective expressions of religious struggle. Even in one of the most oriental of our religions, virtue is to be found in the act of chanting a prayer or counting the beads.

The true oriental, on the contrary, finds equal virtue in almost, if not complete, cessation of movement. His religious life is made up of a half-mystical, half-emotional withdrawal from all types of sensory impression and from all modes of bodily or muscular performance. A common criticism of the instrumental theories of knowing has it that the American temper which favors technical skill and continued overt activity has simply sought for philosophic justification through the identification of knowing and action. From one point of view it is certainly characteristic of the American scene that intelligence expresses itself through technical and behavioral channels. It is pointed out with regret that there is, outside of the so-called menace of a technocracy, no intrinsic American culture. The implication is that a highly skilled and coldly intellectual or experimental solution of social, economic, and other problems is far to be preferred to a mystical attitude which pays more attention to alleged eternal verities than to sanitation, medicine, and other practical arts of control.

These several ways of throwing suspicion upon emotional modes in reaction have found liberal support in some of the behavioristic treatments of common affections. Watson, for example, finds that a vast number of family and personal difficulties are directly associated with the tendency of mothers and nurses to overemphasize certain aspects of the affective life. Beginning with the argument that such stimuli as stroking the skin, rocking, petting, or tickling erogenous zones lead directly to that form of behavior called the love reaction, Watson argues that parents do their best to make their children completely and abnormally dependent upon adults. This dependence then becomes a common source for a great many other types of inefficient and antisocial responses.

Among the results of infantile coddling are to be numbered such adult reactions as lack of initiative and self-reliance, a tendency toward infantilism, that is, a tendency to perpetuate the intimate details of motherly care, and direct barriers in the way of effecting friendly relations with strangers, especially in the case of females who are unprepared to face the marriage ceremony. The remedy for this situation, according to Watson, is to be found in the elimination of all actions and attitudes that would favor the development or spread of the love reaction. The same argument can be used with respect to all types of fears, all modes of expressing resentment, rage, jealousy, and other forms of emotional response.

The heroic measures suggested by Watson stand in close affiliation with one of the principal arguments of psychoanalytic psychology. Much of this psychology is based upon the proposition that the early emotional experiences of children, even though they may be forgotten at the conscious level, continue to exist in the unconscious in such a form that they can and do, whenever the conditions are favorable, reappear in experience and in behavior in such a way as to lead to almost complete functional disorganization. Some phases of this problem have already been considered in previous chapters, and the entire problem will be raised for discussion again in the chapter on adjustment and mental hygiene. In the meantime, it is only necessary to point out that, from the point of view of psychoanalysis, a satisfactory education could be achieved only when there was a more or less complete sublimation of emotional experiences during the early period of development.

3. *The "Higher" Feelings:* It is obvious that the various questions and problems raised by the situations just described cannot be dismissed easily from any study of the problems of education. The general inference is that emotionalized types of response have little or no part to play in the educated life of contemporary man. The moment this inference is made, however, one comes directly upon all of those modes of behavior which have to do with the appreciation of art, with the development of friendly loyalties, with all types of devotion, and with all phases of the religious experience.

Any adequate appreciation of the problems here raised for discussion depends, therefore, upon the relations that may obtain between the so-called emergency emotions and the finer sentiments and aesthetic feelings. It is customary, for example, to limit the word "emotion" to such behavior-patterns as rage, fear, anger, jealousy, and the like. The word "mood" is used to include the milder forms of such attitudes as pleasure, happiness, joy, depression, melancholy, anxiety, worry, and apprehension. The feelings commonly

THE DEVELOPMENT OF EMOTIONALIZED ACTIONS

described as social and moral have to do with friendliness, sympathy, kindliness, righteousness, loyalty, and so on. Feelings and attitudes which lead to a proper appreciation of the beautiful in art, sculpture, architecture, poetry, music, drama, and interpretive dancing are usually called aesthetic feelings. The religious feelings include such attitudes as reverence, devotion, and worship. Are all of these feelings and attitudes cut from the same piece of cloth, or do they represent fundamentally different kinds of psychological function?

The first step in answer to this question is taken by recognizing the fact that emotional behavior does appear to be based upon two separate conditions. We have already described these conditions as follows. On the one hand, it is obvious that the nervous system, which is the principal instrument for mediating psychological functions, is immersed in the most intimate way possible in an ongoing and dynamic set of physiological functions. On the side of experience, this would seem to mean that no human experience could be detached from a background of feeling created by the sympathetic or the autonomic system. On the side of behavior, it would mean that no single act or attitude could be wholly unresponsive of the general level of physiological functioning.

On the other hand, the body contains special organs, the function of which is to control the reserve energies of the body. The very process of making these reserve energies available in reaction brings with it significant types of change throughout the body. These changes may be expressed either in experience or in behavior. The James-Lange theory of the emotions seems to say something about the way in which they might be expressed in experience. All studies on the expression of the emotions are ways of showing how the bodily changes may display themselves in the antecedents of behavior and in the instruments by means of which reaction becomes possible.

The second step in answering the question asked above is taken in the demonstration that feelings and emotions, on one side, and energized responses or postures, on the other, may become readily associated with almost every other type of psychological function. In short, human beings appear to be more educable with respect to their emotions and attitudes than with respect to specific skills or with respect to the acquisition of knowledge. This means that every accomplishment of human beings, whether manual or verbal, whether by way of skill or by way of concept, may acquire some specific emotional fundus.

In view of this circumstance it becomes possible to relate the simpler and more primary feelings with aesthetic, social, and religious sentiments. One of the most competent students of the sentiments, for example, describes them as fairly permanent systems of emotional dispositions toward some objective. In writing of a typical sentiment, for example, Shand remarks: "In the love of an object, there is pleasure in presence and desire in absence, hope or despondency in anticipation, fear in the expectation of its loss or destruction, surprise or astonishment in its unexpected changes, anger when the course of our interest is opposed or frustrated, elation when we triumph over obstacles, satisfaction or disappointment in attaining our desire, regret in the loss, injury, or destruction of the object, joy in its restoration or improvement, and admiration for its superior quality or excellence. And this series of emotions occurs, now in one order, now in another . . . when the appropriate conditions are present." [45]

This is to say that, with respect to a given object, a certain system of emotional reactions may become so habitually attached that it will appear whenever the object is presented either directly or in symbolic form. The same thing appears to hold true with respect to all of the other human sentiments. The flag, for example, is often cited as an object around which a precise array of postures and experiences of the emotionalized type may become so intimately organized as to make it a dominant object in the regulation of whole groups of individuals.

4. *Aesthetic Feelings:* From the highly general way in which we have spoken of some of these matters, the student will get the impression that here is a field of research in which a great deal is yet to be done. In this impression he will be correct. As a single illustration, we may take the religious feelings and sentiments. To be sure, serious efforts have been made to gain some account of the experiences of the mystic, and other phases of the religious life have entered in one way or another into the laboratory, but no one feels that the last word has been said about any of these matters.[46]

Of the various types of sentiments and of "higher feelings" that might be studied, the aesthetic feelings have received most attention. A part of these studies has been concerned only with the way in which aesthetic feelings develop in the classroom. As an example we may take an examination of the extent to which school children appre-

---

[45] Shand, A. F., "Character and the Emotions." *Mind*, 1896, V, 203-226. See p. 218.
[46] Cf. James, W., *The Varieties of Religious Experience.* New York: D. Appleton-Century Co., 1912, *passim*. Also Bennett, C. A., *The Dilemma of Religious Knowledge.* New Haven: Yale Univ. Press, 1931.

THE DEVELOPMENT OF EMOTIONALIZED ACTIONS 217

ciate literary masterpieces. The experimenter laid before his subjects Byron's poem entitled *The Destruction of Sennacherib*. The subjects were asked to write out a summary of certain portions of this poem in their own language. The summary was then judged in terms of the degree of comprehension revealed with respect to the original poem. It was discovered that the average ninth-grade pupil was able to comprehend not more than one-half of the original material, and that approximately forty per cent of the important words were unfamiliar.[47]

One of the inferences drawn from this study was that English teachers undertook often to present literary material to their students which was not only too difficult for them, but which lay beyond their aesthetic judgments. Some light on the way in which these judgments grow in the later teens is shown by the following study. A recognized piece of poetry was modified in three ways: first, by increasing its sentimental quality; second, by making it more commonplace and matter-of-fact; and third, by destroying the meter. These three variations, together with the initial stanzas, were printed upon a single page and presented to a series of subjects. The subjects were asked to mark the best and the worst stanza.

Thirteen such pages were presented to subjects in the fifth and other upper grades, up to a group of graduate students in English. From the fifth grade to the eighth grade, the judgments of the subjects were scarcely better than a mere guess. Clear evidence of literary discrimination did not appear until the upper levels of college work were reached. In short, there was every evidence that the development of literary discrimination must proceed rather slowly under current methods of teaching. Of the several factors involved in this study, lack of meter was detected earlier than other departures from the standard.[48]

As another illustration, we may take ability to judge paintings. The experimental material consisted of a set of fifty famous paintings and of a parallel set in which some modification of the paintings had been made. Four groups of subjects were tested, viz., high school students, college undergraduates, students of art, and members of the art faculty. It was found that college undergraduates were eight points better than high school students, that college art students were five and one-half points better than college under-

---

[47] Irion, T. W. H., "Comprehension Difficulties of Ninth-grade Students in the Study of Literature." *Teachers Coll. Contrib. to Educ.*, 1925 (No. 189).
[48] Abbott, A., and Trabue, M. R., "A Measure of Ability to Judge Poetry." *Teachers Coll. Rec.*, 1921, XXII, 101-126.

graduates, and the members of the art faculty were six and one-half points better than the college art students.[49]

As we have remarked, these and other studies take a given type of instruction in the field of aesthetic judgments for granted. There is some evidence to show that greater competence can be developed by special methods of teaching. As a typical instance, we may take a study which asked a group of children to make certain drawings. The drawings were then rated according to merit. Appreciation was tested by using a series of sketches similar to the sketches made by the children. Each of the subjects was asked to check the sketch he considered the best. The subjects were made up of children drawn from three different schools, the one school standing in a neighborhood of fairly high socio-economic level where a special effort had been made to develop appreciation, a second school being called average, and a third school being called poor. The data showed that children from the first school had developed a sense of artistic appreciation much earlier than students in the other schools. Moreover, the level of excellence in judgments of this type was much higher for these students.[50]

There are, no doubt, many features of the appreciation of art and of aesthetic judgments which are hereditary in their origin. This fact holds true, in particular, of the feelings that may be aroused by different colors, different combinations of colors, tones, patterns of tones, and differences in form or patterning. It still remains true, however, that these possible hereditary factors in aesthetic appreciation are highly subject to modification through training. If, then, a teacher can come to some judgment about the value of the aesthetic feelings in a technical culture like our own, we may be assured that any teaching effort expended in this direction will bring results.

In a great many communities, teachers of music, of painting, and sometimes even of literature face an inertia created by the fact that a group which is intensely interested in invention and commerce holds the aesthetic feelings somewhat in disdain. It can even be said that all types of aesthetic appreciation are nothing more than escape mechanisms and that they should have no part, therefore, in

---

[49] Meier, N. C., "A Measure of Art Talent." *Psychol. Monog.*, 1928, XXXIX, 184-199. See also Stumberg, D., "A Study of Poetic Talent." *J. Exper. Psychol.*, 1928, XI, 219-234.

[50] Whitford, W. G., "Empirical Study of Pupil-ability in Public-school Art Courses." *Element. School J.*, 1919, XX, 33-46, 95-105. See also, Carroll, H. A., "A Preliminary Report on a Study of Interrelationship of Certain Appreciations." *J. Educ. Psychol.*, 1932, XXIII, 505-510.

the school program. This attitude is, perhaps, a natural consequence of a culture which has just passed the pioneering stage and which has not yet developed the sort of leisure which contributes most freely to the "higher feelings."

READINGS

The author ought to apologize, perhaps, for attempting to write out a chapter on the nature of emotionalized action when the whole field is so full of confusion and distortions of fact. As we have said, however, the discovery that the attitudes and postures commonly called emotional can be transferred by processes of training from one situation to another marks one of the outstanding discoveries of recent years, and the educational significance of this fact requires some treatment of problems like those mentioned in the present chapter, even though the treatment does not appear satisfactory.

One of the most useful points of departure for the study of emotionalized actions is to be found in Darwin, C., *The Expression of the Emotions among Men and Animals*. New York: D. Appleton-Century Co., 1872. This book is important because it furnishes the background for so much of current comment and criticism. A broad but confusing picture of beliefs and of points of view about the nature of the emotions is to be found in Reymert, M. L. (Ed.), *Wittenberg Symposium on Feelings and Emotions*. Worcester, Mass.: Clark Univ. Press, 1928. A picture of the experimental attack that is now being made on these problems must come from a study of the periodic literature. The text references can be used for this purpose.

An adequate description of the bodily basis of emotionalized actions is furnished by Murchison, C. (Ed.), *Handbook of General Experimental Psychology*. Worcester, Mass.: Clark Univ. Press, 1934. See Chapter V, "Hunger and Thirst" (by W. B. Cannon); Chapter VI, "Emotion: I. The Neuro-Humoral Basis of Emotional Reactions" (by P. Bard); and Chapter VII, "Emotion: II. The Expressions of Emotion" (by C. Landis). One of the most suggestive books in the field has been written by Cannon, W. B., *Bodily Changes in Pain, Hunger, Fear, and Rage* (2nd ed.). New York: D. Appleton-Century Co., 1929.

Any appreciation of the nature of mood and emotion will have to come, perhaps, by way of inference from experimental studies. Suggestive sources are Sherman, M., and Sherman, I. C., *The Process of Human Behavior*. New York: W. W. Norton Co., 1929; Jones, M. C., "Emotional Development," in Murchison, C. (Ed.), *A Handbook of Child Psychology*. Worcester, Mass.: Clark Univ. Press, 1933, Chapter VI. Those who wish to push the matter further will find an abundant opportunity in the list of references appended to Jones' chapter.

It is not possible, perhaps, to get a complete picture of the nature of emotionalized actions, and neither is it possible to see the extreme educational significance of the experimental work that is being done without taking some account of perversions and abnormalities in emotionalized responses. A basic source for an approach to this group of problems is furnished by Bentley, M., and Cowdry, E. V. (Editors), *The Problem of Mental Disorder*.

New York: McGraw-Hill Book Co., 1934, *passim*. Other helpful sources are Sherman, M., *Mental Hygiene and Education*. New York: Longmans, Green and Co., 1934; Morgan, J. J. B., *Keeping a Sound Mind*. New York: The Macmillan Co., 1934; and Symonds, P. M., *Mental Hygiene of the School Child*. New York: The Macmillan Co., 1934. As we have promised in the text, we shall devote a special chapter to this phase of the problems of emotionalized action.

By inference at least, judgments and inferences concerning the knowledge of emotionalized conduct in the normal processes of living can be gained from the books just mentioned or from Martin, E. D., *Meaning of a Liberal Education*. New York: W. W. Norton and Co., 1926; or from Woodbridge, F. J. E., *The Son of Apollo*. Boston: Houghton Mifflin Co., 1929. Many important inferences can be drawn also from Paulhan, F., *The Laws of Feeling*. (Trans. by C. K. Ogden.) New York: Harcourt, Brace and Co., 1930.

The following references will be found useful in further studies of the higher feelings: Terman, L. M., and Cox, C. M., *Genetic Studies of Genius*, Vol. II. *The Early Mental Traits of 300 Geniuses*. Palo Alto: Stanford Univ. Press, 1926; Hartman, G., and Shumaker, A. (Editors), *Creative Expression: The Development of Children in Art, Music, Literature, and Dramatics*. New York: John Day Co., 1932; Mursell, J. L., *The Psychology of Secondary School Teaching*. New York: W. W. Norton and Co., 1932, Part I.

CHAPTER SEVEN

THE DEVELOPMENT OF PROBLEM-SOLVING

I. Commonsense Views of Thinking

1. *Introduction:* There are, perhaps, no features of the growth pattern that receive more comment from parents and teachers than those that are named by the words "thinking," "reasoning," or the ability to solve problems. By long tradition, the faculty of reason is man's chief claim to superiority over the lower animals, as well as his nearest approach to the divine. We give honor and distinction to those persons who have used their powers of thought to invent a new tool, to make a new discovery in the laboratory, or to find some clever way out of a difficult or perplexing situation. Much that we call culture or civilization is said to be a sum of the "thoughts" that men have had. It is no wonder, then, that teachers and parents often display an unusual interest in the nature of thinking or of problem-solving and in the methods that can be used to train children to acquire larger measures of this ability. Where it is lacking, we use every means that we can to create it, and where it is present we are equally desirous of making it more efficient.

For example, those movements in education sometimes described as "progressive" and those methods of teaching suggested by the phrase "the project method" mark the attempts of teachers and administrators to get away from teaching practices that depended too greatly upon the sheer processes of learning.[1] Most of the books in geometry and algebra contain, at the end of each formal demonstration, a series of projects which are called original exercises, the inference being that, if sufficient learning has taken place, the student ought to exercise himself forthwith in the ability to apply the results of his learning to new or untried situations. The desire to develop problem-solving ability is so great and so persistent that a student may, even when he reaches the higher levels of education, find courses in logic which have, as a part of their function, an increase in the faculty of reason or at least an improvement in reasoning ability that will make it more reliable.

[1] Cf. Stevenson, J. A., *The Project Method of Teaching*. New York: The Macmillan Co., 1921, *passim*.

As we have already seen, social concern about this phase of the growth pattern has been so great that teaching methods that promote the power of reflection have been used to the disadvantage, if not to the total neglect, of emotional training and even of character training, for it is only during recent years that the secular school rather than the religious school has given any thought at all to character and personality traits.[2]

It is the purpose of this chapter, therefore, to find out what the process of solving problems consists of and how this process may be aided by teaching methods. This task requires of us that we clear the ground of a good many faulty opinions about the nature of thinking, for it is only within the present century that experimental work of a truly effective type has been carried out on this particular feature of the whole growth pattern.[3] This means that our daily conversations with one another about thinking and reasoning are full of faulty opinions, prejudices, half-way realizations of the truth, and other considerations that have stood as a serious obstacle in the way of a perspective on the whole matter. The opinions that seem to be the most confusing are (i) that thinking is equivalent to remembering or recalling, (ii) that thinking is equivalent to sign learning or to the use of associations that have already been learned, (iii) that thinking is equivalent to imagination or random reflection over past experience, (iv) that thinking is equivalent to the process of proving by means of logic the truth of a discovery, and (v) that thinking is a purely mental affair which does not directly concern the body or even the nervous system.[4]

2. *Thinking and Remembering:* There is, perhaps, no misuse of the terms "thinking" or "reasoning" which is more common and more beside the mark than that which identifies it with memory or reminiscence.[5] Even when a child is very small, we sometimes wonder what it is thinking about if it appears to be pensive or in any other way to have taken what we commonly describe as a thoughtful attitude. Later on, it is almost certain that, during an examination period, when a group of students is confronted with a series of questions, we will say that the students are being asked to think. The reader has only to examine his own reactions to an

[2] Cf. Hartshorne, H., *Character in Human Relations.* New York: Charles Scribner's Sons, 1932.
[3] Cf. Peterson, J., "Learning in Children," in Murchison, C. (Ed.), *Handbook of Child Psychology.* Worcester, Mass.: Clark Univ. Press, 1933, Chapter X.
[4] Cf. Dewey, J., *How We Think* (2nd ed.). Boston: D. C. Heath and Co., 1933, Chapters I and II.
[5] Cf. Bartlett, F. C., *Remembering: an Experimental and Social Study.* London: Cambridge Univ. Press, 1932.

# THE DEVELOPMENT OF PROBLEM-SOLVING

examination situation in order to discover that, if he refers to himself as a thinking person, the chances are that he is doing nothing more than attempting to recall those verbal habits or skills which he has been asked to learn "by heart" earlier in the course.[6]

To be sure, recall of this type is a performance which aids us a great deal in getting along both in the schoolroom and out of it. As a matter of fact, human beings are so superior to all of the lower animals both in the variety of things they can recall and in the length of time that may elapse between original learning and recall, as to make adequate comparisons almost fruitless. It must be clear, however, that the sheer recall of something that has been learned at some prior time, while fully deserving of the descriptive terms "memory" and "recollection" cannot be described as thinking. It makes no difference whether the word "memory" is used to name the series of ideas that may "pass through one's head" in response to a question or whether it refers to the implied verbal comments aroused by the present situation.[7] In either case, a train of associations or a series of verbal skills describe something that has been acquired by the student during his previous training and which can now be used to very good purposes. The point is that true thinking seems to require something more than sheer recollection.

3. *Thinking and Sign Learning:* The use which we make of sign learning approaches more nearly the true nature of thinking than sheer remembering. As we shall see in a later chapter, sign learning implies that, through experience, one object may point to, signify, or imply the existence of another object or call for the arrival of an event which cannot happen at the moment.[8] When, for example, we go to a street corner to wait for a car, our behavior cannot possibly be explained unless we know from other sources that standing upon a street corner and all of the movements required to get there have been aroused by the fact that the street corner or a signboard or some post is a signal that a bus will pass that way. To be sure, this is a type of memory or the result of previous learning, for, without such learning, it is not conceivable that either a signboard or a corner could serve as a signal for an object or event

---

[6] Cf. Lang, A. R., *Modern Methods in Written Examinations.* Boston: Houghton Mifflin Co., 1930, *passim.*

[7] The student should refer again to the distinctions that have been drawn between manual and verbal skills in Chapter Two.

[8] Cf. Bode, B. H., *Conflicting Psychologies of Learning.* Boston: D. C. Heath, 1929, *passim.*

that will almost certainly arrive but which is not present at the moment.

A great many of the difficulties or perplexities into which we get may be handled in this manner. If, having been caught in a sudden rainstorm, we blame ourselves because we were so stupid as not to have taken an umbrella, we give witness to the fact that the dark cloud on the horizon could have been taken as a sign of coming rain. In somewhat the same way we solve the problems of driving along a highway. A piece of yellow board with some words printed on it is certainly not an automobile or a train. We may, however, avoid a possible accident upon the highway if we take a board or the words printed on it as a suggestion of the fact that there is possible danger ahead.

Many of the lower animals are almost as efficient as we are in their use of sign learning.[9] We would be lowly creatures indeed if we were always obliged to react to objects just as they arrive. We have escaped lowliness simply because sign learning enables us to prepare for contingencies. It lifts us out of direct contact with objects and events and enables us to prepare for the future. When, therefore, we say that sign learning is not genuine thinking we do not mean to diminish the importance of this type of learning for daily conduct. Indeed, we would be much happier and even more intelligent if we used sign learning more frequently than we do. But true problem-solving differs mightily, as we shall try to show, even from the most elaborate levels of sign learning.

4. *Thinking and Imagination:* Still more like problem-solving, at least in our common opinion, is that psychological operation known as imagination.[10] Imagination runs all the way from random daydreaming through the really creative activity of small children during their play periods to thoughtful planning about our conduct for the morrow. Without raising again the question of the relation between imagination and the use of our verbal skills, let us say that the least fruitful forms of imagination, viz., random daydreaming and fantasies, are simply trains of implicit verbal comments or of ideas which follow one another with only such order or sequence as previously established associative connections might require. The point is that, after a sufficient amount of experience, one may fall into a fairly passive or inattentive attitude so far as external objects

---

[9] For a summary of some of the literature, see Heron, W. T., "Complex Learning Processes," in Moss, F. A. (Ed.), *Comparative Psychology.* New York: Prentice-Hall, Inc., 1934, Chapter XI. See also Chapter XII.

[10] Cf. Titchener, E. B., *The Elementary Psychology of the Thought Processes.* New York: The Macmillan Co., 1909, *passim.*

and events are concerned and allow one's verbal symbols to reconstruct in a more or less random fashion the events through which we have already passed.

As we have seen, children may resort frequently to imaginative play during which they use their vocal apparatus in much the same way that they would use manual types of action. There is no particular goal to be reached save the sheer pleasure brought about by activity. To be sure, some of the verbal play of small children may be compensatory in the sense that the child sees objects and events or achieves successes which could not be seen or achieved by direct overt action.[11] In the main, however, it is not fruitful to call this type of verbal play problem-solving although there are some respects in which it might be made to contribute largely to real processes of discovery. Even in the case of thoughtful planning, as in making out a schedule for work to be done during the following day, we cannot be sure that true problem-solving is involved. As a rule, the making out of a schedule or formulating plans for a future vacation merely require the use of the results of sign learning and a tentative outline in verbal terms of the things that we might like to do in overt manual or bodily action.

5. *Thinking and the Syllogism:* In advance of a more positive statement of the nature of true thinking, it will be a little difficult to make the student see that thinking is not equivalent to logic, inference, deduction and other formal features of what is often called the power of reason. Our textbooks of logic tell us that human beings are at their best whenever they can lay down a set of propositions and then, by a series of logical inferences, draw reliable conclusions from the original propositions.[12] We shall try to show, as we proceed with the various phases of this chapter, that logic is a device which we use in order to prove or demonstrate the essential validity or correctness of the discoveries made during actual thinking. In other words, logic is something that we do to a discovery in order to make the discovery convincing to someone else.[13] It is not a description of the process of discovery itself.

This means that it is fruitful to draw a distinction between the psychological operations involved in problem-solving, on the one hand, and a logical demonstration which makes our discoveries con-

---

[11] Cf. Robinson, E. S., "The Compensatory Function of Make-believe Play." *Psychol. Rev.,* 1920, XXVII, 429-439.

[12] Cf. Robinson, D. S., *The Principles of Reasoning.* New York: D. Appleton-Century Co., 1930, *passim.*

[13] Cf. Carmichael, R. D., *The Logic of Discovery.* Chicago: Open Court Publ. Co., 1930, *passim.* Also, Meyerson, E., *Identity and Reality.* (Trans. by K. Loewenberg.) New York: The Macmillan Co., 1930, p. 6.

vincing, on the other. To be sure, there are a great many places in books on teaching method where it is assumed that a logic of demonstration is equivalent to a genuine process of discovery. Such subjects as geometry, for example, depend so largely upon the processes of demonstration that we suppose we have finished our obligations to children so far as problem-solving is concerned whenever we have subjected them to a rigorous course in geometry.[14]

As we shall try to show later on, the demonstrations which are included in a book on geometry are methods of convincing the student that some unnamed person was, no doubt, right in the discovery that he made. As a particular instance let us take the Pythagorean theory. We do not know, of course, just what happened when Pythagoras discovered the fact that the square erected upon the hypothenuse of a right-angle triangle is equal to the sum of the squares erected upon the other two sides. The discovery, however, was made. Moreover, it is now possible to prove by logical means that this theorum is correct if we make the same assumptions that Euclid made in setting up his whole system. Now the pupil in the classroom learns this demonstration. It very rarely happens that he makes the discovery for himself. That is, very few pupils ever face the perplexity which must have faced Pythagoras and neither do they experience the same sudden insight which Pythagoras must have experienced. It is, then, one thing to prove the correctness of an insight or learn how to decide whether insights are valid or not and quite another to achieve the original insight.

6. *Thinking and the Mind:* The last confusion about the nature of thinking which is of concern to us at the moment may be stated as follows. By long tradition it has been taken for granted that thinking or reasoning is a purely mental process, a something that goes on in one's head which probably does not involve either the body or the nervous system.[15] In other words, commonsense opinion has it that, after the nervous system and the sensory apparatus have furnished the mind with a proper amount of information, the mind can reorganize this information, relate one proposition to another, discover meanings and implications, and finally yield a conclusion or judgment.[16] Throughout this entire process, it is assumed that the mind has been inherently or intrinsically logical in its opera-

---

[14] Cf. Young, J. W. A., *The Teaching of Mathematics in the Elementary and the Secondary School.* New York: Longmans, Green and Co., 1906, *passim.*
[15] De Wulf, M., *Scholasticism Old and New.* Dublin: M. H. Gill and Son, 1910, *passim.*
[16] Cf. Lewis, C. L., *Mind and the World Order.* New York: Charles Scribner's Sons, 1929, *passim.*

tions. Given sufficient information and given a sufficient critical examination of the correctness of the information and of the validity of all inferences drawn from it, the conclusion that is reached must be final and unassailable.[17] In short, reason is a process which goes on in the mind and which, if properly safeguarded by logic, will enable a person to arrive at some final truth. When the truth has once been attained, the mind may then convert its operations into action by using the vocal apparatus to announce a judgment or by using the other muscles in the body to adjust the individual to the perplexing situations which originally gave rise to the problem-solving functions.

There is one phase of this doctrine about the nature of thinking which is of great importance to the teacher, for it says that thinking is not so much a psychological operation which can be acquired by a child as it is an innate faculty or power which is present from the very beginning and which can be exercised to good advantage in direct proportion as the amount of information which is available to the child is increased. As long as experimental studies of the nature of thinking were limited to human subjects, it was not possible to gain any information upon which some other statement of the nature of thinking could be based, for rational processes at the human level are so complex and subject to so many variable conditions that experimenters have been almost at a loss as to how to proceed.

More recently, however, as an outcome of studies on the way in which animals solve problems, it has been found that certain complex types of learning display a great many features which are highly suggestive of the operations through which human beings go when they actually reach some new judgment.[18] One of the first results of these experiments has been to show rather clearly that thinking or problem-solving is neither purely mental in character nor is it wholly detached from some of the other types of psychological operation which we have already described. It is almost certain, for example, that thinking is a process which involves unique types of relationship between stimulus-patterns, on the one hand, and of response-patterns, on the other. It is a function which rests upon the fact that certain events may transpire in the nervous system between the initial stimulus-pattern and the final or consummatory

---

[17] For a splendid illustration from the history of psychology, see Titchener, E. B., *Systematic Psychology: Prolegomena.* New York: The Macmillan Co., 1929, Chapter I.

[18] Cf. Köhler, W., *The Mentality of Apes* (Trans. by E. Winter). New York: Harcourt, Brace and Co., 1925, *passim.*

reaction to this pattern.[19] We must, therefore, now that we have cleared the ground of common prejudices and faulty opinions about thinking, pass on to a more positive statement as to just what is implied by this term.

II. THE NATURE OF PROBLEM-SOLVING

1. *Introduction:* There are two reasons why we have given some preference to the phrase "problem-solving" rather than to the more familiar terms "reasoning" and "thinking." In the first place, these more familiar terms have had a very long history, a part of which lies in psychology and a part of which lies in religion and in theology.[20] It is this history which has assumed that thinking is something that can go on in a mind which, by its very nature, is already strictly logical in character. In short, then, thinking and reasoning are so weighted down with meanings derived from theories about the ultimate nature of the mind and from theories about the native functions of the soul as to make them almost useless in any discussion of the types of function they refer to but which have been studied in terms of experimental data.

In the second place, as we have mentioned just above, studies on the nature of problem-solving where human adults were the subjects gave no results that could be called significant.[21] As a matter of fact, it often happened that a subject would respond to a problem or to a pair of statements simply by saying "yes" or "no" and without being able to report on any of the events which led up to these judgments. Let the student, for example, try to report on the events that intervene between the following statement and his judgment with respect to the statement. The statement is: "The next great war will be waged entirely with poisonous gas and with toxic bacteria." The chances are that, if the student has said either "yes" or "no," he will be able to report about his process of reflection only that he said over to himself: "The next great war" . . . "chemistry" . . . "airplanes" . . . "Yes!" or "No!"[22]

There is, of course, nothing about this report that reveals what happened psychologically when the judgment was made. Certainly,

---

[19] Cf. Franz, S. I., "The Neurology of Learning," in Moss, F. A. (Ed.), *Comparative Psychology*. New York: The Ronald Press, 1934, Chapter VIII.
[20] Cf. Boring, E. G., *A History of Experimental Psychology*. New York: D. Appleton-Century Co., 1929, *passim*.
[21] Titchener, E. B., *Experimental Psychology of the Thought Processes*. New York: The Macmillan Co., 1909, *passim*.
[22] For analogous reports, see Titchener, E. B., *op. cit.,* pp. 92 ff.

THE DEVELOPMENT OF PROBLEM-SOLVING 229

there is no symptom of logical discourse and it often turns out that judgments of this type are made in the absence of almost all antecedents that could be called relative to the problem. A student might easily have twiddled his thumbs and still have arrived at the same judgment. When, however, some one of the lower animals is placed in a problematic situation, the situation itself can be made simple enough to lend itself to complete description. Moreover, the nervous apparatus of the animal can be described with sufficient accuracy so that the experimenter can know just what the animal may be able to use in its problem-solving activities.[23] Finally, the actual behavior of the animal may also be fairly simple and related in such a definite way to the character of the stimulus-situation as to reveal fully what must have transpired between the time when the stimulus was presented and the successful response was made. In short, then, the term "problem-solving" has acquired a definite meaning derived out of specific experimental situations. These experimental situations seem to reveal so many fundamental facts about the possible character of thinking at the human level that the phrase "problem-solving" recommends itself, at least for the present, in preference to the older terms "thinking" and "reasoning."

We shall now try to describe some of the operations which either contribute to or which lie in a region immediately adjacent to, true problem-solving. As we do this, the student must remember that human thinking is an even more complex process than we have been able to picture. He must realize also that fruitful experimentation in this field is just now coming to the point where experimenters can feel that they are asking questions, the answers to which will be really suggestive so far as the nature of thinking is concerned. It will not be possible for us, therefore, to say anything final about the nature of thinking and it is highly probable that some of the things we shall say will ultimately be shown to be wrong or to consist of an actual misinterpretation of the facts. The task of teaching children how to use their problem-solving functions more frequently and more adequately, however, is so important a phase of the whole teaching program that one can well afford to make a few mistakes in the attempt to make the art of problem-solving a more common feature of average schoolroom procedure.[24]

2. *Tools:* By common agreement one of the surest signs that real thinking has occurred is to be found in the invention and use

---
[23] Lashley, K. S., *Brain Mechanisms and Intelligence.* Chicago: Univ. of Chicago Press, 1929, *passim.*
[24] Cf. Mursell, J. L., *The Psychology of Secondary School Teaching.* New York: W. W. Norton and Co., 1932, *passim.*

of tools. By a tool we mean any object or device which serves as a medium of contact between a person and a situation. In order that an object or device shall be used as a tool, it is necessary that the person involved shall see the significance of, or the relation between, the object and the situation that is presented.

As an example, let us take some instances of the use of tools by the lower animals. In one of a series of brilliant experiments carried out by Köhler the following situation was described.[25] Outside of a cage and beyond the reach of a chimpanzee housed in the cage there is placed the desired piece of food. Within the cage there is a stick. If the chimpanzee is to get the food, it is necessary that it shall see the relation between the use of its arms for the purpose of reaching, on the one hand, and the position of the food, on the other. When chimpanzees were confronted with this situation almost all of them were able to solve the problem by grasping the stick and using it as a tool for the purpose of drawing the food within reach. The subjects were most successful when the stick lay within the same field of vision as did the food. If, however, the stick were placed at the back of the cage where the chimpanzee could not see it without turning away from the food, the problem became much more difficult. In this case, it was required of the subject that the stick which might occupy a prominent place in one perceptual pattern had to be taken out of that pattern after the pattern itself had been replaced by a new pattern, viz., the one containing the food. The ability to do this is so important a feature of human modes of thinking that we shall give closer attention to it in a moment.

Sometimes chimpanzees are able actually to manufacture a tool if nothing appropriate is already at hand. In one of Köhler's experiments, for example, the cage contained the branch of a tree. In this case the solution of the problem could be achieved only if the chimpanzee were able to fashion a tool by breaking off a part of one of the branches, and using it as a stick.[26] The problem of creating a tool can be made still more difficult by placing within the cage two shorter sticks, neither one of which is long enough to reach the food. Or it may be that a short stick can be placed within the cage and a long stick outside of the cage. In this case the chimpanzee would have to use the short stick in order to draw in the long stick before the food could be reached. In the former case, the

[25] Köhler, W., *op. cit.*, pp. 69 ff.
[26] *Ibid.*, pp. 103 ff.

THE DEVELOPMENT OF PROBLEM-SOLVING 231

chimpanzee would be required to fit the two sticks together in such a way that a long stick could be created out of two pieces. The sticks used in these experiments were bamboo poles and had been chosen in such a manner that the end of the smaller one could be fitted into the opening in the larger.

The first solution of this problem came apparently quite by accident, but on subsequent occasions the subjects not only fitted two sticks together in this manner but where a proper fit was not possible, the end of the smaller stick was chewed off until it did fit into the larger one. It seems clear from these experiments, then, that chimpanzees at least can put objects in such a relation to a stimulus-pattern that they will become useful as tools or instruments for reaching an objective not otherwise attainable.

Behavior of this type is, of course, fairly common at the human level. It is revealed over and over again in the play activities of children, where building blocks and other objects are used in clever ways.[27] We could, if we had the time, review the psychological side of the whole history of human invention in order to show how relations between objects which cannot be acquired by learning have suddenly appeared and led to the discovery of a new tool. Some features of the history of invention will be discussed below, but in this connection it should be remembered that inventions may be made not only with respect to mechanical devices but with respect to methods of work as well. If a man devises a new method of working, he has created just as significant an invention as he has if he discovers some new medium that will effect contact between himself and some object or situation around him. We may say, then, that any statement of the nature of problem-solving must take account of the invention and the use of tools.[28]

3. *The Delayed Reaction:* We have already considered another type of performance which stands close to problem-solving and which may have an intimate bearing upon the frequency with which the problem-solving attitude is taken. We refer here to the ability displayed by all human beings and by some of the lower animals as well whenever they react to an object which has once been present but which at the time of the reaction is actually absent.

The simplest instances of behavior of this type come from what are known as delayed reaction experiments among the lower ani-

---

[27] Cf. Curti, M. W., *Child Psychology.* New York: Longmans, Green and Co., 1931, Chapter IX.
[28] Cf. Mumford, L., *Technics and Civilization.* New York: Harcourt, Brace and Co., 1934, *passim.*

mals.[29] Let us say, for example, that a white rat has learned to know that food is always to be found in that box of a group of three or more which is lighted. This skill can usually be acquired rather quickly. During the training period, one box out of the group is lighted, whereupon the subject is permitted to explore until it has learned to accept the light as a sign or signal of the presence of food. Now, however, let us suppose that the subject is retained in the starting box while the food box is lighted, and that it is also retained in the starting box for a given period of time after the light has been extinguished. The question put up to the rat is whether or not it can still go directly to its food. If it does not, we may draw the inference that it has no machinery for reacting to an object which, though present but a moment before, is now actually absent. On the contrary, if the rat is able to find its food, we must conclude that it does have some machinery by means of which adequate reactions to an absent object are made possible.

In the experimental situation just described, it was found that white rats could react adequately to the food box if the interval between the moment when the light was extinguished and the moment when the rat was released from the starting box did not exceed ten seconds.[30] It was noted, however, that the subject was more apt to be successful if, during the ten-second interval, its body remained orientated toward the food box. If, during the ten-second interval, the rat changed its position, it was very apt to make a mistake. It was inferred, therefore, that the white rat could react to an absent object with the help of a bodily set or posture.

When the same experiment was carried out with some of the higher animals as subjects, it was discovered that such postures or sets were not at all necessary. To be sure, the subjects were greatly helped if the head were properly orientated; but even this partial posture was not essential to success.[31] The higher the animal the longer the interval could be between the extinction of the light and the release from the starting box. Moreover, the higher the animal the less frequently the subject was forced to depend upon some posture or set of the body which could be observed by the experimenter. In later experiments on the white rat it was discovered that even these subjects could exceed the ten-second interval named

---

[29] Cf. Munn, N. L., *Animal Psychology*. Boston: Houghton Mifflin Co., 1933, pp. 357 ff.

[30] Hunter, W. S., "Delayed Reaction in Animals and Children." *Behav. Monog.*, 1913, II (No. 6).

[31] Loucks, R. B., "Efficacy of the Rat's Motor Cortex in Delayed Alternation." *J. Comp. Neurol.*, 1931, LIII, 277-305.

at first. It was also discovered that postures or sets of the body, observable to the experimenter, might undergo even major modification without hindering the performance.[32]

Behavior of this type is, of course, a very common feature of all human action. There is, however, a great difference between human beings and the lower animals. As we have seen, the interval during which an object may be absent in the case of a white rat, if it is to react to the object, is fairly short. Chimpanzees can carry out actions of this type after several hours have elapsed. In our own cases, however, there appears to be no time limit. Small children resemble animals because the interval between the stimulus and the response must also be short, but after the sixth or eighth year the interval increases very rapidly so that a mature person seems to be freed altogether from any dependence upon the time factor.

Sometimes we speak of behavior of this type as the result of the great debt we owe to our past experience. As a rule, no human being can react again to an object that was presented to him at some time prior to his third year. We express this fact by saying that we have few memories which extend beyond the third year. Then, too, there are always some experiences which, for all intents and purposes, are forgotten, but there is plenty of evidence to show that forgetting of this type is only a practical forgetting rather than a real loss of ability to behave in response to objects that are no longer present. The only instances where such loss really seems to be permanent lies in the various forms of aphasia.

We may, then, accept the ability to respond to objects which are not present at the moment of response as a characteristic feature not only of human but of animal behavior as well. This much is easily determined. It is quite a different matter, however, to describe the machinery by means of which such behavior becomes possible. Older theories of human nature handled the problem very well. It was said by them that any sense impressions made upon the sensory apparatus would be conducted into the central nervous system whereupon they could be converted into memory images or into ideas. If, then, an animal could have ideas left over from his past experience, these ideas, upon revival, might serve as internal sources of behavior. In the case of the white rat in the delayed reaction experiment, for example, we might say that the rat can still find its way to the food box because an idea of the location of the food box remains in the mind of the animal after the "real" food

---

[32] Cf. Honzik, C. H., "Delayed Reactions in Rats." *Univ. Calif. Publ. Psychol.*, 1931, IV, 307-318.

box has disappeared. Such a theory would make it possible to describe two kinds of actions, viz., those that are perceptual or sensori-motor and those that are ideational or ideomotor. The student will find, therefore, a great many references to ideomotor action and to ideomotor learning in most of the books which he reads.[33]

This theory would serve very well to account for our responses to objects that are not present, if some way could be found to explain how sense impressions in the sense organs or nervous currents in a nervous system could be translated into memory images or into ideas. If an explanation for this fact could be discovered, then the same explanation might be used to show how it happens that an idea or a cluster of memory images which, by definition, are mental in character could have an effect upon the motor nerves and thus produce action.

This is not the place, however, to enter into a detailed discussion of a very difficult problem in psychology. The student must be satisfied to have the question settled for him by the statement that all of the experimental evidence which is now available supports the conclusion that memory images and ideas are not mental entities which can exist apart from events that have taken place in the nervous system.[34] This conclusion requires that we look at the nervous events themselves in order to see whether they are actually adequate to account for the behavior which has been observed under experimental conditions.[35]

For this purpose, let us look again at the behavior of the white rat in the delayed reaction experiment. Let us suppose that the words "posture," "set," or "orientation" may refer not only to an actual overt posture of the whole body or to some particular part of the body, but that they may refer also to implicit postures, the best examples of which are to be found in the use of the verbal apparatus. As the reader already knows, if he were placed in a situation like that in which the white rat is placed, he would, during the interval between the stimulus and the opportunity for making a response, say to himself, either out loud or by implicit speech (that is, in thought), that the "box in which the food is placed is the second one to the left." If he were to use implicit language habits for

[33] Cf. Thorndike, E. L., "Ideo-motor Action." *Psychol. Rev.*, 1913, XX, 91-106; James, W., *Principles of Psychology.* New York: Henry Holt and Co., 1890. Vol. II, pp. 522 ff.
[34] Cf. Lindworsky, J., *Experimental Psychology.* New York: The Macmillan Co., 1931, pp. 208 ff. Also Fox, C., *The Mind and its Body.* New York: Harcourt, Brace and Co., 1932, *passim.*
[35] Cf. Hunter, W. S., *op. cit., passim* and especially pp. 20-21 ff.

THE DEVELOPMENT OF PROBLEM-SOLVING 235

this purpose no experimenter would be able to tell whether he had been postured or set toward the food box or not. As matters stand, however, when the opportunity for action actually arises the situation becomes a sign or signal for a revival of the former verbal posture, viz., "The food box is the second one to the left." The person, then, would go directly to that box.

This explanation of the way in which reactions to objects not actually present take place in human beings does not, at first sight, appear applicable to such an animal as the white rat because commonsense tells us that it does not use its vocal apparatus for this purpose. It is a mistake to suppose, however, that the verbal apparatus is the only device that can be used in this symbolical way.[36] As a matter of fact, almost any group of muscles can thus be used, and it is even possible that there are some conditions under which the nervous system itself can be prepared to react in one way rather than in another. It will hardly be possible, however, to complete this discussion of the use of words or "thoughts" until we have described certain other types of behavior which stand near true problem-solving.

4. *The Field of Thinking:* We may now bring these several considerations together in order to see how they locate the general area of events within which true problem-solving will take place. Let us say that we have before us some particular person or some particular animal subject. The subject is in the presence of a whole series of environmental objects or events which may become sources of action to him. Under normal conditions, there will be certain parts of this total environmental pattern which will be more effective than other parts in initiating and regulating behavior at any particular moment. In addition to all of the objects and events that are actually present, some of them, by virtue of past experience or by virtue of learning, will have become signs of the existence of other objects which are not actually present or which cannot occur until some future moment.

In addition to the objects that are actually present or which are pointed toward or signified by these objects, there is another whole class of objects which are merely symbolized by sets or postures of the body and especially by explicit and implicit movements in the vocal apparatus. In the case of a human subject, the number and variety of these symbolized objects will be just as large as one's vocabulary or as one's memories. The student knows these objects

[36] Cf. Hunter, W. S., *Human Behavior.* Chicago: Univ. of Chicago Press, 1928, pp. 67 ff.

as ideas. Although our own preference has been to think of ideas in terms of speech reactions or, certainly, as intimately dependent upon speech reactions, it is not necessary to decide one way or the other as far as a discussion of the general area is concerned within which problem-solving can take place.

Now these three classes of objects constitute all of the objects which either directly or indirectly can become sources of action for any particular person. The point we are making will become a little clearer, perhaps, if we state the situation as some of the older psychologies would state it. According to an older point of view, we may think of any subject as being surrounded by a large number of objects and events which are recognized as existing outside of the subject himself and which have become truly environmental in the sense that they can, whenever attention or interest shifts in their direction, become sources of action. In addition to all of these objects and events, however, the older psychologies would say that there is a whole array of mental objects or of ideated objects. These are objects which were said to exist in one's own head. They are the objects which one observes in daydreaming, in imagination, in the making of plans for the morrow, or even in thinking. Now from this same point of view the two groups of objects which we have named, that is, those outside of the body which are called real, plus those inside of the body which are called mental, make up all of the objects with which human beings can become familiar. The principal difference between this older way of describing the nature of objects lies in the fact that the class known as mental objects is now being described in terms of implicit verbal speech or in terms of other postures, sets, or attitudes.[37]

Now let us suppose that a subject who is potentially acquainted with a considerable number of objects of the type described above, begins to respond to them. Since all of them are already attached by suitable nervous connections to adequate modes of response, the person of whom we are speaking would get along very well in the world that he knows providing none of the objects ever came to his attention in any other temporal order or in any other spatial pattern than those in which they were originally placed. In order to illustrate what we mean, let us return again to the chimpanzee which is required to get food which lies beyond its reach. The normal response to food would, of course, consist in making those move-

---

[37] Cf. Hunter, W. S., "Anthroponomy and Psychology," in Murchison, C. (Ed.), *Psychologies of 1930*. Worcester, Mass.: Clark Univ. Press, 1930, Chapter XIV, especially pp. 292 ff.

THE DEVELOPMENT OF PROBLEM-SOLVING 237

ments which are necessary to seize it and to swallow it. Even when the food is too far to be reached, normal conditions might enable the chimpanzee to run along the ground, climb out on a limb, or swing from one branch to another. It happens, however, that the chimpanzee is behind the bars of the cage. The food cannot be reached. This is a situation for which the animal has no previously acquired mode of response. It is a situation which may never have appeared before. Obviously, a chimpanzee would not be able to get its food unless it could make use of some hitherto undescribed form of behavior.

In order to see what this behavior is, let us turn our attention for a moment to the stick that lies on the ground in the cage. The stick, likewise being a familiar object to the chimpanzee, has had attached to it by previous training more or less appropriate modes of response. It is, at the very least, an object that can be grasped or that can be thrown. Up to this point, however, it is not an object that can be used in order to get food. With more or less speed, however, the stick is actually transformed from something to be handled or thrown into an object that can be used as a tool in order to reach food. In other words, a long piece of wood lying on the ground and otherwise closely tied into a particular perceptual pattern is suddenly lifted out of that pattern and put into a significant relation with another object which likewise has been lifted out of its particular context and given a new signifying function.[38]

It is in this situation that we discover the essential nature of problem-solving. In other words, problem-solving occurs when some object of either of the classes described above is taken out of the particular configuration in which it has always appeared and united into a new configuration with some object which likewise has hitherto remained within its own configuration. A stick which heretofore has remained merely as an object of regard or as something to be grasped or thrown suddenly acquires a new meaning. This new meaning makes of it an instrument or a tool by which food can be gained.[39] Likewise the food becomes food that can be got with the aid of a stick.

There are several words in common use which we freely apply to events of this type. When, for example, we suddenly see a relationship between two objects or two situations which has not been

[38] Cf. Koffka, K., *The Growth of the Mind*. New York: Harcourt, Brace and Co., 1924, pp. 179 ff.
[39] Cf. Wheeler, R. H., and Perkins, F. T., *Principles of Mental Development*. New York: T. Y. Crowell Co., 1932, Chapter XX. For further information, see Munn, N. L., *op. cit.*, Chapter VII.

in existence before, we frequently report that we have had a "hunch." Many a student has reported, after a long period spent in the review of a set of facts, and upon describing a peculiar event that may have taken place during his period of study, "All of a sudden it occurred to me that . . ." or, "Just at that point the notion struck me that . . ."

In a later chapter, we shall have occasion to describe more fully this speedy feature of problem-solving. We shall find that it is related to a type of learning now known as learning by insight. This phrase refers to that stage in the total process of learning when a relationship between situations which hitherto have been wholly divorced from one another suddenly emerges. In the case of learning how to get out of a puzzle box, for example, the animal subject makes a great many different types of movement. Let us assume that all of these movements are in response to some phase of the stimulus-situation, save that they coalesce with one another because of the high motivation induced by hunger and because of the presence of emotional factors. During the course of these random movements, one of them becomes effective or adequate in the sense that it opens the door and the animal is able, therefore, to get to the food. From this time forward, the amount of time required for the solution of the problem and the number of errors made become markedly less. There are even occasions when the number of errors decreases to zero almost immediately. Such results can be achieved, of course, only if the subject has "seen" the significance of the button on the door or the string hanging from the middle of the box. This significance converts the button or the string into a tool which can be used to open a door or lead to food.[40] In other words, even "trial-and-error" learning sometimes gives the appearance of yielding insights.

We are now in a position to draw an important distinction between three processes, viz., true problem-solving, ordinary learning, and that type of operation known as logical discourse or logical thought. True problem-solving we have defined as a more or less quick appreciation of the relationship between situations or parts of situations which hitherto have not been related to each other. Learning, on the other hand, may be either (i) a process by means of which previous acts of learning are conjoined into a more complex pattern, or (ii) a process by means of which a newly discovered movement system may be brought to a higher level of skill or

[40] See the criticism of Thorndike's explanation of animal learning in Koffka, K., *op. cit.*, pp. 159 ff.

THE DEVELOPMENT OF PROBLEM-SOLVING 239

efficiency through continued practice, or (iii) a process by means of which one object or event may become a signal for the existence of another or for its subsequent appearance. It is this third form of learning which resembles most nearly true problem-solving.[41]

Under ordinary school conditions, however, sign learning is not a consequence of insights which the students themselves have achieved but a result of teaching methods which already name for the student the signs which any given object should have. As an example, let us take once more the Pythagorean theorem. It would be possible to teach this particular segment of geometry by laying before the student in appropriate places and at appropriate times all of the preliminary stimulus-patterns that must have been present before the theorem actually occurred to Pythagoras. That is, all of the significant facts might be presented to the student so that he too might have an insight, that is, make a sudden discovery or see, for the first time, a series of relationships which hitherto had not obtained for him.

As most teaching actually goes, however, the theorem is learned by quite other methods. As a matter of fact, the theorem is actually stated as the result of someone else's discovery, and then the student is required to learn the logical steps by means of which the discovery can be proved. Neither a statement of the theory nor the learning of a series of logical steps, however, is equivalent to the emergence of a form of relatedness between hitherto unrelated items. This means that, as the student learns the various steps in the proof of the theorem, one step becomes a sign for the next, not because these signs have been discovered, but because he has been told that that is what they mean.

It is at this point that learning by insight or true problem-solving differs markedly from logical thought. As an illustration we may take the experience of a famous mathematician, Poincaré, who reports that as he was about to step into an omnibus, it suddenly occurred to him that there are certain significant relationships between two sets of equations known to mathematicians as the Fuchsian equations, on the one hand, and some of the non-Euclidean geometries, on the other.[42] This sudden "hunch" which Poincaré reports became the starting point for a long series of mathematical studies. In the papers which Poincaré has published bearing upon

[41] See the discussion of theories of learning by Tolman, E. C., in Moss, F. A. (Ed.), *Comparative Psychology*. New York: Prentice-Hall, Inc., 1934, Chapter XII.
[42] Poincaré, H., *The Foundations of Science*. New York: The Science Press, 1929, pp. ix ff.

these researches, there is, of course, a great deal of logical discourse. Poincaré lays down certain propositions and draws inferences, which, in their turn, become propositions for further inferences, and so on. If, then, one were to take the published papers of Poincaré as a description of the psychological events that occurred when the basis for these papers was laid, it would appear that much thinking must be of the logical type. There is, however, a very great difference between the logical discourses which Poincaré used in order to prove his discoveries to other people and the actual events which occurred when the discoveries were made. Let us infer, then, that the real essence of problem-solving is to be found in the insight or the hunch rather than in the methods that are used to prove the essential correctness of an insight or a hunch to some other person.

One of the first functions of logical discourse is to create beliefs rather than to discover new knowledge. This is not to say, of course, that a person may not, during a period of logical thinking, see more or less suddenly, types of relatedness which have not occurred to him before. It is even possible that, during a period of random daydreaming, insights of the greatest importance may appear. One cannot be certain of one's insights, however, until they lead to conviction, that is, until it has been shown that they will actually work.

In an illuminating experiment, for example, where there was no stick in the cage, the chimpanzee undertook to drag the food within reach by breaking off some of the fronds from a potted palm.[43] The fronds, of course, were too light to move the food and the chimpanzee had recourse, therefore, to a rug which was thrown over the food. The rug worked, whereas the fronds did not. If we could credit a chimpanzee with states of conviction or belief, it might be fair to say that it would believe in the rug but not in the fronds.

At a more complex level, the question as to whether or not an insight or a relationship will work depends upon a tremendous number of other factors. It is one of the functions of logic to test insights in order to see whether they are actually useful. A great many people, of course, have insights or see relations that will not stand serious examination and they must, therefore, be laid aside. Since men of science and philosophers are extremely careful in checking up on their insights, it is natural that they should lay con-

---

[43] An extremely interesting and suggestive study of experiments like these on an ape brought up under surroundings equivalent to a home is furnished by Kellogg, W. N., and Kellogg, L. A., *The Ape and the Child*. New York: McGraw-Hill Book Co., 1933. This book is heartily to be recommended to teachers who are interested in the genetic phases of their work.

THE DEVELOPMENT OF PROBLEM-SOLVING

siderable emphasis upon a logical procedure that will demonstrate the truth or the value of a discovery.[44] In short, then, logical demonstration is a necessary consequence to discovery, but this is not to say that the primary function of the teacher, so far as problem-solving is concerned, is to show students how to prove the validity of their discoveries. The most important thing is to teach them how to make discoveries.

III. THE BASES OF PROBLEM-SOLVING

1. *Introduction:* This has been a long and in some places difficult statement of the nature of problem-solving, but the study which we are now going to make of the circumstances under which problem-solving may be trained or developed would not be convincing unless the student could get a good picture of the situation out of which insights actually arise.

If we can look back over the last section with an eye to the section as a whole, we ought to be able to see one fundamental picture, viz., that problem-solving takes place whenever any two situations, objects, inferences, signs, or concepts are brought together into a configuration which hitherto has not been in existence.[45] Let us simplify the picture in the following way. Suppose we were to forget that there is any such thing as remembering; that is, suppose we were to assume that, once an experienced object had been present, it continued to remain present as a part of our external environments. This means that the environment, as we commonly know it, would contain not only the objects which are being perceived at this particular moment, but also all of the objects and all of the relationships between objects which have been perceived in times past. Now, as we have said above, there could be no problem-solving if these objects never appeared to us in any other configuration or in any other temporal sequence than that in which they first appeared. This simply means that all experienced objects or all experienced clusters of objects, both spatial clusters and temporal clusters, would have become related to types of action that would be more or less appropriate to them.

This situation is not changed even though we recognize the fact that some objects are objective whereas others appear to be mental. There are, however, several reasons why such a situation does not obtain. In the first place, no matter how long a person lives, he will

---

[44] Cf. Carmichael, R. D., *op. cit., passim.*
[45] Koffka, K., *op. cit.,* Chapter IV.

never have seen everything there is to see. This means that there will always be objects and situations for which there are no previously acquired pattern of response.

In the second place, objects are continually shifting their spatial locations. We have only to think of the rapidly shifting positions of a group of cars on a highway in order to remind ourselves of an immense number of other respects in which the spatial configurations of objects are changing. This means that clusters of objects will always appear, even to the most experienced of persons, which have not appeared before in that particular configuration. If we are to react adequately to them, it may be required of us that we integrate them or discover new types of relationship in them which are not obvious at the start.

In the third place, objects and situations are continually changing their pattern as far as temporal order of presentation is concerned. Some event which has, on one occasion, occurred before another may, on a subsequent occasion, occur after the other. Here, too, a new total situation is created and it may be required of us, before we can react to it adequately, that we discover relationships between the parts of it which have remained obscure.

2. *Freedom from a Temporal Order:* All of these considerations hold true, in particular, of that class of objects which, for the sake of simplicity, we have called mental objects. More than one person has called attention to the fact that the brain is a device which frees man in a unique way from the temporal order.[46] A part of this freedom is secured by memory because memory means that, instead of going back to the scenes of former experience, we can carry these scenes with us. Freedom from temporal sequence is also furnished by sign learning which enables us to take a present situation or a present object as a portend of the future.

As a rule, the experimental scientist is a man who does a very large amount of his thinking in conjunction with the discovery of relatednesses in the objects that are actually before him. The philosopher, however, carries the world outside of him into his study. To be sure, he surrounds himself with a great many books and other sources of suggestion about information that he may have forgotten. The psychological operations, however, which the two men use in their thinking are fundamentally alike, for the one is coming upon unexpected relationships between perceptually sensed objects

---

[46] For a good discussion of this feature of behavior, see Haldane, J. S., *The Sciences and Philosophy*. Garden City: Doubleday, Doran and Co., 1929, Chapter IX.

THE DEVELOPMENT OF PROBLEM-SOLVING 243

whereas the other is coming upon unexpected relationships between ideationally sensed objects. If either of these two men were limited to worlds in which the spatial and temporal configurations of objects were absolutely fixed, there would neither be any occasion for problem-solving nor for the existence of discoveries that might demand an explanation.[47]

3. *Teaching Problem-Solving:* Now we must turn from the nature of problem-solving to those features of the whole process which can be modified or controlled by the teacher in order to bring a child to greater excellence. We do not mean to say by this that problem-solving is a faculty which we can develop and which we can then use as we might grasp a tool in order to turn out a certain product. It is more nearly the truth, perhaps, that insights are something that happen to a person rather than something for which he definitely goes in search. In other words, no student can simply sit down in a chair and say either to himself or to the world at large, "Go to, now, I will have a thought." On the contrary, he must learn how to use himself and the situations around him in such a way that insights will emerge. It is in this respect that the teacher can be of great aid, for just as it is his business to outline the conditions under which other features of the growth pattern flourish, so he must furnish the conditions under which insights can appear. What, then, can the teacher in the schoolroom do in order to prepare the way for discoveries?

A. CURIOSITY: One of the first items to be considered is not so much a duty placed upon the teacher as it is a special aptitude which students are said to possess, for there are some persons who suppose that the beginnings of problem-solving rest in a special instinct known as curiosity. This instinct has had its origin, of course, partly in the behavior of animals which are known to be attracted by lights, colors, or by other unusual objects, and partly by the common tendency among children to tear things apart, to ask numerous questions, and otherwise to pry into the situations around them.

Outside of these commonsense observations, there seems to be no substantial basis for saying that there is a special instinct of curiosity which will lead inevitably to problem-solving. If an animal is attracted by an object, we may simply say that this object has, for the moment, become prepotent over other objects in directing the postures or even the actions of the animal. In the case of curious children, it is possible to appeal to normal processes of motivation rather than to a special instinct. If a child asks a great many

[47] Cf. Dewey, J., *op. cit.,* Part II, *passim.*

questions, or if it is persistent in tearing things apart in order to see how they are made, or if it goes exploring all over the neighborhood, it must do so because some primary or secondary desire can be satisfied by these measures. In short, if curiosity marks a starting point for problem-solving, we must use the word only to name a whole cluster of results achieved by motivated conduct or by the operation of the conditions which give rise to acts of attention and to interests.

From one point of view, of course, a week-old infant may be said to be curious about a bright light or about a rustling paper. We describe its behavior as an act of curiosity rather than as an act of attention or of interest because the bright light or the rustling paper may remain prepotent over other sources of stimulus for a fairly long period of time. As the child grows older, its parents, its teachers, and its playmates furnish plenty of sources of satisfaction as a consequence of asking questions and of prying into the objects around it.

Not a great deal of experimental work has been done on the development of curiosity, except as curiosity represents one feature of interest. Even in these cases, however, the attempt has been made to detect the presence or absence of curiosity rather than to trace the conditions under which it develops.[48]

B. MEANINGS: The function of the teacher in the promotion of problem-solving appears much more clearly in connection with the development of meanings and with the creation of verbal substitutes for meanings. As we have seen, meanings may be of two types, viz., the primary and the secondary. Primary meanings are created simply by converting larger and larger portions of the irrelevant segment of the environment of the child into relevant or effective segments. The student will recall that these two phases of environmental situations are distinguished from each other because relevant environmental objects or situations can really become effective in initiating and directing the course of action. This process goes on with great speed throughout the whole period of development. So, too, does the process of discovering adequate verbal symbols for primary meanings.

Secondary meanings are made up of the objects or events which are pointed to or signified by primary meanings. When we say that a cloud may become a sign of rain, the cloud itself is a primary meaning whereas the signified rain may be a secondary meaning.

---

[48] Cf. Bühler, C., *Kindheit und Jugend* (3rd ed.). Leipzig: Hirtel, 1931, pp. 216 ff., and *passim*.

THE DEVELOPMENT OF PROBLEM-SOLVING 245

A cloud may acquire a great many other secondary meanings. It can signify or point toward a change in one's plans for the day or a change in the weather other than that leading toward rain. It is one of the chief functions of learning to see to it that primary objects shall be given as many secondary meanings as possible. The study of the nature of problem-solving which we have made in the last section indicates clearly enough that the opportunity for seeing relations between different stimulus-patterns must increase in direct proportion as these patterns are enriched in their pointing or their signifying value.[49]

The most important phase of the development of meanings, both of the primary and of the secondary types, lies in connection with those features of objects and events which are named by such words as "concept formation," "abstraction," "discrimination," and "comparison." All of these words refer to different phases of the same series of operations. As we have seen in an earlier chapter, children make most of their responses to objects as objects. They possess a very scanty ability to react effectively to those respects in which a variety of objects may resemble one another, even though small differences obtain between them.

Among the concepts which are most familiar in the schoolroom are those of number and other abstractions such as beauty, truth, size, distance, time, goodness, and the like. It must be clear, of course, that before such concepts can be created, children must be fairly advanced in their ability to discriminate particulars out of a larger configuration, draw comparisons between these particulars, and discover, amid differences, those respects in which a variety of objects resemble one another.[50]

For each of these phases of the relevant environment, adequate verbal symbols must be acquired. As we have implied above, the total effect of these types of learning is tremendously to widen the field within which new types of relatedness can occur. Processes of learning see to it that we acquire modes of reaction to a great many particulars in an entire environmental field, but if the environmental field were to remain wholly stable, both in its spatial and in its temporal arrangement, there would be no demand upon the child for further learning. We have tried to show above, however, that

---

[49] Cf. Bode, B. H., *Conflicting Psychologies of Learning*. Boston: D. C. Heath and Co., 1929, Chapter XV. Also, Bode, B. H., "Consciousness and Psychology," in Dewey, J., *et al.*, *Creative Intelligence*. New York: Henry Holt and Co., 1917, Chapter V.

[50] The best treatment of some of these concepts has been given by Judd, C. H., *The Psychology of Social Institutions*. New York: The Macmillan Co., 1926, *passim*.

the environmental field is not stable in its spatial and in its temporal arrangement. New situations are constantly being presented to every person. These situations cannot be handled effectively unless their various parts are brought together in a significant relation to one another.

It is sometimes remarked that there is a very great difference between concrete thinking, that is, problem-solving in the presence of concrete situations, as opposed to abstract thinking, that is, problem-solving with respect to ideational situations. As we have already pointed out, the difference between these two types of thinking must be a difference created only by a difference in the types of objects contemplated.[51] In the one case, the objects are truly environmental, in the sense that they lie outside of the thinker; in the other case, the objects are "mental," in the sense that they are remembered or that they are revived with the aid of implicit speech.

It is important to note that both of these types of thinking can go on to best advantage only if the objective environment, on the one hand, and the domain of "mental objects," on the other, are supported by as many aids to memory as possible. To be sure, a philosopher may sit down in the quiet of his study in order to solve problems without the help of such stimulus-patterns as would favor the recall of forgotten facts. Even the philosopher, however, surrounds himself with a good many books, index cards, notes, and appropriate objects and events which will aid him in laying out an environmental field within which new types of relatedness may have a chance to emerge.

C. GUIDANCE IN THINKING: Let us conclude, then, that a teacher may render a great service to the development of problem-solving by acting as a manipulator of appropriate stimulus-situations. In the classroom, for example, it is the teacher's function to place materials on the blackboard, recite groups of facts, assign readings or excite discussions which will widen the environmental field beyond the limits ordinarily made possible by single acts of attention or by limited interests. As we have seen in one of our illustrations above, some chimpanzees were able to solve the problem of getting food which lay beyond reach only when the stick to be used was placed within the same field of vision with the fruit. In other words, the experimenter in this case had promoted the possibility of problem-solving by arranging the whole stimulus-pattern in such a way that a new type of relatedness could hardly fail to appear.

The teacher is in a similar position. It is his task to arrange

[51] Cf. Dewey, J., *op. cit.*, Part Three, *passim.*

THE DEVELOPMENT OF PROBLEM-SOLVING 247

stimulus-situations in such a way that similar types of relatedness will be promoted. To be sure, he can go to an extreme by pointing out the relatedness in advance of its discovery by the child. If he were to do this, he would be like the experimenter who would go so far as to press the stick in the hand of the chimpanzee and actually help it use the stick in reaching for the food. It is to be doubted, however, whether this method will actually promote an attitude on the part of any learner which would be favorable to high degrees of independence in discovering relationships for himself.[52]

D. FAULTS IN TEACHING: It is at this point that so many methods of teaching can be criticized because of their failure to make due allowance for the development of problem-solving. Instead of preparing situations so that relationships will easily emerge, teachers are inclined to furnish not only the situations but all of the relationships as well. They do this, in part, because their classes are so large that they cannot spend the time that is necessary to create a problem-exciting situation; in part, because they have been overinfluenced by the laws of learning which have seemed to simplify so greatly the complexities of teaching procedure; in part, because it has been supposed that the growth pattern can be brought to completion through the use of learning situations alone; in part, because most teachers, especially in the elementary grades and in the high schools, have to carry a very heavy teaching load; and, in part, because there is really a dearth of active intellectual interest among teachers themselves.

It is obvious that, if teachers ask questions in such a way that an adequate answer can be given simply by word of mouth, that is, because the answer has already been written out and learned by the student, nothing is really gained save an additional piece of rote memory information. To be sure, the addition of such information is, as we have tried to say above, one of the fundamental prerequisites for problem-solving, but this fact marks, by no means, the end of the obligations which are placed upon the teacher so far as the promotion of growth in all of its dimensions is concerned.

E. CONFIGURATIONAL COMPACTNESS: If the real nature of problem-solving is described by the fact that some part or phase of one configuration of events must be lifted out of its particular configuration and placed into a new setting with another part or phase of a totally different configuration of events, an obstacle in the way of problem-solving may be created by the tightness or compactness with

[52] Cf. Koffka, K., *The Growth of the Mind*. New York: Harcourt, Brace and Co., 1924, pp. 314-319 and *passim*.

which the parts are imbedded in the original situations. As an illustration of this fact, we may take the achievement of the chimpanzee in breaking off a branch of a tree in order to make a tool out of it. Under ordinary conditions a branch is so intimately a part of a total configuration that we might not concede enough ability to a chimpanzee to extract it from the context in which it has been placed.

An experimenter might make this problem much more difficult by erecting a latticework along the back wall of the cage. The chances are that the various pieces of wood used in this latticework would be so deeply imbedded in the total lattice configuration that no chimpanzee could possibly "think" of disrupting the configuration by taking a single piece from it. A human being, however, would probably think of this device for solving his problem. We may infer, then, that a teacher must use a great deal of skill when he manufactures total fields of a problem-solving type. If the field contains configurations which are compact in the sense that the parts of a given field cannot easily be extracted from the whole field, the problem will not be solved.[53]

As an illustration of this feature of teaching, let us take some of the difficulties that face a detective when he tries to solve a crime. The whole field of objects before him is made up of his numerous clews. As every reader of fiction knows, the author can easily describe a set of circumstances in which an essential clew is so deeply buried as totally to escape both the observation of the reader and the observation of the detective. It may turn out that the solution of the whole crime depends upon the ability of the detective finally to see the relationship between one particular phase of a set of circumstances and all of the other clews that have been assembled from other sources.[54]

We may, if we wish, think of a teacher as though he were the author of a detective story. It is his business to furnish students with as many of the clews as are necessary to solve the "crime." The students are the detectives. They have been thrown into a problem-solving attitude by the very perplexity or the lack of meaning embodied in the various facts presented. The teacher may, of course, write a poor story, that is, an impossible story, because he has left some of the clews so tightly imbedded in a larger configuration of facts that students simply cannot extract the parts out of the whole. It is at this point that the real effectiveness of a teacher, so

[53] Cf. Wheeler, R. H., and Perkins, F. T., *Principles of Mental Development.* New York: T. Y. Crowell Co., 1932, Chapter XX.
[54] Dewey, J., *op. cit.,* Chapter I.

THE DEVELOPMENT OF PROBLEM-SOLVING 249

far as problem-solving is concerned, will be revealed. He must keep himself sensitive to the relative compactness of whole groups of facts and where the compactness is too great he must modify the situation accordingly.

This feature of teaching skill is so important that we can afford, perhaps, to give one more illustration of it.[55] Let us suppose that an experimenter has just placed a rat which has never had any dealings with a complex maze in the starting box to the maze. At the end of the maze there is a liberal supply of food. The rat is hungry. In other words, it is motivated to behavior with respect to the situation presented. Now this situation is, of course, a problem to the experimenter. He sees that the rat is at the beginning of a series of pathways, some of which lead into blind alleys, whereas others lead to the goal.

Obviously, however, this is not a problem for the rat. After a few trials, however, it does become a problem. The experimenter himself might make it a problem by furnishing some of the essential clews. He might, for example, allow a rat to explore the maze rather freely before the real test series begins. He might even allow the rat to find food in various portions of the maze. One of the functions of preliminary trials of this sort is to give direction to the hunger motive.

Now if we may apply these same considerations to an actual teaching situation, we may say that teachers often present problematic situations to their pupils which are problematic to the teacher but cannot possibly be problematic to the pupil. Artistry in handling such a situation would require that the teacher furnish not only a problematic situation but a sufficient number of clews to give direction to the pupils.

F. FREQUENCY OF PROBLEM-SITUATIONS: These considerations lead us naturally to another phase of teaching skill so far as problem-solving is concerned. Obviously, if students are to learn what the problem-solving attitude is and if they are to grow more mature in using problem-solving methods rather than other methods for handling situations, they must be faced with problematic or perplexing situations as frequently as possible.[56] To be sure, not all teaching can be of this type. The number of things that have to be learned by any person who wishes to take a part in our own com-

---

[55] Cf. Köhler, W., *Gestalt Psychology.* New York: Liveright Publishing Corp., 1929, *passim.*
[56] Cf. Watson, J. B., *Psychological Care of the Infant and Child.* New York: W. W. Norton and Co., 1928, *passim.*

plex society is simply immense. As a matter of fact, the number is so great that teachers have usually resorted to sheer processes of learning out of self-defense. They have found it easy to set up learning situations and to measure the results of learning situations simply by counting the number of correct responses that can be made to a variety of questions.

One must, of course, have a good deal of sympathy with the teacher whenever this method is chosen; but clearly it is not a method which promotes in any way whatsoever the problem-solving attitude or disposition. It seems reasonable to expect, therefore, that in schoolroom procedure, a greater effort should be made to convert at least a few learning situations into problematic situations. To say the same thing in another way, there is nothing gained either by the student or by the social group into which he will enter after he has finished his education if teachers and parents go out of their way to deprive him of all opportunities for real thinking.

IV. Sources of Training

1. *Introduction:* Most persons have, as a rule, three different methods of meeting new situations. In the first place, they may try to employ some older habit or skill in response to the situation. In the second place, and especially where situations are highly complex, or where they take on the proportions of an emergency, many people respond at an emotionalized level. In the third place, a new situation may be met in terms of a problem-solving attitude.[57]

We have tried to say in the preceding section that our normal methods of teaching greatly emphasize the first of the methods mentioned above. That is, we have taken it for granted that processes of education are finished whenever a person has acquired all of the habits and skills that are necessary to meet most of the situations in which he may be placed. The second type of action has been left almost completely to informal methods of training. This fact holds true, in particular, of those places where emotionalized forms of action enter into our so-called personality or character traits. The third type of action in the face of new situations appears to be limited to those favored few who, in spite of emphasis upon rote learning and in spite of informal training in emotionalized actions, have

---

[57] The situation is really much more complex than this. Cf. Fisher, V. E., *Introduction to Abnormal Psychology*. New York: The Macmillan Co., 1929. Chapters V-VII.

THE DEVELOPMENT OF PROBLEM-SOLVING 251

somehow managed to get through to maturity with a great deal of respect for, and an actual amount of talent in, true thinking.

It is easy, of course, to say that these favored few owe their superior reasoning ability to heredity, but, as we have tried to say in so many different places, this particular type of appeal to heredity is almost without significance. There must be some special sources of training for problem-solving which can account for the few highly competent problem-solvers that actually emerge out of the educative process. It is our task in this section to find out what these sources of training are.

2. *Preschool Training:* Let us argue at the outset that adequate sources of promoting high problem-solving ability are certainly not to be found during the preschool years. At this time, of course, children are presented with more new situations than will ever be the case again unless they become exceptionally well-informed and lead an aggressive intellectual or academic life. Their responses for meeting these situations, however, are particularly limited. They do not have, for example, a sufficient number of habits and skills, either of the manual or of the verbal type, to take care of the situations to be faced.

Similarly, they do not have enough information—that is, a sufficient environmental field—which can be drawn upon for responses of the problem-solving type. This leaves them with emotionalized forms of action. Emotionalized forms of action, however, are not a source either of comfort or of satisfaction to the parents. When, therefore, a small child begins an emotionalized response to a difficulty or a complexity, the parents and the nurse remove the difficulty as soon as they can rather than help the child to solve it in a reasonable way.

As a typical instance, we may use an illustration from another writer.[58] The perplexity is as follows. A rod with which a child is playing has rolled under a chair. The child reaches between the rungs of the chair for the rod, grasps it by the middle, and undertakes to draw it out. Since the rod is longer than the rungs, it will not come. The emotionalized reaction to the complexity assumes the proportions of a tantrum. The parent, in handling the situation, simply solves the problem for the child by taking the rod out endwise.

It must be clear to the student that the child itself has gained nothing from this experience, save what it could learn by imitation.

[58] Cf. Watson, J. B., *op. cit.,* pp. 186 ff.

On the second or third occasion, the child itself might solve a similar problem by grasping the stick at the end rather than at the middle. It has discovered the relationship between two different objects not for itself, however, but in the form of a typical learning situation. There is nothing about such a learning situation that would increase its disposition toward a problem-solving attitude on another occasion.[59]

We do not mean, of course, to place too much emphasis on this particular instance. We must, however, take the instance as a symbol of an attitude which is common to most parents and to a great many teachers. Where children resort to emotionalized types of action, our first effort is to save ourselves inconvenience and annoyance by removing the source of the emotion as quickly as possible. One might, of course, try to take advantage of such a situation in order to teach the child something about self-control and thus suppose that we are making a contribution to its character education; but not even this result occurs often enough to place any value upon our attitude.

As we have said above, the actual elimination of as many perplexing situations as possible is not the only source of our neglect of the problem-solving disposition, for we not only remove situations but we hasten the process of habit development as much as possible under the thought that we are really making the child more self-contained or more capable in its adjustments to situations. Habit, however, means increasing fixity and hence increasing safety or dependability of response. It does not imply that type of flexibility or meaningfulness which contributes so much to true thinking.

3. *Progressive Schools:* The reaction to the strict adherence to rote learning as a primary method of teaching took place toward the end of the last century with the creation of what is called the progressive school.[60] Further moves in the same direction have been described as project methods of teaching.[61] Both of these changes reflect, in part, an attempt to place students in learning situations which are alleged to be more real in character and which will invite them to learn habits and skills and acquire meanings as a consequence of a practical undertaking.

Let us suppose, for example, that the project set for a given class

---

[59] Cf. Stevenson, R. R., "Difficulties in Problem Solving." *J. Educ. Res.,* 1925, XI, 95-103; Thorndike, E. L., and Upton, C. B., "An Experiment in Learning an Abstract Subject." *J. Educ. Psychol.,* 1922, XIII, 321-329.

[60] Cf. Burton, W. H., *Introduction to Education.* New York: D. Appleton-Century Co., 1934, Part III.

[61] *Ibid.,* Chapter IX.

THE DEVELOPMENT OF PROBLEM-SOLVING 253

is to buy, take care of, and study a living animal. If the animal is to be bought, familiarity with certain arithmetical operations is required. These operations are said to be learned quickly because they are placed in close relation to a task in which the children may be deeply interested. Buying the animal may also involve perplexities and difficulties. The children must, for example, find the necessary amount of money. This may require a considerable degree of cleverness in creating salable materials, in devising simple chores that will be paid for, and in saving pin money which may have been given to them for some other purpose.

Once the animal is bought, a great many problems arise in connection with its care and with the art of housing it. Similarly, observations on the behavior of the animal and even attempts at developing a few tricks may, in their turn, create further opportunities not only for acquiring useful verbal and manual skills but for favoring the relationships between different features of the total situation.

Altogether, then, project methods of teaching have recommended themselves to a certain number of school systems because they have actually seemed to give training in other ways than those implied by rote learning. It is still too early, perhaps, to pass any judgment upon the real effectiveness of such methods, for they have not been in operation long enough and with a sufficient number of children to make reliable studies of the product possible. It seems fair to say, however, that a wisely arranged project carried through to completion, while certainly minimizing the functions of rote learning, does lead to some improvement in the problem-solving attitudes.

4. *School Subjects:* Most of the studies on the sources of training for thinking have been concerned with the possible effects of common school subjects. Among the subjects cited most frequently in this connection are various phases of arithmetic, algebra, and geometry.[62] These subjects recommend themselves, in particular, because they seem to call for abstract thinking as opposed to concrete thinking. Practically all of the objects used in mathematics and all of the operations involved are of the mental type rather than of the environmental type. The concept "1," for example, is not a concept for which an environmental example can be found. Then, too, the experimental sciences are frequently said to make their contribution to problem-solving because they develop the power of observation. As we have seen above, problem-solving thrives most

[62] Judd, C. H., *Psychology of High School Subjects.* Boston: Ginn and Co., 1915, *passim.*

readily when the whole environmental field out of which insights can be gained has been highly enriched. In so far, then, as the experimental sciences—say, physics, chemistry, and biology—increase the environmental range of a child, just so far will they contribute to problem-solving.

Let us, however, look at some of these considerations in more detail. The basis of mathematical study is to be found, of course, in arithmetic.[63] The first skills which a child may acquire in this field will probably be simple counting skills. The child must, however, pass this stage in the use of numbers or else it will simply not be able to use the conceptual framework within which all mathematical operations are placed. This fact may be illustrated in simple processes of multiplication and addition. The child may, of course, learn the multiplication table by heart without ever understanding what is involved. It is almost needless to say that, behind so formal a matter as $7 \times 9 = 63$, number relationships are involved which are constant even though the numbers themselves may change.[64]

We shall leave out of account the various studies that have been made upon the difficulty of different number combinations and the effect of the distribution of drill periods and the amount of drill periods in the formal teaching of arithmetic.[65] Our main concern is with the way in which arithmetical situations may serve the teacher in his efforts to improve problem-solving. After the elementary operations have been learned, these operations may be put into all sorts of combinations which leave some one feature of the whole pattern unknown. As we have seen, it is out of such a situation that new types of relatedness will emerge. If a student is to solve one of the so-called originals in arithmetic or in any of the higher branches of mathematics, he must know the meaning of each of the concepts involved and be able to "play" with these meanings in an imaginative way until the right relationship appears. A student may, to be sure, try to apply a previously learned formula to some new situation, but he will not often be successful unless he has actually discovered the principles caught up in the formula. It has been shown, for example, that many grade-school children do not

[63] Judd, C. H., "Psychological Analysis of the Fundamentals of Arithmetic." *Suppl. Educ. Monog.*, 1927 (No. 32).
[64] Brownell, W. A., "The Development of Children's Number Ideas in the Primary Grades." *Suppl. Educ. Monog.*, 1928 (No. 35).
[65] Cf. Thorndike, E. L., *The Psychology of Arithmetic*. New York: The Macmillan Co., 1922, *passim*. See also Clapp, F. L., "The Number Combinations: Their Relative Difficulty and the Frequency of Their Appearance in Textbooks." *Univ. of Wisconsin Bureau Educ. Res. Bull.*, 1924 (No. 2).

THE DEVELOPMENT OF PROBLEM-SOLVING 255

solve arithmetical problems in terms of the problem-solving functions at all.

The inference is that their teachers must have adhered more closely to processes of rote learning than to invitations to the emergence of insights.[66] These and other features of problem-solving appear to still better advantage in algebra and in geometry for it is in these fields that the student must get still farther away from concrete objects and events and deal almost wholly with abstractions. Just as he will learn the multiplication table, however, so he may acquire considerable facility in reading and reciting formulae. That is, he will develop considerable skill in the making of implicit verbal responses even when he comes to the so-called originals.

Learning of this type, however, should not be confused with the psychological processes that should predominate after rote learning has been finished. The essence of problem-solving does not lie in the recitation of previously learned material. On the contrary, it lies in an imaginative play with respect to ideas or implicit verbal reactions with the hope that out of some new combinations of these materials a new type of relatedness may be discovered.[67]

The real value of mathematics, then, in the development of the problem-solving functions, does not lie in the sheer use of mathematics as mathematics. Whatever we know about this field at the present time has come from research men who have done more than simply learn what their predecessors have discovered. In other words, every book in arithmetic, algebra, or geometry is a repository of the results of someone else's thinking. Whatever training the student gets, therefore, in problem-solving would depend upon the way in which the teacher presents this material. If he presents it simply as something to be learned, it is only the exceptional student who will go beyond his learning to the discovery of new meanings.

On the other hand, if the teacher presents previously discovered meanings in much the same way that they must have appeared to the people who first discovered them, he will be asking his students to do over again that which has been done in the history of thinking. It is not intended, of course, that every student shall discover everything for himself. There is, however, a great gap between learning processes that are purely repetitive in character and learning processes that offer some opportunity for the discovery of new meanings.

[66] Monroe, W. S., "How Pupils Solve Problems in Arithmetic." *Univ. of Ill. Bull.*, 1928, XXVI (No. 23).
[67] Touton, F. C., "Solving Geometric Originals." *Teachers Coll. Contrib. to Educ.*, 1924 (No. 146), pp. 66-82.

READINGS

The most useful book for any teacher who is looking toward improvement in methods of promoting the problem-solving functions, is Dewey, J., *How We Think* (2nd ed.). Boston: D. C. Heath and Co., 1933. Further material of this same sort is to be found in Buermeyer, L., *et al.*, *An Introduction to Reflective Thinking*. Boston: Houghton Mifflin Co., 1923; Keyser, C. J., *The Human Worth of Rigorous Thinking*. New York: Columbia Univ. Press, 1925. An astonishingly suggestive book of a more popular nature has been written by Dimnet, E., *The Art of Thinking*. New York: Simon and Schuster, 1929. See also Boas, G., *Our New Ways of Thinking*. New York: Harper and Bros., 1930.

The author feels that the distinction between the logic of demonstration and the more flexible and creative processes of problem-solving should be taken seriously by the teacher. The logical side of problem-solving can be found in Robinson, D. S., *The Principles of Reasoning*. New York: D. Appleton-Century Co., 1930, and in Bode, B. H., *An Outline of Logic*. New York: Henry Holt and Co., 1910. The classical work in this field is, of course, Mill, J. S., *A System of Logic*. New York: Longmans, Green and Co., 1884. The other side of the picture is furnished by Bode, B. H., *Conflicting Psychologies of Learning*. Boston: D. C. Heath and Co., 1929, *passim;* Köhler, W., *Gestalt Psychology*. New York: Liveright Publishing Corp., 1929.

The work of the introspective school on the nature of thinking is to be found in Titchener, E. B., *The Experimental Psychology of the Thought Processes*. New York: The Macmillan Co., 1908. Also, *Textbook of Psychology*. New York: The Macmillan Co., 1910, pp. 505-547.

Suggestive material concerning the development of the problem-solving functions in children can be found in Piaget, J., *Judgment and Reasoning in the Child*. New York: Harcourt, Brace and Co., 1928. Also, *The Language and Thought of the Child*. New York: Harcourt, Brace and Co., 1926.

It has been the purpose of this book to use the facts of animal psychology in a study of educational psychology, not because animals represent simpler levels of human performance but because work of this type contributes to the genetic point of view. There is no place, perhaps, where the work in this field is more replete with suggestions than in the case of studies on the way in which the lower animals solve problems. Much of this material is readily accessible in Munn, N. L., *Animal Psychology*. Boston: Houghton Mifflin Co., 1933, Chapters VI and VII. An even more suggestive treatment is to be found in Moss, F. A. (Ed.), *Comparative Psychology*. New York: Prentice-Hall, Inc., 1934. See especially Chapter XI, "Complex Learning Processes" (by W. T. Heron), and Chapter XII, "Theories of Learning" (by E. C. Tolman). A most remarkable book bearing on these problems is Kellogg, W. N., and Kellogg, L. A., *The Ape and the Child*. New York: McGraw-Hill Book Co., 1933. The teacher will find it useful, perhaps, to illustrate the nature of problem-solving by asking his students to engage in the following exercise: Let him select any one of the numerous popular books which outline simple tasks for a detective. The student should be instructed to take account of the nature of the materials that he uses in his analysis of the problems and to remark especially the way in which the various items of a total situation, when patterned now in one way and then in another, furnish the opportunity for insights.

Some suggestive experimental studies are as follows: Clem, O. M., and Hendershot, B. A., "Some Difficulties Involved in Solving Verbal Problems in Elementary Algebra." *Mathematics Teacher,* 1930, XXIII, 141-147; Powell, J. J., "A Study of Problem Material in High School Algebra." *Teachers Coll. Contrib. to Educ.,* 1929 (No. 405); Stevenson, P. R., "Difficulties in Problem Solving." *J. of Educ. Res.,* 1925, XI, 95-103; Thorndike, E. L., and Upton, C. B., "An Experiment in Learning an Abstract Subject." *J. of Educ. Psychol.,* 1922, XIII, 321-329; and Wood, B. D., and Bell, J. C., "Solution of Problems in Geometry." *J. of Educ. Psychol.,* 1920, XI, 316-326.

CHAPTER EIGHT

THE DEVELOPMENT OF PERSONALITY AND CHARACTER

I. SHORT-TIME AND LONG-TIME VIEWS OF HUMAN NATURE

1. *Introduction:* A short-time inspection of human conduct normally gives us the impression that the whole stream of behavior is simply a collection of specific or local responses and attitudes to equally local stimulus-situations. We get the impression, also, that specific movements stand, as a rule, in close correlation with specific stimulus-situations. At any single moment, for instance, any one of the persons around the student may be seen to take an attitude or to make some precise reaction to another person or to a particular object. During the presentation of a single stimulus-pattern on the athletic field, an athlete will be observed to make some particular response to that pattern, such as tackling a runner, throwing a ball, hitting at a ball, or defending himself from attack. In response to a question formulated by the teacher, the student in the classroom will make a specific response, either in verbal form, or in manual form at the blackboard, or in postural form. Let us say again, then, that short-time views of human nature give the impression that conduct and experience are made up of a vast number of stimulus-response patterns which appear to be unrelated to one another and to be in no way expressive of the general character or quality of the individual as an individual.[1]

A. TRENDS OF BEHAVIOR: The reaction psychologies and all of the various forms of behaviorism have shown a tendency to take human nature in this piecemeal manner. The reduction of all human behavior to reflexes and combinations of reflexes is a case in point. The description of elementary mental processes such as sensations, images, and simple feelings may be taken as another case in point.

All such impressions of discreteness or of specificity of response break down, however, whenever one takes a long-time view of

---

[1] This is a feature of the study of human nature which leads easily to oversimplified concepts. The belief that all human action can be reduced to responses to stimuli (the S-R formula) is a case in point. Compare, for example, Wheeler, R. H., and Perkins, F. T., *Principles of Mental Development.* New York: T. Y. Crowell Co., 1932, with Gates, A. I., *Psychology for Students of Education.* New York: The Macmillan Co., 1930.

human nature. Under such conditions, it will be observed that single or local responses are almost always imbedded in a total trend or in a total organization of behavior.[2] The stream of conduct is highly patterned or configured. To describe a single reaction is a little like attempting to describe the characteristics of a single piece on the chess board and to suppose that this single piece tells the whole story of attack and defense. Obviously, any account of the single piece must find its proper setting furnished by all of the other pieces in play at the moment.

B. PERSISTENT STIMULI: We have already described several aspects of human behavior which move in the direction of the problems to be discussed in this chapter. We have found, for example, that such terms as "interest," "motive" and "purpose" are more compatible with a long-time inspection of behavior than they are with a short-time inspection of it. If the persistent observer of a human subject is patient enough, he will discover that there are dozens of different actions over a period of a day, a week, a month, or even of several years, which may all be related in some distinctive and intimately contingent fashion to a single but perduring stimulus-situation. Interests and motives describe the fact, then, that human behavior is not as discrete or as partitioned as a more limited view of it would seem to suggest.

Long-time views of the stream of action give us still other impressions of the pervading interrelatedness in behavior. On the one hand, the student can easily see among his fellows that some modes of reaction, certain mannerisms, and certain postures appear over and over again. Such recurring reactions are often so persistent and insistent as to give further evidence of some sort of organization or integration in the total behavioral stream of an individual. It may be observed, for example, that one person will have a distinct preference for a given class of objects in the total range of the effective environment, whereas another person will have a distinct preference for another class. Occasionally one will come upon men who appear to favor definite patterns of emotionalized action, while others prefer quite another disposition. These differences are often related to a definite set of actions and postures which display among themselves a total patterning or integration which will be specific to each particular person.

2. *Personality:* It is with respect to such considerations as these that the problems of "self," "personality," and "character" are to be

[2] Hence the long life of the "self" psychologies. Cf. Calkins, M. W., *A First Book in Psychology* (4th ed.). New York: The Macmillan Co., 1914, *passim.*

located and defined.[3] Since preferences for types of motivation and types of emotional expression are more easily observed and have a greater social significance than are preferences for other types of psychological talent, it often happens that the problems of self, personality, and character are closely identified with emotional balance. Then, too, on account of the close affiliation between certain attitudes and postures, on the one hand, and general social stability, on the other, it has come about that the words self, personality, and character have acquired both a moral and a theological significance. Some of the older varieties of psychology, and especially those which have been used by theology, have contributed to this inflection of the problems of character. If human beings have a soul which is the seat of their personality, and if the soul is taken in a religious rather than a secular sense, the disciplining or training of the soul must have a moral rather than a secular import.[4]

3. *Animal Personalities:* Some of the problems of personality will appear to better advantage if we consider them briefly from the genetic point of view. Long-time views of the reactions and attitudes of the lower animals yield the same impression about the total character of behavior as we get from a long-time view of human behavior. Those who have worked most consistently with the lower animals often remark that some subjects are livelier than others or that household pets may be characterized as dependable or aggressive and as sullen or kind in nature. Köhler's chimpanzees, for example, differed from one another greatly in their personality traits. Tercera was described by Köhler as something of a coquette. Sultan is said to have had an obstinate streak. Techego, being the oldest and the strongest of the group, was described as commanding respect. Rana was stupid and in her whole manner dependent and unlively.[5] It is possible, of course, to find individual acts which, in their total character, deserve descriptive terms of this sort, but most frequently they are terms which spring out of long acquaintance with the lower animals. They are terms which describe general trends in the total stream of behavior of the animal.

4. *Infant Personality:* Human infants may also be described at a

[3] Cf. Symonds, P. M., *Diagnosing Personality and Conduct*. New York: D. Appleton-Century Co., 1931, *passim*.
[4] A major source of theory, fact and experiment about the nature of character can be found in Hartshorne, H., May, M. A., *et al.*, *Studies in the Nature of Character* (3 vols.). New York: The Macmillan Co., 1928-1930.
[5] Köhler, W., *The Mentality of Apes*. New York: Harcourt, Brace and Co., 1925, pp. 306 ff. Cf. Tinklepaugh, O. L., "Social Psychology of Animals," in Moss, F. A. (Ed.), *Comparative Psychology*. New York: Prentice-Hall, Inc., 1934, Chapter XIV.

DEVELOPMENT OF PERSONALITY AND CHARACTER

very early age in terms of the total character or individual quality of their behavior. Shortly after birth, for example, some infants are described as much livelier than others. "Docility," "aggressiveness," "irritability," "stubbornness," and "phlegmatic" are further words which appear to characterize the dispositions of new-born infants.[6] The chances are that these words describe traits which are immediately related to the physiological condition of the infant, for it is hard to see how an infant which is suffering from indigestion or malnutrition could behave so as to give the impression that it was docile or sweet-tempered. In any case, physiological conditions are quickly supplemented by a vast number of social agents.[7] These agents promote the development of some attitudes or dispositions and inhibit the development of others. It has been shown that the necessary routines of eating and sleeping begin to play their part at a very early age. This is true, in particular, of the emotional phases of individual development, for, as we have seen, various modes of emotional expression become associated with new stimulus-situations at an exceedingly rapid rate during the early stages of infant development.

5. *The Genetic View:* The genetic point of view has, then, a number of different questions to ask about the origin and development of persistent habits of expression, on the one hand, and of the total character or quality of behavior, on the other. It may ask, first, about the total number of different character or personality traits which may be present at any given age level. This same question could be asked about any of the lower animals. Both empirical observation and experiment show that most of the lower animals are as limited in this respect as are new-born infants.[8] As the stream of behavior becomes more complex and the various psychological dimensions of the individual expand, the opportunity for the development of persistent patterns of conduct expands in proportion. In spite of the work that has been done, however, only a few items of information are available on this problem, and these few are limited to human psychology rather than to the lower animals.[9]

[6] Cf. Murphy, G., and Murphy, L. B., *Experimental Social Psychology.* New York: Harper and Bros., 1931, Chapter VI.
[7] Wooley, H. T., "Eating, Sleeping, and Elimination," in *A Handbook of Child Psychology* (Ed. C. Murchison). Worcester, Mass.: Clark Univ. Press, 1931, Chapter II.
[8] Hempelmann, F., *Tierpsychologie.* Leipzig: Akad. Verlagsgesellschaft, 1926, Chapter XI.
[9] Cf. Curti, M. W., *Child Psychology.* New York: Longmans, Green and Co., 1931, Chapter XIV. Also Morgan, J. J. B., *Child Psychology.* New York: Farrar and Rinehart, 1934 (rev. ed.), *passim.*

In the second place, the genetic point of view keeps an open eye for the genesis and development of the more general properties and dimensions of that total system called the individual. In the preceding pages we have frequently taken the attitude that every system of events, whether it be physical, biological, or psychological, has total properties and characteristics which are not defined when parts of the system have been isolated and properly characterized. This same attitude will be taken in our treatment of the problems of self, personality, and character. A human being is a biological and psychological system of exceeding great complexity. As we have said, short-time views of this system at work in its environment will give plenty of instances of specific types of reaction. A long-time view of the same system, however, reveals general traits or properties which seem to characterize the system as a whole.

Popular language has given us such contrasting descriptive phrases as "thin personalities" and "men of parts." These phrases do not refer to any particular act. On the contrary, they say something about the total character or quality of human beings as separate entities. It may be that experimental psychology must, for the time being, remain rather vague in its attempts to identify the properties of the whole individual, but of one thing we may be fairly sure: Both psychology and education must take this phase of the problem of human nature as a major problem. It is a problem that must be solved before educators can say that they are able to cross over the line which seems to divide formal education from informal education. As we have seen, the processes of informal education probably have a more direct effect upon the development of character and personality traits than has ever been the case with formal instruction. Continued research on the psychological foundations of education seems to offer some hope of changing this situation.

II. Contemporary Definitions of Personality

1. *Traditional View of Personality:* Most definitions of personality have, as a common point of departure, the older rational psychology out of which contemporary psychology has grown. The older view had it that man has a mind and is a character from the moment of birth onward. By virtue of the act of creation, man's character was said to be intrinsically good and to have, therefore, an inherent moral quality. But the accidents of secular living brought him down from his high estate, and it has been supposed ever since

DEVELOPMENT OF PERSONALITY AND CHARACTER 263

that human beings are intrinsically immoral and antisocial.[10] As we have seen, the conflict between certain types of tissue need, on the one hand, and comfortable social living, on the other, still furnishes adequate reason for saying that a human being may be inherently antisocial, but so far as science is concerned, it is now commonly agreed that human beings are, in their very essence, neither moral nor immoral.

If this fact may be granted as a working hypothesis, then psychology and education must search for proper ways of defining the nature of personality so that the growth or development of personal character will become as significant to education as is the growth or development of any other psychological trait. That is, partly because of the advance of experimental science and partly because of the development of the secular point of view toward almost every human problem, neither psychology nor education has thought it worth while to continue to approach the problems of selfhood and of personality in the manner suggested by theologies and philosophies. We must, therefore, describe some of the contemporary substitutes for the older points of view.[11]

2. *Personality and Instinct:* We may consider, first, the argument that self, personality, and character—assuming that these terms can be used almost, if not quite, synonymously—are bundles of specific virtues having an instinctive or hereditary foundation. This mode of describing the self is perhaps more nearly synonymous with the older point of view than it is with contemporary points of view, for it assumes that every individual possesses by nature a set of tendencies to act in virtuous ways, just as he may possess a set of tendencies to behave in parental ways.

It goes almost without saying that such virtues cannot undergo direct description. In this respect they stand on the same footing with other types of psychological or subjective entities. When a person behaves in a kindly way, this point of view would say that the kindliness of the act derives from the virtue of kindness rather than from the social significance of the act or from any intent which the person himself may have entertained. It would seem to follow, then, that the instinctive or hereditary virtue called kindness could be exercised or trained by the doing of kindly acts just as, in the older scholastic forms of education, the exercise of any mental function would lead to an increase in the strength of that function.

[10] Read the delightful account of the Christian epic in Santayana, G., *Reason in Religion.* New York: Charles Scribner's Sons, 1928, Chapter VI.
[11] A suggestive survey of all of these problems can be found in Hartshorne, H., *Character in Human Relations.* New York: Charles Scribner's Sons, 1932, *passim.*

A number of objections might be offered against this theory of the nature of the self and of its virtues. In the first place, it is clear that it stands on exactly the same foundation as do all other types of instinctive or hereditary traits. In a certain social setting, a given act may be described as kind, honest, courageous, thoughtful, or generous. It is assumed that such acts can be explained by attributing them to an inherited trait or tendency which, in its turn, stands just as much in need of explanation as does the original act. So much has been said in the preceding pages about this device that we need not push our present objection to it any further.

In the second place, the actual observation of behavior shows that, if there are specific virtue-traits, then these virtue-traits are exceedingly sporadic in their activity. It is easy to see, even from the most casual inspection of behavior, that most persons can be honest, kind, or courageous in some situations, and dishonest, thoughtless, and cowardly in others. One of the criteria of an instinct is its universality with respect to all of the members of a given species, but this criterion is open to question in the case of a great many alleged instincts, and it is much more open to question with the so-called virtues.[12]

Even though we were to grant the fact that a person who was honest in one situation might be honest in a majority of such situations, we still could not grant that self or character is a complex of a group of instinctive urges. We may, for example, take such virtues as kindness, courage, loyalty, and persistence. It goes almost without argument that these virtues might be just as characteristic of a thief as of an honored member of society. With respect to his comrades and even with respect to his victim, a thief can be courageous, patient, loyal, and persistent, but certain social groups would not be willing to attribute to such an individual the high character denoted by the words mentioned. It would seem, then, that any definition of self in terms of instinctive traits or virtues does not get into the heart of the problem.[13]

3. *Personality and the Nervous System:* The first experimental psychologies were not much more helpful in this situation than was the instinct psychology. For the most part, introspective psychology has not known what to do with the problems of self or character, since it was not possible to find any distinctive group of mental

[12] Cf. Watson, G. B., "Virtues *versus* Virtue," *School and Soc.*, 1927, XXVI, 286-290; Coe, G. A., "Virtue and the Virtues," *Religious Education*, 1912, VI, 485-492.
[13] For a system of psychology based upon the "self," see Calkins, M. W., *A First Book in Psychology* (4th ed.). New York: The Macmillan Co., 1914.

processes which were attributively selflike in character.[14] It had to follow, then, that selfhood was one of the practical and philosophical deductions which might be made from the personal reference or meaning which sometimes accrued to other types of sensory processes. In considering the problems of selfhood, therefore, where they were considered at all, introspective psychology had to go to habit performance and occasionally to such physiological devices as the determining tendencies.

Titchener, for example, writes of the self as follows:

"There seems to be no doubt that *the individual nervous system possesses, over and above its special habits, susceptibilities, tendencies, and activities, a characteristic mode of functioning at large;* so that a common or general factor enters into all the special intellectual responses that are called forth by particular situations. It is not easy to make this result clear to the reader, mainly because no one has as yet a clear idea of what the common or general factor is; we have good evidence that it exists, but we can say very little more about it. Different names have been given to it: 'energy of attention,' 'general ability,' 'intellective energy,' 'general intelligence'; but they indicate the way in which it manifests itself, and not its own nature; the best name for the present is the vague 'general common factor.' We do not know, either, upon what it depends: on blood-supply, perhaps, or on the arrangement of nervous structures, or on some individual 'quality' of the nervous elements, or perhaps on something else that we cannot even guess at. What it does is to hold a man's intellectual traits together and to enter into the exhibition of them all; *it is thus, from the psychological point of view, a sort of supreme determining tendency, guiding all mental processes whatsoever into the channels of intellectual selfhood.* Whether there is a like general factor on the emotive side, and whether 'emotive energy' is of the same kind as this 'intellective energy,' cannot be said." [15]

4. *Personality and Behavior:* By long tradition and by common consent the words "self," "character," and "personality" have applied more directly to some intrinsic quality of a person than to his overt reactions, but, oddly enough, the behaviorist has contributed more directly to our knowledge of the "self" and to arts of practical control, than have any of the forms of introspective psychology. As the student knows, the behaviorist finds it convenient to make an initial appraisal of human behavior in terms of patterns of stimulus and patterns of response. A vast part of the material of behavior-

[14] See, however, Calkins, M. W., "The Self in Scientific Psychology." *Amer. J. Psychol.,* 1915, XXVI, 495-524.
[15] Titchener, E. B., *A Beginner's Psychology.* New York: The Macmillan Co., 1916, pp. 310-311.

istic psychology is made up of stimuli of short duration which are placed in a one-to-one relation with responses of equally short duration. Long chains of response may be organized under timewise sequences of stimulus-situations, but such sequences do not possess the qualities or properties that distinguish them as features of character or self. In addition to short-time stimuli, there are, as we have just said, certain types of long-time stimuli which can be called motives.

Up to this point, it would seem that behaviorism might well be able to do without the concept of the self, but there are, with respect to short-time stimuli and responses and even with respect to motives, certain characteristics or properties of response which deserve most earnest attention and study. Any given person, for example, may show, during a long-time period, distinct preferences for types of response, slight mannerisms in response, preferred postures and attitudes, and favorite levels of emotion which will be characteristic of him rather than of the stimuli which excite him to action. In other words, it seems possible to describe the behavior of human beings in at least three ways which go beyond the description which appears adequate at the simpler S-R level.

A. PERSISTENT HABITS: In the first place, a long-time view of human nature shows the presence of habits and attitudes which are extraordinarily persistent and insistent. By being insistent, we may mean that certain habits which have been acquired through the normal processes of learning intrude themselves over and over into situations to which they may or may not be particularly adapted. By persistency we may mean that certain habits and skills, which likewise have been acquired through normal processes of learning, endure over longer periods of time than the amount of practice which has been devoted to them would seem to require. Thus we say it is characteristic of a certain person that he will always walk at a faster tempo than other individuals. Rate of walking is, of course, a pace habit that has been acquired in early childhood, and in so far as it possesses the qualities of persistence and insistence, that is, in so far as it characterizes all of the walking which the individual does and intrudes itself into other types of situation as well, it may be said to be a personality trait.

An example of this sort of characterization of behavior is given by studies on what has been called the A-S reaction. In answer to the question, "Are you embarrassed if you have greeted a stranger whom you have mistaken for an acquaintance?" the subject is given an opportunity to check one of three replies, viz., "very much,"

DEVELOPMENT OF PERSONALITY AND CHARACTER

"somewhat," or "not at all." In answer to the question, "At a reception or tea, do you seek to meet the important person present?" the subject may check either "frequently," "occasionally," or "never." These and scores of other questions are asked for the purpose of securing a rating of the relative ascendency or submissiveness of the behavior of the subject. Ascendency and submissiveness are thus inferred to be properties or attributes of behavior-patterns, the measurement of which might throw some light upon the character of the individual.[16]

B. PREFERENCES: In the second place, a long-time view of behavior shows, with respect to any particular person, a preference for some modes of actions rather than for others. Freeman, for example, appears to argue that there may be differences between individuals with respect to will temperament, emotional temperament, moral disposition, and aesthetic sensibilities.[17] Will temperament, for example, refers to those characteristics of behavior which are described by such words as "energetic," "cautious," "timid," "phlegmatic," "reckless," "persistent," and "vacillating."[18] Emotional temperament relates to such traits as pessimism and optimism, enthusiasm and apathy, and the like.[19] Moral disposition is described by such words as "honest," "truthful," "charitable," "obedient," "helpful," and "considerate." Aesthetic sensibility has to do with the appreciation of form and design, the affective character of poetry, the appreciation of music, and the like.

In other words, if an individual were continually energetic and persistent, he might be called a strong character, and if he were persistently timid or vacillating, he might be called a weak character. Likewise, he might have a happy disposition or a moody disposition. If he were honest, truthful, charitable, obedient, helpful, and considerate, we would say of him that he had a good character, while dishonesty, untruthfulness and stinginess would be indicative of poor character.[20]

C. TOTAL PATTERNING: In the third place, it is possible, again by taking a long-time view of the behavior of an individual, to come to some judgment about the total organization or total patterning of

---

[16] Allport, G. W., and Allport, F. H., *A-S Reaction Study*. Boston: Houghton Mifflin Co., 1928, *passim*. See also Allport, G. W., "A Test for Ascendence-submission." *J. Abnorm. and Soc. Psychol.*, 1928, XXIII, 118-136.
[17] Freeman, F. N., *Mental Tests*. Boston: Houghton Mifflin Co., 1926, p. 192.
[18] Downey, J. E., *The Will Temperament and Its Testing*. Yonkers: The World Book Co., 1923, *passim*.
[19] Pressey, S. L., "A Group Scale for Investigating the Emotions." *J. Abnorm. Psychol.*, 1921, XVI, 55-64.
[20] Hartshorne, H., *op. cit.*, Part II.

his stream of behavior. This is a device which has been used frequently both by introspective and by behavioristic psychologies. As we have seen, Titchener describes the self as the total organization of the mental processes that may be associated with any particular nervous system. Somewhat the same path was chosen by the behaviorist. To quote from Watson:

"Psychologists and psychiatrists often have the task of rating the individual as a member of society, passing judgment on him as a whole from the standpoint of how well or how poorly he functions in his present environment, to form estimates of how smoothly he would react to a new environment and to specify the necessary changes in his equipment which would make for present and future adjustment. . . . In making such estimates or inferences we use the term 'personality' or 'character' as a convenient way of expressing the fact that we are looking at the individual not from the standpoint of how well or how poorly any particular emotion, instinct, or group of habits he possesses may function, but from that of how the organism as a whole works or may work under changing conditions." [21]

5. *Summary:* We shall assume in what follows that all three of these ways of approaching the problems of self and character are not only psychologically but educationally significant. In the first place, there are times and occasions when pertinent facts about the self or character of an individual may be stated in terms of the persistency and insistency of certain habits and in terms of the social properties or traits which these habits and attitudes may possess. In the second place, we may agree with commonsense in the argument that certain acts and habits are more indicative of character than are others. There is considerable ground for the argument that this characteristic may be put upon certain habits by the fact that human beings have to make a great many of their reactions within a social setting. Since the interests of society are better served by some performances than they are by others, the foundations for a choice among individual behavior patterns is laid. In the third place, it is not now possible to get away from the idea that the properties of total configurations of the stream of behavior have an important theoretical and practical significance. We may say again that every human being is in several respects a highly organized system of actions and experiences. It ought to be possible to characterize such a system in fairly precise ways and, in so far as this is done, personality may be defined.

[21] Watson, J. B., *Psychology from the Standpoint of a Behaviorist.* Philadelphia: J. B. Lippincott Co., 1924, p. 412.

DEVELOPMENT OF PERSONALITY AND CHARACTER

III. SPECIFICITY AND CONFIGURATIONISM IN PERSONAL DEVELOPMENT

1. *Introduction:* The three ways of approaching the problems of personality described in the last section mark, in reality, only two ways. On the one hand, there are those definitions of personality which adhere to specific traits or acts and, on the other hand, those which emphasize certain characteristics or properties of the total stream of conduct. The doctrine of specificity is a product, perhaps, of the S-R psychology because this sort of psychology studies all human behavior in terms of specific stimulus-response sequences. Symonds, for example, states it as his opinion that "from a review of all the skillful and ingenious methods for testing conduct directly that have been devised, the conclusion stands out above all others that conduct is very specific." [22]

This is the view of human nature which we will meet in the chapter on the transfer of training. The view can be opposed, of course, by the argument stated above which lays emphasis upon the total patterning or configuration of conduct. That is, a long-time view of any single person misses the details of specific response, but gains a general impression of the total quality of character of a man's life.

It seems necessary, at least for the present, to keep these two views of personality or character separate from each other. This procedure is advisable, in part, because no methods have been found for measuring pattern, configuration, or total quality. On the other hand, specific methods can be used for the isolation and description of specific types of reaction to specific situations. It would be a mistake, however, to suppose that personality or character should be defined in one way simply because this way offers the only chance of making direct and immediate measures of character.

2. *Experimental Studies:* Some light is thrown on this problem by recent studies of the nature of specific character traits. It is possible, of course, to place a group of subjects in a large variety of situations, the reactions to which may have some moral or ethical significance. Among the situations that have been used for this purpose are failing to return overchange, failing to return borrowed property, failing to return an extra dime found in testing materials, failing to return all the coins used in the test, various forms of cheat-

---

[22] Symonds, P. M., *Diagnosing Personality and Conduct.* New York: D. Appleton-Century Co., 1932, p. 352.

ing in an examination, cheating in scoring one's own paper as shown by comparison of carbon or wax copy of the original with corrected copy, peeping in a task which was to be done with the eyes closed, unfair methods used in party games, faking a solution to a puzzle, receiving aid in solving puzzles after having been placed under honor to receive no aid on a test taken at home, overstatement in connection with books read, overstatement of knowledge, overstatement about one's conduct to win approval, false statements to cover cheating, willingness to receive a tip for insignificant favors, the degree to which a subject chooses to work for his own score rather than for a group score, efficiency with which one works when striving for an individual prize as compared with degree of striving for a group prize, the degree to which the subject may display egotism, anger, malice, diffidence, shrewdness, brutality, envy, impatience, and the like when the experimental situation requires that two or more persons work together in standardized test situations, persistence in finishing a story when the end is printed in such a way that it is difficult to read, persistence as shown by constancy of work in a monotonous task, self-control in the presence of a temptation to begin working too early on a task, and so on.[23]

Each of these situations, when made concrete and presented to a sufficient number of subjects, will furnish statistical data not only on the distribution of moral and ethical traits among children but upon some features of their development as well.

In commenting upon the way in which moral behavior appears in children, Jones writes as follows:

"One of the first facts which one notes in the inspection of the behavior of children in controlled situations involving a moral problem is that they do not fall into two groups: the good and the bad, or the truthful and the untruthful. There are individual differences in morals just as truly as there are individual differences in general intelligence or in knowledge of history. In a scale of truthfulness, for example, children have been found to distribute themselves from one end representing great deceitfulness to the end representing great truthfulness. Moreover, there is no place on this scale where one can, with any factual justification, draw a line which can be said to separate the untruthful

[23] Cf. Voelker, P. F., "The Function of Ideals and Attitudes in Social Education: An Experimental Study." *Teach. Coll. Contrib. to Educ.*, 1921 (No. 112); Hartshorne, H., and May, M. A., *Studies in the Nature of Character* (3 vols.). New York: The Macmillan Co., 1928-1930. Slaght, W. E., "Untruthfulness in Children: Its Conditioning Factors and Its Setting in Child Nature." *Univ. Iowa Stud.; Stud. Char.*, 1928, I (No. 4); Jones, V., "Children's Morals," in *Handbook of Child Psychology*, Murchison, C. (Ed.). Worcester, Mass.: Clark Univ. Press, 1931, Chapter XIII.

from the truthful. At first glance one might suggest drawing the line at the truth, the whole truth, and nothing but the truth. Such a standard can be defended in some of the simpler situations, and if we make truthfulness co-extensive with truthfulness in certain simple situations, then we do find a considerable number who would satisfy this standard. But such a line or standard cannot be set up for practical usefulness in the distribution of truthfulness taken in its wider meaning, because it would not hit within the distribution of normal children. To see the justification for this statement, one has only to think how the various moral traits—if we consider them for the moment as unities—get in one another's way. Truth-telling at times conflicts with loyalty to our group; truth-telling to the limit may conflict with courtesy and gratitude to our host or benefactor; truth-telling to a sick person may conflict with helpfulness." [24]

IV. PERSONALITY TYPES AND TRAITS

1. *Introduction:* It is a simple fact of mathematics that the number of different patterns into which a series of items may be thrown increases enormously with an increase in the number of items. We might, for example, have 100 different items which were to be grouped into patterns or sets where the sets are to be made up of any five items. This would mean that the total number of combinations or sets of items would be reached through the following operation, viz., $100 \times 99 \times 98 \times 97 \times 96$ divided by $5 \times 4 \times 3 \times 2 \times 1$. It is clear that any increase in the total number of items or in the number of items that were to be thrown into combination with one another would vastly increase the patterns that could result.

This is, so to speak, illustrative of the nature of the difficulty which stands in the way of any attempt to describe types of personality traits. Every growing person becomes a locus for an enormous variety of skills, attitudes, and experiences, any one of which may enter into any pattern with some of the others at any particular moment. This is to say that differences in personality may grade into one another by almost imperceptible changes. Just as the animal kingdom is made up of specimens which cut across the lines drawn by the word "species" as almost to rob this word of its distinctive meaning, so individual differences merge into one another. Attempts have been made, however, to classify personality traits in such a way as to make their investigation easier, but it must be realized that most of these classifications are an entirely arbitrary matter done merely for convenience in discussion.

2. *Differences in Imagery:* One of the first attempts to describe

[24] Jones, V., *op. cit.*, Chapter XIII, p. 483.

type differences among human beings centered around the question of imagery. It was Galton, apparently, who first discovered the fact that scientific men may differ widely from one another in the types of images which they used most frequently.[25] It was supposed, subsequent to Galton's discovery that "individual minds differ widely in the nature and frequency of their characteristic 'image processes.'" Visual and auditory images are of common occurrence, although the auditory image appears, as a rule, to be associated with actual innervation of the larynx, that is, with kinesthesis.[26]

One consequence of these differences was the attempt to label different people with respect to their prevailing type of imagery. Among the types named were the visualizers, the audiels, and the motiles. As studies on imagery continued, however, it turned out that the type of imagery employed by any one person might vary with the nature of the task and that there were a large number of intermediate cases. As a matter of fact, the number of intermediate cases became so great as to lead Thorndike to say, "Instead of distinct types there is a continuous gradation. Instead of a few 'pure' types or many 'mixed' types, there is one type—mediocrity. Instead of antagonism between the development of imagery from one sense and that from other senses there is a close correlation."[27] Thorndike concluded, therefore, that there could be only one type, a type which joins all men one to another in a continuity of variation and describes a man by stating the nature and amount of his divergences from the central mode.[28]

For a time it was supposed that the question of imaginal types might be of some considerable importance to education, because some of the psychological functions ought to proceed more advantageously with one type rather than with another. Visually minded persons, for example, might be expected to have a certain advantage in painting or sculpture, whereas auditorily-minded individuals might be at an advantage in music. For a time, all attempts to find a significant correlation between imaginal types, on the one hand, and efficiency in using various modes of psychological function, on the other, quite failed.[29] There are, however, types of psychology which

[25] Galton, F., *Inquiries into Human Faculty and Development*. London: The Macmillan Co., 1883, *passim*.
[26] Titchener, E. B., *op. cit.*, p. 199. See also Titchener, E. B., *Lectures on Experimental Psychology of the Thought Processes*. New York: The Macmillan Co., 1909, pp. 7 ff.
[27] Thorndike, E. L., *Educational Psychology*. New York: Columbia Univ. Press, 1914, Vol. III, p. 374.
[28] *Ibid.*, p. 376.
[29] Cf. Murphy, G., *General Psychology*. New York: Harper and Bros., 1933, pp. 338-345.

DEVELOPMENT OF PERSONALITY AND CHARACTER 273

are based upon the argument that differences in imaginal type may have some functional significance.[30]

The nature of this problem may be stated, perhaps, as follows. Such individuals as Helen Keller are, of course, quite devoid of visual experience, both at the sensory level and at the imaginal level. We may, then, inquire whether the absence of visual imagery makes any difference in the effectiveness of Miss Keller's thinking. There is no evidence that this is the case. One might draw the inference, therefore, that the presence or absence of certain types of imagery is irrelevant to the effectiveness of certain psychological functions. But in the absence of proper evidence, this question may well be left undecided.

3. *Physical Types:* More recently, other methods and facts have been used in order to gain some insight into the derivation of personality types. Among the various circumstances which have been used for this purpose we may consider primarily physical traits, mental traits, special capacities, general knowledge and technical skill, temperament, volition, and character.

Among the physical traits which are frequently used to designate differences in personality are height, weight, build, appearance, facial expression, health, stamina, and other properties and traits of the various bodily functions. Kretschmer, for example, recognizes four types of individuality called, respectively, the asthenic, the athletic, the pyknic, and the dysplastic types.[31] These types are distinguished from one another by their bodily build, muscular development and placement of weight on the body, shape of the face and hands, and character of the skin and hair.

The asthenic individual is of average height, being relatively tall for his weight. This means that he is thin, with a long, narrow, shallow chest. His shoulders are broad compared with the diameter of the chest. The muscles are thin and poorly developed, the skin thin and loosely attached to the underlying tissues and the face long and narrow.

The athletic type is similar to the asthenic, save that all of the structures are thicker, firmer, and more robust; the shoulders are heavy, the chest is broad, the skeleton is heavily built, the muscles are thin, and so on. The pyknic type is characterized, for the most part, by an increase in the volume of all of the body cavities. The

---

[30] Cf. Carr, H. A., *Psychology*. New York: Longmans, Green and Co., 1925, *passim*.
[31] Kretschmer, E., *Physique and Character* (Trans. by W. H. J. Sprott). New York: Harcourt, Brace and Co., 1925; Paterson, D. G., *Physique and Intellect*. New York: D. Appleton-Century Co., 1930.

head is large, the chest voluminous, the abdomen full, the face round, and the complexion ruddy. The dysplastic type includes, for the most part, marked deviations from the normal, the deviations usually standing as a sign of some sort of disturbance of the various glands of internal secretion.[32]

Certain temperamental differences are associated with these various types. According to Kretschmer, the cyclothymic temperaments are said to "wear their emotions on their sleeves." This means that they are apt to fluctuate in mood from joyful excitation to extreme depression. At more ordinary levels, the cycloid is sociable, good-natured, friendly, genial, and a "hale fellow well met." The schizophrenic temperament or schizoid is unsociable, quiet, reserved, serious, and apt to be eccentric; his emotional life is usually repressed. Kretschmer has argued that there is a marked relationship between these two types of temperament and differences in physique. The asthenic and athletic types of bodily build go with the schizoid temperament; that is, the tall, thin man tends to be reserved, sensitive, and unemotional; the pyknic type, on the other hand, goes with cycloid temperaments. The fat, well-developed person is said to be genial, friendly, and easy to meet.

4. *Chemical Composition:* A wholly different attack on the problem of the relation between personality traits and physical characteristics has been made by Cleeton and Knight. A total of 122 different physical measurements were made on thirty different subjects. Such traits as judgment, intelligence, frankness, will power, ability to make friends, leadership, originality and impulsiveness were rated by a group of competent judges, and the results pooled in such a way as to make the ratings fairly reliable. When the correlations between the physical measurements and the character traits were computed and averaged, no sign of contingent relationship could be discovered.[33] It is inevitable, of course, that a manner of living should make such differences in facial expression and other bodily characters as would be reflected by a change in the tonus of the muscles or a change in general body metabolism, but it does not seem likely that the dependence of psychological traits upon body structures could go much further than this.[34]

It still remains to be seen how far experimental methods can go in

---

[32] Mohr, J. G., and Gundlach, R. H., "The Relation between Physique and Performance." *J. Exper. Psychol.,* 1927, X, 117-157.

[33] Cleeton, G. U., and Knight, F. B., "Validity of Character Judgments Based on External Criteria." *J. Appl. Psychol.,* 1924, VIII, 215-229.

[34] Cf. Dunlap, K., "The Reading of Character from External Signs." *Scient. Mo.,* 1922, XV, 153-165.

DEVELOPMENT OF PERSONALITY AND CHARACTER

correlating the chemical condition of the body with various types of psychological function. The studies of Cannon have shown, of course, that there are certain biochemical mechanisms which have much to do with the determination of such functions as pain, rage, fear, and hunger.[35] Some investigators have been inclined to argue that this sort of chemical correlation between the body, including its several functions, and psychological function may come ultimately to an expression of psychological phenomena in chemical terms.[36]

As a typical piece of research in this field, we may take Rich's study of correlations between a variety of biochemical tests and a series of personality ratings. The subjects included eighteen graduate students in psychology, thirty undergraduate members of a fraternity, and 303 children who had passed through the behavior clinic of the Institute for Juvenile Research in Chicago. The tentative conclusions drawn by Rich from his series of studies run as follows, viz., (1) acid in the urine and in saliva tend to characterize the less excitable persons, whereas the more excitable persons tend to neutrality or alkalinity; (2) acidity, as measured by formol titration and high alkali reserve in the blood, seems to characterize the less aggressive subjects, and vice versa; (3) creatinine in the blood and its excretion in the urine seems to be related inversely to emotional excitability; and (4) no clear-cut relationship between phosphorus metabolism and personality traits is demonstrated, although the evidence suggests that definite relationships might be shown through further experimentation.[37]

Among the physical conditions underlying the development of personality traits which have been utilized beyond available experimental evidence are the ductless glands.[38] Research has gone just far enough, perhaps, to show that there is some sort of relationship between the endocrine mechanisms and personality traits, but it still remains to be seen how these relationships can be particularized. It is known, for example, that the administration of the active principle from the thyroid gland can, in a few cases, transform that form of idiocy known as cretinism into a more normal set of functions.[39]

[35] Cannon, W. B., *Bodily Changes in Pain, Hunger, Fear and Rage* (2nd ed.). New York: D. Appleton-Century Co., 1929, *passim*.
[36] Cf. Needham, J., *The Skeptical Biologist*. New York: W. W. Norton and Co., 1930, pp. 130-153.
[37] Cf. Rich, G. J., "A Biochemical Approach to the Study of Personality." *J. Abnorm. and Soc. Psychol.*, 1928, XXIII, 158-175. Also, "Body Acidity as Related to Emotional Excitability." *Arch. Neur. and Psychiat.*, 1928, XX, 589-594.
[38] Cf. Berman, L., *The Glands Regulating Personality*. New York: The Macmillan Co., 1921, *passim*.
[39] Tredgold, A. F., *Mental Deficiency*. London: William Wood, 1908, pp. 251 ff. See also, Hoskins, R. G., "Endocrinology," in Bentley, M. (Ed.), *The Problem of Mental Disorder*. New York: McGraw-Hill Book Co., 1934, Chapter XI.

276 INTRODUCTION TO EDUCATIONAL PSYCHOLOGY

It has not been possible to detect any significant correlations between disturbances of glandular function and I.Q.'s.[40] Obviously, then, a great deal of work needs to be done in this field if more precise correlations between glandular dysfunction and various phases of the intelligence quotient and of personality are to be discerned.

V. THE DEVELOPMENT OF PERSONALITY TRAITS

1. *Introduction:* The most significant feature of the contemporary approach to the problems of personality and character lies in the fact that most traits are seen to be the product of training. A demonstration of this inference, however, is to be found primarily in the origin and development of such traits in order to see how changes can be brought about in them. In general, the development of character is one phase of the problem of learning. This is obviously true of skills and habits which become both persistent and insistent in the total stream of behavior of a person. It must be true, also, of those acts, whether emotional, moral, or aesthetic, which gain some of their particular qualities by virtue of the social setting within which they occur.

2. *Introversion–Extroversion:* It is commonly believed, of course, that a great many of these features of behavior are innate or hereditary. Lusty crying on the part of a new-born infant, for example, has been taken as a sign of independence or of temper; and in the same way, quiet repose has been taken as a sign of a sweet disposition. It has been shown, however, that no such correlation exists. Furfey gained a rating of the fretfulness, quietness, irritability, and other traits from seventy-five infants during the first few hours. These judgments were compared with corresponding traits of the same children when they had reached the ages of eighteen to twenty-four months. No significant correlation between the two sets of judgments was discovered.[41]

It is more reasonable to expect that the behavior of new-born infants is initiated pretty largely by the organic conditions which obtain at birth. Almost immediately, however, the processes of learning are brought to bear upon the reaction patterns of the infant. Marston, for example, has examined the origin of those behavior

---

[40] Fox, E. J., "Influence of Glandular Therapy on the Intelligence Quotient." *Ment. Hygiene,* 1928, XII, 90-102.

[41] Bonham, M., and Sargeant, M. K., "A Study of the Development of Personality Traits in Infants Eighteen to Twenty-four Months of Age." Master's Thesis, Catholic Univ. of America, 1928.

DEVELOPMENT OF PERSONALITY AND CHARACTER

traits and tendencies known as extroversion and introversion.[42] Among the traits which are said to be characteristic of the introvert are self-depreciation, sensitiveness to the opinions of others, reticence, absentmindedness, meticulousness, moodiness, self-consciousness, imaginativeness, and dislike of prominence in groups. The extrovert has traits which are the opposite of these, and he is more apt to be interested in external realities than in feeling and thought.[43] Marston studied, for example, the trait of compliance and its opposite by noting a child's reactions to the request that he open a box with fastenings so complicated that the task was impossible for him. Degree of interest in external objects was measured by recording the number of stops made by a child when it was permitted to explore an animal museum which it had never seen before. Altogether twenty such traits were thus examined. It turned out that the traits were dependable enough to argue that they must be fairly well established within the first five years. Bühler has shown that some of these tendencies may be established by the end of the first year.[44]

3. *Jealousy:* As a further illustration of the early appearance of special dispositions, we may take a study of jealousy. This study was based upon 70 children whose behavior was observed in connection with the birth of an additional member of the family.[45] Jealous behavior displayed itself in the following ways, viz., by direct bodily attacks on the younger sibling, by ignoring the presence of the sibling, and by denying its possession. It was noted that, in some cases, definite changes of personality would appear when a new member of the family was added. These changes were described as an increase in temper, the development of a negative attitude, an increase in daydreaming, and an increase in shyness and timidity. There was no evidence in this study that older children who had been told about the coming birth of a brother or sister were any the less likely to develop a jealous attitude.

[42] Marston, L. R., "The Emotions of Young Children, An Experimental Study in Introversion and Extroversion." *Univ. of Iowa Stud. in Child Welfare*, 1925, III, 3, pp. 7-99.
[43] Jung, C. G., *Collected Papers on Analytical Psychology*. London: Baillière, 1917; Freyd, M., "Introversion and Extroversion." *Psychol. Rev.*, 1924, XXXI, 74-87; Heidbreder, E., "Measuring Introversion and Extroversion." *J. Abnorm. and Soc. Psychol.*, 1926, XXI, 21-34.
[44] Bühler, C., "Die Ersten sozialen Verhaltungsweisen des Kindes," *Sociol. und Psychol. Stud. über das Erste Lebensjahr*, pp. 1-102; Verry, E. E., "A Study of Personality in Pre-school Play Groups." *J. of Social Forces*, 1925, III, 645-648; Wooley, H. T., "Personality Studies of Three-year-olds." *J. Exper. Psychol.*, 1922, V, 381-391.
[45] Sewell, M., "Some Causes of Jealousy in Young Children." *Smith. Coll. Studies in Social Work*, 1930, I, 6-22.

The development of jealousy has an important bearing upon some of the problems which the teacher has to face, not only in the schoolroom, but on the playground as well. Once the attitude has been developed, it is almost inevitable that it will be transferred to other persons and to other situations. If it does, in fact, contribute to shyness, timidity, an increase in daydreaming, or an increase in temper, these dispositions too can be transferred to other situations. The optimal time for the appearance of jealousy lies between the ages of eighteen and forty-two months. It is at this time, perhaps, that a child would feel most keenly any loss of preference displayed toward it by its parents. In other words, the development of jealousy might be a product of feelings of overdependence upon parents which were induced by the attitudes of the parents themselves. If the child were brought under the influence of a teacher toward whom no such feelings of dependence could be manifested, problems of a social and personal nature might develop at once.

4. *Obstinacy:* Facts of similar import come out of studies on the attitude known as obstinacy. In general, obstinacy may be defined either as a negative attitude toward commands of parents and teachers or as persistence in a type of action even when the situation which would normally prompt a given type of action has been greatly modified. It looks as though the obstinate attitude develops most frequently among preschool children whenever they are ignored for a period of time, or when commands forbidding them to engage in preferred types of activity become too numerous.[46]

It has been urged by some that negative attitudes of the obstinate sort are often the result of the attempt of a child to overcome a feeling of inferiority. The point is that, if a child accustomed to attention does not receive sufficient attention, it will attempt to express its dominance by saying "No" at every opportunity and by going its own way, irrespective of the commands or suggestions that have been given to it. If simpler forms of negative attitude are not adequate to the situation, the pupil may respond by long periods of retreat from the teacher and from other pupils and by sulkiness.[47]

5. *Leadership:* A complex of social traits which has received much attention in recent years is described by the term "leadership." It looks as though the dominance of one child over another may receive some impetus fairly early in life, if, in the first social contacts that are established, one infant is physiologically more mature

---

[46] Cf. Reynolds, N. M., "Negativism of Preschool Children." *Teachers Coll. Contrib. to Educ.*, 1928, No. 288.

[47] Sherman, M. M., *Mental Hygiene and Education.* New York: Longmans, Green and Co., 1913, Chapter V, *passim.*

DEVELOPMENT OF PERSONALITY AND CHARACTER 279

or more aggressive than another. There is some evidence to show that, among adults, most leaders are taller than the average and more robust in other aspects of stature. A great many other qualities have been attributed to more dominating persons.[48]

In one of the first experiments on leadership, a considerable number of subjects were divided into groups of four each. A variety of pictures were presented to each of the subjects, the subjects then being questioned about the objects in the pictures. Some of the questions were pertinent to these objects, while others were "catch" questions. It was assumed that certain persons in each of the groups of four might take the lead in answering questions quickly or in detecting the "catch" questions. In a second series of observations, the subjects were reshuffled into groups of four so that each group contained one of the subjects who had taken the initiative in the previous test. It was thus possible to compare the initiative of a given person in one group as contrasted with his initiative in another group.

Considerable amounts of information were gained concerning the way in which leadership could be expressed.[49] Among other things, it was found that the person who took the initiative in one group was very apt to do so in another as well. Moreover, it was found that children having initiative of this type were apt to be rated either first or last in such factors as dress, health, social status, quality of schoolwork, boldness in conduct, and fluency in speech. The nonleaders gained an average rank in these respects. The teachers of these children mentioned the more aggressive pupils about twice as often as they did the others.[50]

6. *Ethical Traits:* The problem of the development of ethical traits is tied up closely with a series of traditions about the origin and nature of conscience. As a rule, it has been implied by the word "conscience" that every person could achieve, sooner or later, an innate sense of right as opposed to wrong. It might follow from this belief that a person who was honest in one situation would be honest in all situations.

At the same time, however, it has been assumed that conscience could be trained. Were this true, it ought to follow that those relationships between stimulus-situations and responses which can be described as moral or ethical would fall into a normal probability

---

[48] Griffith, C. R., *Introduction to Applied Psychology.* New York: The Macmillan Co., 1934, Chapter X.
[49] Terman, L. M., "A Preliminary Study of the Psychology and Pedagogy of Leadership." *Ped. Sem.,* 1904, XI, 413-451.
[50] For a further study, see Caldwell, O. W., and Wellman, B., "Characteristics of School Leaders." *J. Educ. Res.,* 1926, XIV, 1-13.

curve. This has, as a matter of fact, been found to be the case. When, for example, a large number of children are confronted with a variety of situations in which cheating is possible, a very few will be found to react honestly in a large number of cases, and a large number will be found to react in an honest way in an average number of cases. These same facts appear to hold true of other types of ethical and moral traits.[51]

A number of attempts have been made to discover where such traits have their origin and how they change under the influence of teaching situations. Among other things, it has been shown that moral traits appear more frequently among the more intelligent than they do among unselected groups. Subjects with a high intelligence quotient, for example, excel unselected groups in every one of the traits that have been measured.[52] It looks as though moral and ethical traits become fairly stable at an early age. To say the same thing in another way, it might be expected that, given special training in them, the relative number of instances in which dishonesty, untruthfulness, and selfishness appear would decrease as the child grows older. It looks, however, as though major decreases do not occur. To be sure, as children grow older, the number of situations in which ethical as opposed to unethical actions may appear, increase greatly. If, however, allowances are made for this fact, ethical and moral traits appear to be as constant as is the intelligence quotient.[53]

It is now quite certain that environmental situations in the form of home life, the character of childhood associations, moving picture attendance, and types of reading stand in a fair measure of correlation with scores gained from measures of moral and ethical traits. One investigator, for example, has attributed about ninety per cent of disorders in conduct to poor training and discipline in the home.[54] Another investigator has found that broken homes contribute freely to faulty moral behavior.[55] The same facts appear to hold true of the quality of a child's playmates.[56]

[51] Cf. Slaght, W. E., "On Truthfulness in Children: Its Conditioning Factors and Its Setting in Child Nature." *Univ. of Iowa Stud. in Char.*, 1928, I (No. 4).

[52] Cf. Terman, L. M., et al., *Genetic Studies of Genius*, Vol. I: *Mental and Physical Traits of a Thousand Gifted Children*. Palo Alto: Stanford Univ. Press, 1925, pp. 515 ff.

[53] For a summary of the literature, see Jones, V., "Children's Morals," in Murchison, C. (Ed.), *Handbook of Child Psychology* (2nd ed.). Worcester, Mass.: Clark Univ. Press, 1933, Chapter XI.

[54] Cf. Paynter, H., and Blanchard, P., *Educational Achievement of Children with Personality and Behavior Difficulties*. New York: Commonwealth Fund, 1928, *passim*.

[55] Cf. Thomas, W. I., and Thomas, D. S., *The Child in America*. New York: A. A. Knopf and Co., 1928, *passim*.

[56] Wellman, B. L., "The School Child's Choice of Companions." *J. Educ. Res.*, 1926, XIV, 126-132.

DEVELOPMENT OF PERSONALITY AND CHARACTER

There are, of course, a great many other factors which have a bearing upon this problem but space will not permit us to consider them all. The student can see, however, that most of the traits that have been mentioned in this section owe their origin not so much to formal school situations as they do to more informal types of training. One might take the attitude, of course, that a secular school has no obligations toward this feature of the whole growth pattern, but this attitude can scarcely be justified, since it is not possible for the teacher to take no attitude at all. Even though no attention is paid to teaching situations having a moral or ethical value, the very lack of attention implies that an attitude has been taken.

VI. THE INFLUENCE OF SPECIAL FACTORS ON THE DEVELOPMENT OF CHARACTER TRAITS

1. *Hereditary Factors:* As with so many of the psychological functions, the problems of self, character, and personality force both psychology and education to take some position with respect to the relative influence of heredity and environment in giving shape to a human being. There are those who would argue that most, if not all, of the essential ingredients of personality are subject to hereditary factors, but more recently the impression has been growing that an experimental education should push to the very limit the analysis of possible environmental influences.[57]

As an approach to this problem of the influence of the environment on the development of character, we shall do well to distinguish factors which are presumably hereditary from possible environmental factors. We may remark, in the first place, that personality traits may be partly dependent upon certain anatomical, physiological, and chemical properties of the body. In so far as these anatomical, physiological, and chemical properties are subject to hereditary determination, it might be said that the personality traits that depend upon them could also be subject to hereditary determination.

This does not exhaust, however, the meanings which are attached to hereditary determination by a great many authorities. Since prevailing motives to action often reflect the general character of a person and since some of these prevailing motives spring out of fundamental tissue needs, further support for the hereditary hypothesis might be gained. Moreover, it has been argued that heredity equips

[57] For a survey of the literature, see Murphy, G., and Murphy, L. B., *op. cit.*, *passim.*

282 INTRODUCTION TO EDUCATIONAL PSYCHOLOGY

different persons with a variety of instinctive tendencies to action, many of which are distinctly social in character. Various amounts of the herding instinct, for example, or of the possessive, acquisitive, and aggressive instincts would make a difference in the so-called personality of an individual.

It is possible to think of the physiological and chemical determinants of personality traits in two ways. In the first place, it has been argued that some of the bodily features which represent, so to speak, products of preferred types of chemical activity in the body are not only indicative of but diagnostic of personality differences. The size of a person's chin, the color of his hair, or some of the principal features of his total bodily stature are obviously products of a chemical condition of the body. In the second place, it is possible to search out the primary chemical conditions themselves in order to see whether there is any relation between these conditions and the appearance of personality traits. In so far as such correlations can be discovered, it might be argued that personality has a derived hereditary component. In addition to these factors, however, there are a great many other determinants of personality, some of which are a product of accidents at birth and some of organizations of environmental materials in such a way that they will become effective in promoting certain traits to the exclusion of others.

2. *Physical Condition:* We may pass over quickly some of the more general physical conditions that are said to favor or disfavor character dispositions. There seems to be sufficient reason to believe that general good health or vitality may contribute to the development of such traits as cheerfulness, impulsiveness, optimism, and aggressiveness. This belief lies behind all of the attempts that are now being made to insure proper nourishment, good teeth, healthy throat conditions, and other hygienic care both in the schoolroom and out of it.[58] Low degrees of vitality or poor health are said to favor lack of confidence, introversion, moodiness, slowness, and pessimism. There are, to be sure, a great many exceptions to be made to these common beliefs, but in general they appear worthy of the most serious levels of attention.

Specific anatomical and physiological characteristics have been related to personality traits in two different ways. On the one hand, it has been argued that special physical defects may result in the creation of a personality trait which will compensate for the

[58] Cf. Fisher, V. E., *An Introduction to Abnormal Psychology.* New York: The Macmillan Co., 1929, Chapter VI.

DEVELOPMENT OF PERSONALITY AND CHARACTER 283

defect.[59] Adler, for example, writes of some of the aggressive attitudes taken by children as follows:

"If we trace the history of this aggressive attitude back to childhood we always come upon the outstanding fact that, throughout the whole period of development, the child possesses a feeling of inferiority in its relations both to parents and the world at large; . . . this feeling of inferiority is the cause of his continual restlessness as a child, his craving for action, his playing of rôles, the pitting of his strength against that of others, his anticipatory pictures of the future, and his physical as well as mental preparations. The whole potential educability of the child depends upon this feeling of insufficiency. . . . Thus the child arrives at the positing of a goal, an imagined goal of superiority, whereby his poverty is transformed into wealth, his subordination into determination, his ignorance into omniscience, and his incapacity into artistic creation. The longer and more definitely the child feels his insecurity, the more he suffers either from physical or marked mental weakness, the more he is aware of life's neglect, the higher will this goal be placed and the more faithfully will it be adhered to." [60]

Adler's argument is, of course, based entirely upon clinical and empirical evidence, but a certain amount of justification for it has been found with the aid of test scores. Faterson, for example, finds a slight though definite degree of relationship between "organ inferiority" and "feelings of inferiority," such as were described by Adler.[61] Obviously, however, problems of this sort must be considered in still greater detail. The second phase of the relationship between organic structures and personality traits is to be found in the argument that there is an aggressive brow, a weak chin, an intelligent forehead, and the like.

It is hardly the function of an educational psychology to consider the problems of character analysis from the empirical point of view, but so many teachers suppose that they can, from a casual inspection of face, form, and manner, proceed to a correct judgment concerning the personality traits of their students, that some consideration of the matter is demanded. The tendency of teachers to use these superficial methods is often aided by the general credulity of uneducated persons and by the publication and wide sale of certain

---

[59] Adler, A., *The Neurotic Constitution* (Trans. by B. Glueck and J. E. Lind). New York: Moffat, Yard, 1917. See also Adler, A., *A Study of Organ Inferiority and Its Psychical Compensation* (Trans. by S. E. Jellife). New York: Nervous and Mental Diseases Publ. Co., 1917.
[60] Adler, A., *The Practice and Theory of Individual Psychology.* New York: Harcourt, Brace and Co., 1924, p. 37.
[61] Faterson, H. F., *Some Implications of the Normal Inferiority Complex.* Thesis from the Univ. of Minn., 1928.

types of books which claim to describe short-cut methods of character analysis.[62]

As an example, we may take a series of common prejudices about the temperamental traits of blondes versus brunettes. It is argued, for instance, that blondes are positive, dynamic, driving, aggressive, domineering, impatient, active, quick, hopeful, speculative, changeable and variety-loving. Brunettes are said to be characterized by the opposite traits. These assertions have been put to a test by Paterson and Ludgate. A group of 94 judges was asked to rate 187 blondes and 187 brunettes who were well known to the judges in terms of such traits as are mentioned above. The results showed clearly enough that the traits were distributed almost equally among both types of complexion.[63] The same conclusions were drawn from a study of 152 successful salesmen who were about equally divided as to dominant complexion.[64] Most of the attempts to diagnose character traits by facial expressions have failed.

3. *Intelligence:* The third set of factors which have been said to exert an influence on personality traits involves differences in intelligence. For a long time it has been supposed that the exceptionally bright child is likely to be physically inferior, unduly serious, a trifle introspective, and perhaps unpopular with his playmates. None of these assertions can be supported by the evidence that is now available.[65] It sometimes happens that a dull child born of very bright parents or having brothers and sisters differing greatly in intelligence may suffer modifications of personality as a result of his family associations. This factor, however, may easily be exaggerated, as is shown by a study of adjustment during a five-year period of 68 retarded children. Very little correlation was found between the degree of retardation and the level of social adjustment.[66] In a study by Powers, who used the Marston introversion-extroversion rating scale, it was found that the development of character per-

---

[62] Blackford, K. M. H., *Reading Character at Sight.* New York: Independent Corp., 1918. See also, Adams, H. F., "Psychological Gold Bricks." *Scribner's Mag.*, 1921, LXX, 94-101; Dunlap, K., "The Reading of Character from External Signs." *Scientific Mo.*, 1922, XIV, 153-165.

[63] Paterson, D. G., and Ludgate, K. E., "Blond and Brunette Traits: A Quantitative Study." *J. Person. Res.*, 1922, I, 122-127.

[64] Kenagy, H. G., "Do Blonds Make the Best Salesmen?" *Sales Manag.*, 1923 (Feb.), pp. 325-326.

[65] Terman, L. M., *Genetic Studies of Genius.* Vol. I: *Mental and Physical Traits of a Thousand Gifted Children.* Palo Alto: Stanford Univ. Press, 1925-1926. See also Hollingworth, L. S., *Gifted Children.* New York: The Macmillan Co., 1926.

[66] Kinder, E. F., and Rutherford, E. J., "Social Adjustment of Retarded Children," *Mental Hygiene*, 1927, XI, 811-833.

DEVELOPMENT OF PERSONALITY AND CHARACTER

sonality traits is also, to a considerable extent, independent of the I.Q.'s of the subject.[67]

4. *Family Relationships:* A fourth factor that has been alleged to have some effect upon the development of character traits is the position of a child in the family. Only children, for example, are supposed to be surrounded with dangers that come from the lack of companionship, or from standing at the center of attention and of affection. It has been said that the only child is apt to be selfish, lacking in initiative, overemotional, nervously unstable, and quite unable to get along with companions of its own age. On the other hand, it is argued that the oldest child in a family may be aggressive and domineering, while a younger child is apt to develop an inferiority complex in the face of the older brothers and sisters. Here, too, popular opinion seems to have exaggerated the situation. Such studies as can be made upon relationships of this sort seem to suggest that, as a group, only children are normal in their development.[68]

5. *Social Factors:* By all odds the most important factor having to do with the development of character and personality traits is the social environment. It used to be thought that a large share of the undesirable traits of children must be hereditary. The appeal to heredity is, as we shall try to show, obviously a refusal to recognize the importance of informal education operating outside of the home and the schoolroom.

The facts that are now available force the conclusion that crimes brew readily in regions of poverty, congestion, and ignorance.[69] Moreover, one of the great contributions of psychoanalysis to education has been the demonstration that maladjustments are the offspring of early childhood experiences and conflicts. Both of these factors are obviously signs of ignorance and unintelligence in the control of education rather than evidence either for inbred perversion, instincts, or the inscrutable ways of Deity. A number of studies have shown that a considerable proportion of delinquent boys and girls come from homes of the poor. In one such study, 69 per cent of the girls and 38 per cent of the boys were found to have come from the lowest class, the "very poor," the class in which

---

[67] Powers, N. E., "Application of the Marston Introversion-Extroversion Rating Scale," *J. Educ. Psychol.*, 1928, XIX, pp. 168 ff.; Foster, J. C., and Anderson, J. E., *The Young Child and His Parents: A Study of 100 Cases.* Minn.: Univ. of Minn. Press, 1927.
[68] Goodenough, F. L., and Leahy, A. M., "The Effect of Certain Family Relationships upon the Development of Personality." *Ped. Sem.,* 1927, XXXIV, 45-71.
[69] Thomas, W. I., *The Unadjusted Girl.* Boston: Little, Brown and Co., 1923, p. 100.

there existed not merely destitution but destitution accompanied by degradation or destitution caused by degradation.[70]

Another study of delinquency areas in a large city has shown that there are zones of transition between resident sections and those of business and industry. These slums, or semislum areas, represent regions of social chaos filled with cheap rooming houses and tenements, an unwelded mixture of racial groups and other unfortunate social conditions. All of the evidence seems to suggest that no very great amount of character can grow out of an educational program ordered along these lines.

Obviously, the point of departure for the organization of the environment for the development of character lies either in the home or in the schoolroom. Sufficient evidence has already been advanced to show that the early home environment is probably the most effective agent for the establishment of personality and character traits that the child will ever have to meet. The school situation is sometimes highly effective, and there are those who would argue that it should become still more effective than is the case at present.[71] It is being pointed out more and more frequently, for example, that the personality or character traits of children cannot easily rise above the level already attained by the teachers. This is to say that the teaching staff in any institution presents a personality background to instruction in the more specific subjects, so that the processes of incidental learning may be promoted thereby.

The direct contribution to character and personality traits made by the curriculum itself will depend upon the attitude which is taken by the teachers toward the problem of the transfer of training. As we shall see, there has been a long tradition to the effect that some of the subjects in the curriculum are there partly because of their disciplinary effect. In addition to the actual acquisition of knowledge, students were supposed to learn neatness, persistence, honesty, and other similar traits. This assumption has, of course, been seriously questioned, but it does appear that experimental methods are actually adequate to the character of the problem. It still remains to be seen, therefore, just what effect the normal curriculum may have on personality traits. The same argument holds true of extracurricular activities. Various types of competition in athletics,

---

[70] Cf. Breckenridge, S. P., and Abbott, E., *The Delinquent Child and the Home.* New York: Charities Publ. Com., 1912. See especially, pp. 70-74. Also, Burt, C. L., *The Young Delinquent.* New York: D. Appleton-Century Co., 1925, pp. 62, 65 and *passim.*

[71] Cf. Kilpatrick, W. H., et al., *The Educational Frontier.* New York: D. Appleton-Century Co., 1933, *passim.*

DEVELOPMENT OF PERSONALITY AND CHARACTER

for example, have been supported by a strong belief in their value for the training and development of character. One might say offhand that extracurricular activities are in the same situation as are curricular studies, the amount of transfer from such a game as football, for example, depending upon the extent to which coaches and others generalize football experiences to the total good of the individual.

In large-scale production, however, it is not possible for each teacher to become directly effective with individual pupils. A great many school systems have been forced, therefore, to supplement the classroom by the creation of special personnel clinics wherein idiosyncrasies of personality and character, problem children, and underprivileged children can receive special types of instruction. It is not unusual to have a physician, a psychologist, a psychiatrist, and a nurse available through the school clinic. Since the problems have increased greatly in recent years we shall devote a special chapter to them.

READINGS

One of the quickest modes of approach to some of the older views of the nature of the self and of personality is to be found in Calkins, M. W., *A First Book in Psychology* (4th ed.). New York: The Macmillan Co., 1914. If the student were to read hurriedly through this book and then compare it with Hartshorne, H., *Character in Human Relations.* New York: Charles Scribner's Sons, 1932, he would see at once the great change that has taken place in our view of the nature of the self. The book by Hartshorne is, for the most part, a review and interpretation of the monumental survey of this whole problem. See Hartshorne, H., and May, M. A., *Studies in the Nature of Character* (3 vols.). New York: The Macmillan Co., 1928-1930.

As in so many other places, so here, there is a difference in opinion as to the relative value of specific types of conduct versus configuration or patterning in conduct. The work of Hartshorne mentioned above emphasizes the specific features of the stream of behavior insofar as these features have personal or characterlike qualities. The configurational point of view is well presented in Wheeler, R. H., and Perkins, F. T., *Principles of Mental Development.* New York: T. Y. Crowell Co., 1932, Chapter XII. The student will find it profitable to read also the first chapter of this book. One of the standard sources of information concerning personality types is by Kretschmer, E., *Physique and Character* (trans. by W. H. J. Sprott). New York: Harcourt, Brace and Co., 1925. The psychology of personality types is closely related to organic factors contributing to personality. These matters are discussed in Paterson, D. G., *Physique and Intellect.* New York: D. Appleton-Century Co., 1930. See also, Stockard, C. R., *The Physical Basis of Personality.* New York: W. W. Norton Co., 1931.

Authoritative information on various contributory factors to the development of personality can be found in Murchison, C., *Handbook of Child*

Psychology. Worcester, Mass.: Clark Univ. Press, 1933. See especially Chapter III, "Emotional Development" (by M. C. Jones); Chapter IX, "The Social Behavior of Children" (by C. Bühler); Chapter XXII, "The Child with Difficulties of Adjustment" (by P. Blanchard); and Chapter XXIV, "The Primitive Child" (by M. Mead).

It is not easy to separate the development of personality traits from their social implications. A rich mine of information about this phase of personal development is to be found in Murphy, G., and Murphy, L. B., *Experimental Social Psychology.* New York: Harper and Bros., 1931. If the student has not already considered some of the references on mental hygiene listed at the end of the last chapter, he should take this occasion to make use of them now, for a complete view of the development of the self cannot be had apart from some knowledge of maladjustment.

The development of social, ethical, and moral traits, together with their relation to citizenship and to other objectives of the educational program, is just now producing a large literature. Any one of the following references will be found helpful: Boorman, W. R., *Developing Personality in Boys.* New York: The Macmillan Co., 1929; Charters, W. W., *The Teaching of Ideals.* New York: The Macmillan Co., 1927; Coe, G. A., *What is Christian Education?* New York: Charles Scribner's Sons, 1929; Fishback, E. H., *Character Building for Junior High School Grades.* Boston: D. C. Heath and Co., 1930; Maller, J. B., "Cooperation and Competition." *Teachers College Contrib. to Educ.,* 1929 (No. 384); Shand, A. F., *The Foundations of Character.* London: The Macmillan Co., 1914; Symonds, P. M., *The Nature of Conduct.* New York: The Macmillan Co., 1928.

The most useful survey of tests and measures of personality and character traits has been compiled by Symonds, P. M., *Diagnosing Personality and Conduct.* New York: D. Appleton-Century Co., 1931. See also, Symonds, P. M., *Psychological Diagnosis in Social Adjustment.* New York: American Book Co., 1934.

A further discussion of the various environmental factors that contribute to personality and character traits may be expected in a later chapter. Some of the more important references are as follows: Thomas, W. I., and Thomas, D. S., *The Child in America.* New York: A. Knopf, 1928; Burt, C., *The Young Delinquent.* New York: D. Appleton-Century Co., 1925; Slawson, J., *The Delinquent Boy.* Boston: R. C. Badger, 1926; Healy, W., and Bronner, A., *Delinquents and Criminals: Their Making and Unmaking.* New York: The Macmillan Co., 1928; Healy, W., *Mental Conflicts and Misconduct.* Boston: Little, Brown and Co., 1917; Healy, W., et al., *Reconstructing Behavior in Youth: A Study of Problem Children in Foster Families.* New York: A. Knopf, 1929; Germane, C. E., and Germane, E. G., *Character Education.* Newark: Silver, Burdett and Co., 1929.

PART TWO

ORIGINAL NATURE AND LEARNING

CHAPTER NINE

THE PROBLEMS OF ORIGINAL NATURE

I. Directed Growth Patterns

1. *Introduction:* The sketchy picture which was drawn in the first chapter of some of the main features of a human growth pattern does not give much more than a suggestion of the vast amount of work that is being done in the field. It used to be said that the first decades of the present century saw parents, educators, and psychologists becoming, for the first time, child-conscious, but, as we now look at these decades, it is clear that adults were child-conscious only at an anecdotal or, at the best, a descriptive level.[1]

It is an amazing thing, of course, to find that, even though children have been trained in some fashion or other ever since living creatures became essentially human rather than essentially animal, no serious attempt has been made, until the present decade, to examine the processes of child development with the aid of experimental methods. Men have been far more interested in the material objects and events around them than they have in the psychological and socializing events that transform a new-born infant into a mature person who is ready to play a worth-while part in the social scene.

A more objective interest in child psychology was promoted by the theory of evolution, but the first child psychologies, while rich in observation and inference, were, after all, nothing more than diaries of the various things which children were actually found to be doing in a home environment. There was little attempt to discover whether the home and the playground conditions which surround the growth process could be altered for the purpose of modifying the whole pattern and for bringing intelligent guidance to bear upon it. Now the journals, both those specifically devoted to child research and those devoted to the general problems of psychology, are

[1] Cf. Anderson, J. E., "The Methods of Child Psychology," in Murchison, C. (Ed.), *Handbook of Child Psychology* (2nd ed.). Worcester, Mass.: Clark Univ. Press, 1933, Chapter I.

filled with experimental material which cannot help but become of major importance to the educator.[2]

Much of this experimental literature goes to make up that sequence of events which has been described in the first chapter as the growth pattern. In order to keep this pattern before us, let us suppose that we were to make a continuous moving picture of a human being from the moment of conception to the attainment of full maturity. Let us suppose, moreover, that we were to make this record according to the principles used in filming the growth of a plant. That is, let us expose a few feet of film every few days so that our final record will summarize, in a small number of minutes, the whole process that requires twenty or thirty years. With such a filming of human growth before us, we would have a basis for getting a perspective upon the whole pattern, for it is clear that this is a pattern which can be described as a pattern. The first chapter was intended to give, with the aid of words rather than with the aid of a moving picture film, a general view of the pattern.[3]

2. *The Directedness of the Pattern:* One of the essential features of this pattern is that it is observably continuous. Its continuity is made up, not by the gradual addition of one item to another, but by a forward movement of an astonishingly complex and highly configured series of events. There is, however, another feature of the growth pattern which is of primary importance to the teacher. Every growth pattern appears to be directed. It has what the mathematician would call a vectorial quality. Living systems appear to be going somewhere in particular.

This is not to say that all children are proceeding in the same direction toward exactly the same goal, except in so far as most of them will become normal or typical human beings. On the contrary, children will become human beings who differ from one another in a great many respects. Some will become professors, some will become workers, and some will become criminals. When, however, we set up a profession or an occupation as a goal toward which the growth pattern is directed, we are using, as the basis of difference between persons, the services rendered by the use of our psychological functions rather than differences in the quality of the psy-

[2] For example, the *Journal of Genetic Psychology, The Genetic Psychology Monographs, Child Development, The Journal of Comparative Psychology,* and *The Journal of Educational Psychology.* In addition, there are many special series of monographs from research laboratories and many equally important foreign journals.

[3] A more nearly complete picture has been drawn by Goodenough, F. L., *Developmental Psychology.* New York: D. Appleton-Century Co., 1934.

chological functions themselves. It is more important to note that the growth pattern is directed in the sense that all normal human beings come to goals which can be measured in terms of high or low competence irrespective of the situations in which variable degrees of competence are to be used.

This is a phase of education, however, which will concern us later on in our study. For the present, let us devote ourselves to the fact that growth patterns are directed. When we say this, what, precisely, do we mean? Where is directedness to be found? Who or what is it that determines the direction? Why should it happen that some people appear to be directed toward distressingly low levels of competence, and why is it that other people appear to be directed toward extremely satisfying measures of high competence? Or, if we wish to think of directedness in terms of services rendered, why is it that some persons are directed toward the legal profession, the teaching profession, or toward the medical profession, while other persons are directed toward the workshop, the grocery store, or the railroad right-of-way?

3. *Hereditary Factors:* As we have implied in several chapters, two definite answers have been given to these questions. On the one hand, there is the answer which is furnished by the words "heredity" and "original nature." This answer says that the child is already fairly mature in some of its psychological operations at the moment it is born. It even says that the child is, at the moment of conception, as old as its parents, for this moment determines what traits and talents will stand at the foundation of everything that the child can do. In other words, the fertilized ovum of the newborn child is almost as old as its instincts, its native dispositions, its inherent reflexes, and its other unlearned capacities will allow it to be. If we say that every human being, either at birth or shortly thereafter, is equipped with a large variety of action-patterns or of tendencies to the formation of these patterns without the aid of particular learning situations, then all human beings, like many of the lower animals, are fairly mature even before they have begun to live. In short, this answer to the questions asked above would say that the growth pattern is directed primarily by factors which are resident in the hereditary constitution of the individual.[4]

4. *Learning Situations:* The second answer to the questions asked above is furnished by the guiding and promoting influence

---

[4] This answer is accepted most whole-heartedly, perhaps, by the eugenicists. See, for example, Popenoe, P., and Johnson, R. H., *Applied Eugenics.* New York: The Macmillan Co., 1933, Chapter I and *passim.*

of learning situations. In other words, the term "learning" is a term which is often paired with the phrase "original nature," as though there were some things about the vectorial features of human growth which must be attributed solely to original nature, the other things being attributable solely to learning. It is even argued that learning situations are much more fundamental in their effect on the growth pattern than hereditary factors can ever be.[5]

The student will see almost at once that he will not be able to read himself into the daily tasks of the teacher until these two sources of influence on the growth pattern have been examined in considerable detail. If the growth pattern gains most of its directed quality from hereditary agents, it must follow that human nature is uneducable in direct proportion to the intensity and variety of the hereditary agents. Likewise, if the growth pattern gets a considerable share of its directed quality from those environmental agents which are called learning situations or from the general buffering action of our modern climates of opinion, and if we may assume that a considerable number of learning situations are under the control of parents and teachers, it would follow that every person is highly educable, and that the direction which the educative process takes must be a problem of exceptional social importance.

5. *The Purpose of This Chapter:* It is the purpose of this chapter, and of the one that follows after, to make an appraisal of the facts which support the first of the two answers mentioned above. In other words, we propose to study the concept of original nature and all of the correlative terms that go with this concept, viz., heredity, instinct, innate ideas, hereditary tendencies, and all other types of native components of human nature. The three chapters which follow have, as their main purpose, a survey of the field of learning. This survey will include the major varieties and theories of learning, the "laws" of learning, and those general principles which are now known to serve as means of promoting the efficiency of the learning process. We must study also the extent to which the results of learning may be transferred from one situation to another.

As a result of our study of the two groups of agents which are alleged to give direction to the growth pattern, we ought to be able to say with some degree of assurance what parts of human nature are educable and what parts are not educable. It is hardly necessary to assert again that this is an extremely important problem for,

---

[5] Many students of sociology are strongly inclined toward environmental influences. See, for example, Hiller, E. T., *Principles of Sociology.* New York: Harper and Bros., 1933, *passim.*

if human nature is generously educable, this fact also should be known. It should be known for two reasons in particular. As educability increases, the responsibility of the teacher increases. Moreover, as educability increases, the alleged instinctive foundation for political systems, economic theories, and fundamental types of social organization must be changed. In short, a marked difference will be made in some parts of educational philosophy.

II. The Evidence for Psychological Inheritance

1. *The Commonsense View of Heredity:* When we take a longtime or a genetic view of human nature, there emerges a definite pattern of events which we have called the growth pattern. This growth pattern, after it is finished, appears to have been directed toward a specific goal. We are asking whence the directedness comes. There are those who would say that most of it comes from the hereditary components of human nature.

The general argument in favor of this answer may be stated as follows. Any survey of human conduct and experience will show that there is a large number of stimulus-connection-response patterns which do not appear to have any relevant learning or educational career behind them. In the case of the new-born child, the lack of a relevant educational process is obvious enough, for neither teachers nor parents can gain access to the child before it is born. We may say, then, that if the terms "original nature" or "heredity" are used to account for the behavior of the new-born infant, they are sometimes used not because it has been demonstrated that the actions of a new-born infant are really original or hereditary, but only because they are actions that have become observable for the first time.

It is clear that no one of these first observable actions should be called native or original until it has been shown that directive forces of the environmental type could not have had any effect upon them. Even after the child grows older, it will display many types of action and attitude which appear to have no relevant educational history behind them. Neither parents nor teachers, for example, set up a series of special learning situations in order to make children afraid of the dark or in order to make introverts out of them. Nevertheless, many children are afraid of the dark, and they are afraid in the presence of a good many other objects and situations as well. Likewise, some children are introverts, while others are extroverts. Moreover, they display a rich variety of other attitudes and dispositions, many of which are highly socialized in character, even though no educative process leading to them can be named either by their parents or their teachers.

Finally, our commonsense observations tell us that some persons seem to be more adapted to certain professions or to certain occupations than they are to others. Most children, for example, are given at least a few lessons at the piano or at some other musical instrument. Not all children, however, become musicians. A few become extremely competent. They may even become more competent than their earlier training can account for. The inference is that there must have been driving agents or factors behind the growth patterns of these children which directed them toward one type of competence rather than toward another.[6]

We are under an obligation, then, to name in more detail the actual evidence which supports the view that hereditary agents can give direction to the growth pattern. This evidence is of several different types. In the first place, there is an argument drawn from older definitions of psychology to the effect that the mind is a species unto itself and that it must, therefore, have properties or characteristics which distinguish it from all other entities. In the second place, there is the existence of all of those forms of behavior, both among men and animals, that have been called instinctive. In the third place, even our casual inspections will tell us that children are more apt to resemble their parents than they are to resemble other people. It is possible to measure degrees of resemblance, and these measurements favor the importance of heredity. In the fourth place, it is asserted that if a child has gained an I.Q. of 132 when it is six years of age, its I.Q. will stand almost, if not quite, at this same level at all subsequent ages, even though its environment has passed through major changes. In other words, since the I.Q. tends to remain constant, it must remain constant because of directive forces in the hereditary constituents of human nature which resist the environment. In the fifth place, even though children may be brought up in what are often called "identical" environments, they still differ from one another not only in degrees of competence, but in choice of occupation. These differences are sometimes highly resistant to alteration through practice, and it may be inferred, therefore, that they must owe their origin to the directive power of heredity.[7]

[6] Cf. Seashore, C. E., *The Psychology of Musical Talent.* Boston: Silver, Burdett and Co., 1919, *passim.*
[7] Some of the more important literature in this field which is, at the same time, readily accessible is as follows: Jennings, H. S., *The Biological Basis of Human Nature.* New York: W. W. Norton and Co., 1930; Schwesinger, G. C., *Heredity and Environment.* New York: The Macmillan Co., 1933.

THE PROBLEMS OF ORIGINAL NATURE

2. *The Doctrine of Innate Ideas:* The student has, no doubt, been somewhat perplexed by the fact that so little has been said in previous chapters about mind or consciousness, while so much has been said of stimulus and response. Commonsense opinion has it that it is the primary business of the teacher to train a person's mind and not to tell him how to react to situations. Our omission of references to the mind, however, has been intentional, for it has proven much more helpful to think of psychological and of educational problems in terms of modes of action in the presence of stimulus-situations than it has been to think of them in terms of mental processes. This means that modern psychology differs in certain essential respects from older forms of psychology, where a great deal of emphasis was placed upon the mind and upon its innate or intrinsic qualities.[8]

We shall consider some phases of the nature of psychology later on. In the meantime, there is one feature of older views that bears upon our present task. It used to be asserted that the mind was a distinct species unto itself. This view argued that a mind must be really a mind wherever it is found and hence, when it was said that new-born infants or the lower animals possess minds, it had to follow that these minds were of the same species as the minds of which adults speak. In other words, even though some of the incidental features of mental life may change, its essential character or its essential traits or properties or powers cannot change. The mind of the infant, therefore, must be just like the mind of the adult, save that it is smaller in dimension. It would follow from this definition of the mind that one can know the main outlines of the child mind whenever the main outlines of the adult mind have been drawn. This is to say that child psychology is automatically finished whenever a complete psychology of the adult mind is written.[9]

It is not this feature of the definition of psychology as the science of mind, however, to which we wish to draw attention at the present moment. On the contrary, we wish to remind the student of the fact that if the mind is a species unto itself, then there must be certain properties or traits or characteristics of the mind which exist

---

[8] In the last chapter of Part III, we shall try to see how the problems of educational psychology shift as definitions of the science of psychology shift. Either now or later, the student can consult with profit either Boring, E. G., *A History of Experimental Psychology*. New York: D. Appleton-Century Co., 1929, or Flugel, J. C., *A Hundred Years of Psychology*. New York: The Macmillan Co., 1933.
[9] Cf. Baldwin, J. M., *Mental Development*. New York: The Macmillan Co., 1906, Chapter I. Also Weld, H. P., *Psychology as Science*. New York: Henry Holt and Co., 1928, *passim*.

as inevitable or intrinsic properties of it. In other words, the mind has, by definition, an original nature.[10] In the history of philosophy this original nature has expressed itself in the doctrine that every child comes into the world with certain innate ideas, that is, ideas which do not have to be learned through experience. The more serious student of philosophy will remember that, in addition to these innate ideas, some philosophers have supposed that the mind can be characterized by certain fundamental types of operation, or that there are inborn categories within which experiences will be classified as fast as they arrive. Among the innate ideas that have been mentioned most frequently are the ideas of space and of time. It has even been urged that there are innate ideas of justice and of right and wrong.[11]

We do not propose to debate this question at the present moment. It is clear, however, that if minds are essentially the same wherever they are found, and if they have certain intrinsic functions or ideas which exist wholly apart from the accident which places them in one human body rather than in another, or in a human body rather than in the body of an animal, the problem of original nature is solved as soon as it is stated. In all essential respects, we must be what we are, because the mind is a species among other species and distinguishable from them in terms of properties of functions which are inherent to it. In a later chapter we shall try to show why it is that modern psychology has departed from this point of view. For the present we may simply remark that the question of native traits versus acquired traits cannot be settled in terms of a theory about human nature which is not in keeping with the trend of experimental research.

3. *Human and Animal Instincts:* A second source of arguments in favor of original nature springs from the observed fact that many of the lower animals appear to adjust themselves to their environments almost wholly by the use of inherited or inbred patterns of behavior known as instincts. It is pointed out, for example, that ants, bees, and social wasps are so well equipped with instincts that, as soon as they emerge from their cocoons, they are able to meet almost every situation in a wholly adequate manner. Moreover, the social life of ants and bees has often been pointed out as a model against which human societies can be compared only to the disadvantage of the latter. There is a division of labor among the various

[10] Consult the articles "mind" and "consciousness" in Hastings' *Encyclopedia of Religion and Ethics*. New York: Charles Scribner's Sons, 1928.
[11] Cf. Klemm, G. O., *A History of Psychology* (Trans. by E. C. Wilm and R. Pintner). New York: Charles Scribner's Sons, 1914, *passim*.

members of the colony and an ability to cope with situations which almost certainly, so it is said, cannot be attributed to any training process.[12]

A. ANIMAL INSTINCTS: The widespread appearance of instincts in the lower animals has made it appear probable that human beings must also be moved to action by tendencies toward behavior that are unlearned. This can be said, of course, without overlooking the fact that human beings differ from the lower animals in the extent to which they make use of intelligence. As a matter of fact, it is sometimes argued that the difference between the lower animals and human beings is created solely by the relative extent to which each group depends upon instinct as opposed to intelligence. The lower animals, for example, are not often credited with operations which are truly intellectual in character. Man, however, while being instinctive in a great many of his performances, can, nevertheless, modify his instincts and supplement them with the use of his intelligence.[13]

In any case, it has been the custom in educational psychology to begin a discussion of the field with a statement of the instincts which are probably basic to the educative process. Three such lists have become almost standard equipment in many of the books on educational psychology. There is, first of all, a set of some forty which was assembled by William James.[14] This list includes such items as acquisitiveness, collectiveness, gregariousness, and rivalry or emulation, in addition to more frequently cited items such as instinctive fears, anger, pugnaciousness, and the like.

A similar list has been made out by Thorndike.[15] This is the list, perhaps, which has been followed out more extensively than any other. McDougall, using, at one and the same time, the methods of logic and the methods of casual observation, has arrived at a list of seven primary pairs of instincts and emotions, several more general tendencies being added as a supplement to these primary pairs. There is, for example, an instinct of flight with its emotion of fear, a pugnacious instinct with its emotion of rage, a mating instinct with its emotion of love, and so on.[16] Were one to review all of

---

[12] Wheeler, W. M., *Ants*. New York: Columbia Univ. Press, 1910; Morgan, C. L., *Habit and Instinct*. London: E. Arnold, 1896.
[13] Cf. Morgan, C. L., *Instinct and Experience*. New York: The Macmillan Co., 1912, passim.
[14] James, W., *Principles of Psychology*. New York: Henry Holt and Co., 1890. Vol. II, Chapter XXIV.
[15] Thorndike, E. L., *Educational Psychology*. New York: Columbia Univ. Press, 1913. Vol. I: *The Original Nature of Man*.
[16] McDougall, W., *Social Psychology*. New York: J. W. Luce, 1916, Chapter III.

the studies that have been made upon performances of human beings that are alleged to be instinctive, the total number of instincts that have been attributed at one time or another to human nature would run into the hundreds.[17]

B. INSTINCTIVE URGES: Up to this point we have spoken of instincts as though the word should be used to name either any unlearned pattern of behavior which appears in response to basic stimulus-patterns or as a name for innate sets of connections between sense organs and muscles which can be tapped whenever the right situations appear. There is, however, still another way in which the word may be used. If the term "instinct" referred only to behavior-patterns or to nervous connections between stimuli and responses, it could be said that all human behavior must be nothing more than response to stimuli. As we have seen just above, however, some of the older views about psychology held that the mind serves as a source of energy or a directing power in the conduct of affairs.

Some psychologists have thought it wise not to abandon this notion of effective agency. McDougall, in particular, has argued in this way by asserting that the word "instinct" should properly be applied not to behavior or to nerve connections, but to driving forces of an unlearned character. Since, however, the word "instinct" has already been used so often to name behavior-patterns, on the one hand, and inbred nervous connections, on the other, McDougall has introduced a new term for the driving forces behind human action. It is his argument that all human and animal action is action that is purposive, in the sense that it is directed consciously and intentionally toward a goal. There are, therefore, *hormic* tendencies which lie at the root of whatever shall be called the original nature of human beings.[18]

C. THE EVIDENCE FROM INSTINCTS: It will not be possible for us to discuss this particular type of evidence for original nature intelligently until we have looked more carefully at the machinery by means of which hereditary factors can be passed on from parents to offspring. It is pertinent to inquire at this time, however, what the character of the evidence is upon which the doctrine of instinctive action is based. That is, we ought to know whether psychologists and educators have actually examined the entire history of actions which are said to be instinctive in order to discover where

[17] Bernard, L. L., *Instinct, A Study in Social Psychology*. New York: Henry Holt and Co., 1924, *passim*.
[18] Cf. McDougall, W., "The Hormic Psychology," in Murchison, C. (Ed.), *Psychologies of 1930*. Worcester, Mass.: Clark Univ. Press, 1930, Chapter I.

such acts began and how they have acquired the particular form they possess when we see them in operation.

It seems fair to say that the evidence for instinctive behavior at the human level is of two types. The first line of evidence comes from observations on the lower animals. These observations have been made, however, not with the aid of experimental methods nor from the desire to write out the whole history of action, but only in order to account for some of the amazing things which animals are known to do by inventing a word. Before the theory of evolution had become a general scientific principle it was easy to divide the lower animals from men by saying that the former had been endowed by their Creator with "frozen" intelligence whereas the latter are peculiarly endowed with intelligence.[19] After the theory of evolution had become a general scientific principle, that is, after it was possible to say that human beings, like the lower animals, are a part of the natural order, it was easy to assume that all of those types of action in human conduct which do not have an obvious educational history must, therefore, be as original as is instinctive behavior among the animals. In other words, if human beings can be placed upon the tree of life, some evidence of intelligence ought to be found in at least the higher of the lower animals, and some evidence of instinct in men.[20]

The second source of evidence in favor of instincts has already been stated in the first chapter. Any inspection of human conduct will reveal a large number of actions and tendencies to action which have no obvious or relevant period of training behind them. In view of this circumstance, it has been easy to say that such modes of action cannot possibly owe their origin to previous training. In other words, they must be original or native.

It is not often that human beings fall into a logic that is quite as bad as this, but the facts named above, together with the commonsense observation that a new-born infant does a great many things which it could not possibly have been taught to do will serve, perhaps, as an excuse for bad logic. As long as it is assumed that a new-born infant miraculously begins living in a mature way at birth, then anything that it does at or shortly after birth must be attributed to some other agency than training. In short, then, the evidence in

[19] For the meaning of the phrase "frozen" intelligence, see Bergson, H., *Creative Evolution* (Trans. by A. Mitchell). New York: Henry Holt and Co., 1911, *passim.*
[20] The principle of genetic continuity has rendered great service to many psychologists. See, for example, Bentley, M., *The Field of Psychology.* New York: D. Appleton-Century Co., 1924, Chapter XX.

favor of the existence of instincts is, in and of itself, not very convincing. It cannot be convincing until experimental methods have been applied to the entire genetic history of every type of human and animal conduct. This fact is somewhat disturbing when we realize the enormous use that has been made of instincts in educational theory and practice.[21]

D. THE THEORY OF RECAPITULATION: There is one further phase of current theories about instinct which should receive at least a brief description. It has been known for some time that each human being, during the first few weeks, and even during the first few months of development, follows a growth pattern which is very much like the growth pattern pursued by the lower animals. All living creatures, for example, begin with a single cell or with the fusion of two incomplete cells. Among all save the very simplest animals, growth depends, in part, upon a multiplied number of cell divisions, the first division yielding two daughter cells, the next four, the next eight, and so on. Moreover, at a slightly later stage of development the human embryo appears to have followed the growth pattern of some of the lower animals to such an extent that it is hard to distinguish it from, say, the embryo of a fish, a bird, or a chimpanzee.[22]

This similarity between growth patterns has furnished the basis for a law known as the law of recapitulation.[23] The law argues that human beings in their physiological development tend to pass through some of the major stages in the development of the lower animals. It is not of this side of the law of recapitulation, however, that we mean to speak, for the law has been translated into psychological terms. The argument has been simply this. Any survey of the psychological development of a child will show types of behavior and tendencies toward behavior which seem certainly to be an echo of the behavior of the remote ancestors of men.

As a simple example, we may take the grasping reflex. As the student knows, even a new-born infant will, if a rod is placed across the palms of its hands, grasp the rod and cling tightly to it even though the infant is lifted from its bed and is compelled, therefore, to support its own weight.[24] Since there was a time in the imme-

[21] As, for example, all of the educational psychologies which have followed Thorndike's position. Cf. Thorndike, E. L., *op. cit., passim.*
[22] Cf. Lull, R. S., and others, *The Evolution of Man.* New Haven: Yale Univ. Press, 1922, Chapter II and *passim.*
[23] Better known in biology as the law of biogenesis. Cf. Haldane, J. B. S., and Huxley, J., *Animal Biology.* Oxford: The Clarendon Press, 1927, pp. 79 ff.
[24] Cf. Watson, J. B., *Psychology from the Standpoint of a Behaviorist.* Philadelphia: J. B. Lippincott Co., 1924, pp. 261 ff.

diate ancestry of man when grasping the branches of trees seemed to be a necessary skill, it has seemed logical to suppose that the grasping reflex in the human infant must be an echo of the grasping skills of man's Simian ancestors.[25]

We have space for only one comment about this phase of the theories which argue that reflexes and instincts support the doctrine of original nature. It seems to be fairly clear that the environmental conditions under which life had its origin and has enjoyed its continuance have been fairly stabilized for a long period of time. These measures of stabilization touch more than temperature and food conditions. They touch the very balance that has been struck between all of the chemical elements.[26] Were the temperature of the earth to be raised by any considerable amount, an entirely new balance between the chemical elements would be brought into effect.

If, then, we grant the general stability of environmental conditions, even though we recognize wide variations within this stability, it would be necessary to explain, not the similarity that obtains between the growth patterns pursued by different animals, but marked dissimilarities in these growth patterns. In other words, the theory of recapitulation is a theory created by the supposed fact that certain influences must be at work, other than the mere stability of nature in making the prenatal growth pattern of human beings resemble early stages in the growth pattern of the lower animals. It is, of course, a simple thing to say that the original part of human nature is a summary or condensation of the previous experiences of the race, but when this is said, one must recognize that the basis for saying it is purely speculative and in a great many respects highly fanciful.

4. *Family Resemblances:* A third source of argument in favor of original nature comes from marked similarities between offspring and their parents. This is a fact which is too obvious to require supporting arguments. It is, however, a fact which may explain too much rather than too little. The student can easily see that, if a child does not resemble its own parents more nearly than it resembles other mature persons, then one may go to the grandparents or to the great-grandparents for evidence of hereditary transmission. The reader of these lines, for example, may have blue eyes. If neither of his parents has blue eyes, he will look to his grandparents for evidence of hereditary transmission. If neither his

---

[25] Cf. Hall, G. S., *Adolescence* (2 vols.). New York: D. Appleton-Century Co., 1904, *passim*.
[26] Cf. Henderson, L. J., *The Fitness of the Environment.* New York: The Macmillan Co., 1913, *passim*.

father's nor his mother's parents have blue eyes, he may pass on to uncles and aunts or to great-uncles and -aunts. If he continues his search far enough, he will almost always find somewhere in the family line a pair of blue eyes. He will, then, be inclined to say that he must have got his own blue eyes from this distant relative. Clearly, there is no feature of one's body or of one's psychological functions which could not be duplicated somewhere in a family tree, if one examined the tree long enough. We may draw the inference, then, that a theory which explains the origin of every trait is subject to some suspicion, simply because it explains too much.[27]

A. HEREDITARY GENIUS: There is, however, a more serious phase of heredity. Since human nature is so complex in its structures and functions and since the processes of human mating do not lend themselves easily to experimental control, it has become more or less popular to abbreviate studies in the field of human heredity by making statistical comparisons between the measurable traits of parents and the measurable traits of offspring.

This was one of the major contributions of Galton, both to the science of heredity and to the art of education.[28] Galton selected, for example, a large number of eminent men in Great Britain for the purpose of asking this question: How many eminent relatives do these men have? It was necessary also to study an equal number of persons who were not eminent in order to find out how many eminent relatives they might have. The motive behind this question was simply the following, viz., if eminent men are more apt to have eminent relatives than obscure men, there must be some truth in the statement that "blood will tell."

Galton's studies were wholly favorable to the belief that psychological functions have a hereditary basis. It has long been known that many of the physical traits of a person are directly inheritable as, for example, eye color, hair color, stature, and even predispositions toward certain diseases. The evidence for the hereditary transmission of physical traits had already been convincing enough in the case of the lower animals and in the case of plants. As a matter of fact, the evidence was so clear that it was possible to name some of the laws which appear to govern the processes of heredity.[29] Gal-

[27] The student will find much interest in a chapter on "Biological Fallacies and Human Affairs" in Jennings, H. S., *The Biological Basis of Human Nature.* New York: W. W. Norton and Co., 1930, Chapter IX.
[28] Cf. Galton, F., *Hereditary Genius.* London: The Macmillan Co., 1869. Also, *Inquiries into the Human Faculty and Its Development.* London: The Macmillan Co., 1883.
[29] As, for example, the Mendelian Laws. See Hurst, C. C., *The Mechanism of Creative Evolution.* New York: The Macmillan Co., 1932, Chapter I.

ton's studies were significant because they extended to psychological functions the principles that had already been discovered in connection with physical traits.

One of the principal conclusions that may be drawn from Galton's studies runs as follows. To cite only one concrete case, he found that the son of a distinguished judge had about one chance in four of becoming distinguished, while the son of a man picked at random from the population as a whole had about one chance in one thousand of becoming equally distinguished. Later studies carried on with a different group of distinguished men appear to show that, in the United States, only one person in five hundred has a chance to be a near relative of one of the thirty-five hundred eminent men in this country. The eminent men considered, however, are related to one another, not in the ratio of one to five hundred, but in the ratio of one to five.[30] The inference is plain. It must be that the attainment of distinction rests upon some innate qualities which are passed on from generation to generation.

B. TWIN RESEMBLANCE: Since Galton's time an immense number of studies have been carried out on other features of the relation between traits and degrees of blood kinship. It is possible, for example, to discover how closely identical twins resemble each other as compared with the resemblance of ordinary brothers and sisters. Most of the evidence from this source leads to the conclusion that hereditary factors must be far more important than environmental factors, because twins that are brought up in what may be called different environments still resemble each other more closely than brothers and sisters who are brought up in what is commonly called the same environment.[31]

C. FOSTER CHILDREN: Parallel evidence can be drawn from studies on foster children who have been placed at a very early age in homes differing in social status from that maintained by their own parents. Since such children develop traits and levels of intelligence which make them more nearly resemble their own parents than their foster parents, it may be argued that heredity must exercise a more important influence on their growth patterns than environment does.[32]

D. INNATE INFERIORITY: The most striking evidence in the field of family resemblance comes from studies on strains in which there

[30] Woods, F. A., "Heredity and the Hall of Fame." *Pop. Sci. Mo.*, 1913, LXXXII, 445-452.
[31] Much of this evidence has been summarized by Schwesinger, G. C., *op. cit.*, pp. 175 ff.
[32] *Ibid.*, pp. 247 ff.

has been marked inferiority. There was, for example, one Martin Kallikak who gave rise to two lines of descendants, the one by a more or less talented mother and the other by an unsocially disposed and feebleminded mother. The family histories of these two lines are pretty well known. They show that feeblemindedness, and a great many forms of antisocial behavior as well, appeared much more frequently in the descendants of Martin Kallikak and the feebleminded mother than they did among the descendants of the other strain.[33]

E. THE NATURE OF THE EVIDENCE: It would not be proper to leave these sources of evidence in favor of the hereditary components of behavior without making one or two comments concerning the general nature of the evidence. In the first place, the student should be a little cautious in moving too readily from evidence in favor of the hereditary transmission of physical traits to the possible transmission of psychological traits. There can be no doubt, of course, about the hereditary transmission of a nervous system. By long repute and because of direct experimental knowledge, the new-born infant possesses a more plastic or a more educable nervous system than is possessed by any of the lower animals. In other words, the human infant is a past master in gaining profit from earlier experience. When we infer, therefore, from studies on the inheritance of physical traits, that psychological traits ought to be equally inheritable, we are saying that new-born infants not only inherit a nervous system from their parents but that they inherit a nervous system which is already lacking in plasticity. The greater the amount of emphasis placed upon the inheritance of psychological traits, the greater the amount of fixity rather than of plasticity that we must impute to the new-born infant.

5. *Constancy of the I.Q.:* Let us assume for the moment that there is some feature of human action or some cross-sectional view of a variety of actions which requires the special term "intelligent." Let us assume, also, that it is possible to secure fairly reliable measures of intelligence. Then, if any considerable part of intelligence owes its origin to hereditary factors, it ought to follow that the ratio between measures of intelligence and chronological age (called the intelligence quotient or I.Q.) should remain fairly stable over a period of years. That is, environmental changes ought not seriously to modify innate intellectual quality.

To be sure, it is known that measures of intelligence of very

[33] Cf. Goddard, H. H., *The Kallikak Family.* New York: The Macmillan Co., 1912 (1921).

young children are apt to be highly variable. It is known also that the number of points which a child can gain on an intelligence test depends upon its age at the time the test is taken. For example, the addition of one month during the first year increases the relative intelligence of a child by about eight points. At eight years, the addition of one month to its chronological age would increase its relative intelligence by only one point. In general, however, if a child who is six years of age has an I.Q. of 132, this same child will have approximately the same I.Q. when he is one, two, five, or ten years older.[34]

As we shall see, there are a considerable number of sources of unreliability in tests of intelligence, but if due allowance is made for these sources, a variation of as much as five points from the first test to a later test could still be interpreted as supporting the alleged constancy of the I.Q. It may be inferred, then, that if the I.Q. of a child tends to remain constant from an early age to maturity, even though changes have taken place in its general environment and in its schooling, there can be only one explanation, viz., a constancy in the hereditary components of intelligence.[35] This is, as a matter of fact, an explanation that is commonly adopted by experimenters in this field.

6. *Individual Differences and Training:* It is hardly necessary to convince the student that human beings differ widely from one another not only in all of their measurable traits but in non-measurable traits as well.[36] These differences appear very early in the growth pattern and they continue without any diminution during the entire course of development. Children in the same family differ greatly from one another even though it can be said that the environmental conditions must have been fairly constant for all of them. It has not been possible as yet to describe the actual amount of such differences; but many persons concerned with this field of research are inclined to infer that the most talented persons must be at least twice as good as the least talented.[37] The very fact that people do differ from one another, even though the environment appears to have remained constant, can be taken, therefore, as an

---

[34] A summary of the work in this field has been prepared by Nemzek, C. L., "The Constancy of the I.Q." *Psychol. Bull.*, 1933, XXX, 143-168.

[35] Cf. Terman, L. M., "Introduction to Nature and Nurture, Their Influence on Intelligence." *27th Year Book Nat. Soc. for the Study of Educ.*, Bloomington, Ill., 1928.

[36] Cf. Dodge, R., *Human Variability*. New Haven: Yale Univ. Press, 1931.

[37] Cf. Wechsler, D., "The Range of Human Capacities." *Scient. Mo.*, 1930, XXXI, 35-39. See also Hull, C. L., *Aptitude Testing*. New York: World Book Co., 1928, pp. 33 ff. and *passim*.

argument in favor of significant hereditary components in human nature.

There is, however, a still more convincing phase of the data on individual differences. Let us suppose that we have a group of subjects each of whom has been measured in a number of different traits. Each of the traits will be found to stand at a lower level in some of the subjects than in others. Now let us give those subjects who have a small measure of competence in a given trait special practice in that particular trait. We may, if we wish, give all of the subjects the same type and the same amounts of practice. If individual differences are a product of training rather than of hereditary factors, it ought to follow that those persons who stand low in a given trait would improve more rapidly than those persons who already stand high in it. Moreover, the total effect of the practice periods ought to level out the differences between the subjects used in the experiment.

When studies of this type are actually made, it turns out that the differences between the subjects remain almost as great as they were before the experiment began. To be sure, some of the poorer subjects will have made more progress than the others simply because they have farther to go; but there is no evidence that special training seriously modifies the range of the differences that are known to obtain between different people.[38] One seems justified in drawing the inference, therefore, that five-talent men, two-talent men, and one-talent men are not a product of training. They must be a product of directive hereditary factors.

III. The Problems of Original Nature

1. *Introduction:* We have now given the student an exceedingly brief picture of a few of the facts which seem to support the argument that much of human nature owes its quality to hereditary processes. We have been particularly brief in the case of the constancy of the I.Q. and in the case of the effect of practice on individual differences because these are topics that can be discussed to better advantage in subsequent chapters. Our immediate task is to see how the type of information which has just been cited fits into our general inquiry after the hereditary agents which are alleged to give precise direction to the growth pattern.

Of one thing we may be sure, viz., that there are a good many

[38] Ewert, H., "The Effect of Practice on Individual Differences When Studied with Measurements Weighted for Difficulty." *J. Gen. Psychol.*, 1934, X, 249-285.

people who will hold that the facts we have just cited mark the conclusion of a problem.[39] They will say that the powerful influence of heredity in giving character or quality to the growth pattern has been amply demonstrated. Not only has the general fact been demonstrated, but there are those who will say that the relative value of hereditary as compared with environmental forces can be estimated. In interpreting the results of one study, for example, of two hundred children who had been adopted at birth or within the first year into homes that were somewhat better than their own, the influence of heredity was credited with seventy-five or eighty per cent of the level of intelligence achieved.[40] The home environment was credited with approximately seventeen per cent. This ratio has, of course, appeared to be too favorable to heredity to a good many persons and hence, motivated more by the chance factor than by an examination of the experimental material, they would urge at least a fifty-fifty ratio.

It does not seem likely that the problems of original nature versus training can be solved this easily. As a matter of fact, it is possible to show that such considerations as have been advanced in the last section mark merely the beginning of a problem rather than its culmination. They set one of the points of departure for an appraisal of all of the factors that may give direction to the growth pattern, the other points of departure being made up of queries (i) about the experimental methods that are used in this field, and (ii) about methods of interpreting results. We propose, therefore, to look at each of the sources of evidence mentioned in the last section with the attitude of a doubter rather than with the attitude of a believer. We do this not because we propose to doubt hereditary factors, but merely to help the student to get a clearer picture of the many factors which must enter into any discussion of the original nature of human beings.

2. *The Reaction Against Instincts:* We shall not say anything more, at the present moment, about the native or intrinsic properties of minds since this is a question that will concern us in a later chapter. All of the problems connected with instinctive behavior and with hormic urges, however, must receive serious consideration. As we have implied, most of the lists of instincts now commonly used in the various arts and sciences represent nothing more than empirical observations and anecdotal comments upon the "un-

---

[39] See, for example, Davenport, C. B., "Child Development from the Standpoint of Genetics." *Scient. Mo.*, 1934, XXXIX, 97-116.
[40] Popenoe, P., and Johnson, R. H., *op. cit.*, p. 3.

learned" behavior of both animals and men.[41] The reaction against instinct theories was signalized in part by a paper which asked in a straightforward manner: Are there any instincts?[42] This question had been raised, partly, because social psychology, under the influence of McDougall, had been inclined to base practically all types of communal living upon an instinctive foundation and, partly, because of the gradual emergence of a truly genetic view of human and animal nature.

In any case, the question which was thus asked prompted immediately a direct experimental attack upon the whole problem. The purpose of the experiments was to trace the origin and development of typical instinctive patterns back to periods in the growth pattern antecedent to birth.[43] At the same time, a large number of attempts were made to trace the origin and course of development of personality or character traits, for it was in this field that instinct theories had flourished most readily.[44] As the student will remember, we have already commented upon this fact, for there is very little about formal processes of teaching which leads to excellence in personality or character traits, even though there may be a great deal about informal education which has a bearing upon the problem. Since, however, no one has intended to develop certain types of attitudes in the same way that they have intended to develop the senses and the intellect, it has been easy to assume that most personality traits must be instinctive and hence hereditary.

A. AN EXPERIMENT ON AN ANIMAL INSTINCT: Some of the main features of the growth pattern at the human level have already been described in the first chapter. In addition to this material, we shall cite two further illustrations showing the general character of the work that is now being done. The one illustration will be drawn from the behavior of one of the lower animals and the other from human behavior.

In a series of brilliant experiments on the common salamander (*Amblystoma*), Coghill has worked out some of the main facts about the development of swimming and walking movements.[45] The

---

[41] Bernard, L. L., *op. cit., passim.*
[42] Dunlap, K., "Are There Any Instincts?" *J. of Abnorm. Psychol.*, 1919, XIV, 307-311. See, also, "The Identity of Instinct and Habit." *J. of Phil.*, 1922, XIX, 85-99.
[43] Cf. Stone, C. P., "Maturation and 'Instinctive' Functions," in *Comparative Psychology* (Ed. F. A. Moss). New York: Prentice-Hall, Inc., 1934, Chapter II.
[44] Cf. Murphy, G., and Murphy, L. B., *Experimental Social Psychology*. New York: Harper and Bros., 1931, *passim.*
[45] Coghill, G. E., *Anatomy and the Problems of Behavior*. New York: The Macmillan Co., 1929, *passim.*

first movements of this animal appear as slow pendular movements of the head from one side to the other. This movement is the result of the contraction of groups of muscles which lie just behind the head. Within a few hours, muscle cells along the two sides of the animal increase in number and proceed gradually to maturity. The result is that a movement which starts in the head region can travel down the length of the animal toward the tail end. After a time these movements become related to one another in such a way that those taking place on one side of the body will not be finished before the head has begun to move in the other direction. The effect of this is to throw the animal ultimately into an S-shaped coil. As the movements become speedier, the body will, of course, exert pressure against the water and thus the animal swims.

The whole period of development of these swimming movements can be divided into five stages. There is, first of all, a non-motile stage in which stimuli applied directly to the muscle cells will lead to muscular contraction and hence to an observable response. In the second stage, movements characteristic of the first stage can be induced by touching the skin of the animal at any part of the body. In the third stage, there is an increase in the extent of the contraction and in its power. The fourth stage is reached when there is a reversal in the head end before the movement which is traveling down the length of the body has been finished at the tail end. It is at this stage that the swimming movements begin. During the final stage the whole pattern of movement is speeded up and swimming becomes really effective.

All five of these stages of development appear to stand out as nothing more than a progressive individuation or a progressive expansion of a growth pattern which has been integrated from the very first. As we have seen in the first chapter, a part of this pattern is created by the fact that even an unfertilized egg cell is not a mere collection of parts. Although there may be no structures for them, there will be a functional head end and a functional tail end in any growing cell. After clusters of cells have appeared, development in the head end takes place faster than it does in the tail end. This fact holds true not only of muscles but of the development of the nervous system as well, for movements in the head end of the salamander occur even before nerve connections have been established between the surface layers (that is, sensitive areas) and the central nervous system. This means, of course, that the coördinating activities of the nervous system acquire some of their properties either from the total integration of the developing system or from the fact that movement is already under way in this system.[46]

These inferences are strongly supported by the subsequent development of limb movements. The limb buds for the fore legs appear before the limb buds for the hind legs. These limb buds are an intricate part of the growing system and as soon as movements in the head end begin, the limbs must also move. Gradually, as the limbs actually take mature form, and as nerve connections are established between them and the central nervous system, more specialized limb movements emerge out of the previous patterns of movement. Since the pendular movements of the head would move the forward limb buds alternately forward and backward, this pattern of movement becomes a fundamental pattern in the salamander. Obviously, alternating movements of the limbs would give rise to walking movements.

The casual observer, in looking at the development of the salamander, and especially in looking at its swimming movements, would say that the salamander was obviously swimming because some instinctive urge had driven the whole pattern in that direction. Exactly the same inference could be drawn from walking movements. As Coghill's studies have shown, however, swimming movements are a by-product of an initial and highly integrated system of vital energies out of which specialized functions progressively emerge. Any object whatsover, moving from one "S" form to another would, when placed in water, move with respect to the water. Likewise, any object with appendages integrated into a total pattern of movement in the manner described by a developing amblystoma would, if placed upon a solid surface, walk.

We have, then, in Coghill's studies, the beginnings of a search after the dynamic conditions under which behavior-patterns find their origin and pass through their earliest stages of development to a more mature level. The conclusion is obvious, viz., that an anecdotal or empirical comment about an instinct is one thing and a search into the dynamics of the growth pattern is quite another. It seems to be clear that neither the psychologist nor the teacher can be wise about the original nature of animals or of human beings until researches of the type carried out by Coghill have been applied to all forms of "instinctive" action.[47]

[46] Coghill, G. E., "Individuation versus Integration in the Development of Behavior." *J. Gen. Psychol.*, 1930, III, 431-435; "The Structural Basis of the Integration of Behavior." *Proc. Nat. Acad. Sci.*, 1930, XVI, 637-643.
[47] The literature in this field is already large. See Stone, C. P., *op. cit., passim.*

B. AN EXPERIMENT ON A HUMAN INSTINCT: As an example of instinctive performance at the human level, we may take any one of the common fears of children. Most persons are convinced that children are instinctively afraid of the dark. This is rather a strange conviction, especially in view of the fact that the first nine months of a human being's life are spent in almost complete darkness. Moreover, small infants are kept in the dark as much as possible even during the daytime. There is, then, an adequate stimulus to the appearance of an instinctive fear of the dark from the very first were such an instinct a part of original nature. Fears of the dark do not manifest themselves, however, for variable periods after birth. Since no one deliberately teaches an infant how to acquire his first fear of this type, it can easily be assumed that fear of the dark is a timed instinct. As the student knows, many attempts have been made to show that some instincts will not appear until the time is ripe for them to appear.

In a series of experiments upon this problem, Watson was able to show that fears of the dark must certainly be acquired.[48] His first discovery was that a new-born infant has no such fears. Moreover, under suitable learning situations, he was able to describe the circumstances under which an object or event which hitherto has not excited an emotionalized action of this sort readily acquires the ability to do so. This discovery implies, of course, that an emotionalized type of action had been attached to a new stimulus and we may well inquire, therefore, what the original emotionalized action was.

During the early stages of experimentation in this field, it seemed that at least three fundamental types of emotionalized action must still be called instinctive.[49] Now, however, it is pretty clear that the primary situation which excites an emotionalized form of response is one that transpires suddenly or unexpectedly.[50] That is, the sheer intensity of the stimulus-pattern itself serves as a shock to the infant, the responses being just those that we ought to expect were the nerve energy generated in the sense organs to be distributed widely over the whole action system. At this stage in the growth pattern, therefore, it is not possible to say that a child has any emotions. It does have, however, a generalized mode of augmented re-

[48] Watson, J. B., and Rayner, R., "Conditioned Emotional Reactions." *J. Exper. Psychol.*, 1920, III, 1-14.
[49] Watson first argued for primary emotions of three types, viz., fear of loud sounds, anger at being restricted in movement, and "love" on being rocked, tickled, or soothed.
[50] For a summary of the literature see Jones, M. C., "Emotional Development," in Murchison, C. (Ed.), *op. cit.*, Chapter VI.

sponse to unexpected situations which may serve as the starting point for more specialized patterns of response to discrete situations.

As we shall see, these patterns of response are closely related to the action of some of the glands of internal secretion and principally to the adrenal glands which make available to the organism reserve supplies of energy. Within a few months after birth, some action-patterns of the emotionalized type are closely attached to equally specialized stimulus-patterns, and if an external observer knows what the reaction is, on the one hand, and what the stimulus-pattern was, on the other, he can describe the behavior as a particular emotion.

There are, of course, scores of other experiments in this field but space forbids that we refer to all of them.[51] Were the student to examine them, however, he would find that they all point in the same direction. They point, first, to the fact that it is fruitless to talk about instincts where the entire genetic history of the behavior-pattern in question is not known. They point, secondly, to the fruitfulness of basing some of the main considerations of educational psychology upon the genetic point of view. They point, in the third place, to the fact that the growth pattern is a product of many co-operating factors, some of which are intrinsic to that particular system of events known as the living system and others of which are a product of the environmental system in which the living system is placed. Finally, they point to the fact that no type of behavior should be called innate or instinctive until it has been shown that intrinsic processes of development are sufficient to account for the particular form and quality of the trait in question.

3. *Criticisms of Studies on Family Resemblances:* We shall, of course, refer to some of these conclusions later on in the chapter and especially in the section on the nature of development. We turn, therefore, to the next source of evidence, viz., family resemblances. As we have seen, our commonsense observations about the similarity between children and their parents can be supported by a vast number of statistical comparisons based upon measurable traits. It is argued that these similarities must be accepted as testimony in favor of heredity because there are no other circumstances surrounding the growth pattern which could possibly lead to such similarities. This is a fairly common type of scientific fallacy, for as soon as one way has been discovered of explaining a given set of facts, it is easy to suppose that this one way is the only way.

[51] Consult the references in Moss, F. A. (Ed.), *op. cit.,* Chapter II.

THE PROBLEMS OF ORIGINAL NATURE 315

A. "IDENTICAL" ENVIRONMENTS: The first comment to be made about statistical comparisons between members of the same family is simply this. Up to the present time, no serious examination has been made of the real meaning of the phrase "identical environments" as opposed to the phrase "different environments." In experimental studies on the psychological traits of twins, for example, it is sometimes argued that twins ought to be alike, not only because they have a common hereditary background, but because they are brought up in identical environments. The word "identity" when used in this connection, can only mean, however, that the twins are brought up in the same house, with the same parents and, perhaps, with the same playthings. The student will see at once that it is one thing to describe samenesses of this order and quite another to describe samenesses that are functional in character.[52]

As a single instance, let us look in on a pair of twins when they are just being punished for misbehavior. One might argue that, since each of the twins is being punished, this particular phase of their environments has been identical. It is easy to see, however, that identity may have no meaning whatsoever in this connection for both twins cannot readily be punished at the same time. The one must be, or usually is, punished before the other. This means that the functional value of punishment for the one may stand on an entirely different level than the functional value of the punishment for the other.

Other illustrations of the difficulties involved in arriving at a precise definition of identical environments can be illustrated by ordinary siblings, by only children, and by studies on the effect of birth order on development. It is easy to say, of course, that the second child in a family is brought up in the same environment that surrounded the first child, and yet the very addition of the second child may modify the functional significance of all of its home situations by a tremendous amount. Studies that have been made on the effect of birth order show clearly enough that some of the differences between brothers and sisters are certainly due to their status as a first-born child or as a later-born child.[53] The very parents are functionally different in their relations to the second child than they were in their relations to the first.

---

[52] Cf. Lewin, K., "Environmental Forces," in Murchison, C. (Ed.), *op. cit.,* Chapter XIV. Also, Isaacs, S., "The Experimental Construction of an Environment Optimal for Mental Growth," in Murchison, C. (Ed.), *op. cit.* (1st ed.), Chapter V.

[53] Cf. Jones, H. E., "Order of Birth," in Murchison, C. (Ed.), *op. cit.,* Chapter XIII.

All of these considerations hold even more clearly of so-called identities in schoolroom situations and of playground conditions. To be sure, a number of children may be kept together throughout a series of grades. They may have even the same teacher and the same playmates through a period of years; but it seems almost fair to say that samenesses of this type have no meaning whatsoever so far as psychological growth is concerned. Psychological growth may rest more intimately upon the general features of environments of children than upon a superficial identity among particular objects.

In his contemplation of the problems of this chapter, the student must be ever mindful of the fact that environmental factors may certainly become potential forces or agents in giving direction to the growth pattern. When, however, he reads of an experiment in which it is shown that people continue to differ widely from one another, even though they have been subjected to identical environments, he must remember that the phrase "identical environments" does not as yet have any defensible meaning. It has no defensible meaning, simply because not enough is known about the functional value of environments to enable anyone to be intelligent about the matter. To be sure, those features of an environment which are called learning situations and which are employed most frequently in the schoolroom, are used to good effect, but these situations constitute, perhaps, a minor fraction of the total number of situations which must exert a promoting and guiding influence on the growth pattern.

B. THE EXPERIMENTAL PROBLEM: With respect, then, to the evidence in favor of the importance of heredity which is based upon statistical comparisons between members of the same family, let us conclude that the information now available marks simply the beginning of research. It happens, as we shall see, that students of genetics have found, in the germ plasm, a set of structures which appear to stand in a one-to-one relation to the presence or absence of certain traits both in parents and in their offspring. These structures are the only visible signs of immediate continuity between parents and their offspring. It has been easy to assert, therefore, that they constitute the only basis upon which degrees of similarity might be made to rest. This is like saying that, since the sun can be observed to rise only on clear mornings, clear air must, therefore, be the only reason why the sun rises.

Obviously, a teacher who is seriously interested in promoting and guiding the growth of the pupils under his care can hardly afford to resort to logic of this type. Even though little is known about identity in environments, one should not grasp eagerly for any explanation whatsoever and thus delay the course of adequate experimentation.

4. *The Interpretation of the Constancy of the I.Q.:* The same considerations hold true of the so-called constancy of the I.Q. There is, of course, a certain amount of evidence which shows that the I.Q. does not vary a great deal from one year to the next. Children grow, to be sure, in their intelligence, but they are also growing older in age. Since the ratio between these two types of change tends to remain constant even though environmental situations have changed, one may conclude that hereditary factors constitute the primary sources of explanation.

It is barely possible, however, that the environment may offer just as much inertia to change as the hereditary mechanisms do. After all, most of the children in any given community have to learn a common fund of skills which are taught to them in much the same way from one generation to the next. The very conditions under which they live imply that they will bring to their learning tasks degrees of motivation which will represent the prevailing tempo of living. Having adopted a tempo at an early stage in the growth pattern, the chances are that this tempo will persist as a fairly constant feature of their psychological nature.

There is, however, another phase of the constancy of the I.Q. which has an important bearing on these problems. Even though we have said above that the functional value of different environments for promoting growth is as yet quite unknown, it is nevertheless possible to make a trial-and-error search for environments which are superior to a normal home environment or for those home environments that are better than others.[54]

Either by direct intention or by implication, this is the situation in some of the more modern preschool clinics. It has proven of interest, therefore, to compare the intelligence quotients of children who have spent a considerable amount of time in a preschool clinic with the intelligence quotients of children from families of the same socio-economic level who have had the schooling of normal children, that is, ordinary home and classroom schooling. In one of the most significant of these studies, it has been shown that the children brought up under the "more favorable" environment of the preschool clinic increased their I.Q.'s by from twenty to thirty points.[55]

[54] There is already a large literature in this field. See Schwesinger, G. C., *op. cit., passim.* Also, any good Sociology.
[55] Wellman, B. L., "Some New Bases for the Interpretation of the I.Q." *J. Genet. Psychol.,* 1932, XLI, 116-126.

The subjects from whom this fact was drawn had spent a number of hours a day in the preschool clinic and had been examined at periodic intervals over a number of years.

It is not possible as yet to say in just what respects the environment furnished by the preschool clinic was superior to a normal home environment or to the average schoolroom environment. The significance of the fact, however, is clear. The functional value of the preschool environment for promoting the growth pattern of certain children was certainly greater than the functional value of the other environments. The chances are that both environments included the same objects and they may have included many identical methods of using objects. There must have been, however, in the one environment a more effective way of promoting the growth pattern so far as test intelligence is concerned.

5. *Individual Differences and Acquired Fixity:* In view of these considerations, it is necessary to refer only briefly to the existence of individual differences and to their relative resistance to practice. It is simply a good scientific principle that any given set of facts ought to be viewed in the light of all possible modes of explanation instead of attributing the set to a mode of explanation that seems, at first sight, the most obvious one. New-born infants are, of course, not alike. They do resemble one another, however, much more nearly than they will when they become mature persons. If the moment of birth really marked the beginning of the growth period and if infants were actually found to differ greatly from one another at this zero point, one would have to attribute the differences between them to other than environmental factors. As we have seen, however, birth is not the beginning of the growth pattern. Environmental and quasi-environmental factors have been operative in this pattern from the moment of conception. From one point of view even fertilization itself can be taken as an instance of environmental influence for the male cell is certainly foreign to the ovum.

There is one other feature of individual differences which will give us a good deal of thought in later chapters and especially in our study of the transfer of training. As the student knows, curves of growth rise rapidly during the first few years and then taper off in what appears to be a plateau. We may infer from this fact that most of the psychological functions of a child must reach a level near to maturity rather early in life. Let us take only a single instance of this, viz., the preferred rate at which a child will work. This preferred rate is a function, in part, of the tempo of its habits and, in part, of the degree of its motivation. Nothing is known at

THE PROBLEMS OF ORIGINAL NATURE

the present time about the conditions surrounding an infant or a small child which contribute to the fixation of preferred rates of working. It seems to be clear, however, that if environmental factors are assumed to have a different functional value, both with respect to tempos of work and with respect to degrees of motivation, some of the differences between individuals might easily be explained as a result of these different functional values of a supposedly identical environment. As we have intimated, we shall consider this possibility in much more detail later on. For the present, we must be satisfied with a general conclusion, viz., that the evidence which has been advanced in favor of a dominant hereditary factor behind human conduct and experience marks more nearly the beginning of a problem than its conclusion.

IV. The Logic of Research on Hereditary Factors

1. *Introduction:* The student will not have been able to understand all of the comments made in the last section nor will he see their full significance unless he has already studied in detail the science of genetics, for it is this science which describes the machinery by means of which the traits of parents are passed on to their offspring. Since some of the more general facts about the science of genetics are necessary to our description of the problems of original nature, in so far as they concern the teacher, we shall now devote a few paragraphs to them. Even though an experimenter were to discover that some offspring are an exact photographic reproduction of their parents, this fact would be meaningless unless there were some bridge, so to speak, over which parents could pass to their offspring. This bridge is said to have been discovered. It consists of a relatively small number of physiological units which serve, at least among the lower animals, as a visible means of continuity from one generation to the next. The science of genetics is largely concerned with the nature and functions of these physiological units.[56]

2. *The Importance of Chromosomes:* For the purposes of the present chapter, each new person may be said to begin his existence when an ovum in the body of the female is fertilized by a spermatozoön which has come from the body of the male. In preparation for this event, both the male and female germ cells will have passed through a period of change which is of considerable significance to the study of the mechanisms of heredity. At one stage in its his-

[56] Cf. Hurst, C. C., *The Mechanism of Creative Evolution.* New York: The Macmillan Co., 1932.

tory, for example, the ovum can be shown to include in its nucleus a few segments of material which, because of the effect of certain dyes upon them, have come to be known as chromosomes (colored bodies). It turns out that these segments of material, that is to say, the number of chromosomes, is fairly constant for every species. In human beings, the number is forty-eight.[57]

At a certain stage in the life history of a germinal cell, it can be seen that the material in the nucleus of the cell thickens markedly and that it appears to arrange itself in twenty-four pairs of chromosome material. Soon after this point is reached, the whole cell structure will divide into two parts, each of which will contain half of the chromosomes that were in the parent cell. In other words, cell division of this type differs somewhat from ordinary cell division for, as a rule, all of the chromosomes split lengthwise so that each of the daughter cells will have just as many chromosomes as did the parent cell. After the division which reduces the number of chromosomes by half, one of the daughter cells is prepared to receive the male cell. In the meantime, the male cell will have passed through a similar process so that it, too, bears only half its normal complement of chromosomes. It is obvious that, when the male cell fuses with the female cell, the chromosome supply of the new cell is brought back to the original number, viz., forty-eight, as in the human species.

From this brief reference to a very complex process, we gain one clear impression, viz., that the only physical material which is actually held in common by the newly developing individual, on the one hand, and by its father and its mother, on the other, is the chromatin material plus, perhaps, a certain amount of the surrounding cellular stuff.[58] It has seemed fair to conclude, therefore, that the chromosomes form the bridge, so to speak, over which the traits and talents of the parents must pass in order to reach the offspring.

The chromosomes themselves, of course, are extremely complex substances and there is considerable evidence to show that they really consist of chains of still smaller units known as genes. When appropriate experimental methods are used, it has been possible to correlate the presence or absence of certain genes or certain groups of genes with the presence or absence of definite somatic (bodily) traits. This is not to say that a single gene can be thought of as the sole

---

[57] On occasion there will be a forty-ninth chromosome which is usually called the x-chromosome. This x-chromosome is thought to play an important part in determining the sex of a new individual.

[58] The whole of the ovum is, of course, continuous from mother to child. Moreover, it is known that the ovum, like all other cell structures, is a highly organized pattern of events or of fields of energy, and this fact is thought to play an important part in the whole developmental process.

agent responsible for the appearance of a given somatic trait, but only to furnish more detailed information about the complex relationships that may obtain between chromosome material, on the one hand, and the high correlation between the traits of parents and offspring, on the other.[59]

3. *The First Principle of Genetic Research:* It is not our purpose to write out in any greater detail the vast number of facts that are now known about the so-called mechanisms of heredity. Such information can be gained easily enough by looking into any one of the authoritative books on the subject.[60] There are, however, certain general principles of research and a few major assumptions about this research that are of great importance to any adequate appraisal of the meaning of original nature.

Let us examine, first, the procedure which was followed by one of the first students of heredity, viz., Mendel, in his initial discovery of a simple ratio which obtains between some of the traits of parental stock and the appearance of these same traits in offspring. For this purpose, it is necessary to distinguish between traits that may be called recessive, on the one hand, and dominant, on the other. As the student knows, there are two varieties of the common garden pea, the one a tall variety and the other a short variety. Now it happens that, when the tall variety is crossed with the short variety, all of the garden peas in the first generation are tall. That is, the gene factors, whatever they are, which make for tallness are dominant over the gene factors, whatever they are, which make for shortness. In the second generation, however, the short variety appears again. It appears, however, in a ratio of one to three with respect to the tall variety.[61]

Our interest, however, is not so much in this ratio or in any of the other ratios that have been computed as in the logic of the method employed in order to discover them. Let us generalize the above situation in the following way. For this purpose, we shall represent the traits of one of the parents by the following symbols, viz., a_1, a_2, a_3, a_4, ... a_n. Likewise we may symbolize the traits of the other parent by the symbols b_1, b_2, b_3, b_4, ... b_n. When these parents possessing these several traits (the total number remaining unknown) are mated together, the traits of the offspring

[59] Cf. Morgan, T. H., *The Scientific Basis of Evolution.* New York: W. W. Norton and Co., 1932, *passim.*
[60] Cf. Morgan, T. H., "The Mechanism of Heredity," in Murchison, C. (Ed.), *A Handbook of General Experimental Psychology.* Worcester, Mass.: Clark Univ. Press, 1934, Chapter II.
[61] This is the simplest of the so-called Mendelian laws. See *Ibid.*, references at end of chapter.

will be some combination of the traits of the parents. We might say, for example, that the traits of one of the offspring will include the following items, viz., a_1, a_3, b_1, b_2, b_4, . . . a_n, b_n.

The student will see at once that the method being used here is exactly like the method that had been used by Galton. One may note, first, the traits which the parents are known to possess. It is possible that one may even go so far as to measure the traits in suitable terms. After the offspring have appeared, their principal traits can also be noted and, as in studies like Galton's, the traits themselves may be subjected to measurement. Now when correlations are calculated between the traits of offspring and the traits of their parents, it is discovered that the degree of correlation, that is to say, the degree of resemblance, increases almost in direct proportion to the increase in the degree of blood kinship. Twins resemble one another much more closely than do ordinary brothers and sisters while ordinary brothers and sisters resemble one another almost as closely as any one of them resembles either one of their parents. All of these resemblances are much greater than are the resemblances between one group of children and an unrelated group of parents or between one group of children and another group.[62] In short, then, the discovery of significant degrees of correlation between the traits of offspring and the traits of parents is one of the fundamental principles upon which most studies of the mechanisms of heredity must depend.

4. *The Second Principle of Genetic Research:* This discovery might not have become of any great value either to psychology or to education if it had not been for the discovery of still another type of correlation. As we have pointed out above, there is, at certain stages in the life history of each person, a cluster of substances which act, so to speak, as a bond of continuity between parents and offspring. Now these substances, that is, the chromosomes, are supposed to consist of a large number of smaller units known as genes. As a result of studies on the mechanisms of heredity in the lower animals, it can be asserted that the presence or absence of certain genes or the presence or absence of certain clusters of genes will explain why degrees of correlation between the presence of certain traits or clusters of traits in parents and in offspring are possible.

In the case of the garden pea mentioned above, it can be assumed that, since the chromosomes in the seeds of the garden pea are essentially continuous from one generation to the next, one of these chromosomes or some cluster of genes in the chromosomes must be re-

[62] Cf. Schwesinger, G. C., *op. cit., passim.*

THE PROBLEMS OF ORIGINAL NATURE 323

sponsible for tallness as opposed to shortness. Moreover, there are times when two tall peas give rise to the short variety, the inference being that the gene factors responsible for shortness have managed to become operative to the exclusion of other gene factors. Work of this type has gone on so far that, in one case, at least, viz., the little fruit fly called Drosophila, it has been possible to say just where, in each chromosome, certain genes must lie.[63]

Here again, however, we are not so much interested in the experimental facts as in the logic that underlies the experimental methods. And the logic is simply this. In addition to significant degrees of correlation between the traits of parents and the traits of offspring, there are equally significant degrees of correlation between the traits of offspring and parents and the presence or absence of certain types of germinal material.

5. *The First Assumption of Genetic Research:* This, then, is the second major fact that has to be considered by students of original nature. It is a fact which has enabled the geneticist to explain a great many things about heredity, and it has also brought to hand a very important tool for controlling the outcome of various types of mating in plants and among the lower animals. It has even been urged that one could, through the science of eugenics, greatly increase the physical and mental quality of the human race by processes of controlled mating.[64]

These results can be achieved, however, not solely because of the facts that have been mentioned up to this point but as a result of two important assumptions which are said to grow out of the facts. In the first place, it is sometimes assumed that the structures in the germinal plasm which vary as the traits of different persons vary are the essential causative agents in the appearance of these traits. In other words, chromosomes or the genes of which they are made are sometimes spoken of as forces which reside in ova and spermatozoa and which make it certain that offspring shall be a composite picture of their immediate parents.

This way of looking at the nature of genes and chromosomes has now been definitely discarded by most biologists, but, as we have seen, it is still tacitly implied by a great many psychologists who try to interpret such data as have been considered in the earlier part of this chapter.[65] When, for example, a psychologist speaks of the

[63] Morgan, T. H., *op. cit., passim.*
[64] Cf. Popenoe, P., and Johnson, R. H., *Applied Eugenics.* New York: The Macmillan Co., 1933.
[65] Cf. Jennings, H. S., *op. cit.*, Chapter IX.

constancy of the I.Q. as though the I.Q. must be constant because of the hereditary constitution of the person in question, it is easy to assume that an important psychological fact is a product of agents or forces which reside in genes or chromosomes. Most biologists now recognize the fact that the genes or the chromosomes represent one of the essential preconditions for, rather than the causes of, the appearance of any set of traits. We shall see in a moment just how the phrase "an essential precondition of" differs from the word "cause."

6. *The Second Assumption of Genetic Research:* A second theoretical addition to the facts of genetics may be stated in the following way. There are those who will argue that, since some traits (usually physical) appear to stand in a definite relation to the presence or absence of certain structures in the germinal plasm, all other traits, even though they be psychological rather than physical in character, must possess a similar relationship.[66] This is an assumption about the meaning of heredity that is made most frequently by psychologists.

It is hardly necessary to argue, of course, that the development of a nervous system must, in some way or other, be contingent upon the presence of germinal factors which serve as preconditions for its appearance and growth. Some psychologists are not satisfied, however, with so meager a statement. They would, on the contrary, like to argue that the nervous system is guided in its growth not merely as a physical piece of apparatus with certain properties of its own but as a collection of pathways of conduction which make it inevitable, even in advance of experience, that some stimulus-situations will result in particular response-patterns.[67] The instinct theory, for example, at least in some of its forms, requires just this theory of the nature of nervous growth.

7. *Summary:* We have, then, in this section, two groups of facts and two sets of assumptions drawn from the science of genetics. The first fact is that degrees of correlation between parents and offspring in both casually observed and in measured traits vary in almost direct proportion to the degree of blood kinship. The second fact is that there is a measurable degree of correlation between the traits of parents and offspring, on the one hand, and the presence or absence of certain substances in the germinal cells, on the other.

[66] Cf. Holmes, S. J., *The Trend of the Race.* New York: Harcourt, Brace and Co., 1921, *passim.* Also Hogben, L., *Genetic Principles in Medicine and Social Science.* New York: Harcourt, Brace and Co., 1934, *passim.*
[67] Cf. Thorndike, E. L., *Educational Psychology.* Vol. I. *The Original Nature of Man.* New York: Columbia Univ. Press, 1913. Chapter I and *passim.*

THE PROBLEMS OF ORIGINAL NATURE

When we say that this is a fact, it should be admitted that it is by no means so certain as is the first. Chromosomes, of course, can be seen sometimes with the naked eye and easily enough under the microscope. The actual existence of genes has been tentatively verified by recent researches. Since, however, chromosomes, or the genes of which they are composed, stand as the most important source of continuity between parents and offspring, the second type of correlation mentioned above appears highly credible.

The two assumptions we have before us are as follows. First, it has sometimes been assumed that, since chromosome material is the only visible bond of union between parents and offspring and since there are high degrees of correlation in traits where there is close kinship in blood, the chromosomes must contain the causative agents or the necessary preconditions for the appearance in offspring of the traits in question. The second assumption is that, since this first assumption is almost certainly true of some traits (mostly physical), it is, therefore, inevitably true of all traits both physical and psychological.

We might infer from these considerations that the problem of the original nature of human beings is a closed problem, for, if a piece of machinery has been discovered whereby parents may photograph themselves, as it were, in their children, the major traits and dispositions of children must be inevitable. In opposition to this point of view, we have tried to show that the discovery of some of the mechanisms of heredity marks the beginning of a problem rather than its end, for we have not yet considered any of the questions which arise when we think of the relation between chromosome (or gene) material and its environment.

The student will see at once that this relationship has an important bearing on the problems of this chapter. We might, of course, say that chromosomes (or genes) are substances which have no environment at all. As a matter of fact, some persons appear to be convinced of this possibility for they argue that chromosome material cannot be affected by environmental agents. They argue, too, that the chromosomes are self-sufficient in producing both physical and psychological traits. The evidence cited at the beginning of this chapter is their authority. It must be admitted, however, that chromosomes (or genes) are just as truly surrounded by an environment as are all other substances. The natural inference is that the chromosomes themselves may derive some of their properties from their environments. In any case, it is important that we consider this possibility for a moment. This is the task of the next section.

V. CHROMOSOMES AND THEIR ENVIRONMENTS

1. *The "Part" vs. the "Whole":* It will be convenient, during the course of the present section, to think of all of the objects or events which make up the world as we know it as belonging to one or the other of two systems. Let us, for the sake of brevity, speak of x-systems, on the one hand, and of y-systems, on the other. An electron, for example, is a definite object or event which stands in close relation to other similar objects or events. The electron itself we may call an x-system, and we may think of all of the other systems around it as making up its y-system, that is, the total environment within which the electron is placed. From one point of view, a molecule, likewise, is a single entity or an x-system which has, as a part of its environment, or as a part of its y-system, all of the molecules around it. In the same way, we may speak of a cell as though it were an x-system placed in the midst of a great many other cells which would, therefore, stand as a part of its y-system. Yet again, a human being can be thought of as an x-system, while all of the objects and events which surround him can be thought of as making up his y-system.

In other words, any single part of the whole pattern of events which make up the word as we know it can be taken *as a part* and set off from the rest of the whole pattern.[68] We do not intend to say, of course, that it is possible to conceive of an electron, a molecule, a cell, or a person as being able to exist without any kind of an environment whatsoever. On the contrary, the whole universe is simply too complex to be thought of or to be handled as a single unit and men of science always proceed, therefore, to think of it partwise rather than whole-wise. For our present purposes, any of the parts which are extracted from the whole can be designated as an x-system and everything else that is not thus extracted can be thought of as the y-system.

2. *The Inertia of Parts:* Now there are a number of questions about the relationship between any given x-system and its relevant y-system that bear directly upon the topic of this chapter. In the first place, the student will see at once that x-systems may differ greatly from one another in their relative inertia. He has learned

---

[68] This is a fundamental aspect of all modern sciences. The world as we actually observe it is too complex and too intimately interrelated to be studied as a unit. Hence scientific men resort to the method of analysis. They take the world piece by piece.

in chemistry, for example, that there are certain chemical elements such as neon and argon which are called inert elements, simply because they do not react easily with other elements. Oxygen is called an active element because so many different compounds can be manufactured out of it.

High degrees of inertia, however, are not limited to chemical elements. Compounds of these elements may also offer resistance to change. As we shall see in a moment, chromosome material appears to be highly inert. In other words, it tends to remain fairly constant even though the environment in which it is placed is seriously modified. The nervous system, on the contrary, taken as an x-system of events, is highly active or, as we have said in another place, highly plastic. It is extremely subject to change through the influence of learning situations. Our first thought, then, is plain. X-systems display various degrees of inertia or of resistance to change under the influence of modifications in their respective y-systems.

3. *Field Relationships:* In the second place, it is quite clear that no x-system can ever be put in a state of total isolation from some sort of a y-system. This fact is so obvious as hardly to merit special attention; but it is, at the same time, a fact that is frequently forgotten. An electron is always in an environment furnished by other electrons and protons. An atom is always in an environment made up of other atoms or of some of the field properties created by the presence of these atoms. Cells possess, as a part of their environments, other cells and also the general medium in which they live. Every human being stands in an environment furnished, in part, by other human beings and, in part, by the objects and events which make up his non-socialized surroundings.

4. *The Origin of Intrinsic Properties:* With these two features of the relation between x-systems and y-systems before us, we are prepared to ask where x-systems obtain the properties or characteristics which define them as x-systems. It is clear, of course, that it would not be possible to identify any given x-system unless the system were stable enough to admit of repeated observation and description. What, however, do we mean by stability? That is, what do we mean by the properties or characteristics of an x-system which identify it as a system which can be extracted for the moment from the particular y-system, that is, the particular context, in which it is placed.

A. THE DOCTRINE OF ESSENCES: There are at least two answers to these questions. In the first place, it may be argued that all x-systems derive their properties or characteristics out of their own intrinsic nature. Another way to say this is that every x-system is a species unto itself. It is just in the nature of things that it shall be what it is. It will remain true to its own species no matter how its environment, or the y-system which surrounds it, is changed. To be sure, there may be changes in its accidents, that is, in its superficial properties, but not in its essential character.[69]

We have already run across this point of view, for it is sometimes said that the mind is what it is, simply because it is in the inherent nature of the mind to be that way. We have run across this same argument, also, in the preceding sections of this chapter for it has been assumed by some students of heredity that the particular x-system known as germinal plasm possesses an intrinsic and species-like nature which is relatively immutable. Human beings do produce human beings and not figs and thistles. No amount of change in the context of human chromosomes could alter them so that they would give rise to figs and thistles.

B. THE DOCTRINE OF CONFIGURATIONAL PATTERNS: In the second place, it is possible to say that x-systems gain their distinguishing properties or characteristics by virtue of the relations which they sustain to their y-systems.[70] In other words, it can be argued that any x-system will be what its y-system permits it to be. As an example of what may be said in behalf of this argument, let us remind ourselves of some of the changes that would take place in the objects around us were one feature of the whole environment of the earth to be changed. The earth, as we know it at the present time, is made up of a very large number of solid objects such as rocks, stones and bricks, of semisolid objects such as vegetable and animal matter, and a great many other viscous substances, of liquid objects such as water, and of gaseous objects such as air, hydrogen, and marsh gas. It is our general belief that all of these objects can be distinguished from one another because each of them possesses properties or characteristics which are intrinsic to them as objects. As the student knows, however, water may be changed into ice or into a gas. Likewise, iron may be changed into a liquid. In short, water and iron appear to change their essential character. These

---

[69] The student of philosophy will recognize this as the distinction between *essences* and *accidents*. See the article *Species* in Hastings, J., *Encyclopedia of Religion and Ethics*. New York: Charles Scribner's Sons, 1928.

[70] The Gestalt psychologies have attempted to work out all the problems of human nature in terms of relationships or configurations. For an application of the method to education, see Wheeler, R. H., and Perkins, F. T., *Principles of Mental Development*. New York: T. Y. Crowell Co., 1932.

changes are brought about by altering certain parts of the environment (that is, the temperature) within which water and iron have achieved a normal state of equilibrium.

Now let us suppose that the average mean temperature on the surface of the earth were to be raised one thousand degrees. It is hardly necessary to argue that, under these circumstances, the alleged intrinsic or inherent properties of all of the x-systems about which we know anything at all would be markedly changed. Very few solid substances, for example, would be left; and there would be a notable increase in the variety and in the total volume of the several gases. That unique series of x-systems which we call living animals would disappear altogether. In other words, the chances are that a change of one thousand degrees in the mean temperature would make it forever impossible for the x-systems which we call the chemical elements ever to fuse into that particular pattern of events which can be defined as a living organism.

C. APPLICATION TO PROBLEMS OF HEREDITY: There are, then, at least these two ways of answering the question stated above, viz., Where do x-systems gain the properties or characteristics or functions by virtue of which they can be extracted from the whole order of nature and identified as parts of the whole? Now let us apply these two answers to that particular system known as germinal plasm or, more accurately, to that particular series of x-systems known as chromosome material. There are, of course, a great many facts which seem to argue that chromosomes are highly stable or inert systems. They resist change. The various subsystems, of which each chromosome is a sum, stand in such a complete state of equilibrium with other subsystems that the pattern of the whole cannot be easily modified. This assertion is proved by the fact that all of the experiments that have sought to establish the inheritance of acquired traits have turned out as failures.[71] If it could be shown that a change in the body or even a change in the immediate environment of the germinal material itself could bring about a permanent change in the structure or patterning of the chromosomes, it would have to be admitted that the chromosomes are not as inert or as resistant to change as they are now thought to be.

In short, then, we may safely conclude that germinal material is inert material. It is like such chemical elements as neon and argon which do not combine readily with other elements. It is to be contrasted with the element oxygen which does combine readily with

[71] Jennings, H. S., *op. cit.*, Chapter XV; Morgan, T. H., "Are Acquired Characters Inherited?" *The Yale Rev.*, 1924, XIII, 712-729.

itself and with a great many other elements. The student will see at once, however, that this is not equivalent to saying that chromosomes possess properties or characteristics which are intrinsic to them and, therefore, wholly unrelated to the y-system within which they are immersed. On the contrary, we propose to argue that the word "heredity" does not describe any agents or forces which lead to the creation of given traits, but rather that the word should refer to the relative inertia of germinal material. Let us argue, also, that the inertia of germinal material is an expression of a state of quasi-equilibrium which has been reached among a great many x-systems because the y-systems in which these x-systems have been placed is also in a state of quasi-equilibrium. As we have said above, a major change in the temperature of the earth would completely modify the types of x-systems that could exist on it. It is almost certainly true that the x-systems we know as a set of chromosomes could not possibly exist were the temperature of the earth to be raised one thousand degrees.

5. *The Inertia of Germ Plasm:* We do not mean to imply, however, that chromosome material is absolutely and irretrievably inert. There are several pieces of evidence which show that this cannot be true.

A. EVOLUTION: The first is furnished by the theory of evolution itself. That particular combination of chemical elements known as human germinal material did not exist a billion years ago. Apparently, it did not exist even five hundred thousand years ago. The theory of evolution asserts, nevertheless, that there has been continuity in the stream of life from the very beginning to the present time. In short, living forms have undergone an immense number of changes. The biologist ascribes most of these changes to mutations. The word mutation means that, because of some alteration in the patterning of the subsystems which make up chromosome material, traits other than those that could have been developed if germinal material had remained absolutely inert have appeared. Some of these traits have promoted the adaptation of the animal to its environment, and the animal has been able, therefore, to outlive its fellows. To be sure, we may say that the changes which take place in germinal material and which give rise, therefore, to mutations are changes which express an inner urge, but the evidence does not support this view. On the contrary, there has been variation and natural selection and thus life has moved forward.

B. MASS-ATTACKS: In the second place, it is now known that changes may be brought about in the total pattern of the germ plasm

THE PROBLEMS OF ORIGINAL NATURE 331

if X-rays of a given length, intensity, and duration are made a part of the y-system of the germ plasm.[72] Most of the mutations which result from this source are lethal, that is, they lead to the death of the offspring. Some of them, however, are not lethal. Moreover, the mutations thus produced can be passed on from generation to generation. There is only one way to interpret these facts. If X-rays of a certain type are put into the y-system—that is, into the environment of the germ plasm—some alteration is made in the germ plasm whereby a new level of equilibrium among its various parts is reached. That this level is fairly stable is revealed by the fact that animals having this particular hereditary constitution breed true to type. There are, however, other ways of gaining the same results. Changes in the prevailing temperature around germinal material may effect changes in the rate of mutation. It is possible that such chemicals as alcohol will also have a permanent effect on the pattern of germinal material.[73] It is clear, then, that the x-systems known as germinal material are not absolutely and irrevocably unmodifiable. It must be clear, also, that the properties or characteristics which distinguish a given piece of germinal material may be derived not from what it is as germinal material but from the nature of the environment in which it is placed. If the environment is changed, the germinal material itself will change until a new state of quasi-equilibrium is reached. This means that any experimenter could make anything he desired out of a particular piece of germinal material if only he could find out how to work with objects that are as small as molecules, atoms, and electrons and protons. The methods of present-day science, however, have not reached this measure of refinement. To be sure, when X-rays are brought into the environment of germinal material or when the temperature is changed, the experimenter can make a mass-attack upon the germ plasm; but if, instead of a mass-attack, he could knock a single electron out of the way or rearrange the pieces of which an atom is made, he would certainly be able to modify what we call the intrinsic properties of germinal material. In other words, he would bring about a new state of balance between a given x-system, on the one hand, and its y-system, on the other.

[72] Muller, H. J., "Artificial Transmutation of the Gene." *Science,* 1927, LXVI, 84-87. Also, "Radiation and Genetics." *Amer. Nat.,* LXIV, 220-251.
[73] Stockard, C. R., and Papanicolaou, G., "A Further Analysis of Hereditary Transmission of Degeneracy and Deformities by the Descendants of Alcoholized Mammals." *Amer. Nat.,* 1916, L, 65-88, 144-177; *J. Exper. Zool.,* 1918, XXVI, 119-226; McDowell, E. C., and Vicari, E. M., "Alcoholism and the Behavior of the White Rat." *J. Exper. Zool.,* 1921, XXXIII, 209-291; 1923, XXXVII, 417-456.

C. AN ILLUSTRATION FROM CHESS: This fact is so important that we can well afford to illustrate it in another way. Let us suppose that we have just begun to play a game of chess. The game does not begin with chaos. On the contrary, the pieces are already arranged on the board. They are, so to speak, in a certain definable state of equilibrium with respect to one another. Just the moment that white makes the first move, however, this state of equilibrium is disturbed. It will remain disturbed until black makes a countermove.

Those students who are chess players will see at once, however, that the state of equilibrium which obtained between white and black before the game began, differs in certain essential respects from the state of equilibrium which obtains as soon as white and black have made their first moves. In the first place, the particular way in which white has opened the game makes it almost necessary for black to meet white's move. In short, the move that black can make is made, so to speak, with the permission of white. In the second place, the initial moves made by white and black determine, to a large extent, what many of the future moves must be. If this is not the case with the first moves, it is almost certainly the case after two or three moves, for, at this point, the general pattern of strategy of the game has been set.

If, now, we may think of chromosomes as though they were black's pieces and of the environment as though it were made up of white's pieces, it will follow that any given amount of chromosome material must be in a state of quasi-equilibrium with its environment. Where the environment is fairly stable, there will be no occasion for a disturbance of this equilibrium. In the case of X-rays and prolonged changes in temperature, however, a disturbance is created. White, so to speak, has made a move. Black, to continue the analogy, responds by an alteration in the pattern of its pieces. From this time forward white and black, that is to say, heredity and environment, are in a constant effort to maintain a state of quasi-equilibrium which will preserve the integrity of both of them.

6. *The Principle of Buffering:* We now have the following picture of the relationship between the germ plasm, on the one hand, and the environment within which it is placed, on the other. The germ plasm of any particular person is an x-system of events which gains its particular properties or characteristics as a result of a state of equilibrium which has been reached with the "permission" of the y-system around it. Now it happens that it is not easy to gain access

to the germ plasm. The difficulty is created, in part, by the inability of the chemist to work at subatomic levels and, in part, by the fact that the states of equilibrium which obtain between germ cells and the environments in which they have been placed are extremely stabilized. It is well known, for example, that the very existence of life depends upon a balance which has been reached in the relations between water, carbon dioxide, and nitrogen on the surface of the earth.[74] The range within which this balance can be maintained is extremely limited. It depends, in part, upon the mean annual temperature of the surface of the earth. Factors of this type are not, however, easily subject to control.

Now let us see whether some way cannot be found for gaining a larger perspective on the interrelatedness of x-systems and y-systems. One possibility is furnished by the word "buffering." This word comes from the physiology of respiration and of metabolism and it refers to all of the events or operations involved in keeping the acid-base value of the blood at a proper equilibrium. It would be too long a story to tell of the tremendous complexity of these operations; but the main fact is that, when the system becomes too acid, there are certain substances which will buffer the acids, that is, stand between them and the possible damage they might do if left free to act. The same operation takes place when the system becomes too alkaline.[75]

We do not desire, however, a picture of a particular type of physiological function but a general picture of the way in which different systems act and interact with one another, each buffering the other in such a way that a state of quasi-equilibrium or even of dynamic equilibrium can be maintained. If the student will think of two bodies in contact with each other which differ greatly in temperature, he will be thinking of two systems in a state of quasi-equilibrium. Stable equilibrium so far as these two systems are concerned will not be reached until both are of the same temperature. Germinal cells, then, and the organism which grows out of them, are in a state of quasi-equilibrium with their environments. Buffering describes the interrelatedness or the reciprocal action between the two systems. By analogy, we may say that the growth pattern is being continually buffered by the environment in which it is placed.

[74] Cf. Henderson, L. J., *op. cit.*, Chapter II.
[75] Cf. Gould, A. G., and Dye, J. A., *Exercise and Its Physiology*. New York: A. S. Barnes and Co., 1932, Chapter VII and *passim*.

7. *Summary:* We may conclude from the above discussion that the germ plasm is essentially stable in its functions and that the offspring which issue out of it will continue to resemble their parents to a greater or less extent just so long as the environment of the germ plasm "permits" it to have no other type of internal organization than it has at the moment of fertilization. The term "heredity," therefore, does not describe a force which is resident in the germinal system and which compels children to resemble their parents. On the contrary, it describes a state of equilibrium which has been reached in germinal material because of a state of equilibrium in the environment of that material. There are only two groups of circumstances known at the present time which suggest the possibility of changing this stability. The one is furnished by making a mass-attack on the chromosomes through the use of X-rays or temperature changes, and the other is furnished by some theory of natural variation or mutation. Evolution means, of course, that there has been a constant repatterning of the environment of germinal plasm so that this material has been able to "grow" or to change in its capacity to produce given sets of organs and functions.

There is one further consideration which must be kept in mind as we proceed in the next chapter to discuss the original nature of human beings. Throughout our description of possible types of relationship between x-systems and y-systems it must be assumed that any y-system will be composed of factors which are either relevant or irrelevant. As an illustration we may think of an amoeba as an x-system which has been placed in a suitable y-system by the experimenter. It can be shown that the behavioral properties of an amoeba may be modified by certain types of change in its y-system, say, temperature changes, or various chemical substances, but it has not been shown that a printed page such as the reader now has before him can in any way become an effective part of the environment of an amoeba. In other words, it would not be worth while to carry out an experiment on legibility if an amoeba were used as a subject. Such an experiment can, however, be carried out on school children. This experiment is possible with school children because a printed page has become an effective or relevant phase of the total environment of such subjects. Before printed matter could become an effective agent in the environment of an amoeba, it would be necessary that the whole series of concomitant changes in x-systems and y-systems which have translated amoeba-like individuals into humanlike individuals (a series of changes which is described by the theory of evolution) would have to take place again.

Let us look at this proposition in another way. On the one hand, it might be possible to argue that amoebae cannot react effectively to the printed page because they are intrinsically, or by native endowment, different from human beings. They do not possess a visual apparatus like the human apparatus. Neither do they possess all of the devices which bring certain types of visual stimuli into conjunction with appropriate verbal and other responses. It must be clear, however, that both amoebae and human beings have come to be what they are through the "permission" of their respective contexts. This is to say that environments or y-systems—and x-systems as well—have had a history. It is the function of the various phases of genetic science to describe histories of this type. Such a history shows clearly enough that, as x-systems and y-systems change, factors in a y-system that were once effective may become ineffective, whereas factors that were once ineffective may become effective. One cannot make the leap from an amoeba to a human being by one immense saltation. On the contrary, all of the genetic sciences must presuppose the passage of lengthy periods of time for this purpose. The point we are trying to make here will become a little clearer perhaps as we now pass on to a study of some of the general features of a particular genetic sequence, viz., the development of a human individual.

VI. Some Major Features of Development

1. *Temporal Sequences:* It is now necessary to bring some of the propositions discussed in the last section to bear upon the general problem of development. Up to this point, we have spoken as though an x-system and a y-system were under observation for a single moment of time during which there was no change or movement in them. That kind of an x-system which we have called the germ plasm is not, however, a motionless system. On the contrary, it begins, as soon as it is fertilized, to pass through that timewise process of becoming to which the words "growth" or "development" are commonly attached. Since growth or development must always take place within an environment, we are still faced with the question as to whether there are factors intrinsic to the germ plasm which determine the course of the growth pattern or whether this pattern takes a particular form by "permission" of its environment. A pure doctrine of heredity would say, of course, that a great many aspects of any developmental trend are determined by the inherent nature of the chromosomes or genes from which development starts.

A pure environmentalist, on the contrary, must argue that the growth pattern is solely a product of environmental agents and factors.

The growth process to which we have just referred is, of course, a temporal process. The x-system of which we have been speaking is an x-system which has not only a momentary character but a longitudinal or timewise character as well. By the same token, the y-system in which any given growth pattern is placed also has a timewise or longitudinal character. If we follow the general argument presented in the last section, we should now see that the growth process of an individual may take a particular course, not because it is its own inherent nature to do so, but with the "permission" of its surrounding y-system, where both the x-system and the y-system are moving forward in time.

2. *Types of Environment:* In order to discuss this proposition intelligently, it will be fruitful to distinguish at least three different aspects of the y-systems which surround each human growth pattern.

A. THE PHYSICAL ENVIRONMENT: There is, first of all, that aspect of the context which may be described as physico-chemical. In other words, the fertilized ovum and the organism which issues out of it is deeply imbedded in physico-chemical systems furnished by the cytoplasm and the general medium in which the whole cell is immersed. Later on, this medium is supplemented by the food and the oxygen which are supplied by the mother. As we have seen above, these y-systems may be, in part, relevant and, in part, irrelevant. That is, some are really effective in their influence on a developing x-system and some are not effective.

B. THE PSYCHOLOGICAL ENVIRONMENT: There is, in the second place, a phase of the environment which can be called psychological. This environment is made up of those objects and events which have acquired the power to call forth reactions of the psychological type. When, for example, a person is called upon to discriminate between lights of different intensities, such an act is called a psychological function. The two lights may still be described as a part of the physico-chemical context of that person; but they have, in the meantime, acquired a new status, viz., their psychological status. So far as we know at the present time, neither the germ plasm nor the growing foetus are in any way affected by environmental factors of a psychological character. Somewhere, however, between the time just before birth and the time after birth, the psychological parts of the context do become effective.

THE PROBLEMS OF ORIGINAL NATURE 337

C. THE SOCIAL ENVIRONMENT: In the third place, there is another sector of the environment which, for practical purposes, can be distinguished both from the physio-chemical and the psychological phases. This phase is called the social environment. Here again, those parts of the total surroundings of a growing person which may be called social are not known to be effective either at the germinal stage, at the prenatal stage, or even at the new-born stage. Shortly after birth, however, social situations do become an effective part of the situations around the growing individual.

3. *Environmental Control: Physical Methods:* We are now ready to ask the most important question which the general story of growth and development presents to students of psychology and of education. This question runs as follows: To what extent can the growth pattern of any individual be changed or modified by changing or modifying the y-system within which the x-system runs its timewise course? At first sight, it will appear that we have already answered this question, for we have said that any x-system will be that which its y-system permits it to be. The question we have asked should, then, take the following form, viz., Can an experimenter change the y-system around any growing individual so that this individual will become something other than he would have become if left to a "natural" course of events?

The student of genetics will answer this question by saying that the internal organization of the genes and chromosomes has predetermined the growth pattern and the ultimate traits of the individual. The extreme environmentalist would say that no growing x-system can be left to itself for this would almost be the same as saying that growth could take place independently of an environment. Since growth cannot take place under these conditions, the environmentalist can point to any situation whatsoever and say of that situation that it must have been determinative in making the individual what he is.

A. INADEQUACY OF PHYSICAL METHODS: It seems possible to offer another answer to the question raised above. This answer assumes that the whole problem of heredity versus environment turns on a question of scientific methodology. Let us grant, for purposes of argument, that any x-system is what it is and will become what it becomes by "permission" of its context. It turns out, however, that the contexts of some x-systems, both at some particular moment and during any particular segment of their history, are not open to control by any of the methods which science now knows how to use. This fact is true, in particular, of the history of an individual when he is at the gene or chromosome stage. There is sufficient reason to believe that the genes are tremendously complex molecules or clusters of molecules to which access cannot be had. When the chemist is dealing with such simple molecules as a molecule of water, he can direct his experimental methods upon the molecule in such a way as significantly to alter it. He may, so to speak, take away one atom of oxygen and put in another. He does this, to be sure, not with individual molecules but rather with whole groups of molecules.

Even the chance of making a mass-attack on such molecules as are found in living tissues, however, is denied him for the situation is so complex that he can do practically nothing about it. He may, of course, make a mass-attack upon the germ plasm by irradiating it with X-rays, by changing its temperature, or by making certain other changes in the medium in which it lives. These latter devices are used most frequently by the dietician who hopes to get at the effective physiological environment of a growing individual by changing the diet of the mother. It is known, for example, that, in regions where drinking water is devoid of iodine, the growth processes in the thyroid glands will not take a normal course. The dietitian may, therefore, change the diet of the mother by adding iodine to the salt which she uses. In this case, a change in the y-system of the foetus often makes for, rather than against, the normal maturation of the thyroid glands. Since the development of the nervous system depends, in part, upon the proper functioning of the thyroid glands, the dietitian may even hope to exert some control over the growth of the nervous system. In the case of irradiation, of temperature changes, and of diet, however, there is no possibility of localizing action so that definite control over the individual can be secured when he is still an ovum or a foetus. In short, hereditary factors will be dominant.

B. CONSEQUENCES OF THE INADEQUACY OF PHYSICAL METHODS: In view of the hopeless situation in which men of science are placed with respect to the earliest stages of growth, it has seemed appropriate to say that the environment of the germ plasm or of the embryo has nothing to do with the course of its development. Obviously, however, this is a false conclusion. The only conclusion which seems justified is that the methods of science are not adequate to the problem. Fortunately, the geneticist has found a way out of this difficulty. Since neither he nor other men of science can identify and separately control different segments of the environment of the germ plasm, they must ask whether the relative stability of the environment manifests itself in any other way. It is sheer good luck that such manifestations can be discovered. They are discovered in the very stability of the component parts of the germ plasm itself. Everything that we know about genes or chromosomes points to the fact that they are relatively immutable not only at the moment at which they are observed but in the conditions which they seem to establish for the whole growth process. In view of this fact, it has become possible to work out some of the statistical correlations between the presence or absence of genes and the presence or absence of traits in the adult. It is these correlations which make up the science of genetics.

In other words, the geneticist takes advantage of one single point in the whole pattern of development where two systems, viz., an x-system and a y-system, have come into a fairly stable and observable equilibrium with each other. It would seem to follow that, whenever any investigator finds a way of disturbing this equilibrium, he will have found a way of modifying the germ plasm. We may say again that one such way has been found, for X-rays and similar agents do disturb the stability of germinal material. The experimenter must, however, go much further than this before it can be said that any sort of control is being exerted over hereditary processes. It would be necessary to localize such irradiation in specific parts of germinal material and to show that such specificity was related to the presence or absence of given traits before one could conclude that one had, at length, achieved control over hereditary processes.

C. THE MEANING OF HEREDITY: These considerations lead us to the possibility of giving the word "heredity" a new meaning. We have already discarded the possibility that heredity is a force. We mean to discard the proposition, also, that heredity describes anything that is intrinsic or native to germinal stuff. On the contrary, the word "heredity" describes the fact that there is a residual inertia in germinal plasm. This residual inertia is permitted of the germ plasm because of the correlative stability of the y-system within which it is placed.

4. *Environmental Control: Psychological Methods:* We have, however, considered only half the picture. We have said above that there are other phases of the environment which may become effective in regulating the growth of all such x-systems as living creatures. Immediately upon birth, if not before, that unique type of environment which we call a learning situation becomes highly significant in promoting and guiding the growth pattern. Shortly

after birth, situations which merit the name "social" become equally significant. It turns out, therefore, that the psychologist can easily be called an environmentalist since he works most readily from the point of view of a y-system which is psychological and social in character.

In this respect, he is to be contrasted with the geneticist. Because of the reasons named above, the geneticist must attack the growth pattern at one single point in its total history, viz., before the individual has become too complex and before many of the events which he might wish to view are covered up by skin and other tissues. The psychologist would be in a highly favorable position if, instead of having access only to stimulus-situations and to responses, he could have access to the events that take place in the cortex and in other parts of the brain as growth continues. Unfortunately, however, access cannot be had to these events and he must remain satisfied, therefore, with rearrangements of the psychological and social environments of animals.

This aspect of the problems we are considering will come in for more detailed discussion in the three chapters which are to be devoted to the nature of the learning process and to the various conditions under which environmental situations can be made most effective in promoting the growth of the individual. For the time being, we may say that learning is a type of growing. It falls, therefore, in the total pattern of events that we have been describing during this chapter. Moreover, it shows why the psychologist can easily be tempted to take the environmentalist's horn of the dilemma created by the two words "original nature" and "training."

5. *Summary:* We may summarize our argument up to the present time in the following way. Any growing individual is always in an environment. At any single moment of the growth pattern, the individual will be intrinsically that which his environment permits him to be. Since the whole order of nature has achieved a large degree of stability, it follows that growth patterns are not very apt to deviate largely from one another. A small amount of deviation, studied as it can be in the germ plasm and in a correlation between the germ plasm and adult traits, is called heredity. It may also, however, be called environment, as indeed it is, by the psychologist who undertakes to control the environment in the form of learning situations and in other forms as well. The degree of control which can be exerted over any growth process is a matter of scientific method. It turns out that there are no scientific methods which are really effective at early stages of development. The psychologist and

the educator, however, are fortunate enough to have methods which are useful during the latter stages of development.

This brief summary will become more meaningful, perhaps, if we apply what has just been said to some of the evidences for heredity which were described at the beginning of the chapter. We may take as a single example the so-called constancy of the I.Q. Obviously, this constancy can be explained equally well either by using such terms as the geneticist would use or by using such terms as the psychologist would use. In the former case, the constancy would be attributed to factors in the germ plasm; but, as we have tried to say, these factors represent a level of inertia or of stability which is permitted of germinal material by its context. In the latter case, the constancy of the I.Q. is a reflection of the constancy of the environment of any individual.

It will not be possible for us to say all that should be said about the phrase "the constancy of the environment" at this point. Of two things, however, we may be sure. On the one hand, the word "constancy" derives no significance whatsoever so far as the presence or absence of certain objects is concerned. That is to say, constancy must imply the functional part which objects and events play with respect to the individual. Without considering these matters further, it can be seen at once that there is not now enough evidence concerning the functional value of different kinds of environments either as total stimulus-situations or as temporal sequences of situations to enable the psychologist to be anywhere near as intelligent in his discussion as is the geneticist.

READINGS

The primary sources of information about the matters discussed in this chapter can be found in Jennings, H. S., *The Biological Basis of Human Nature*. New York: W. W. Norton and Co., 1930, and in Schwesinger, G. C., *Heredity and Environment*. New York: The Macmillan Co., 1933.

As the text has pointed out, biologists emphasize for the most part the hereditary factors in the growth pattern. This disposition is most clearly displayed in Morgan, T. H., *The Scientific Basis of Evolution*. New York: W. W. Norton and Co., 1932. The contrasting disposition of the sociologist, in particular, and of the social sciences, in general, is displayed in Rice, S. A. (Ed.), *Methods in Social Science*. Chicago: Univ. of Chicago Press, 1931. This book is strongly to be recommended to students of education, for even that phase of education known as educational psychology goes beyond the problems of original nature and learning. Education is a social agent which requires high measures of familiarity with social, physiological, and other cultural materials.

The more serious student of the mechanisms of heredity should consult some such book as Hurst, C. C., *The Mechanism of Creative Evolution.* New York: The Macmillan Co., 1932. Other books which are, perhaps, more accessible are Conklin, E. G., *The Direction of Human Evolution.* New York: Charles Scribner's Sons, 1921; Guyer, M. F., *Being Well Born.* Indianapolis: Bobbs-Merrill Co., 1916; Newman, H. H., *et al., The Nature of the World and of Man.* Chicago: Univ. of Chicago Press, 1927; Walter, H. E., *Genetics.* The Macmillan Co., 1930.

There are several places where the student may find an adequate survey of the instinct theory and of the several varieties of instincts. See, for example, Wilm, E. C., *The Theories of Instinct.* New Haven: Yale Univ. Press, 1925; McDougall, W., *Social Psychology.* Boston: J. W. Luce, 1916; Bernard, L. L., *Instinct; A Study of Social Psychology.* New York: Henry Holt and Co., 1924; and Drever, A., *Instinct in Man: A Contribution to the Psychology of Education.* (2nd ed.). London: Cambridge Univ. Press, 1921.

Data from the experimental study of "instinctive" performances is better found in the original articles. Cf. Kuo, Z. Y., "Giving Up Instincts in Psychology," *J. Phil.,* 1921, XVIII, 645-664; Kuo, Z. Y., "How Are Our Instincts Acquired?" *Psychol. Rev.,* 1922, XXIX, 344-365; Watson, J. B., "What the Nursery Has to Say About Instincts," in Murchison, C. (ed.), *Psychologies of 1925.* Worcester, Mass.: Clark Univ. Press, 1926, pp. 37-58; Carmichael, L., "Heredity and Environment: Are They Antithetical?" *J. Abnorm. and Soc. Psychol.,* 1925, XX, 245-260.

Notable books which did much to establish the instinct theory are Fabre, J. H. C., *The Hunting Wasps.* New York: Dodd, Mead and Co., 1915, and Peckham, G. W., and Peckham, E. G., *Wasps, Social and Solitary.* Boston: Houghton Mifflin Co., 1905. See also Hingston, R. W. G., *Problems of Instinct and Intelligence.* New York: The Macmillan Co., 1928. A fruitful study of instincts from the experimental point of view can be found in Tolman, E. C., *Purposive Behavior in Animals and Men.* New York: D. Appleton-Century Co., 1932, Chapter XX.

The original source material for the theory of recapitulation is to be found, of course, in Hall, G. S., *Adolescence* (2 vols.). New York: D. Appleton-Century Co., 1904, *passim.* More accessible material, perhaps, is to be found in Partridge, G. E., *Genetic Philosophy of Education.* New York: The Macmillan Co., 1912.

The standard references on hereditary genius and inferiority are Galton, F., *Hereditary Genius.* London: The Macmillan Co., 1869; Galton, F., *Inquiries into the Human Faculty and its Development.* London: The Macmillan Co., 1883; and Goddard, H. H., *The Kallikak Family* (Rev. ed.). New York: The Macmillan Co., 1921. All of this material is splendidly surveyed in Schwesinger, G. C., *op. cit., passim.*

The student should also refer to the book by Schwesinger for an adequate treatment of such topics as the constancy of the I.Q., the resistance of individual differences to practice, and the developmental psychology of twins. The first two of these topics are also presented in a fruitful way by Viteles, M. S., *Industrial Psychology.* New York: W. W. Norton and Co., Chapters VI, VII, and *passim.*

One phase of the configurational point of view upon which our own study of the relations between heredity and environment has been based can be found in Wheeler, R. H., and Perkins, F. T., *Principles of Mental Development*. New York: T. Y. Crowell Co., 1932. See also Wheeler, R. H., *The Laws of Psychology*. New York: D. Appleton-Century Co., 1933, and Köhler, W., *Gestalt Psychology*. New York: Liveright Publishing Corp., 1929.

The student who wishes to go further afield into the general biological background of human growth and development will find abundant material in Thompson, J. A., and Geddes, P., *Life: Outlines of General Biology* (2 vols.). New York: Harper and Bros., 1931. A similar survey of the domain of biology has been written by Wells, H. G., Huxley, J. S., and Wells, G. P., *The Science of Life*. Garden City: Doubleday, Doran and Co., 1930. A shorter book of excellent quality has been written by Haldane, J. B. S., and Huxley, J., *Animal Biology*. Oxford: The Clarendon Press, 1927.

CHAPTER TEN

THE ORIGINAL NATURE OF MAN

I. Psychological Inheritance

1. *Introduction:* One of the main conclusions to be drawn from the last chapter is simply this, viz., all of the problems of the variety and extent of original nature cannot be settled until much more is known about the course of prenatal development than is the case at present. The first chapter has shown us, to be sure, that work in this field is being hastened as fast as possible and already there are a few general inferences which may be drawn from the facts now on hand. Prenatal development, however, is an extraordinarily complex process, just as complex, in fact, as is post-natal development.

Every cluster of atoms in the germ cell represents a field of energy which must stand in variable degrees of quasi-equilibrium with other clusters. All appear to be coöperating with one another in a larger pattern which must be, in part, a product of the subpatterns involved and, in part, a product of the buffering action of the physico-chemical environment within which the developing system is immersed.[1] If it were possible to work with events at subatomic levels as easily as it is to work with them at grosser levels, facts about the dynamics of development would come, perhaps, much more quickly and with much greater assurance. As matters stand, the experimenters in the field of genetics are limited to mass-attacks on the germ plasm and to statistical statements about the results of these attacks. It is almost certain that, if direct access could be had to the events that take place in a germ cell, just as access can be had to the movement of pieces on a chess board, an experimenter could make almost anything he desired out of a given set of chromatin material.

It is not necessary, however, to bring all the possible researches in the field of genetics to an end before saying something about the minima of original human nature. That is, in the light of the facts which have already been presented, what is there about human

[1] Cf. Wheeler, R. H., *The Laws of Human Nature.* New York: D. Appleton-Century Co., 1933, *passim.*

nature which almost certainly can be attributed to the inertia of germinal material? In terms of a rough analogy, we do not for a moment say that a copper wire has a special instinct or an innate tendency which leads it to conduct an electric current. Conductivity is a property of copper which we attribute, to be sure, to the nature of copper as copper but which is really derived from those features of the environment of copper which permit electrons and protons to assume the particular mode of stability described by "copperiness." In the same way, we do not propose, in this chapter, to describe special instincts but only to name what appear to be the essential psychological properties of that type of stuff of which human beings are made.[2]

In general, the stuff is living material. This living material, however, has been brought together in a way which is made permissible to it by the environment in which it has been placed. It is organized into structures and these structures have certain functions. The functions are just as inevitable or as innate as are the structures. Sometimes, however, the relatedness of structures gives rise to functions which require the subsequent development of appropriate structures. With respect to these structures and functions, there are certain properties or characteristics which must be accepted as inevitable. These inevitable features of living organisms would constitute, then, the minima so far as original nature is concerned.

2. *What is Psychological Inheritance?:* Even before we search out these minima, however, there are certain questions about human beings that must be asked and answered. For example, when we say that a human body is made up of structures which have intrinsic properties or functions, just what sort of structures and functions are we speaking of? During the last chapter, for example, we gave some of the evidence which leads men to believe that psychological inheritance is just as real a type of inheritance as is physical inheritance. What, however, can we mean by the phrase "psychological inheritance"? Is it implied that some structures and functions are purely physical in character, whereas others are purely mental in character, or must we limit the word "heredity" only to physical events?

A. MENTAL INHERITANCE: The student will see at once that some of the earlier forms of psychology would have had considerable

[2] Just as, for example, the biologist tries to work out the vital properties of living tissue. He can, of course, say that life is due to an intrinsic vital principle, but this argument has not proven useful. See Haldane, J. S., *The Sciences and Philosophy.* Garden City: Doubleday, Doran and Co., 1929, *passim.*

difficulty in answering this question. If the phrase "psychological inheritance" means that psychological traits can be passed on from one generation to the next as psychological traits, it must follow that there are mental genes and mental chromosomes which act in ways that are analogous to real genes and chromosomes. The work of Galton, which was referred to in the last chapter, makes it appear that children who are superior in psychological matters are more apt to come from superior parents than from inferior parents. Genetic continuity between the *minds* of the parents, on the one hand, and the *minds* of the children, on the other, could only be established, however, by machinery which is like the physical machinery.

To talk about mental chromosomes or genes, however, has seemed nonsense. This means that some of the older psychologies did not even attempt to solve the problem of inheritance in this way. As a matter of fact, they used an entirely different way to do it. They assumed that the mind of a child must be implanted in the body at some particular moment during the developmental history of the body.[3] There are those who have chosen the moment of conception for this implantation, while others have chosen the moment of birth. Obviously, however, this device does not help us very much in our questions about the original nature of man, for if minds are added to bodies at some time during the developmental process, and if minds are a species unto themselves, the problem of original nature is solved as soon as it is formulated. If children resemble their parents more nearly than they do any other adults, they must do so in the accidents of mind, rather than in the species or quality of mind. To be sure, minds might differ from one another, partly because some of them are of the order of five talents while others are only of the order of one talent, and partly because the instrument through which they could become effective, viz., the body, is a more nearly perfect instrument in some cases than others. Aside, however, from actual differences in talent, all of the variations that are known to obtain between different people would have to belong to the accidents of mind rather than to its species.

B. THEORIES OF MIND-BODY RELATIONSHIPS: A second answer given to the questions asked above runs as follows. It may be taken for granted that the science of genetics describes the only mechanisms that are necessary to account for psychological inheritance. Each new child, therefore, would be equipped with a proper assortment of muscles, the normal number of sense organs, and a nervous

---

[3] See the article "Traducianism" in Hastings, J., *Encyclopedia of Religion and Ethics*. New York: Charles Scribner's Sons, 1928.

system which could be used for all of the ordinary types of integration between sense organs and muscles.

Inheritance of this type would provide for psychological inheritance in terms of any one of the various theories that have been offered for the relationship between mind and body.[4] As the student already knows, the mind-body problem has always been a very perplexing problem not only in psychology and in philosophy but in education as well. If we assume that there is a mind which is of a different species than the body, then we will most certainly be perplexed by the question as to how these two different species of things can have an influence on one another. The mind which, by definition, is immaterial and without dimensions, is said to have an effect upon nerves or upon muscles which, by definition, are material and mensurable.

This difficulty has been evaded sometimes by appealing to the doctrine of psychophysical parallelism and sometimes by saying that mind and body represent two different aspects of a single entity. Parallelism would assert that, for some reason which lies beyond the ken of human beings, those mental processes which are appropriate to any given level of development or of training simply keep pace with correlative events in the sense organs, the nervous system, and the muscles. The parallelist, then, could say that there is no particular service to be rendered by the phrase "psychological inheritance." He can describe the factors which lead to the development of the body with all of its special organs and simply assume that, by virtue of some mystery which cannot be made known, appropriate types of experience will occur. In this, he will be supported by making use of the comparative equation. This equation says, in general, that the mind of a lower animal is to its body as the mind of a person is to the human body.[5]

Those who believe in the double-aspect theory are a little more fortunate so far as psychological inheritance is concerned since, according to this theory, our own inner view of ourselves gives us the mind part of ourselves, whereas our view of someone else gives us the body part. As the bodily parts begin to develop, then, the inside view would likewise develop. Moreover, it would have to develop in quantity and in variety in direct relation to the character of the developing physical parts.

[4] Cf. McDougall, W., *Body and Mind*. New York: The Macmillan Co., 1920, *passim*.
[5] Cf. Bentley, M., *The Field of Psychology*. New York: D. Appleton-Century Co., 1924, Chapter XX.

C. THE SCIENCE OF BEHAVIOR: The student already knows, perhaps, that psychologists have turned definitely away from these problems. We shall not be able to give all of the reasons for the newer points of view until we come to Chapter Twenty. We must, however, anticipate this chapter to the extent of saying that definitions of the science of psychology in terms of mind or consciousness have simply not proven useful.[6] It would take no argument to show that the mind of a new-born infant is not open to observation. Neither can one say with assurance anything about the nature of its mental life, if it has one.[7] These same assertions hold true also of adults.

If the student has any doubts about this matter, let him undertake to describe the mind of one of his friends. He will have no question, of course, about his own mindedness, that is, about the fact that he does have a personal or private view of what he calls his own intimate experience; but he certainly cannot get a glimpse of the private view which his friend has of his experience. The only facts that are available about infants and adults are facts concerning the nature of stimulus-situations to which they can be observed to give a discriminable response. When, for example, the infant reacts to a lighted object by reaching for it, we may say, of course, that the infant is seeing the object simply because we know that we would be seeing it if it were presented to us. This, however, is surely an inference drawn from the facts rather than a statement of fact, for all that we actually observe is the lighted object and the directed response of the infant toward the object. In short, then, it is much more fruitful in child psychology and in general psychology, as well, to describe the unique types of relationship that are set up between stimulus-patterns and responses than it is to make precarious analogies drawn from our own private view of ourselves.

As we have said, these problems about the nature of psychology will concern us in more detail in a later chapter. We raise them here only in order to point out that modern psychology is more properly described as the science of behavior. If we do this, direct meaning can be given to the phrase "psychological inheritance." The behavior which the psychologist describes is obviously psychological rather than physical. It is characterized by a unique set of

---

[6] Cf. Heidbreder, E. F., *Seven Psychologies.* New York: D. Appleton-Century Co., 1933, *passim.*

[7] Cf. Washburn, M. F., *The Animal Mind.* The Macmillan Co., 1926, Chapter XII.

properties which distinguish it from the behavior of non-living objects.[8]

Now it happens that it is the function of some of the structures which make up a human body to bring about various types of movement in the body. These movements are always made in response to, and appear to be directed toward, definite stimulus-patterns. It becomes pertinent to inquire, therefore, what types of movement and what types of relatedness to stimulus-patterns are innate or intrinsic to the kind of organism which human beings represent. If human beings, like some of the lower animals, have sense organs, if they have mechanisms by which movements can be made, and if they possess pathways of conduction between sense organs and muscles, what properties or characteristics of these devices are there which can be called native or hereditary or unlearned?

II. The Minima of Original Nature

1. *Introduction:* Let the student be warned that the whole stream of behavior in its relation to the stream of environmental situations is an exceedingly complex but configured whole. Were our powers of description great enough we might take it as a whole; but for purposes of experimental work and discussion it must be broken into parts. The first part of Chapter II has given us a brief description of seven such parts. There is nothing sacred about this number or this mode of treatment. It is intended to serve only the practical purpose of enabling us to dip into the whole range of human nature at convenient places.

2. *Examples of Original Nature:* Now we must try to find out what features of each of the sections listed earlier are innate in the sense that they are intrinsic properties of human nature. That is, in any statements about original nature, what is the least that can be said? It will be convenient to make this statement in terms of each of the segments of the whole stream of action described in another connection.

A. ACTION PATTERNS: There is, first, the fact that it is a native or natural trait of all animals to respond to appropriate excitation by taking a posture or by making some sort of movement.[9] That is

[8] Cf. for example, Tolman, E. C., *Purposive Behavior in Animals and Men.* New York: D. Appleton-Century Co., 1933, *passim;* Bentley, M., "Psychology for Psychologists," in Murchison, C. (Ed.), *Psychologies of 1930.* Clark Univ. Press, 1930, Chapter V; Hunter, W. S., "The Psychological Study of Behavior." *Psychol. Rev.,* 1932, XXXIX, 1-24.
[9] Cf. Freeman, G. L., *op. cit.,* Chapter I.

to say, no living creature has to be taught how to respond to a stimulus. It is a property of muscular tissue to contract and the mechanical arrangement of muscles with respect to the bones makes bodily movement inevitable. There is, however, every reason to suppose that the initial movements of any living creature are extraordinarily diffuse or highly generalized. They may even be called unorganized if they are compared to the movements an adult would make under similar circumstances.[10] In some cases at least, these movements take place independently of external sensory stimulation and they furnish, therefore, the setting within which an environment, acting by way of a specific stimulus-situation, can achieve a part of its effectiveness in perfecting behavior-patterns.

The initial change that takes place in the development of behavior is by way of a process of individuation whereby movements that can be called reflexive are differentiated out of more general types of response.[11] In the human embryo, a part of this process has already taken place, but the more elaborate organization of muscle twitches into systems and patterns of response to particular stimulus-patterns is certainly a product of environmental coöperation.

In general, then, we may say that no living creature has to learn the art of contraction. Contractility is a property native to muscle tissue.[12] What is done with this property depends pretty largely upon the character and frequency of the stimulating agents which come to excite it. That is, precise habits and skills depend upon the buffering action of a y-system.

In addition to these properties and functions it is commonly argued that the nervous system is equipped with tendencies toward more precise actions or modes of behavior which are totally unlearned. There are, for example, such reflexes as the grasping reflex and the Babinski reflex which appear at or soon after birth and for which there could have been no training of the type commonly thought of in connection with education.[13] It is also asserted that there are other more general tendencies in the nervous system of the order of instinctive tendencies. What are the facts?

With reference to reflexes, we have already found reason to believe that simpler movements often issue out of more general or

[10] Review the discussion of this matter in Chapter One.
[11] Cf. Carmichael, L., "Origin and Prenatal Growth of Behavior," in *Handbook of Child Psychology* (Ed. C. Murchison), 1933, Chapter II. See also, Pratt, K. C., "The Neonate," *ibid.*, Chapter III.
[12] Cf. Gould, A. G., and Dye, J. A., *op. cit.*, Chapters I-VI.
[13] Cf. Rabinger, A., and Keschner, M., "Theory of the Mechanism for the Babinski Toe Phenomenon." *Arch. Neur. and Psychiat.*, 1926, XVI, 312-318.

more complex movements during a process of individuation. Individuation of this sort may rest, in part, upon dynamic conditions within growing tissue but in part, also, upon the directing and promoting influence of environmental factors. Obviously much research still needs to be done on this problem even though it is clear that the difficulties which stand in the way of proper experimentation are almost insurmountable.

It may be that further studies upon the growth and development of patterns of behavior in the lower animals will throw light on the nature and extent of organization within the brain brought about by special stimulus agents; but for the time being, we seem to be limited almost entirely to the behavior which we can actually observe after birth. It stands to reason, of course, that various parts of the central nervous system must sustain relations to one another that are just as natural and as definite as the relation of a pair of eyes to a nose or a nose to a mouth.[14] We would count it strange indeed if any of these organs were displaced from what we call their natural setting. No one has thought it worth while, however, to argue that the two eyes should be separated by the bridge of the nose or that a wealth of hair should grow on the head rather than upon the middle of the back because eyes and hair follicles have an instinct to become located as they actually are. On the contrary, we suppose that the general patterning of growth events is strictly a function of the dynamic processes involved in growth processes which are both hereditary and environmental. The same kinds of processes put a cerebrum, a cerebellum, a thalamus, and other brain structures in what we call their proper relation to one another. It must be true, also, that individual nerve cells or, at least, colonies of such cells may have not only an anatomical but a functional relation with one another which are expressive of the organization of the whole growing system. Within the limits suggested by such a relationship it would be reasonable to suppose that certain types of natural preferences for pathways of conduction would antedate all training. Pending a further investigation of the matter, it could be said that the grasping reflex and the Babinski reflex, to take only these two as examples, suggest the existence of such preferred pathways of conduction.[15]

B. PERCEPTUAL SKILLS: In the second place, no living creature has to learn how to be nervously excitable in the presence of light

[14] Cf. Murchison, C., *op. cit.*, Chapter III; Lashley, K. S., *Brain Mechanisms and Intelligence.* Chicago: Univ. of Chicago Press, 1929, *passim.*
[15] See, however, Givler, R. C., "The Intellectual Significance of the Grasping Reflex." *J. Phil.*, 1921, XVIII, 617-628.

waves, sound waves, touch and pressure, temperature or chemical substances such as odors and tastes.[16] In other words, the dynamic process of growth has seen to it that every normal human embryo is equipped with a complete array of receptors, each of which is potentially related to a set of effectors. It is known, for example, that there is a time when a group of cells taken from any part of a developing egg will adapt itself to its environment and produce what that environment calls for in the whole pattern. After a time, the trend of growth of any particular group of cells becomes fixed, and it will then proceed to develop an eye or a limb irrespective of its context.[17] The possession of eyes and of other receptors in a particular relation to other organs and structures, therefore, is a matter of the dynamics of heredity and of growth and not a matter of training. As in the case of muscular movement, most of these structures come to a fair degree of perfection without dependence upon stimulating agents in the environment, but the way in which they are to be used and the degree of refinement in perception must be largely a matter of environmental coöperation with the hereditary factors.[18]

This argument certainly holds true of the conscious modes of experience which are known to accompany a proper stimulation of the various receptors. No one has ever supposed that a new-born infant has to learn how to experience color qualities when the visual apparatus is stimulated or how to experience auditory qualities when the auditory apparatus is stimulated. The same considerations hold true for the other receptors. If one chooses to say that the possession of a certain type of conscious experience in conjunction with the excitation of a certain set of physical instruments is instinctive or native, then certainly a case can be made out for the existence of an original nature of the psychological type. It goes almost without saying, however, that the phrase "original nature" has not ordinarily been used in this way.

C. FACILITATION AND INHIBITION: In the third place, no human infant has to learn how to facilitate the events set up in the brain tissue by some stimuli and inhibit the events set up by others in order to create that shifting relationship between potency and impotency called attention.[19] It does not do at all to say that attention is a faculty or power whose history dates back to the trait of some

---

[16] Troland, L. T., *The Principles of Psychophysiology*. New York: D. Van Nostrand Co., 1930, Vol. II: "Sensation," *passim*.
[17] Cf. Morgan, T. H., *Experimental Embryology*. New York: Columbia Univ. Press, 1927, *passim*.
[18] Jennings, H. S., *op. cit.*, Chapter III.
[19] Cf. Freeman, G. L., *op. cit.*, Chapters XVI-XXI.

particular gene. On the contrary, attention seems to depend upon the sort of integration and coöperation which is possible to such physical systems which have a brainlike character. It may never be possible to describe all of the circumstances under which some patterns of energy in the brain achieve dominance over others and thus promote reactions to some stimulus-situations rather than to others. The results of such variable relationships, however, cannot be denied, since even very young children do actually "attend to" some objects and "attend from" others without learning how to do so.

Among the factors that serve this purpose, we may mention certain properties of stimulus-situations themselves. A very intense stimulus, for example, may create a brain field which will dominate other brain fields. It looks as though new or unexpected stimulus-patterns may have the same effect. It has already been noted that stimulus-patterns which have been reacted to on some previous occasion will achieve preference over others, but this is to imply that learning of some sort has already taken place. It is exceedingly difficult to give any precise meaning to the phrase "biological advantage" but there can be no doubt about some preferences which owe their origin solely to the fact that they serve the interests of the reacting individual.[20]

D. THE BODILY ENERGIES: The picture which we have already drawn of the way in which the bodily energies, on the one hand, and the general tonus of the living system, on the other, may enter into the quality of modes of reaction is, of course, highly inadequate. It seems to be clear, however, that the rate at which a given person will live, that is, his fundamental rate of metabolism, on the one hand, and his possession of glands of internal secretion which regulate the reserve supplies of energy, can depend in no way upon learning situations. In short, it is a part of the original nature of man that those features of attitude and action which he will describe as pleasant or satisfying, on the one hand, and as unpleasant or annoying, on the other, are unlearned.

Given equipment of this type, however, a great deal yet remains to be said concerning the way in which the equipment will be used in variable situations. As the total range of the effective environment increases, and as additional modes of action are acquired, all sorts of situations and actions which hitherto may have had no affective or emotional quality will acquire such quality.[21]

[20] Cf. Freeman, G. L., *op. cit.*, Part III.
[21] As we have indicated in Chapter VI, the clearest evidence of this fact comes from studies on emotional maladjustments. Cf. Sherman, M., *Mental Hygiene and Education.* New York: Longmans, Green and Co., 1934, *passim.*

As a precise illustration, we may take a case that has been cited in several different places. A great many children display a marked fear of darkness. Before a proper examination of this fear, it was easy to say that it was instinctive or that it was a reflection of the long experience of the race in dark caves where a dangerous situation might develop at any time. The chemical and physiological equipment which will make a person afraid in these or in other situations is certainly hereditary, but the situations which will actually tap this equipment are able to do so largely because of the effect of learning situations.

E. MOTIVES: The native and the acquired factors in motives are almost of the same order as is the case with emotionalized types of action. No child has to learn how to move the walls of its stomach at a time when the tissues stand in need of new supplies of food. Neither does the child have to learn how to fall asleep or to assume other resting postures as a response to the presence of excess toxic products in its system. In other words, the whole pattern of growth which has already been described gives each child an equipment of organs and functions which are dependent upon hereditary factors. From this point forward, however, situations which have not been related in any way whatsoever to the satisfaction of the bodily desires can, under the influence of learning situations, acquire an intimate degree of relationship.

F. PROBLEM-SOLVING: In the sixth place, living creatures are very rarely put in a place where their natural equipment is totally adequate to every situation. In spite of its general stability, the environment is enormously variable, and this means that every stimulus-situation has new components or properties for which an untrained person will have no precise reactions. Several methods of escape from such situations are possible. The person may, for example, try another movement. It is sometimes said that the emotions are symptomatic of situations where the normal mechanisms of response are not adequate. On other occasions, however, a perplexity is solved or a difficulty is met by the sudden creation of a new mode of response.

We frequently say that the schoolroom teaches children how to think. It would be better, perhaps, to say that it teaches them how to use the mechanisms that make thinking possible, for no child has to learn how to bring about that kind of short-circuiting in nerve tissue which makes insight possible.[22] Even where thinking goes on by way of a stream of associations, it cannot be said that learning

---

[22] Cf. Freeman, G. L., *op. cit.*, Chapters XIX and XX. Also, Köhler, W., *Gestalt Psychology*. New York: Liveright Publishing Corp., 1929, *passim*.

makes the initial fact of association possible. It happens to be one of the properties of fields of force in the brain that they should, whenever they come to be related together in any way, tend to sustain such a relationship.

G. PERSONALITY: In the seventh place, if it were ever possible for us to practice a given skill and then become completely unable to live through any further experience whatsoever, the chances are that we should never forget the thing last practiced. In other words, forgetting is one way of describing the fact that the experiences of the present moment always supervene upon a fund of experiences already had.[23] Conversely, experiences which have been lived through prior to the present hour may react upon the present and help to eliminate, to wipe out, or otherwise to change what has taken place in it.

In the field of learning, this principle has been called the law of retroactive inhibition. In its most general form, the law would state that the experience of the present moment reacts upon past experiences so as to limit their effectiveness whereas past experiences interfere with the present so as to modify its effectiveness. Thus a mechanism for forgetting is provided.[24] But forgetting is never complete. In the sense that every experience means activity on the part of a nervous system—which is the common factor behind all experiences—any present performance must become more than a reflection of a present stimulus. It is a reflection of that stimulus and of the whole past history of a brain. In other words, then, the unlearned mnemonic functions of the brain inevitably mean that the brain is taking on a total character under the influence of experience. No child has to learn or otherwise acquire this property of brain tissue. Children may become one kind of a person or character and this will be dependent upon their training; but the fact that they can become a character or person at all is dependent upon their heredity.

In other words, it is sometimes possible, in a long-time study of any individual, to recognize behavior-patterns which have a unique consistency and persistency about them. In spite of all of the small changes that may take place in the experience of the individual and in spite of the new situations into which he may fall, there is still a total trend in his behavior which marks him indelibly as being one

---

[23] This fact is often used as a basis for educational considerations. Cf. Leary, D. B., *Living and Learning*. New York: R. R. Smith, Inc., 1931, *passim*.

[24] For titles concerning theories of forgetting, see McGeoch, J. A., "The Psychology of Human Learning: A Bibliography." *Psychol. Bull.*, 1933, XXX, pp. 60-61.

person and not another.[25] It is this persistence and consistency of behavior which we call character or personality.

Certain analogies for the persistence of organization in spite of change among the items which make up the organization are to be found in chemical systems and in a great many organic systems. It is one of the unexplained puzzles of physics and physiology that the organization, say of an atom, a molecule, an amoeba, an earthworm, or a human being, should maintain its stability in spite of constant change in the materials that make up the whole system. In an atom, for example, one electron may be knocked off and a new one take its place or, on occasion, even the nucleus may be shattered and a new nucleus started; but in spite of this change in material the total integrity of the whole pattern persists. Even though all of the changes wrought by education are accounted for, and even though, after six or seven years, practically the entire chemical constitution of the human body has been changed, there still remains a persistence of form or identity of total organization which cannot be mistaken. As we have said, no person learns through experience that it is worth while to cherish such an organization. This is a feature of growth or development which is implicit within organic and physical systems.[26]

H. PLASTICITY: There is one further feature of the whole growth pattern which certainly displays a large amount of dependence upon hereditary factors. This feature is named by the word "plasticity."[27] That is, no infant has to learn how to make its nerve tissue plastic enough to undergo some sort of functional modification during use and stable enough to retain its own history. In spite of the many physical analogies which we have for the so-called mnemonic properties of matter, it is not yet possible to say just what has happened when a physiological system reacts to a situation, partly in terms of factors intrinsic to that situation, and partly in terms of factors dependent upon the history of the system.[28] The second repetition of an act is never a photographic copy of the first. It must be conceded that children do not acquire this mnemonic property of nerve tissue by experience or by conscious effort. Plasticity

[25] Cf. James, W., *Principles of Psychology*. New York: Henry Holt and Co., 1890, Vol. I, Chapters IX and X.
[26] Cf. Eldridge, S., *The Organization of Life*. New York: T. Y. Crowell Co., 1925, *passim*.
[27] Cf. Fiske, J., *The Meaning of Infancy*. Boston: Houghton Mifflin Co., 1909, *passim*.
[28] Interesting sidelights are thrown by such papers as the following, viz., Rashevsky, N., "Learning as a Property of Physical Systems." *J. Gen. Psychol.*, 1931, V, **207-229**.

and the mnemonic functions dependent upon it are just as inevitably properties of nerve tissue as contractility is of muscle tissue.

1. SUMMARY: In general, then, we may say that the processes of heredity shall have the same meaning for psychology as they have for physiology. Just as no child has to learn how to acquire a pair of legs or a set of teeth so no child has to learn how to acquire sense organs, a nervous system, muscles, glands of internal secretion, processes of facilitation and inhibition, mnemonic functions, modes of short-circuiting and of association, or tendencies toward total patterning in action. All of these traits and properties of the nervous system are a product of the dynamics of growth, and growth, in turn, is a reflection of coöperation between one set of physico-chemical events called genes and another set of physico-chemical events called the environment.

III. HEREDITARY NEURAL CONNECTIONS

1. *Introduction:* We have now given the student a list of some of the psychological features of human nature which appear to constitute the minimum that can be attributed to native constitution. It will be realized, of course, that the first two classes of innate properties are classes which deal almost entirely with situations, on the one hand, and with modes of response, on the other, to the exclusion of types of connection between these terminals. It is to be taken for granted that nerve connections between stimulus-patterns presented to any part of the sensory apparatus and the responses made to these stimulus-patterns must exist. It is for this reason that we speak of sensori-motor learning, for it must never be assumed that stimulus-patterns have any meaning apart from the intimate relation they sustain to motor organs.[29] As a matter of fact, where stimulus-patterns do not have such relationship, they are not stimulus-patterns at all, but parts of the irrelevant environment of a person.

Let us agree, then, that sensori-motor patterns furnish the general matrix of conditions within which all other psychological and educational problems are to be found. After having described the total variety of objects and events which can become effective in initiating and regulating the behavior of a person and after having taken full account of all of the variable modes of response that can be made to these stimulus-patterns, the rest of the problems of psychology

[29] Cf. Dewey, J., "The Reflex Arc Concept in Psychology." *Psychol. Rev.*, 1896, III, 357-370.

and of education refer not to other stimulus-patterns or to other action-patterns, but to the unique types of relationship which are observed to obtain between these correlated pairs of events. In the case of attention, for example, the psychologist discovers his problems, not because he discovers evidence of some special faculty or agent, but because relations between stimulus-patterns and responses are actually set up which give evidence of selection or of prepotency. When a person who is surrounded by a considerable number of stimulus-patterns and who is capable of making a variety of responses to them actually uses only one pattern of response to a single stimulus-pattern, it is imperative that the conditions be described under which selection of this type can be made possible.

These considerations hold even more clearly of the relations between stimulus-patterns and action-patterns which give rise to the phenomena of motivation. Here again, we may think of motivation as the result of inbred or native drives, or we may think of it in terms of the enduring and persistent value of particular stimulus-situations in initiating and regulating behavior. Motivation is a problem for the psychologist, not because there is some hypothetical driving power behind human action, but because there are certain conditions which guarantee that some stimulus-patterns will actually endure as initiating and controlling influences.

Let us assume, then, that the inevitable properties or characteristics of living systems do give rise to some such statement of original nature as has been outlined in the last section. This statement constitutes, as we have said, a series of minima. Now we must find out how much further it is possible to go. That is, we must look at the nervous system itself or at the connections that may be established between sense-organs and response-organs, for it is in the nature of these connections that most people find the most convincing evidence for original nature. Those, for example, who believe in native reflexes or instincts will argue that connection patterns must be so mature at birth that certain types of stimuli will lead almost certainly to precise modes of response. More precisely, then, what is the evidence in favor of the existence of any considerable number of unlearned connections?

2. *The Meaning of "Organism"*: A partial answer to this question is given by the fact that the nervous system is a complex integration of parts. The student is already familiar with the most important of these parts, viz., the cerebrum with its outer layer of nerve cells which is called the cortex, the cerebellum, the thalamus which stands almost at the upper end of the old brain, the medulla,

THE ORIGINAL NATURE OF MAN 359

the spinal cord, and the clusters of nerve cells (ganglia) which lie alongside the spinal cord throughout its entire length.[30] In addition to these more commonly known parts, the anatomist has been able to identify a tremendous number of other parts or centers.

Now we could, if we wished, think of the whole nervous apparatus as a simple collection of parts, each of which has grown up more or less independently of other parts and as having no essential kinship with them. This manner of thinking, however, would be contrary to the facts, for, as we have said over and over again, every growing system is, from the very first, an integrated system. If the student will think again of the concepts which we have attached to the phrases "x-system" and "y-system," we may say that every part of the nervous apparatus can be thought of as an x-system which has gained some of its characteristics as an x-system because it is surrounded by or has grown up in an environment furnished by other parts of the nervous apparatus and by other parts of the body. It is almost too obvious to say that a new-born infant does not appear as a collection of pieces which have to be put together by the physician. On the contrary, the new-born infant is an organism. This means that, if we speak of parts at all, we do so simply because it is more convenient in science to give our attention to one thing at a time while assuming that other things remain constant.

Let us grant, then, that the nervous apparatus of a new-born infant is a configured whole. Emphasis must be placed upon the word "configured," simply because nothing occurs in nature which can be described as chaotic. If we say that the nervous system is a configured whole, it follows that the parts of which we speak so easily in conversation are parts which sustain a membership relation to other parts. In short, no new-born infant has to learn how to cause impulses which are set up in the retina to be conducted along the optic nerves to an optic center in the brain and thence to other correlation centers, and eventually to muscles. The very conditions of growth guarantee that nervous excitations will spread throughout portions of the system in the manner described.[31]

3. *The Maturation Factor:* It is one thing to say this, however, and quite another to argue that the particular pattern of excitation created by a particular stimulus-situation will be conducted to that particular configuration of motor organs which will enable the person

---

[30] Cf. Herrick, C. J., *An Introduction to Neurology.* Philadelphia: W. B. Saunders Co., 1931 (5th ed.), *passim.*
[31] Cf. Parker, G. H., *The Elementary Nervous System.* Philadelphia: J. B. Lippincott Co., 1919, *passim.*

concerned to respond in an adequate way to that situation on the very first occasion. In some of the lower animals, of course, the evidence appears to bear out this possibility, but even in the case of the lower animals, it will be necessary to describe all of the dynamic factors involved in the growth pattern and to describe, also, the chemical and other environmental circumstances which may give guidance to the quick individuation of precise modes of action before the possibility is accepted.

As an illustration, we may take some of the studies that have been made on the maturation of the pecking instinct in chicks.[32] These experiments required that some newly hatched chicks be placed in total darkness for variable periods of time and thus deprived of adequate stimuli to the pecking movements. Their behavior, when compared with the behavior of chicks which had been allowed to peck from the moment of hatching, can be used to illustrate the dependence of the pecking instinct upon learning processes, on the one hand, and upon maturation, on the other. Now, if pecking were instinctive in the sense that a stimulus object like a piece of grain will inevitably and invariably lead to accuracy in movement in bringing the beak to the grain and in swallowing it, newly hatched chicks ought to display high skill in the performance. The experiments show, of course, that they are fairly awkward. As a matter of fact, they actually hit the grain only a small percentage of the time. At the end of three or four days, however, their skill has increased so greatly that they may be successful on the first attempt as frequently as ninety per cent of the time.[33]

In other words, chicks appear to acquire facility in pecking at objects on the ground by trial-and-error learning. To be sure, chicks which have been kept in total darkness for two or three days start at a slightly higher level of skill, and they learn much more rapidly. At the end of four or five days, chicks which have been kept in darkness for three days will be just as skilful as chicks which have been allowed to peck from the very first. There is, then, a maturation factor in the development of the pecking instinct, but even this maturation factor does not necessarily imply more precise connections between excitations in the visual receptors, on the one hand, and conduction to precise muscle groups, on the other, than those

[32] Cf. Shepard, J. F., and Breed, F. S., "Maturation and Use in the Development of an Instinct." *J. Anim. Behav.*, 1913, III, 274-285; Moseley, D., "The Accuracy of the Pecking Response in Chicks." *J. Comp. Psychol.*, 1925, V, 75-97.
[33] For comparable experiments, see Carmichael, L., "The Development of Behavior in Vertebrates Experimentally Removed from the Influence of External Stimulation." *Psychol. Rev.*, 1926, XXXIII, 51-58; 1927, XXXIV, 34-47; 1928, XXXV, 253-260.

THE ORIGINAL NATURE OF MAN

made possible by the total configuration or patterning of the various parts of the nervous apparatus.

Moreover, it is clear that the initial pecking action of a newly hatched chick has a history which may be pertinent to the degree of skill already shown. For example, the chick pecks its way out of the shell. This fact implies that movements of the head are not only possible while the chick is still within the shell but that head movements have probably occurred for some time prior to the moment of hatching. As we have seen in the first chapter, any movements made during the embryonic period may become powerful agents in establishing connections which contribute to the whole problem of configuration.[34]

4. *Plasticity:* We are led to conclude, then, that the nervous system as a whole, being a configured or patterned unit, may have certain general properties or characteristics over and above those which have already been described. There are two of these general properties which have played a large part in educational theory and practice. One of them we have already referred to, viz., plasticity. By plasticity we mean that human infants are highly educable, or that they are easily subject to growth under the influence of learning processes, or that there is a minimal amount of prior fixity in the connections between the sensory apparatus and the motor apparatus. Plasticity is, therefore, a general property of neural connections which would stand naturally in conflict with the alleged existence of previously established reflexes and instincts. At the same time, however, it is a concept which almost demands the unlearned configurations which we have assumed to hold true of the various parts of the nervous system.

If it is more likely that excitations of the visual apparatus will find their way through the nervous system over portions of the system that are more appropriate to lighted objects than over those portions of the nervous system that would be more appropriate to sounding objects or to pressures, temperatures, or changes in balance, we do not also say that the potential character of these connections must imply a vast number of highly specific patterns of conduction. The visual-motor pattern is an unlearned feature of the types of integration characteristic of that kind of stuff we know as nervous stuff. We may say, therefore, that these potentialities are innate or hereditary simply because they are an inevitable part of the configurational element in the nervous apparatus. The partic-

[34] Cf. Child, C. M., *The Origin and Development of the Nervous System.* Chicago: Univ. of Chicago Press, 1921, *passim.*

ular uses to which these potentialities will be put must certainly rest upon learning situations.

As we have seen, the total field of events laid before a new-born infant is highly lacking in particulars. It is a *ground* out of which *figures* will emerge. Likewise, the responses which a new-born infant makes to the initial ground materials are diffuse or highly generalized. As fast as specific types of conduction between the retina and the motor apparatus are established under the influence of learning situations, particular lighted objects, that is to say, particular figures, will emerge out of the previous field and become related in definite ways to particular modes of response. It is this type of individuation which gives rise to the concept of plasticity. One might say that there is no guarantee at birth or at any time prior to birth that an excitation of the visual apparatus may not pass into any part of the nervous system whatsoever.

In other words, the concept of plasticity might mean the total absence of all preferred lines of conduct. The absence of all preferred lines of conduct, in turn, would mean that the various parts of the nervous system are really not configured at all. This is a conclusion which does not appear to be justified by the facts. Even the unfertilized ovum is a configured system of events and as the organism emerges out of the ovum, every part of the developing pattern becomes a functionally significant part of the environment of each of the other parts. It is guaranteed from the beginning, therefore, that potential degrees of relatedness must be accepted as a part of original nature.[35]

5. *Intelligence:* A second general property of human nature which has played a large part in the art of teaching and which is attributed to innate factors is known as intelligence. We shall, of course, devote an entire chapter to a study of the nature of intelligence and of methods of measuring intelligence, but it will be helpful at this point if we think, for a moment, of intelligence as a general feature of original nature.

This general feature has been described in a number of different ways. For example, it may be said that intelligence depends upon the total number of cells in the brain, but especially on the total number in the cortex.[36] It is known, for example, that the nerve cells (or neurones), which are really mature and hence useful in psychological operations, grow out of a more primordial cell known

[35] Cf. Jennings, H. S., *The Biological Basis of Human Nature.* New York: W. W. Norton and Co., 1930, *passim.*
[36] Cf. Herrick, C. J., *op. cit.,* Chapters X, XIX-XXI.

THE ORIGINAL NATURE OF MAN

as the neuroblast. It has been shown that, in the case of certain types of feeblemindedness, an ample supply of neuroblasts is present, but that some unknown circumstances have hindered the further development of the neuroblast into a functionally mature neurone. In any case, it is possible to say that the intelligence of a person may depend upon the total number of active neurones present in the brain and especially in the cortex.[37]

Since the number of neuroblasts or of mature neurones must be dependent upon hereditary factors, it would seem to follow that intelligence itself must be primarily dependent upon hereditary conditions. Arguments against this conclusion would serve no good purpose, for no known methods of training can alter the total number of nerve cells that will be available for the proper development of the major psychological operations. On the contrary, it is easy to say that chemical conditions such as might be furnished by variations in diet and all of the other factors that have to do with buffering between x-systems and y-systems might have a profound influence upon the total number of nerve cells available. In other words, there is not much that can be said about the real value of hereditary factors in the creation of the total number of nerve cells that will be available for use until researches on the dynamics of the growth pattern have been carried to a point far ahead of the present situation.

Almost the same considerations hold true of those theories which argue that intelligence depends upon a particular fund of nerve energy. As we shall see, in our discussion of the nature of intelligence, there are certain facts which suggest the existence of such an energy supply.[38] The operation of the central nervous system, like the operation of all of the other parts of the body, does involve the expenditure of energy, but since there are serious strictures placed in the way of adequate experimental work on nerve energies and the various patterns into which they may fall, this phase of theories about the nature of intelligence does not lend itself readily to intelligent discussion.

A pretty good argument can be made out for the proposition that intelligence must be related in an intimate way to the limits of plasticity. It still remains to be seen whether some persons are actually more plastic, that is to say, more educable, than others. A part of plasticity would depend, of course, upon the total amount

---

[37] Cf. Lashley, K. S., *Brain Mechanisms and Intelligence*. Chicago: Univ. of Chicago Press, 1929, *passim*.

[38] Cf. Spearman, C., *The Nature of "Intelligence" and the Principles of Cognition*. London: The Macmillan Co., 1927, *passim*.

of nerve tissue available. It would depend, also, upon the rate at which original degrees of plasticity have been converted into degrees of fixity. If the nervous system has acquired any considerable measure of fixity—say, types of connections that are established between particular patterns of stimulus and particular patterns of response—real efforts are required to destroy this fixity and to establish some new habit. This fact is embodied in the old saying that habits tend to become highly automatized and to resist change through further learning.

As we shall try to show in our study of the transfer of training, limitations may be placed upon intelligence by the fact that many of the more fundamental aspects of our psychological functions reach a practical level of efficiency which is far removed from a physiological or a theoretical limit. This means that the average person might use a low level of efficiency for a good many different purposes but that an expansion in the services rendered to him, that is to say, an increase in his intelligence could be brought about only by raising the level of efficiency in fundamental respects. The student will probably not see all that is implied in these remarks; but we put them in at this place because we wish to remind him that a very important part of his work as a teacher will depend upon the skill he uses in drawing a distinction between essential psychological growth, on the one hand, and the services rendered to a person and to society by the use of attained levels of growth, on the other.

IV. General Principles of Development

1. *Maturation:* If we were to study, in a more serious way, all of the facts that have a bearing upon this and the preceding chapter, it would be required of us that we go to the fields of embryology and, in particular, to a whole series of studies on the unlearned equipment of the lower animals.[39] Enough has been said, perhaps, to show the reader that the word "heredity" and certainly the word "instinct" must receive a new interpretation or at least a renewed emphasis upon certain features which have been present in every study of these problems but which have not been recognized for their full value. These features spring out of the configured character of the whole growth process and out of the dynamic events that are involved in this configuration.

One witness to the change that is taking place in the discussion

[39] Cf. Needham, J., *Chemical Embryology* (3 vols.). Cambridge: Cambridge Univ. Press, 1932.

of instinct and heredity is furnished by the word "maturation."[40] The word maturation means that such events as have been described in the last and in other sections come into existence and are organized into a definite developmental pattern because of the operation of the same factors that lead to the physical development of each new individual. As we have seen, these include the organization or polarization of the ovum prior to fertilization, the factors which control the nature of cell division, and all of those features of subsequent development which are dependent upon the relation which any single cell maintains with other cells in the whole developmental pattern.

The word "maturation" ought to include, however, the effects of learning. The set of factors just mentioned gives shape and form to the basic structures in the body and to many of the basic adjustments which each person is called upon to make in his particular habitat; but learning processes may go a long way toward refining, extending, individualizing, and otherwise increasing the appropriateness of these basic adjustments to particularized environmental situations. If, then, we were to place, on the one hand, all of the factors that are now known to serve as preconditions of the whole growth pattern, and if we were to place, on the other hand, the growth pattern itself as a consequence of these directing and guiding conditions, the result could be described as maturation.[41]

2. *Causative Principles of Development:* It would be reasonable to suppose that, if a typical growth pattern has been described, one might be able to look at the pattern as a whole in order to say whether it displays any general features or characteristic properties. If a total view of the growth pattern were to reveal such general properties that ought to be described, they might serve not only the interests of genetic psychology but the interests of the teacher as well. As a matter of fact, some of them already serve the interests of the teacher, for the very organization of the school system, in general, and the organization of curricular sequences, in particular, are based upon the premise that the early part of a whole growth pattern differs in several essential respects from the latter part. Teachers have not always been clear about this matter, however, for

[40] Cf. Gesell, A., "Maturation and the Patterning of Behavior," in Murchison, C. (Ed.), *op. cit.*, Chapter IV.

[41] The word "maturation" has not as yet been clearly defined. There are some writers who appear to use it as a direct synonym of the older instinct hypothesis and even as a synonym for the hereditary agents which play their part in the whole growth pattern. Cf. Stone, C. P., "Learning: I. The Factor of Maturation," in Murchison, C. (Ed.), *A Handbook of Child Psychology.* Worcester, Mass.: Clark Univ. Press, 1934, Chapter VIII.

they have supposed that the educative process should begin with simple matters where simplicity has been the result of a logical dissection of more difficult matters rather than of a search for genetically prior types of accomplishment. We propose, then, in this section to glance briefly at some of the things that can be said at the present time about the general principles of development. We shall consider, first, some of the explanatory principles that are sometimes used to account for the course of mental development.

A. INHERITANCE OF ACQUIRED CHARACTERS: In addition to the factors that have already been mentioned as having a bearing upon the growth pattern, a number of special causative agents have been named. One of these is known as the doctrine of the inheritance of acquired characters.[42] This doctrine states that any particular growth pattern at the present time will receive a part of its directional quality from the fact that its immediate ancestors gained great skill in some particular performance or brought about some other change in their bodily or somatic structures and functions. In explaining the tendency for certain types of ability to run in families, it is often said that superior achievements of the first person in the sequence predetermined other persons in the sequence toward the same ability.

A great many experiments have been performed in this field, but the results have invariably stood on the negative side.[43] From information the student now has, he ought to be able to see clearly that the development of special skill in piano playing, athletics, or a given profession could have no influence upon his hereditary dispositions, unless some way could be found whereby such skills could be made a really effective part of the environment of the germ plasm. At the present time, no possible source of contact between a bodily or psychological skill, on the one hand, and the germ plasm, on the other, has been discovered. It looks as though the nature of growth processes were such that a discovery of this sort is wholly improbable. We may infer, therefore, that the growth pattern does not get any part of its directional quality from the special accomplishments of the immediate parents.

B. THE THEORY OF RECAPITULATION: We have already referred briefly to the theory of recapitulation. The student will recall that this theory attributes a part of the directional quality of an individual growth pattern to the influence exerted upon it by the previous

---

[42] Cf. Osborn, H. F., *From the Greeks to Darwin* (2nd ed.). New York: Charles Scribner's Sons, 1929, Chapter V.

[43] Cf. Morgan, T. H., "Mechanisms and Laws of Heredity," in Murchison, C. (Ed.), *op. cit.*, Chapter II.

history of the race. If there is a grasping reflex, this reflex owes its origin to the fact that some of the immediate ancestors of man depended upon it in their favorite habitat. If the growing child displays unexplainable fears or otherwise gives expression to attitudes and dispositions for which there is no obvious antecedent in its training, one may appeal to echoes of fearful experiences among man's ancestors or to other major crises in racial history.[44]

The study of embryology has shown rather clearly that some of the earlier stages in the development of the human embryo copy, so to speak, some of the earlier stages in the development of other animal species. Then, too, there are a number of vestigial organs, and there may be vestigial functions dependent upon these organs which must be expected as an echo of previous modes of living. It has not been shown, however, that the biological form of the theory of recapitulation can be translated "word for word" into a psychological form.[45]

This fact is not quite so important to teachers today as it was a decade ago, for some of the educational inferences drawn from the theory of recapitulation have already passed out of use.[46] The most significant fact about this theory for our purposes is the emphasis which it placed upon the genetic point of view. Now that the experimental laboratory is proving so productive, most persons find it more fruitful to go to the laboratory than to speculations about recapitulation of the psychological sort.

C. VARIATION AND NATURAL SELECTION: At the present time the psychologist is inclined to accept whatever the biologist has to say concerning the value of variation and natural selection as explanatory concepts.[47] The student will remember from his study of biology that variations from the general pattern or type may be brought about (i) by change in food, climate, the use or disuse of particular organs, or by such other environmental conditions as will lead to fluctuations, (ii) by new configurations of hereditary factors which are already present in the germ cell, and (iii) by rather sudden alterations in the germinal material which will lead to true mutations. It is now commonly thought that mutations have furnished the primary source of directedness in racial growth patterns. Those muta-

[44] Hall, G. S., *Adolescence* (2 vols.). New York: D. Appleton-Century Co., 1903, *passim*.
[45] Cf. Haldane, J. B. S., and Huxley, J., *Animal Biology*. Oxford: Clarendon Press, 1927, pp. 82 ff.
[46] Cf. Partridge, G. E., *Genetic Philosophy of Education*. New York: The Macmillan Co., 1912.
[47] Cf. Newman, H. H., *Evolution, Genetics and Eugenics*. Chicago: Univ. of Chicago Press, 1925, *passim*.

tions that would lead to some organ or function that would promote the welfare of an animal would be preserved, whereas those animals that were not benefited would be lost in the struggle for existence.[48]

The attempt to apply the principles of variation and selection to psychological facts may be illustrated by a study of the functional services of the conditioned reflex.[49] We shall find in a later chapter that conditioning makes it possible for one particular stimulus-pattern which has not hitherto called out a given reaction to become associated with this reaction simply by appearing in close temporal relation to its proper stimulus-pattern. In other words, one object or event may come to serve as a sign of the existence of another object or event. One might infer from this fact that an organism which could use signs to good advantage would have a chance of surviving, where another animal might perish. Other features of conditioning have been related to survival value in somewhat the same way.

3. *Descriptive Principles:* Of still greater importance to the teacher are those principles which are strictly descriptive of the whole growth pattern. It is still too early to state how many of these principles there are, and in some cases the evidence that is offered in favor of a given principle is scanty indeed. We may, however, suggest briefly their nature.[50]

A. INCREASING COMPLEXITY: The principle of increasing complexity has been carried over almost directly from biology. The principle states that most developmental sequences pass from a relatively simple beginning to an exceedingly complex terminus. If we think of the number side of the picture alone, each human being begins with a single cell and ends as a configured pattern including multiplied millions of cells. Some of the older views of psychological development made use of this same fact. It was said, for example, that behavior must have its origin in a relatively small number of simple reflex movements, the more complex types of movement being created by the addition of one reflex to another. In the same way, complex forms of perception and of conception are said to have their origin in a few experiences which represent the simple elements of mental life.[51]

[48] Consult, however, Hogben, L., *The Nature of Living Matter.* New York: A. A. Knopf, 1932, Part II.
[49] Hull, C. L., "A Functional Interpretation of the Conditioned Reflex." *Psychol. Rev.,* 1929, XXXVI, 498-511.
[50] Cf. Hollingworth, H. L., *Mental Growth and Decline.* New York: D. Appleton-Century Co., 1927, Chapter XVII.
[51] Titchener, E. B., *A Textbook of Psychology.* New York: The Macmillan Co., 1910, *passim.*

We shall see in a moment that the situation is not quite so simple as this, but, in general, a survey of schedules of development, either on the side of the body or on the side of psychological performance, gives the impression of increasing complexity. The best illustration of this fact, so far as the teacher is concerned, is to be found in the increasing amount of material that is finding its way into the curriculum. Knowledge, of course, is ever on the increase, and for a long time it has been impossible for any single person to become acquainted with more than two or three sectors of the whole range of information. The so-called "enrichment" of the curriculum, however, has increased with great speed during the present century. A part of this movement owes its origin, apparently, to the discovery, near the turn of the century, that the disciplinary value of certain types of subject matter was not so great as had been supposed. This discovery meant, of course, that a competent person would have to become acquainted with more material rather than increase his stature as a learning person. This phase of the educative process is so important that we shall devote a later chapter to it.

B. DIFFERENTIATION AND SPECIALIZATION: It is almost impossible to speak of the principle of increasing complexity without saying something at the same time of the principle of progressive differentiation and specialization. This principle is, in many ways, related to the process of individuation which has been described in earlier chapters. It names the fact that most genetic processes begin with a generalized structure and function out of which the specialized structures and functions emerge. As an almost classical example, we may take the comparisons that can be drawn between a single-celled animal like the amoeba and an organism like the human being. As the student knows, an amoeba is at one and the same time a mouth, a set of sense organs, a digestive apparatus, a nervous system, and a muscular system.[52] In the human being, however, each of these functions is associated with some particular structure or group of structures.

Other examples of progressive differentiation and specialization have appeared in each of the chapters of Part I. In the development of perception, for example, we have seen how particular figures may emerge out of a field. Likewise, more particularized or specialized movements emerge out of general types of movement. Many teaching procedures illustrate this same principle for it is often said that

[52] Cf. Jennings, H. S., *The Behavior of the Lower Organisms*. New York: Columbia Univ. Press, 1906, *passim*.

370 INTRODUCTION TO EDUCATIONAL PSYCHOLOGY

that teacher proceeds wisely who looks from generalized principles toward details.

D. THE PRINCIPLE OF ORGANIC QUALITY: Every genetic pattern is made up of a great many coöperating parts. The principle of organic quality would state that each of these parts is duly related in quality to the whole. They are essentially members of the whole. Illustrations of this fact are to be found in the story of evolution where the appearance of some particular structure or function has called for the almost simultaneous appearance of supporting structures and functions.

The best illustration of this principle, perhaps, is to be found in degrees of correlation among different psychological functions. For a time, it was supposed that those persons who are excellent in one respect must compensate for their excellence by being poor in a great many other respects. This tradition has held true, in particular, of precocious children. Terman has shown, however, in his studies on large numbers of such children, that if an individual ranks high in some particular respect, he is very apt to rank high in all other respects as well.[53] To be sure, there are a great many exceptions to this principle; but, in general, it appears that any level of excellence which obtains in one set of functions will obtain with respect to all functions.

E. THE PRINCIPLE OF VARIED TEMPO: We have already remarked the fact that every growth process is an essentially continuous process. Continuity, however, does not require an even tempo. Growth may take place much more rapidly at some times than it does at others.[54] These variations differ greatly from one child to another. In general, however, it has been possible to draw curves of developmental schedules which show positive acceleration during the early parts of the growth pattern and negative acceleration in later parts.[55] To be sure, changes in acceleration or changes in the tempo of growth depend to some extent on the methods that are used in plotting growth curves. In the case of learning, for example, it is possible to show that the first portions of certain types of learning proceed rather slowly. After the essential steps have been taken, the rate of progress increases. Almost every method of plotting learn-

[53] Terman, L. M., et al., *Genetic Studies of Genius.* Palo Alto: Stanford Univ. Press, 1925-30 (3 vols.).
[54] Baldwin, B. T., "The Physical Growth of Children from Birth to Maturity." *Univ. of Iowa Stud. in Child Welfare,* 1921, I (No. 1).
[55] Cf. Goodenough, F. L., *Developmental Psychology.* New York: D. Appleton-Century Co., 1934, *passim.*

ing curves, however, shows decreasing rate of growth as a practical limit of efficiency is reached.

The principle of varied tempo is one of the factors that lies behind our earlier statement to the effect that the preschool years are exceedingly important years as far as teaching effort is concerned. If the preschool child and the grade school child are reaching practical limits of efficiency at a rapid pace, it must follow that the learning situations which are brought to bear upon them ought to be of such a character as to lead to as high a level of practical efficiency as possible. In other words, the plasticity with which the child begins is quickly converted into larger measures of fixity. If these various degrees of fixity have been reached, further periods of learning become increasingly difficult. One witness in favor of this fact is to be found in the disappointing measure of success that attends efforts to reëducate delinquent children.

F. THE PRINCIPLE OF SERIAL ORDER: Even though there may be large individual differences in the rate at which growth may be proceeding at different times in different children, it is almost invariably true that every growth pattern is subject to a definite schedule. In an earlier chapter, for example, we have cited an experiment on the gradual development of skill in grasping. The experimenter, in this case, undertook to describe specific stages of development. Different children may pass through these different stages at different rates but it is significant to note that each of the stages is normally present and describable.

The same fact holds true of the development of language. The experimenters are not altogether certain as yet about these stages, but it seems to be quite clear that, irrespective of the rate at which the stages are passed, each child is committed to a definite schedule of events in the acquisition of his verbal skills. One important consequence of this schedule may be stated as follows. If a child has not yet passed a given stage in its growth pattern, special practice periods will not be of any profit to it. In this connection, the student will recall an experiment cited earlier which showed that special practice in climbing stairs and in handling a cube did not place one twin ahead of the other twin in degree of skill.

G. SUMMARY: These are only a few of the general principles of development which have been explicitly stated by some writers or implied by others. The time has not yet come, perhaps, when even the principles described above can be given the full experimental support that they ought to have. This, however, is not the main point. On the contrary, the student should realize that the growth pattern does involve a schedule of events which can be described or characterized as though it were a single, coherent whole. The description is of importance to the teacher because teaching is a timewise process which should be geared to the schedule of events which makes up the growth pattern. It will never be possible, of course, to gear teaching processes adequately to the growing child until specific stages in the whole growth pattern have been accounted for and the general features of the pattern used as a basis of suggestion for sequences in the curriculum, for changes in the difficulty of problems, and as a basis for measuring the effectiveness of teaching methods.[56]

V. Original Nature and the Art of Teaching

1. *Introduction:* We may now seek to summarize the data and the various interpretations of data which have been presented in the last two chapters. In the first place, we have sought definitely to shift the burden of proof from one point to another, so far as the general problems of heredity are concerned. Heretofore, many students of education have been inclined to admit that modes of conduct or of experience which are not obviously due to the influence either of parents or teachers must, therefore, be due to heredity. This means that the burden of proof for showing that those phases of conduct or of experience which are to be removed from the class of hereditary products to the class of environmental products must rest upon the environmentalist. The various things that we have had to say about original nature have changed this situation. We are concluding from the facts presented in the last two chapters that all phases of conduct and experience are to be taken as a result of particularized learning situations or of the general buffering action of the environment until the contrary has definitely been shown.

In the second place, we have sought to place considerable emphasis upon the dynamic character of the growth pattern. We have conceived this growth pattern as the outcome of two systems of events, the one of which we have identified as an x-system, and the other of which has been identified as a y-system. This identification has served the purpose merely of showing that, in matter of fact, no such identification is possible, for x-systems derive their properties and traits very largely through the buffering action exerted upon them by y-systems. This is to say that both x- and y-systems are

[56] Cf. Wheeler, R. H., and Perkins, F. T., *Principles of Mental Development.* New York: T. Y. Crowell Co., 1931, *passim.*

intimately coöperating events which cannot fruitfully be divorced from each other.[57]

We may, if we wish, say that the word "heredity" describes a special type of agency resident in that particular class of x-systems known as germinal material, whereas the word "environment" describes similar forces resident in that class of y-systems known as learning situations. However, both of these ways of speaking obscure the essential configuration or patterning that must always obtain within any cluster of events. If a biologist were able to exert sufficient control over the y-systems which immediately surround any given type of germ plasm, that is, if he were able to change the buffering action exerted on germ plasm so that the germ plasm itself could become something different than it is, there would no longer be any question of the relation between heredity and environment.

The point is that, save for mass methods of attack upon the germ plasm, such as changing the temperature or of irradiating it with X-rays, no experimenter can handle effectively events of the order that obtain during the early stages of development. As it happens, events at this level do display fairly large measures of stability or of resistance to change. Hence, given any particular germinal plasm and given a reasonable stability in the environment, a certain species of animal is destined to appear. Heredity, therefore, becomes a word which describes the inertia or resistance to change of germinal material. Environment, on the contrary, is a word which describes the possibility of change. If X-rays could actually be directed upon some particular molecule in the germinal plasm or even upon some particular atom so as to produce controlled changes in the atom or in the molecule and hence in the individual that grows out of this changed material, we should certainly speak of the experiment as an environmental alteration of original nature. The whole growth pattern, then, is subject to some sets of conditions which are highly resistant to alteration. It is also subject to conditions which are readily changed. Hence the artificial contrast between heredity and environment.

2. *Logic and Practice:* It would seem to follow from these considerations that we have not really modified the essential problems of original nature and training at all. From a practical point of view, we are still where we were when we began, for we must still say that there are some things about human beings that are inevitable

[57] Cf. Wheeler, R. H., *The Laws of Human Nature.* New York: D. Appleton-Century Co., 1933, *passim.*

whereas other things are subject to the guiding action of teachers and parents. Older ways of looking at the relation between heredity and environment have resulted in exactly this same conclusion. It seems important to note, however, that a difference in the method of arriving at a given conclusion, while it may make no difference in actual practice, must make a marked difference in the general philosophy behind actual practice. Teachers will still have to go about their work knowing that some features of human action are beyond the ordinary influence of the educative processes. It must be recognized, however, that all native or inevitable features of the growth pattern are native or inevitable solely because of limitations placed upon scientific method; for it is one thing to see the limitations of a scientific method and quite another to suppose that there are hereditary forces or agents which, because of their very nature, lie wholly outside of all possibility of control.

3. *Particular and General Environments:* We may now apply these considerations to later stages in the growth pattern. Before birth, it is almost impossible to exert any control whatsoever over the environment which surrounds the new person save where mass-attacks of the type described above are used. After birth, the environmental situations are of such a character that many of them can be controlled.

It is still pertinent to ask, however, whether there is any phase of the environment which is so inert or so resistant to change as to offer the same obstacles to control as is the case during the prenatal period. In order to illustrate the point which we wish to make, let us draw upon a distinction which is frequently used by Gestalt psychology. This distinction was used in our study of the development of perception. In any given act of perception it has been noted that the perceptual field may be divided into two parts, the one part known as the *ground* and the other part known as the *figure*.[58] In drawing this distinction between figure and ground, the Gestalt psychologist intends only to point out, first, that figure and ground are two phases of a single pattern of objects and, second, that the properties or characteristics of a figure derive, in part, from the ground upon which it is placed, while the properties or characteristics of the ground derive, in part, from the nature of the figures appearing on it.

If now we may apply this distinction to environments, we may say that environments are of two types. There is that type of en-

[58] Cf. Koffka, K., *The Growth of the Mind.* New York: Harcourt, Brace and Co., 1924, Chapter IV.

vironment which furnishes, so to speak, the ground within which other parts of the environment, viz., the figures, that is, particularized learning situations, find their place. Now it is the primary function of a school to provide learning situations which are of the "figure" type. These learning situations are specific segments of the environment of a particular child which are raised, for the time being, out of the total climate of opinion in which the child lives. They are used for the purpose of developing, in answer to them, adequate modes of response. Even though we may say that a child in the schoolroom is totally absorbed in learning a particular skill, say the fundamental operations of arithmetic, and thus appears to disregard the ground upon which these particular learning situations are placed, it can never happen that particular situations are actually independent of a background. The child, even while learning a particular skill, is still under the influence of a total climate of opinion furnished by the culture within which he lives.

The student can see readily enough that it is possible to shift learning situations rapidly. A child may learn poetry at the beginning of one hour and arithmetical operations toward the end of the same hour. In other words, the school program shifts rapidly so far as environmental "figures" are concerned. The ground out of which these figures emerge, however, does not change rapidly. This is simply another way of saying that each person lives in a generation where, save for the accidents of war or of sudden revolution, the whole background of environmental influences marks a fairly stable component of the whole period of development.

As a major illustration of this fact, let us refer for a moment to the differences between our own highly secularized and highly industrialized environment as compared with the intensely religious environment of the Middle Ages. We can, of course, read about the education of children during the Middle Ages, and we can make some attempts to appraise the total quality of the culture which lay in the background of the scholastic period. We can point out the fact that children were taught arithmetical operations in the Middle Ages in much the same way as they are being taught at the present time. It is clear, however, that even so special an act of learning as is required in the study of arithmetic can be, and has been, placed upon two entirely different cultural grounds. The ground which prevailed during the Middle Ages was, as we have said, intensely religious in import.[59] The ground in which we live, however, is in-

[59] Cf. Taylor, H. O., *The Medieval Mind* (2 vols.). London: The Macmillan Co., 1927, *passim*.

tensely secular and highly industrialized. Our own secular or industrialized ground has prevailed, as a more or less permanent feature of every educative process, for a good many generations. Even though there have been varying currents in our total climate of opinion, no one can doubt at all the essential inertia or fixity of the general qualities of that climate of opinion.

It would seem to follow from these considerations that teachers can be effective in giving direction or guidance to the learning process only with respect to specific types of learning situations. They cannot easily change the whole climate of opinion under which a child is growing. This means that there will be some features of the growth pattern which are just as fixed as is the climate of opinion under which growth takes form.[60]

One of the conclusions to be drawn from these considerations runs as follows. Some of the constancies that are to be found in environments are exactly commensurate with the constancies commonly described by heredity. If we say that heredity describes some of the more inert features of the growth pattern, then we ought also to be able to speak of "social heredity." This phrase would refer to the facts we have just mentioned, viz., to the persistent and unchanging character of the total climate of opinion in which any particular generation or even two or three generations may be brought up. Neither hereditary factors of the physical or of the social sort are inevitable, however, solely because they represent forces which lie wholly beyond human control. On the contrary, they lie beyond control, simply because they represent features of the growth pattern which are highly resistant to any of the experimental methods now available.

If a way could be found of changing, during the entire period of infancy and of childhood, the whole cultural background of a group of subjects, there is no doubt at all but that an equally significant change might be wrought in the psychological character of the subjects upon whom the experiment was tried.[61] As an illustration of this possibility, let us take the difference between such a group as the Eskimos, on the one hand, and the residents of any community in the United States, on the other. Eskimos differ from citizens of the United States neither in the size of their brains nor in the potential power of these brains to do work of an academic or of an inventive character. To be sure, we shall find in our chapter on

---

[60] For a study of changing climates of opinion, see Randall, J. H., *The Making of the Modern Mind*. Boston: Houghton Mifflin Co., 1926, *passim*.
[61] This is, in part, the function of propaganda. Cf. Dunlap, K., *Civilized Life*. Baltimore: The Williams and Wilkins Co., 1934, Chapter XI.

individual differences, that certain variations in psychological function can be correlated with differences in racial origin. Human beings the world over, however, are very much alike, at least in their potentialities. Eskimos, however, do not have a literature, and neither have they built up the same levels of culture as is the case with citizens of the United States. They learn, however, to read and sometimes to write, they have a language, and they have developed a wide variety of skills which are adequate to the demands placed upon them by the physical features of their environments. In spite of all of this, however, it seems that an immense amount of potential nerve energy is simply going to waste among such peoples. If it is wastage, it must be attributed to differences between them and us in climates of opinion, rather than to a difference in the character of specific learning situations or in the teaching methods that are used with respect to these situations.[62]

There is another feature of stability versus change in environments which will become of greater importance to us later on in the book. It is known that the rate of learning sometimes depends upon the order in which various parts of a learning situation are presented. If we may generalize on this fact, it becomes possible for us to see that the general order in which environmental situations become effective in initiating and regulating growth patterns may offer just as many signs of stability or inertia to change as the actual objects and events do which make up a typical environment. At the present time, for example, there is implied, in our whole manner of teaching, a definite order for the processes of schooling. After a preliminary period spent in the home and in the kindergarten, children pass from one grade to another where each grade, as a result of tradition, supplies a given type of information. Anyone who would undertake seriously to alter the temporal sequences which now prevail in our modern systems of education would be hailed as a radical, as indeed those persons were who interested themselves, during the later years of the last century, in progressive education.[63]

One may argue, to be sure, that the temporal sequence which is now used in most school systems is a sequence which, by trial-and-error methods, has been derived from those hereditary sequences which bring the child to given levels of maturity. This, however,

[62] The problem of race differences is, of course, a very complex and difficult one. Cf. Garth, T. R., *Race Psychology.* New York: McGraw-Hill Book Co., 1931.
[63] Cf. Burton, W. H., *Introduction to Education.* New York: D. Appleton-Century Co., 1934, Part VI.

is by no means certain. In any case, we have found a good many places in the preceding chapters where the order of presentation of environmental situations may make a notable difference in the way in which these situations can become effective in promoting the growth pattern.

READINGS

Background material for the study of psychological inheritance can be found in Kelly, T. L., *Crossroads in the Mind of Man*. Palo Alto: Stanford Univ. Press, 1928; Kelly, T. L., *The Influence of Nurture Upon Native Differences*. New York: The Macmillan Co., 1926. A suggestive article has been written by Bentley, M., "Mental Inheritance," *Pop. Sci. Mo.*, 1909, LXXV, 458-468. See also Kelly, T. L., "The Inheritance of Mental Traits," in Murchison, C. (ed.), *Psychologies of 1930*. Worcester, Mass.: Clark Univ. Press, 1930, Chapter XXIII.

As the text has indicated, points of view concerning original nature vary from one extreme to the other. On the other side, we may place Thorndike, E. L., *Educational Psychology* (3 vols.). New York: Columbia Univ. Press, 1913, and McDougall, W., *Social Psychology*. Boston: J. W. Luce, 1916; and on the other side, Dashiell, J. F., *Fundamentals of Objective Psychology*. Boston: Houghton Mifflin Co., 1928, Chapter VIII, or Watson, J. B., *Behaviorism*. New York: W. W. Norton and Co., 1929, Chapters V to VIII.

It is almost implied in any serious study of the hereditary foundations of behavior that some reference be made to the essentials of physiological psychology. The most suitable place for this information, perhaps, is Freeman, G. L., *Introduction to Physiological Psychology*. New York: The Ronald Press, 1934.

Further studies on the general principles of development are almost certain to follow the present intensive examination of the experimental facts. This holds true more directly, perhaps, of descriptive principles of development than of explanatory principles. On the side of explanation, the following references may be useful: A short but adequate survey of the doctrine of the inheritance of acquired characters has been written by Morgan, T. H., "Mechanisms and Laws of Heredity," in Murchison, C. (ed.), *A Handbook of General Experimental Psychology*. Worcester, Mass.: Clark Univ. Press, 1934, Chapter II. The doctrine of variation and natural selection is presented in an illuminating way by Haldane, J. B. S., and Huxley, J., *Animal Biology*. Oxford: The Clarendon Press, 1927, Chapter X to XIII. The more avid reader will desire to consult the large surveys of biology by Thompson and Geddes and by Wells, Huxley, and Wells, which were mentioned in the readings at the end of the last chapter. The text has not mentioned one explanatory principle of development which is just now very much in vogue, viz., the doctrine of emergent evolution. Cf. Morgan, C. L., *Emergent Evolution*. New York: Henry Holt and Co., 1923; Wheeler, W. M., *Emergent Evolution and the Development of Societies*. New York: W. W. Norton and Co., 1928.

As the student knows, most of those forms of psychology described as functionalism had their origin in the doctrine that the gradual appearance of psychological traits must have possessed a marked survival value. Functionalism is, then, the type of psychology which is, so to speak, more biological than some of the other types. In this connection, see Carr, H. A., *Psychology*. New York: Longmans, Green and Co., 1925. See also, Carr, H. A., "Functionalism," in Murchison, C. (ed.), *Psychologies of 1930*. Worcester, Mass.: Clark Univ. Press, Chapter III.

At the present time there are only general indications as to the range and variety of possible descriptive principles of development. A considerable number of such principles have been listed by Hollingworth, H. L., *Mental Growth and Decline*. New York: D. Appleton-Century Co., 1927, Chapter XVII. See also Anderson, J. E., and Goodenough, F. L., *Experimental Child Study*. New York: D. Appleton-Century Co., 1931, Chapter II.

Background material for the emphasis which has been placed in the text on environmental factors is furnished by a wide variety of studies on the socio-economic status of homes, on the influence of institutions and of foster homes on development, and on attempted surveys of cultural levels. Many of these facts will be considered in a later chapter. The student will find Chapter IV of Schwesinger, G. C., *Heredity and Environment*. New York: The Macmillan Co., 1933, very helpful in this connection.

CHAPTER ELEVEN

MAJOR VARIETIES AND THEORIES OF LEARNING

I. The Significance of Learning

1. *Introduction:* It is to be hoped that, during this long study of the difficult problems of original nature, the student has not lost sight of the two principles which lie behind the whole of this second part of our study of educational psychology. These two principles may be described as the principle of essential continuity in the growth pattern and the principle of directedness. He ought to recall that, at the beginning of Chapter Nine, it was said that the growth pattern is not only a definable course of events, but that it appears to be moving toward a particular goal as well. Even though they arrive at different levels of skill or at different occupations, most infants, nevertheless, arrive at the destination named by the phrase "a normal adult human being."

At the beginning of Chapter Nine it was also said that the teacher must know where directedness in the growth pattern has its origins, both directedness toward adulthood in general and directedness toward a given quality of adulthood. It has been stated that there are two possible sources of directedness, viz., those furnished by factors which are alleged to be intrinsic to the germinal plasm and those furnished by factors which can be called environmental. We have now covered some of the more important facts that have a bearing upon the directedness furnished by hereditary factors, but we still have before us all of the facts which have to do with the use of the environment as in controlled learning situations, on the one hand, and as a source of general background buffering, on the other.

The general setting of this next phase of our study of educational psychology may be stated somewhat as follows. First, let us remind ourselves again of those persons who appear to believe that the development of the unborn child can have no bearing upon its later education. Let us remind ourselves, also, of the persons who hold that the history of a child between the moment of birth and the moment of its entrance into the formal school system is without major educational significance. In contrast to both of these points of view, we have brought forth evidence to show that growth processes which are definitely psychological in character begin long before birth. In other words, let us say again that one of the dominant features of the growth pattern is its essential continuity. The psychological operations which are visible at birth are cut from exactly the same piece of cloth as are the prenatal events. The act of birth, when it is normal, involves a few changes in physiological function such as an alteration in the method by which oxygen is supplied to the blood stream and in the method of obtaining food, but it is not fruitful to exaggerate a change in the mechanics of metabolism at the expense of overemphasizing an alleged lack of continuity between prenatal and post-natal behavior.[1]

To be sure, the changes in the stream of behavior of a child that take place after birth are obviously much more dependent upon environmental events of the psychological and social types than they were before, but it is important to remember that the growing child has not been sheltered from an environment at any time during the prenatal period. From the moment of conception or from any other moment which can be chosen as a tentative "zero" point for development, the new individual has been fully immersed in a complex but highly effective contextual system. The character of this system changes somewhat after birth, but it would be a mistake to suppose that this change marks a qualitative rather than a quantitative change.

2. *Environmental Influences:* If we may begin with the fact that the new-born child is still within an environment furnished by all of the objects and events which surround it, then we may say that, during the preschool years (and from that time forward as well), considerable portions of this total environment become transformed into psychological and social systems or into particular stimulus-patterns which become increasingly effective in guiding and promoting the growth of the child. To be sure, the unborn infant is well insulated from lighted objects, from sounding objects, from tasty or odorous objects, from socialized objects, and from all of the various configurations into which these agents may be placed. The removal of this shelter does not, apparently, modify in any way whatsoever the nature of the changes which take place within the nervous system of the child itself.

[1] There is, to be sure, a theory about the birth act which makes of it a major trauma from which many persons will never recover. See Freud, S., *New Introductory Lectures on Psychoanalysis.* New York: W. W. Norton, 1934, *passim.* See, also, the discussion below, Chapter Eighteen.

Before birth, the child has been growing under the influence of dynamic factors which are an essential feature of its own tissues and of the physico-chemical environment in which it is placed, but it must be remembered that the conditions which favor growth are the same after birth as they were before. That is, the body of the child, including its nervous system, can be described as a very complex series of dynamic events which are surrounded by an equally complex set of contextual objects and events. Between these two sets, there is a progressively unstable equilibrium out of which the growth pattern emerges. Neither before birth nor afterwards does the child grow solely because there is some mysterious incentive to growth within its own body or within its chromosomes.

It is still more important to recognize the fact that the child does not grow of its own initiative until it is born and that then, after birth, it continues to grow because of the sole influence of environmental agents. It cannot be said too many times that the entire growth pattern takes on a particular form and a particular direction because of the constant interplay of dynamic events, some of which are vital or organic, and some of which are environmental.

3. *Learning and Growing:* With these things in mind, we may pass on to the statement that, for certain practical reasons, it is worth while to think of the growth-promoting effects of the environment in a special way. This special way has been signalized by the invention and common use of a large number of words. There is, first of all, the word "learning." The histories of education and of psychology are full of words having a similar import, viz., "habit," "skill," "memory," "remembering," "imagery," "imagination," "recall," "recognition," "association of ideas," "profit from past experience," "reminiscence," and "reflection." [2]

In one way or another, each of these words refers to the fact that the actions and attitudes of a person may be changed under the influence of what have come to be known as learning situations. Take, for instance, the attempts of a small infant to stand on its feet. As everyone knows, the first movements which the infant makes are awkward, ill-timed, and wholly inadequate to the result that is desired. The general situation in which the child is placed, however, invites it constantly to renewed attempts. The invitation is accepted with the result that, even within a few days or a few hours, the total character of the movements will be modified or changed.

[2] Definitions of these words are exceedingly variable. A good perspective on most of them, however, can be found in Dunlap, K., *Habits, Their Making and Unmaking.* New York: Liveright Publishing Corp., 1932.

MAJOR VARIETIES AND THEORIES OF LEARNING

A learning process makes it possible for the child to grow into a standing position.[3]

From one point of view, it is fair to say that, prior to the act of standing, the movements of the infant have been *immature* rather than awkward. After a standing posture has been achieved, we may say that the child has become more *mature,* or that it is *older* in its modes of acting. Its muscles may have increased in strength; but there is a fact about learning to stand which is of much more importance to education than sheer increase in the strength of the muscles. This fact is that some change has been wrought in the nervous system, both in its structure and in its functions. As we shall see, this change may imply an actual process of growth in some parts of the nervous system in the sense that nerve connections have been established which were not in existence up to that moment.[4] Even where growth does not call for new tissue or new types of connection, it must certainly demand new levels of function or new modes of relatedness between nerve elements which were already in existence.

4. *The Importance of Teaching:* It is hardly necessary to convince the student, perhaps, that all of the phenomena of learning must be of major importance to the teacher and to the whole teaching process. If we may revert again to the distinction we have drawn between the relevant and the irrelevant phases of the total environment of a child, we can say that the relevant environment of a new-born infant is rather small whereas the irrelevant environment is very large. As time goes on, that is, as the growth pattern follows its normal course, larger and larger portions of the whole environment are transformed into a truly effective environment. This effective environment is made up of lighted objects, sounding objects, movements, relationships, and of all of the other configurations of events which we as adults are able to distinguish and to react to.[5]

Now it happens that there is one person whose particular business it is to stand as a source of supply for specific environmental situations of the relevant or growth-promoting type. This person is the teacher. When the child enters the schoolroom, it becomes the business of the teacher to invent and to organize specific learning situa-

[3] Cf. Shirley, M. M., "Locomotor and Visual-manual Functions in the First Two Years," in Murchison, C. (Ed.), *Handbook of Child Psychology.* Worcester, Mass.: Clark Univ. Press, 1933, Chapter V.
[4] Cf. Coghill, G. E., "The Growth of Functional Neurones and Its Relation to the Development of Behavior." *Proc. Amer. Phil. Soc.,* 1926, LXV, 51-55.
[5] Consider again, Bentley, M., "Environment and Context." *Amer. J. Psychol.,* 1927, XXXIX, 54-61.

tions to which the child shall be invited to respond over and over again. The child is invited to make these responses because it is known that, with their aid, learning or growing will take place.[6] In other words, it is known that the child will become older and older with respect to a learning situation in almost direct proportion to the number of times it responds to that situation. The teacher can and does become a substitute for an order of events which, without him, would occur more or less haphazardly as in informal education and in that type of training which results from the general buffering action of our prevailing climates of opinion.

Not only is this true but those persons who have lived in the past have, through the exercise of their psychological functions, notably modified, and added to, the world in which we live.[7] As a single instance we may take language. There was a time in the history of human beings when language and all of the environmental objects which language has made possible, viz., dramas, novels, histories, essays, documents, and laws, were neither a part of the relevant nor of the irrelevant environments of any human being. Now, however, language stands out as a very important part of the environment of every child.

Language, however, is only one of the many additions and modifications which characterize the modern world. There are the inventions and all of the other objects which make up our technical culture.[8] It is the teacher who is responsible for organizing this material and laying it before a growing child with the hope that the child, like its parents before it, can become more mature with respect to the adult world. The teacher, of course, draws many learning situations from organized curricula. As a matter of fact, a curriculum is a special way of grouping and listing things to be learned.

If, then, we say that learning is, in a good many respects, to be identified with growth, it follows that the teacher becomes one of the main agents for promoting growth after the child enters the school system. This fact must not be emphasized too strongly, however, for the student must ever be mindful of the pervading character or of the buffering action of that part of the relevant environment which always lies in the background of every growth pattern. Even though the child is not in a schoolroom, it is still surrounded

---

[6] Burnham, W. H., "The Significance of Stimulation in the Development of the Nervous System," *Amer. J. Psychol.,* 1917, XXVIII, 38-56.

[7] Cf. Wundt, W., *Elements of Folk Psychology* (Trans. by E. Schaub). New York: The Macmillan Co., 1916; Judd, C. H., *The Psychology of Social Institutions.* New York: The Macmillan Co., 1926, *passim.*

[8] Cf. Mumford, L., *Technics and Civilization.* New York: Harcourt, Brace and Co., 1934, *passim.*

MAJOR VARIETIES AND THEORIES OF LEARNING

by objects and events which play their part in promoting its growth.[9] In other words, it is not fruitful to draw too sharp a distinction between formal and informal education where formal education refers to the growth processes that occur in the schoolroom and informal education refers to growth processes that occur outside the schoolroom under the general influence of relatively unorganized portions of the environment.

II. TYPES OF LEARNING

1. *Introduction:* There has been a marked disposition among students of educational psychology, and even among psychologists themselves, to suppose that tidy formulas for teaching, based upon experimental work, can be put into operation in the schoolroom in order to relieve the teacher of a large amount of personal attention to the growing children under his direction. This feeling has been supported, first, by the description of what are said to be several different types of learning. Each of these types is sometimes offered as the fundamental way in which psychological growth may be promoted. There are, in the second place, many oversimplified appeals to the neural changes which take place when new skills are being acquired. Finally, there is, in education, a marked degree of confusion between the nature of learning and some of the conditions under which learning will be promoted. Of these three factors we may give our attention for a moment to the third, although all of them will be found to have a bearing upon the problems of this and of the following chapter.

A. THEORY AND PRACTICE IN LEARNING: The student will easily see that it is one thing to discover the essential nature of learning or to explain progressive changes in the stream of behavior under the influence of learning situations by an appeal to the nervous system and that it is quite another thing to state some of the conditions which will favor change rather than hinder it. At the present time not enough is known about the fundamental *nature* of learning so that the psychologist can be of positive help to the teacher.[10] It may be doubted whether it is essential that the teacher should know what learning really is.

We may, however, on the basis of the researches that have now

---

[9] Cf. Kawin, E., *Children of Preschool Age.* Chicago: Univ. of Chicago Press, 1934, *passim.*
[10] Cf. Lashley, K. S., "Learning III: Nervous Mechanisms in Learning," in Murchison, C. (Ed.), *A Handbook of General Experimental Psychology.* Worcester, Mass.: Clark Univ. Press, 1934, Chapter X.

been finished, give the teacher a certain sense of caution in the use of theories which mark a premature attempt to say how learning actually takes place. It is for this reason that the present chapter will be given over to a study of various types of learning and to a statement of some of the current theories as to the nature of learning, for nowhere, in the whole field of educational psychology, is it so essential to distinguish fact from theory. The next chapter will consider the various ways in which the learning process may be guided and controlled to good advantage in the schoolroom.

B. MODES OF CLASSIFYING LEARNING PROCESSES: One of the most frequent ways of classifying the various types of learning does not depend upon a question of types at all, but upon the different psychological operations which are most obviously changed by the process. It is said, for example, that there are certain fundamental differences between motor learning, perceptual learning, ideational or associative learning, and rational learning.

When changes take place in the action systems of a person, that is, in his habits and skills, the changes are classified as examples of motor learning.[11] Similarly, when a person becomes more accurate in the use of his perceptual apparatus, it is said that perceptual learning has become effective.[12] The main difference between perceptual learning and motor learning, on the one hand, and ideational or associative or rational learning, on the other, is said to lie in the fact that the former are more bodily or organic in character, whereas the latter are more mental or truly psychological.[13] In associative learning, for example, a person is said to have profited from past experience whenever he learns how to bring ideas together into new patterns.[14] As we shall see, however, ideas are closely related to bodily movements and especially to movements and postures in the vocal apparatus. In other words, from one point of view rational learning is also motor learning.[15]

In any case, it does not look at the present time as though proc-

---

[11] One of the first studies of motor learning was made by Bryan, W. L., and Harter, N., "Studies in the Physiology and Psychology of the Telegraphic Language." *Psychol. Rev.*, 1897, IV, 27-53; 1899, VI, 346-375. A review of much of the literature in this field has been prepared by McGeoch, J. A., "The Acquisition of Skill." *Psychol. Bull.*, 1929, XXVI, 457-498.

[12] The classical experiment in this field was done by Judd, C. H., "Practice and Its Effects on the Perception of Illusions." *Psychol. Rev.*, 1902, IX, 27-59.

[13] Cf. Thorndike, E. L., "The Effect of Practice in the Case of a Purely Intellectual Function." *Amer. J. Psychol.*, 1908, XIX, 374-384.

[14] Reed, H. B., "The Essential Laws of Learning or Association." *Psychol. Rev.*, 1927, XXXIV, 107-115.

[15] Dashiell, J. F., "A Physiological Behavioristic Description of Thinking." *Psychol. Rev.*, 1925, XXXII, 54-73.

MAJOR VARIETIES AND THEORIES OF LEARNING

esses of learning which are classified according to the places in the body where they become effective offer much advantage either to education or to psychology. We must turn, therefore, to a study of different aspects of the learning process which are commonly accepted as representing a true difference in type or character. These different aspects have been described as rote learning, trial-and-error learning, the association of ideas, conditioning, sign learning, and insight.

2. *Rote Learning:* Tradition has it that most of the learning which takes place in the schoolroom must be of the rote memory type. Let us say, for example, that a child is being asked to learn the multiplication table. For this purpose, lists of numbers will be presented to him with the instruction that he must repeat them to himself, over and over again, until they have become automatic, that is, until they have been learned by heart. Given some preliminary instruction and guidance, together with some knowledge of the general principle involved, most children could multiply two single-digit numbers by each other through the lengthy process of adding them the proper number of times. This means, of course, that multiplication is a shorthand method of adding, but the child who has learned the multiplication table ought to be able to take the multiplication of any two numbers below twelve or fifteen as a routine matter. Given a pair and he ought to report the answer "without thinking."

As a further illustration of rote learning, we may choose the processes involved in learning how to recite a piece of prose or a series of stanzas from a poem. It is commonly argued that skill in recitation can be acquired simply by reading the poetry or the prose over and over again until the entire thing has been committed either to memory or to the nervous system. In learning of this type, sheer repetition and such factors as primacy and recency seem to be important.[16]

A. COMMENTS ON ROTE LEARNING: There are three things to be said about the rote memory type of learning. In the first place, it is clear that a vast amount of change in conduct and experience is actually brought about in this way. If we wish to fix a fact "in the mind," as the saying goes, we repeat it over and over again until we can recall it "at will." That is, we can recall it whenever any stimulus-pattern is presented to us which was in any way associated

[16] Consult James' famous chapter on habit. James, W., *Principles of Psychology.* New York: Henry Holt and Co., 1890. See Vol. I, Chapter IV.

with the fact when the initial learning process was under way.[17]

In the second place, it is clear that rote memory holds a good many points in common both with motor learning and with associative learning. We may, for example, suppose that each of the words in the poem will excite ideas in our minds and that these ideas are fastened together by some adhesive, the exact nature of which has not been discovered. On the other hand, it is equally clear that each reading of the material to be learned calls for a stream of action in the vocal apparatus, in the eyes and, perhaps, in other parts of the body. When the prose is finally learned to the point where we can, as we commonly put it, say it "by heart," uttering the first word appears to act as a sort of signal for the second, the second for the third, and so on. In short, the vocal apparatus has acquired a skill in much the same way that any other group of muscles in the body may acquire a new skill.[18]

In the third place, rote learning presupposes a considerable amount of previous learning. The child, for example, who is asked to learn the multiplication table, has already learned how to "see" the various numbers in the table and he has learned, too, how to discriminate one printed number from another. This means that a considerable amount of perceptual skill must be taken for granted. The person who learns a piece of prose likewise has learned how to say each of the words of which the prose is composed, and he may even have learned how to say some of the combinations of words which are included in it.

B. ROTE LEARNING NOT A TYPE OF LEARNING: In short, then, rote learning appears to describe, not so much the processes of acquiring a new skill as a process of fusing previously acquired skills into a single or continuous pattern. We have already said, of course, that this process of putting older skills into new patterns is highly important in teaching, for throughout the grades, and even at the high school level, pupils find an immense number of things which have to be "learned by heart." That is, they have to be so thoroughly automatized that they will run their several courses without reflection and at times almost without intention.

Rote learning is, then, important to the teaching process but it is not perhaps as important as a description of the way in which wholly new skills rather than new patterns of previously acquired skills are

[17] Cf. Carr, H. A., "Time Relationships in the Formation of Associations." *Psychol. Rev.*, 1919, XXVI, 465-473; Cason, H., "Specific Serial Learning." *J. Exper. Psychol.*, 1926, IX, 195-227, 229-324.
[18] Cf. Dashiell, J. F., *Fundamentals of Objective Psychology*. New York: Houghton Mifflin Co., 1928, Chapter XV.

MAJOR VARIETIES AND THEORIES OF LEARNING

secured. For example, a new-born infant cannot say the number "eight." The ability to speak this word requires a fine degree of integration among a great many different members of the body. How is this integration brought about? What do the processes of growth which lead to such a skill involve? What circumstances can be brought to bear upon the process in order to hasten it? These are questions which cannot be answered by rote learning alone.

3. *Trial-and-Error Learning:* One of the principal ways of answering the questions just asked has been offered by a type of growth commonly known as trial-and-error learning.[19] This expression had its origin in studies on the way in which some of the lower animals acquire their habits and skills. As the phrase implies, most living creatures will respond to a new situation by making more intense movements or by making more different types of movements than are actually necessary in order to meet the situation effectively.

A. ILLUSTRATIONS OF TRIAL-AND-ERROR LEARNING: We have already seen, to take only a single example, that a small child will, when it attempts to reach for an object, move not only its arms and fingers, but its feet, its head, and some of the muscles in its face, as well. If we consider only the foot movements, it can easily be shown that, as the child grows older, both the number and intensity of these movement decrease.[20] We might say that, in advance of actual success in reaching for an object, a child does not "know" what movements will be required of it in order to get hold of the object. It must, therefore, try out a considerable variety of movements on the chance that one or more of them will be successful. Whenever one or more of them does become successful it will, according to laws to be described below, become more firmly attached to the stimulus-situation, while all other movements will tend to disappear.

The student himself can think of many illustrations of a similar course of events.[21] He may recall, for example, that the first time he attempted to serve a tennis ball, he made more movements than were actually necessary to a proper service. Moreover, he will no doubt remember that all of his movements were awkward and ill-

---

[19] Hull, C. L., "Simple Trial-and-Error Learning: A Study in Psychological Theory." *Psychol. Rev.*, 1930, XXXVII, 241-256; Starch, D., "A Demonstration of the Trial and Error Method of Learning." *Psychol. Bull.*, 1910, VII, 20-23.
[20] Cf. Curti, M. W., *Child Psychology*. New York: Longmans, Green and Co., 1931, pp. 169 ff.
[21] Cf. Snoddy, G. S., "An Experimental Analysis of a Case of Trial and Error Learning in the Human Subject." *Psychol. Monog.*, 1920, XXVIII (No. 78).

timed. During subsequent attempts, useless or irrelevant movements disappeared while the movements actually necessary to the task were retained. When a high level of skill is finally reached, the exceptional tennis player realizes that every motion is of just the right type for a particular task and that it is correctly timed and coordinated with every other motion. Even in the case of adult trial-and-error learning, then, we may say that the learner does not "know" in advance just exactly what moves he must make in order to be successful, and his trial-and-error efforts, therefore, turn into an attempt to discover, by chance, the right combination.[22]

B. PRINCIPAL FEATURES OF TRIAL-AND-ERROR LEARNING: It will be helpful, perhaps, to recite in more detail some of the essential features of trial-and-error learning.[23] In the first place, it must be taken for granted that the learner has some reason for wishing to change his mode of reaction to a situation. That is, trial-and-error learning must be motivated. If the events which surround a child were left to their "natural" order, a great many associations would be established between them, and a nondescript array of skills would, no doubt, emerge. But, in trial-and-error learning, it is necessary that the learner shall wish to attain a desired goal. The influence of the factor of motivation on learning will be discussed in the next chapter.

In the second place, it is often said that trial-and-error learning requires a problematic situation, that is, a situation which cannot be met adequately by using skills that have already been acquired. The tennis player, for example, knows how to throw a ball into the air, how to maintain an upright posture, and how to swing such an object as a racket. He does not know, however, how to fuse all of these partial skills into the new pattern that will be required of him. It is possible that, under some conditions, the learner cannot even define the character of the problem.

This is a situation which has often held true in studies on animal learning. When a white rat is placed in a maze without any previous experience with mazes, it cannot by any stretch of the imagination "know" that food is to be found somewhere in the maze. When, therefore, it starts its trip of exploration through the maze, it will make a great many "wrong" movements; but these movements will be wrong only in the sense that they lead to the wrong goal so far as the experimenter is concerned. The actions cannot

[22] Cf. Hamilton, G. V., "A Study of Trial and Error Reactions in Mammals." *J. Anim. Behav.*, 1911, I, 33-66.
[23] Cf. Curti, M. W., *op. cit.*, Chapter III.

MAJOR VARIETIES AND THEORIES OF LEARNING 391

be wrong for the rat until some relation has been established between a problematic situation and a means for resolving the situation.

In the third place, trial-and-error learning involves varied attack or multiple effort. This feature has already been emphasized sufficiently, perhaps, in our original illustrations of trial-and-error learning. As we have just said, varied attack may take the form which is characteristic of an adult who has a general idea as to the goal he wishes to attain or it may take the form represented in the early stages of maze learning where the animal does not "know" what the goal is.

In the fourth place, trial-and-error learning is characterized by the progressive elimination of wrong responses and an equally progressive fixation of right responses. This is, perhaps, one of the crucial features of this type of learning. At any rate, some of the most important theories about the nature of learning have been devised for the special purpose of explaining why wrong movements drop out and right movements persist. We shall examine these laws later on in the present chapter.

4. *Associative Learning:* The attempt to make a special type of learning out of the principles of varied attack, and out of the gradual selection of right responses and the elimination of wrong responses, came as a result of studies on the way in which the lower animals acquire new skills.[24] This means that trial-and-error learning holds many features in common with motor learning. Motor learning, however, appears to describe something that happens to muscles rather than to minds; and the real concern of the teacher is with mental, rather than with physical, changes. There ought, therefore, to be a type of learning which is "truly" psychological in character.

A. ORIGIN OF ASSOCIATIONISM: This type is known as associationism. As early as Aristotle, it had been noted that the stream of experience was not a chaos.[25] On the contrary, it was commonly reported to possess a high degree of orderliness and coherence. In his examination of the mental life, Aristotle sought to describe the conditions under which orderliness could arise. He noted that a part of it might be accounted for by the tendency of one idea to call up another. Following a suggestion which may have been made by Plato, Aristotle said that a coherent sequence of ideas will arise (i) because some ideas tend to resemble others, (ii) because two or

---

[24] Cf. Morgan, C. L., *Habit and Instinct.* London: Arnold, 1896, passim.
[25] Cf. Warren, H. C., *A History of the Association Psychology.* New York: Charles Scribner's Sons, 1921, *passim.*

more ideas may occur at the same time, and (iii) because some ideas may be similar to or contrasted against others. In other words, it was assumed that ideas are entities or things made up of mental stuff and subject to adhesion to one another in much the same way that physical objects may be fastened together.

B. LAWS OF ASSOCIATION: The three principles named above furnished the basis for the first laws of association.[26] These laws have always been held in high regard by psychologists and especially by educators, for they pointed out some of the conditions under which changes could be made in the "purely" mental phases of human nature. If ideas can follow one another in experience according to the laws of similarity, identity, contrast, or contiguity, then one might easily change human nature by ordering the sequence of the events that are presented to a growing child in accordance with the principles suggested by the laws.[27]

One of the particular advantages of associative learning was alleged to reside in the chance that it gave for a simple story of the origin of all ideas and concepts. Locke, who was one of the great English philosophers of the seventeenth century, took this point of view. Prior to Locke, it had been supposed that some ideas (e.g., the concepts of space, time, causality, and Deity) must be non-learned or original. Locke undertook to show that, granted the laws of association, one could start with a person who had had no experience whatsoever and gradually build up, by the addition of one idea to another, the whole pattern of the events which take place in an adult mind.[28] This philosophy of associationism has had a long history, especially in England, where almost two centuries were devoted to the completion of the system of thinking begun by Locke.[29]

There are, however, certain considerations which seem to throw some doubt upon associative learning as an adequate picture of the way in which changes may be wrought in human nature. Even Locke himself could not depend wholly upon associative learning for, in addition to the connection of ideas established by the initial connection of external events, Locke paid some attention to a trait of mind known as the faculty of reflection. The faculty of reflection, for example, rendered the service of furnishing the stream of

---

[26] Cf. Carr, H. A., "The Laws of Association." *Psychol. Rev.*, 1931, XXXVIII, 212-228.

[27] Bolton, T. L., and Haskell, E. M., "Knowledge from the Standpoint of Association." *Educ. Rev.*, 1898, XV, 474-499.

[28] Cf. Warren, H. C., "Mental Association from Plato to Hume." *Psychol. Rev.*, 1916, XXIII, 208-230.

[29] Cf. Warren, H. C., *A History of the Association Psychology*. New York: Charles Scribner's Sons, 1921, *passim*.

experience with certain ideas or concepts which could not have had their origin in a simple accumulation of ideas.

C. CRITICISMS: More recently further serious criticisms have been made of associative learning. During the middle of the last century, a major part of the system of teaching based upon associative learning was rendered obsolete by the development of the theory of evolution.[30] Locke had assumed that the psychological furniture of an adult person could be acquired simply by a mechanical summation of experiences. The doctrine of evolution, however, meant that psychological development must be a genuine process of becoming rather than a process of simple addition. Since becoming or growing is a process that starts before birth and is essentially continuous with the events that take place after birth, the "white sheet of paper" which Locke had assumed as the starting point of the mind must already be marked in definite ways by factors which are intrinsic to the growing organism. That is, a child may not have had, before birth, any experiences in Locke's sense of the word; but the very fact that it is a growing organism means that it may well possess certain predispositions in advance of immediate experience. This is a feature of the growth pattern which we have already considered in the previous chapter.

In the second place, the theory that changes in human nature are brought about principally by associative learning assumes that ideas are mental events or existences which can be bound together in groups by the use of some sort of psychological cement. It will not be fruitful to raise at this point the perplexing question as to what ideas really are, although the student may, if he wishes, dip ahead into Chapter Twenty, where these matters are discussed. For the present it is necessary only to point out that there are many types of modern psychology which can say important things about the process of changing human nature without making use of the concept of ideas. This fact was recognized even by those who continued the history of associationism for it was said that the laws of association could be described just as easily in terms of nervous events as in terms of ideas. That is, one might say that any two nerve processes which occur at or nearly at the same time, will have a tendency to become associated together in such a way that the excitation of the one will result in a revival of the other.[31]

---

[30] The most destructive criticism of the older form of associationism was made by Ward, J., Article "Psychology" in the Encyclopaedia Britannica, 11th Edition, 1911.

[31] Bentley, M., *The Field of Psychology.* New York: D. Appleton-Century Co., 1924, Chapter V. Also, Robinson, E. S., *Association Theory Today.* New York: D. Appleton-Century Co., 1932, *passim.*

We shall return to this possibility in a moment. The main fact which ought to be pointed out is that the associations which are described by the laws of association are not so much associations between ideas as between objects. That is to say, one idea does not call up another. On the contrary, one object may remind a person of another. Associative learning would undertake, then, to describe the way in which objects acquire this ability to point to, suggest, or imply other objects.[32]

D. NEURAL ASSOCIATIONS: More recently the older laws of association have been converted into a more general form simply by saying that, whenever any two psychological activities have taken place at or near the same time, a relation will be established between them so that the appearance of the one will tend to excite the other.[33] The phrase "psychological activity" may be left undefined, or it may refer to almost anything which human beings do or experience. If the traditional laws of association are transformed in this way, then it becomes imperative to discover the stuff of which associative connections are made. Is this stuff physiological or is it psychological? Moreover, what factors determine when and how the stuff shall be used?

An answer to the first of these questions will be given in the next section. A part of the answer to the second question is suggested by the following fact. Let us say that a teacher has written the word "become" and the word *"werden"* on the blackboard. As the student knows, there will be a tendency for all of the persons who see these two words to associate the one with the other. That is, the German word *"werden"* will have a tendency to point to or to signify the English word "become" and, likewise, the English word "become" will have a tendency to point to or signify the German word "werden." Obviously, however, there are a great many other events in the total stimulus-situation which obtains at this particular moment of learning. Simultaneously and contiguously with "become" and *"werden,"* there is the teacher, the piece of chalk, the blackboard, the lights in the room, the temperature, and dozens of other objects and events. How does it happen that *"werden"* becomes associated with "become" rather than with a piece of chalk, with the teacher, or with any of the other objects named above?[34]

[32] Cf. Titchener, E. B., *A Textbook of Psychology*. New York: The Macmillan Co., 1910, pp. 365 ff.
[33] This is sometimes called the principle of redintegration. See Hollingworth, H. L., "General Laws of Redintegration." *J. Gen. Psychol.*, 1928, I, 79-90.
[34] Cf. Köhler, W., *Gestalt Psychology*. New York: Liveright Publishing Corp., 1929, Chapter III and *passim*.

MAJOR VARIETIES AND THEORIES OF LEARNING

This question seems to imply that mere contiguity in space and time is not a sufficient answer to the questions about the nature of associative learning. Attempts have been made, therefore, to find out why associative learning appears to be so selective in its character. One answer is that those objects or events will be associated with one another which have the trait or property of "belongingness."[35] That is, *"werden" belongs* to "become" much more strongly than it *belongs* to a piece of chalk or to the blackboard. It is not so easy to see, however, that any progress has been made by this subterfuge. As a matter of fact, *"werden"* and "become" *are* more frequently associated with each other than they are to any other part of the whole stimulus-pattern. This means that they do belong to one another; but to say that they belong to one another because they have the property of "belongingness" is scarcely meaningful. Obviously, something further must be said about the nature of learning, if associative learning is to be described as a major source of change in human nature. We shall return to this problem later on in the chapter.

5. *Conditioning:* Associative learning began as a theory which proposed to describe the way in which one idea may call up another. It is, therefore, a type of learning which assumes the existence of ideas, that is, of mental or psychological objects which differ from physical objects in highly important respects. The student has already gained the impression, however, that a great many things of psychological import can be said without making use of purely mental objects. In other words, the recent history of psychology is full of accounts of the way in which people behave rather than of the way in which they think.[36]

Toward the end of the book, we shall try to write out, in a brief manner, some of the changes that have taken place in modern psychology in order to show how these changes bear upon problems of teaching. Now, however, we mean only to admit the fact that contemporary psychology and much of contemporary teaching is more objective than it used to be. As a matter of fact, there are a great many persons who hold that both psychology and education should be completely objective in the sense that they should study only the stimulus-situations which are known to excite a reaction. More-

---

[35] This is a word which has recently been used by Thorndike to supplement some of his earlier theories as to the nature of learning. It will be considered in more detail later in the present chapter. Cf. Thorndike, E. L., *Human Learning.* New York: D. Appleton-Century Co., 1931, Chapter I and *passim.*

[36] Cf. Heidbreder, E. F., *Seven Psychologies.* New York: D. Appleton-Century Co., 1933.

over, it becomes necessary to study all of the modes of reaction of which human beings are capable. Any discovery, then, that would enable people who are interested in an objective account of human nature to translate older subjective points of view into the more objective language of men of science would be hailed as a major discovery.[87]

A. NATURE OF CONDITIONING: This discovery is said actually to have been made. It has given rise to a type of learning known as learning by conditioning. The original experiments were simple and straightforward.[88] The student knows, if he has ever had a dog for a pet, that a piece of meat placed upon the tongue of the dog will bring about a rapid increase in the flow of saliva. We may call the situation described by the phrase "a piece of meat on the tongue of the dog" as an original or "unconditioned" stimulus. Likewise, we may call the increased flow of saliva an original or "unconditioned" response to the stimulus. Now it may be that the student has seen an increased flow of saliva take place in his pet not only when it is actually chewing the meat but even before the meat has been taken into its mouth. The stimulus-situation in this case is now visual rather than chemical but the response remains about what it was before.

In other words, a stimulus which, prior to experience, must have called forth some other response, has now acquired the capacity to call out a response not hitherto associated with it. To say the same thing in another way, a response which was "natively" or originally connected with some particular stimulus-pattern has now become conditioned to a new stimulus-pattern. Not only can responses be conditioned to new stimuli, but the same stimulus can be conditioned to variable responses. In other words, the associative type of learning has been translated into purely objective terms. There is no phase of learning by conditioning which involves the use of ideas, memories, or other types of purely mental events.[39]

If this inference seems to go beyond the facts, we may take still another illustration. Let us say that a bright object has been placed before an infant. Under normal conditions, the infant will attempt

[87] Cf. Hogben, L., *The Nature of Living Matter*. New York: A. A. Knopf, 1932, Chapter I and *passim*.
[88] Cf. Pavlov, I. P., *Conditioned Reflexes* (Trans. by G. V. Anrep). London: Oxford Univ. Press, 1927, *passim*.
[39] Cf. Humphrey, G., "The Conditioned Reflex and the Laws of Learning." *J. Educ. Psychol.*, 1928, XIX, 424-430. Also, Smith, S., and Guthrie, E. R., *General Psychology in Terms of Behavior*. New York: D. Appleton-Century Co., 1921, *passim*.

MAJOR VARIETIES AND THEORIES OF LEARNING

to reach for the object. An adult, however, will often say a word in response to the object rather than reach for it. He may even speak the word in the absence of the object, whereupon another person will attempt to produce the object. Now it can be shown by experiment, and even by casual observations of children, that both the sound of a spoken word and the actual act of uttering a word will be substituted either for the reaching movements toward an object or for an object that is not present during the process of the development of language responses. In other words, a conditioning may take place here after much the same fashion as was described above.[40] There has been, however, no reference to ideas, memories, concepts, or other mental events.

In view of these considerations, learning by conditioning has offered itself as an objective way of writing out the main facts that used to be described by associative learning. Moreover, it has offered itself as the fundamental type of all learning. As we shall see, it has been possible to explain trial-and-error learning and rote learning in terms of progressive conditionings.

B. EXPERIMENTAL FACTS: There are a number of facts about learning by conditioning which must be mentioned before any critical comments are offered. In the first place, it now seems possible to say that almost any stimulus-pattern whatsoever can be conditioned to any response-pattern.[41] This fact has already become of very great significance to us in our attempt to take account of the changes that may be wrought in emotionalized forms of action.

In the second place, conditioning is a type of learning which appears at all levels of human development and among all of the higher animals.[42] This fact has brought great comfort to those who interpret all of the problems of psychology in terms of the stimulus-response formula, for it shows that the learning process can be described in ways that hold true equally of human beings and of the lower animals. To be sure, human beings and the lower animals appear, on occasion, to use trial-and-error methods; but associative learning has always seemed to be more psychological or mental than trial-and-error learning. If associative learning, therefore, can be wholly replaced by conditioning, it becomes possible to say that changes in human nature can be brought about by the same processes

---

[40] Cf. Hunter, W. S., *Human Behavior.* Chicago: Univ. of Chicago Press, 1928, *passim.*
[41] For experiments in child psychology, see Razran, G. H., "Conditioned Responses in Children." *Arch. Psychol.,* 1933 (No. 148).
[42] Cf. Liddell, H. S., "The Conditioned Reflex," in Moss, F. A. (Ed.), *Comparative Psychology.* New York: Prentice-Hall, 1934, Chapter IX.

which issue in changes in the nature of the lower animals.[43] Moreover, studies on the way in which the lower animals learn can be translated immediately into human learning, because the learning processes among the lower animals do not differ in kind from those that take place in human beings. They are, as a matter of fact, simpler and hence can be studied more exactly. It is for this reason, perhaps, that animal psychology has entered so largely into some surveys of educational psychology.[44]

In the third place, conditioning takes place most readily when the two events to be related to each other occur almost, if not quite, simultaneously.[45] This feature of conditioning has been much studied so that it is now possible to say, in terms of the number of repetitions required, how fast the process will be when the conditioned stimulus appears before the unconditioned stimulus, when the two are simultaneous, and when the conditioned stimulus comes after the unconditioned stimulus. The most favorable rate of learning obtains when the third relation is used.

This is one of the facts about conditioning that can be of great importance to the teacher. Let us suppose, for example, that unsocial conduct on the part of a child is to be punished. The ideal time for punishment, if punishment is to be corrective rather than retributive, would be just at the time the act is actually under way or immediately thereafter. It frequently happens, however, that a considerable delay occurs between an unsocial act and the punishment for it. This means that the child will be negatively conditioned, not to the unsocial act, but to some one of the dominant features of the situation which obtains at the moment the punishment is administered. Since one of the parents is usually responsible for punishment, it may easily happen that a child will become negatively conditioned to one of its own parents rather than to the act.[46] This unfortunate result appears most readily during the earlier years. As the child grows older and as it acquires the ability to relate objects and events which are separated in time, punishment which is markedly delayed may still be conditioned to the unsocial act. The significance of this change in the nature of the circumstances under which learning by conditioning becomes effective will appear to good advantage in a moment.

[43] Cf. Hunter, W. S., "Experimental Studies of Learning," in Murchison, C. (Ed.), *op. cit.*, Chapter XV.
[44] For example, Sandiford, P., *Educational Psychology*. New York: Longmans, Green and Co., 1928.
[45] Cf. Hull, C. L., "The Factor of the Conditioned Reflex," in Murchison, C. (Ed.), *op. cit.*, Chapter IX.
[46] Cf. Curti, M. W., *op. cit.*, Chapter V.

MAJOR VARIETIES AND THEORIES OF LEARNING

A fourth feature of conditioning has another important bearing upon the nature of learning and upon the way in which learning situations may be used in the schoolroom. As we have seen, rote learning and trial-and-error learning are time-consuming processes. If a poem is to be recited easily and accurately it must be read over and over again until the sequence of words will follow almost of its own accord. If an animal is to find its way through the maze, much time is consumed in fixing the right responses and eliminating the wrong responses. In conditioning, however, it frequently happens that the unconditioned stimulus may become a substitute for an original stimulus after a single repetition.[47] In other words, conditioning is a process which takes place quickly. To be sure, there are times when conditioned and unconditioned stimulus-response patterns must be presented simultaneously for hundreds, and even thousands, of times, before the one can be substituted for the other. But these cases are rare. In general, then, learning by conditioning can be described as a quick type of learning in contrast to the somewhat lengthy processes of rote learning and trial-and-error learning.[48]

C. CONDITIONING AND "BELONGINGNESS": There is some evidence to show that the readiness with which conditioning may be effected depends upon the "belongingness" of the two stimulus-response patterns. If the belongingness is highly natural, the conditioning may take place rapidly. For example, in some of the early experiments in this field, it was found that the subjects acquired conditioned responses rather slowly and that they frequently answered the whole situation as though they were hysterically disposed.[49] This result was explained by saying that the conditions of the experiment had not been sufficiently controlled. In other words, the animals had been placed in a situation where there were too many obvious stimulus-agents, any one of which might have been the "right" agent so far as the subject was concerned. The animals acted very much as though they did not "know" what the experimenter wanted them to do. When, therefore, the experimental situation was more definitely controlled in the sense that it contained only two dominant stimuli, the one being the unconditioned pattern and the other the pattern to be conditioned, the process of learning took place rather quickly. In experiments on human beings,

---
[47] Hull, C. L., *op. cit.*, pp. 424 ff.
[48] See, however, Hilgard, E. R., "Conditioned Eyelid Reactions to a Light Stimulus Based on the Reflex Wink to Sound." *Psychol. Monog.*, 1931, XLI (No. 184).
[49] Pavlov, I. P., *op. cit.*, p. 49.

conditioning takes place more slowly when the connection between the two stimulus-patterns is left undefined. Where there is any doubt about the "belongingness" of two patterns, the one will easily and quickly become a substitute for the other.[50]

D. CRITICISMS OF CONDITIONING: These facts suggest one of the possible differences between conditioning and rote, or trial-and-error, learning. If, in his study of German, the student were asked to establish a connection between *"werden"* and "become," the chances are that the learning process would be completed in a single repetition. When, however, the two words *"werden"* and "become" are a single pair in a large list of words, the connections that are established between the single pair may suffer interference from the connections established between other pairs according to principles to be described in the next chapter. In short, rote learning and trial-and-error learning may be slow processes because they are intimate mixtures of learning and forgetting. Although we do not often realize it, any single act of learning exerts an important influence on other acts of learning. This influence reaches both forward and backward in time. When it reaches backward, it interferes with previously acquired habits, and when it reaches forward it places obstacles in the way of future learning.

When, therefore, attempts are made to condition an animal under circumstances which leave the two major stimulus-situations undefined, learning by conditioning has many marks in common with rote learning and even with trial-and-error learning. On the other hand, when rote learning or trial-and-error learning involve simple tasks, that is, tasks that are just as simple as those which obtain when conditioning takes place rapidly, they tend to resemble the speed aspect of conditioning. The implications of these facts for the teacher are clear. We shall study them in more detail in later chapters, but it is obvious that a great many learning situations in the schoolroom are time-consuming not because learning itself is a sluggish process, but because the learning task is so complex or so ill-defined as to create a large amount of interference between learning and forgetting.

It was said at the beginning of this section that learning by conditioning has commended itself to psychologists and to teachers, partly because it explains a good many actual instances of learning, and partly because it offers itself as an objective way of studying

---

[50] Cf. Liddell, H. S., and Anderson, O. D., "A Comparative Study of the Conditioned Motor Reflex in the Rabbit, Sheep, Goat, and Pig." *Amer. J. Physiol.*, 1931, XCVII, pp. 539 ff.

MAJOR VARIETIES AND THEORIES OF LEARNING 401

events which hitherto have been highly subjective or mental. There are, however, certain criticisms of this type of learning which must be considered before one can accept it as *the* method by which all human growth of the psychological sort takes place.

In the first place, it has been shown that the results of conditioning are not necessarily permanent. Let us suppose, for example, that a conditioned response to a loud noise has been set up. Under certain circumstances, many children will respond to a loud noise by crying and by masslike movements that are sometimes described as a "fear" response. If a furry object is presented to a small infant at the moment a loud sound is made, the furry object will quickly acquire the capacity to call forth the responses formerly made only to the loud sound. Now, let us suppose that the furry object is presented over and over again to the child without the loud sound. It turns out that, after a few repetitions, the child will "forget," so to speak, its acquired reaction and return to some former type of reaction. In other words, the sheer repetition of the conditioned response without support from the original stimulus will lead to its extinction.[51] If the newly conditioned response is reinforced at appropriate intervals by the original stimulus-response pattern, it will remain fairly stable.

This fact may be illustrated by drawing again upon the illustration used above. When a child is punished for an unsocial act, a repetition of the situation which produced the act may come eventually to call forth the act as though there had been no punishment. Thus, punishments must occur more or less frequently, if a given situation is to lose its effectiveness as a source for unsocial behavior. The student knows, however, that there are times when a learning period results in changes in human nature which are really permanent. As a rule, the highest degrees of permanence come as a result of long-continued practice. We never forget, for example, how to write, how to maintain an erect posture, or how to use words properly. If the learning process which results in such a high degree of stability is to be explained by conditioning, then we must suppose that repeated acts must be supported at fairly frequent intervals by original or unconditioned stimulus-response patterns. It is difficult to discover stimulus-response patterns that would play this part with respect to some of our more stable skills.

A second feature of conditioning which throws some doubt upon its value as an exhaustive description of the nature of learning is to

---
[51] Hull, C. L., *op. cit.*, pp. 436 ff.

be found in the fact that the conditioned response is not always like the original response.[52] Let us say, for example, that a white rat is being conditioned to jump over a barrier. The act of jumping after conditioning is to be compared with its jumping behavior under normal conditions. It has been shown that these two acts are different from each other even though the stimulus-situations which lead to them are, to all intents and purposes, identical.[53] In other words, the newly acquired response may be a different type of response from that which occurred before the conditioning took place. This fact means that there must be some feature about learning which makes it possible for acts to acquire new properties which will make them more nearly adequate to the situation. It has not been shown that pure conditioning will explain the modifications of this type.

In general, then, we may say that learning by conditioning appears to describe one of the ways in which changes in psychological nature can be produced. It still remains to be shown, however, that conditioning is *the* theory of learning for which psychology and education have been in search.[54] As a central fact, we may accept the proposition that, under certain circumstances, two stimulus-patterns which are presented to a subject almost, if not quite simultaneously, will be conjoined with one another in such a way as to allow one of them to excite a response which previously has been called out only by the other. In other words, conditioning implies a new theory of the way in which associative learning takes place. The new theory would require some mechanism in the nervous system by means of which pathways of conduction which are excited almost, if not quite simultaneously, may be fused into a single pattern.[55]

Surrounding this central fact, there are the variable factors mentioned above, viz., the time relations between two stimulus-patterns, the circumstances which favor conditioning in one direction rather than in the other, the number of repetitions required to effect the change, the experimental extinction of change in the absence of the unconditioned stimulus, the dependence of conditioning upon the relevancy or obvious connection between stimulus-patterns, and the

---

[52] Cf. Liddell, H. S., *op. cit.,* pp. 279 ff.
[53] Warner, L. H., "An Experimental Search for the 'Conditioned Response.'" *J. Genet. Psychol.,* 1932, XLI, 91-115.
[54] Cf. Tolman, E. C., "Theories of Learning," in Moss, F. A. (Ed.), *op. cit.,* Chapter XII.
[55] Cf. Adams, D. K., "A Restatement of the Problem of Learning." *Brit. J. Psychol.,* 1931, XXII, 150-178. Also, Tolman, E. C., *op. cit.,* pp. 390 ff.

modifications that actually take place in the response-patterns themselves.

6. *Sign Learning:* During our study of rote learning, trial-and-error learning, associative learning, and conditioning, the student has felt, no doubt, that we have always been just on the point of saying something really significant about learning, but that we have actually missed the opportunity to do so. In rote learning, for example, we have found that previously acquired skills can be put together in sequences where the one member of the sequence seems to serve as a sort of signal for the next member. In trial-and-error learning, we have just barely missed saying that errors will be made until that point in the whole process is reached when some particular feature of the situation will stand out as the significant feature so far as solving the difficulty is concerned. In associative learning, it is certainly true that one idea can act as a signal for the revival of another, or if the laws of association are translated into neural terms, it looks as though one state of excitement in the nervous system, because of its previous togetherness with another state, can act as a signal for the reestablishment of the other state. The same facts hold true of learning by conditioning. Where the experimental situation is left undefined, the subject acts as though he did not know what was required of him. If, however, he is aided by the experimenter who makes two particular stimulus-patterns stand out above all of the others, the one quickly acquires the ability to call out a response which was not previously associated with it. This response may not be, of course, the original response but almost any response which will serve nearly the same purpose. It will be a response which has the same functional value for the subject of the experiment.

These and other features of learning have recently laid the basis for a new type of learning which has been called "sign learning." [56] When we say that sign learning is a new type, it is not implied that psychologists recently have found a hitherto unsuspected type of learning. On the contrary, reference is made only to the fact that attention has been directed to a feature of a great many learning situations which, though taken for granted by other types of learning, has not really been emphasized as it should be.

A. ILLUSTRATIONS: As an illustration of what we mean by sign learning, let us take the following instance. A person who is driv-

[56] Cf. Tolman, E. C., in Moss, F. A. (Ed.), *op. cit.*, Chapter XII. Also, *Purposive Behavior in Animals and Men.* New York: D. Appleton-Century Co., 1932, *passim.*

ing along a highway will have learned what to do when another car actually appears on the road ahead of him. Let us say that the car has cut in sharply from a side road. It may not be necessary at all, in any particular case, that such a car must actually be present in order that the driver will prepare to set his brakes or develop an attitude of caution. On the contrary, any object or situation which in any way resembles the objects present the first time that a car cut into the road, may serve as a sign of the possible entrance of a car. A row of fence posts or a line of telephone poles may acquire this sign function. A great many other features of a highway may also acquire such a function. A dip in the road ahead, a sharp turn in a line of telephone poles, an actual sign post, or any one of a number of other objects may acquire a signifying or a pointing-to function which will imply the possible presence of some obstruction along the highway. The responses which the driver makes to these signs may not be anything like the original response of actually setting the brakes. Instead, the driver may simply change his posture or he may redirect his attention so as to "get more" of the sign situation in order to discover exactly what is being pointed toward.[57] It might be, for example, that the telephone poles actually curve away from the road; but, on closer inspection, it is discovered that the fence posts continue straight ahead. In short, within a complex situation, a great many different objects do actually acquire some sort of "belongingness" to other objects which are either present or implied.

As we have already seen, there are certain phases of conditioning which look in this same direction. The infant who has learned to make a sucking response to the presence of the nipple in its mouth, may be conditioned to the sight of the bottle or to the sight of the mother. Upon seeing the bottle or the mother, however, it does not immediately begin the sucking response. On the contrary, it may make any one of a number of other movements, some of which are anticipatory, to be sure, of the sucking response but some of which may be totally unrelated to this particular movement. Even in the original experiments on conditioning, it was clear that an increased flow of saliva brought about by the sight of the food, the sound of a bell, or the placing of ice on some part of the body called for other modifications of behavior than those described by the phrase "an increased flow of saliva." It can be shown that in addition to the flow of saliva the conditioned stimulus will induce an attentive pos-

[57] Cf. Bode, B. H., *Conflicting Psychologies of Learning.* Boston: D. C. Heath and Co., 1929, Chapter XV.

MAJOR VARIETIES AND THEORIES OF LEARNING

ture, the rate of breathing will be modified, and other changes brought about in the whole action system.[58]

In short, then, learning by conditioning appears to be a type of learning which has emphasized only one feature of a very complex process. Not only is there a new stimulus which has been associated with an older response, but this response and the whole posture or attitude in which it is placed is of a different character than the original or unconditioned response. Under certain circumstances, as, for example, in rote learning, the number of signs that are to be established has already been furnished by the stimulus-situation itself. If, for example, one is to learn by heart the sequence of words: "What is so rare as a day in June! Then, if ever, come perfect days," the very words that are printed in the book presuppose the nature and the direction in which sign learning shall proceed.

In trial-and-error learning, however, there is no such previous determination. Then the sign must be discovered. The thing that is pointed to must be set into proper relation with the thing that will do the pointing. In short, a significant type of "belongingness" must be created. It is necessary, then, to find out what the origins of "belongingness" are and just what is implied by the term. These questions will be considered in the next section.

7. *Learning by Insight:* Let us say that a small child has been placed in the following situation. Just in front of it there is a highly desired plaything. The plaything, however, cannot be grasped because of a wire screen between it and the child. Moreover, there are side walls which act as barriers against the act of reaching or running around the screen. Behind the child there is no obstruction. The problem placed before the child is to get to the desired object.

If we may draw upon the several types of learning previously described, it would be possible for the child to react to the situation in any one of the following ways. It might make a variety of efforts to reach through the holes in the screen, break the screen down, push over the side walls, climb over one of the walls, climb over the screen, cry with vexation, or turn its back upon the desired object and escape from its compartment by running around the rear end of one of the two side walls. Of these various attempts to get the object, there is only one that is successful, viz., the last. After getting around the rear end of one of the walls, the child can turn forward, run along the outside of the compartment, and pick up the object.

[58] Liddell, H. S., *op. cit.,* pp. 279-280.

On the second occasion the child, especially if it is very young, may do many of the things that it did before, but the chances are that it will hit upon the successful series of movements much more quickly. In brief, it will appear to have learned how to get to the desired plaything by a trial-and-error method. If, however, an older child is placed in such a situation it will proceed immediately to the solution of the problem. The chances are that an older child would size up such a situation by noting almost immediately the relation between the screen and the side walls, on the one hand, and the opening at the rear of the compartment which offers a means of escape to the object, on the other. Even in this case, however, there might be a certain amount of trial-and-error effort in the sense that the child would use eye movements and perhaps some verbal movements in sizing up the situation. It would have to turn around, for example, in order to explore the whole region before the solution to the problem could arrive. In general, however, an older child would display a minimal amount of exploratory activity and proceed almost immediately to the solution of the problem. Even a chimpanzee can solve a problem of this type with surprising speed.[59]

From one point of view, then, the act of learning how to get to an object by a roundabout method can be explained as trial-and-error learning. It may also be described as an example of rote learning for, even though the number of repetitions is small, a very young child will quickly acquire the ability to choose the roundabout method rather than the fruitless methods of scaling the wall or of attempting to tear down the screen. It is even possible to explain the above example of learning by conditioning. The primary stimulus is, of course, the desired plaything. The primary responses might include better adjustment of the visual apparatus or movements of the body and the arms toward the desired object. In the nature of the case, however, this reaction-pattern is blocked. The whole situation offers, however, a number of other stimulus-patterns which may become temporary substitutes for the primary object. One of these situations is the opening at the rear of the compartment. If, then, the opening at the rear of the compartment can be interpolated between the desired plaything and the movements actually necessary to get hold of it, the child will learn how to get out of its difficulties.

There is one further feature in this whole learning situation which has attracted a great deal of attention. This feature is found in the fact that an older child can quickly see the relationship between an

[59] Köhler, W., *The Mentality of Apes.* New York: Harcourt, Brace and Co., 1925, *passim*.

MAJOR VARIETIES AND THEORIES OF LEARNING   407

opening at the end of the compartment and the getting of the object. This means that separate features of the total configuration of events which hitherto have not entered into a meaningful relation with one another suddenly acquire such a relationship. Moreover, the new configuration which is fashioned out of component parts of an older configuration calls forth almost immediately a new configuration of response. In both of these respects, speed seems to be one of the essential characteristics. Even though some trial-and-error movements are made, they belong to the whole situation in the sense that they furnish a part of the groundwork within which the process of refashioning or reconstruction takes place.

This type of learning has recently been called "learning by insight." [60] In short, learning by insight describes the fact that human beings and a good many of the higher animals may discern more or less quickly the essential relationship between hitherto unrelated parts of a total configuration of events and will have, on the spur of the moment, a mode of response which will be adequate to the new stimulus-pattern so that the problem or the difficulty supplied by the new pattern will be solved.[61]

A. EXPERIMENTAL RESULTS: Most of the experimental work on learning by insight has been carried out with the lower animals.[62] As a typical illustration, let us take the behavior of a chimpanzee which is confronted with the problem of getting hold of a piece of fruit which lies so far away from the bars of its cage that it cannot be reached by extending an arm through the opening between the bars. Let us also assume, however, that a stick is lying on the ground between the chimpanzee and the fruit but within easy reaching distance. After a certain amount of fruitless effort most chimpanzees will quickly solve the problem by grasping the stick and using it as a tool for pulling the fruit within arm's reach. A problem of this type will be solved most quickly if the stick is within the same field of vision with the fruit. That is to say, if the stick is placed at the back of the cage and out of sight of the chimpanzee when it is looking at the fruit, the problem becomes more difficult. The point is that the piece of fruit is one part of a total configuration of events which does not, and cannot, include a stick until the whole configuration has been made over. This process of making

---
[60] *Ibid., passim.* See also, however, Yerkes, R. M., "The Mental Life of Monkeys and Apes." *Behav. Monog.*, 1916, III (No. 12).
[61] A negative view is expressed by Hunter, W. S., "Learning: IV, Experimental Studies of Learning," in Murchison, C. (Ed.), *op. cit.*, pp. 509 ff.
[62] Köhler, W., *op. cit.*, Chapter II. The initial experiments of this type were done, however, by Hobhouse, L. T., *Mind in Evolution.* New York: The Macmillan Co., 1901.

over a situation requires that a stick or the branch of a tree or any other object that can be used as a tool shall be put into a significant functional relation with the fruit. Apparently, this functional relationship is not created by trial-and-error methods, although trial-and-error may precede it. It certainly is not created by rote learning. It still remains to be seen whether it can be created by the process of conditioning.

For these reasons, learning by insight has been offered not only as a distinctive type of learning but as the one way in which all learning may take place.[63] For example, we have already said that rote learning may require time and thus differ from learning by insight in the amount of time required simply because the learner attempts to place too many words in functional relationship at one and the same moment. It might be argued, therefore, that the events which place *"werden"* and "become" into a single unit actually do take place immediately and would be permanent were it not for the fact that the connections between *"werden"* and "become" are interfered with by the connections that must be established between other pairs of words.

Likewise, trial-and-error learning may involve many fruitless trials simply because the learner has not been able to identify those parts of the total situation which should be placed in a significant functional relationship to one another. Whenever this discovery is made, fruitless efforts disappear. The learner proceeds immediately to the solution of the task. Finally, learning by insight can be related to conditioning because of two of the features of conditioning described above, viz., the quickness with which the process takes place and because of the requirement that the two stimulus-response patterns to be conditioned to one another must occupy such a dominant place in the total experimental situation, that they will acquire with respect to one another the property of belongingness.[64]

B. SUMMARY: We have now laid out for inspection some of the principal facts regarding the major types of learning. The time has not yet come to say the final word about these various types and neither shall we be able to give the student a well-rounded theory of learning. There is, however, one consideration that must be taken into account before we pass on to a description of the principal laws of learning. This consideration arises out of the question as to whether learning by insight describes the same type of psychological

[63] Cf. Köhler, W., *Gestalt Psychology.* New York: Liveright Publishing Corp., 1929, *passim.*
[64] Cf. Hunter, W. S., *op. cit.,* pp. 561 ff.

operation as is described by rote learning, trial-and-error learning, and conditioning.

For the present, we shall assume that insight describes a type of learning which, in human nature, should fall more naturally in a chapter on the nature of thinking or reasoning. In other words, learning by insight is not a type of learning at all, but a totally different mode of psychological function. It is for this reason that we have considered this phase of the problem in an earlier chapter. We are still left, however, with rote learning, trial-and-error learning, and learning by conditioning. The question is whether these terms mark fundamentally different ways in which human nature may be changed or whether they simply stand for different ways of looking at one and the same process. Although it will not be possible to settle this question at the present time, further comments upon it must be postponed until we have outlined a few of the laws which are said to characterize psychological growth under the influence of learning situations.

III. The Laws of Learning

1. *Introduction:* The next chapter will show us clearly that it is not necessary to know the full nature of a given process before a certain amount of practical control can be exercised over it. In other words, we shall see that the teacher can do a great many things toward promoting and guiding growth through learning, even though he is not able to say all that should be said concerning the essential nature of learning.

The person who uses psychology as an aid to teaching, however, must be warned to distinguish clearly between the facts that are known about increased efficiency in learning, on the one hand, and the so-called laws of learning, on the other. For the most part, these laws have had their origin in one or more of the types of learning described in the last section. In the case of rote learning, for example, we have said that a poem or a piece of prose can be committed to memory simply by reading material over and over again. It has been easy to assert, therefore, that the necessity for repetition should be elevated to the rank of a law. A good many books will say, therefore, that, other things being equal, practice makes perfect.

2. *The Law of Exercise:* From a more formal point of view, we may speak of the law of exercise. This law was first definitely formulated by Thorndike:

"To the situation, 'a modifiable connection being made by him between a situation S and a response R,' man responds originally, other things being equal, by an increase in the strength of that connection. By the strength of a connection is meant the probability that it will be made when the situation recurs. Greater probability that a connection will be made means a greater probability for the same time, or an equal probability for a longer time." [65]

A. THE SYNAPSE: It is clear from this statement of the law of use or of exercise that a definite assumption has been made concerning the nature of the nervous events which underlie learning processes.[66] As is commonly known, the nervous system is made up of an immense number of cellular units called neurones. A typical neurone bears some resemblance to a bulbous plant. The bulb itself is analogous to the central cell structure. The roots of the plant may be taken as analogous to a bunchy group of fibres arising from one side of the central cell body. These fibres are called dendrites. The flowering portions of the plant are somewhat less like a fibre with branching fibres which may arise from the other side of the cell and stretch for considerable distances into other portions of the body. This fibre with its collaterals is called the axone.

It has been assumed that these neurones are arranged in such a way in the nervous system that the axone of one neurone comes into more or less intimate contact with the dendrites of another.[67] Thus a path of conduction may be established between a sense organ on or within the body, through the central nervous system, to a muscle cell. Since the nervous system is made up of an immense number of neurones it is easy to believe that a tremendous number of pathways may exist between sense organs and muscles. The nerve currents are presumed always to flow from dendrites to the cell body and out of the axone into the next dendrite.

The important features of this theory of the nature of nerve action are as follows. In the first place, it is assumed that each of the connections which may be established between a sense organ and a muscle fibre is an independent unit somewhat like the telephone line that connects one subscriber with another. In the second place, the law of exercise named above requires that changes in the readiness with which such a pathway may conduct an impulse must depend upon a change that takes place in the pathway itself. The

---

[65] Thorndike, E. L., *op. cit.*, pp. 171-172.
[66] Cf. Gates, A. I., *Elementary Psychology*. New York: The Macmillan Co., 1925, Chapter X.
[67] Sherrington, C. S., *The Integrative Action of the Nervous System*. New Haven: Yale Univ. Press, 1906, Chapter I and *passim*.

chief region in which such changes are possible is called the synapse —that is, that point where the axone of one neurone comes into close functional relationship with the dendrites of another. The law of exercise assumes that the synapse may offer a certain amount of resistance to the passage of a nerve current. If, however, a passage has once been effected, the law would say that the resistance offered at the synapse has been slightly decreased, thus raising the chances that the same pathway will be used again on another occasion. If practice periods have been sufficiently numerous, the resistance offered by the synapses may almost, if not quite, disappear, in which case the movements made in response to a particular stimulus-pattern will have become thoroughly habitualized. This theory of the operation of the nervous system is now being subjected to serious criticism.[68]

B. FREQUENCY: There are two corollaries which are often mentioned in connection with the law of exercise. The first of these is known as the law of frequency.[69] This corollary simply affirms more emphatically a principle already implied by the law of exercise, viz., that, other things being equal, the more frequently a connection is exercised, the less resistance it will offer to functional connections between sense organ and muscle fibre. In other words, learning cannot take place all at once. The first repetition of an action means that the nerve connections leading to the act are a little stronger than they were before. As time goes on, the connection is made stronger and stronger.

C. RECENCY: A second corollary is known as the law of recency.[70] This law would say that, other things being equal, the more recently a nerve current has travelled a given pathway, the stronger will be the connections used. It is in the law of recency that provision is made for the phenomena of forgetting. If a connection between a sense organ and a muscle fibre has not been made recently, the law of recency would imply that the connection had been weakened either because of the mere passage of time or because of other factors which need not concern us at the moment.

3. *Criticisms of the Law of Exercise:* The law of exercise and its corollaries has played a very large part in modern methods of teaching, first, because there are so many obvious facts which seem to lend support to it, and, secondly, because the theory of the nervous

[68] Cf. Lashley, K. S., "The Theory that Synaptic Resistance is Reduced by the Passage of the Nerve Impulse." *Psychol. Rev.,* 1924, XXXI, 369-375.
[69] Gates, A. I., *op. cit.,* p. 255.
[70] *Ibid.,* p. 256.

system upon which it is based is so simple and straightforward as to lead easily to conviction. There are, however, a number of considerations which create serious doubts about the validity of the laws. One of these considerations has already been mentioned in our study of conditioning. The student will remember that there are occasions when a conditioned response will be weakened rather than strengthened by continuous exercise. That is, the child which has learned to react to a furry object in the same way that it has previously reacted to a loud noise will quickly abandon its newly acquired mode of response and return to an older mode unless the newer response is fortified occasionally by the simultaneous presentation of the original stimulus-object.[71]

This is, however, only one of the circumstances which throws doubt upon the significance of the law of exercise. Other circumstances are as follows. It has long been known that the repeated use of any member of the body makes that member less ready for action rather than more ready for action. Changes of this type have often been described by adaptation and fatigue. When, for example, the eye is repeatedly stimulated with a bright light it becomes less rather than more sensitive to further stimulation. Continuous temperature applied to the skin makes the sense organs in the skin less rather than more sensitive to thermal stimulus.[72] When a group of muscles is used over and over again in the execution of a simple task, these muscles become less ready for action rather than more ready. Even in the nervous system, it can be shown that the system is less ready to conduct for short intervals of time after exercise. To be sure, nervous tissue recuperates quickly, but even under the best interpretation, the alleged improvement of a function described by the law of exercise or of use stands in opposition to the phenomena of adaptation and of fatigue.[73] This opposition has been supported recently by direct experiments upon the effect of repetition upon certain types of skills. In the case of some skills it has been shown that repeated use of the skills is an almost certain means of destroying them. Consider, for example, the common error of writing "hte" for "the" on the typewriter. This faulty habit has actually been corrected by intentionally writing "hte" over and over again.[74]

In other experiments, especially of the trial-and-error type, it has been shown that an animal may choose the wrong pathway much

[71] Cf. Hull, C. L., *op. cit.*, pp. 436 ff.
[72] Cf. Titchener, E. B., *op. cit.*, pp. 71 ff.
[73] Cf. Robinson, E. S., *op. cit.*, *passim*.
[74] Dunlap, K., "Repetition in the Breaking of Habits." *Scient. Mo.*, 1930, XXX, 66-70.

MAJOR VARIETIES AND THEORIES OF LEARNING 413

more frequently than the right pathway and yet this fact does not prevent the animal from learning how to solve the problem.[75] Let us take, for example, a simple maze in which one pathway ends in a blind alley and the other leads to food. Obviously an animal may run into the blind alley more frequently than into the food alley for any entrance into the food alley terminates the experiment. The actual data in such experiments show clearly that the wrong response is exercised more frequently than the right response. According to the law of exercise, then, it is the wrong rather than the right response that should be learned. Some measure of escape from this predicament is offered by the law of recency. Since any entrance into a food alley will presumably be the last choice made by the animal it ought to influence the choice made on the next trial.

4. *The Law of Effect:* The use of the principle of recency in this way has not answered all of the difficulties raised by the inadequacy of the law of exercise or of use. Experimenters went rather quickly, therefore, to other principles which might support the law of exercise. The principle used most frequently has been elevated into a law and is called the law of effect.[76]

In order to sense the meaning of this law, let us take an actual learning situation. Let us say that a child has been asked to learn how to solve a simple mechanical problem. As we have seen, it will attack the problem by making a large variety of random or chance movements. Among all of these movements, there will be one which solves the problem. If the puzzle is more difficult, the child will have to hit upon the right combination of movements before it can be solved.

Now it may be argued that those movements which are unsuccessful will annoy the child, whereas a glow of satisfaction will attend the making of the right movements. The law of effect argues that states of annoyance certainly do nothing to stamp in the connections that have been made and which lead to behavior which is annoying. There are some who would say that states of annoyance actually prevent the establishment of such connections, even though they may be used more frequently than others.[77]

On the other hand, states of satisfaction or of pleasure are said to favor the fixation of the pathways which have been used for producing behavior which leads to satisfaction. When, therefore, the

---

[75] Cf. Koffka, K., *The Growth of the Mind.* New York: Harcourt, Brace and Co., 1924, pp. 158 ff.
[76] Thorndike, E. L., *op. cit., passim.*
[77] For a critical survey of this whole problem, see Cason, H., "Criticisms of the Laws of Exercise and Effect." *Psychol. Rev.,* 1924, XXXI, 397-417.

child makes a variety of attacks upon its problem, it may see no relation between a movement and the solution of the problem. If, however, a given movement actually leads to the solution of the problem, it will be covered with a halo of satisfaction, and the connections that lead to it will be strengthened. All of the other connections that have been used during trial-and-error attempts will be left unstrengthened or will be actually weakened.

The law of effect has exerted a marked influence upon teaching methods in the schoolroom, for there are so many features of schoolroom learning which favor the law of exercise.[78] Neither teachers nor psychologists have been anxious to give up the law of exercise, and consequently the law of effect has proceeded to clear the way of all difficulties.

Let us consider, for example, the following experiment. Let a white rat be placed in a situation where there is a choice of four pathways, all of which lead to the same goal. The pathways differ, however, in length or in time consumed, or in the effort involved. One pathway, for example, may be very long, another may lead through a chamber where the rat can be delayed, and a third may offer an obstruction. It has been shown that white rats will invariably choose the path which involves the least time and the least effort, even though some of the other pathways have been traversed more frequently than the shorter pathway.[79] In this case the law of effect offers itself as a means of defense for the law of exercise because it says that the state of satisfaction which is associated with a quick and easy solution to the problem will stamp in some connections rather than others.

5. *Criticisms of the Law of Effect:* From a superficial point of view the laws of exercise and of effect seem to account for a great many learning processes.[80] The laws can be stated so simply and they are given so much support by our commonsense opinions that we can easily accept them and proceed to teaching operations with some confidence that they will actually work in the schoolroom. As with the law of exercise, however, so with the law of effect, there are a number of rather disturbing sources of doubt.[81]

In the first place, the connections that are said to be established between a stimulus-situation and the adequate response to that situation are physico-chemical events in the nervous system. States of

[78] Cf. Gates, A. I., *op. cit.*, Chapter VII and *passim.*
[79] Kuo, Z. Y., "The Nature of Unsuccessful Acts and Their Order of Elimination in Animal Learning." *J. Comp. Psychol.*, 1922, II, 1-27.
[80] Gates, A. I., *op. cit.*, Chapter VII.
[81] Cason, H., *op. cit., passim.*

satisfaction and of annoyance, however, are commonly described as mental states. They are ways of feeling. If, then, the law of effect is a true law of learning, we must find out how a mental state can exert an influence upon the physical and chemical processes that occur in the nerve tissue. Since this is a direct return to the traditional problem of the relation between mind and body, attempts to solve it look no more promising than the attempts that have been made to solve the mind-body problem.[82] As a matter of fact, it is now commonly thought that the mind-body problem is an artificial problem created by wrong ways of asking questions.

We shall look at this problem in more detail in a later chapter. In the meantime, it may be pointed out that a way of escape is provided if we say that satisfaction and annoyance are not only mental states but that they are also descriptive of different bodily attitudes or conditions. We might say, for example, that a state of annoyance means that the chemical condition of the blood and of the nervous system is different from the condition which obtains when a person is satisfied or pleased. As we have seen, there is some reason to believe that the general chemical tone of the body does change from time to time. Moreover, changes in chemical tone may bring about considerable changes in the general quality of action.[83] It has not been shown, however, that a change in quality of action has any bearing upon the question as to whether a series of connections will or will not be strengthened.

If the law of effect is a valid law of learning, it ought to follow that the memories of a person should be almost, if not quite, exclusively pleasurable or happy memories. That is, we ought not to be able to recall any experiences or to use any skills that had been acquired during states of annoyance or during periods when profound degrees of unhappiness were present. There is some evidence to show that, of the memories which are spontaneously recalled, a slight majority imply states of satisfaction or of pleasure.[84] Even a casual inspection of our recollections, however, will show that we have a great many memories of unpleasant events. Moreover, any athlete can report that he spends a considerable number of unhappy practice periods in acquiring high levels of skill. These facts would enable us to say that the law of effect may be useful on some occasions, but they enable us to say also that the law of effect is not a dominating law of learning. Even if we agree that the

[82] Cf. Tolman, E. C., *op. cit., passim.*
[83] Young, P. T., *op. cit., passim.*
[84] For reference, see McGeoch, J. A., "The Psychology of Human Learning: A Bibliography." *Psychol. Bull.,* 1933, XXX, p. 47.

law of exercise will overcome the effects of annoyance or unhappiness, we have not escaped all of our difficulties for some of our most intense recollections are certainly recollections of unhappy events which occurred but once.

Further light upon the law of effect has been thrown by a series of experiments in which deliberate attempts have been made to acquire skills in the face of states of annoyance. A group of subjects, for example, was asked to learn a maze which consisted of thirty pairs of holes arranged in irregular order on a punchboard.[85] The subjects were divided into five groups. The first group was asked to avoid that hole of each pair which caused a buzzer to sound when a stylus was pushed into it. The second group was asked to select that hole of each pair which caused the buzzer to sound. A third group learned the maze when the wiring was reversed so that the buzzer sounded on the opposite hole of each pair as compared with the tasks assigned to the first two groups. A fourth group was instructed in the same way as the first two groups save that, in addition to the buzzer, the subjects received a shock through the stylus. In other words, this group learned to avoid the hole in each pair of holes which gave a buzz but which gave no electric shock. The fifth group was asked to select that hole in each pair of holes which buzzed and which gave an electric shock.

The best performance was turned in by the last group and the second best performance by the second group. The poorest performance came from the first group. In other words, the results stood in direct contrast to the results that should have appeared if the law of effect holds true. The sounding of the buzzer, of course, can hardly be described either as a reward or a punishment, but it does emphasize the fact that the response that has just been made is either right or wrong. In other words, it emphasizes one hole in a pair rather than the other. When, therefore, such an emphasizer appears in conjunction with a correct response, this response is acquired more quickly than when it is attached to an incorrect response. An electric shock, likewise, may serve as an emphasizer as well as a punishment. In any case, when the electric shock was introduced in connection with wrong responses it caused a state of distraction and kept the subjects from remembering that the responses were wrong. Similarly, when the shock was introduced after right responses, it might cause distraction in some cases or

[85] Tolman, E. C., Hall, C. S., and Bretnall, E. P., "A Disproof of the Law of Effect and a Substitution of the Laws of Emphasis, Motivation and Disruption." *J. Exper. Psychol.*, 1932, XV, 601-614.

MAJOR VARIETIES AND THEORIES OF LEARNING

serve as an emphasizer in others. In short, then, this experiment seems to show clearly that there must be other factors in learning than sheer repetition and effect. We do not mean to say that these factors are always emphasizers, on the one hand, or distractors, on the others, but only to argue that the laws of exercise and of effect probably make too simple a matter out of the learning process.[86]

IV. A Theory of Learning

1. *Introduction:* The student has felt, no doubt, that our study of the various types of learning, on the one hand, and of the laws of learning, on the other, has led neither himself nor the author to any particular conclusion. He need not be troubled by this feeling, however, for this is just where theories about the nature of learning stand at the present time. Ten years ago it was thought that some of the main outlines of this section of the science of psychology had been drawn in final form and that future experimenters were needed only to fill in the details of the picture. Since the main facts were known, it was urged that the teacher could safely proceed to use these facts in the schoolroom. Now, however, both psychologists and educators are less certain than they were of the true nature of learning, although, as we shall see in the next chapter, they are not any less certain about the rules or principles which can be used in order to get results from learning periods.[87]

2. *Points of Similarity:* It will not do, perhaps, to leave the whole question of the nature of learning quite so open as we have left it and we shall, therefore, try to give form to our present knowledge about this field by making several general statements. In the first place, the question as to whether there are several fundamentally different types of learning or whether the alleged types of learning are different ways of describing a single fundamental process cannot be answered at the present time. To be sure, a great many attempts have been made to show that trial-and-error learning is a more complicated form of learning by conditioning.[88] Obviously, the person who is placed in a complex situation will make a good many tentative responses to the various features of that situation. Since it is

---

[86] For a more extended analysis of these features of learning, see Tolman, E. C., *Purposive Behavior in Animals and Men.* New York: D. Appleton-Century Co., 1932, Chapters XXI-XXIII.
[87] Cf. Lashley, K. S., "Learning: I, Nervous Mechanisms in Learning," in Murchison, C. (Ed.), *Foundations of Experimental Psychology.* Worcester, Mass.: Clark Univ. Press, 1929, Chapter XIV. See especially, p. 561.
[88] Guthrie, E. R., "Conditioning as a Principle of Learning." *Psychol. Rev.,* 1930, XXXVII, 412-428.

not clear to him, however, which responses are truly significant with respect to the essential parts of the total stimulus-pattern, he will behave in a semi-emotionalized manner. The frantic efforts of some of the lower animals, for example, to solve certain types of problems obviously give evidence of emotional factors in the total behavior-pattern. Even during such periods, however, the curve of learning, as measured by time consumed or as measured by number of errors, may drop suddenly when significant relations between the goal and the means to the goal are seen. This drop in the learning curve can be attributed to insight, but it has also been attributed to a process of conditioning whereby one part of the whole stimulus-pattern is substituted for the whole.

We have already discovered that learning by conditioning has a good many properties in common with learning by association. The chief difference between the two, perhaps, lies in the fact that learning by conditioning is dependent upon a physiological theory of the way in which the nervous system acts when associations are established. The older theories of association often implied that learning by association must be a purely mental affair. Since experimental psychology has moved steadily away from entire dependence upon concepts which are in any way related to the existence of minds or of ideas, learning by conditioning has been hailed as a major achievement not only for psychology but for education as well.[89]

Certain similarities have also been pointed out in connection with the relative quickness with which conditioning may take place, on the one hand, and those types of learning which can be called insightful, on the other. The natural inference is that the physiological events which take place during conditioning must also be present when stimulus-patterns are reconstructed so as to bring together parts of them which have not hitherto stood in an intimate relation with one another. One of the lower animals can use a stick in order to reach food which otherwise would lie beyond its reach because the stick and the food are taken, so to speak, out of their own configurations and placed in a new configuration.

It is one thing, however, to cite instances of similarity and of dissimilarity among the several types of learning described above and quite another to note some of the practical outcomes of the use of various types in schoolroom procedure. A careful survey of the events that go on in the average schoolroom suggests that teaching

[89] Hogben, L., *op. cit.*, Chapter I.

MAJOR VARIETIES AND THEORIES OF LEARNING

procedures are centered pretty largely around rote learning, on the one hand, and trial-and-error learning, on the other. From the first grades to the last years in an institution of higher learning, teachers are accustomed to lay before their pupils specific stimulus-situations made up of facts to be learned. It is desired that the student in the schoolroom shall acquire facility to recite these facts either in a recitation or in an examination. In general, it is desired that students shall learn how to make the right responses to the situations presented to them, not because they have any sense of what is right or appropriate, but simply because they have learned in routine fashion what is normally expected of them.

The schoolroom itself, therefore, is taken up pretty largely with the rote memory type of learning.[90] As we have shown, however, rote learning is a type of learning which is superimposed upon considerable measures of prior learning. Even the first-grader who learns to repeat a simple poem is making use of verbal skills the fundamental features of which have been learned long since. In some of the newer schools, to be sure, where so-called progressive methods of teaching are used, there is a greater amount of learning by trial-and-error and even of learning by insight.[91] Trial-and-error learning appears to best advantage, perhaps, in playground activities and in drawing, painting, and in the manual arts. Even here, however, the child is not actually acquiring new motor and perceptual skills. On the contrary, he is putting older skills and certainly some of the essential properties of these skills into new patterns.

When we said above that the ordinary school program is centered pretty largely around rote learning and trial-and-error learning, we spoke advisedly even though we have also argued that learning by conditioning is a type of profit from experience which probably has more consequences for the future success of a person than these others. This apparent discrepancy in our statements can be explained in the following way. The chances are that learning by conditioning comes into the schoolroom and into the preschool educational program, not so much by intent or by formal recognition on the part of teachers and parents, as by indirection and through informal methods of training. Neither parents nor teachers intentionally try to teach children how to be shy of other children, how to be afraid of the dark, how to have inferiority complexes, or how to

[90] Cf. Freeman, F. N., *How Children Learn.* Boston: Houghton Mifflin Co., 1917, *passim.*
[91] Cf. Burton, W. H., *Introduction to Education.* New York: D. Appleton-Century Co., 1934, Part III and *passim.*

develop any of the other attitudes and dispositions that make up the constitution of those children who are commonly called problem-children.[92]

As we have seen, the common failure in recognizing the types of learning which have been responsible for all of these traits is one of the facts that lies behind the alleged existence of instincts and the alleged importance of heredity. If no one has intentionally tried to teach a child how to be jealous or overly competitive or shy during the recitation period, these dispositions, so it is said, must obviously be due to the child's original nature. We must conclude, then, that learning by conditioning is a type of learning which is extremely common throughout the whole period of growth.[93] It is, however, a type of learning which belongs to informal education rather than to formal education. So long as teachers and parents suppose that the products of informal education, that is, the products of learning by conditioning, are instinctive or are a part of the original nature of children, they will remain more or less helpless in the presence of such traits. If, however, parents and teachers can begin to realize that all of the traits to be described in some of the later chapters and, especially, in the chapter on the socialized person, are the result of definite learning processes, they will be in a position where they can become more effective in reeducating and retraining the child. As we have implied in several places, one of the major tasks of higher education is to remedy or correct the faults of earlier education.

3. *Points of Dissimilarity:* As we speak of similarities between the various types of learning described above, we must not forget some of the possible dissimilarities. There is, for example, a marked dissimilarity between learning by insight and all of the other types of learning.[94] This dissimilarity is to be found in the fact that learning by insight seems to involve just what the word implies, viz., an intuitive realization of the relationship between stimulus-patterns which hitherto have not appeared to be related to each other.

In this connection, let us consider again the concept of "togetherness." Objects may be put together by the teacher simply through presenting them at the same time and in such a context that they will seem to have closer relations with each other than they will with any-

[92] Cf. Watson, J. B., *Psychological Care of Infant and Child.* New York: W. W. Norton and Co., 1928, *passim.*
[93] Cf. Hull, C. L., *op. cit., passim.*
[94] Cf. Tolman, E. C., "Theories of Learning," in Moss, F. A. (Ed.), *op. cit.,* Chapter XII.

MAJOR VARIETIES AND THEORIES OF LEARNING

thing else. These relations must, however, be perceived by the learner. Now the perception of relationships lies more in the direction of problem-solving or of reasoning than it does in the direction of learning. This is certainly true of rote learning and of trial-and-error learning. In the case of rote learning, a person may sometimes be more or less witless about the meaning or significance of the series of events being learned. If he is not witless during the actual learning process, he may be almost, if not quite so, during the period of recitation. There is, however, nothing witless in learning by insight. On the contrary, learning by insight is, so to speak, "witful."

These are some of the considerations which led us to the nature of learning by insight in our chapter on problem-solving. There is, however, one further general statement to be made about learning. It has been pointed out a good many times that a typical learning curve has a good many features in common with growth curves.[95] Even a growth curve showing the way in which weight is increased from early infancy to adulthood looks very much like a learning curve drawn either from animal learning or from human learning. This fact, together with a number of others, has suggested the possibility that learning and growing may be analogous terms. We speak, to be sure, of psychological growth as well as of physical growth. It may be, however, that learning is simply another way of describing psychological growth, the word growth itself being a more general term which might include both physical and psychological growth.[96]

The concept that is intended when we say that learning and growing are analogous terms may be illustrated by referring briefly to some of the older theories of the nature of learning and memory. It was once said that learning and memory were processes which had some similarity to the process of depositing a sum of money in a bank or to the process of filing a letter away in a cabinet. In short, learning included two factors, viz., the practice factor which led to memories or learnings and the memories and learnings themselves which were to be stored away, pending a proper occasion for their use.[97] Teachers were inclined to say, therefore, that the mind or the brain could act as a storehouse. It was even argued at times that there must be a considerable number of nerve cells in the brain which

[95] Ariens Kappers, C. U., "The Logetic Character of Growth." *J. Comp. Neurol.*, 1919, XXXI, 51-67.
[96] Cf. Freeman, G. L., *Introduction to Physiological Psychology*. New York: The Ronald Press, 1934, Chapter XXIV.
[97] For a discussion of this matter, see James, W., *Principles of Psychology*. New York: Henry Holt and Co., 1890, Vol. I, Chapters IV, XIV, and XVI.

were the particular places where given memories could be filed away. This older view of a storehouse of memories did not imply that the brain itself was actually changed by practice, in the sense that it had become a more mature psychological instrument. It could not even be said that the mind was an abler instrument simply because somewhere in the cellars of the mind a vast number of items had been stored away for future reference.

There is another feature of this whole review of learning and memory which is important in any theory of the nature of learning. If either the mind or the nervous system can be described as filing cabinets or safety deposit vaults within which memories and learnings are to be stored, the implication is that these memories and learnings can, for considerable periods of time, remain wholly passive, pending the time when they will be recalled. If we may continue the analogy with a storage vault, the implication is that the vast number of items put away in the storage vault makes no essential change in the edifice itself.[98] A bank, for example, so far as external observation is concerned, is the same whether the vaults are full or empty. Clearly, however, the functions of the bank may change markedly with the amount of capital put away in the vaults.

In other words, the analogy which we are using breaks down if we suppose that surplus funds are not merely passive, as is the case with memories and learnings. If, however, we think of learning and growth as analogous terms, it must follow that previous experiences actively and progressively change the character of each person. The more he lives the more certain it is that he will be a different sort of psychological instrument from moment to moment. So far as this idea is concerned, it makes no difference whether learning falls into various types or not. The point is that learning of any type expresses itself in the progressively changing quality of the psychological instrument which we call a mature person.

This is, perhaps, one of the most arresting facts that has come out of recent studies on the nature of learning. It is a fact which resembles, in a good many respects, the conditions under which nerve tissue develops during periods of stimulation.[99] As we have seen in an earlier chapter, the very excitations which pass through the nervous system modify in essential respects the growth pattern of that system. There is no sense of the word in which such excitations can be stored away in a relatively passive condition, awaiting the time when they will be called forth for further use.

[98] Cf. James, W., *op. cit.*, Chapters IV and XVI.
[99] Cf. Wheeler, R. M., and Perkins, F. T., *op. cit.*, Chapter XIX.

MAJOR VARIETIES AND THEORIES OF LEARNING   423

It has not been possible for us, in this connection, to say very much about the changes in our theories of nerve action which new studies in the field of learning require. We may, however, report, in brief, that the older telephone-exchange idea of nerve function has now given way to an idea which more nearly resembles some of the field concepts familiar to the physicist.[100] If we think of the whole brain as a complex pattern of energy or of fields of force within which variations in equilibrium may take place, then we can say how it happens that a total state of equilibrium at the present moment, resulting as it has from past experience, may sustain an active relation to future experience. There is no question at all about parts of the brain field lying dormant, awaiting the time when they can be used again.

4. *Conclusion:* In view of the facts that have now been presented, it would be unwise to take any final position on the question as to whether there are several different types of learning. For practical purposes, however, it will be worth our while to distinguish at least three features of all learning processes. We do this only because there are times, in the schoolroom, when one of these features should be emphasized more than another.

Everything considered, it looks as though the essential nature of learning will be found in the neighborhood of that type described above as sign learning. In other words, there are a great many circumstances under which one object or event may become a sign of another, point to it, or otherwise signify it.[101] Trial-end-error learning seems to describe the behavior of a learner during those periods when he has not yet discovered the one feature of a complex situation which "belongs" to, points toward, or serves as, a sign of another. In puzzle-box experiments, it is frequently not possible for the subject to perceive "belongingness" because there is nothing about a latch to be lifted or a string to be pulled that will help the animal to place it in a single configuration with the getting of food.[102] The same behavior can be observed in experiments on conditioning where the experimental situation is of such a character as to give the animal no clew or suggestion whatsoever as to the possible "belongingness" of various parts of the whole situation. When, however, the experimental conditions are so arranged that two stimulus-patterns are really "figures" upon a "ground" furnished by the

[100] Lashley, K. S., *op. cit., passim.*
[101] Cf. Tolman, E. C., in Moss, F. A. (Ed.), *op. cit.*
[102] Koffka, K., *op. cit.*

whole setting of the experiment, the one may quickly become a sign or signal for the other.

Some of the facts that have a bearing upon the way in which previously discovered signs or signals will be forgotten have been presented in this chapter. Other facts will be considered in the next chapter. In the meantime, it should be pointed out that a discovered "belongingness" between two or more patterns can be lost. One of the chief methods for preventing losses is to be found in rote learning. In other words, there are times when the sheer repetition of sequences of action, both at the manual level and at the verbal level, will make the "belongingness" between the various parts of these sequences more stable or more secure. No one has been able to say with any assurance as yet just what happens in the nervous system when security of this sort is established. This, however, is not an important matter so far as the teacher is concerned. The main point is that, during processes of rote learning, types of relatedness can be so firmly fixed that only an unusual set of circumstances will destroy them.

Some light is thrown upon this phase of rote learning by experiments on what is commonly known as overlearning. In the study of animal learning, for example, it is frequently taken for granted that the first successful, that is, the first errorless, performance or the first three successful (errorless) performances can be taken as the criterion of learning. The fact that errors will continue to appear after this criterion has been reached can be explained in terms of the interference which one part of a long learning task creates with respect to another part. In any case, for certain purposes, the subjects in an experiment may be invited to practice a successful response for long periods of time beyond either of the criteria just mentioned. This sort of practice is known as overlearning. It appears to establish connections so firmly that no ordinary set of circumstances will interfere with the connections. In brief, then, rote learning leads to response-patterns of the habit type.

In the third place, learning by insight describes a feature of the whole process of learning which resembles in a good many respects the sign learning feature, but which differs from sign learning in the sense that one or more parts of the single configuration of circumstances may enter into a new pattern with one or more parts of another configuration. As we have suggested, this type of learning ought not, perhaps, to be called learning at all. On the contrary, it should be designated as problem-solving. It is this possibility which has led us to devote a special chapter to the nature of problem-solving and to point out some of the possible relations between learning by insight and those events that have commonly been known as thinking or reasoning.

READINGS

This chapter has been provided so abundantly with footnotes that the student will need, perhaps, no further guidance in his outside reading. Of most general use, perhaps, are Dunlap, K., *Habits: Their Making and Unmaking*. New York: Liveright Publishing Corp., 1932; Wheeler, R. H., and Perkins, F. T., *Principles of Mental Development*. New York: T. Y. Crowell, 1932, Chapters XIII to XX; Tolman, E. C., *Purposive Behavior in Animals and Men*. New York: D. Appleton-Century Co., 1932, Chapters XXI to XXIII, and Moss, F. A. (ed.), *Comparative Psychology*. New York: Prentice-Hall, Inc., Chapters VIII to XII.

One of the most illuminating surveys of the nature of learning is by Lashley, K. S., "Learning: III. Nervous Mechanisms in Learning," in Murchison, C. (ed.), *A Handbook of Experimental Psychology*. Worcester, Mass.: Clark Univ. Press, 1934, Chapter X. See also Chapter VIII. "Learning: I. The Factor of Maturation" (by C. P. Stone); Chapter IX. "Learning: II. The Factor of the Conditioned Reflex" (by C. L. Hull), and Chapter XI. "Learning: IV. Experimental Studies of Learning" (by W. S. Hunter).

CHAPTER TWELVE

ENGINEERING THE LEARNING PROCESS

I. Theory and Practice

1. *Introduction:* It is a fortunate thing that a certain measure of control can be exerted over objects and events in advance of complete knowledge about their real nature or of the ways in which they may properly be explained. It is still more fortunate that control can sometimes be made effective where alleged knowledge about the nature of the events involved is almost certainly wrong. If the engineering sciences, for example, had to wait upon "complete" knowledge of all of the materials and processes that are in common use, society would have to sit down in pious resignation until the course of research had come more nearly to a successful conclusion than is the case at present.

As an example of the way in which events and materials may be engineered in advance of any true knowledge about them, let us take illuminating engineering. There are now two theories as to the nature of light, the one maintaining that it behaves as though it were made up of particles, and the other maintaining that it behaves in ways analogous to sound waves. It has not been necessary to settle this difficult experimental and theoretical problem in advance of any attempt to illuminate a room properly. As every teacher knows, a schoolroom can be lighted so as to favor efficient work by everyone in it.[1] A second illustration is to be found in the use which modern industry has made of electricity. There are a number of theories as to what electricity may be, but a generous measure of practical control over an electric current in no way waits upon the discovery of the intrinsic nature of electrical energy.

For our own purposes, the best example of the discrepancy between the ideal of complete or final knowledge, on the one hand, and the immediate arts of practical control, on the other, is to be found in the study of human nature itself. From the very earliest times to the present, societies have always acted as though they were able

---

[1] Cf. Viteles, M. S., *Industrial Psychology*. New York: W. W. Norton and Co., 1932, pp. 482-492; Humphries, F. H., *Artificial Sunlight* (5th ed.). London: Oxford Univ. Press, 1929.

to engineer, with more or less success, the behavior of individual persons; and individuals, likewise, have often been successful in bending groups of people to their wills; but even the most successful levels of guidance and control have not waited upon a complete story of the nature of human nature.

There are, at the present time, two major theories about men and their doings which appear to stand as far apart as possible.[2] The study of mental processes, on the one hand, and of the reactions of muscles and glands, on the other, represent points of view in psychology which can scarcely be brought together into a composite picture; and yet adherents of both types of psychology have long been able to account for many features of human nature, make certain types of predictions with respect to it, and otherwise control and guide it in a good many practical ways. Even the most primitive men made use of certain facts about action, perception, habit, problem-solving, and personality in order to organize group behavior. This is to say that they acted as though they were practical psychologists even though they had none of the information that is now available.[3]

The fundamental processes used by teachers in guiding and promoting growth stand in this same situation. As we have seen in the last chapter, there are several different ways of classifying these processes. Men speak, for example, of rote learning, trial-and-error learning, conditioning, and of insight. It may be that each of these expressions represent fundamentally different ways in which psychological growth may be promoted. On the contrary, they may describe different aspects of a single method of producing changes in human nature. At the present time, much of the evidence seems to point in this latter direction. This is certainly the case if we say that learning by insight is more akin to problem-solving than it is to profit from past experience through sheer practice. Even so, it still remains true that research men have not come much nearer to a statement of what takes place in nerve tissue during periods of learning than they were before the researches began. In spite of our ignorance, however, the learning process is a process that can be facilitated and controlled by the use of certain guiding principles. It is this fortunate fact which is full of promise to education and

[2] Cf. Heidbreder, E. F., *Seven Psychologies.* New York: D. Appleton-Century Co., 1933, *passim.*
[3] The most convincing evidence in support of this assertion is furnished by the biographies of such men as Confucius, Alexander the Great, Genghis Khan, Julius Caesar, and the like. The biographical notes and letters of Benjamin Franklin are full of practical psychological information.

to the other arts which cherish the hope of making men more competent during their mature years than they were on the day that they were born.

2. *Purpose of the Chapter:* It is the purpose of the present chapter to review some of the experimental facts which might make the task of engineering the learning process an easier and more intelligent task. As we approach these facts, it becomes pertinent to ask whether the guides to efficient learning bear a more intimate relation to any one of the various "types" of learning than they do to any of the other types. This question is to be answered in the affirmative. Most of the facts that are now known about efficient control of growth through profit from experience center upon those types of learning described by the phrases rote learning and trial-and-error learning, or learning through steady practice.[4]

If we may assume, as we have in the previous chapter, that rote learning and trial-and-error learning represent an attempt on the part of a person to complete in too short a time a task which is altogether too large for him, it may turn out that the engineering principles now to be discussed really apply to conditioning and to insightful learning as well as to repetitive learning. As matters stand, however, rote learning and trial-and-error learning are the types of learning which are actually used most frequently in the schoolroom, in the factory, and in almost every other place where profit from past experience is secured. Pending the course of future research which shall clear up such problems, we turn to the methods of engineering human growth through learning without further prejudice as to the type of learning involved.[5]

II. Whole versus Part Learning

1. *Introduction:* For all practical considerations, the learning situation is usually made up of a coherent and identifiable segment of stimulus material. We may be asked to learn a poem, run through a maze, acquire a new manual or verbal skill, develop a stance, attain a good posture, or solve a particular problem. Each of these expressions refers to an organized unit or segment of the environment and, at the end of the learning process, each unit ought to call for an equally organized pattern of response. It becomes perti-

[4] Cf. Gates, A. I., *Psychology for Students of Education* (rev. ed.). New York: The Macmillan Co., 1930, Chapter II and *passim.*
[5] One of the most useful and suggestive books in this field is Dunlap, K., *Habits, Their Making and Unmaking.* New York: Liveright Publishing Corp., 1932. See especially Chapter VI.

nent to inquire, therefore, whether the learning situation thus selected can be used most economically as a single unit or whether efficiency is better served by dividing the total unit into smaller parts. In this latter case, the student would learn each of the parts and then assemble them once more into the full unit. In short, we may ask whether it is better to learn a poem, a German-English vocabulary or a new skill in terms of large units or whether all such units should be separated into smaller parts.

In answering a question of this type, we may wish to know not only about efficiency with respect to the actual course of the learning process itself, but with respect to the degree and accuracy of retention for various intervals after the learning process has come to "completion." In general, the results of the hundreds of the experiments that have been done on this problem seem to say that, subject to the conditions named below, the whole method of learning is more economical than the part method, both with respect to the time consumed during the learning process itself and with respect to the degree of retention at various intervals after learning has taken place.[6]

2. *Historical Note:* The initial experiments to be done on any type of learning gave some suggestion as to the superiority of the whole method over the part method.[7] One of the first direct studies of the whole-part method made use of poetry and nonsense syllables. In one phase of this experiment, Steffens allowed his subjects to study such material without definite instructions, save that they were to commit it to memory as fast as they could. The subjects used a part method in the sense that they studied a few lines, added a few more, then repeated the first lines, added the second group to the first, and so on. In another part of the experiment, the subjects were required to learn poetry and nonsense syllables by repeating the entire unit from beginning to end at each reading. When the method naturally chosen by the subjects (the part method) was compared with the whole method, it was found that the latter procedure had effected a saving of nine per cent in the time consumed during learning. In the use of nonsense syllables the natural method adopted by the subjects was superior during the first ten days,

[6] Cf. Douglass, H. R., "A Summary of the Experimental Data on Certain Phases of Learning." *Ped. Sem.*, 1927, XXXIV, 92-117; McGeoch, G. O., "The Whole-part Problem." *Psychol. Bull.*, 1931, XXVIII, 713-739. This second title contains an excellent summary of this whole field of research.
[7] Ebbinghaus, H., *Memory* (trans. by H. A. Ruger and C. E. Bussenius). New York: Columbia Univ. Press, 1913. The original study, *Ueber das Gedächtnis*, was published in 1895.

but during the last twenty-four days, the situation was reversed.[8]

Pyle and Schneider used longer sections of material, the method in general being the same as that adopted by Steffens. Their conclusions run as follows:

". . . Without any exception, the method of the whole is more economical than is the part-method, and . . . the saving is much greater in the case of the long units, which required more than one sitting. The greatest saving in the short units was about eleven per cent in the twenty-line and the fifty-line units. In the larger units the saving was about twenty per cent in one sixty-line test and twenty-two per cent in the other, seventeen per cent in the 120 line test and twenty per cent in the 240 line test." [9]

As the researches have begun to pile up on this aspect of learning, it has turned out that the whole method is to be preferred over the part method only with respect to certain types of materials and with respect to certain subjects. As a matter of fact, a general survey of the literature seems to suggest (i) that the more meaningful the material is, the more efficient the whole method, (ii) that the more intelligent or quick the learner, the more efficient the whole method, and (iii) that learning of any sort is dependent to some extent on the magnitude of the unit to be acquired. Each of these modifications of the whole method of learning is worthy of further study.

3. *Meaning:* It has long been known that the relative effectiveness of whole versus part methods depends upon the nature of the material that is used. Ephrussi, for example, found that the whole method was superior to the part method except when nonsense syllables and vocabularies were used as the learning material.[10] As the student may know, nonsense syllables were introduced into the experimental psychology of learning, partly in order to simplify the conditions under which rate of learning may be measured, and partly in order to make comparisons between one learning process and another possible.[11]

When nonsense syllables are used in comparison with meaningful material, they seem to create the same sort of problem, save in an

---

[8] Steffens, L., "Experimentelle Beiträge zur Lehre vom ekönomischen Lehrnen." *Zsch. f. Psychol.,* 1900, XXII, 321-382.

[9] Pyle, W. H., and Schneider, J. C., "The Most Economical Unit for Committing to Memory." *J. Educ. Psychol.,* 1911, II, 133-142. See also Lakenan, M. E., "The Whole and Part Methods of Memorizing Poetry and Prose." *J. Educ. Psychol.,* 1913, IV, 189-198.

[10] Ephrussi, P., "Experimentelle Beiträge zur Lehre vom Gedächtnis." *Zsch. f. Psychol.,* 1904, XXXVII, 56-103, 161-224.

[11] Cf. Glaze, J. A., "The Association Value of Non-sense Syllables." *J. Genet. Psychol.,* 1928, XXXV, 255-267.

extreme form, as is created by the existence of meaningful material which differs from time to time in difficulty. In laboratory experiments, then, it is fruitful to compare not only nonsense syllables with meaningful material but to compare material at simpler levels of difficulty with material of greater difficulty. Sawdon, for example, using as his subjects boys who stood on about the same level of intelligence, was able to show that the whole method was superior when the material to be learned (poetry) was easy, rhythmical, and well unified by a plot running through the material. When, however, the passages to be learned were more difficult, the whole method was not so satisfactory. Furthermore, it was discovered that, if the time for learning was fairly limited, the part method became more effective.[12]

Meaningful material is to be distinguished from nonsense material partly in terms of the fact that all of the words in a poem or in a paragraph have a significance or a type of relatedness which is a product of their membership in a total configuration. It is possible, then, to emphasize the "belongingness" or "form quality" of meaningful material as opposed to nonsense material in order to discover the relative effectiveness of whole versus part methods under such conditions. An investigation of this type has been made by Guilford.[13] That is, Guilford was interested in finding out whether the presence of form or significance actually increased or decreased the rate of learning. It was discovered that learning becomes more efficient in direct proportion to an increase in the form or patterning of the material to be learned. It seems to be clear, then, that learning by wholes is to be preferred to learning by parts in direct proportion to the meaningfulness of the material or in direct proportion to the extent to which the learner can discover some sort of form or patterning that will unite discrete materials into a significant whole.[14]

4. *Intelligence:* As we have said above, learning by wholes appears to be dependent also upon differences in intelligence. In a study which used 113 college students who were asked to learn sections of poetry, Reed found that the whole method was superior for only twenty-six of his subjects.[15] Thirty-one subjects did best

[12] Sawdon, E. W., "Should Children Learn Poems in Wholes or Parts?" *Forum Educ.*, 1927, III, 182-197.
[13] Guilford, J. P., "The Rôle of Form in Learning." *J. Exper. Psychol.*, 1927, X, 415-423.
[14] For a discussion of this whole problem from the point of view of education, see Wheeler, R. H., and Perkins, F. T., *Principles of Mental Development.* New York: T. Y. Crowell Co., 1932, *passim.*
[15] Reed, H. B., "Part and Whole Methods of Learning." *J. Educ. Psychol.*, 1924, XV, 107-115, 248-249.

when they used the part method, that is, when separate stanzas were learned first as units and then the stanzas consolidated into the whole poem. Fifty-six students did best when they used what has been called a progressive method, that is, when the first stanza was learned, then the next, then the first and second together, then the third, then the first three together, and so on.

Similar results were gained by Pechstein who used the maze rather than nonsense syllables or poetry. Both white rats and college students served as subjects. The mazes were so arranged that they could be divided into four sections. Four modes of organizing the learning process were adopted, viz., the pure part method, the progressive part method, the direct repetitive method (where the first part was learned and then followed by the second part, and so on), and the reversed repetitive method wherein the fourth part was learned first, the third second, and the first added on as fast as each successive part was learned. The results showed clearly enough that both the progressive and indirect repetitive methods were superior to the undivided whole method; but it was discovered also that the higher the intelligence of the subjects (as measured by I.Q.) the more effective was their use of the undivided whole method.[16]

5. *Practical Conclusions:* It seems to be clear, then, that the effectiveness of the whole method is dependent upon one or more individual factors. One of the factors used in the experiment just cited is the intelligence factor, but it must be true that other factors such as the subject's age (which would also involve intelligence), the amount of training he has had, and other similar circumstances, will enter into the situation. In any case, we may summarize the experiments described up to this point somewhat as follows. The part method appears to be best for learners who have a low I.Q. and for material which is so difficult that the learner is not able to grasp its general significance or to gain a general perspective over it. It is not possible for very many people to bring a series of nonsense syllables into a coherent or meaningful whole and any failure on this score seems to work against the effectiveness of the whole method.[17]

It is not wise, perhaps, to try to draw too many inferences from such conclusions.[18] In the first place, practical experience has shown that learners of low intelligence, that is, those who are not in insti-

[16] Pechstein, L. A., "Whole versus Part Methods in Motor Learning: A Comparative Study." *Psychol. Monog.*, 1917, XXIII (No. 99). Also, "The Whole versus Part Methods in Learning." *Stud. Educ.*, 1926, XV, 181-186.
[17] McGeoch, J. A., "The Influence of Associative Value upon the Difficulty of Nonsense-syllable Lists." *J. Genet. Psychol.*, 1930, XXXVII, 421-426.
[18] Cf. Wheeler, R. H., and Perkins, F. T., *op. cit.*, pp. 279-286.

tutions for the feebleminded, should not be asked to meet learning situations which, when taken as single units, stand beyond their comprehension. This same consideration ought to hold true of students of average or even of superior intelligence. The experiments which we have cited certainly show that the process of learning is hindered or is cumbersome whenever the learning situation surpasses the ability of the subject to comprehend it.[19] The use of complex or difficult learning situations satisfied, to be sure, an older type of education wherein it was supposed that the more severe the intellectual exercise the greater the effectiveness of the exercise. We shall have to consider this phase of the problem of learning in the next chapter. In the meantime, we may conclude that the teacher who does not devise learning situations commensurate with the learner's level of maturation and comprehension is using poor judgment.[20]

A. THE VALUE OF NONSENSE SYLLABLES: This conclusion may be used as a source of earnest question concerning the relevance to education of experiments on learning which make use of nonsense syllables. It raises a question also concerning the relevance to education of experiments on learning among the lower animals, and especially of experiments which are of a strictly mechanical type. Both types of experimentation have been justified on the grounds that they attack the learning process at a much simpler level than can be reached in the case of human learning.[21] This is, to be sure, a reasonable argument, but one may well ask whether an attempt to learn meaningless material can say anything significant about the unique circumstances which distinguish meaningful or intelligent learning from other varieties of learning.

After all is said and done, the student in the classroom does not learn witlessly unless the teacher is obtuse enough to lay out unintelligent situations. In short, then, educational psychology may take simplified forms of the learning process for what they are worth; but it should keep an eagle eye open for all of those aspects of human learning which make it distinctive.[22] It is barely possible that studies intended to lead to a more successful engineering of the learning process which make use of incoherent or nonsense material

[19] Cf. McGeoch, J. A., and Oberschelp, V. J., "The Influence of Length of Problem and of Transfer upon Rational Learning and Its Retention." *J. Gen. Psychol.,* 1930, IV, 154-168.
[20] Cf. Lough, J. E., "The Development of Memory in School Children." *Psychol. Rev.,* 1903, X, 154-155.
[21] Cf. Munn, N. L., *An Introduction to Animal Psychology.* Boston: Houghton Mifflin Co., 1933, p. xii and *passim.*
[22] Cf. Wheeler, R. H., and Perkins, F. T., *op. cit.,* Chapter XX and *passim.*

may be quite beside the point. This argument is important not only in the present setting but in any adequate appreciation of the problems of transfer of training. We shall return to it, therefore, in a later chapter.

B. THE AMOUNT OF MATERIAL: There is still another aspect of learning which has a direct bearing upon the use of whole versus part methods. It is easy to see that a subject of low intelligence might discern the total meaning or form of small amounts of material and yet remain quite incompetent with respect to larger units. It is easy to see, also, that even a very capable learner might lose the thread of coherency in a unit of material, if the material were very extensive. In short, then, both the specific problem of whole versus part learning and the general problem of the relation between length of material and speed of learning would depend upon the size of the unit used. One aspect of this problem has been studied by Lyon.[23] Nonsense syllables, digits, poetry, and prose were used as the learning material. The material differed in length. Certain significant differences were also made in the way in which the time available was spent. Among other results it was found that, whereas it might take only five minutes to learn twenty-four digits, two hours and thirty-four minutes might be required to learn 200 digits. That is, the ratio between the lengths of the two sets of material was as one to eight, whereas the ratio between the times taken to learn the two sets was as one to thirty-one. It would seem fair to draw the inference that, as material is increased in length beyond the power of the individual to grasp it as a unit, the learning time mounts very rapidly. Similar results have been obtained by Robinson and Heron.[24]

6. *Conclusion:* It thus appears that the principle of learning by wholes rather than by parts is wrapped up with a large number of related factors and that it is intimately dependent upon the fundamental nature of learning. It appears, also, that the principle might be used as a symptom of the genetic course of learning and, perhaps, of maturation in other respects as well, for the total units that can be learned most effectively by young children are much smaller than those which can be learned by older individuals. The same sort of relationship is to be found between size of unit and intelligence.

[23] Lyon, D. O., "The Relation of Length of Material to the Time Taken for Learning, and the Optimum Distribution of Time." *J. Educ. Psychol.,* 1914, V, 1-9. See, also, Skaggs, E. B., "The Relation of Length of Material and Number of Repetitions Needed to Learn." *J. Gen. Psychol.,* 1929, II, 150-152.
[24] Robinson, E. S., and Heron, W. T., "Results of Variations in Length of Memorized Material." *J. Exper. Psychol.,* 1922, V, 428-448.

ENGINEERING THE LEARNING PROCESS

In short, then, learning by wholes versus learning by parts would seem to suggest that something more than sheer repetition is involved since the repetition factor is always conjoined with a range of comprehension factor. There is no reason to doubt but that continued research will greatly clarify these several problems.

III. THE DISTRIBUTION OF PRACTICE AND REST PERIODS

1. *Introduction:* If a learning program could be so wisely arranged that the learner would never face a situation that was too difficult for him, that is, if all learning could be of the quick or insightful type which is described so frequently by Gestalt psychology, there would be no question of the relation between practice periods and rest periods. That is to say, there would be no such relation unless it were found desirable to interrupt single acts of complete learning by short rest intervals.

In actual practice, however, very little profit from past experience is actually instantaneous. The existence of rote or purely repetitive learning, on the one hand, and the argument that trial-and-error learning constitutes a unique type of learning, on the other, emphasize the fact that processes of learning hold many properties in common with growth or maturation. One of the most important of these common properties lies in the fact that both are somehow contingent upon the passage of time.[25] Growth is not instantaneous and neither is trial-and-error learning or repetitive learning. Under the impetus of certain types of practice, the structures involved in repetitive learning maturate or in some other way become changed so that a skill emerges out of awkwardness. It becomes important to inquire, therefore, how the period of maturation or growth through learning may best be handled. Should one force the process as is frequently done in the growing of vegetables by the aid of artificial light or is this type of learning functionally dependent upon the passage of a given amount of time and therefore resistant to forcing?[26]

2. *Experimental Results:* As is so often the case in the field of learning, the first studies on this problem go back to Ebbinghaus. Ebbinghaus laid out six lists of nonsense syllables, each made up of twelve items. Each of these lists was learned at a single sitting with

---

[25] Cf. Filter, R. O., and Held, O. C., *The Growth of an Ability*. Baltimore: Warwick and York, 1930, *passim*.
[26] Cf. Gesell, A., "Maturation and the Patterning of Behavior," in Murchison, C. (Ed.), *Handbook of Child Psychology* (2nd ed.). Worcester, Mass.: Clark Univ. Press, 1933, Chapter IV.

an average of 68.3 repetitions per list. Twenty-four hours later the relearning of the list required an average of 6.8 repetitions per list. When, however, similar lists of syllables were learned to the point of one correct recall on each of three successive days, 37.9 repetitions, distributed over a period of three days, gave essentially the same degree of retention after twenty-four hours as did 68.3 repetitions in immediate succession.[27] Yost was the first investigator to make a more thorough study of this problem. His results confirmed those secured by Ebbinghaus. Not only did he find that concentrated repetitions of the material led to poorer retention than did the distribution of the same number of repetitions but he was able to show, also, that the effectiveness of distributed work was not to be explained by the lesser degree of fatigue that might be developed because of a shorter but more intensive work period.[28]

These facts, gained as they were from human subjects, have been verified in the case of animal experimentation. Ulrich, for example, caused white rats to practice at the skill of lifting a latch in order to enter a box and secure food. The rats were given one, three, and five trials daily. Other experiments made use of a maze and of an inclined plane box. The general conclusion drawn from these experiments was that the more infrequent the trials the more economical the learning as measured by the total number of trials. Obviously a greater number of days would be required with greater distribution of effort.[29]

Warden's experiments likewise made use of a maze. Four groups of subjects were trained with one trial per day, the length of the interpolated interval varying from six hours for one group to three days for another group. The results showed that the interpolation of a twelve-hour "rest" period was the most favorable condition for learning no matter whether it occurred after one, three, or five consecutive trials. It was determined, moreover, that one trial is to be preferred to three or five trials under all of the conditions established during the experiment.[30]

It is not as yet known how far the distribution of work periods may be carried, and neither has the optimal amount of material to be used at any single sitting been determined. In an experiment by

[27] Ebbinghaus, H., *op. cit., passim.*
[28] Yost, A., "Die Assoziationsfestigkeit in ihre Abhängigkeit von der Verteilung der Wiederholungen." *Zsch. f. Psychol.,* 1897, XIV, 436-472.
[29] Ulrich, J. L., "Distribution of Effort in Learning in the White Rat." *Behav. Monog.,* 1915, II (No. 10).
[30] Warden, C. J., "Distribution of Practice in Animal Learning." *Comp. Psychol. Monog.,* 1923, I (No. 3).

Perkins, lists of nonsense syllables were given sixteen repetitions. These repetitions were divided into periods of one, two, four, and eight readings. The intervals were one, two, three, and four days in length. There were, then, sixteen different combinations of repetitions and intervals. The results showed clearly enough that one reading of the nonsense syllables on each successive day until sixteen days had passed was the most economical type of learning where learning was measured by the number of nonsense syllables that could be recalled after a two weeks' interval. Under these conditions the subjects recalled 79 per cent of the syllables. Two readings of the list for eight days gave a retention value of only 43 per cent; four readings a day for four days gave a retention value of 25 per cent; and eight readings a day for two days gave a retention value of only 9 per cent. In other words, when the total time devoted to learning was held relatively constant, shorter work periods widely distributed proved to be most advantageous.[31] This study may be compared with a similar study on logical material. Austin asked his subjects to read logical material either once a day for five successive days or five times at one sitting. When the results were computed for immediate recall, it was found that concentrated effort was very slightly superior to distributed effort; but after a two weeks' interval, distributed effort was superior to concentrated effort by 24.13 per cent.[32]

3. *Explanations of Distributed Effort:* These few examples, drawn almost at random from scores of studies on the relation between concentrated and distributed practice periods, show clearly enough that distributed effort leads to much greater economy in learning.[33] Various theories have been proposed to account for this fact. The Müller and Pilzecker theory of perseveration argues that the neural events developed during practice persevere for an appreciable length of time after the practice periods have come to an end. It is inferred that the neural events thus set going will be retained to better advantage if they are allowed to become "fixed" without interference.[34]

Lashley, on the contrary, has argued that there may be no single

---

[31] Perkins, N. L., "The Value of Distributed Repetitions in Rote Learning," *Brit. J. Psychol.*, 1914, VII, 253-261.
[32] Austin, S. D. M., "A Study in Logical Memory," *Amer. J. Psychol.*, 1921, XXXII, 370-403.
[33] A very useful list of titles on this and other features of learning has been prepared by McGeoch, J. A., "The Psychology of Human Learning: A Bibliography." *Psychol. Bull.*, 1933, XXX, 1-62.
[34] Cf. Müller, G. E., and Pilzecker, A., "Experimentelle Beiträge zur Lehre vom Gedächtnis," *Zsch. f. Psychol.*, 1900, Erg. 1.

438 INTRODUCTION TO EDUCATIONAL PSYCHOLOGY

explanation of the increased efficiency of distributed effort. He has been able to show, for example, that the behavior of white rats in learning to run a maze shows less diversity of action during concentrated trials than is the case during distributed effort. In other words, concentrated trials call for the repetition of the same type of errors. Moreover, concentrated effort may bring into the situation such factors as fatigue and loss of interest.[35]

Still another theory has been advanced by Snoddy. Snoddy remarked that, as practice periods continued, his subjects altered the character of their response to the maze. Whereas at first they had been cautious in striving for accuracy, they soon became careless and strove for greater speed. This meant, of course, a spread of movement and a loss of coördination which Snoddy called the "irradiation pattern." Distributed practice periods would, of course, eliminate this factor in the learning process.[36]

This explanation of the higher value of distributed learning is favored also by Wheeler.[37] Wheeler argues, moreover, for the influence of such factors as the growth potential. Since it is the growth potential that is raised by stimulation and which is resolved by maturation and since maturation takes time, the introduction of rest intervals between work periods would serve three purposes, viz., "(1) to permit a replenishing of the lower energy supply; (2) to overcome the effects of overstimulation, which are faulty energy distributions, and (3) to permit maturation with its increased differentiation of energy patterns." [38]

4. *Conclusions:* Regardless of the arguments over the fundamental nature of learning, it still remains true that practically all of the learning that takes place in the schoolroom is of the same general type that has been studied in such experiments as we have mentioned. This form of learning is, therefore, a function of the passage of time. It would seem, then, that the massing of effort would be unlikely to hasten the kind of change or growth involved in learning. As we have already seen, in our discussion of the relations between maturation and learning, practice periods administered to small children who are just on the threshold of some major accomplishment are not effective in hastening the development of

---

[35] Lashley, K. S., "A Causal Factor in the Relation of the Distribution of Practice to the Rate of Learning," *J. Anim. Behav.,* 1917, VII, 139-142; "A Simple Maze: With Data on the Relation of the Distribution of Practice to the Rate of Learning," *Psychol. Bull.,* 1918, I, 353-367.
[36] Snoddy, G. S., "An Experimental Analysis of a Case of Trial and Error Learning on a Human Subject," *Psychol. Monog.,* 1920, XX (No. 124).
[37] Wheeler, R. H., and Perkins, F. T., *op. cit.,* pp. 339 ff.
[38] *Ibid.,* p. 339.

skill. A major portion of the facts, then, both experimental and theoretical, seem to support the conclusion that distributed effort is a more efficient way of engineering the process of learning than is concentrated effort.

It becomes necessary, at this point, to insert a word of caution. The principle that learning becomes more efficient, the greater the distribution of the practice periods, has been determined by taking a concise bit of material and keeping this material identical from one training period to the next. It need not follow that a lesson in geography or history should be subject to the same principle. The hour spent in the study of geography is not spent by going over and over again the same limited amount of material. On the contrary, it represents a total practice period within which there may be a good many shifts in the nature of the material to be learned. As Dunlap remarks of this fact, "The conditions are essentially different from those in the verse-learning, and results of the experiments under the one condition cannot be directly applied to the work under the other conditions. Unfortunately, most of the 'principles of learning' formulated for school work, and supposedly based on psychological experiments, entirely overlook these essential conditions, and although they may accidentally be correct, they have no scientific basis." [39]

IV. Types of Inhibition

1. *Introduction:* It is only with the greatest difficulty that engineers have been able to develop telephone transmission so that more than one message can be sent over a given wire at the same time. If telephone wires were of such a character that they preserved in their own structure a history of all the messages that had been transmitted, the chances are that they would soon become totally unsuited for such work. In any case, we get a truer picture of telephonic communication when we think of a system of wires, each of which is, for the moment, the bearer of a single message and which then returns to a neutral state in preparation for a second message, none of its previous history being retained.

There was a time when the nervous system was thought of in this same way except that the individual paths of conduction in the nervous system did somehow have the property of conserving their own history.[40] There were, however, such an immense number of

[39] Dunlap, K., *op. cit.*, p. 101.
[40] Cf. Dewey, J., "The Reflex Arc Concept in Psychology." *Psychol. Rev.*, 1896, III, 357-370.

possible connections in the whole system that a normal lifetime could scarcely make use of them all. This theory of nerve function was acceptable because it was simple; but it has now been shown that the nervous system does not act after the fashion of a telephone system. On the contrary, there is considerable reason to believe that large areas of the system are in use during any given stimulus-response situation.[41]

As an illustration, we may take one of Lashley's experiments on learning in animals. Lashley taught a monkey how to open a latch box with its right hand when its left hand and arm were paralyzed by an operation in the right cerebral hemisphere. After the problem had been learned, the monkey's right hand and arm were paralyzed by an operation on the left cerebral hemisphere. In the meantime, the left side of the body had recovered its normal functions. The subject was able successfully to open the latch box with the unpracticed left hand and arm. This experiment would seem to indicate that a *monkey,* rather than a set of connections in the nervous system, had learned how to open a box. The results also suggest that the nervous system functions in some other manner than that described by isolated connecting fibres.[42]

From these considerations we can infer that several processes of learning which make use of a common mechanism may be subject to interference simply because any present process of learning must be superimposed upon previous processes or stand in the way of a future process. This type of interference is known as inhibition.[43] Retroactive inhibition describes the general fact that any single process of learning may exert an adverse influence on material that has already been learned. Mutual and reciprocal inhibition describe the interference that may occur between two simultaneous periods of learning. Forward inhibition describes the fact that a present act of learning may place an obstacle in the way of future attempts to learn.

If we were to extend these several concepts to all of the phenomena covered by the terms "learning" and "forgetting," we might say that any act of learning whatsoever interferes in some way or other with almost every other act of learning. This sort of inter-

---

[41] Cf. Lashley, K. S., *Brain Mechanisms and Intelligence.* Chicago: Univ. of Chicago Press, 1929, *passim.*

[42] Cf. Lashley, K. S., "The Retention of Motor Habits after the Destruction of the So-called Motor Areas in Primates." *Arch. Neurol. and Psychol.,* 1924, XII, 249-276. See also the discussion of the nature of learning in Koffka, K., *The Growth of the Mind.* New York: Harcourt, Brace and Co., 1924, Chapter IV.

[43] Much of the information about this topic has been assembled by Skaggs, E. B., *The Major Forms of Inhibition in Man.* Chicago: Univ. of Chicago Press, 1931.

ference could not take place if each specific learning process involved its own particular conduction paths. Since the evidence seems to show that whole sections of the nervous system may function as a unit, any one of its states must be superimposed upon preceding states. This same structure is called upon to perform an exceedingly complex variety of services. That it cannot do so easily is remarked by the phrase, "retroactive inhibition."

2. *Experimental Results:* The first experimental work on this problem of interference was done by Müller and Pilzecker.[44] Typical experiments in this field usually take the following form. There is, first, some definite learning task which is followed by some other task which is called the interpolated material. Following the completion of this second task, recall for the material first learned is asked for or the initial task is done over again. Müller and Pilzecker used nonsense syllables for the initial learning material. The interpolated material consisted either of other nonsense syllables or of the study of landscape pictures. In order to draw comparisons concerning the effect of different types of interpolated material on learning, other subjects were asked to "do nothing" after each learning period. In the nine experiments performed by Müller and Pilzecker, definite evidence of a retroactive process which worked detrimentally upon the preceding learning was found. It appeared that if the interpolated work was introduced immediately after the original learning, the retroactive effect was greater than if it was introduced after six minutes of rest. Moreover, the more intense the effort during the intervening period, the greater the detrimental effect.[45]

This initial work was sufficient to establish retroactive inhibition as a definite obstacle in the way of efficient learning. Subsequent work has sought to find out what the more precise conditions are which favor or disfavor the retroactive effect. Tolman, for example, studied the affective value of materials on degree of retroaction, the effect of caffeine, and the relation between degree of inhibition and changes of efficiency during the day.[46] Words, numbers, and nonsense syllables were used as the initial learning material. The interpolated activity consisted of learning either tables of numbers or colored consonants. It was found that lists of words which were pleasant were less susceptible to inhibition than were

---

[44] Müller, G. E., and Pilzecker, A., "Experimentelle Beiträge zur Lehre vom Gedächtnis," *Zsch. f. Psychol.*, 1900, Ergbd. 1.
[45] Cf. McGeoch, J. A., *op. cit.*, for titles of experimental work in this field.
[46] Tolman, E. C., "Retroactive Inhibition as Effected by Conditions of Learning," *Psychol. Monog.*, 1917-1918, XXV (No. 107).

words that had an indifferent affective quality. Subjects who had taken a small amount of caffeine were less subject to inhibition than they would have been otherwise. Finally, it was shown that material learned during inefficient hours of the day showed greater effects of inhibition than did lists of words learned during the more efficient hours of the day.[47]

Robinson has also studied some of the factors involved in retroactive inhibition. One of his main purposes was to ascertain whether or not similarity between the initial learning task and the interpolated work increased or diminished the retroactive effect. The original learning involved the use of eight four-place numbers. The interpolated activity consisted in learning eight nonsense syllables, memorizing a series of twenty consonants, learning poetry, multiplying four-place by four-place numbers, and reading simple prose.

It is not easy to say offhand how similar or dissimilar this interpolated activity was with respect to the original activity; but it is fairly clear that learning a second series of four-place numbers is more like the first learning of such a series than the reading of prose would be. In any case, Robinson was able to show that the factor named by degree of similarity was the most important factor in retroaction. He found practically no inhibition, for example, when the learning of eight four-place numbers was followed by the reading of simple prose.[48]

The situation with respect to similarity is not quite so simple, however, as these results appear to make it. Further studies have shown that there is a certain combination of like and unlike elements in the learning and in the interpolated task which produces the greatest amount of inhibition. It is sometimes difficult to say just what this combination shall be, but in any case retroactive inhibition is brought to a minimum if a learning task is followed by a task which differs as far as possible from the initial task.[49]

Sufficient evidence has been gained to show that the amount of retroactive inhibition increases in inverse proportion to the degree of original learning. That is, if an initial task which has been but barely learned is followed by some other task, recall for the barely

---

[47] As the student knows, efficiency shows wide diurnal variations. Cf. Hollingworth, H. L., "Variations in Efficiency During the Working Day." *Psychol. Rev.,* 1914, XXI, 473-491.

[48] Robinson, E. S., "Some Factors Determining the Degree of Retroactive Inhibition," *Psychol. Monog.,* 1920, XXVIII (No. 128).

[49] Skaggs, E. B., "Further Studies in Retroactive Inhibition," *Psychol. Monog.,* 1925, XXXIV (No. 161).

learned material will be greatly interfered with. On the contrary, if the initial material is highly overlearned the degree of retroactive inhibition decreases accordingly.[50] Moreover, it has been shown that the amount of interference varies with the quickness with which a subsequent task is begun. Work that is introduced immediately after the initial learning produces the greatest amount of inhibition.[51] To say the same thing in another way, when the greatest efficiency is sought for any particular learning situation, it should be followed by as complete a state of relaxation as possible.

3. *Practical Consequences:* The importance of these various studies for education can hardly be overestimated.[52] A day's work in a schoolroom, for example, is a temporal interval. A great many different types of activities have to be crowded into this interval. The phenomena of retroactive inhibition would seem to indicate that an optimal sequence of activities could be devised which would create during the day the least amount of interference. It is clear, of course, that the nature of learning makes it forever impossible to escape all interference. The phenomena of forgetting are, no doubt, to be accounted for, partly, in terms of such interference. This is not to say, however, that optimal conditions could not be discovered which would subject the learning tasks of any one day or of any one period to the least amount of interference. It is clear, then, that teachers and administrators must accept the responsibility of seeing to it that experiments of the order we have mentioned—and which have been done, for the most part, in the laboratory—are repeated with respect to actual periods of instruction in the schoolroom.[53]

4. *Associative Inhibition:* In addition to the sort of inhibition just described, there are a great many other places where similar phenomena are to be discovered. There is, for example, that kind of inhibition which is called associative inhibition. Retroactive inhibition describes the fact that a later learning activity may interfere in some way with an earlier activity. Associative inhibition, on the contrary, describes the fact that an earlier learning may interfere with later learning. These facts were also examined by

[50] McGeoch, J. A., "The Influence of Degree of Learning upon Retroactive Inhibition," *Amer. J. Psychol.*, 1929, XLI, 252-262.
[51] Skaggs, E. B., *op. cit.*, Chapter III.
[52] Cf. Gengerelli, J. A., "Mutual Interference in the Evolution of Concepts." *Amer. J. Psychol.*, 1927, XXXVIII, 639-646.
[53] Cf. Reed, H. B., "Distributed Practice in Reading." *J. Educ. Psychol.*, 1924, XV, 248-249.

Müller and Pilzecker.[54] Further studies have been made by Kline,[55] by Bergstrom,[56] and by Culler.[57]

These experiments have shown that associative inhibition, like retroactive inhibition, depends, in part, upon the degree of the initial learning. It depends, also, upon general attitude and attention. If, having established associations between two given situations, one then tries to reassociate one of the initial situations with a third, associative inhibition will be considerably minimized if full attention is paid to the new task and the old association forgotten as far as possible.[58]

Among the other places where interference may occur, there are to be mentioned affective and emotional situations,[59] cognitive types of reproduction,[60] and the relation between inhibition and transfer of training.[61] We may say again, then, that the phenomena of inhibition in one form or another exercise a marked and significant influence upon all aspects of learning, retention, and recall. In view of this fact it would seem to be essential that educational psychology should acquaint itself thoroughly with the facts.

V. Learning and Recitation

1. *Introduction:* We have already met the fact that learning is a form of doing. It would seem to follow from this proposition that the processes of learning would become most effective in direct proportion to the amount of relative activity engaged in during the process. As we have seen, this is an especially important feature of that type of learning described as rote learning, on the one hand, and as trial-and-error learning, on the other. This is not to say, of course, that learning is a process whereby we practice, on the first occasion, the precise thing we hope to do on the last occasion. On

---

[54] Müller, G. E., and Pilzecker, A., *op. cit., passim.*
[55] Kline, L. W., "An Experimental Study of Associative Inhibition." *J. Exper. Psychol.,* 1921, IV, 270-299.
[56] Bergstrom, J. A., "Experiments upon Physiological Memory by Means of the Interference of Associations." *Amer. J. Psychol.,* 1893, V, 356-369.
[57] Culler, E. A., "Interference and Adaptability." *Arch. of Psychol.,* 1912, III (No. 24).
[58] Cf. Dashiell, J. F., "An Experimental Isolation of Higher Level Habits." *J. Exper. Psychol.,* 1924, VII, 391-397.
[59] Meltzer, H., "The Present Status of Experimental Studies in the Relationship of Feeling and Memory." *Psychol. Rev.,* 1930, XXXVII, 124-139; Harden, L. M., "The Effect of Emotional Reactions upon Retention." *J. Gen. Psychol.,* 1930, III, 197-221.
[60] Shephard, J. F., and Fogelsonger, H. M., "Studies in Association and Inhibition." *Psychol. Rev.,* 1913, XX, 290-311.
[61] Webb, L. W., "Transfer of Training and Retroaction." *Psychol. Monog.,* 1917, XXIV (No. 104).

the contrary, learning has a rather intimate kinship with growth or maturation. The mechanisms involved in learning develop with respect to a stimulating situation and one of the necessary features of maturation is exercise.

2. *Experimental Studies:* Some of the experimental work having to do with this mode of effecting economy in learning runs as follows. We may consider, as most relevant to education, a series of experiments upon the effect of recitation, for recitation means action, at least in the vocal apparatus. Kühn gave three types of material to his subjects, viz., (i) vertical rows of twelve nonsense syllables, (ii) vertical rows of twelve one-syllable substantives, and (iii) short verses. One group of subjects merely read and reread the material until each person in the group was satisfied that the material had been learned. The other group recited the material whenever it wished. In general, the subjects who had recited the material were superior in rate of learning. Their superiority showed most clearly, however, with respect to the nonsense syllables. It was least in the case of the verses. The same facts held true when, after twenty-four, forty-eight, and ninety-six hours, the material was relearned.[62]

A variety of questions can be asked about the general fact thus established in Kühn's experiment. We might wish to know, for example, just when, with respect to learning, recitation should begin in order that it may be most effective. Witasek has answered this question. The subjects learned lists of nonsense syllables arranged in ten pairs in each list. Some subjects read the list aloud. Others listened as the experimenter spoke one word of each pair, the learner trying to recite the second member of the pair. In all variations of the experiment the recitation group was superior to the reading group. The reading method, moreover, was found to be subject to the law of diminishing returns, for its value declined very rapidly after the first six repetitions. From then on, for a considerable period of time, recitation stood out as the better method, but ultimately it, too, became subject to the law of diminishing returns.[63]

One of the most comprehensive studies on recitation has been made by Gates who, instead of using laboratory procedures, worked directly with school children under schoolroom conditions, and with methods common to the schoolroom. The material to be learned

[62] Kühn, A., "Über Einprägung durch Lesen und durch Rezitieren." *Zsch. f. Psychol.*, 1914, LXVIII, 396-481.
[63] Witasek, S., "Über Lesen und Rezitieren in Ihre Beziehungen zum Gedächtnis." *Zsch. f. Psychol.*, 1907, XLIV, 161-185, 246-282.

was of three types, viz., nonsense syllables, unconnected material, and connected material fashioned after the biographical sketches in *Who's Who*. The subjects were divided into groups which were distinguished from one another in terms of the relative amounts of reading and recitation used. One group spent the entire time in reading, while another group used only the recitation method. Several other groups progressively decreased the amount of reading time with a proportionate increase in the amount of recitation.

The results showed, in general, that, as the amount of recitation was increased, the average recall also increased. When eighty per cent of the time was devoted to recitation, for example, and only twenty per cent to reading, the recitation method proved twice as effective as a pure reading method. Of the six ratios between reading and recitation which were used, number five proved to be most advantageous for subjects in the sixth, seventh, and eighth grades, whereas number four proved most efficient for subjects in the fourth and fifth grades. Method five consisted of twenty per cent reading and eighty per cent recitation, whereas method four consisted of forty per cent reading and sixty per cent recitation.[64]

It is not as yet certain, however, that these results can be transported directly into the schoolroom. Gates' study, for example, shows that recitation is more efficient with respect to nonsense syllables than with respect to the biographical material. In other words, the value of recitation would seem to depend upon the meaningfulness of the material used. This fact raises a very important question about learning for it seems to suggest that there may be some significant difference between ideational learning, on the one hand, and motor learning, on the other.[65]

It ought to be clear that skill in golf, typewriting, handwriting, and other motor accomplishments cannot be increased simply by hearing someone talk about the skill. Neither can it be increased by inactive imitation or wishful thinking. The person who desires really to become expert in any sort of motor skill thinks nothing of spending a good many hours in practice, and he thus gives witness to the fact that motor learning at least is certainly dependent upon action. In the case of ideational or associative learning, however, the student is asked to take *thought* about the matter. Let us say

[64] Gates, A. I., "Recitation as a Factor in Memorizing." *Arch. Psychol.*, 1917, VI (No. 40).
[65] Johnson, H. M., "A Simpler Principle of Explanation of Imaginative and Ideational Behavior and of Learning." *J. Comp. Psychol.*, 1927, VII, 187-235; Peterson, J. C., "The Higher Mental Processes in Learning." *Psychol. Monog.*, 1920, XXVIII (No. 129).

# ENGINEERING THE LEARNING PROCESS

that he has just read this page up to this point. The act of reading, together with the act of comprehension, will have given him a certain amount of information. He may now close the book and review this information, as the saying goes, in his head. Neither the student himself, nor anyone else, can doubt but that reviews of this type make some contribution to learning. The contribution appears to be made, however, in the absence of activity unless "taking thought" can be described as activity.[66]

There is no one, perhaps, who would say that taking thought about a matter implies no activity at all. Students of psychology disagree widely from one another, however, in the way in which they attempt to describe this activity. As we have seen, there are some who will limit the activity entirely to mental processes. Others believe that the mental processes are simple concomitants of events in the nervous system and in the muscles, especially in the muscles in the vocal apparatus. Still others believe that action in the vocal apparatus is the most essential feature of ideational or associative learning. It has been most fruitful to use as a working hypothesis either the second or the third of these opinions. In other words, if recitation is to make learning more effective, the recitation may be of the common verbal type where the student actually speaks out that which he is attempting to learn or it may be of the implicit type in which he speaks over to himself that which he is in the process of learning.[67]

3. *Learning and Understanding:* There is still another phase of the relation between activity and rate of learning. This relation may be expressed by saying that there is a difference between the actual skill possessed by a person and his general good judgment in using the skill in an appropriate way. In taking account of the profit that seems to come from past experience during what may be called the off-season period of training, it has been remarked that a continuous practice period may be subject to the law of diminishing returns. That is, more recent periods of practice are less fruitful in actually bringing about an improvement in skill than were earlier periods of practice. If the learner has discontinued his practice for several weeks or for several months, however, it has been noted that, on resuming his training, he will appear to be more pro-

---

[66] The student will see that here again we are touching upon the relation between mental processes and behavior. See above, pp. 65 ff.
[67] Thorndike, E. L., "Ideo-motor Action," *Psychol. Rev.,* 1913, XX, 91-106; Barlow, M. C., "The Rôle of Articulation in Memorizing." *J. Exper. Psychol.,* 1928, XI, 306-312; Heidbreder, E. F., Problem Solving in Children and Adults." *J. Genet. Psychol.,* 1928, XXXV, 522-545.

ficient than he was at the end of his last training period. Moreover, it will sometimes appear that he is more proficient than he will be for several subsequent occasions. The inference is that, during the interval, a considerable amount of actual improvement in a person's skills may have taken place even though the skills themselves have not actually been practiced.[68]

There are several ways in which this apparent profit from training during periods when training is not actually under way may be explained. In the first place, it is clear that many persons disobey the principle of distributed effort in their attempt to acquire a new skill. It can be shown that failure to distribute practice periods properly may create a considerable amount of interference and it may also lead to training in bad habits as well as in good habits. Furthermore, long-continued periods of training easily become subject to fatigue effects.

In the second place, it is hardly possible to say that no training at all takes place during off-season periods. This training may be of two sorts. On the one hand, a learner may actually rehearse, by word of mouth, the manual movements he ought to make in order to do the thing well that he has been practicing. As we shall see in a later section of this chapter, this factor has sometimes been used to explain the value of primacy as a means of learning. The law of primacy states that those parts of a learning task which occur first are learned more readily than other parts. On the other hand, a learner may, during an off-season period, rehearse not so much the actual movements he intends to make as the variable situations in which such movements might be used.

As a typical illustration, let us think of an athlete who has practiced his skills intensively during the season of play and who then suspends most of these habits until the next season. During the interval, he will naturally recall his previous experiences, including the way in which he has behaved under a great many different circumstances. It not infrequently happens that such an athlete will try to imagine himself in play again; but he will now use himself and his skills to much better advantage than he did when games were actually under way.

Obviously, any imaginative attempts of this sort to improve the quality of one's game might lead readily to an increase in what may be called good judgment. In other words, habits and skills are to

---

[68] William James has carried this fact into modern psychology in the saying that we learn to skate in the summer time and to swim in the winter time. Cf. James, W., *Principles of Psychology*. New York: Henry Holt and Co., 1890, Vol. I, p. 110.

be valued not only in terms of their absolute perfection as habits and skills but in terms of the total situations in which they may be placed. One man may be ever so skilful in a variety of movement patterns and yet quite fail to capitalize on his skill simply because he does not know when to use one skill and when to use another. Another person, much inferior in aptitude, may actually surpass his more skilful comrade, solely because he is able to make the very best use of such measures of skill as he actually possesses.[69]

4. *Summary:* Let us draw the conclusion, then, that all forms of learning can be increased greatly in effectiveness in direct proportion as the learner takes an active part in the learning process. In short, learning is doing. To be sure, many students give the appearance of letting information pass in one ear and out of the other, but even where such an extreme degree of passivity occurs, something will be retained. It will be retained, that is, if the information has actually entered one ear, for the very act of perception is really an act. It implies a readjustment of the mechanisms of hearing and, perhaps, even a favorable posture of the body. Truly effective learning, however, requires still more intensive forms of favorable posture. The learner must have the intent to learn and he must, moreover, make some sort of response to the stimulus-patterns that are presented to him.[70]

The converse of these facts is brought out in the studies that have been made on the effect of manual guidance during learning processes. If there is any time when a student might be wholly passive with respect to a learning situation, it would occur when the teacher or some other person moves the bodily members of the learner in the way in which they should be moved. As a typical case, let us take that method of teaching the art of writing which requires either that the teacher shall move the arms and fingers of the learner or which requires that the learner shall trace a copy through transparent paper. Almost all of the studies that have been carried out in this field show that rate of learning and degree of retention are not aided by this method of instruction. In some cases they are actually impeded.[71]

[69] Unpublished data from the University of Illinois Laboratories for Research in Athletics.
[70] Sanderson, S., "Intention in Motor Learning." *J. Exper. Psychol.*, 1929, XII, 463-489; Eliasberg, W., "Recent Work on the Psychology of Forming Concepts." *Psychol. Bull.*, 1923, XX, 427-437.
[71] Carr, H. A., "The Influence of Extraneous Controls in the Learning Process." *Psychol. Rev.*, 1919, XXVI, 287-294; Twitmyer, E. M., Visual Guidance in Motor Learning." *Amer. J. Psychol.*, 1931, XLIII, 165-187.

VI. Motivation and Learning

1. *Introduction:* There was a time when teachers took it for granted that processes of learning were subject to only one principle, viz., the intent or the "will" of the learner to master the material presented to him. During the earlier stages of the development of experimental psychology, this method of increasing the efficiency of learning processes came to be looked upon with considerable suspicion for the term "will" implied something about the nature of the mind which was not compatible with the trend of experimental work. Now, however, subject to certain reinterpretations, the intent or the "will" of the learner is known to exert a marked influence upon rate of learning. As a matter of fact, the experimental work in this field is so large that we shall be able to sample only a part of it.

2. *Incidental Learning:* In understanding the relationship between motivation and rate of progress it is necessary to remind ourselves of a possible distinction between true learning and the effects of mere practice, where there is no intent to learn. There is some reason to believe that inattentive repetition of an act will simply make the act more automatic. Learning, however, is best described as a progressive modification of behavior rather than a progressive fixation of any given response. Even in cases where the learner is more or less witless regarding the learning process, certain progressive modifications can take place, for action in the nervous system is more than coextensive with "conscious" action.

This is shown by the phenomena of incidental learning. Myers, for example, asked a group of subjects to judge some of the minor characteristics of certain familiar objects such as a dollar bill or a coin. It was assumed by the experimenter that most persons have learned such characteristics only as an incident to other types of learning, say, the value of a coin, its size and its relation to other types of money. The reports of his subjects showed clearly enough that incidental learning, as measured in this way, was highly subject to error, but that the size of the error decreased with an increase in the age of the subjects. In further experiments, Myers asked his subjects to read words under conditions that seemed to be foreign to the real purpose of the experiment. During subsequent recall both children and college students resembled one another with respect to incidental memories; but in delayed recall the older group was markedly more efficient. In other words, the older group gave evidence of having seen and noted more than was the case with the younger children.[72]

The effectiveness of incidental learning has come into education through an attempt to answer the following question, viz., Can children acquire the details of a multiplication table to best advantage through direct practice or as an accessory to actual arithmetical operations arising in conjunction with practical tasks? The experiments have shown that primary arithmetical operations are often learned to best advantage by incidental rather than by direct means.[73] The same question and the same answer relate to skill in reading, in spelling and even to certain types of information.

Incidental learning, then, does take place, but its degree of excellence is to be explained in terms of the maturity of the subjects rather than in terms of the method. It is to be explained also in terms of the fact that the subjects in such experiments as we have cited knew the nature of the experiments. Evidence in favor of incidental learning does not prove that all learning proceeds to best advantage under these circumstances. We must, then, examine the evidence regarding intent and special incentives to learning.

3. *Incentives:* Among the specific ways of providing an incentive for learning, we shall consider such factors as the knowledge of results, the effect of rewards and punishments, and the effect of social stimulation or rivalry.

A. KNOWLEDGE OF RESULTS: With respect to the effect of a knowledge of the results achieved on learning, Book and Norvell asked 124 college students (i) to practice the simple muscular act of drawing the letter "a," (ii) to locate and cross out certain letters in a list of unrelated Spanish words, (iii) to substitute letters for a page of digits, and (iv) to multiply mentally one two-place number by another. The subjects were divided into two groups. The experimental group was instructed to count the score in the several experiments and it was also given a number of other special incentives. The control group was kept in ignorance of the score and it had no special incentive.

After the experiment had continued for fifty trials, the instruc-

[72] Myers, G. C., "A Study of Incidental Memory," *Arch. Psychol.,* 1913, IV (No. 26). See also Brown, W., "Incidental Memory in a Group of Persons." *Psychol. Rev.,* 1915, XXII, 81-85. Shellow, S. M., "Individual Differences in Incidental Memory." *Arch. Psychol.,* 1923, X (No. 64).
[73] Kirkpatrick, E. A., "An Experiment on Memorizing versus Incidental Learning," *J. Educ. Psychol.,* 1914, V, 405-412. See also Willoughby, R. R., "Incidental Learning," *J. Educ. Psychol.,* 1929, XX, 671-682; 1930, XXI, 12-23; Franz, S. I., and Houston, H. E., "The Accuracy of Observation and of Recollection in School Children." *Psychol. Rev.,* 1896, III, 531-535.

tions for the two groups were changed so that the first group was now deprived of information concerning success whereas the second group was given such information. The results showed clearly enough that those individuals who knew about their progress and who were subject to certain other incentives, made the greatest gain in all of the tasks. When, however, the instructions were changed, the relationship between the two groups was altered. The group that had been uninformed about rate of progress surpassed the other group as soon as it was given information about rate of progress. These results held true not only with respect to speed but with respect to accuracy as well.[74]

B. PUNISHMENT: The effect of punishment on rate of learning has been studied by Bunch. The subjects in this experiment were asked to learn a maze. During the course of learning some of the subjects received a shock whenever they made a wrong move in the maze. Punishment of this type served to decrease the number of trials necessary to learn the maze by fifty per cent over the number of trials necessary in the absence of an electric shock. The total time and the number of errors were also decreased.[75]

The situation with respect to punishment is not quite so simple, however, as this experiment would seem to indicate. Hamilton has shown, for example, that in discriminating small distances, punishment, on the one hand, and reward, on the other, do not help the subject to increase in accuracy.[76] A part of this variation from a general principle is due, apparently, to the ratio between the intensity of punishment and the difficulty of the task. Where the punishment stands out of all proportion to the task, it may serve as a distraction or even as a source of inhibition against learning rather than as an incentive.[77]

Experiments of this type stand, as we have seen, in close relation to one of the major laws of learning known as the law of effect. In general, this law states that learning processes will be aided whenever they are accompanied by or terminate in a feeling of satisfaction. There are some experiments which show that learning can be

[74] Book, W. F., and Norvell, L., "The Will to Learn: An Experimental Study of Incentives in Learning." *Ped. Sem.*, 1922, XXIX, 305-362; Deputy, E. C., "Knowledge of Success as a Motivating Influence in College Work." *J. Educ. Res.*, 1929, XX, 327-334; Spencer, L. T., "The Effects of Practice Without Knowledge of Results." *Amer. J. Psychol.*, 1923, XXXIV, 107-111.
[75] Bunch, M. E., "The Effects of Electric Shock as Punishment for Errors in Human Maze Learning." *J. Comp. Psychol.*, 1928, VII, 334-359.
[76] Hamilton, H. C., "The Effect of Incentives on Accuracy in Learning as Measured on the Galton Bar." *Arch. Psychol.*, 1929, CIII (No. 73).
[77] Vaughn, J., and Diserens, C. M., "The Relative Effects of Various Intensities of Punishment on Learning and Efficiency." *J. Comp. Psychol.*, 1930, X, 55-66.

ENGINEERING THE LEARNING PROCESS

made more profitable, however, even when the right response rather than the wrong response is punished. This is simply to say that the factor of punishment can never be used as the sole factor in any experiment. A subject may, for example, be given a strong intention to learn, or he may be motivated through a knowledge of the results he is attaining, even though he is punished for doing the right thing.[78] In the face of punishment, a meaningful relation between the different parts of a stimulus-pattern or a sufficient emphasis upon related parts will be sufficient to secure strong associative connections.

There are a great many studies in the field of animal psychology which look in this same direction. As a matter of fact, it is sometimes urged that the use of punishment, on the one hand, and the use of reward, on the other, lend themselves to more accurate measurement with animal subjects than with human subjects, for the conditions surrounding learning processes among the lower animals are often simpler and much more straightforward in character. As a typical example of the sort of thing that may be done, let us suppose that white rats are given a choice of four paths to food, viz., a short alley, a long alley, an alley involving confinement, and an alley involving an electric shock. Apart from the fact that the short alley was eventually chosen by most subjects, it appeared that the path involving an electric shock was eliminated twice as quickly as the path involving confinement.[79]

C. REWARD: Most teachers already know that rewards may be used as strong incentives in learning. The major difference between our commonsense beliefs about the effect of rewards and our experimental knowledge lies in the way that experimenters have been able to place incentives of this type on a quantitative basis. As a typical example of the use of a reward at the animal level, we may take the following experiment. The subjects were white rats. Four groups of subjects learned the maze, one group receiving no punishment for errors, one group receiving punishment from the very beginning of the experiment, one group receiving punishment for errors after the maze had been half mastered, and one group receiving punishment for errors after the maze had been three-fourths mastered. A reward consisting of food was given at the end of each trial.

[78] McGeoch, J. A., "Forgetting and the Law of Disuse." *Psychol. Rev.*, 1932, XXXIX, 352-370. See also, Tolman, E. C., Hill, C. S., and Bretnall, E. P., "A Disproof of the Law of Effect and a Substitution of the Laws of Emphasis, Motivation, and Disruption." *J. Exper. Psychol.*, 1932, XV, 601-614.

[79] Kuo, Z. Y., "The Nature of Unsuccessful Acts and Their Order of Elimination in Animal Learning." *J. Comp. Psychol.*, 1922, II, 1-27.

454   INTRODUCTION TO EDUCATIONAL PSYCHOLOGY

Those subjects that were punished for wrong responses and rewarded at the end of the trials did better than those that merely received a reward. When punishment was introduced later in the experiment, it was more effective in reducing errors than the entire absence of punishment.[80]

The same value for reward holds true of human learning. Chapman and Feder, for example, offered certain rewards for excellent performance in such acts as simple addition, a cancellation test, and a substitution test where figures were to be substituted for numerals. The subjects were thirty-six boys and girls in the fifth grade. One group of subjects differed from another by knowing the results of its effort for the previous day and by receiving special credit in the form of stars. The motivated group was found to be distinctly superior to the nonmotivated group in every respect.[81]

Another experiment on fifth-grade-school children ran as follows. The work assigned consisted of ten-minute exercises in multiplication three days a week for a period of seven weeks. On the eighth day of the experiment it was announced before each trial that a small box of chocolate bars would be given to those subjects who completed a certain number of problems. The required number was marked on the sheet given to each child. This number was chosen with respect to the presumable ability of a child as measured by the preliminary trials. The number of trials required per day was gradually increased. At one period during the experiment, a social incentive in the form of rivalry was introduced as were also other types of incentive. The results indicated clearly that the chocolate bar had indeed served as a marked incentive for the performances of the motivated children were fifty-two per cent above the level of the control group.[82]

D. SOCIAL STIMULATION: Social stimulation may take any one of several different forms. The subject, for example, can simply work in the presence of another subject, or several subjects may work in coöperation with one another or one subject may be placed in direct competition with another. All of these various forms of social stimulation have been brought under experimental control.

[80] Valentine, R., "The Effects of Punishment for Errors on the Maze Learning of Rats." *J. Comp. Psychol.*, 1930, X, 35-53. See also, Thorndike, E. L., "Reward and Punishment in Animal Learning." *Comp. Psychol. Monog.*, 1932, VIII, pp. 1 ff.
[81] Chapman, J. C., and Feder, R. B., "The Effect of External Incentives on Improvement." *J. Educ. Psychol.*, 1917, VIII, 469-474.
[82] Leuba, C. J., "A Preliminary Experiment to Quantity an Incentive and Its Effects." *J. Abnorm. and Soc. Psychol.*, 1930, XXV, 275-288. See also Chase, L., "Motivation of Young Children." *Univ. Iowa Stud.: Stud. in Child Welfare*, 1923, V (No. 3).

ENGINEERING THE LEARNING PROCESS

As an example of the first form, we may take an experiment in which the subjects simply worked in one another's presence without attempting to emulate one another. Groups of from three to five persons were asked to work on several different types of association test and upon a thought problem. It was concluded from this experiment that the presence of other persons increased the speed of free association, that slow persons were more favorably affected than fast workers, that social stimulation was more effective in the early stages of the task than it was in late stages, and that more ideas of a personal nature appeared when a person was working alone than when he was working with a group.[83] A more practical experiment of the same general type has shown that achievement in writing compositions and doing arithmetical sums under the social conditions of the classroom surpasses achievement in solitary work at home.[84]

When people work in a coöperative enterprise, the product of the whole group is apt to surpass the product of any single person as compared with the success that a person would achieve had he been working alone. On the other hand, however, it frequently happens that socialized effort creates many inhibitions and conflicts which will interfere with rate of learning. As a typical experiment in this field, we may take the results gained from a group of subjects who had been asked to work in committees of from three to ten persons on a problem of constructing words out of a key word. The results indicated that individual subjects were able to do much better when they were members of a group than they were able to do when they worked alone. Even though such subjects do not know how well other subjects are working, they appear to derive an incentive from the situation simply by knowing that other persons around them are working.[85]

Another study in this field was carried out in the following way. The subjects worked in groups of four. One set of instructions asked the groups simply to get as much done as possible without attempting to surpass fellow workers. Another set of instructions placed special emphasis upon the attempt to compete against other workers. Every one of the subjects achieved greater success when competing against another subject than when he was not competing.

---

[83] Allport, F. H., "The Influence of the Group upon Association and Thought." *J. Exper. Psychol.*, 1920, III, 159-182.
[84] Schmidt, E., "Experimentelle Untersuchung über die Hausaufgaben des Schulkindes." *Abhl. zur Psychol. Päd.*, 1904, I, 181-300.
[85] Watson, G. B., "Do Groups Think More Efficiently Than Individuals?" *J. Abnorm. and Soc. Psychol.*, 1928, XXIII, 328-336.

The gain brought about by rivalry amounted to about twenty-six per cent.[86]

One of the best experiments in this field was carried out in the following way. The Courtis test of addition was given to 145 children in the fourth and fifth grades of a public school. The children were then divided into two equivalent groups in respect to age, sex, and initial ability. One of these groups was asked to add numbers as quickly and as accurately as possible. The other group was divided into two sub-groups also equated with respect to ability. The experimenter explained this fact to these two groups and asked them to try to surpass each other. The name of the winning group was announced on the following day, and each child belonging to this group was asked to rise as his name was called. The experiment was continued under these conditions for five days. The results showed clearly that rivalry had acted as a strong incentive. The younger children profited more from the course of the experiment than the older children did.[87] Likewise, children of inferior ability improved more rapidly under the incentive of rivalry than superior children. In all cases, there were some tendencies toward a decrease in accuracy of work.

E. SUMMARY: Since all of the problems suggested by the words "incentive," "desire," "motive," and "purpose" have received more extended treatment in an earlier chapter, we shall leave this matter at this point. The student ought to be convinced, however, that there are a great many factors which can be used by the teacher in order to increase the effectiveness of periods of learning. It would be a mistake, of course, to suppose that there is any type of human effort which is totally devoid of the influence of motivation. To say the same thing in another way, it would be a mistake to suppose that motives, urges, desires, and purposes constitute a special class of psychological facts which operate during only a part of the time. The fact is that almost, if not quite, all features of human behavior could be discussed in any book that undertook a thorough treatment of the nature of motives.[88] In other words, then, when we say that

[86] Whittemore, I. C., "The Influence of Competition on Performance: An Experimental Study." *J. Abnorm. and Soc. Psychol.*, 1924, XIX, 236-253. See also Sims, V. M., "The Relative Influence of Two Types of Motivation on Improvement." *J. Educ. Psychol.*, 1928, XIX, 480-484.

[87] Hurlock, E. B., "The Use of Group Rivalry as an Incentive." *J. Abnorm. and Soc. Psychol.*, 1927, XXII, 278-290. See also Maller, J. B., "Coöperation and Competition; an Experimental Study in Motivation." *Columbia Univ. Contrib. to Educ.*, 1929 (No. 384).

[88] Cf. Troland, L. T., *The Fundamentals of Human Motivation*. New York: D. Van Nostrand Co., 1928, *passim*.

learning processes do profit from an increase in the incentive or because of a special intent to learn, we are simply recognizing the fact that there are times when incentives and purposes can be made more obvious or more intense than they are at other times.

VII. Order of Presentation

1. *Introduction:* As the reader knows, a very large part of the information about processes of learning which teachers use in the schoolroom has come from a study of the way in which the lower animals profit from past experience.[89] The white rat has been used more extensively for this purpose than almost any other animal. Similarly, the maze has been one of the favorite pieces of apparatus not only for white rats but for a good many other animals as well.[90]

Let us suppose that we have just placed a white rat in any one of the mazes that are now in common use. We are to study rate of learning by taking account of the time consumed in running from the entrance to the reward chamber, by taking account of the number of errors or by taking account of the total number of trials necessary to run through the maze without error for three consecutive occasions. After the results are all in, we may examine them in order to see whether any particular parts of the maze have been learned in advance of other parts. It will be discovered that most white rats have a tendency to learn the first parts and the last parts of the maze somewhat in advance of the middle parts.[91] Other more recent experiments have shown that the last parts of the maze are learned more quickly than the first parts. As a matter of fact, there are times when it appears that errors are eliminated in a reverse direction, those nearest the food box being eliminated first, and those lying farther away being eliminated in order of distance from the food box.[92]

These and other facts have lent support to two principles of learning. These principles are known as the principle of primacy and the principle of recency. The principle of primacy states that that part of a total learning task which occurs first will be learned more

---

[89] For considerations involved in applying the results of animal experimentation to human learning, see Yerkes, R. M., "Concerning the Genetic Relations of Types of Action." *J. Comp. Neur. and Psychol.*, 1915, XV, 132-137.

[90] Cf. Munn, N. L., *An Introduction to Animal Psychology.* Boston: Houghton Mifflin Co., 1933, *passim.*

[91] Munn, N. L., *op. cit.*, pp. 335 ff.

[92] Spence, K. W., "The Order of Eliminating Blinds in Maze Learning by the Rat." *J. Comp. Psychol.*, 1932, XIV, 9-27. See also Hull, C. L., "The Goal Gradient Hypothesis and Maze Learning." *Psychol. Rev.*, 1932, XXXIX, 25-43.

rapidly than those parts which occur later. The evidence for this principle is, however, somewhat contradictory. In one series of experiments, for example, a group of subjects was asked to learn lists of nonsense syllables. It was found that syllables occurring at the beginning and at the end of the whole list held a marked advantage over the intermediate syllables, the advantage for those at the end being greater than those for the beginning.[93]

Another experimenter has argued that the apparent influence of primacy is due to other factors among which there may be named the principle that, other things being equal, the stronger a connection is the oftener and so the earlier it will show itself.[94] Then, too, the first part of a new learning task may be either novel or more clearly impressed than other parts. In general, however, most experimenters are inclined to accept at least some measure of influence from primacy and recency factors.[95]

It is not of primacy and recency themselves, however, that we wish to speak. On the contrary, these two alleged laws of learning are a part of a still larger principle, viz., that rate of learning and degrees of retention may depend upon the order in which the various parts of a total learning situation are presented. Moreover, the efficiency of learning at one time during the whole growth pattern may depend, in part, upon the nature of preceding learning periods and upon the order in which these preceding learning periods have been presented.

As a general illustration of the principle we are trying to uncover, let us take an incident from the schoolroom experience of the reader himself. He has found, no doubt, after having listened in company with his fellow students to a lengthy explanation of a series of facts, that there are some persons in the class who understand forthwith the material that has been presented. There are other students, however, who do not understand what has been said. Now, it is easy to say that those who understand must be brighter than the others, but obviously, understanding may come to some simply because the order of presentation of the material has been of the right order for some of the people in the class and of the wrong order for other people.

[93] Robinson, E. S., and Brown, M. A., "Effect of Serial Position upon Memorization." *Amer. J. Psychol.*, 1926, XXXVII, 538-552.
[94] Thorndike, E. L., "The Influence of Primacy." *J. Exper. Psychol.*, 1927, X, 18-29.
[95] Cf. Peterson, J., "The Backward Elimination of Errors in Mental Maze Learning." *J. Exper. Psychol.*, 1920, III, 257-280; Warden, C. J., "Primacy and Recency as Factors in Cul-de-sac Elimination in a Stylus Maze." *J. Exper. Psychol.*, 1924, VII, 98-116.

To be sure, the order of presentation which is right for some people may secure a part of its rightness from the fact that these people have already acquired information pertinent to the material being discussed, whereas other people do not possess this information. Even apart from previous information, however, it is still possible that order of presentation, in and of itself, may make for or against adequate understanding. Those teachers who have tried several different orders of presentation of the same subject matter are witnesses to this fact for they realize that it is not always possible to tell in advance just how a given subject should be introduced in order that it may be made plain to a group of students.

In the writing of this book, for example, the author has arranged the chapters in at least a half a dozen different sequences. Moreover, in his teaching experience, he has introduced each of the topics in each of the chapters in a good many different ways. He has made a serious attempt to arrange the chapters and the order of presentation of each of the topics in the chapters in a sequence that will make the book easily understood by most of the persons who study it. Even as the book stands, there will be some people who will find it a very difficult book, not solely because the material has been presented in an awkward way, but also because the particular order of presentation which has been chosen does not "click," so to speak.

Aside from such features of order of presentation as are reflected in the principles of primacy and recency not much has been done in this field of research. At a much earlier stage in the growth pattern, however, there are a few experiments which suggest the nature of the problem. Let us suppose, for example, that we are to study the development of muscular control in a pair of twins. Let us say that one of the twins is subjected to a program of daily training in how to climb stairs and in methods of grasping such an object as a small cube. The other twin is deprived of special training in these modes of reaction. After four weeks of training (age fifty weeks), the first twin had learned to climb a staircase with considerable skill. The other twin, however, at the age of fifty-three weeks was able, without any previous training, to climb the same staircase with almost the same skill displayed by the first twin. After two weeks of training, this subject could not be distinguished from the other in ability even though the other had begun training seven weeks earlier and had had three times as much training.[96]

[96] Gesell, A., and Thompson, H., "Learning and Growth in Identical Infant Twins: An Experimental Study by the Method of Co-twin Control." *Genet. Psychol. Monog.*, 1929, VI, 1-124.

The same results were obtained from the study of motor control in handling a small cube. Even though one of the twins received no special practice it was able, toward the end of the period of observation, to handle the cube with just as much skill as did the twin which had received a relatively large amount of special training. In other words, these results indicate that training cannot become really effective in advance of proper maturation. To say the same thing in another way, certain types of skill cannot be acquired to the best advantage unless they take their proper serial position in a whole pattern of developmental events, some of which prepare the way for later training periods.[97]

These facts appear still more clearly in studies on the relationship between growth and the development of language. The training of one twin began at eighty-four weeks and continued through the eighty-eighth week. The training program for the other twin began with the eighty-ninth week. These age levels were chosen because they represented a point in the average growth pattern when language responses were just beginning to appear. A close check of the development of a vocabulary revealed the fact that both of these twins passed through identical stages of development. The second subject, however, was slightly in advance of the first throughout the period of observation. In other words, the experimenter concluded that a training period which began with a maturity advantage of five weeks was more effective than a training program which was begun before the subject was ready for the acquisition of verbal skills.[98]

In experiments of this type, the word "maturation" is sometimes used as a synonym for heredity.[99] That is, learning processes of certain types cannot be really effective until the subject is old enough to let them be effective. If we were to assume, however, that the whole growth pattern is a forward-moving series of changes brought about, in part, by hereditary factors and, in part, by processes of learning, that is, if we were to assume that learning itself is a type of growth or a means for promoting growth, it would follow that the results of such experiments as we have just described must be

[97] Hilgard, E. R., "Learning and Maturation in Preschool Children." *J. Genet. Psychol.*, 1932, XLI, 36-56; Jersild, A. T., *Training and Growth in the Development of Children*. New York: Columbia Univ., Teach. Coll., Bur. Publ., 1932, *passim*.
[98] Strayer, L. C., "Language and Growth: The Relative Efficacy of Early and Deferred Vocabulary Training Studied by the Method of Co-twin Control." *Genet. Psychol. Monog.*, 1930, VIII, 209-319.
[99] Cf. Stone, C. P., "Learning: I, The Maturation Factor," in Murchison, C. (Ed.), *op. cit.*, Chapter VIII.

representative of a situation that obtains throughout the entire growth pattern. In other words, any present act of learning must depend, in part, for its effectiveness upon the level of skill that has been reached as a result of previous acts of learning. The moment we say this, however, we run into difficulties for there are no experiments which have been directed toward this particular problem. We must appeal to tradition and to commonsense.

Among the traditions which give support to an essential relation between order of presentation and efficiency in learning, there is common practice in the construction of curricula. The student knows, of course, that children are supposed to learn their three R's before they try to learn anything else from the so-called "content" courses. Likewise, they are supposed to learn certain parts of arithmetic before they learn other parts.[100] Arithmetic usually precedes algebra and algebra precedes some of the so-called "higher" forms of mathematics. The inference is that the average curriculum actually presents genetic series of events in an order of presentation which is the best possible so far as its growth-promoting functions are concerned.

As a more specific illustration of this point, let us take methods of teaching reading. The traditional method required that the pupil should learn first the letters of the alphabet, then some of the simpler words, and finally some of the simpler phrases into which words may be cast. The logic behind this order of presentation is fairly simple. Since books are made of chapters, chapters of sections, sections of paragraphs, paragraphs of sentences, sentences of words, and words of letters, it must follow that letters are the simplest elements in the act of learning how to read. Being the simplest elements, they must, therefore, be genetically prior elements. Consequently, reading ought to begin with those materials that are most simple and conform, therefore, to a genetic point of view. It takes only a casual observation of early language skills, however, to see that the first words spoken by the child are certainly not letters, and neither are they really words. On the contrary, they are phrases. The functional unit in language is either a phrase or a word-phrase. When this fact was discovered, methods of teaching reading were changed. The child now begins with those elements of language which are functionally and genetically, rather than logically, prior to the whole art of reading.

[100] For a study of order of difficulty, see Clapp, F. L., "The Number Combinations: Their Relative Difficulty and the Frequency of Their Appearance in Textbooks." Univ. of Wisconsin, Bur. of Educ. Res., 1924 (No. 2).

462 INTRODUCTION TO EDUCATIONAL PSYCHOLOGY

The conclusion we wish to draw from these considerations runs as follows. The growth pattern is an essentially continuous pattern. Moreover, it is a pattern which displays a principle known as the principle of serial order of development.[101] Not much is known about the details of this serial order, but its existence is full of suggestion for methods of increasing the efficiency of learning processes. If the teacher has to work with a pattern of events which is truly genetic in character it is clear that the order in which learning situations are presented to students must be an order commensurate with the growth pattern. On some occasions, the first part of a learning task may be learned more quickly than later parts and under other conditions the later parts may be learned more quickly than earlier parts. As we have said, however, these serial-position effects are a fairly minor phase of a much more comprehensive problem. The chances are that, when researches upon the whole growth pattern have given a more accurate picture of this pattern, and when the relation between order of presentation and efficiency of learning has been worked out in more detail, teachers will be in a much better position than they are at the present time to promote psychological growth.

VIII. Retention and Recall

1. *Introduction:* If learning is a word which refers to the procedures through which one must go in order to advance oneself in skill or to increase one's range of information, the words "skill," "habit," "knowledge," and "information" would describe the products, so to speak, of the learning process.[102] At the end of a period of practice which has been organized according to the principles already described, the learner will have grown into a type of competence or into a level of maturity which certainly makes a different person out of him, but which will, on some occasions, make a better person out of him. That is, he will have become a more effective psychological instrument.

The learning process itself, however, does not mark the limits of a teacher's interest in bringing about changes in his students. If everything that we learned were to be used only once and then discarded, teaching effort would be much simpler than it is. It turns out, however, that some of the improvements which are made in

---

[101] This principle has already been discussed in connection with other general features of the growth pattern in Chapter Ten.
[102] Cf. Dunlap, K., *op. cit.*, Chapter VII.

human nature ought to be permanent. The skill that an athlete acquires during one season of training, for example, will be of great service to him if it is retained during the off-season period and can be used to good advantage when the next season opens. We must, therefore, inquire about some of the conditions which will guarantee the permanence of an attained level of skill or a memorized series of facts.

2. *Measuring of Retention:* Since learning is a type of growth, it ought to follow that the changes in the body or in the nervous system that result from practice periods should display themselves in some recognizable form. If, for example, learning means reduced resistance at synapses, a direct measure of the permanence of this reduction might be gained if some way could be found to experiment upon the conduction of nerve impulses. This way has not been found, either with respect to synapses or with respect to any other theory of nerve function. It is necessary, therefore, that the degree of retention or the relative durability of the changes brought about by learning processes must be measured in terms of recall or in terms of remembering.

One of the principal ways of measuring the strength of retention requires a direct comparison between original levels of skill or ranges of information and attained levels of skill or ranges of information after a given period of time has elapsed. There is some evidence to show that forgetting takes place much more rapidly during the first few hours after a practice period has been finished than it does at later times. As a matter of fact, some efforts have been made to draw curves of forgetting.[103] These curves are apt to be a mere image of the rate of learning although the forms, both of the curve of learning and of the curve of forgetting, will vary greatly, depending upon the way in which experimental data are plotted.[104]

A second way of measuring the degree of retention makes use of the process of relearning. In this process the learner is required to repeat the original training exercise as many times as are necessary to bring a skill or a range of information back to the original level of excellence. Obviously, the amount of relearning that is required will depend upon the amount of overlearning that took place during the original practice period and upon the length of time

[103] Anderson, J. P., and Jordan, A. M., "Learning and Retention of Latin Words and Phrases." *J. Educ. Psychol.*, 1928, XIX, 485-496.
[104] Cf. Bean, C. H., "The Curve of Forgetting." *Arch. of Psychol.*, 1912, III, No. 21. Also Finkenbinder, E. O., "The Curve of Forgetting." *Amer. J. Psychol.*, 1913, XXIV, 8-32.

that has elapsed between the original learning and the relearning.[105]

The indirect measure of recall in these and in other ways is not, however, the most important feature of retention, so far as teaching effort is concerned. On the contrary, after it is recognized that processes of forgetting seriously modify previous learning, one must try to find out what factors will increase the durability of changes rather than decrease them. In general, of course, we may say that all of the conditions which increase the efficiency of the original learning processes ought to lead to longer retention of the practiced material. Other things being equal, a proper distribution of practice periods, the introduction of appropriate rest intervals, the intent to learn, and other similar factors will manifest themselves in a heightened degree of retention. There are, however, certain other considerations which enter into this picture. Some of them are specific, but most of them are exceedingly variable and up to the present time beyond practical means of control.

It is highly probable that the degree of retention will increase in direct proportion to the amount of previous overlearning. Similarly, material that has barely been learned will, other things being equal, quickly be forgotten.[106] The student will remember that overlearning has variable meanings depending upon the criteria that are laid down for learning. If the first successful repetition of an act is counted as learning, then further repetitions can be described as overlearning.

In general, it looks as though the degree of retention both for almost immediate recall and for delayed recall stands in a more or less direct ratio to the number of repetitions of the material. If the learning task is simple enough, retention for all of the material will be complete after a single repetition. With more complex materials, however, the learning of some parts of the total will interfere with the learning of other parts. A learner may stop short, then, of perfect reproduction and yet have gained some advantage from his practice. The amount of this advantage appears to depend, among other factors, upon the original rate of learning. It looks as though the best learners, where the term "best" is applied

[105] Myers, G. C., "Some Correlations between Learning and Recall." *J. Educ. Psychol.*, 1916, VII, 546-547; Brown, W., "Effects of Interval on Recall." *J. Exper. Psychol.*, 1924, VII, 469-474.
[106] Krueger, W. C. F., "The Effect of Overlearning on Retention." *J. Exper. Psychol.*, 1929, XII, 71-78; 1930, XIII, 152-163. See also, Tolman, E. C., "The Effects of Overlearning upon Short and Long-time Retentions." *J. Exper. Psychol.*, 1923, VI, 466-474.

ENGINEERING THE LEARNING PROCESS

to those persons who learn most quickly, enjoy more enduring levels of retention than slow learners.[107]

All of the facts that have just been mentioned, together with a great many more that have a bearing upon this field, are subject to a series of variable conditions about which many reports have been made but with respect to which small measures of control can be exercised. The student already knows, for example, that he can recall some items of information and scenes from his earlier life which were not practiced and for which there was no special intent to learn. This fact has been brought out in a variety of studies upon early childhood experiences.[108] These studies indicate that there must have been some factors surrounding the presentation of situations during childhood which were much more important for insuring retention over a long period of time than many that have been discovered in the laboratory.

Among the possibilities, there is the influence of affective tone on retention. It has been shown, for example, that unpleasant experiences are apt to be inhibited.[109] The evidence on this matter, however, is highly conflicting. The law of effect would suggest that most persons ought to be more free in their recollection of pleasant experiences than they are in the recollection of unpleasant experiences, but the studies that have been made upon the affective tone of learned material have not shown this to be the case.[110] The safest inference to be drawn from these studies is, perhaps, that affective tone does make some difference in the relative retention of an experience, but that a good many circumstances touching the relation between feeling tone and the learning process are yet to be discovered.

Another factor which has an occasional bearing upon retention is perseveration. This word describes the fact that, during a learning process or even during a casual experience, some item of information or some series of movements will gain dominance over everything else and persist in a recurring form for considerable periods of time.[111] Not the least of the variable factors in reten-

[107] Lyon, D. O., "The Relation of Quickness of Learning to Retentiveness." *Arch. of Psychol.*, 1916, V (No. 34). See also, Gates, A. I., "Correlations of Immediate and Delayed Recall." *J. Educ. Psychol.*, 1918, IX, 489-496.

[108] Gordon, K., "A Study of Early Memories." *J. Delinq.*, 1928, XII, 129-132; Titchener, E. B., "Early Memories." *Amer. J. Psychol.*, 1900, XI, 435-436.

[109] Anderson, A. C., and Bolton, F. J., "Inhibition of the Unpleasant." *J. Abnorm. and Soc. Psychol.*, 1925, XX, 300-302.

[110] Jones, H. E., "Emotional Factors in Learning." *J. Gen. Psychol.*, 1929, II, 263-270; Thompson, R. H., "An Experimental Study of Memory as Influenced by Feeling Tone." *J. Exper. Psychol.*, 1930, XIII, 462-468.

[111] Foster, W. S., "On the Perseverative Tendency." *Amer. J. Psychol.*, 1914, XXV, 393-426.

tion is the time factor itself. Some students of learning processes have implied that the passage of time itself could serve as a source of destruction to previously acquired skills. The student will see at once, however, that time can scarcely be used as a causal agent. At least, there is no other place in the domain of science where it is known that time can have a causal relation of this sort.[112] The chances are that laws of retention, instead of being explained by the sheer passage of time, ought to be explained by the other events that take place between original learning and subsequent recall. We have already seen, for example, that one period of learning may have an important influence upon previous periods and upon future periods as well. Then, too, most students do not realize that lack of practice is, from some points of view, just as much a learning process as is an actual practice period. In other words, we can learn not to use certain skills or not to recall certain information just as we learn to use them. The athlete, for example, who ends one season of competition, may let several months pass without using any of the skills that he has acquired. This must mean that he has acquired the habit of not using these skills. In any case, it is a well-recognized fact that the occasional exercise of any functions that have been acquired through training will serve greatly to keep these functions in serviceable order.

3. *Recall:* It is usual to think of recollection or of remembering in two ways. On the one hand, a person may repeat word-for-word some set of information which has been acquired at a previous time or he may use a highly overlearned skill as effectively as he did at the end of a consecutive practice period. For example, a person has learned how to swim. The chances are that he will never forget at least the rudiments of the skill. Something may be lost in grace or in speed or in endurance, but other things being equal, a person who has not been in the water for a great many years will know how to handle himself in case he is capsized. This sort of recollection may be called direct.

The second form of recollection or of remembering sometimes does not even bring back the rudiments of a skill or any of the facts that have been learned. The rememberer will, however, have a feeling of familiarity or of recognition. He will realize that there was a time when he did know a certain set of material even though none of the material can actually be recalled. A great many experiments have been performed upon the recognition factor in learning, but

---

[112] Robinson, E. S., *Associative Theory Today.* New York: D. Appleton-Century Co., 1932, pp. 77 ff.

aside from the fact that recognition is an obvious feature of recall, little is known of the circumstances which make it possible.[113]

In general, all of the circumstances which favor speed of learning and durability in retention will favor completeness of recall and the degree of confidence which a person has in the correctness of recognized material.[114] Other things being equal, recall will be aided if there is placed in the situation inviting recall as many of the factors that were present during the original learning as possible.[115] This fact has been recognized in our commonsense methods of aiding memory. If we cannot recall on the spur of the moment a given fact or the full details of an earlier episode, we search around, so to speak, for near relatives of the material we wish to remember. One student of these matters has argued that most of the phenomena of learning and of recall are of this nature. The term "redintegration" is used to describe the fact that one feature of the total situation which obtained at the time the original learning took place may serve as an adequate source of recall at some subsequent time.[116]

The student will have been impressed, perhaps, by the fact that many of the studies that have been made on learning concern short learning periods and relatively short intervals between learning and recall. In the schoolroom, however, some learning periods may be long-drawn-out. Moreover, the period of time that elapses between schoolroom learning and any possible use of the materials learned may be fairly long. In some of the studies that cover these longer periods of time, it has been shown that memory for details is distressingly evanescent.[117] Even so short an interval as a summer vacation may interfere rather seriously with some types of subject matter.[118]

The chief remedy for forgetfulness over longer periods of time lies, of course, in considerable degrees of overlearning and in those modes of review and of repetition which are a part of the method

[113] Woods, E. L., "An Experimental Analysis of the Process of Recognizing." *Amer. J. Psychol.*, 1915, XXVI, 313-387.
[114] Lund, F. H., "The Criteria of Confidence." *Amer. J. Psychol.*, 1926, XXXVII, 372-381; Jersild, A. T., "The Determinants of Confidence." *Amer. J. Psychol.*, 1929, XLI, 640-642.
[115] Pan, S., "The Influence of Context upon Learning and Recall." *J. Exper. Psychol.*, 1926, IX, 468-491.
[116] Hollingworth, H. L., "General Laws of Redintegration." *J. Gen. Psychol.*, 1928, I, 79-90.
[117] Eikenberry, D. H., "Permanence of High School Learning." *J. Educ. Psychol.*, 1923, XIV, 463-481.
[118] Garfinkel, M. A., "The Effect of Summer Vacation on Ability in the Fundamentals of Arithmetic." *J. Educ. Psychol.*, 1919, X, 44-48. See also Noonan, M. E., "Influence of the Summer Vacation on the Abilities of Fifth and Sixth Grade Children." *Teachers Coll. Contrib. to Educ.*, 1926 (No. 204).

of distribution of effort. As we have seen, practice periods may follow rather quickly upon one another during the early part of a learning process, but later on, after longer intervals have elapsed, they are just as effective. The sheer forgetfulness occasioned by long intervals is to be compensated for, however, by the fact that absolute forgetting is probably not possible. If we say that learning is a form of growth, no type of experience can be had without some resultant change in the quality or character of the organism as a psychological instrument. A student who leaves his years of school training, therefore, may not be able to remember all of the details that he actually wrote down on some particular examination, but he most certainly is, from the psychological point of view, a more mature instrument than he was at any particular stage during his whole training period. This feature of schooling will be stated in a more convincing form in the next chapter.

READINGS

The text of this chapter has provided more references than the student will be able to use, but he should not, on that account, disregard them. They have been listed partly in order to let the student know where certain types of information are to be found, and partly to guide his choice of supplementary readings. An excellent general survey of the facts discussed in this chapter can be found in Dunlap, K., *Habits: Their Making and Unmaking*. New York: Liveright Publishing Corp., 1932, Chapters VI, VII, and VIII. An equally good account has been supplied by Robinson, E. S., "Work of the Integrated Organism," in Murchison, C. (ed.), *A Handbook of General Experimental Psychology*. Worcester, Mass.: Clark Univ. Press, 1934, Chapter XII. See also Robinson, E. S., *Practical Psychology*. New York: The Macmillan Co., 1926.

Both the teacher and the student will miss an account of the practical applications of the facts described above, but the limitations of space and the abundance of excellent books in the field have prompted the author to leave these matters for more general reading. Among the references that may be found useful are Bird, C., *Effective Study Habits*. New York: D. Appleton-Century Co., 1931; Book, W. F., *Economy and Technique of Learning*. Boston: D. C. Heath and Co., 1932; Muse, M. B., *An Introduction to Efficient Study Habits*. Philadelphia: W. B. Saunders and Co., 1929; Werner, O. H., *Every College Student's Problems*. Newark: Silver, Burdett and Co., 1929; and Whipple, G. M., *How to Study Effectively*. Bloomington: Public School Publ. Co., 1927.

CHAPTER THIRTEEN

THE TRANSFER OF TRAINING

I. SPECIALIZATION AND GENERAL TRAINING

1. *Introduction:* The last three chapters have been filled with facts and suggestions which touch the processes of education not only in the schoolroom where the teacher comes face-to-face with the results of original nature and of training, but in the study of the philosopher, as well, who tries to search out and identify the aims, goals, or objectives which must be reached if society is to gain the most benefit from its educated members. If a native endowment marks the limit beyond which some persons cannot go or if it specifies, in advance of experience, the particular interest or vocation of a student, no teaching method or philosophy of education can evade what is, from one point of view, a rather serious measure of helplessness in the face of nature. On the contrary, if native endowment furnishes only the tools or instruments with which the teacher can work, then both teaching methods and the definition of ultimate aims or goals can free themselves from the determinism that appears to reside in too much emphasis on hereditary constitution.[1]

We have not as yet, however, brought out one of the principal implications of the relation between original nature and training no matter how this relation may be defined. Everyone will agree that the educative process has its special function to perform with respect to native endowment, but men will not agree as to the scope and value of this function.

We may approach this disagreement in the following manner. The student will recall that the first chapter was given over to a study of the general course of preschool development for it is during this period that education has its beginnings. In spite of the various situations in which children are placed during the first three years of their lives, it is fairly clear that a fundamental similarity

[1] This whole problem has been discussed by Bagley, W. C., *Determinism in Education.* Baltimore: Warwick and York, 1925, *passim.* See also Burton, W. H., *Introduction to Education.* New York: D. Appleton-Century Co., 1934, Chapter III.

runs through all of them. In any given community, every child learns to carry out the same kinds of actions, to adjust himself to the common run of objects, and to develop similar groups of social traits.[2] There is an increase in the similarity of learning situations as soon as a child gets into the grade schools. This similarity, created as it is by set curricula, persists throughout the grades and well into the high school. Sometimes, at the high school level, and almost surely at the college level, learning situations tend to become more dissimilar. This means that the educative process has become more and more specialized. The student will realize, however, that specialization during the higher levels of education is not created so much by emphasis upon the use of different psychological functions as it is by the use of widely divergent types of learning situations.

2. *Identities in Training:* As an example of this fact, we may take the cases of two students, the one majoring in mathematics and the other majoring in history. These two subjects differ from each other in what may be called their content; but they resemble each other in the fact that both of them require a liberal use of such principles of effective learning as were discussed in the last chapter. They require, moreover, essentially the same perceptual skills. We propose, by this statement, to draw a distinction between the meaning or the content of situations that may be presented to a growing person and the psychological functions of the person that are exercised by these situations. The point is that, irrespective of the content of the course in the high school or college curriculum, every student receives exercise in all of the psychological traits of which he is a sum. To be sure, a single situation may emphasize some traits rather than others; but the total effect of the teaching program is to call into action most of the talents possessed by a person. We shall conclude, then, that the educative process has within it a large amount of identity so far as psychological operations are concerned, although there may be great variety in the services rendered by these operations.

The students who come through an educative process stand in marked contrast to these identities. As every teacher knows, some graduates of a high school or a college are versatile in their skills, well informed about the objects and events around them, more or less stable in their personal development, socially adaptable, and

---

[2] For a picture of a typical community, see Lynd, R. S., and Lynd, H. M., *Middletown, a Study in Contemporary Culture.* New York: Harcourt, Brace and Co., 1929.

highly energetic. Others, on the contrary, are dull-witted, awkward, uninformed, socially maladjusted, and scarcely able to take a fruitful place in the social order. If we think of these two types as normal extremes, we may say that a few persons fall beyond either extreme. Moreover, the mid-region between the extremes is filled with persons differing in quality but tending to concentrate around an average. In addition to differences of this type, some graduates will be highly skilled in specific vocations. Of these we may say either that they have been specially gifted or specially trained or that they might have been able to achieve an equal amount of competence in any other subject to which an equal amount of attention had been given.[3]

3. *Differences in Training:* As we have seen in Chapter Ten, everyone is compelled to agree that differences of the order just named are dependent to some undetermined extent upon a native or hereditary factor. It is not our purpose, however, to raise this difficult question again. On the contrary, we shall ask how the process of education is related to the differences described above. There are some who would say that the schoolroom is a device for promoting the hereditary factors, disciplining them, and otherwise aiding them to come to more adequate expression. The new-born infant, of course, is not a very effective psychological instrument. The task of education, supported as it is by the normal processes of growth, is to make as good a psychological instrument out of each person as it can.

For a long time, it has been taken for granted that any given learning situation would be just as effective as any other. This is certainly true at the preschool level, for no one has ever supposed that a child living in a mountainous district suffered any disadvantages over a child living in the prairies so far as the development of the visual functions is concerned. Teachers have usually argued that reading, writing, and arithmetic must be fairly effective aids to growth when formal schooling is first begun.

4. *Formal Discipline:* At higher levels the same argument has lain behind the selection of the subjects to be put into the curriculum, although curriculum makers have always had a preference for those subjects that could be described by the word "difficult."[4] As we shall see in a later chapter, some men have long believed that the

---

[3] Cf. Griffitts, C. H., *Fundamentals of Vocational Psychology.* New York: The Macmillan Co., 1924, *passim.*
[4] This is one of the implications in Flexner's study of universities. Cf. Flexner, A., *Universities, American, English, German.* London: Oxford Univ. Press, 1930, *passim.*

mind of a new-born infant is weak and untrained. Since hard work is known to increase the strength and stamina of muscles, it was easy to suppose that hard mental work would likewise increase the strength and stamina of the mental tissues. Since, however, some persons have had to be born with fewer native endowments than others, no amount of exercise or training could take them beyond a given level. In any case, there is a long-standing belief to the effect that the mind can be given a general training no matter what types of exercise the teacher may use.[5]

5. *Particular Discipline:* This answer to the question of the relation between individual differences and education has now been replaced by another. There are those who will assert that the training of the mind is not a general matter at all. On the contrary, it is asserted that the schoolroom can train a person only in those particular situations in which the person happens to be placed. If, for example, a student learns how to acquire information and skill in the field of history this does not mean at all that he will have become a more effective instrument in the field of mathematics.

If we were to apply this argument to the training of the muscles of the body, it would be necessary to say that a man who had greatly increased the strength of arm, shoulder, and back muscles by throwing dirt out of a pit would not be able to use this strength in the act of rowing a boat, felling a tree, or lifting a load. To be sure, the analogy here is not so simple as it may appear, for the acts of digging a ditch, on the one hand, and of rowing a boat, on the other, do not depend on strength alone. Both acts require a certain amount of special skill in using strong muscles. We should say, therefore, that a man who has learned how to throw dirt out of a ditch would not, on that account alone, have learned how to row a boat. We should have to go even further than this. We should have to say that a man who had learned how to throw dirt out of a ditch would not be able even to learn how to row a boat any more quickly than he would had he not previously learned the other skill.[6]

6. *The Nature of the Controversy:* As we shall see during the course of this chapter, experiments in the laboratory and in the schoolroom are beginning to suggest a way of effecting a compromise between these two points of view. Before we recite some of the experiments, however, it will be instructive to see how these two points of view have tried to argue one another down. Those who

---

[5] See the Report of the Committee of Ten on Secondary School Studies. New York: American Book Co., 1894, p. 43, and *passim.*
[6] This whole problem has been reviewed by Orata, P., *The Theory of Identical Elements.* Columbus: Ohio State Univ. Press, 1928.

say that education or training may be general in its nature point to the successful or highly competent graduates of high schools or colleges and to the rigorous training which these persons have received during their years of schooling.[7] They will even go further than this, for they will say that the older educational processes which included such "difficult" subjects as Latin, Greek, and mathematics were much more effective than is the case at the present time. Then, too, odious comparisons will be drawn between education in France, in Germany, in England, and in the United States.

The reply to such arguments often takes the following form. Those who assert that training is specific in character will argue that older methods of teaching did not do much more than act as a selective agent. In other words, they will think of the schoolroom as though it were a sieve through which the more talented students could pass, while the less talented students were dropped by the wayside. One of the inferences of this reply is clear. It can be said that those persons who are well endowed by nature achieve success in later life, irrespective of the training they may get in a school system. The conclusion to be drawn from this possibility is clear, for if the exceptional student and the successful man will arrive at their respective goals even though they have not submitted themselves to the rigorous discipline of a school system, the folly of spending three billions of dollars for the construction of an educational sieve can scarcely be exaggerated.[8]

7. *Purpose of the Chapter:* The main task of this chapter, then, ought to be clear. Students do differ from one another greatly during their entire period of training. After their formal education is finished, they differ greatly from one another in the success which they achieve in adult life. Do they owe their success to the fact that education has made a more effective instrument out of them or because they have been specifically prepared to excel in an equally specific vocation? Is there such a thing as general training or must one be limited in one's competence to those actions which have been tutored in the schoolroom? Is the curriculum, as it stands at the present time (and as it has stood in the past), an expensive colander through which the more talented will pass or does the measure of training which one gets in the schoolroom actually change the quality of a person so far as his psychological traits are concerned?

[7] Cf. Schwesinger, G. C., *Heredity and Environment.* New York: The Macmillan Co., 1933, pp. 66 ff.
[8] Cf. Kilpatrick, W. H., *et al., The Educational Frontier.* New York: D. Appleton-Century Co., 1933, *passim.*

Everyone will grant that long periods of practice devoted to a specific skill will make a person highly competent in that skill. This fact is so plain that the social group could direct its tutorial energies toward this goal with a high degree of skill and efficiency.[9] It is not this phase of the relation between training and original nature, however, about which we must inquire. On the contrary, we wish to know, first, whether the special interests and aptitudes of a child are so deeply innate that they cannot be overruled by education and, second, whether having received special training in some particular skill, a student will have become, in any sense of the word, a better and a more versatile instrument for the acquisition of new skills and new knowledge. If interests and aptitudes are native the teacher ought, as early in the life of the child as possible, to search them out and help the child to make the most of them.[10] If, however, a growing child can actually learn how to generalize his interests and aptitudes, a good teacher might hope to lay a broad foundation of ability upon which more specialized interests could later be established.

II. Experimental Studies on Transfer

1. *Introduction:* It is hardly necessary to say that these questions and the answers to them stand high among the important problems, not only of educational psychology, but of social philosophy as well. The student will realize, of course, that they are a part of the general phenomena of learning. They arise out of the question as to how a present act of learning stands related to previous periods of growth, on the one hand, and to future periods of growth, on the other.

In order to get as clear an answer as possible to this question we may take the following situation. Here is a student who now faces, for the first time, the study of the German language. We may assume that this student has already studied Latin, Greek, and French in addition to his own mother language. We may assume also that he has studied all of the other subjects which fall in a typical curriculum. The question we have to ask is simply this: How will the task of studying German be related to the previous study of other languages and what effect will knowledge and skill in the use of German have upon some further task such as the study of Italian?

---

[9] This goal is actually being approached in industry. Cf. Viteles, M. S., *Industrial Psychology*. New York: W. W. Norton and Co., 1932, Chapter XX.
[10] Cf. Symonds, P. M., *Diagnosing Personality and Conduct*. New York: D. Appleton-Century Co., 1931, Chapter VII.

THE TRANSFER OF TRAINING 475

2. *Relationships Between Learning Periods:* There are six possible answers to these questions. In the first place, it may be that the study of German will help a person to recall some of the material that has been learned in times past. As we have seen in the last chapter, a present situation may aid recall whenever there is anything about the present situation that can be associated with previously acquired materials.[11]

In the second place, learning German at the present time may prevent recall of previously acquired materials. This type of interference has already been described by the phrase "retroactive inhibition."[12] In the third place, the process of learning how to use the German language may be aided because the student has acquired a general ability to study languages through his work on Latin, Greek, and French. This answer would imply that learning processes which have taken place during the previous history of the student will have a beneficial effect upon his present undertaking simply because the student has become a more mature instrument.[13] In the fourth place, it is possible that the study of German at the present time may be hindered by previous language studies. This relationship between one learning task and another has been described by the phrase "mutual interference."[14] In the fifth place, the relation between the study of German and the future study of some other language may be like the situation described in the third answer. That is, the student who now acquires facility in the use of German may find that the subsequent study of Italian will receive benefit from his present study of German. Finally, it is possible that a study of German at the present time may prevent rather than aid future learning activities.

Of these six types of relation between one learning situation and another we are concerned in this chapter with the third and the fifth. That is, we wish to find out how far the task of learning German at the present moment will be aided by a previous study of language (or of any other subject matter) and how far achievement in German at the present time will promote learning at some future time.[15] As we have seen, there are some persons who would say that the task of learning German will be a highly specific

---

[11] For references to this matter, see McGeoch, J. A., "The Psychology of Human Learning: A Bibliography." *Psychol. Bull.,* 1933, XXX, pp. 47 ff.
[12] See above, Chapter Twelve, pp. 439 ff.
[13] The last part of the present chapter will be concerned with this proposition.
[14] See above, pp. 443 ff.
[15] For a discussion of related problems, see Robinson, E. S., "Work of the Integrated Organism," in Murchison, C. (Ed.), *A Handbook of General Experimental Psychology.* Worcester, Mass.: Clark Univ. Press, 1934, Chapter XII.

task and that one should not expect, therefore, either to receive any profit from previous learning or to lend any support to future learning. On the contrary, other persons hold that certain types of learning are general in their effect of gaining profit from previous skills and lending profit to future undertakings. The experimental laboratory must decide this issue. Moreover, in case there are any general profits from learning it must name the conditions under which these profits can be gained.[16]

3. *Cross-Education:* We may begin with some of the experiments that have been done on what is commonly called cross-education. These experiments have to do with the extent to which special training on one side of the body may lead to improvement on the other side of the body. Since there is a right and a left arm or a right and a left eye such studies can be carried out rather directly. We might, for example, ask a group of subjects to exercise the muscles of the fingers, wrist, and forearm on the right side of the body and then find out whether any improvement in strength had been effected in the left hand, even though it has not been exercised.[17] Then, too, we may study various types of performance such as quickness of tapping with the hands and feet, accuracy at tapping with the hands, tossing one or more balls, tracing objects from a mirror, and the like.[18]

As a typical illustration of the way in which such experiments are carried out, let us take the following. Two groups of subjects, after having been equated for ability, were asked to trace the mirror image of a star. The one group, called the training group, was first given one trial with the nonpreferred hand and then fifty practice trials with the preferred hand. The experiment for this training group ended with another trial for the nonpreferred hand. The control group began likewise with a trial for the nonpreferred hand, but then turned to a rest period of one hour. The experiment for the control group likewise ended with another trial for the non-preferred hand. The difference between the two groups, then, was

---

[16] Cf. Hunter, W. S., "Learning: IV. Experimental Studies of Learning," in Murchison, C., *op. cit.*, Chapter XI.
[17] Scripture, E. W., Smith, T. L., and Brown, E. M., "On the Education of Muscular Control and Power." *Stud. Yale Psychol. Lab.*, 1894, II, 114-119.
[18] Davis, W. W., "Researches in Cross-education." *Stud. Yale Psychol. Lab.*, 1898, VI, 6-50; 1900, VIII, 64-108; Thorndike, E. L., and Woodworth, R. S., "The Influence of Improvement in One Mental Function upon the Efficiency of Other Functions." *Psychol. Rev.*, 1901, VIII, 247-261, 384-395, 553-564; Starch, D., "A Demonstration of the Trial and Error Method of Learning." *Psychol. Bull.*, 1910, VII, 20-23; Ewert, P. H., "Bilateral Transfer in Mirror-drawing." *Ped. Sem.*, 1926, XXXIII, 235-249; Bray, C. W., "Transfer of Learning." *J. Exper. Psychol.*, 1928, XI, 443-467.

created by the fact that the one group spent an hour practicing for skill in drawing with the preferred hand, while the other group spent an equal period of time at rest.

When proper comparisons were drawn between the sets of data it was found that the nonpreferred hand had increased approximately thirty-six per cent for time and twenty-one per cent for errors, because of the practice that had been given to the preferred hand.[19] In other words, practice administered to one part of the body had been transferred to another part. Almost all of the experiments that have been done in this field have supported this conclusion.

The same facts hold true for exercise in the use of the visual functions. In one experiment in this field the left eyes of white rats were blindfolded whereupon they were trained to avoid the brighter of two lights in a problem box.[20] As soon as the subjects were able to make this distinction successfully for thirty consecutive trials, the blindfold was transferred to the right eye. Even though this eye had not been subjected to practice, all of the subjects continued to discriminate between the two lights as correctly as they had done before.

In another series of experiments the left arm and hand of a cebus monkey were paralyzed through a small operation performed on its brain. The subject was then trained to open a latch box with the right hand. When the necessary coördinations had been learned, the right hand and arm were paralyzed by an operation similar to the one named above. In the meantime, the animal had recovered the use of its left hand. When the latch box was presented to the subject, it fumbled clumsily at the catches with its right hand and then, without further delay, opened the latch successfully with the untrained left hand. In both of these cases then almost a complete transfer of the learned response from one organ of the body to another had taken place.[21]

There can be no doubt, then, but that training of one member of the body may promote skill in another part of the body. The degree of transfer is not always complete, but it is significant to know that a considerable amount of transfer may actually take place. To reach this conclusion, however, is one thing and to name the conditions under which such transfer becomes possible is quite another.

[19] Ewert, *ibid.*, p. 248.
[20] Cf. Lashley, K. S., "Vicarious Function After Destruction of the Visual Areas." *Amer. J. Physiol.*, 1922, LIX, 44-71.
[21] Lashley, K. S., "Studies of Cerebral Function in Learning. V. The Retention of Motor Habits After the Destruction of the So-called Motor Areas in Primates." *Arch. Neur. and Psychiat.*, 1924, XII, 249-276.

The student will realize this fact if he will only recall some of the experiments described in the last chapter which showed that the learning of one habit may seriously interfere with the learning of another. We must, then, pass on to other aspects of the experimental literature, for so important a question as the possible transfer effects of training must be examined from every point of view.

4. *Laboratory Studies on Transfer:* Until the turn of the present century, both teachers and students of the philosophy of education had simply taken it for granted that the transfer effects of training were fairly large. This belief was held, in particular, by teachers of mathematics, Latin, Greek, and other cultural and disciplinary subjects. A marked change in opinion took place, however, shortly after the publication of the following studies.[22]

In the first major experiment, two investigators sought to find out how practice in the estimation of areas, lengths, and weights would affect estimations of similar factors when slight differences in form and size were introduced. In the initial series of experiments the subjects were asked to estimate the areas of rectangles varying from ten to one hundred square centimeters in size. All of the subjects practiced this skill until marked improvement had been achieved. Similar tests were made of the ability to estimate weights varying from 120 to 1,800 grams, to estimate lines varying from .5 to 1.5 inches in length, and to perceive words containing "e's" and "s's" and other letters of the alphabet.

After these initial practice periods, changes were made in the stimulus-objects. When, for example, areas of the original size but of different shape were presented to the subjects, their skill in estimation was only forty-four per cent as great as it had been for the original material. Likewise, when the areas were increased from 140 to 300 square centimeters, the transfer of perceptual skill was limited to thirty per cent. As a result of these experiments, the authors concluded that "(i) improvement in any single mental function need not improve ability in functions commonly called by the same name—it may injure it; (ii) improvement in any single mental function rarely brings about equal improvement in any other function, no matter how similar, for the working of every mental function-group is conditioned by the nature of the data in each particular case; and (iii) the general consideration of the cases of retention or of loss of practice effect seems to make it likely that

---

[22] The initial study was made by James. Cf. James, W., *Principles of Psychology.* New York: Henry Holt and Co., 1890, Vol. I, pp. 666-668.

spread of practice occurs only where identical elements are concerned in the influencing and influenced functions."[23]

These experiments have been followed by a vast number of other experiments using a great many different kinds of material. In the field of memory proper and in addition to the James' experiments, the following researches may be mentioned. Ebert and Meumann have made the most elaborate study of the amount of transfer between memory practice on a series of nonsense syllables and various other types of learning, such as immediate memory for numbers, letters, words, permanent memory for prose, poetry, and the like.[24] The results made it appear that there was a large amount of transfer. Dearborn, however, remarks that Ebert and Meumann did not use a control group with respect to which the experimental group could be compared. When this was done, the amount of transfer discovered by Ebert and Meumann was reduced to a much smaller value.[25] Fracker based his studies on ability to remember various combinations of four degrees of loudness in a sound.[26] The four sounds were presented in various combinations and the subjects were to recall the order in which the sounds had been heard. The attempt was then made to see whether increased ability in this skill was carried over to memory for various combinations of four shades of grey, nine tones, eight shades of grey, four tones, geometrical figures, nine sets of numbers, arm movements, and poetry. In general, it was found that the amount of transfer to memory functions which were like the training series was considerably greater than it was for memory functions unlike the training series. Sleight used such functions as the following, viz., remembering and reproducing the location of points in circles, remembering two series of two dates, each associated with their corresponding events, learning a series of eight nonsense syllables, learning a stanza of from eight to twelve lines of poetry, learning a passage of prose, reproducing the content of a passage of prose, remembering locations on a map, remembering dictated sentences, memory span for letters, and

[23] Cf. Thorndike, E. L., and Woodworth, R. S., "Influence of Improvement in one Mental Function upon the Efficiency of Other Functions." *Psychol. Rev.*, 1901, VIII, 247-261, 384-395, 553-564. For a statement of the conclusions of this experiment, see Thorndike, E. L., *Educational Psychology*. New York: Columbia Univ. Press, 1913, Vol. II, pp. 398-399.
[24] Ebert, E., and Meumann, E., "Ueber einige Grundfragen der Psychologie der Gedächtnisses." *Arch. f. d. ges. Psychol.*, 1905, IV, 1-32.
[25] Cf. Dearborn, W. F., "Experiments in Learning." *J. Educ. Psychol.*, 1910, I, 373-388.
[26] Fracker, G. C., "On the Transference of Training in Memory," *Psychol. Rev. Monog.*, 1908, XXXVIII, 56-102.

remembering names.[27] Four groups of subjects were equated in ability, whereupon three of the groups were trained in three special ways while the fourth group had no special practice. The amount of transfer was almost negligible and Sleight concluded, therefore, that "there appears to be no general memory improvement as a result of practice nor any evidence for the hypothesis of a general memory function." Coover and Angell have studied the effect of training on imagery of various types. They, too, found scant evidence for transfer.[28] Dearborn measured the effect of practice in learning a vocabulary and poetry upon ability to memorize various other sorts of materials.[29] Winch studied the effect of memorizing poetry and of working arithmetical problems on the recall of a passage of historical prose. Some practice effect was discovered.[30]

A great many other experiments have followed the path suggested by Thorndike and Woodworth in that they have depended upon perceptual discriminations rather than upon memory proper. Coover used material somewhat like the Thorndike material and found a somewhat larger transfer effect than his predecessor had found.[31] Kline asked nine subjects to practice for fourteen days, thirty to forty-five minutes daily, in cancelling "e's" and "t's" on pages of prose. Each of the subjects had been tested before and after each practice in cancelling nouns, verbs, prepositions, pronouns, and adverbs. A control group of eight subjects was tested in like manner without the practice series. The discovery that the practice group did not gain as much as the unpracticed group was explained by the tendency to cross out words containing "e's" and "t's" instead of crossing out the required part of speech.[32] Bennett asked sixteen pupils to discriminate shades of red, yellow, green, and orange and differences in the pitch of tones before and after training. The training period lasted for four minutes during which the subjects made discriminations between shades of blue. A considerable

[27] Sleight, W. J., "Memory and Formal Training." *Brit. J. of Psychol.,* 1911, IV, 386-457.
[28] Coover, J. E., and Angell, F., "General Practice Effect of Special Exercise." *Amer. J. Psychol.,* 1907, XVIII, 327-340.
[29] Dearborn, W. F., "Experiments in Learning." *J. Educ. Psychol.,* 1910, I, 373-388.
[30] Winch, W. H., "The Transfer of Improvement of Memory in School Children." *Brit. J. Psychol.,* 1908, II, 284-293; 1910, III, 386-405; Winch, W. H., "Accuracy in School Children as Improvement in Numerical Accuracy Transfer." *J. Educ. Psychol.,* 1910, I, 557-589; 1911, II, 262-271.
[31] Coover, J. E., "Formal Discipline from the Standpoint of Experimental Psychology." *Psychol. Rev. Monog.,* 1916, XX (No. 3).
[32] Kline, L. W., "Some Experimental Evidence on the Doctrine of Formal Discipline." *Bull. State Normal School,* Duluth, Minn., 1909.

amount of transfer was discovered.[33] Bair attempted to measure transfer by training subjects in one function and then determining the effect of this training upon the progress which the subjects made in acquiring skill in other functions. Some improvement was shown.[34]

Judd and his students studied the effect of information about the principle of refraction upon learning to hit a target. To quote:

"One group of boys was given a full theoretical explanation of refraction. The other group of boys was left to work out experience without theoretical training. These two groups began practice with the target under twelve inches of water. It is a very striking fact that in the first series of trials the boys who knew the theory of refraction and those who did not, gave about the same results. That is, a theory seemed to be of no value in the first tests. All the boys had to learn how to use the dart, and theory proved to be no substitute for practice. At this point the conditions were changed. The twelve inches of water were reduced to four. The differences between the two groups of boys came out very strikingly. The boys without theory were very much confused. The practice gained with twelve inches of water did not help them with four inches. Their errors were large and persistent. On the other hand, the boys who had the theory, fitted themselves to four inches very rapidly." [35]

Webb studied the effect of learning one maze upon the rate of learning others. Both white rats and human beings were used as subjects, and it was found that the learning of one maze does have a beneficial effect on the mastery of subsequent maze situations, the amount of transfer being dependent, in part, upon the degree of simplicity of the two maze patterns.[36]

5. *Transfer in School Situations:* In addition to these experiments of a formal laboratory type, a great many studies have been made upon transfer in practical school situations where the material to be studied has consisted of parts of the curriculum and of pupil attitudes supposed to be developed in the schoolroom. Let us briefly run through some of the experiments that have been performed. In one of the first, Squire found that neatness developed in arithmetic papers upon the demand of the teachers was not transferred

---

[33] Bennett, C. J. C., *Formal Discipline.* New York: Teachers Coll., Columbia Univ. Press, 1907, *passim.*
[34] Bair, J. H., "The Practice Curve: A Study in the Formation of Habits." *Columbia Univ. Contrib. to Phil., Psychol., etc.,* 1902, IX (No. 3).
[35] Judd, C. H., "The Relation of Special Training to General Intelligence." *Educ. Rev.,* 1908, XXXVI, 28-42. See esp. p. 37.
[36] Webb, L. W., "Transfer of Training and Retroaction." *Psychol. Rev. Monog.,* 1917, XXIV (No. 104).

482 INTRODUCTION TO EDUCATIONAL PSYCHOLOGY

to language and spelling papers.[37] In another experiment, however, where the ideal of neatness was emphasized before a class, it was found that neatness would become effective to some extent in other classes.[38] The general results of studies on the relationship between formal grammar versus ability to use language seem to show that there is little transfer from the one situation to the other. Hoyt,[39] Briggs,[40] and Starch[41] have studied this problem. More evidence for transfer from training in arithmetic to reasoning in arithmetic has been forthcoming. Starch, for example, found such evidence.[42] Latin has been, perhaps, most studied. Swift examined the relation between Latin versus German on progress in learning Spanish.[43] Perkins studied the effect of emphasizing the derivation of English words from Latin upon the efficiency of Latin instruction.[44] Harris studied the relation of a study of Latin to spelling English words.[45] Starch has studied the effect of Latin versus German on the progress of students in the university.[46] The general outcome of these experiments seems to suggest that the transfer effect of Latin is much smaller than classical students have hoped for, the amount almost invariably standing below twenty per cent. Similar studies on the transfer effect of geometry have been more favorable. Rugg has concluded from such a study that a semester of descriptive geometry increases the student's ability to solve problems although the amount of the transfer is increased by an increase in similarity between problems to be solved and the problems included in the training course.[47]

[37] Cf. Bagley, W. C., *Educational Values.* New York: The Macmillan Co., 1911, p. 188.
[38] Ruediger, W. C., "The Indirect Improvement of Mental Functions Through Ideals." *Educ. Rev.,* 1908, XXXVI, 364-371. See also, "Mental Discipline." *School and Soc.,* 1915, II, 251-252.
[39] Hoyt, F. S., "Studies in the Teaching of English Grammar." *Teachers College Record,* 1906, VII (No. 5).
[40] Briggs, T. H., "Formal English Grammar As a Discipline." *Teachers College Record,* 1913 (No. 41).
[41] Starch, D., "The Measurement of Achievement in English Grammar." *J. Educ. Psychol.,* 1915, VI, 615-626.
[42] Starch, D., "The Transfer of Training in Arithmetic Operations." *J. Exper. Psychol.,* 1911, II, 209-13.
[43] Swift, E. J., "Studies in the Psychology and Physiology of Learning." *Amer. J. Psychol.,* 1903, XIV, 201-251.
[44] Perkins, A. S., "Latin as a Vocational Study in the Commercial Course." *Classical Journal,* 1914, X, 7-16.
[45] Harris, L. H., "A Study in the Relation of Latin to English Composition." *School and Soc.,* 1924, XIX, 171-172.
[46] Starch, D., "Further Experimental Data on the Value of Studying Foreign Languages." *School Rev.,* 1917, XXV, 243-248, and the like. For further references, see Starch, D., *Educational Psychology,* New York: The Macmillan Co., 1927, Chapter XV.
[47] Rugg, H. O., "The Experimental Determination of Mental Discipline in School Studies." Baltimore: Warwick and York, 1916.

One of the most elaborate studies carried out in an actual school situation made use of some eight thousand school children, none of whom knew that they were being used as the subjects of an experiment. The children were practiced in their actual school work, the test performance consisting of an intelligence test which was given at the beginning and at the end of the school year. The subjects were divided into groups in such a way that only one item of the curriculum was different with respect to two groups. On the whole, it was found that the amount of transfer from different subjects was not so great as easily to be discerned. The school subjects, when arranged in a descending order from high value to low value, stood as follows: French, chemistry, trigonometry, physics, general science, Latin, bookkeeping, physical training, arithmetic, geometry, algebra, history, music, shop, Spanish, English, drawing, business, civics, biology, dramatic art, stenography, economics, cooking, and sewing. In every case, however, the transfer effect was rather small. As a general conclusion to the experiment, Thorndike wrote as follows:

"By any reasonable interpretation of the results, the intellectual value of studies should be determined largely by the special information, habits, interests, attitudes, and ideals which they demonstrably produce. The expectation of any large differences in general improvement of the mind from one study rather than another seems doomed to disappointment. . . . The chief reason why good thinkers seem superficially to have been made such by having taken such school subjects, is that good thinkers have taken such studies, becoming better by the inherent tendency of the good to gain more than the poor from any study. . . . When the good thinkers studied Greek and Latin, these studies seemed to make good thinking. Now that the good thinkers study Physics and Trigonometry, these seem to make good thinkers. . . . After positive correlation of gain with initial ability is allowed for, the balance in favor of any study is certainly not large. Disciplinary values may be real and deserve weight in the curriculum, but the weights should be reasonable." [48]

From this brief summary of the more important experimental methods of attack upon the problem of formal discipline, we may draw the following conclusions. In general, it is not fair to say that either laboratory or practical experiments in the schoolroom have demonstrated the absence of transfer of training. On the contrary, some small measure of transfer is usually found but by no means in so large a proportion as the traditional theory had argued for. In the second place, it seems fairly clear that the training value

[48] Thorndike, E. L., "Mental Discipline in High School Studies." *J. Educ. Psychol.*, 1924, XV, 1-22, 83-98.

of different subjects is not so great as had been supposed. The traditional theory has always based its claim on the proposition that mathematics and the classics have exceptional advantages as disciplinary subjects. The experiments just examined seem to deny the possibility.

III. EXPLANATION OF TRANSFER

1. *Introduction:* We must now try to draw out of this survey of the results of some of the experiments on transfer of training those general principles or considerations which are, after all, much more important to the teacher than the experiments themselves. The student has gained the impression, no doubt, that many of the experiments in this field have been for the distinct purpose of showing that there is no transfer from one situation to another. This is certainly true of all of the early experiments. Educators have had the habit of justifying some of the more difficult subjects in a curriculum on the grounds that even though these subjects gave students nothing that they could use in an immediate and practical way, they must, nevertheless, contribute materially to the general psychological competence of the student. In other words, then, the first experiments on the transfer of training were specifically designed to show that educators had been wrong in these matters and that the time had come when the curriculum should be changed so as to make it of more practical value to students.

In spite of the motive which lay behind this early work, however, most of the experiments we have cited have actually shown at least small amounts of transfer. Even in the initial work of Thorndike and Woodworth, the subjects seemed to have profited a little by their special training in particular situations. It is important to notice, however, that the amount of transfer from one situation to another varies rather regularly with the character of the experimental conditions. In general, those experimental conditions which include practice on specific and easily measurable functions show a minimal amount of transfer, whereas those which are less specific display a relatively large amount of transfer. We shall comment upon this fact a little later.

The first task of this section is to take account of some of the explanations that have been offered of the amounts of transfer actually discovered. The very fact that experimenters should be called upon to explain the transfer effect of training is, in itself, an interesting comment upon them and their work, for it shows clearly enough that they have approached this group of problems with a definite bias. Instead of allowing the burden of proof to rest upon those who would argue that there is no transfer, the burden of proof has been placed upon those who would argue that there is.

As we have said above, educators have, by long tradition, simply assumed the existence of transfer. This assumption was made because the mind was supposed to be the principal subject of the educative process, and it seemed reasonable to suppose that if the mind is a particular species having inherent or intrinsic traits and functions, these traits and functions must be much feebler in small children than they are in adults. To say that discovered amounts of transfer from one situation to another must be explained is simply to assume that transfer is an unusual or unexpected thing rather than the usual or the expected thing.

The theories which are used most frequently to account for transfer of practice from one situation to another are as follows, viz., the theory of identical elements and the theory of general generalized habits. The difference between these two theories implies certain important facts about methods of explanation which are adequate to this particular group of problems. Furthermore, it will be helpful to say a few words about the relation between transfer and learning, on the one hand, and transfer and the growth pattern, on the other.

2. *The Theory of Identical Elements:* The theory of identical elements as an explanation for observed degrees of transfer is based upon the argument that two or more learning situations may include part processes that are the same in two situations.[49] As an illustration we may take the skills involved in multiplying one three-place number by another. The chances are that before multiplications at this level are undertaken, a child has already learned how to multiply a single digit by another. This skill is, in part, one of the products of having learned the multiplication table. After multiplication has been completed, it is necessary to resort to addition. Let us suppose that the act of addition involves finding the sum of seven and nine. It may be pointed out, however, that the average child will already have acquired some considerable degree of skill in adding these two numbers. It would seem to follow that, if the complete task of multiplying one three-place number by another involves the addition of nine and seven, multiplication will be increased in effectiveness in proportion as skill has already been acquired in adding these numbers. It ought to follow, then, from the theory of identical elements that transfer will take place from one situation to another in direct

[49] Cf. Thorndike, E. L., *The Principles of Teaching.* New York: A. G. Seiler, 1906, pp. 243 ff.

proportion to the number of these identical elements. Since the number of identical elements between any two situations might be fairly small, it would be reasonable to suppose that the transfer effect would likewise be small.

A. THE MEANING OF IDENTITY: Up to this point, the theory of identical elements seems to be very simple and straightforward. There are, however, a good many questions to be raised by the exact meanings which can be attached to the word "identical." It is one thing, of course, to say that the figure 9, printed in a list of adding exercises in an arithmetic book, is identical with the figure 9 written on a piece of paper during the course of an exercise in multiplication; and it is quite another thing to attach the word "identity" to objects which may have the same functional value for the organism.[50] For example, a child might acquire some skill in accurate throwing, now by using a ball, and again by using some of its playthings. There is, of course, no similarity between a ball and a doll unless similarity is defined in terms of the functional operations through which the child goes in reacting to these two objects. Both, of course, may be thrown and the repeated throwing of either might lead to a considerable improvement in accuracy.

This identity of function is, perhaps, an identity implied above in our illustration from arithmetic. The psychological operations involved in adding nine to seven during an adding exercise are identical with the psychological operations involved in adding nine to seven during the course of an act of multiplication. There is, however, a further source of complexity in any definition of identity, for the doctrine, as we have stated it up to this point, seems to imply that every learning situation is to be understood in terms of its parts rather than in terms of the situation as a configured whole.

This is a phase of learning, and of all psychological operations, for that matter, which has been much emphasized by that type of psychology known as Gestalt psychology or as configurationism.[51] Let us suppose, for example, that we are conducting an experiment upon the ability to identify geometrical forms. During the first part of our experiment, we use very simple forms such as the angles which two or three lines might make with one another, or the spaces that might be inclosed by three or four lines. After a considerable amount of practice, we now bring some of these simpler geometrical

[50] Experiments on animals are beginning to throw some light on this problem. Cf. Munn, N. L., *Animal Psychology*. Boston: Houghton Mifflin Co., 1933, pp. 244 ff.

[51] Cf. Wheeler, R. H., and Perkins, F. T., *op. cit.*, pp. 318 ff.

figures into large complexes. We wish to find out whether previous practice in identifying geometrical forms contributes anything to the identification of more complex forms.

Experiments of this type show that there is no transfer from the simpler situation to the more complex situation, even though the complex situation contains nothing but geometrical forms with which the subject is wholly familiar.[52] The point is that when the simpler forms are brought together into more complex units, there is a tendency for a person to take the more complex units as single configured wholes in which the parts lose their identity. In other words, the parts of which the configured whole is made now have a different functional value for an observer.

B. FUNCTIONAL IDENTITY: We may draw the inference from these experiments that the theory of identical elements is not so simple as it appears at first sight. As a matter of fact, it may not be possible to speak with real intelligence about the theory of identical elements until many further discoveries have been made bearing upon the meanings that ought to be attached to functional identity. There must be, of course, a good many psychological operations which do involve functional identities and from this point of view it is fair to assume that discovered measures of transfer of training can be explained, in part, at least, by the number of these functional identities.

Even in very simple types of learning identities may be achieved by wholly different means. As a case in point, let us take an experiment in conditioning a white rat to jump over a barrier.[53] When the subjects in this experiment were allowed to jump over the barrier without the influence of a conditioned stimulus, their behavior-pattern was usually of such form that it could be described in considerable detail. When, however, the same subjects jumped over a barrier after having been conditioned to a painful stimulus, the jumping was similar to the previous behavior-patterns only in the sense that the rats actually got over the barrier. The types of muscular coördination involved and the general form of jumping behavior differed in certain essential respects from the initial behavior. In other words, these subjects had not been conditioned simply by attaching a stable pattern of response to a new stimulus-situation. On the contrary, the new situation had led to a new

[52] Gottschaldt, K., "Ueber den Einfluss der Erfahrung auf die Wahrnehmung von Figuren." *Psychol. Forsch.*, 1926, VIII, 261-318; 1929, XII, 1-87.
[53] Cf. Warner, L. H., "An Experimental Search for the Conditioned Response." *J. Genet. Psychol.*, 1932, XLI, 91-115.

action-pattern which served approximately the same purpose as had been served by the older action-pattern.[54]

C. THE S-R FORMULA: There is one further feature of the theory of identical elements which ought not to go unmentioned. This theory is based, apparently, upon another theory about the fundamental character of all psychological operations. This theory is usually expressed in what we may call the S-R formula.[55] The S-R formula asserts that all human conduct (and all animal conduct as well) can be described in terms of the stimuli that are presented to a subject, in terms of the responses which the subject makes to these stimuli, and in terms of the connections which are established between stimulus and response. The function of education would be to create and solidify as many new connections as the normal conditions of life would seem to warrant.

In other words, it is implied that all learning is connection-forming.[56] It is implied, moreover, that connection-forming is a result that can be achieved only after the learner has made a number of efforts to meet a situation, some of which are most certainly wrong but one or more of which may be right. The right actions are said to be stamped in under the influence of states of satisfyingness which are supposed to accompany successful behavior. Subsequent stages of the learning process can be described, then, as a process of overlearning in the sense that the right connections are made more and more inevitable. If we think of the nervous system in terms of a system of wires between sense organs and muscles, overlearning would imply that these wires offer less and less resistance to the passage of nerve currents. Similarly, if we think of connections as channels of conduction, then overlearning would imply that the channels are dug deeper and deeper through practice.[57]

This view of the nature of learning implies that the end result of practice periods is greater and greater fixity of response rather than greater plasticity, flexibility, or intelligence in response. A person who had a great many habits could, of course, be called intelligent in the sense that he had learned how to make the right reactions in response to a great variety of situations. If we assume that one

[54] Cf. Tolman, E. C., "Theories of Learning," in Moss, F. A. (Ed.), *Comparative Psychology*. New York: Prentice-Hall, Inc., 1934, Chapter XII, *passim*.
[55] Cf. Gates, A. I., *Psychology for Students of Education*. New York: The Macmillan Co., 1930, *passim*.
[56] Thorndike, E. L., *Educational Psychology*. New York: Columbia University Press, 1913, Vol. I, *passim*.
[57] Lashley, K. S., "The Theory That Synaptic Resistance Is Reduced by the Passage of the Nerve Impulse." *Psychol. Rev.*, 1924, XXXI, 369-375.

situation differs from another only in terms of complexity, that is, if we assume that one situation is simply an assemblage of other situations for which adequate reactions have already been learned, it must follow that a reaction to a new situation could be intelligent in direct proportion to the number of the older connections already established.

It now seems to be fairly certain that situations do not differ from one another in this simple quantitative way. As we have implied above, every situation is an entity in itself in the sense that it is a configured pattern of events which must be reacted to as a pattern.[58] In other words, no person can ever learn how to respond to all of the situations which may be placed before him even in the most stable types of environment. We may well inquire, therefore, whether the word "learning" really exhausts the types of change that may take place during human growth. If it does exhaust these changes, the theory of identical elements as a source of transfer of training might be made acceptable. Moreover, experiments on the transfer of training which require of the subjects that they shall become more and more automatic in their responses would be adequate to the nature of the problem described by the phrase "the transfer of training." On the contrary, if learning does not exhaust the changes possible in human nature, it will be necessary to inquire how these other types of change are related to the problem of transfer. Moreover, it will be necessary to inquire about modes of experimentation that can be called adequate to this field. A description which has already been given of that type of learning sometimes called insight suggests that the transfer of training cannot be explained wholly in terms of identical elements.

3. *Generalized Habits and Attitudes:* Among the experiments on the transfer of training that have been attempted, there are two which stand out as being markedly different from the others. These two ask the subjects not merely to exercise themselves in certain specific ways, but to make use of information and attitudes which form a background, as it were, for the more specific learning tasks.

The first of the experiments just mentioned was done by Woodrow. Woodrow's experiments made use of three groups of subjects who were divided in such a way as to approximately equal one another in ability.[59] One group, the control group, had no special training whatsoever. A second group, known as the practice group,

---

[58] Cf. Wheeler, R. H., and Perkins, F. T., *op. cit., passim.*
[59] Woodrow, H., "The Effect of Types of Training upon Transference," *J. Educ. Psychol.*, 1927, XVIII, 159-172.

was given material to memorize but without any special guidance or instruction as to fruitful methods, helpful attitudes, and the like. This group went through the following program, viz., twenty minutes memorizing poetry, twenty-five minutes memorizing poetry, twenty-eight minutes memorizing nonsense syllables, twenty minutes memorizing nonsense syllables, nineteen minutes memorizing nonsense syllables, twenty-five minutes memorizing poetry, twenty minutes memorizing poetry, and again twenty minutes memorizing nonsense syllables. In other words, a total of 177 minutes during eight periods of work was devoted to practice without special guidance or instruction. The third group, which was called the educated group, likewise worked through eight periods. In the first period, seven minutes was devoted to an exposition of the rules and thirteen minutes to memorizing poetry. The second period gave seven minutes to exposition of rules and eighteen minutes to memorizing poetry. The third period of twenty-eight minutes was devoted to an exposition and illustration of rules of learning. The fourth period gave five minutes to a review of the preceding period and fifteen minutes to the learning of nonsense syllables. The fifth period gave nine minutes to a "blackboard talk" on the meaning of secondary associations and ten minutes to learning of nonsense syllables. The sixth and seventh periods were devoted to the learning of poetry. The eighth period was spent in a review of methods and the situations in which to use them. The total amount of time spent in the eight periods was again 177 minutes.

Among the methods and devices given to the educated group were the use of the whole method, the use of actual recitation instead of mere rereading, methods for using rhythms, groupings, meaningful clues, and the like. Tests to determine the amount of transfer were given before and after practice to all three groups, viz., the control group, the practice group, and the educated group. Woodrow drew the following conclusions from his experiments:

"The facts given establish very definitely certain conclusions. They show unequivocally that the training group did much better than the practice group in every one of six end-tests, which were related to each other only to the extent of an average intercorrelation, after correction for attenuation, of 38.3 per cent. The percentage of gain in the end-tests averaged 31.6 higher for the training group than for the control group.

"This greater gain on the part of the training group was obtained, in spite of the fact that drill in memorizing was given to the training group with no other material than that employed with the practice group. It was produced by using the drill material primarily as material with which to conduct practice in proper methods of memorizing, and, further, by explaining these methods and calling attention to the ones which should be employed when new kinds of memorizing were undertaken. In short, the experiment shows that in a case where one kind of training—undirected drill—produces amounts of transference which are sometimes positive and sometimes negative, but always small, another kind of training with the same drill material may result in a transference, the effects of which are uniformly large and positive.[60]

There can be no doubt about these results. As the data show, the educated group enjoyed the advantage of more than ten times as much transfer as did the practice group. In other words, we have here a demonstration of the advantage not only in learning but in teaching method of supplementing the process of mechanical learning with a general understanding of methods and situations. Even a critic of transfer effects has recognized this fact in the remark: "Insight into new situations and ability to transfer reactions to them is brought about only by careful education in which various situations are properly introduced and the proper reactions exercised." [61] This is a remark that could not be made if one were to limit onself to a study of stable and fixed connections between S and R or to the insertion into different situations of identical elements.

Further evidence on this problem is brought by Meredith's experiment on the amount of transfer from practice in the definition of scientific terms to the definition of more ordinary terms.[62] Here, too, three equivalent groups were used where equivalence was based on scores on intelligence tests and teachers' estimates. Group A, the control group, was given no special training, Group B, the practice group, received routine training in the art of defining scientific terms, and Group C, the training group (equivalent to Woodrow's educated group) was trained in definition, the extent of the training amounting to three periods of discussion of approximately ten minutes each. These periods included practice in defining and a critical analysis of definitions. The training presented was thus not a simple unitary process, but a combination of several activities involving the higher coördinating functions of the brain. The results of the experiment showed clearly enough that Group C, the trained group, had the advantage of a relatively large amount of transfer.

[60] Woodrow, H., "The Effect of Types of Training upon Transference," *J. Educ. Psychol.*, 1927, XVIII, p. 171.
[61] Gates, A. I., *op. cit.*, p. 442.
[62] Meredith, G. P., "Consciousness of Method as a Means of Transfer of Training." *The Forum of Education*, 1927, V, 37-45.

We may conclude, then, that when a student is asked to learn poetry or prose while being instructed about methods of learning and while being reminded of devices that can be used to hasten learning, he is certainly approaching his problem from a different point of view than are those subjects who do not change their general set or attitude from one learning period to another.

A. OVERLEARNING: In order to catch the full significance of the issue raised by the theory of generalized habits and attitudes, on the one hand, and the theory of identical elements, on the other, let us take the following situation. Let us say that we have two groups of subjects. The one group is to learn, as did James, the first 158 lines of Hugo's *Satyre*. It is proposed to measure not only the amount of time required to learn these lines but the number of repetitions which must precede the first perfect recitation from memory. After this initial test, let us ask this group of subjects to spend an hour a day for a full month in learning nonsense syllables. At the end of this special practice period, we return to another 158 lines of the *Satyre*. Both during the practice period and in the final learning period, we again measure time consumed and number of repetitions necessary to the required levels of achievement.

We may now say that, if there is transfer of training, the practice spent in learning nonsense syllables ought to have strengthened the memory functions so that the second set of 158 lines from the *Satyre* could be learned more readily than the first set. The only instruction given to this group of subjects is the following, viz., to learn this material as fast as it can. It must be clear that, when a group of subjects approaches a learning problem under these conditions, they approach it with an attitude or with learning habits which have been acquired and stabilized during previous learning periods. They will possess, for example, tempos of working and degrees of motivation which represent a more or less permanent way of going about learning tasks.

To be sure, none of the subjects possessed these permanent ways as new-born infants. They would not even have possessed all of them during the first years of schooling. Somewhere along the line, however, all of them will have become so habitualized or stabilized that they represent a permanent part of each learner's psychological equipment. They describe how efficient the learner is as a learner. It would seem to follow from these considerations that nothing has been done to the subjects of this first group during the month of practice to alter their efficiency as learners. In other words, they have simply learned nonsense syllables for a month with the same attitudes, the same methods of working, and the same dispositions which prevailed during the initial learning period and which will also prevail during the final learning period. If any change has been wrought at all in them, the change will be toward greater fixity of the supplementary habits and attitudes previously acquired. To say the same thing in another way, the efficiency of these subjects as learners, because of the practice through which they have passed, will have become all the more stable or inexorable.

B. GENERALIZED HABITS: Now let us compare the subjects in this group with the subjects in another group. The task assigned to the subjects in the second group will be exactly the same as it was for the first group. There is an initial 158 lines of Hugo's *Satyre,* an hour a day for a month spent in learning nonsense syllables, and a final set of 158 lines from the *Satyre.* During the month of practice, however, the experimenter gives to the subjects in this second group a number of lectures about methods of learning, rates of reading, distribution of practice periods, the influence of motivation on learning, and other hints and suggestions concerning the most effective ways of using practice periods. These instructions are given not only at the start of the training period but they are repeated frequently during its entire course.

The student will see at once that the subjects in this second group are exercising themselves in two different respects. On the one hand, they are exercising themselves in the learning of nonsense syllables. In this respect they are to be compared with the subjects in the first group. On the other hand, however, the subjects in the second group will exercise themselves with respect to the accessory habits, attitudes, and dispositions involved in learning. In other words, they are exercising themselves with respect to those psychological functions which determine the practical efficiency of a person as a learner.

It seems to be clear, for example, that if the subjects in the second group change their previous levels of motivation during the practice period, they will approach the final learning task after having become a different kind of psychological person. Similarly, if they have acquired, during the training period, a new method of reading material or of reciting it, they will bring to the final learning task a different degree of competence than they possessed during the initial learning task. In short, they will be, at the end of the training period, a different sort of person than they were at its beginning. Their efficiency as learners will have been increased. They will have reached new levels of competency in the use of some of those psychological operations which add to the capacity of a learner as a learner. This, then, seems to be the essential difference between the theory of identical elements and the theory of generalized habits and attitudes.

C. FEATURES OF A RELEVANT EXPERIMENT: This difference raises two very important questions. In the first place, we must examine the relevancy of some of the methods that have been used in experiments in this field for getting results that are really significant. It is clear that, if an experiment is set up in such a way as to make it impossible to get results which will bear upon the problem in hand, the experiment is quite beside the mark. It says nothing either for or against the transfer of training. In the second place, we must inquire about the relation between the transfer of training and the nature of psychological growth. If it is true that some types of practice serve only to make a person more automatic at a given level of efficiency while other types of practice actually allow him to grow older or more mature or more efficient in his psychological functions, this fact should be noted and applied to the problems of the transfer of training.

4. *Experimental Methods:* The first of the questions just asked can be answered rather quickly. The student has only to look back over the description of some of the experiments in the field of transfer of training in order to realize that they have not been at all devised to meet the requirements of this problem.

A. FUNCTIONS AND SERVICES: As an argument in favor of this statement, let us refer again to the distinction that can be drawn between the major psychological functions possessed by a person and the services rendered either to him or to his social group by the use of these functions. As a specific example, we may take reading. As we have seen, reading is a psychological operation that involves a great many different factors, one of the most important of which lies in the skill with which the reader may use his eye muscles. The rate of reading, primarily, and the speed of comprehension, secondarily, depend upon the number of times the eyes come to rest on each line of printed material, upon the duration of these pauses, and upon the number of times the reader has to look back in order to pick up a word or a phrase that has been missed.

Now this skill, being a constituent part of the total operation known as reading, acquires a given level of excellence not so much because of precise practice periods in developing it but more as a by-product of actual reading exercises. The chances are that fairly definite tempos of movement and equally definite habits of fixation are acquired long before the child has finished his grade school work. In other words, with respect to this phase of the operation known as reading, most persons will have achieved what has been called a behavior constancy. They will have learned to move their eyes at a given rate and in given form. This rate and this form probably represent the most favored or most normal condition for any particular person. They represent a level of fixity which has been reached during the period between infancy and late childhood. In short, they represent a level of efficiency in the use of the eyes which is quite satisfactory for all of the normal needs of a particular person and he proceeds, therefore, to use this level of efficiency for a good many other different purposes. He may read poetry or prose or he may watch a football game or try to follow the tricks of a sleight-of-hand performer. To be sure, if he has not learned how to use his eyes with a high level of efficiency, a great many things on the football field, on the highway, or in the theater will escape him.

B. AN EXPERIMENT ON SERVICES: Now let us suppose that we are about to conduct a study of the transfer of training, where reading is the psychological function to be measured. We choose a group of subjects, each one of whom has attained some particular level of efficiency in the use of his visual apparatus. We set up the experiment in the following way. We find out, first, how fast each of the subjects can read a standardized selection of prose. This measure, if taken carefully, ought to give us an index of efficiency in the use of the eyes during the act of reading.

The subjects will differ widely from one another, of course, in efficiency. There will be some who can read with high levels of comprehension at least twice as fast as others. Having established these facts, we invite each of the subjects to a long training program. Some of them will be asked to read poetry, others to read prose, still others to read nonsense syllables, and yet another subgroup to read a foreign language. We may even set up an experimental situation involving many moving parts and give a subgroup of subjects practice in observation under the conditions prescribed.

Let us say that these practice periods continue for a considerable period of time. At the end of the training period we take a new measure of rate of reading. As many of the experiments cited earlier in this chapter have indicated, we shall probably find that our subjects are not significantly better—that is, more efficient—at the time of the final test than they were at the time of the first test. In other words, it will appear that there has been no transfer of training. It may even appear that practice in reading nonsense syllables shows just as little transfer as practice in reading poetry or prose.

The student can see, however, that this whole experiment simply does not meet the issue raised by the question as to whether training can be transferred or not, for the subjects used in the experiment have not taken advantage of the training period actually to increase their efficiency in reading. On the contrary, they have simply used the habit-resources of which they are already in possession in such a manner as to make these resources more fixed than they were at the beginning. Having acquired a given level of skill in the use of the eyes they proceed to practice at this level.

Now practice of this type serves only that phase of learning known as overlearning. The chances are that, when a child first undertakes to use its eyes in an act of observation, it makes a good many movements which are not necessary. As we have seen in our study of varieties of learning, the proper movements emerge out of the whole complex of movements by some such principle as trial-and-error, with the gradual selection of appropriate movements. After the appropriate movements have been discovered, however, they may be exercised repeatedly in order that they may become well fixed or habitualized. Most of our habits, for example, are acquired modes of response which have emerged out of more immature patterns of response and which have become highly automatic and wholly dependable simply because they have been overlearned.

In the experiment just described, therefore, we have not invited our subjects to acquire any new skills or to reach any new levels of efficiency. We have simply asked them to become more automatic or more stabilized in a series of skills which they have already acquired. To be sure, overlearning does make some contribution to efficiency. This fact holds true, in particular, in the transition period during which a person is just moving from a barely learned skill to a well-automatized habit. We ought, then, to expect a small amount of transfer of training even in the type of experiment described above. It would not be reasonable to expect, however, a very large amount of transfer unless the training period which is placed between the initial measure of skill and the final measure of skill covers a period of years. The years to be covered should certainly stand early in the growth pattern.

C. AN EXPERIMENT ON FUNCTIONS: Now, let us suppose that we perform the experiment described above under the following conditions. First, let us measure the rate at which a five-year-old child can read. We may then allow this child to practice the art of reading for the next seven years. When it is twelve years old, we can take another measure of its rate of reading. We shall find, of course, that it can now read much faster than it could on the first occasion. In this case, the amount of transfer would be very large. We would have no hesitancy at all in ascribing the superior achievement of a twelve-year-old child to the training period through which it had passed. We may assert again, then, that many of the experiments which have been carried out in the attempt to discover degrees of transfer from one situation to another are simply inadequate to the problem for they do not take account of the growth factor.

If we draw this conclusion, we ought to describe a type of experiment that would be suitable. This we have already done. We have said above that, if a group of subjects is carried through a training program which really modifies the quality of its psychological operations, this training program will certainly throw light upon the extent to which transfer is possible. In more detail, if the subjects named above could be given types of practice which would lead to new habits in rate of eye movement, in number of fixations per line, in number of regressive movements per line, and in all other features of the total act of reading, they certainly would be able to read faster and with greater degrees of comprehension after their training than before. As a result of their training, they would become a different type of psychological instrument. Certain fundamental skills would have been brought to a higher level of efficiency. These skills would serve the person who possessed them to better advantage.

In any case, the results of such experiments as those conducted by Woodrow and Meredith result in much higher degrees of transfer from a training period to a test period than is the case with other types of experiments. It is hardly worth while to discount experiments of this type because they cannot be carried out with the same degree of accuracy as experiments of the other type. Even when we say this, however, the student will see that some of the loss in experimental exactness is simply due to a failure to locate exactly the intrinsic character of the problems created by transfer of training.

5. *Growth and Transfer:* The whole argument we are making concerning the transfer of training can be brought to still clearer expression if we try to discover some of the relations between changes in the growth pattern, on the one hand, and the transfer

of training, on the other. The student will recall that a very real test of the transfer of training would be available if we were to assume that studies on transfer were carried out with young children and if the training period included several months or several years rather than a few days or a few weeks.

Compare, for example, the levels of efficiency which are displayed by a new-born infant, on the one hand, and those that are displayed by a person in early maturity, on the other. As we have seen, it is scarcely possible to attach the word efficiency to the new-born infant at all. It displays practically no maturity in the use of its psychological functions. It has no highly developed skills either at the motor level or at the perceptual level. Its emotionalized forms of response are almost completely undifferentiated. It does not solve problems, and its motives are limited almost entirely to its primary tissue needs. Between the hour of birth, however, and an hour selected at random during its twentieth year, a tremendous amount of training will have taken place. The subject of our experiment will have profited from this training by having become more mature in the use of his psychological functions.

At any given age, all of these functions will have achieved measurable levels of efficiency. This means that, at any particular age level, a given level of efficiency can be used for a good many different purposes. The older a child becomes the more efficient it will be until that stage is reached in its whole growth pattern where skills and attitudes have reached an acceptable or optimal level of efficiency.

A. LIMITS OF IMPROVEMENT: In studies on learning, it has sometimes been helpful to think of the possible limits of learning. These limits are usually described as being set by physiological factors. In any given case, then, we may say that there is a physiological limit beyond which a person cannot pass. There is, however, a wide difference between the physiological limit and the practical limit of learning. The point is that most children reach a practical limit fairly early in the growth pattern.

The practical limits for different psychological functions vary, of course, between wide extremes. One such variability is commonly recognized in the development of problem-solving. As a rule, teachers are inclined to say that human beings do not really become problem-solvers until the late years of adolescence. With these considerations before us, the following conclusion seems to be warranted, viz., that any experiment on the transfer of training which takes a practical limit for granted is simply not relevant to the problems raised by the transfer of training. On the contrary, any experiment which presupposes a possible lifting of the practical limits is a relevant experiment. Moreover, it is an experiment in which considerable degrees of transfer will appear.

B. TRANSFER OF PERSONS: We may say all of this in another way. The theory of identical elements sometimes implies that transfer is to be explained because a part of one situation is identical with a part of some other situation or with the whole of it. This theory also says, however, that sets of connections may be transferred from one situation to another. If we expand this doctrine, we may say that the real heart of the problem created by transfer of training is to be found in the fact that a person is transferred from one situation to another. If the person that is transferred is not a different kind of a person, that is, if he is not the sum of several new levels of practical efficiency, there will be no transfer.

On the contrary, if he is a different kind of a person, that is, if the practical limit of his various efficiencies has been materially raised, there will be transfer. The transfer will be increased in direct proportion to the increase in the practical limits of learning. This conclusion is so obvious that those persons who have made transfer a difficult problem can be excused, for it is always easy to overlook the obvious. So long as teachers leave out of account the essential character of the growth pattern and so long as they fail to see the difference between the relative excellence of a psychological function as compared with the different services which these functions may render, the problem of transfer will appear difficult. When, however, we recognize the fact that the growth pattern is a pattern made up of a constantly increasing measure of efficiency in the use of the psychological functions, an increase which is directly attributable to training periods, transfer is easily demonstrated.

C. LIMITS OF TRANSFER: We still have to inquire after the presumable limits of transfer, for it is important to know what advantages are to be gained from any particular training period. In general, we may say that the limits of transfer are set by the extent to which preschool education has already led to fixity in psychological operations. The student will recall that we have already discussed the relations between fixity and plasticity in the first chapter. The new-born infant is almost wholly plastic. It is highly amenable to training. At various points in its growth pattern, however, initial levels of plasticity are converted into practical levels of fixity. If a learning situation makes no attempt to convert an attained level of fixity back into a more plastic condition looking toward a new level of fixity no transfer will appear. On the contrary, if a given training period actually raises the level of attained fixity, transfer will almost certainly appear.

6. *Conclusion:* There is, perhaps, no feature of the whole field of educational psychology which more richly deserves the serious attention of experimenters and teachers than the phase that has been discussed in this chapter. Even at the expense of exaggerating the situation a little, we may say that the issue involved is simply this: Shall education lead to the development of a large number of specialized skills and habits of action or shall it make more effective psychological instruments out of people? At the present time it appears to be doing both. The first years of schooling are obviously directed toward the improvement of the growing child as a psychological instrument. The item that is transferred from one situation to another when growth has taken place most rapidly is the child itself. At higher levels, however, teachers often give the impression that they have abandoned this particular goal of teaching effort and have turned to the task of taking a psychological instrument as it stands and equipping it with as many specialized traits and skills as they can.

The query which we have raised in this chapter is simply this: Can the teacher carry over into the higher forms of education the methods that are used at the lower levels? In other words, is it possible really to increase still further the maturity of people who enter the high school and the college so that they will, in their high school and college work, give the impression that they are able to do the work assigned to them? It seems fairly safe to say that an answer to this query cannot be gained by experimental procedures which lead to greater and greater fixation of methods of working at levels which have already reached the practical limit of excellence. Whatever the cause, there are a great many teachers at the upper levels who are beginning to feel that the students who come under their direction have neither the psychological stamina nor the methods of working which seem to have characterized a great many students a generation or so ago.

READINGS

The problems discussed in this chapter are conspicuous in the sense that they have not received the thoroughgoing appraisal which has been given to other departments of research in educational psychology. There is, as the footnotes in this chapter have indicated, an astonishing array of experimental evidence, but no one has as yet examined methods of research, balanced one set of conclusions against another, or brought to bear upon the whole problem data from researches in other fields looking toward a systematic survey of this particular problem. A beginning in this direction has been made by Orata, P., *The Theory of Identical Elements.* Columbus: Ohio State Univ. Press, 1928. Further critical studies of this type are urgently needed.

Good surveys of the experimental literature are to be found in any of the textbooks on educational psychology. Consider, for example, Pressey, S. L., *Psychology and the New Education.* Harper and Bros., 1933, Chapter XIV; Dunlap, K., *Habits: Their Making and Unmaking.* New York: Liveright Publishing Corp., 1932, Chapter VI. Wheeler, R. H., and Perkins, F. T., *Principles of Mental Development.* New York: T. Y. Crowell Co., Chapter XVII.

The student will find suggestive points of view about this and other phases of the learning process in Bode, B. H., *Conflicting Psychologies of Learning.* Boston: D. C. Heath and Co., 1929, *passim.* See also, Bode, B. H., *Modern Educational Theories.* New York: The Macmillan Co., 1927, Chapter IX and *passim.*

CHAPTER FOURTEEN

THE ART OF TEACHING

I. Science and Practice

1. *Introduction:* It was said in the preface that students and teachers often fail to get the practical help for which they have hoped from books on educational psychology because these books do not seem to be talking about the things that actually happen in a classroom. The reader may feel, perhaps, that this was certainly the case with all of the chapters that made up the first part of our study, for every one of them was heavily loaded with psychology rather than with methods of teaching. Throughout this second part, more attention has been given to schoolroom problems; but even so, our study has been definitely psychological rather than pedagogical.

2. *The Genetic Point of View:* The author has not made much of an attempt to avoid this procedure, for two reasons. In the first place, when we base the art of teaching upon the genetic point of view, we assume that many of the questions that will arise at any particular age level cannot be answered unless one knows something about the origin and developmental history of the factors involved. We can think of nothing that is more practical, therefore, than a view of teaching methods based upon the whole growth pattern.

It may be that not enough facts have been presented actually to give the reader a feeling for the growth pattern rather than a casual acquaintance with it, but the student may be sure that he has not got all he should out of the previous chapters, unless he has been able not only to learn facts, but also to see human growth in its proper perspective. A great teacher is made not so much by the actual information about psychology that he may have acquired as by his real appreciation of the forward-moving character of human nature.

In the second place, the practical part of educational psychology cannot help but call for knowledge about a great many different types of experimentation. It seems fair to say that the main out-

THE ART OF TEACHING 503

lines of educational psychology were first established by Thorndike in the publication of his notable three-volume work.[1] We could, of course, assume that the foundations that were thus laid, and which were based on the psychology that was then available, are permanent and that further textbooks in educational psychology should become more and more practical, in the sense that they should actually describe the relations between Thorndike's initial work and actual problems of teaching. The student is now fully aware of the fact, however, that the science of experimental psychology has moved along pretty fast since 1913.[2]

If, then, our own study of methods of promoting the growth pattern has seemed to be weighted more heavily with psychology than it is with practical teaching problems, a defense is to be found by saying that new points of view in the one science upon which education must be based require this procedure.

3. *The Teacher's Point of View:* We cannot, however, devote the entire book to psychology. We pass, therefore, in this chapter to a general picture of the teaching situation. Many of the basic facts about learning which the teacher ought to know have been presented in the preceding chapters. We have tried to find out how old a child is when it is born and how old it has become when first it enters the schoolroom. We have done this not only with respect to the whole pattern of development, but with respect to seven of its major features. At every point we have tried to show how the original inertia to change which finds its source in the germinal system can be overcome by the appropriate use of learning situations. Although the psychologist is not yet in a position to state exactly what learning is, the teacher may, nevertheless, take advantage of certain general principles which will promote growth. It has been the purpose of the last thirteen chapters to see what the main course of growth is with respect to essential features of the whole pattern and to relate processes of growth to those schoolroom subjects upon which most experimental work has been done.

It would be easy to suppose that the major part of our study of educational psychology has thus been finished, but, as we shall see in a moment, there is much more to be said. Let us turn our atten-

[1] Cf. Thorndike, E. L., *Educational Psychology.* New York: Columbia Univ. Press, 1913 (3 vols.).
[2] Cf. Murchison, C. (Ed.), *A Handbook of General Experimental Psychology.* Worcester, Mass.: Clark Univ. Press, 1934. Were the student to compare this volume with, say, Titchener, E. B., *Textbook of Psychology,* New York: The Macmillan Co., 1910, a survey published at about the same time as Thorndike's work, he would see the great change that has come over the face of psychology.

tion for a moment to an actual teaching situation. The student already knows that the teacher is only one part of a very complex situation. Another part is furnished by the growing child. Still other parts are furnished by the previous history of this child and by all of those learning situations which do not come under the direct influence of the teacher himself.

Now we may ask whether there are any attitudes, methods, or procedures in the teaching situation as a whole that will make a teacher more serviceable. It is one thing, of course, to know the facts, and quite another to know how to put the facts into practice. It is the task of the present chapter to look more carefully at common practices than at facts. In other words, the chapter will serve in some respects as a summary of Parts I and II, and yet it will add to these parts by looking through them to the general features of an actual teaching situation.[3]

As we go about this task, there is one fact that cannot receive too much emphasis. Every teaching situation is a particular situation. Even though we may try to standardize the process of learning by bringing children into large groups and by trying to remain as objective as possible in our attitudes toward each member of the whole group, it still remains true that each teacher-pupil relationship is probably the only one of its kind.[4] It represents a configuration of factors and events which cannot be handled by rule. To be sure, the teacher may have as a part of his background a general knowledge about such facts as have been considered in the previous chapters, but it is upon his own insight into teaching situations that he must depend for good judgment or good sense in applying the general facts to the particular case.

II. THE FUNCTIONS OF THE TEACHER

1. *Introduction:* In order to get a broad view of the functions of the teacher, let us pick up the whole growth pattern once more at some such convenient point as the moment of birth. As we have seen, the neonate stands, as it were, within a total context of things, a considerable portion of which will be gradually converted into an effective environment. The neonate, for example, knows nothing about its body or of the objects around it. It has no information

---

[3] Cf. Burton, W. H., *Introduction to Education.* New York: D. Appleton-Century Co., 1934, Chapter XXIII.
[4] Kilpatrick, W. H., *Foundations of Method.* New York: The Macmillan Co., 1926.

concerning the history of its own or the history of other countries. It has no appreciation of music, literature, and art. It is still unacquainted with the major philosophies and with the other great ideas which enter into that whole pattern of things known as culture or as civilization. It is devoid of all types of social-mindedness. In short, its environment is at first made up of a very limited number of objects and events which have almost no significance as compared with adult modes of living.

If the neonate were left to itself, that is, if it could survive during the first two or three years without aid and guidance from its parents, it would proceed to convert at least a part of its context into an effective environment.[5] The chances are, however, that only those portions of the context which are natural or physical would be so converted. Fortunately, we have a pretty good example of education which proceeds in this direction, for there was discovered in the seventeenth century a wild boy in one of the forests of Aveyron who had been subjected to just this type of training. The studies that have been made on this subject show clearly enough that educative processes which consist only of chance contacts with natural objects and events do not do very much toward promoting the growth pattern.

2. *The Rôle of the Teacher:* The same sort of conversion of context into environment takes place in the most primitive forms of education.[6] Here, to be sure, there are no special teachers, but newborn infants are not simply cast into the wilderness to live alone. They are surrounded by adults who see to it that the child gains information about particular parts of its total surroundings. It is not our task to appraise this form of education. On the contrary, we simply wish to remind the student that the adults around the child can and do become agents or intermediaries, as it were, between the child and its total context. They are persons who, having made some decisions about the matter beforehand, select those parts of the context which shall become truly environmental in character. Moreover, they see to it that growing children actually become more or less competent in their modes of reaction to these environmental situations.

The teacher is simply an extenuation of this idea of an agent between the total context which surrounds the child and the child

[5] Cf. Humphrey G., and Humphrey, M., *Itard's The Wild Boy of Aveyron.* New York: D. Appleton-Century Co., 1932.
[6] Cf. Monroe, P., *A Textbook in the History of Education.* New York: The Macmillan Co., 1918, Chapter I.

itself. His task is a little more difficult, however, than the task of a parent in a primitive society, for socialized living has added tremendously to the surroundings of modern children. Even though they know nothing about the social phase of their contexts when they are born, they must, nevertheless, expect to have a considerable portion of this context converted into a truly effective environment before they have gone very far.

Now, it is simply not possible for every child to learn everything that there is to be known. Not only is it not possible, but there are some who would say that socialized living has created some things which are positively harmful. As an example, we may take the present world conflict between the various forms of socialism or communism as opposed to capitalism. It is inferred in those schools supported by capitalistic systems that socialistic and communistic ways of thinking and all social institutions of the communistic sort should not become a part of the effective environment of the oncoming generation. Similarly, school systems supported by socialistic governments are forbidden to teach any of those facts that might contribute to a capitalistic form of government.[7] A still better illustration, perhaps, is to be found in the long-drawn-out conflict between science and religion. Men have made scientific discoveries, but it is often inferred that these discoveries, or at least some of them, should not be converted into the status of a relevant environment.

If, then, the teacher is one of the agents or intermediaries by means of which selected portions of the total environment may be converted into a truly effective environment, it must be assumed that he is well grounded in social philosophy or in educational philosophy, or that he is simply a henchman of someone else who is thus grounded. Even where this is not true, that is, where the teacher is allowed unlimited amounts of what is commonly known as academic freedom, he still finds one of his major functions in the selection of things to be taught.[8]

3. *Psychological Growth:* This is, however, only one-half of the picture. The long-drawn-out process of converting an environment or of any portion of it into an effective environment implies that a child is gradually gaining such mastery over its psychological functions that the transformation can really take place. This means that a learning situation is not only a device for converting an irrelevant

---

[7] Cf. Trow, C. W., *Character Education in Soviet Russia* (Trans. by P. D. Kalachov). Ann Arbor: Ann Arbor Press, 1934.

[8] Cf. Parker, S. C., *Types of Elementary Teaching and Learning.* Boston: D. C. Heath and Co., 1923.

context into an environment but a device, also, for increasing the excellence of our psychological functions.

As we have seen, a new-born infant has practically no serviceable habits or skills. Not even its sense organs are functionally mature in the sense that it can distinguish very many of the minor parts that make up a total stimulus-pattern. It has no habits of attention, no cultivated interests, only a limited number of primary tissue needs, no facility for problem-solving, no balance in its emotionalized action, and, apart from direct expressions of bodily condition, no rich and intimately organized personality traits. It is, therefore, one of the functions of the teacher to use learning situations not only for the purpose of converting an irrelevant context into an environment, but for the purpose of actually enabling the child to become more mature as a psychological instrument.

The most of this maturity is reached at a very early age. It is for this reason that some of the early grades are given almost entirely over to the so-called tool subjects. It is inferred that these subjects are being taught not for the information which is to be gained from them, but for the increasing maturity that will come out of them.[9] It is not possible as yet to say when a child reaches maturity as a psychological instrument, but it is almost certainly true that the amount of growth that takes place after the child enters the schoolroom is probably less than that that takes place before he enters the schoolroom.

4. *Types of Teaching Effort:* We may now summarize these considerations by saying that the teacher has two primary functions. In the first place, he stands as an intermediary between the irrelevant context and the truly effective environments. In the second place, he is one of the primary aids in the process of converting an immature or inefficient psychological instrument into a more mature and increasingly efficient psychological instrument. It is still necessary, however, to define a little more carefully the exact character of the mediation between context and environment which the teacher should supply. Of the many different methods which have been used to define this function of the teacher, we shall choose only three.

A. THE TEXTBOOK TEACHER: In the first place, it is often said that the teacher has almost satisfied his obligations to the social group if he provides the content, that is, the material that is to be learned, reminds the students of the methods that ought to be used

[9] Parker, S. C., *General Methods of Teaching in Elementary Schools.* Boston: Ginn and Co., 1919.

for learning this material, and then adopts whatever disciplinary measures that are necessary to guarantee actual learning.[10] This is almost to assume that the teacher is a textbook, as though he had no other obligation than to become a source of written and spoken words which should be learned by heart, much as one might learn the material in this book. In extreme cases, it might be argued that it is not often the function of the teacher to remind the student of the best methods of learning. In other words, it could be assumed that the teacher ought to take these things for granted simply by supplying the material to be learned and measuring the results of learning effort. Teaching of this type is often found at the higher levels of instruction under the plea that a student who has attained early maturity ought to be thrown upon his own resources.

The student will see at once that this method of defining the mediating functions of a teacher can be seriously criticized, especially when it is applied to teachers at the lower levels. As an illustration, we may refer the reader again to the latter part of the discussion on the transfer of training, where it was pointed out that experimental and teaching procedures which take a given level of excellence for granted could not possibly lead to transfer save in so far as identical elements are involved. If it could be assumed that children will not have a tendency to stop at a practical level of development, that is, if it could be assumed that their effectiveness as psychological instruments goes on increasing in direct proportion to the number of times the instruments are used, a teacher might simply serve as a source of content and let his profession go at that. As we have found, however, children do reach a practical level of competence in the use of their psychological instruments.[11] They reach levels of speed in work and habits of work which are simply overlearned rather than improved through additional exercise. Let us infer, therefore, that this first description of the functions of the teacher is not sufficient.

B. ACTIVE TEACHING: A second possible way of defining the functions of a teacher is directly suggested by what we have just said. In other words, the teacher can stand not only as an intermediary between an irrelevant context and environment, but he can actually bend learning situations toward the goal of increasing psychological competence. This means that, in addition to his position as a source

[10] Cf. Thayer, V. T., *The Passing of the Recitation.* Boston: D. C. Heath and Co., 1928, *passim.*
[11] This feature of teaching has been emphasized by Judd, C. H., *Psychology of Secondary Education.* Boston: Ginn and Co., 1927.

of content or as a source of material to be learned, the teacher becomes a source of motivation. This implies, of course, that the teacher shall know what motives are, where they have had their origin, and how they may be transformed from the level of primary desires to the level of intentions and purposes. It seems to be quite clear that both the quality and speed of work depend as much upon the incentives that are offered as they do upon particular methods of procedure. The inference is, then, that the teacher is not only an intermediary between context and environment, but also that he should be a source of the directed energy necessary to achievement of particular types.[12]

C. THE "HALO" EFFECT: This, however, does not exhaust the matter. A part of the content which teachers furnish is factual or informative in character. For example, teachers require of the students that they shall learn something about history, literature, mathematics, science, and philosophy. Once a student has learned how to read, he can go to books just as readily as to a teacher. There is, however, another type of content which cannot so easily be put down in books or stated in definite sentences. This is content which is furnished by the personal quality or character of the teacher himself. That is, the teacher is a person. He is the center of special interests, preferences for various types of emotionalized action, and various degrees of organization in personality and character traits.

Even though many teachers will say that it is their business to teach only their own subject matter, it is never possible for them to escape from the proposition that they themselves must be an inevitable part of the teaching situation.[13] If, for example, a teacher reports that it is only his business to teach his particular subject matter, he has already taken, at least by implication, an attitude toward those features of the whole teaching situation which are not exactly content, which cannot be written down in books, but which are, nevertheless, highly effective in giving quality and richness to the student-teacher relationship.

5. *Summary:* These considerations lead us directly into the topic which we shall discuss in the next section. Before we pass on to this section, we may summarize what has been said in the present section in the following way. Our summary shall include not only the facts now being considered, but some of the facts already presented in preceding chapters.

[12] Cf. Morrison, H. C., *The Practice of Teaching in the Secondary School.* Chicago: Univ. of Chicago Press, 1931.
[13] Cf. Wheeler, R. H., and Perkins, F. T., *Principles of Mental Development.* New York: T. Y. Crowell Co., 1932, Chapter XXVI.

In the first place, it is clear that a teacher must have an intimate knowledge about each one of his students. A part of this knowledge will come from experimental studies on differences in intelligence and upon differences of other types, but a great part of it will come from direct knowledge of the way in which students conduct themselves in the classroom situation. Perhaps, one illustration will be sufficient. It is hard to see how the average teacher could hope to make himself really effective as a medium between context and environment if he did not know something about the primary interests of the students in his class. It has already been implied that passage to new types of material can be made most readily by connecting the new material with some earlier and rather deep-running interest.[14]

In the second place, it cannot be said too often that the first years of a growth pattern are years in which major emphasis should be placed upon improved quality in psychological operations. One method of achieving this end lies in a varied curriculum. We do not mean to say that students should be asked to study superficially a large number of different things, but only that a sufficient variety be presented to them to keep them always on the forward edge of psychological effort. To be sure, there are a good many occasions where growth requires a large amount of simple overlearning, but the monotonous repetition of the same materials does not appear to serve this purpose.[15]

One of the best means of promoting psychological growth lies in language studies. Words are, as we have found, symbols for objects and for the multifarious relations that obtain between objects. At a primitive level of living, words are not necessary, simply because all of the problems that have to be met can be met in manual actions. We live, however, in the world of ideas. This means that we cannot expect to become competent with respect to this world unless we are in possession of the instruments by means of which it can be handled. These instruments are, for the most part, words. It seems reasonable to infer, therefore, that every effort should be made early in the period of growth to enrich the vocabulary not only through the sheer acquisition of a vocabulary, but through the development of the meanings conveyed by written and verbal language.[16]

[14] Cf. Thorndike, E. L., *The Principles of Teaching*. New York: A. G. Seiler, 1906.
[15] Cf. Parker, S. C., *Types of Elementary Teaching and Learning*. Boston: Ginn and Co., 1923.
[16] Cf. Woodring, M. N., and Sabin, F. E., *Enriched Teaching of Latin in the High School*. New York: Columbia Univ. Press, 1930.

This proposition leads directly to a third general feature of the psychology of teaching, viz., the great necessity of laying a proper foundation for the emergence of insights.[17] One can, to be sure, take learning simply as a way of committing certain propositions to heart, but the previous chapters have shown us that a teacher cannot really be called successful unless he has, with respect to every learning situation, created as many meanings or signs pointing to other objects as he can. It is not possible to force children to discover every type of significant relationship for themselves. This should not be taken as an excuse, however, for depriving them of the privilege of getting insights on their own account in sufficient number to develop a hunger for insights and to enjoy the excitement of real academic achievement.

III. THE QUALITIES OF A TEACHER

1. *Introduction:* A good many attempts have been made to tease out those particular traits or types of training that would be most apt to lead to success in the teaching profession. It is clear at once that, with respect to these attempts, there are a good many bases of judgment.[18] One might, for example, wish to know something about the administrative skill of a teacher. By administrative skill is meant the ability of a man to mobilize his resources quickly, handle the class with a minimal amount of effort, and otherwise take care of the mechanical side of actual teaching processes.

Then, too, it would be possible to argue that that person who handles the most students with a reasonable degree of success can be called efficient simply because the actual cost per pupil would be less. It goes almost without saying that judgments of the quality of a teacher in terms of cost per pupil would vary widely from judgments made in terms of ethical values. As we have seen just above, these ethical values may be furnished not so much by the content provided by the teacher as by the fact that the teacher himself is an intrinsic part of the teaching situation. Ethical and other personal values are extraordinarily difficult to measure and, as a rule, therefore, most studies upon the qualities of a teacher concern his academic preparation and his knowledge of the methods which pro-

[17] Pressey, S. L., *Psychology and the New Education*. New York: Harper and Bros., 1933, Chapter XV.
[18] Cf. Boardman, C. W., "Professional Tests as Measures of Teaching Efficiency in High School." *Teachers Coll. Contrib. to Educ.*, 1928 (No. 327).

mote the learning process, on the one hand, and motivate it, on the other.[19]

2. *Ratings:* There is still another aspect of this question. If anyone is going to say what the qualities of a good teacher should be, it is very likely that the qualities will reflect the character of the judges rather than the character of the persons judged. Some attempts have been made, for example, to secure ratings of teachers by their pupils.[20] As a rule, a questionnaire is used, but this method is not to be favored, in part, because of the inherent weaknesses of the questionnaire, and in part, because of the inability of pupils to make judgments apart from their prejudices.

The questionnaire has been replaced, therefore, by rating scales which take on almost the form of a standardized test.[21] Some of these rating scales throw light upon the educational program of the pupils, some of them measure the increased social competence of the pupils, while some of them attempt to measure emotional stability and adjustment. In other words, there is a tendency to measure students rather than to measure teachers.

Up to the present time, it has not been found possible to get trustworthy reports from parents upon the value of teachers. Parents do not often see their own children in the schoolroom situation, and neither do teachers go out of their way to untangle home and playground conditions.

3. *Causes of Success and Failure:* In spite of all of these difficulties, a number of attempts have been made to identify the general behavior-patterns of the excellent and the poor teacher. One student of these matters, for example, has found that deficiencies in knowledge of content, errors in method or technique of teaching, unfortunate personal idiosyncrasies, and inability to maintain discipline are four of the major features of a poor teacher.[22] Each of the items mentioned, however, refers not so much to the intrinsic quality of the teacher as a person as to his lack of information in his chosen field.

Among the factors that are alleged to contribute to real success in teaching are the stamina or persistence displayed by the teacher in his own earlier schoolroom attitudes, the early dawn and a marked

---

[19] Cf. Powers, F. F., *Character Training.* New York: A. S. Barnes and Co., 1932, *passim.*

[20] Birkelo, C. P., "What Characteristics in Teachers Impress Themselves upon Elementary and High School Students?" *Educ. Admin. and Supervis.,* 1929, XV, 453-456.

[21] Cf. Symonds, P. M., *Diagnosing Personality and Conduct.* New York: D. Appleton-Century Co., 1931.

[22] Cf. Palmer, G. H., *The Ideal Teacher.* Boston: Houghton Mifflin Co., 1910.

continuation of interest in the teaching profession, the extent to which teachers have engaged in extracurricular activities during their earlier training, and the extent to which they have definitely committed themselves to the teaching profession. In conjunction with this last item, it is often pointed out that many persons have used the teaching profession merely as a stepping stone to some other occupation.[23]

IV. Types of Teaching Procedure

1. *Introduction:* If there are a great many factors which prevent us from getting a good picture of the traits of a successful teacher, there are still more factors which modify our appraisals of proper teaching methods.[24] In general, of course, it is the function of a teaching method to promote learning but, as we have seen, learning may take a good many different forms. It is one thing to promote rote learning or trial-and-error learning, and quite another to place pupils in those situations which will lead to the discovery of meanings and insights.

Moreover, methods of teaching might vary widely with respect to the sort of product that one wishes to gain. There are some methods which lend themselves easily to increased measures of manual skill, while there are other methods which lend themselves more readily to verbal skills or to the symbolic use of language. Then, too, we may wish to throw more emphasis upon the possible transfer effects of learning than we do upon the more immediate outcomes of a learning process.

Finally, it is hardly necessary to say that methods of teaching might vary widely with the ability of the pupils in the classroom, with the general attitude and personal quality of the teacher himself, with the nature of the subject matter to be taught, with the materials such as maps, pieces of apparatus, moving picture cameras, and diagrams that are available and with one's general beliefs about the social values of different types of training.

2. *Recitation Method:* It will not be possible for us to review all of these various factors in detail. On the contrary, we shall confine our attention to three general types of teaching procedure and then ask the student to relate these types to the various purposes to be served by them.

[23] Barr, A. S., *Characteristic Differences of Good and Poor Teachers.* Bloomington, Ill.: Public School Publ. Co., 1929.
[24] Cf. Brueckner, L., and Melby, E. O., *Diagnostic and Remedial Teaching.* Boston: Houghton Mifflin Co., 1931.

As the first type, we may take the drill-recitation method.[25] This is, of course, the oldest of all of the methods of teaching. Before any experiments had been carried out on the nature of learning, it was simply recognized as a plain fact that the more often the movements that are called for by a stimulus-situation are practiced, the easier or the more automatic they will become. After the development of experimental psychology, it was urged that learning of this type should be called rote learning or trial-and-error learning. Moreover, as we have seen in an earlier chapter, it was taken for granted that two laws could be used to justify drill procedure, viz., the law of exercise and the law of effect.

A. DRILL: Now that methods of teaching have been brought more frequently under experimental examination, certain difficulties in plain drill procedure have been made clear.[26] It is argued, for example, that since constant drill means monotonous repetition of the same material, a child must be intensively motivated if it is actually to get its work done. As long as teachers could draw upon a native will power, this did not appear to be much of a problem, but now that some of the main facts about motives and incentives have been discovered, it is obvious that the drill procedure will fail unless the teacher can aid the pupil in the acquisition of proper motives.

One of the most frequent devices for achieving this end is to convert the drill procedure into a sort of a game where the interests and energies which have often been described as a product of the play instinct can be brought to bear on an otherwise monotonous task. It follows that, if the drill procedure is to be used, the responsibility for motivating it during the periods of loss of interest rests squarely upon the teacher. Moreover, since learning of this type proceeds to best advantage where the learning task remains prepotent over all other possible types of action the teacher must see to it that the persons who are being drilled have habits of attention which are adequate to the task.

It is hardly necessary to say again that many of the principles of effective learning, as, for example, distributed practice, learning by wholes rather than by parts (subject to the conditions described earlier), the insertion of frequent rest intervals, and the main facts governing facilitation and inhibition must be strictly followed.[27] The chief difficulty with the older drill method lay not so much in

[25] This method is, of course, directly related to rote memory and trial-and-error theories of learning.
[26] Cf. Thayer, V. T., *op. cit., passim.*
[27] Cf. Gates, A. I., *Psychology for Students of Education.* New York: The Macmillan Co., 1930, *passim.*

the actual use of drill as in failure to modify the drill period according to some of the facts that are now known about effective learning procedures. If pupils have a will, this will ought to carry them as easily through an hour of monotonous repetition as through fifteen minutes of it. If the experimental study of learning has changed this point of view, it has not, on that account, diminished the significance of the whole procedure.

B. RECITATION: The natural counterpart to drill is the recitation. We have already found that learning is favored whenever the learner actually takes an active attitude in the whole situation. To be sure, one may use one's vocal apparatus as in implicit speech and hence give the appearance of ideational or associative learning, but the best results are obtained if students are actually called upon to recite as frequently as possible under classroom conditions.[28]

Some of the main criticisms which have been passed upon the class recitation as a method of teaching run as follows. In the first place, a recitation must come from one person rather than from the group. It may be said, therefore, that the method does not favor coöperative effort. The other students in the room may attend to comments made by the teacher, but it is difficult indeed to motivate them to listen appreciatively while a fellow student is making a recitation.[29]

In the second place, it is often argued that the recitation will be wholly perfunctory in character. It seems that neither the teacher nor the student is doing anything more about it than to accept it as an inevitable phase of classroom activity. Since, by a long tradition, it is assumed that students ought to recite some of the things that they have learned, the recitation becomes a mere stimulus-response affair rather than a vivid piece of conversation between two people.

In the third place, an unsocialized and an unmotivated recitation quite fails to provide an opportunity for training in initiative, originality, and good judgment. This simply means that there is a great difference between parrotlike responses to a question, asked by the teacher, on the one hand, and that active give-and-take which was often called the Socratic method, on the other.

We may infer, then, that some of these faults of the recitative procedure do not reside in the recitation itself but in the ways in

[28] Cf. Bagley, W. C., "The Textbook in American Education." *School and Soc.,* 1931, XXXIII, 356-360.
[29] Douglass, H. R., *Modern Method in High School Teaching.* Boston: Houghton Mifflin Co., 1926, pp. 241-248 and *passim.*

which the recitation is used. The teacher can, of course, allow himself to become an automatic source of questions and allow the students to become the automatic reactors to questions. It may be doubted, however, whether there are any enthusiastic teachers who make use of so degenerate a form of recitation.

Other things being equal, the recitative method is to be recommended to those persons who are gaining their first teaching experience or who are teaching right on the forward edge of their knowledge. Moreover, if recitations are actually socialized in the sense that they call for a real measure of rapport between the teacher and the student, they will automatically avoid some of the worst features of pure rote learning. It is to be taken for granted, of course, that an intimate rapport between the teacher and his students requires a fairly high level of interest and motivation.

3. *Project Methods:* A second method of teaching owes its origin pretty largely to the reactions directed against the more automatic levels of rote learning and recitation. If a teacher simply lays a certain amount of material before his students with the comment that this material be learned, it is almost certain that no contribution at all will be made either to the excellence of the students as psychological instruments or to the exercise of those functions known as problem-solving. In the invention of the problem and project methods, therefore, a direct attempt has been made to emphasize variability of response and the opportunity for the emergence of insights.[30]

A. THE PROBLEM METHOD: In case of the problem method, some general proposition or line of action is suggested to the students. They take this situation as a starting point for a study of all of the factors that may be suggested by the general proposition. It is to be assumed, of course, that the problem will be recognized as a real problem by the students and that, in their attempted solution of it, direct use of the problem-solving functions will be required. It often happens, for example, that teachers will accept apparent solutions of assigned problems under the belief that problem-solving has actually occurred when, as a matter of fact, no inquiry has been made at all concerning the procedures used by the students.

The chief criticism to be lodged against problem methods of teaching lies in the task of coördinating or integrating the whole learning period so that the student will actually arrive at some definable goal. Nothing is to be gained, apparently, simply by allowing students to

[30] Cf. Dewey, J., *The Child and the Curriculum.* Chicago: Univ. of Chicago Press, 1902.

range widely over a variety of tasks which have no inner coherency and which involve no real discipline.[31]

B. THE PROJECT METHOD: The project method of teaching is very much like the problem method, both in its advantages and in its disadvantages. If projects are chosen wisely, they will, perhaps, bring learning processes closer to real situations but, at the same time, it is easy to let a project entice the student in so many divergent types of activity that no real advantage can be gained.[32]

Some of the requirements of a good project have been described as follows.[33] In the first place, it is argued that, since a good many students may work upon different aspects of single projects, a socialized rather than an individualized form of teaching will be favored. It is not to be assumed, of course, in this process of socialization that the project will actually fail to promote individual initiative, for not all of the students will be working upon the project as a whole. On the contrary, each student may be assigned some particular phase of the project and if these assignments are at all equalized and wisely made, every member of the class will have his own particular contribution to the work as a whole.

In the second place, it is argued that the project method, requiring, as it may, some measure of intensive drill, will also lead to an increased use of the problem-solving functions. Since the students cannot read the answer to their project in a book, although they may acquire a good deal of information about it, the opportunity is readily furnished for the emergence of insights. If the student actually runs into a major difficulty or into a blind alley, and if the project is adequately supervised by an alert teacher, such information can be supplied as will recall the student from his plight without, at the same time, robbing him of the chance to make a discovery for himself.[34]

The social feature of the project method of teaching has a good many arguments in its favor. Because of home conditions or of unfortunate accidents on the playground, many children come to the schoolroom with a definite unsocial, if not antisocial, attitude. Since every occupation into which the child may enter after it finishes its formal training will require high measures of proper social

[31] Cf. Bagley, W. C., *Education, Social Progress, and Crime*. New York: The Macmillan Co., 1931.
[32] Bode, B. H., *Modern Educational Theories*. New York: The Macmillan Co., 1927, Chapter VII.
[33] Stevenson, J. A., *The Project Method of Teaching*. New York: The Macmillan Co., 1921.
[34] Palmer, R. P., *Progressive Practices in Directing Learning*. New York: The Macmillan Co., 1929, *passim*.

attitude, anything that the school can do to promote coöperative work will certainly be an advantage.[35] If children in the schoolroom can learn that the success of their own effort may depend upon the efforts of other people, they will have gone a long way toward recognizing their social responsibility in coöperative activities.

4. *Laboratory Methods:* The third major method of teaching is known as the laboratory method. The student will see at once that this is a method which owes its origin to the rapid development of the experimental sciences. One may, of course, try to find out some of the main facts about physics, chemistry, or biology simply by hearing them stated or by learning them by heart, but learning is a kind of doing, and it has been argued, therefore, that the development of the experimental sciences which require a large amount of actual laboratory work satisfy more nearly the requirements of good teaching method than any other part of the curriculum.

During the early days of laboratory methods of teaching this proposition was accepted almost without question, but more recently, under the influence of direct experimental examination of the results of laboratory methods, it has begun to appear that the method has been greatly overestimated.[36]

Among the criticisms that may be directed against the method, let us mention the following. In the first place, actual laboratory procedures take an immense amount of time. For example, in order to learn some of the main facts about the relations between oxygen and hydrogen, facts which might be stated in a very few moments, the student is required to spend many hours in the manipulation of test-tubes, a balance, and other pieces of apparatus. These processes of manipulation may, to be sure, make some contribution to the development of fine manual skills, but one may well wonder whether skills of this order should occupy so large a place in the training program as they now do.

In the second place, the laboratory method of teaching is said to place too much emphasis upon manual learning and not enough emphasis upon ideational or associative learning. If, for example, a student is going to do all of the classical experiments in physics, he will know something about these classical experiments, but he may not be able to place either his manual dexterity or his information about physics into a significant relation even with the technical

---

[35] Cf. Robbins, C. L., *The Socialized Recitation.* New York: Allyn and Bacon, 1920, *passim.*

[36] Downing, E. R., "Summary of Investigations of the Demonstration Method vs. the Laboratory Method." *High School J.*, 1930, XIII, 51-55.

aspects of the world in which he lives. In other words, it is said by some that the value of the laboratory sciences is to be found not in the laboratory procedure itself but in the contribution which scientific facts have made to our current climate of opinion.[37]

The chief argument in favor of laboratory methods of teaching is said to lie in the contribution that they ought to make to an appreciation of the scientific method. As the student knows, this method requires high measures of accuracy, long periods of patient effort, and a rigid adherence to facts.[38] It has been pointed out that there are no virtues which have more importance in our type of living than these. We call our day a scientific day and our culture a technical culture. We entertain the hope that all types of personal and social problems will become much simpler in direct proportion as we apply to them the methods of science rather than the methods of commonsense and of opinion. It may be doubted, however, whether these virtues actually appear from the laboratory method of teaching, simply because students have learned how to handle test-tubes or a balance. On the contrary, the evidence seems to show that they are a product of the teacher's attitude and of other non-laboratory features of laboratory experience.[39]

As the student has already surmised, it is possible to describe other methods of teaching which lie between the three types already mentioned. He will know, too, that there is no precise way of saying which method should be used and neither are there any maxims that can be laid down with respect to any one of the methods. A teaching method is not a process which exists apart from an actual teaching situation. The principal features of an actual teaching situation are, of course, the teacher and the students, and the value which a particular teaching method will have will depend, therefore, upon the way in which the teacher and the student handle themselves. This way is always a particular way in the sense that the teacher-pupil relationship is a unique configuration having its own properties or characteristics. The successful teacher then will always be aware of the total configuration of which he is an integral part and use all of the resources at his disposal to make this configuration as productive as possible.

[37] Cf. Saidla, L. E., and Gibbs, W. E., *Science and the Scientific Mind*. New York: McGraw-Hill Book Co., 1930.
[38] Cf. Horton, R. E., "Measurable Outcomes of Individual Laboratory Work in High School Chemistry." *Teachers Coll. Contrib. to Educ.*, 1928 (No. 303).
[39] Downing, E. R., "Methods in Science Teaching." *J. Higher Educ.*, 1931, II. 316-320.

V. CLASSROOM MANAGEMENT

1. *Introduction:* There are several features of classroom management which are purely administrative and mechanical in character.[40] It is not of these, however, that we wish to speak. On the contrary, let us consider for a moment two or three of the more important psychological factors which have a bearing upon the art of teaching. Of the many factors that will be included in almost any book on classroom management, we shall select only two, viz., the process known as warming-up and some of the psychological features created by differences in class size.

2. *The Warming-up Effect:* We may go to the athlete for a preliminary example of the meaning that can be given to the phrase "warming up." As the student knows, it is never fruitful to jump into a new activity when the muscles and other devices used in athletic skills are "cold." In preparation for a race, for example, the runner will try to make his muscles more limber by going first through a series of stretching and setting-up exercises. He will then run slowly about the track or take two or three starts from his marks before attempting a speed trial. It is known that these preliminary exercises bring about certain changes in all of the bodily operations which support physical effort.[41]

A parallel to these physical processes of warming up may be found in psychological tasks. Let us say, for example, that a student has just passed from a class in history to a class in physics. If the student has observed himself at all during this passage, he will have noted that, as he entered the physics class, there were still echoes of the facts of history standing in the way of attention to the new subject matter. Even though he may be surrounded by pieces of apparatus and other sources of suggestion concerning the new material, his recollection of the events in the preceding meeting of the class and of his actual place with respect to the whole pattern of work to be done will come back to him rather slowly. Shortly, however, his associations seem to "warm up" in much the same way that the muscles of an athlete "warm up."

This fact has long been noted by teachers, and it has earned a special name. The student will recall, no doubt, from his study of the history of education, that the doctrine of the apperceptive mass

---

[40] Cf. Breed, F. S., *Classroom Organization and Management.* New York: The World Book Co., 1933, *passim.*

[41] Cf. Gould, A. G., and Dye, J. A., *The Physiology of Exercise.* New York: A. S. Barnes and Co., 1932, Chapters XXIII and XXIV.

played a very important part in the educational psychology of Herbart.[42] This doctrine pointed out that whenever new material was presented to a person, it would be received more or less easily in direct proportion to the amount of material like it or associated with it that was already present. One very important inference drawn from this doctrine was that instruction drawn from new material would also presuppose some preliminary tuning which would give a student a starting point for comprehension.[43] A favorite maxim of teaching, for example, runs as follows, viz., always pass from the familiar to the unfamiliar. Other maxims are somewhat the same; e.g., "always proceed from the simple to the complex," or "always proceed from the general to the particular."

A number of experiments have been performed on warming-up of the psychological type and these experiments show clearly the teaching advantages of the procedure. Some of these experiments are closely related to that whole field of research which we have already described in connection with our study of set, attitude, and posture. It is simply a plain fact of human nature that learning and comprehension will be favored if the student is already prepared to receive the material to be learned or comprehended.

The experimental facts bearing upon the other maxims mentioned above are not quite so straightforward. If we say that we should proceed from the simple to the complex, some criteria of simplicity and complexity must be discovered. As an example, let us take the concept of God. If a child asks about the origin of some natural object, it may be said that an answer using the word "God" is a simple answer. The concept of Deity, however, is an extraordinarily complex concept. It has been reached as a result of some of the most earnest reflection which human beings have ever been able to devote to any problem. On the other hand, it might be argued that natural explanations of common occurrences might also be simple. If a child asks, "What makes the flowers grow?" and if the answer is given, "The rain and the sunshine make them grow," one might say that rain and sunshine are simple and obvious facts. From one point of view, of course, they are simple; but the relation between rain or sunshine, on the one hand, and the processes of plant growth, on the other, are extremely complex. We may infer, then, that any maxim about proceeding from the simple to the complex or from the complex to the simple requires further

[42] Cf. Burton, W. H., *op. cit.*, Chapter XXIII.
[43] The student will, no doubt, recall the discussion of "set" or "attitude" in Chapters Two and Four.

examination of the relation between these terms and the previous training of the person being taught.[44]

Some light has been thrown upon these maxims by the Gestalt theory of the origin of perception.[45] This theory says that the first perceptions of a child are not made up of a great many parts but of simple figures placed upon an undifferentiated background. The growth of perception requires the gradual emergence of figures out of the background. In other words, particulars become individuated out of generalities. The same process takes place, as we have seen, in the development of behavior. The initial movements of an untutored person are more generalized than his skilled movements. The skilled or particular movements are individuated out of a larger pattern. It seems proper to draw the inference that other types of growth might follow the same course. In other words, a teacher could take some generalized concept even though it were highly complex in its history and in its various meanings and then proceed to particulars. The particulars in this case would be all of the meanings or signs pointing toward other objects.[46]

3. *Class Size:* The second feature of classroom management which we have set for discussion in this section involves some of the problems created by class size. There is a long tradition to the effect that the smaller the class the more effective the teaching process. The arguments in favor of this belief are simple and straightforward.[47] It is said that the teacher can give more personal attention to each member of a small class than he can to several members of a large class. Moreover, he can spend much more time on individual diagnosis and thus make his remedial techniques more quickly effective. It is said, also, that certain advantages are to be gained from the development of a considerable measure of friendship between the teacher and the student. This friendship would reveal some information concerning variations in development, in ability, in interest, in emotionalized forms of action, and in dominant personality traits. Since one of the functions of the teaching process ought to include personality traits as well as sheer information and since the small class lends itself more readily than the large class to excellence in this respect, tradition has suggested that no

[44] Burton, W. H., *op. cit., passim.*
[45] Cf. Koffka, K., *The Growth of the Mind.* New York: Harcourt, Brace and Co., 1924, *passim.*
[46] Bode, B. H., *Conflicting Psychologies of Learning.* Boston: D. C. Heath and Co., 1929, Chapter XV.
[47] Burton, W. H., *op. cit.,* pp. 558 ff.

teacher should be asked to handle more than twenty-five or thirty pupils.

At about the turn of the century, the traditions on class size were seriously upset by a series of experiments which seemed to show clearly that the individual members of large classes learned as much as did the individual members of small classes. In the first major experiment, for example, six thousand children in grades from the fourth to the eighth year were used as subjects.[48] There was some evidence that smaller classes in the upper grades did better than large classes, that small classes were better for dull children than for brighter children, but that, on the whole, a large class was just as good as the small class.

This first study was subject to a great many errors. No attempt was made, for example, to find out whether the students in the different classes were actually comparable to one another in ability. This failure was remedied after the intelligence test became a more reliable instrument.

In recent years, new attempts have been made to uncover the various advantages and disadvantages created by class size and the situation now stands about as follows. It seems to be clear that, so far as those results of learning which are measurable are concerned, class size makes no difference.[49] In other words, if drill procedures are used and if measures are made of the results of rote learning or of trial-and-error learning, members of a large class, even though it be a lecture group, may do just as well as members of a small class.

There are, however, a good many other products of teaching which, though they are not measurable, ought to be recognized as essential to the art of teaching. Let us think, for example, not so much of the outcome of formal methods of teaching which take a given level of excellence for granted as of excellence itself. The student will remember that we have placed considerable emphasis upon those teaching procedures which will actually change the quality of a person as a psychological instrument. In addition to sheer information it is required of an educated person that he have highly serviceable habits of attention, versatile but persistent interests, favorable sources of motivation, considerable aptitude for recognizing and handling in a constructive way difficult or problematic situations, and a dependable variety of personality traits.

[48] Rice, J. M., "Educational Research: A Test in Arithmetic." *The Forum*, 1902, XXXIV, 281-297; 1903, XXXV, 269-293; 1904, XXXVI, 96-114.
[49] Cf. Hudelson, E., *Class Size at the University Level*. Minneapolis: Univ. of Minn. Press, 1928.

To be sure, some of these features of an educated person are now measurable, but some of them are not. The question of the advantage of small classes over large classes cannot be settled, therefore, until a picture can be got of the whole range of human quality. If the results of teaching should be measured solely in terms of habits and skills, on the one hand, and total range of information, on the other, then a great amount of money can be saved to the taxpayer by increasing the size of classes and decreasing the number of teachers. On the contrary, however, if social and personal values are to be included in any appraisal of the results of teaching, one's judgment about these matters must be suspended until further data are available.

VI. MEASURING THE RESULTS OF TEACHING

1. *The Examination:* There is, at the present time, such a vast literature on the methods which can be used in order to measure the results of teaching that we shall do no more than suggest the general nature of the devices used.[50]

The oldest device, of course, is the ordinary examination.[51] Because of a change in the character of examinations during recent years the older type has come to be known as the essay type. As an example, let us take the following statement: "Discuss the relation between original nature and training." A statement of this kind presented to a group of students in educational psychology could easily make up an entire examination. The student would be expected to define the terms "original nature" and "learning" and then arrange such facts as he had learned about them in an order commensurate with the character of the question asked.

Examinations of this type have been defended on the ground that they require of the student not only that he shall recall previous information but that he shall integrate this information in some thoughtful or reasonable way.[52] It is clear too, however, that the essay examination may really miss this point altogether. All too often it turns into a simple exercise of recall. The student will put down on his paper those things which he happens to remember.

---

[50] Cf., for example, Webb, L. W., and Shotwell, A. M., *Standard Tests in the Elementary School.* New York: Ray Long and R. R. Smith, 1932.

[51] Cf. Odell, C. W., *Traditional Examinations and New Type Tests.* New York: D. Appleton-Century Co., 1928.

[52] Cf. Ruch, G. M., *The Improvement of the Written Examination.* Chicago: Scott, Foresman and Co., 1924.

Moreover, he will put them down in the order in which they are recalled.

There is, however, another difficulty created by the essay type of examination. This is a difficulty created by the way in which the teacher will interpret what has been written. As a typical instance, let us take an experiment that was performed on some geometry papers.[53] These papers were sent to 116 different teachers with the request that they be graded as if they themselves had given the examinations. The grades varied from 28 to 91 on a scale of 100. Similar studies have been made by asking the same teacher to grade a set of examination papers at different intervals.[54] The correlations between the two sets of grades were so low as to show that normal processes of grading are extremely subjective in character. A paper that appears adequate to the teacher on one occasion may appear wholly inadequate to him on another.

2. *Objective Examinations:* These difficulties in the essay type of examination have brought about a search for a more objective method of appraising the results of teaching. Objective measures now fall into two groups. On the one hand, there are those measures which are made out by the teacher himself. Instead of asking the students to write as they wish or as they can remember, the examination is made up of a large number of sentences, some of which are right and some of which are wrong, of a number of propositions to which several possible answers have been appended, of a number of incomplete sentences, and the like. The student is simply required to place a check mark at appropriate places provided in the examination paper.[55]

The advantages ascribed to this new type of examination are as follows. In the first place, it enables the teacher to tap the results of his effort at a great many more places than he could if he simply asked five or six more general questions. In the second place, it is argued that the new-type examination makes the teaching process more specific. The student knows, for example, that he will be asked a large number of specific questions and he will be able, therefore, to direct himself more adequately during his learning periods. In the third place, the task of grading a new-type examination is much simplified. The teacher has only to count the number of correct

---

[53] Starch, D., and Elliott, E. C., "Reliability of Grading Work in Mathematics." *School Rev.*, 1913, XXI, 254-259.
[54] Eells, W. C., "Reliability of Repeated Grading of Essay-Type Examinations." *J. Educ. Psychol.*, 1930, XXI, 48-52.
[55] Paterson, D. G., *Preparation and Use of New-Type Examinations.* Yonkers: World Book Co., 1925.

check marks. In other words, he can evade the subjective elements which are alleged to play so large a part in the older essay type. In the fourth place, the new-type examination can be called an objective examination, partly, because it puts the relative performance of different students on a more concrete foundation. If the examination includes 100 or 150 items and if each item can be scored in an objective way, the results of the examination can be thrown into a distribution curve and the teacher may then discover just how reliable the examination was.[56]

3. *Achievement Tests:* Even at its best, however, the new type of examination is not so objective as might be desired. Teachers will differ from one another in the items which they will select and they will not always be careful to phrase propositions so as to avoid all ambiguity. For these and for other reasons a number of specific achievement tests have been devised.[57] For this purpose a number of different teachers must agree as to what the essential parts of any given course are. Let us suppose, for example, that in a course in history it is agreed that one thousand different facts ought to be acquired by the students taking the course. Clearly, an examination asking about all of these facts would be too extensive. If, however, a selected number of facts which are truly representative of the whole group could be brought together and used as a substitute for the group, they could be phrased in a standardized way, tested for reliability, and thus used almost as one might use an intelligence test. As a matter of fact, we shall see in a later chapter that intelligence tests are actually created in this same manner.

In brief, then, a standard test is made up of material that has been carefully selected as a result of curricular research or as a result of the objectives that have been laid down for the teaching of each particular subject. In the case of spelling, for example, a study will first be made of the words that are actually used by the children and adults, both in writing and in speaking.[58] The inference is that it is not necessary to include in the course on spelling a vast number of words for which the child and the adult will have no frequent use. Once these most common words have been discovered, a certain number of them can be cast into a standard test by assuming that they are representative of the whole list and by assuming that they will actually distinguish between adequate spellers and inadequate spellers.

[56] Cf. Odell, C. W., *op. cit., passim.*
[57] Cf. Pressey, L. C., and Pressey, S. L., *Introduction to the Use of Standard Tests.* Yonkers: World Book Co., 1933.
[58] Cf. Webb, L. W., and Shotwell, A. M., *op. cit.,* Chapters X, XI.

At the present time, approximately fourteen hundred tests of this type have been created. These tests involve almost every school subject from the first grade through college. Some of them are much more general than others, some are used primarily for the purpose of diagnosis, and some of them are substitutes for the regular examination. They are created not only for the purpose of measuring achievement in school subjects but for detecting changes in general attitudes, character traits, and various types of social adjustment.[59] If, for example, one wishes to know what the actual interests of any group of children are, he can use a test which will uncover the major interests and describe their relative importance. The same fact holds true of all of the other principal features of the growth pattern.

4. *Nonmeasurable Factors:* In our discussion of class size, it was noted that not all consequences of teaching are measurable. If, for example, it has been decided that a certain number of facts about any given section of subject matter are to be presented to a class and if it is desired to know whether the members of the class will learn these facts just as readily when the class is small as when the class is large, a precise answer can be found. It seems to be fairly clear, however, that the results of teaching ought to reach far beyond this point. As a witness in this direction, we may ask of the student to consider again the probable influence of formal methods of teaching as opposed to informal methods in the development of social and ethical traits. We may ask him too to consider some of the circumstances that surround the growth of aesthetic feelings and sentiments.

Of the various incommensurables that are caught up in any teaching process we shall speak of only two, viz., the contrast between responses that are purely adaptive in character as opposed to responses that reflect good judgment and especially that reflect the meanings inherent in the phrase "social adjustment." As a result of normal processes of training, most students do acquire a very large number of modes of reaction that will serve to adjust themselves to the situations in which they are placed. We may consider, for example, some of the precise skills which an athlete acquires during the course of his training in preparation for a season of competition. As every coach knows, it is not always possible for him to use men who are actually superior in special skills. He will often prefer to use a man with much less skill but who is at the same time more seasoned. His choices in all such cases are determined by

[59] Cf. Symonds, P. M., *op. cit., passim.*

the following factor. Even though a man may have a large measure of accuracy in throwing forward passes, tackling, running the open field, or blocking, it does not follow that he will always exercise good judgment in the use of these skills. To be sure, if the situation met is a familiar situation in the sense that he has learned how to react adequately to it, he may perform well but an average season of competition will present a great many situations which require not only a high measure of skill but a high measure of good sense as to when and how the skill shall be used.

The term "adjustive reaction" then refers to the fact that normal processes of learning will equip men with a large variety of skills and attitudes which are appropriate to the particular situations to which they have become attached. Adjustive reactions of this type, however, are not to be confused with the general adaptability of a man for adaptability is more a product of "seasoning" or of experience than it is of particular learning situations. In other words, the acquisition of special skills or of particular types of information must always be placed upon a background of teaching effort which will look toward those features of the growth pattern which are emphasized by the transfer of training. As we have seen, some measures of transfer can be gained because of the presence of identical elements in two or more situations. The real significance of transfer of training, however, is to be found not so much in the number of identical situations as in the more general attitudes, habits, and dispositions which supply, so to speak, the matrix out of which more specialized actions can emerge.

There is, at the present time, no way to measure this more general feature of teaching effort, save as one attempts empirical estimates of it in terms of what a student does after he leaves the schoolroom. In short, then, the full quality of a teacher's work cannot be discovered until long after the immediate processes of teaching have been finished. Even here, however, it cannot be guaranteed that the more general habits and dispositions of the person are a product of the classroom. The inference is frequently drawn by critics of contemporary education that all too many of these more general products of training are a result of informal education rather than of direct classroom procedure.

The same inferences are drawn with respect to whatever facility a person acquires for adjusting himself to social situations. Every teacher has to face problems of social adjustment from the time the child first enters a schoolroom until it has been graduated. As an example, let us take some of the difficulties that often attend the transition from preschool home life to first-grade work. If the home life has been of such a character as to promote a deep sense of dependence upon the parents, the child coming from this home will enter a schoolroom with no facility at all for adapting itself to a new source of authority or even for adapting itself to its playmates. The chances are that this transition is one of the most difficult that has to be made by the child, but there is every reason to believe that every passage from one grade to another raises social problems of the same sort.

It is sometimes assumed that many of the problems of social adaptation can be handled more fruitfully through extracurricular activities and through fraternity life than they can in the classroom. This feature of education has not received the attention that it deserves, and the field has been wide open, therefore, to extravagant statements, both for and against the influence of these factors. On the one hand, for example, it will be said that extracurricular activities stand as a more important source of training in essential social traits than the classroom. On the other hand, however, many teachers will resent such statements and hold fast to the opinion that the schoolroom itself can do everything that is essential.[60]

Most important evidence bearing upon this matter comes from leaders in the professions or from those who have to employ and seek to place graduates of high schools and universities. With respect to such graduates there is one common report, viz., that they may be ever so well equipped in information and skill but wholly incompetent to adjust themselves to fellow workmen or to the spirit of the profession or to the general temper of an industry. It looks as though some of the major industries have taken this problem more seriously than the teachers have, for the development of personnel offices and studies on methods of following up newly employed persons in order to help them to adapt themselves to their new environments have become increasingly numerous.

READINGS

The topics that have been discussed in this chapter touch phases of education which reach far beyond a survey of educational psychology itself. In the background of the work of the teacher, for example, there is always implied some philosophy of education. A convenient source of information for the philosophy of education is to be found in Burton, W. H., *Introduction to Education*. New York: D. Appleton-Century Co., 1934, Parts I and II.

[60] For references and a suggestive discussion, see Werner, O. H., *Every College Student's Problems*. Newark: Silver, Burdett and Co., 1929, *passim*.

Some of the more important references on methods of teaching are Adams, F., and Brown, W., *Teaching the Bright Pupil.* New York: Henry Holt and Co., 1930; Miller, H. L., *Creative Learning and Teaching.* New York: Charles Scribner's Sons, 1927; Ruediger, W. C., *Teaching Procedures.* Boston: Houghton Mifflin Co., 1932; Kilpatrick, W. H., *Foundations of Method.* New York: The Macmillan Co., 1926; Morrison, H. C., *The Practice of Teaching in the Secondary School.* Chicago: Univ. of Chicago Press, 1931; Parker, S. C., *General Methods of Teaching in High School.* Boston: Ginn and Co., 1920. A short but illuminating study of the development of teaching method is to be found in Burton, W. H., *op. cit.,* Chapter XXIII.

For classroom management, see Breed, F. S., *Classroom Organization and Management.* Yonkers: The World Book Co., 1933.

There is a large literature on the use of the examination as a test of the quality of teaching. See Douglass, A. A., *The American School System.* New York: Farrar and Rinehart, Inc., 1934, Chapter XI. This book will also be found useful in the study of principles of method (Chapter X), the education of exceptional children (Chapter XIV), extracurricular activities (Chapter XVI), and so on.

Further references on methods of appraising the art of teaching will be listed at the end of Chapter XV.

PART THREE

CONCEPTUAL AND METHODOLOGICAL TOOLS OF EDUCATION

CHAPTER FIFTEEN

THE NATURE OF INTELLIGENCE

I. THE NATURE OF CONCEPTUAL TOOLS

1. *Introduction:* We have now drawn as complete a picture of the growth pattern, in so far as it is subject to schoolroom conditions, as our space will allow. Even though we have been forced to look at the whole pattern now in terms of one major feature and then in terms of another, the student will not have forgotten that the growing child is actually the sum of all of the particular things we have been trying to say about him. Not only is this true, but every child is placed in a home, playground, and schoolroom situation, the total character of which is just as important in any adequate statement of his education as is a study of the child himself.

Now we must turn to a group of topics in educational psychology which are a little different in character but which play, nevertheless, a very important part in the daily work of the teacher. These problems, even though they have to do with the growth pattern, are concerned not so much with the way in which a child grows older in its essential psychological features as with certain concepts which have proven useful in taking account of a large number of facts in a very simple way. These concepts are more like tools which the educator may use in his daily work than descriptions of changes in the growth pattern.

As an example, let us take the concept of intelligence.[1] When we say that intelligence is a concept, we imply that it is not a faculty or power or agent of which some people have more than others. We do not even assert that intelligence is one of the primary modes of psychological operation. On the contrary, it is a concept which cuts across a good many different types of operation and which serves, therefore, as a fairly simple device for estimating one person's psychological standing with respect to another's. In other words, intelligence is an appraisal which we make of the way in which students in the schoolroom are getting along with the tasks set before

[1] Cf. Peterson, J., *Early Conceptions and Tests of Intelligence.* Yonkers: The World Book Co., 1925; Young, K., "The History of Mental Testing." *Ped. Sem.,* 1923, XXXI, pp. 1 ff.

them by the teacher. When we point out that one pupil is more intelligent than another we mean that, by using his various modes of psychological operation, he can get more done in a given amount of time or do what he does do at a higher level of excellence. We do not ordinarily mean that he possesses some unique type of psychological operation which, in and of itself, is the intellect or which gives rise to intelligent acts.[2]

2. *Facts and Concepts:* It is hardly wise, however, to draw too sharp a distinction between a description of the growth pattern, on the one hand, and the various concepts or tools which the educator may use in his daily work, on the other. Neither is it worth while to draw too sharp a distinction between the methods that may be used to guide and promote the learning process as opposed to the concepts which are useful in summarizing a very large number of facts, or as opposed to the mathematical and statistical tools which the educator may invent in order to measure the results of his work. Since, however, it is easy to suppose that intelligence is a name for a special faculty and since the use of the word in this connection has brought into education a large amount of confusion, there will be a certain practical advantage in separating the actual description of the growth processes from the various ways in which the outcome of the growth process can be described.

This separation is worth while, in part, because of the distinction we have drawn in several places between modes of psychological operation, on the one hand, and the services rendered to a person (including the quality of these services), on the other. As a typical instance let us take a single act of problem-solving. Although we have no reliable evidence on the matter, it is easy to suppose that a frontiersman may discover a good many relationships between objects and events such as are found in a primitive environment. His very existence often depends upon his ability to gain "hunches" about possible sources of danger, the presence of enemies, the habits of birds and beasts, and about signs pointing toward changes in the weather. Even though he has actually solved no problems, he would, no doubt, develop a remarkable facility for taking almost irrelevant details as signs or symbols of important facts. That is, he must make frequent use of the results of sign learning.

Now this use of fundamental modes of psychological operation might have no value at all to an urban dweller or to an academic man. The services they make possible are not of great social value

[2] Cf. Dearborn, W. F., *Intelligence Tests.* Boston: Houghton Mifflin Co., 1928, Chapters I and IV.

in a more "civilized" community. The academic man, therefore, could easily argue that the frontiersman is not a highly intelligent person, simply because he cannot discover relations between abstractions or otherwise adjust himself wisely to an urban life. Obviously, the difference between the frontiersman and the academic man would consist not so much of a difference in types of psychological function as in the types of information used in solving problems and in the social value of the services rendered.[3]

We shall say, therefore, that intelligence is a concept which cuts across both psychological functions and services rendered. It has, on that account, a highly practical value. Some of the other conceptual and methodological tools which are in constant use by the educator are the concept of the socialized person, the concept of adjustment, the concept of efficiency, and the concept of individual differences. The chief methodological tools of education are, of course, direct experimentation and those principles of statistics which make it possible for the educator to appraise his work, compare one group of subjects with another, judge the reliability of a test or of an examination, and so on.

3. *Purpose of the Chapter:* It is the function of this third part of our study of the problems of educational psychology, then, to make the student more familiar with the nature of these concepts and with the ways in which they may be used in the schoolroom. We shall begin our study of the conceptual and methodological tools of education by making a brief appraisal of the several meanings which can be given to the word "intelligence."

II. CURRENT DEFINITIONS OF INTELLIGENCE

1. *Varieties of Intelligence:* The concept of intelligence is, perhaps, one of the most important tools the educator uses, because it enables him to express in a single word (or in a number) the general outcome of training or the general psychological excellence of children at different stages of development. As we have said above, many persons have supposed that intelligence must name a special mental power which people possess just as they are supposed to possess a brain, a heart, or a pair of eyes.[4] The older psychologies

[3] Similar comments could be made about the difference between the thinking of adults and children. At a simple level, see Gellerman, L. W., "The Behavior of Children and Adults in a Double Alternation Temporal Maze." *J. Genet. Psychol.*, 1931, XXXIX, 359-392. Also Hazlitt, V., "Children's Thinking." *Brit. J. Psychol.*, 1930, XX, 354-361.
[4] Cf. Bode, B. H., *Conflicting Psychologies of Learning*. Boston: D. C. Heath and Co., 1929, Chapter I.

took it for granted that intelligence was one of the intrinsic properties of mind stuff, and before we have finished with this chapter, we shall see that the measurement of intelligence sometimes makes it possible to argue that there must be, in various types of psychological function, a central factor which is not a simple sum of each of the psychological operations taken by themselves. In general, however, we shall try to show that intelligence is not a thing or faculty which people have, but a judgment which is placed upon them by others. Intelligence is one of the properties which we may attribute to the whole quality of getting on in the world, a quality which some persons display more clearly than others.

We must not, however, run too far ahead of our story, for even though we say that intelligence is a way of appraising other people, it is not agreed as to just which of the various psychological traits of which they are a sum should be most emphasized. As we have seen in several of the preceding chapters, it is possible to describe the whole course of human growth in terms of seven major features. These seven major features have been described in detail in each of seven different chapters of Part I.

We may, if we wish, direct our attention primarily (i) to the whole array of skills which a person has acquired, (ii) to the whole variety of objects and situations which have been converted from the status of an irrelevant to the status of a relevant environment, (iii) to the conditions and circumstances under which some objects and events become more important than others in initiating and regulating behavior, (iv) to the circumstances under which behavior may be emotionalized, (v) to the circumstances which make some types of situations effective over long periods of time in regulating behavior, (vi) to the factors that favor problem-solving, or (vii) to the way in which the whole stream of behavior is organized or patterned.

As we have said, a person may be appraised with respect to his excellence in any one of these seven dimensions and the word "intelligence" has been used in the case of all of them, although the fourth, the fifth and the last have been used less frequently than the others.[5] We shall get a better view of all of the facts named by the word "intelligence" if we describe briefly the relation between intelligence and the seven dimensions of behavior around which our whole study of the educative process has been centered.

[5] Cf. Thorndike, E. L., and others. "Symposium: Intelligence and Its Measurement." *J. Educ. Psychol.*, 1921, XII, 123-147, 195-216, 271-275.

THE NATURE OF INTELLIGENCE 537

2. *Motor and Mechanical Intelligence:* In the first place, there are those who would say that intelligence is to be identified either with the properties of action systems or with the number and quality of the services rendered by these systems. The phrase "mechanical intelligence" is a case in point.[6] As it is used in tests of mechanical ingenuity and in definitions of intelligence, this phrase appears to mean that the habits and skills that have been acquired by some children are more serviceable or more appropriate than those which have been acquired by other children.

It is known, of course, that people differ widely from one another in their ability to use their habits and skills effectively. Some people, for example, have a peculiar adeptness for making toys, repairing simple machinery, and otherwise handling the objects around them. Similar things can be said about athletes. If, for example, a football player is able to handle his body well, that is, if he is able to run, dodge, pivot, twist, tackle, and fall cleverly, it may be said of him that he has some general quality or property which deserves special recognition.[7] By common consent, then, it might be said that the athlete in his field and the person who is clever in repairing machinery or in making toys must be more intelligent than those who cannot use their movement systems so effectively.

To be sure, no one would argue that excellence in manual or motor skills is a thing that can be measured independently of other psychological functions. The athlete, for example, can neither dodge nor pivot wisely if he has not already taken account, in a clever way, of the positions which the men on the opposing team occupy in the whole field of vision. This is only to say, however, that the athlete, like the child in the schoolroom, is a total person. When we apply the concept of intelligence to his motor or manual performance, we mean simply to emphasize for the time being one aspect of the whole set of events which makes a game of football possible. The same considerations hold true of other services—industry, for example, where emphasis is laid upon mechanical skill.[8]

3. *Perceptual Intelligence:* In the second place, it is sometimes argued that the concept of intelligence should emphasize, in particular, either the quality of a person in his use of his perceptual apparatus or the total range of objects and events which make up

[6] Cf. Paterson, D. G., and others, *Minnesota Mechanical Ability Tests.* Minneapolis: Univ. of Minn. Press, 1930.
[7] Cf. Brace, D. K., *Measuring Motor Ability.* New York: A. S. Barnes Co., 1927; Seashore, R. H., "Stanford Motor Skills Unit." *Psychol. Monog.*, 1928, XXXIX, pp. 51-65.
[8] Cf. Viteles, M. S., *Industrial Psychology.* New York: W. W. Norton and Co., 1932, Chapter XII.

his environment.[9] Common opinion has it, for example, that that person must be intelligent who has read widely, traveled in distant places, and who has made a large number of acquaintances. Such a person would, of course, be able to measure the range of his effective environment in large terms and if emphasis were being placed upon the extent to which he had converted his context into environment, he might be called highly intelligent.

There is, however, another way in which the effective use of perceptual functions may vary in intelligence. As we have seen above, the normal processes of growth make it possible for a person not only to increase the whole range of objects to which he can respond effectively but they enable him also to draw finer and finer distinctions among objects. Sometimes this ability has been described as an increase in one's powers of observation. It has also been described as an increase in sensory acuity. In addition, there are all of the environmental factors which result from comparison, abstraction and sign learning. One might, then, say that intelligence should be used to identify those persons who have very acute senses or who have acquired a large number of concepts.

This was an assumption that was frequently made in the early days of mental testing. Since some of the older psychologies had already assumed that the senses were, so to speak, the windows of the mind, it seemed logical to suppose that the clearer these windows were, that is, the better vision or the better hearing they afforded, the more opportunity there would be for the mind to reflect upon the materials furnished by sense perception. In any case, some of the first mental tests included tests of visual acuity and of visual discrimination in general, tests of pitch discrimination, and tests of tactual discrimination. These tests were frequently united with tests of manual and motor skill. In one of the first lists of such tests, for example, such items as the following were included, viz., measures of strength of the grip, measures of the speed with which the hand could be moved over a given distance, measures of the smallest distance between two points placed on the skin which could be distinguished as two points, measures of the amount of pressure necessary to cause pain, measures of the smallest differences between two weights which could just be detected, measures of reaction time to sound, measures of the quickness with which the subject could name ten specimens of four different colors, accuracy in bisecting a fifty-centimeter line, accuracy in reproducing a ten-second

[9] As a special instance, consider Seashore, C. E., *The Psychology of Musical Talent*. New York: Silver, Burdett and Co., 1919.

interval, and measures of the number of spoken consonants which could be repeated from memory immediately after presentation.[10]

Except for special purposes, tests of this type have now disappeared almost completely from tests of intelligence or of mental alertness. One reason for this lies in the fact that the degree of relationship between scores in such tests and scores on tests which emphasize other psychological traits are often negligible. This fact holds true also of motor ability tests.[11]

4. *Intelligence and Attention:* In the third place, intelligence has sometimes been defined so as to lay emphasis upon the facts described by the word "attention." As we have seen, attention describes, in general, the circumstances under which stumulus-situations which are external to the body may become prepotent in initiating and regulating behavior. Sometimes these external stimulus-situations gain their potency from the fact that they are intense or involve movement or are unexpected. Sometimes, however, they gain their potency because they have been presented to a person so many times that they can be reacted to out of sheer habit.

The first type of attention is called non-voluntary or spontaneous attention, whereas the second is called voluntary or sustained attention. Since persons differ widely from one another in the degree to which voluntary attention can be sustained, it might be said that intelligence is the power of sustained attention. In one of the first intelligence tests, for example, the subjects were asked to listen to the beats of a metronome and to tell, at a predetermined time, whether or not the rate of the beats had been changed.[12] The argument was that if intelligence involves sustained attention, the brighter subjects ought to be able to tell more quickly than the dull subjects whether or not a change in a rate of beating had occurred. Since the dull children were found to be actually superior to the bright children in this test, it had to be abandoned as a factor in those tests of intelligence which emphasized still other aspects of human nature. It is still commonly assumed, however, that those persons who can devote themselves for a long period of time to a single task must be superior in some respect or other to persons who are absent-minded—that is, to persons whose attention is fluctuating rapidly.

[10] Cattell, J. McK., "Mental Tests and Measurements." *Mind,* 1890, XV, 373-380.
[11] Perrin, F. A. C., "An Experimental Study of Motor Ability." *J. Exper. Psychol.,* 1921, IV, 24-57.
[12] Cf. Binet, A., "Attention et Adaptation." *L'Année psychol.,* 1899, XV, 373-380. Burt, C. L., "Experimental Tests of General Intelligence." *Brit. J. Psychol.,* 1909, III, pp. 168 ff.

5. *Intelligence and Learning:* In the fourth place, a great many students of the concept of intelligence have sought to define it in terms of rate of learning or degree of retention or in terms of some other feature of the learning process. It has been said, for example, that intelligence must depend upon the total amount of information that has been acquired. Another point of view has it that intelligence must be closely related to the speed with which change can be effected in human nature under the influence of learning situations. Here again it is clear that learning can be taken apart from other aspects of the growth pattern and it is not meant, therefore, that learning and intelligence should be synonymous. On the contrary, definitions of intelligence which emphasize the learning factor simply assume that rate of learning, or the total amount of learning, or the length of retention should be the one aspect of human nature that is most important in defining intelligence.[13]

6. *Intelligence and Problem-Solving:* In the fifth place, intelligence is often used so as to include the problem-solving functions. This is, perhaps, by all odds, the most common way of thinking about intelligence for there is a long tradition to the effect that reason is the one distinctive feature of human beings as opposed to the lower animals. Since problem-solving has been defined in an earlier chapter as the ability to respond to new situations by re-creating the situation or by refashioning modes of response so that these modes will be better adapted to the situation, it would follow that intelligence could easily be defined as the ability to meet new situations in a rational way.[14]

Human beings differ, of course, from the lower animals in the extent to which they may make use of tentative verbal responses, in the interval between a stimulus-situation and the final or consummatory response. It is during this period of tentative verbal action, perhaps, that that type of activity which we call reflection occurs. One might, then, say that intelligence is power of reflection. This definition would certainly hold true of the philosopher in his armchair. As a common saying has it, the philosopher is doing everything that he does in his head. The final response will come, of course, when, after the period of reflection has ended, the philosopher proceeds to speak out or write out the results of his delibera-

[13] Cf. Colvin, S. S., "Intelligence and Its Measurement." *J. Educ. Psychol.*, 1921, XII, pp. 136 ff.; Woodrow, H., "Intelligence and Its Measurement." *J. Educ. Psychol.*, 1921, XII, pp. 207 ff.

[14] Terman, L. M., "Intelligence and Its Measurement." *J. Educ. Psychol.*, 1921, XII, pp. 128 ff.; Freeman, F. H., *Mental Tests.* Boston: Houghton Mifflin Co., 1926, pp. 491 ff.

tions. Since reflective thinking is largely abstract in nature, one could even say that intelligence is the ability to do abstract thinking.

7. *Intelligence and Adjustment:* We shall try to show later on that these various ways of defining intelligence emphasize points of view toward psychology which cannot easily be brought into our more modern ways of thinking about human nature. Partly for this reason, and partly because of the development of animal psychology with its concepts of biological adaptation, it has become popular to emphasize the adjustments which problem-solving makes possible rather than problem-solving itself.[15]

The student will recall that human beings may react to a new situation in three different ways. The first would call for a more or less nonadaptive use of older habits and skills, the second would call for emotionalized action, the third would call for problem-solving. Problem-solving might, then, be described as a means of promoting adjustment for, obviously, there are times when neither older habits and skills nor emotionalized forms of action would be adequate to a situation. We might say, then, that intelligence is adaptability to new problems or skill in making new types of adjustment to new demands of the environment.[16]

Problem-solving may also be tentative, however; that is, a new situation may be met in a variety of ways. It would seem to follow that the person who could react to a new situation with the greatest variety of tentative efforts, might have some advantage over persons who do not have such a variety. In any case, there are definitions of intelligence which say that it is a capacity for variability or versatility of response.[17]

8. *Intelligence and Character:* These, then, are the various aspects of human nature which have been emphasized most frequently in current attempts to arrive at a defensible definition of intelligence. The student has already seen, no doubt, a marked absence of any reference to motivation, to personality traits, and even to emotionalized forms of action. Some students in this field appear to be convinced that the concept of intelligence should not include emotional stability, the absence of psychopathic tendencies, the presence of moral disposition or good character, or the presence of any other personality or character traits.[18] In other words, the concept of in-

---

[15] Cf. Pintner, R., *Intelligence Testing*. New York: Henry Holt and Co., 1923, p. 48.
[16] Peterson, J., "Intelligence and Its Measurement." *J. Educ. Psychol.*, 1921, XII, pp. 198 ff.
[17] Edwards, A. S., "Intelligence as the Capacity for Variability or Versatility of Response." *Psychol. Rev.*, 1928, XXXV, 198-210.
[18] Freeman, F. H., *op. cit.*, pp. 486 ff.

telligence has usually been limited to those features of human nature which can be called cognitive or intellectual in character. It is as though a definite line should be drawn between all of the operations which make knowing possible as compared with all of the operations which make feeling possible.

There are two things to be said about this distinction. In the first place, if a distinction is made and if we adhere to it, we are put in the position of trying to say that intelligence must be, after all, some special faculty to classify people apart from the situations in which they actually find themselves. Let us suppose, for example, that a person has learned how to throw with a high degree of skill. This means, first, that he may have good manual intelligence, second, that he may have good perceptual intelligence, third, that he may be able to size up complex situations in which throwing would be an excellent way to resolve the situation. We may assume further, however, that the object to be thrown is not a baseball but a stick of dynamite. From the point of view of the individual himself and from the point of view of the equipment which he uses in his act, the throwing of the stick of dynamite in a crowded street might be defined as highly intelligent. When judged, however, with respect to the people in the street and with respect to political, economic, or cultural conditions, the act of throwing might be highly unintelligent. The decision as to whether to throw or not to throw might be made, not so much in terms of a rational appraisal of all of these factors as in terms of lack of emotional balance or lack of good character. In this case, it is certainly clear that one method of defining intelligence would have to include emotional and personal factors.[19]

In the second place, it is clear that a great many of the traits mentioned above and associated with intelligence depend for their quality upon the motives or incentives which have been present during the growth process.[20] As a matter of fact, we shall try to show later on in this chapter that the score which a person gets from an intelligence test may depend more intimately upon the degrees of motivation which have been present throughout his educational history than upon any of the other psychological factors which appear to be dominant while the test is actually being administered. Clearly, then, we must look more closely at the concept of intelligence in

[19] Cf. Wheeler, R. H., and Perkins, F. T., *Principles of Mental Development.* New York: T. Y. Crowell Co., 1932, pp. 167 ff.
[20] Cf. Peterson, J., *op. cit.,* pp. 450 ff.

order to see just what it involves by way of descriptive usefulness and by way of measurement.

III. Manufacturing an Intelligence Test

1. *The Basis of Intelligence:* One of the quickest ways to get a faithful picture of the nature of the intelligence test and to see what such a test actually measures is to trace out the general logic of the way in which a person would go about it to manufacture such a test.[21] In the first place, it is clear that no one can measure the intelligence of a new-born infant. Even though we were to assume that the infant has a mind which is of the same species as that which it will have later on, nothing can be measured for the mind of the infant is not open to any of the methods we know anything about. It is hardly worth while even to try to measure the intelligence of an infant by measuring its modes of action, for, as we have seen, these are highly general in character and very few of them stand in any significant relation to the stimulus-patterns around it.

The student will do well to remember that even in the case of an adult an intelligence test does not measure the intellect nor any other type of mental process or agent. On the contrary, the adult has come to possess something which the infant does not have, viz., specialized modes of reaction to an immense number of stimulus-situations. One of our first inferences, then, about the nature of intelligence and about its measurement is that intelligence is some sort of a value or concept which is drawn out of a special method of treating stimulus-response patterns. There are, to be sure, some persons who would say that these methods actually throw light upon an intellect or a mental power, just as patterns of light waves point to or signify the existence of stars which lie beyond the reach of direct inspection.[22] We shall, however, look at this possibility later on.

As a child grows older, it will, according to some such picture as has been drawn in the chapters that make up Part II, develop its powers of reacting in an adequate way to a considerable number of stimulus-situations. In order to simplify as much as possible the picture which we wish to draw of the process of manufacturing an intelligence test, we shall direct our attention primarily to modes of action, on the one hand, and to stimulus-situations, on

[21] Cf. Young, K., *op. cit., passim.*
[22] Consider again the considerations presented in pp. 50 ff., bearing upon the psychological significance of behavior.

the other, leaving out of account the unique relations between these two events which give rise to such features of behavior as attention, interest, motivation, emotionalized action, and problem-solving.

2. *Empirical Measures of Intelligence:* Let us suppose that it were possible to make a list of all of the stimulus-patterns which might, under normal conditions, be presented to an average person. This list would include a considerable number of words, both in the printed and in the spoken form. There would be some words which are direct substitutes for objects and a great many others which are substitutes for variable relations between objects. The list would have to include, also, all of the objects that make up an average environment, objects which vary in size, in distance, and in rate of movement. There would be included a great many other people and the ways in which these people act when they become sources of stimulus to another person. The list would include also a considerable variety of situations made up of sequences of patterns of words such as are used to describe laws, customs, manners, and the like. The student will see at once that this list would have to be fairly long.

Now let us suppose that we were to write out a parallel list made up of all of the modes of action, attitude, or posture which, by common consent, might be accepted as adequate responses to all of the situations we have named. This list would not be nearly so long as the other list unless considerable attention were paid to small changes in movement, for, as we have seen in an earlier chapter, there are a few fundamental habits and skills which may be used for a great many different purposes.

Now let us attempt to use this material in order to find out something about the competence or the good sense or the rate of development of a group of children. The first subject which we shall take is a child which is just three years of age. Let us start at the beginning of our list and present one after the other, each of the situations which has been entered as a situation to which some identifiable mode of response can be made. Among other things, we would have to speak or to present to the child in printed form many of the words that are in daily use. We would ask it to identify a large number of objects and otherwise to make a suitable response to all of the other items in the list.

As we go down the list we could make an appropriate sign opposite those items in it to which the child can make a suitable reaction. After a good many days of effort we would probably be able to say with precision just which items in the whole list a normal child can react to in a suitable manner. Now, having finished with one child, let us proceed in the same way with another. At the end of this second effort, we would find, no doubt, that the two children differed greatly from each other in the number of items to which they could properly react. If, for purposes of argument, we say that the first child has been able to make five hundred adequate responses, whereas the second has been able to make eight hundred adequate responses, we might be tempted to infer that these two children stand in the ratio of eight to five so far as competence or excellence or ability to get along is concerned.

It would be possible to carry out this same procedure with children of different ages. We might, as a matter of fact, greatly increase the number of subjects at any given significant age, say three-year-olds, three-and-a-half-year-olds, four-year-olds, and so on, and thus make out a curve showing the rate of increase of competence from one age to the next. We might, for example, after having finished with our first four-year-old discover that he was able to react adequately to just as many situations as did the second of the three-year-olds. We could explain this by saying that the second three-year-old was really more competent than he ought to be considering his age, since he has actually turned in a performance that was equivalent to the performance of an average four-year-old. In any case, with a sufficient number of subjects at any given age level, the average performance for a given age could be determined and thus a normal or typical curve of increasing competence with respect to our list could be drawn.

This is a method of determining the competence or the intelligence of a child at a given age which we actually use in our daily observation of children. Moreover, it is the method which we use in our daily observation of one another. To be sure, we do not draw up a formal list of all possible stimulus-patterns and present them in a given order to the subjects of our experiment. On the contrary, as we live with various subjects and as we see them in action day after day, we get a general impression of their competence or of their intelligence from the average run of their conduct. If a child surprises us by knowing the meaning of certain words which we did not think it knew or by identifying objects or otherwise reacting to them in a way that draws from us some special comment, we speak of the child as a bright child or as having been "mentally" developed beyond its age.

3. *Experimental Measures of Intelligence:* Now it is clear that our commonsense use of the method which we have just described

would take a considerable amount of time. Moreover, it creates the opportunity for a good many errors of judgment.[23] So far as the time factor is concerned, we would not be in a much better position if we actually made a list of all possible stimulus-situations and presented each of the items in the list to a child. We may, therefore, try to abbreviate the method by reducing markedly the length of the list. Offhand, of course, we would know that there are a great many things which a three-year-old child could not, by any stretch of the imagination, be expected to react to adequately. All of these items, then, we might strike out of the list. We would still have, however, a lengthy series of items.

Now let us suppose that we make a drastic cut in the list by selecting a very few items, say, six or eight, which we assume to be well within the range of a three-year-old's competence. After having selected such a list, let us present it to a group of one thousand children. We shall want to know whether all of the children can react adequately to all of the items or whether any of the children can react to any of the items, or whether there will be some children who can react to all, some who can react to none, and a good many who can react to at least half of them. If we were to discover that none of the children in our group could react in an adequate way to none of the six or eight items chosen, we would be justified in assuming either (i) that all of the children were too poorly developed or (ii) that the items which we had chosen were too difficult. Since, however, we are seeking for a set of items which will be representative of a very large group but which will, at the same time, act as a sort of standard of achievement for three-year-olds, we will probably be inclined toward the second assumption.

Let us make, therefore, another list. This time we discover that all of the children can answer all of the items adequately. Here again, we could assume either (i) that all of the children were too highly developed for their age or (ii) that the items we had chosen were too simple. For the reason cited above, we would probably accept the second assumption.

The next step would require that we find a set of six or eight items which would stand somewhere between the extremes already mentioned. That is, we ought to find a set of items, none of which could be reacted to by some of our subjects, all of which could be reacted to by others, and a part of which could be reacted to by

---

[23] See, for example, the discussion of sources of error in judgments of intelligence in Dearborn, W. F., *Intelligence Tests*. Boston: Houghton Mifflin Co., 1928, Chapter I.

the majority. In other words, we would have obtained a list of items which could be taken as a reasonable or representative substitute for a much larger list but which would, at the same time, give us some clew to the average ability of three-year-olds.

4. *The Stanford Revision:* As a typical example of such a list let us name the items that are actually contained in the Stanford Revision of the original Binet-Simon tests.[24] In the Stanford Revision, a three-year-old child is asked to point to several parts of its body, viz., the nose, the eyes, the mouth, and the ear; it is asked to name four familiar objects, viz., a key, a penny, a knife, a watch, and a pencil; if a simple picture has been laid before it, the subject is expected to identify several objects in the picture. A three-year-old should be able to give its sex, give its last name, and either repeat a sentence of seven syllables or repeat three digits in order.

The student will see at once that the sentence, "Where is your nose?" is one of the stimulus-patterns that might have been put into the long list with which we began. Keys, pennies, knives, watches, pencils, and the objects that might be included in a common picture are likewise items that would have been included in our long list. If a key is laid before the child with the question, "What is this?" and the child answers, "A key," it has made a suitable or acceptable response to the situation.

In short, then, the list of items included in the test for the three-year-old child is just such a list as we were searching for above. Not all children can answer all of the items in the test. A good many children can answer all of the items but cannot answer any that belong in the four-year-old list. A few children can answer all of the three-year-old tests and a considerable number of the four-year-old tests as well. It follows, of course, that if the general method described above is used for each age level from the third to the eighteenth year, some norm of performance will have been established for each age level and the test becomes a test of competence or of ability, therefore, simply because it indicates what the average or the normal child can do. Once the norm has been established, it is fairly easy to discover those children who depart from the norm, either on the side of low levels of competence or on the side of high levels of competence.

5. *The Meaning of Test-Intelligence:* It is important that the student understand just what is implied in this procedure if he hopes to see what intelligence means and how intelligence may be

---

[24] Cf. Terman, L. M., *The Measurement of Intelligence.* Boston: Houghton Mifflin Co., 1916.

measured. One thing is fairly certain. The experimenter has not laid out on the table some special faculty or agent which can be called the intellect, the reason, or the mind. On the contrary, he has taken typical samples of the stimulus-patterns with which children at any given age level should be familiar and he has attempted, as a matter of fact, to find out whether they are sufficiently familiar with them to make what we would commonly call an adequate mode of response. The facts that are actually available, then, are facts which come out of the use of stimulus-response patterns. Everything else that is said about the intelligence of a child or of the origins of its intelligence is a matter of inference from these facts.

In the second place, it must be assumed that all of the children who are given an intelligence test must have had the same opportunity to get acquainted with the items used in the test. It is clear that if a child had been brought up in a community which knew nothing about digits it could hardly be expected to repeat even three digits in order. Moreover, a child brought up in a community where there were no such things as keys, knives, or watches would not be able to identify such objects. It even has to be assumed that all of the children who are used in standardizing the test for a given age level speak the same language. To be sure, the test might be translated into another language, but if this were done, it would have to be made certain that an act of translation did not change the character of the items of a test in the sense of implying objects which might not be as familiar to the children of a foreign country as they are to children in the country in which the test has been devised.[25]

A. THE INTELLIGENCE QUOTIENT: We are now ready to take the third step in the manufacture of an intelligence test. We have, up to this point, secured a fairly small list of items, that is, a list of stimulus-patterns, which are representative of the whole class of stimulus-patterns with which a child of a given age might normally be expected to be familiar. Moreover, the items that we have actually chosen are normative items in the sense that they stand on the borderline between all of those items that are completely familiar to children of a given age level and those items which are completely unfamiliar.

Now let us administer this test to two additional children. The first of these children is able to answer three of the items in the first list and one in the second. The second child answers all of

[25] Cf. Boynton, P. L., *Intelligence: Its Manifestations and Measurement.* New York: D. Appleton-Century Co., 1933, pp. 389-412.

THE NATURE OF INTELLIGENCE 549

the items in the first list and two in the second. According to the provisions of the Stanford Revision, each item that is answered correctly is equivalent to two months in what is called mental age. Since the child is already three years of age, we will simply assume that it is also three years old mentally. It does not, however, answer all of the items which should be answered by a normal three-year-old child. Since two of these items are missed, we must deduct four months from its mental age. It has answered, however, one item in the four-year-old list properly. It should, therefore, be given credit for two months. This means that our first child, although it is three years of age chronologically, is only two years and ten months of age mentally. It has been convenient to translate these two values into a single value by stating the ratio between them. If 34, the mental age of the first child in months, is divided by 36, its chronological age, we get approximately .94 or 94, as it is commonly expressed, as the intelligence quotient of this particular child.

The other child, however, has answered not only all of the items in the list for the third year but two of the items in the list for the fourth year as well. He is to be given credit, therefore, for three years of mental age plus four months. Here again, if we calculate the ratio between mental age and chronological age, we get the value of 1.11 or, as it is more commonly stated, 111 as its intelligence quotient. If a child were to answer all of the items on the three-year-old list and none of the items in the four-year-old list it would be just as old mentally as it is chronologically. In other words, the intelligence quotient would be 100. The value 100, therefore, may be taken as a normal level of intelligence or as a base with respect to which variations in intelligence can be measured.[26]

B. INTELLIGENCE AND HEREDITY: We must now inquire still more seriously as to just what we have done. What do we mean when we say that a normal or average child should have an intelligence quotient of 100? What is implied if a child turns up with an intelligence quotient of 130 or better? In what respects is such a child better than the average child? As we have seen, there are some people who find no difficulty at all in giving an answer to these questions. They will say that the child who has an I.Q. of 140 achieves this record because he has a greater hereditary capacity of the intellectual sort than the child who is just normal.[27] The su-

[26] Terman, L. M., *The Measurement of Intelligence.* Boston: Houghton Mifflin Co., 1916, p. 79 and *passim.*
[27] Cf. Terman, L. M., *Genetic Studies of Genius.* Palo Alto: Stanford Univ. Press. Vol. I, 1925; Vol. II, 1930.

perior child and the normal child likewise must have a greater heredity capacity than the child who gets an intelligence quotient of 70.

As an illustration of an argument that is often used in this connection, let us take the following.[28] Two boys go to a creek in search of water, both of them carrying a gallon bucket. It is clear that if one of them dips his bucket into the creek at a shallow place, he will not be able to fill his bucket. The other, however, if he dips his bucket into a pool, will get a full bucket. Now it may be argued that the size of the bucket will neither be increased nor decreased by the amount of water which is dipped up in it. In other words, the amount of water which the two boys will get will not depend upon the size of their buckets but upon the way in which their buckets have been used.

By analogy, then, one may say that the hereditary power known as intellect or intelligence is neither decreased nor increased by the amount of training which the intellect receives or, as it is more commonly expressed, by the amount of information which a person acquires. Since, as we have already pointed out, there is a tendency for the I.Q. to remain constant, it must be that the size of a child's bucket remains constant no matter what changes he may make in his method of using it or in the frequency of its use.

The student can easily see, however, that there is something wrong with this argument for the only information that an experimenter can get about children is information on the amount of water actually picked up. That is, a mental test reveals the actual number of adequate reactions that can be made to a sample list of stimulus-patterns. There is no information at all about either buckets or hereditary intelligence. The norm for performance at each age level is only a statistical and, as it turns out, a rather stable average of what a great number of children are actually found to be doing at the present moment. The variations from this norm are never variations with respect to a standard that has been discovered by some other means than those furnished by the test itself.[29]

We may illustrate this point by assuming that, for purposes of experimentation, we have been granted the power to eliminate all children in the United States of the age of six or below who are known to possess an I.Q. of 90 or less. A year from this time let us say that we give the remaining children the same test as they had before or a similar test. The chances are that all of them will

---

[28] Boynton, P. L., *op. cit.*, Chapter I.
[29] This fact lies at the basis of almost all types of measurement, even those which contribute to physical laws and constants.

receive a score of 90 or above. It is clear, however, that this second test would be meaningless for it would be required of us that we make over again the entire test before we can get a norm or central tendency. We would have to start as we have done earlier in the chapter with a group of typical situations which would stand somewhere between those situations which all seven-, eight-, or nine-year-olds can answer, on the one hand, as opposed to those situations which none of the subjects could answer, on the other.

In short, we would have to search out a new norm. To be sure, this norm would stand at a "higher" level than the norm previously used although we would not be able to see that it was higher if we had already forgotten our previous test and all of the children with low I.Q.'s. In other words, then, an intelligence test is a device which is based upon the average performance of a large number of children who have come through an environmental situation which must be accepted as, in general, a fairly stable and at the same time a fairly representative environment. Any major departure from the norm that is thus secured requires explanation. Just as we have said, one possible source of explanation lies in an appeal to differences in hereditary capacity.

C. SOURCES OF VARIABILITY: Before we can answer this appeal, however, we must raise the question as to whether there are any other sources of possible variations. Among the sources that suggest themselves almost immediately let us consider the following. In the first place, it is now known that the score which a child gets on an intelligence test is not always a measure of its previous rate of learning. It may be a measure of its social and emotional balance.[30] It is well known, for example, that very small children, when placed in a test situation, react to the situation either in a bashful and timid way which means that normal modes of response are blocked or it reacts to the test situation as though it were a game. Some of the instructions that are followed in giving a test to very small children emphasize the fact that the tester must secure, at all costs, some measure of rapport with the child. Even though the tester may feel that he has been successful in doing this, it by no means follows that the child is actually as "free" during the test situation as it would be in using the same stimulus-response patterns during contact with playmates of its own age. The social stability of children, therefore, may be a very important item in bringing about variation in test scores. To be sure, this item is not thought to be

[30] Goodenough, F. L., "The Emotional Behavior of Young Children during Mental Tests." *J. Juvenile Res.*, 1929, XIII, 204-219.

important with older children, but up to the present time it has remained as an unmeasured factor leading to variability.

In the second place, the student will see that tests of intelligence are almost certainly based upon the rate at which children acquire adequate modes of response to the objects and events around them. It is clear also that intelligence tests must assume that all children have the opportunity to become acquainted with approximately the same type of environment. This fact raises a rather important question as to just what we may mean by the phrase "the same environment." In some cases, there can be no doubt at all about sameness. Since all children have eyes, noses, mouths, and ears, it would be strange indeed if, at a fairly early age, they did not learn how to identify and point to these parts of their bodies. In the life which we lead, keys, watches, pennies, and other similar objects are almost certain to be the same from one environment to another. Such objects serve very well, therefore, as indices of rate of learning.

In addition to items of this type, we must also take account of the sameness which is introduced by those slowly moving traditions about the nature of early education. The reader will recall that, on a previous page, we have found it useful to distinguish between stimulus-situations which are temporary or phasic as opposed to those stimulus-situations which exert a constant buffering action on the growth pattern. There is, of course, a good deal of overlapping between these two types; but in speaking of buffering action we merely lay emphasis upon those relatively inert features of the environment named by the words custom and tradition.

At the present time, for example, it is almost customary or traditional that every child shall learn to identify some portions of its environment before others. In the case of language, to take only a single instance, there are a few words which almost every child will learn prior to others. There is no inherent psychological reason why an eighteen-months-old infant should learn to say "daddy," "goodbye," "hello," rather than to say "five cents," "seven," "four," "three," "six," or any other combination of words. The same thing holds true of playthings. There are, of course, a good many variations in playthings; but, for any given period of time, all children have some experience at least with a fairly limited range of such objects. In addition to the actual objects which are presented to it, it seems fair to say that traditions about methods of teaching, degrees of motivation, supplying motives and incentives, and other methods of procedure become just as customary.

As we have pointed out before, it is not possible to be wholly intelligent when we try to identify the meaning of sameness in environmental situations, but it seems to be fairly clear that the possibility of sameness should be inquired into just as seriously as we try to inquire into hereditary factors. Even without this inquiry, we may still say that the methods which are used to devise an intelligence test inevitably presuppose the fact that all children have been within the same environment or that they have been motivated to convert their context into an environment at about the same rate.

It is in this fact that we come upon another of the circumstances that may introduce variability in the scores which different children acquire on an intelligence test. We have already considered the tremendous effect which motives and incentives may have upon rate of learning.[31] If the student has really caught the meaning of our earlier discussion, he will see at once that motives may play a very important part early in life when the conditions are most favorable to rapid learning. If we could but recall our own history before we were three years of age, or if we will actually try to recall some of the situations in which we were placed after we were three, we will certainly realize the fact that incentives for learning were applied with extraordinary degrees of variation. It looks as though some parents leave their children almost to their own devices, whereas others take pains in answering questions, give praise freely, and otherwise surround the learning process with those factors that will have a marked effect upon its rate.

This is, however, not the most important feature of motive and incentive. The parents of a child have already come to a fairly stable level of development so far as their own motives and incentives are concerned. That is, every mature person has achieved fairly stable methods of working and equally stable rates of working. Whether he knows it or not, it is almost certain that these features will act as important parts of the learning situations in which children are placed. They too will come to stabilize themselves at given levels of speed. It is entirely possible, therefore, that some of the differences in I.Q. between children may be attributed to these rates of working or rates of learning.[32]

The principal objection to this source of variation in the I.Q. is found, as we have seen, in the alleged constancy of the I.Q. and in the resistance which individual differences display to modification

[31] Cf. Hurlock, E. B., "An Evaluation of Certain Incentives Used in School Work." *J. Educ. Psychol.*, 1925, III, 145-159.
[32] Cf. Hurlock, E. B., "The Effect of Incentives on the Constancy of the I.Q." *Ped. Sem.*, 1925, XXXII, 422-434.

through practice. The student has already learned, however, that this is not a convincing answer, for, as we have tried to show in our study of the conditions under which learning may be transferred from one situation to another, low measures of transfer can sometimes be explained by the fact that practice periods mean simply a continuation of methods of working which have already become habitualized. Let us suppose, for example, that, after we have measured the I.Q. of a child, we try to change significantly the intensity of the motives and incentives behind its performance. As a rule, we would probably provide, for a short period of time, a strong incentive and thus discover that learning will take place for an equivalent period of time at a much faster rate. This is not to say, however, that the child itself has actually reached a new level of motivation which can be depended upon from that time forward. On the contrary, after the special exercise is over, the average child will drop back to levels of working which, through previous training, have become optimal for him.

6. *Summary:* If the student has read himself into the facts presented in this section, he will be able to see rather easily the inferences that should be drawn from it. In the first place, we have found no evidence at all that intelligence tests in and of themselves measure innate hereditary faculty or power. To be sure, we do not mean to deny any of the things that have been said in Chapter Nine about the factors which give direction and quality to the growth pattern for, as we have seen, there are some features of human nature that do owe their origin to the resistance which the germ plasm offers to change. So far as intelligence tests are concerned, however, the constancy of ratios between mental age and chronological age reflect just as clearly possible constancy of states of inertia in the environment as they do in original nature. Since there is more hope of experimenting with different environmental situations than there is with some of the equilibria which surround the early stages of the growth process, there will be a practical advantage in emphasizing the environmental components of the growth pattern, if only for the purpose of promoting adequate types of experimental work.[33]

The reader may, no doubt, have thought of another way of saying this same thing. If our description of the methods that are used to manufacture an intelligence test is reasonably correct, it must be

[33] Cf. Isaacs, S., "The Experimental Construction of an Environment Optimal for Mental Growth," in Murchison, C. (Ed.), *Handbook of Child Psychology* (1st ed.). Worcester, Mass.: Clark Univ. Press, 1931, Chapter V.

concluded that an intelligence test simply states in a convenient arithmetical way the normal or average rate of learning of a large population. Once a norm has been established, the same test can be given to other persons and thus their rate of learning can be compared with the norm or the standard. Rate of learning may be due either to the inertia of germinal material or to the inertia of environmental systems. We cannot evade the suspicion, however, that a third factor is at least involved, viz., the habitual rate at which a person may work or the stabilized levels of purpose and motivation which have been achieved.

In stating these conclusions in this way, the student may have the feeling that we have come out at exactly the same point at which we would have come if we had based our entire discussion of the nature of intelligence tests on hereditary factors. If, for example, rates of working and stable levels of purpose and motive stand in the way of increased levels of achievement, what difference does it make whether we explain the constancy of the I.Q. and the resistance of individual differences to practice in terms of the above-mentioned type of fixity or in terms of hereditary fixity?

As an illustration, let us take the relation between the performances of high school students and college students. It is known that the correlation between the grades of high school graduates and of college graduates is about equal to the correlation between either set of measures and the measures gained from any one of the standard intelligence tests. In other words, then, a student who has received high grades in high school will be very apt to do well in his college work also.[34] Likewise the student who has stood near the bottom of his graduating class in high school is very apt to do poorly when he gets to college.

Now facts of this sort hold true no matter whether we explain them in terms of heredity or in terms of stabilized methods of working. This, however, is not the main point. If one high school student is superior to another because he has a better hereditary background, there is nothing which college instructors can do for him to lift him above his history. On the contrary, if one high school student is better than another because of better methods of working or because of stronger motives and purposes, and if motives and purposes are, as we have said in an earlier chapter, subject to training, then one of the major functions of the college instructor is to change the quality of the people who come to him rather than

[34] Cf. Thorndike, E. L., "The Permanence of School Learning." *School and Soc.*, 1922, XV, 625-627.

to accept their quality simply as it stands. In other words, the first year in college should have, as one of its aims, an increase in the psychological functions of which each person is a sum. If, however, the freshman is to be made over into a better psychological instrument, this result cannot be achieved simply by furnishing temporary incentives. The whole tempo of one's psychological operations must be changed.

There are two obstacles which will stand in the way of success in this sort of teaching. In the first place, a student who is ready to enter college has already attained high levels of fixity. As our discussion of the transfer of training has shown, the major hope for improvement lies in the attempt to reach some new practical limit of skill. The second obstacle is furnished by the fact that slow rates of learning and low levels of motivation early in life may have led to the construction of such a poor foundation for academic work that no subsequent change in interest or desire can really compensate for the loss. If there has been any truth to an earlier argument that speed of learning sometimes depends upon the order in which learning tasks have been assigned, no amount of zest or of motivation can make up for a loss which has been sustained in the earlier periods of the growth pattern.

Let the student suppose, for example, that he is, at the age of twenty, to try to get a doctor's degree in mathematics. Let him suppose, further, that he has never had very much mathematics. It is quite clear that, no matter how intensively he motivates himself or how much interest he develops in mathematics, he will hardly be able to compete with the person who has saturated himself with mathematics for a period of eight or ten years. A better illustration, perhaps, is to be found in the case of some of the newly rich who attempt to take on the refinement of those who have had gentility bred, so to speak, in the bone. The attainment of true gentility by a rough-and-ready workman may, of course, be achieved; but it is achieved only with great difficulty. This difficulty owes its origin to the fact that foundations for a proper sense of social values have not been adequately laid.

IV. Practical Uses of Intelligence Tests

1. *Intelligence and Achievement:* There is, perhaps, one further comment that should have been made in the last section. It seems to be clear from what has been said that there is, as a matter of fact, no significant difference between an intelligence test and an

achievement test. If, of course, we say that intelligence tests actually do measure an innate factor or power while an achievement test measures how a student has used his innate faculty or power in the study of some particular subject matter, then intelligence tests and achievement tests must be sharply distinguished from each other.

The achievement test, whether it takes the form of an ordinary examination at the end of the course or the form of a special examination like those that are used in industry, would measure the knowledge or the skill of a person with respect to some particular class of stimulus-patterns. At the end of a course in history, for example, the student will be asked to answer certain questions. It is often assumed that the answers to these questions will show the teacher how the student has used himself during the semester, but that they will not reveal the potential capacity of the student.

It is easy to see, however, that an intelligence test shows this same thing save that the intelligence test makes use of stimulus-patterns which cut across a great many of the particular subjects that might be taught either in the schoolroom or on the playground. If we may refer again to the simplest levels of an intelligence test, we shall see that the child which can point to parts of its body and identify a few of the more common objects around it is giving just as much evidence of its achievement in learning as is the student who can identify (or otherwise respond adequately to) a set of examination questions in history.

From this point of view, the intelligence test has a certain advantage over the achievement test for it enables teachers and experimenters to speak more generally of the excellence of a person than they could if they were limited to some particular subject matter. It is not possible for every student to learn all that there is to learn even in the curriculum of a small college. There are, however, certain facts which ought to be the common property of everyone, and if some of these facts are chosen as a source of suggestion about rate of learning and degree of motivation, they will have a more general meaning for the teacher and the experimenter than the special facts that make up some particular course.

2. *Individual Differences:* The most obvious practical use of intelligence tests is found in the discovery of individual differences. Our main discussion of the relation between individual differences and the problems of educational psychology will come in a later chapter. There are, however, certain practical school problems that should be mentioned at the present time. Since the methods which

are used in creating an intelligence test presuppose the discovery of a normal or average achievement for the normal or average child, it is almost certain that any large array, either of direct scores from the tests or of I.Q.'s, will fall into a normal distribution curve. This means that children may be classified into groups according to their ability.

A classification that is used rather frequently in education puts all children having an I.Q. of 135 or better in the class of geniuses, those children having an I.Q. from 110 to 135 in the superior group, those ranging from 90 to 110 in the normal group, those ranging from 40 to 70 in the moron group, those ranging from 20 to 40 in the imbecile group, and those ranging from 20 downward in the idiot group.[35] The same facts may be stated in terms of mental ages. In one instance, for example, it is stated that the mental age of idiots ranges from 0 to 3 years, of imbeciles from 3 years to 5 years and 8 or 9 months, and the mental age of morons from 5 years, 10 months to 8 years, 6 months. These mental ages assume that there is some age which shall be called maturity. During the early days of mental testing, it was assumed that a mental age of twelve or fourteen represented maturity. More recently a mental age of sixteen has been found more acceptable. This is, however, still an open question.[36]

In addition to variations of this type, there are, as we shall discover in the next chapter, certain significant variations between the sexes, between members of different racial groups, and between members of different occupational groups. It would seem to follow, then, that in an ordinary school system any given class, say the third grade, would include a number of persons differing widely from one another in excellence.

As an indication of these variations, let us take the mental age range in years of some of the grades in a typical school system. In the first grade, the mental age of pupils ranged from less than four and one-half to eight; in the second grade there was a range from five to ten and one-half; and in the fourth grade there was a range from seven to fifteen.[37] In other words, in terms of the figures given above, the classes in this school system included persons ranging all the way from the moron level to the genius level. It is

---

[35] Hollingworth, L. S., *The Psychology of Subnormal Children.* New York: The Macmillan Co., 1920, *passim.* See also Pintner, R., "The Feebleminded Child," in Murchison, C. (Ed.), *Handbook of Child Psychology.* Worcester, Mass.: Clark Univ. Press, 1933, Chapter XX.
[36] Corning, H. M., *After Testing—What?* Scott, Foresman and Co., 1926, *passim.*
[37] This whole matter is discussed by Pintner, R., op. cit., pp. 814 ff.

hardly necessary to argue that variations of this type raise important school problems.

3. *Homogeneous Grouping:* As an instance of the general character of the problems raised by differences in excellence, let us consider some of the results of early methods of handling the problem. If a child was not able to pass a given grade, he was asked to repeat the grade. Those children who were distinctly superior to the average were often given double promotions. It might happen, therefore, that retarded children, although increasing in physiological maturity and in chronological age, would be kept in the same room with much younger children. In the same way, superior children, although not so well developed physically nor so old chronologically, would be placed with older children.

There are two rather disturbing consequences of this practice. On the one hand, the retarded children are often subject to maladjustments and other personality difficulties which are much more hazardous than their failure to pass a given grade. For example, badly retarded children often become discouraged by having to remain in the same room year after year. Discouragement in this case means loss of incentive and a thorough weakening in purpose.

On the other hand, those children who are advanced in terms of their mental age rather than in terms of their chronological age find themselves out of touch with the social maturity attained by older children. They may, of course, pass through a normal school system at a faster rate; but this does not mean at all that they are actually profiting more from their schooling.

After the invention of the intelligence test it was assumed that this problem could be solved in particular by the use of homogeneous groupings. In other words, it was assumed that, in a large school system at least, all of those children of about the same I.Q. might profitably be put together in a single class. Once the pupils had been segregated according to ability, the teaching program could be adjusted to the level of the whole group and every group treated as a particular case.

Among the advantages commonly mentioned for homogeneous grouping are (i) ease in teaching, (ii) the adaptation of the curriculum to group needs, (iii) increased satisfaction among pupils, and (iv) reduced percentage of failures.[38] The disadvantages have been listed as follows, viz., (i) a stigma is often placed upon the dull students, (ii) the pupils are placed in an unnatural life situation, (iii)

[38] McGaughty, J. R., "Homogeneous Grouping of Pupils." *Childhood Educ.*, 1930, VI.

560 INTRODUCTION TO EDUCATIONAL PSYCHOLOGY

teachers with special training are required for each group, and (iv) even though divisions are made in terms of I.Q. homogeneous groups are still not homogeneous.[39]

A great many experiments have been made on the effect of homogeneous grouping, but only one conclusion seems defensible at the present time. This conclusion is that the high hopes that were held out for the method during the early days of testing have not been justified.[40] As an instance we may consider the question as to whether a division of pupils in terms of the I.Q. actually leads to the homogeneous grouping. It is clear that this is not the case for even though pupils resemble one another in general excellence, they may still differ greatly from one another in their rate of reading, in their aptness in arithmetic, and in every one of the other functions which they use. It may be, for example, that the student has an intimate friend who, in terms of the I.Q., is almost a twin. This does not mean, however, that the student himself does as well in all of his subjects as his friend does. The chances are that any two persons approximately equivalent to each other in I.Q. will have widely varying interests.[41]

We may draw the general inference, then, that within limits, some of the problems of teaching can be simplified if students are classified according to ability. Whenever any such classification is made, however, it must be remembered that there are a good many other psychological functions and a good many services rendered by these functions which must be taken into account. If a student who has been placed in a low grade section responds to the situation with adverse social and personal attitudes, that is, if his normal development as a member of society is interfered with, no good end has been reached. The method is a little more favorable for superior students, partly because it has been shown that such students are no more liable to the development of maladjustments than others and partly because, with the right types of teaching, such students can be greatly aided in their effort to capitalize upon their resources.[42]

4. *Achievement and Ability:* It often happens that the results of achievement tests fail to correlate significantly with the results of

---

[39] This whole matter has been appraised by Burton, W. H., *Introduction to Education.* New York: D. Appleton-Century Co., 1934, pp. 548-558.
[40] Cf. Purdom, T. L., *The Value of Homogeneous Grouping.* Baltimore: Warwick and York, 1929, *passim.*
[41] Cf. Symonds, P. M., "Homogeneous Grouping." *Teachers Coll. Rec.,* 1931, XXXII, 501-517.
[42] Cf. Keliher, A. V., "A Critical Study of Homogeneous Grouping." *Teachers Coll. Contrib. to Educ.,* 1931 (No. 452).

intelligence tests.[43] As we have said above, this fact may be taken to mean that intelligence tests measure one thing while achievement tests measure another. It may be taken to mean, also, that there are a good many occasions when extracurricular activities or social difficulties actually interfere with achievement. Moreover, when students are taken into a class just as they come, the class may be conducted in terms of the median group of pupils or even in terms of the slower pupils. In either case, there would be a great amount of wastage in teaching effort.

For practical purposes, then, one may draw a working distinction between intelligence tests and achievement tests. If this is done and if the distinction is interpreted in the second way described above, then the intelligence test could be used as a measure of the amount of wastage. Let us suppose, for example, that a given class contains a few students who have an I.Q. below 100 and a great many more who have an I.Q. above 120. If such a class were geared to the duller pupils, the bright ones would be receiving neither the load nor the degrees of motivation that they should have for their own advantage. The same considerations would hold true of a marked difference between I.Q. and achievement created by maladjustments, adverse working conditions or social ineptitude. In all of these cases the I.Q. has served as a standard of comparison and a good many school systems, therefore, have been able to discover sources of poor adjustment or eliminate wastage in teaching effort.[44]

5. *Elimination:* One of the most important phases of wastage in teaching effort is to be found in the cases of those students who are carried on year after year, but who, at the end of their prescribed course, have failed to graduate. In terms of a democratic philosophy of education, it can be argued that every child whose father is a taxpayer has a right to continue in a school system just as long as he wishes. Children are, however, continuously being dropped from school for failures. It might be asked, therefore, whether such persons could not have been detected at an earlier age and dropped before effort, time and money had been expended upon them. This question is particularly pertinent with respect to those students either in the high school or in the university who have managed to hang on until the day of graduation and who then fall by the wayside.

[43] Cf. McPhail, A. H., "The Correlation between the I.Q. and the A.Q." *School and Soc.*, 1922, XVI.
[44] Cf. Boynton, P. L., *op. cit.*, pp. 343 ff.

A good many studies have been made on this problem, and it is quite clear that the largest percentage of failures come to those persons who have received low scores on an intelligence test.[45] To take only a typical instance, it was discovered in one case that forty-eight per cent of the students who left college because of inferior scholastic work were in the lowest fifth on a psychological examination, whereas none of the students eliminated were in the highest fifth.[46]

This fact, then, is plain; but there is another fact which has to be considered. In the study just mentioned, for example, seven per cent of those who failed by the end of the freshman year were in the fourth fifth of the whole group. The inference is that these persons may have failed not because they could not do their work well, but because of other factors. Other studies have shown that students who stand low on an intelligence test may do well not only in their high school but in their university work. The inference is that some favorable change must have been brought about in the working habits or in the motivation of these persons.

In short, then, the significant fact about correlations between success or failure in school and relative standing on an intelligence test is not to be found in the similarities which favor high correlation but in the exceptions which keep the correlation from being any higher than it is. These exceptions appear to furnish the real crux of the teaching problem. If students can actually be transferred from one I.Q. or achievement level to another, the reason for the change ought to be discovered.

6. *Individual Instruction:* In addition to the uses of intelligence test scores which have been described above, a great many attempts have been made to discover whether variations in intelligence stand in any significant degree of correlation with success in the various occupations. Most of these studies have been rather fruitless because of the same factors that operate in the schoolroom. The chief of these is that each schoolroom situation or each student-teacher relation is a single or configured pattern of events where intelligence is only one of the many features involved. In an occupation, for example, which demands as a rule a high level of intelligence a person with a low level of intelligence may be successful if he is able to draw upon his other traits and faculties in a compensatory way. It is known, for example, that salesmen are not, as a

---

[45] Cf. Burwell, W. R., and McPhail, A. H., "Some Results of Psychological Testing at Brown University." *School and Soc.*, 1925, XXII, pp. 48 ff.

[46] Davidson, M. R., and McPhail, A. H., "Psychological Testing in a Women's College." *Person. J.*, 1927, VI, pp. 266 ff.

THE NATURE OF INTELLIGENCE

rule, superior in intelligence but many of them are able to achieve high levels of success because of their more facile ways of adjusting themselves to social situations. The student must, however, go to the special books in this field for further information about this particular use of tests of intelligence.

One of the principal gains that has come to education as a result of measures of intelligence is to be found in the increased emphasis that is now being placed upon individualized modes of instruction. If people actually differ from one another by the margins cited above, it would seem almost certain that any lasting method of education could hardly meet the demands which society has a right to place upon a school system. The differences in I.Q. of which we have spoken are, of course, only a part of the whole picture created by individual differences. In any case, a good many different attempts have been made to individualize instruction. As an example, we may take a very comprehensive series of studies on superior children. These studies had as their primary aim a discovery of the factors which led to superiority in children and in achievement. A scientific study, however, has turned out to be very suggestive for teaching procedures since special methods can be used on persons of high quality both to their own advantage and to the advantage of the social group in which they propose to live. It is not possible to draw final conclusions from these studies for the real test of the diagnoses which have been made will come when superior children have reached a mature level. It will then be worth while to note whether the promise of youth is fulfilled and in what ways.

More specific types of individualized instruction have been tried out in particular school systems. There is, for example, the Dalton plan and the Winnetka plan. In the case of the second, the teaching scheme ran somewhat as follows. Each child was allowed to move along as fast as he could. This meant that no child ever failed to pass a given grade. His goal was reached whenever he had finished a given unit of work. It is clear, of course, that if a child is judged as a success or a failure in his school work, the judgment is usually made with respect to the average of the class rather than to the completion of the task.[47]

The student will see at once that we will begin here to enter the field of individual differences proper. We shall, therefore, continue our discussion of this phase of development in the next chapter.

[47] Cf. Burton, W. H., *op. cit.*, pp. 270-275, 542 ff.

READINGS

The text of this chapter has been supplied abundantly with references to the periodical literature. There are, however, a number of excellent books in this field. Any one of the following may be used extensively for outside readings: Boynton, P. L., *Intelligence, Its Manifestations and Measurement*. New York: D. Appleton-Century Co., 1933; Dearborn, W. F., *Intelligence Tests*. Boston: Houghton Mifflin Co., 1928; Freeman, F. N., *Mental Tests*. Boston: Houghton Mifflin Co., 1926; Pintner, R., *Intelligence Testing*. New York: Henry Holt and Co., 1923; Thorndike, E. L., *The Measurement of Intelligence*. New York: Columbia Univ. Press, 1927.

As a special exercise, the teacher may wish to have some of his students report upon some of the more technical phases of the concept of intelligence. He should consult, therefore, Spearman, C., *The Nature of Intelligence and the Principles of Cognition*. New York: The Macmillan Co., 1927; Spearman, C., *The Abilities of Man*. New York: The Macmillan Co., 1927. A very important contribution to the field of measurements and to theoretical concepts of the nature of intelligence is being made under the direction of Thurstone at the University of Chicago. See Thurstone, L. L., "The Vectors of the Mind." *Psychol. Rev.*, 1934, XLI, 1-32. See also Thurstone, L. L., *The Theory of Multiple Factors*. Chicago: Univ. of Chicago Book Store, 1932.

It has not been possible to consider in detail any of the methodological and statistical tools of education. The principle methodological tool, of course, is the experiment. By inference, at least, knowledge of this tool will come from a survey of Garrett, H. E., *Great Experiments in Psychology*. New York: D. Appleton-Century Co., 1930.

Other methods are discussed by Symonds, P. M., *Diagnosing Personality and Conduct*. New York: D. Appleton-Century Co., 1932, *passim*.

There are many good books on statistical methods. See Garrett, H. E., *Statistics in Psychology and Education*. New York: Longmans, Green and Co., 1926; Kelley, T. L., *Statistical Method*. New York: The Macmillan Co., 1924; Riegel, R., *Elements of Business Statistics*. New York: D. Appleton-Century Co., 1924, Chapters I-VIII, X-XIII, XV, XVI, Appendices; Rugg, H. O., *Statistical Methods Applied to Education*. Boston: Houghton Mifflin Co., 1917; Tiegs, E. W., and Crawford, C. C., *Statistics for Teachers*. Boston: Houghton Mifflin Co., 1930; Williams, J. H., *Elementary Statistics*. Boston: D. C. Heath and Co., 1929.

For readings in the field of tests and measurements any one of the following references will be useful. Greene, H. A., and Jorgensen, A. N., *The Use and Interpretation of Educational Tests*. New York: Longmans, Green and Co., 1929; Madsen, I. N., *Educational Measurement in the Elementary Grades*. Yonkers: The World Book Co., 1930; Pressey, S. L., and Pressey, L. C., *Introduction to the Use of Standard Tests*. Yonkers: The World Book Co., 1931; Tiegs, E. W., *Tests and Measurements for Teachers*. Boston: Houghton Mifflin Co., 1931; Webb, L. W., and Shotwell, A. M., *Standard Tests in the Elementary School*. New York: Farrar and Rinehart, Inc., 1932; Woody, C., and Sangren, P. V., *Administration of the Testing Program*. Yonkers: The World Book Co., 1933.

CHAPTER SIXTEEN

PROBLEMS OF TEACHING CREATED BY INDIVIDUAL DIFFERENCES

I. THE PART AND THE WHOLE

1. *Introduction:* There is, perhaps, no phase of contemporary science which possesses more intrinsic interest or more theoretical import, both for research and for the arts of practical control, than that of the relation between the properties of groups of objects (the Many) as compared with the properties of a single object (the One).[1] Such comparisons are important because the group is not merely a sum of the units of which it is made. In other words, one may know all about the single unit taken as a unit but still be unable to say much about the qualities or properties that will appear when a number of such units are put together into a larger pattern. Likewise, one might know a great deal about the total pattern and yet not be in a position to say much about the parts of the pattern.[2]

As examples of this two-sided fact, we may take the behavior of an electron as compared with the behavior of a cluster of electrons, the behavior of a single cell as compared with the behavior of a colony of cells or of an organism, the behavior of a single animal as compared with the behavior of a herd, and the behavior of a single human being as compared with the behavior of an audience, a committee, or a crowd.

Differences of this type have come up over and over again in the preceding pages.[3] Throughout the whole of Parts I and II, for example, we have sought to describe neither a particular growth pattern nor a particular teaching situation. On the contrary, we have always had before us an average growth pattern and a highly generalized group of teaching procedures. It has been only during the last chapter that the particular case has appeared important, for

[1] Students of philosophy will see at once that this is a famous philosophical as well as scientific problem.
[2] This is the principal fact about nature which has given rise to the Gestalt psychologies. Cf. Köhler, W., *Gestalt Psychology.* New York: Liveright Publishing Corp., 1929, *passim.*
[3] Review again the discussion of original nature in Chapter Nine, and especially the comments that were made on the significance of organization or patterning.

I.Q.'s are always individual and never group facts. It is *this* or *that* child and not a whole group of children, which ranks highest or lowest in a series of measures. In other words, it is not possible to say anything at all about the I.Q. unless a particular numerical value derived from a test has been related to a large number of other numerical values. Likewise, personality is a word that has no meaning at all when applied to a collection of persons. A personality is a single case and not a group case.

The qualities of the individual as opposed to the properties of a group will appear to still better advantage in the field of mental hygiene and adjustment, for the work of the teacher in correcting maladjustments can never be generalized. It is always the particular case in its particular setting that should be under examination and treatment. To be sure, there are a few general principles, even in the field of mental hygiene; but these general principles must always be modified to fit the particular case.[4]

2. *An Illustration from Physics:* We may illustrate the really perplexing nature of the relation between the individual and the group in the following way. As the student already knows, a thermometer is a simple device for measuring what is commonly called the temperature of a substance. All of the substances with which we normally deal, however, are collections of molecules. Temperature, therefore, is only a way of describing one of the statistical properties of a vast number of molecules which are in movement. That is, a single molecule could hardly be said to possess the property described by the word "temperature." Such a molecule might still be in a state of rapid motion, but no measure of a single phase of its motion or even of a whole series of phases could give rise to the concept of temperature. To be sure, one might think of the motion of a single molecule in relation to the motion of the molecules of mercury that are to be found in the bulb of the thermometer, but even here we run into difficulties for the pattern of motion of one molecule outside the bulb presupposes the existence of other molecules. When a large number of molecules are in movement, their group behavior will, on the average, give rise to such points on the temperature scale as the freezing point and the boiling point, but it could not be said of a single molecule that it had either of these characteristics.[5]

[4] For a study of the application of these principles to education, see Wheeler, R. H., and Perkins, F. T., *The Principles of Mental Development.* New York: T. Y. Crowell Co., 1932.
[5] Cf. Swann, W. F. G., *The Architecture of the Universe.* New York: The Macmillan Co., 1934, pp. 54, 210, and *passim.*

If we may generalize upon this single illustration, we should be able to say that all of the alleged uniformities or type cases in nature are uniformities or type cases created by averages which have been struck across a considerable number of particular cases. Any study of the relations between hydrogen and oxygen, for example, is a study based upon the behavior of immense numbers of atoms of these elements. It is generally safe to predict that, when hydrogen and oxygen come together under certain conditions, one or more molecules of water will be formed.

This event happens so regularly that the chemist may describe the event in terms of laws of valence and in terms of the emergent properties of water. To know this fact with respect to large numbers of atoms or of any group of elements is not to know at the same time, however, anything about the behavior, at any given moment, of any one of the atoms. Similarly, to know the behavior of an atom is not equivalent to a study of the simpler elements which make up the atom.

3. *Statistical Averages:* Some of the relationships between the statistical properties of groups and the properties or attributes of individuals can be illustrated by the meaning of the word "measurement." If we are to measure, say, the length of any given object, each successive attempt will differ to a greater or less extent from preceding attempts. Where great care is taken to make what are called accurate measurements, the amount of variation around the mean will be small, but certain variations will always occur, and the length of any object, then, becomes synonymous with the concept of averages gained by statistical methods. Neither the average nor any of the original measurements can be accepted as a "true" measure of the length of the object simply because there are no "true" measures of any object.[6]

In other words, there are no measurements which can be called "objective" measurements in opposition to what are sometimes described as "subjective" measurements. When the conditions for making a series of measurements have been controlled to the finest detail, the range of variation around the mean will be fairly small, but some degree of variation will still be present. The object under measurement is said, then, to have a certain length; but this length is not a length that has been established independently of actual trial-and-error measures. There is no way to draw comparisons

[6] Cf. Bridgman, P. W., *The Logic of Modern Physics.* New York: The Macmillan Co., 1927, Chapter III.

between an allegedly true, or real, length and the average of a large number of measures of length.[7]

When the conditions surrounding any given attempt at measurement are difficult to control, that is, when a discovered mean or average is very large, such measurements are called subjective. In the process of establishing color preferences, for example, a large number of persons are asked to express a preference for colors where each single color is compared with every other color. In this experiment it is possible to control some of the external conditions of observation, but it is never possible to control all of the conditions which obtain within the nervous system of the person making the judgments, even though the instructions given to him have been made as "exact" as possible.[8] It turns out, therefore, that an average color preference is an average accompanied by a wide range of variation. Any single individual judgment may, for certain purposes, be much more important than the statistical average. It has, therefore, certain functions or properties which may or may not be characteristic of the average.

The most famous example of the discrepancy between the single case and the group case is to be found in what is known as the principle of indeterminacy. Certain of the phenomena of light are thought to be related to the fact that some of the electrons in an atom may jump from one orbit to another. At the level of event open to inspection in the physical laboratory, so many such changes of orbit are made that the emission of light from any object can be described in terms of laws. These laws are, however, nothing more nor less than the statistical properties or traits of an immense number of events. They describe the uniformity of nature only because the average result is open to inspection and calculation. When attempts are made, however, to understand the individual case, it turns out that the movements of electrons in their orbits are not only unpredicted but unpredictable. Under certain circumstances, it is possible to say where an electron may be at an assigned moment; but any increase in accuracy with respect to this determination is correlated with increasing inaccuracy with respect to the speed of the electron. Similarly, any increase in accuracy with respect to the

[7] For discussions of the nature of measurements in psychology and education, see Garrett, H. E., *Statistics in Psychology and Education*. New York: Longmans, Green and Co., 1926; Kelley, T. L., *Statistical Method*. New York: The Macmillan Co., 1924.

[8] The student will see in this statement a further reference to the nature of set or attitude. See Freeman, G. L., *Introduction to Physiological Psychology*. New York: The Ronald Press, 1934, Chapter XXIII.

speed of the electron means a proportionate decrease in accuracy with respect to its location.[9]

4. *Individual Differences:* In short, then, the functions, properties, or characteristics of the individual case may differ widely from the functions, properties, or characteristics of the group. This fact gives rise, as we have just said, to some of the most perplexing problems of science. In education, sociology, and psychology, these problems are usually described by the phrase "individual differences." This is a phrase which had its origins in experimental psychology.[10] It is usually thought, therefore, that the problem of individual differences is distinctively a psychological problem. From what has been said, however, it is easy to see that it becomes distinctively psychological only because the conduct and experience of single persons have commonly been held in greater respect than have the properties of groups of persons. This has seemed to mean that the treatment which experimental psychology gives to single subjects as opposed to groups of subjects should bear no resemblance whatsoever to the more general scientific problem of the relation between statistical averages and individual performances.

In any case, it becomes important to know that individual differences with respect to psychological traits stand on the same general scientific foundation as do other types of individual versus group problems.[11] Moreover, the concept of individuality is about the most important concept which human beings know anything about. It is important because we all recognize ourselves as selves or persons.

II. The Problem of Psychological Differences

1. *Individual and Social Psychology:* There are two ways in which experimental psychology has proposed to deal with the problem of statistical averages. On the one hand, it is commonly remarked that social groups possess certain traits or characteristics which do not pertain to the persons who make up the group. Such terms as "loyalty," "patriotism," "sympathy," "kindliness," "suggestibility," "imitation," and "gregariousness" are traits which are said to adhere to the individual whenever he is thought of as sus-

[9] Cf. Swann, W. F. G., *op. cit.*, pp. 168 ff.
[10] Cf. Galton, F., *Inquiries into Human Faculty and its Development.* London: The Macmillan Co., 1883; Stern, W., *Ueber Psychologie der individuellen Differenzen.* Leipzig: J. C. Barth, 1900.
[11] Cf. Dodge, R., *Conditions and Consequences of Human Variability.* New Haven: Yale Univ. Press, 1931, *passim.*

taining a membership relation to a group. Social psychology, therefore, is interested in those aspects of human nature which come to expression when a perspective is gained over large numbers of persons. It is a kind of empirical science which attempts to describe and to classify the properties of group performance.[12]

As we have just suggested, however, these properties may not be predictable from the properties or characteristics of any of the persons in the group. It would seem to follow that a second problem of social psychology has to do with significant distinctions and significant comparisons between the behavior of single persons as opposed to the behavior of groups of persons. The study of individual differences, therefore, limits itself to those psychological operations which are differential with respect to different individuals.[13] To say the same thing in a more general way, it turns out that an individual member of society, like an individual proton or electron, has certain characteristics or traits which cannot be deduced from any statistical study of large numbers of units. Since the conduct and experience of a single person are more important to himself than to any other person, the psychological study of the individual has always taken first place among the psychological sciences. More recently, however, the problems of social psychology have achieved a major position among the psychological sciences as the marked increase in the amount of experimental work readily shows.[14]

2. *Normative Psychology:* A psychology of the individual, however, may still be concerned with traits which are average traits rather than differential traits. The major task of experimental psychology has been to get a picture of the typical, normal, adult individual. It has ever sought to describe the median case, even though a median case has never been found. It has conducted a search for all of those traits and talents that are common to human beings as individual human beings.[15] We have already seen how this type of normative psychology has, in times past, played a very large part in educational method and practice. The typical human adult was alleged to possess certain traits or capacities and from this starting

[12] Cf. Rice, S. A., *Methods in Social Science.* Chicago: Univ. of Chicago Press, 1931.
[13] Cf. Ellis, R. S., *The Psychology of Individual Differences.* New York: D. Appleton-Century Co., 1929.
[14] For example, Murphy, G., and Murphy, L. B., *Experimental Social Psychology.* New York: Harper and Bros., 1931.
[15] For a discussion of the meaning of the word "normal," see Spearman, C., "Normality," in Murchison, C. (Ed.), *Psychologies of 1930.* Worcester, Mass.: Clark Univ. Press, 1930, Chapter XXIV.

point education assumed that small children must possess the same traits and capacities only in a smaller or more diminutive form.[16]

It is hardly necessary to repeat that neither experimental psychology nor education has ever actually met the typical person described in the textbooks of psychology. He is a fictitious construct from the laboratory. He is a person who has been created in much the same way that mythical All-American football teams are constructed. Certain tremendous advantages are to be gained, of course, in having such a normal or typical pattern, but even the most elementary consideration of the problems of education, to say nothing of the problems of the other arts which depend upon experimental psychology, will show that the unit of investigation is the individual himself.

Common observation tells us that each person is the only one of his kind. He has his own particular stature, weight, and facial expression. The rough distinction we draw between geniuses and idiots and the ready way in which we describe all types of special aptitudes, such as mechanical ability, musical ability, and social affability, give testimony in favor of the proposition that the matrix must have been destroyed immediately after each single person was fashioned.

We shall discover in a moment that there is abundant experimental support for these commonsense judgments. In the meantime, it goes almost without argument that such differences create a major problem for education. On first thought, they would seem to suggest that factory methods of mass production must be totally inadequate to the education of single persons. For certain purposes, any particular piece of sheet metal may be just as good as any other piece, but the universality of individual differences would seem to say that no good purpose could be served by attempting to identify two different persons during an educational process.[17]

3. *Types of Individual Differences:* There are, of course, a great many modes of entrance into the detailed problems of individual differences. As we shall see, differences may be described with respect to race, with respect to sex, or with respect to social status. The most fruitful mode of entrance, however, is by way of the several general features of the growth pattern described in earlier chapters. People differ from one another, for example, in all of the traits and characteristics of behavior-patterns. One of the first

---

[16] Review the discussion of this problem in Chapter Ten.
[17] Cf. Thorndike, E. L., *Educational Psychology*. New York: Columbia Univ. Press, 1913. Vol. III: *Individual Differences*.

differences between people ever to be noted and measured accurately was that of speed of reaction.[18] It is now known that there are probably as many reaction times as there are persons. This saying becomes true, of course, only with respect to the units that are used in making the measurements. There are a few men who can run 100 yards in 9.4 seconds. At first thought, it would be easy to say that these athletes must be alike in reaction time and in speed of movement. It is clear, however, that even a tenth of a second may be a gross unit with respect to differences between men that must be expressed, if they are to be expressed at all, in terms of hundredths or even thousandths of a second. These same considerations hold true of other properties of modes of response, viz., accuracy, coördination, and the like. In coördination, for example, there are just as many modes of patterning separate muscle groups into a single coördinated movement as there are persons to make such movements.

Individual differences may also be described in terms of the range of the effective environment.[19] Victims of blindness or of deafness suggest almost immediately one sort of deviation from the normal. But even where all of the sense organs are known to be normal, people still differ from one another in the range and variety of objects to which they may make effective response. As a single illustration, we may take differences with respect to language. There are probably very few persons, if any at all, who know the precise meaning of every word in the English language. There are probably no persons of the white race who know no words at all. Between these extremes fall the remainder who differ from one another not only with respect to the total number of words to which they can react effectively but who differ also in degree of effectiveness itself.

In a complete survey of individual differences we would be compelled to go ahead with respect to the other dimensions of behavior, viz., attention, learning, emotion, problem-solving, motivation, and character. At the level of organization of behavior-patterns described by the words "self" or "character" the problems of individual differences would become particularly significant. The total number of neurones in the nervous system is thought to amount to a sum well over 13 billions. If only a million of these neurones were taken, in all possible permutations and combinations, the total

---

[18] Cf. Garrett, H. E., *Great Experiments in Psychology*. New York: D. Appleton-Century Co., 1930, *passim*. Also Valentine, W. L., *Readings in Experimental Psychology*. New York: Harper and Bros., 1931, *passim*.
[19] Cf. Ellis, R. S., *op. cit.,* Chapters II, III.

number of combinations possible would be described by the number two to the two-millionth power.[20] The nervous system, of course, does not work on the principle of neurones taken two at a time; but this sort of mathematical calculation does give some suggestion of the infinite variety in long-time patterning of organization that might be possible. The chances of finding two individuals who were alike in all of the details of selfhood or character would be about as great as the chance that all of the atoms in a table might move in the same direction at once. Both chances are theoretically possible, but actually impossible.

In addition to the individual differences which can be described in terms of the major dimensions of psychological trait, it has become especially fruitful to use the concept of intelligence. As we have seen, the word "intelligence" is a way of bringing together in statistical form the net result of several different types of psychological function. For certain statistical purposes, it is possible to say that a large number of individuals have the same I.Q. No one has ever supposed, however, that sameness in this connection had any other meaning than that certain practical school procedures could handle a group of individuals of a given I.Q. in much the same way. It is said, for example, that in the population at large, differences of intelligence are distributed as follows. About 1 per cent of the population is said to have an I.Q. below 70, 5 per cent is said to have an I.Q. between 70 and 79, 14 per cent have an I.Q. between 80 and 89, 30 per cent an I.Q. between 90 and 99, another 30 per cent have an I.Q. between 100 and 109, 14 per cent have an I.Q. between 110 and 119, 5 per cent have an I.Q. between 120 and 129, and 1 per cent have an I.Q. over 130.[21] As we have seen, certain school operations can be conducted more efficiently when different individuals are grouped in this way and thus come to be called more or less identical, but such a grouping does not and cannot mean that any two individuals are a mirror image of each other in the traits said to be measured by intelligence tests.

III. AGE, SEX AND RACE DIFFERENCES

1. *Introduction:* For the purposes of experimental psychology and for certain purposes of education as well, the mode of classifying individual differences just described has a great many advan-

---

[20] Cf. Herrick, C. J., *Brains of Rats and Men.* Chicago: Univ. of Chicago Press, 1926, Chapter I.
[21] Cf. Brigham, C. C., *A Study of American Intelligence.* Princeton: Princeton Univ. Press, 1923, *passim.*

tages. There are, however, certain other modes of classification which have a still greater value both for psychology and education. In addition to the fact that each human being differs from every other human being in every trait, it is known that persons of one sex differ from persons of the other sex in certain significant ways. It is known also that persons having different racial derivations differ from one another in certain significant ways. In short, it would be possible to take almost any group of persons—say, lawyers as a class, industrial workers as a class, or individuals of a given height as a class—and attempt to ascertain whether or not certain significant differences were peculiar to that class as a class. Of such classes those represented by age, sex, and race have been studied most frequently.[22]

2. *Age Differences:* It is not necessary to consider in any greater detail than we already have done some of the problems of individual differences created by various age levels. This is, in particular, the major task of genetic psychology. It is at least the problem with which genetic psychology begins, for this branch of the science uses as its materials the progressive changes in psychological function which occur coincident with growth or with increasing chronological age. If, then, we were to review the problem of age differences, we should have to consider again most of the questions that have been discussed throughout the chapters which make up Part I of this book. Since we have frankly adopted the genetic point of view almost our entire study has centered around age differences.

3. *Sex Differences:* A vast amount of work has been done on the question of sex differences.[23] It is obvious, of course, that marked physiological differences owe their origin to the different biological functions of the male and of the female, but it is by no means so certain that these physiological differences are either the occasion of or are correlated with, other sorts of differences in the muscles, in the sense organs, in the brain, or in any of the functions mediated by these pieces of apparatus.[24] It is known, of course, that girls mature somewhat earlier than boys, and that boys are, on the average, taller and of greater strength.[25] This is not necessarily to say, however, that such differences would appear in intimate dependence upon hereditary factors, were all differences in

[22] Cf. Ellis, R. S., *op. cit.,* Chapters IX, X, and XI.
[23] Ellis, R. S., *op. cit.,* Chapter X.
[24] Cf. Dunlap, K., *Civilized Life.* Baltimore: The Williams and Wilkins Co., 1934, Chapter IV. This chapter makes a very good statement of the various social and educational problems created by sex differences.
[25] Cf. Baldwin, B. T., "The Physical Growth of Children from Birth to Maturity." *Univ. of Iowa Stud. in Child Welfare,* 1921, I (No. 1).

INDIVIDUAL DIFFERENCES 575

mode of training eliminated. There is some evidence that women are less variable in tests of different psychological functions than are men, but even here final judgment must be suspended. It is sometimes argued that men are apt to be more intellectually inclined, while women are apt to be intuitionally inclined. Here, again, however, a statement of possible difference between the sexes does not say whether the difference is due to hereditary factors or to educational and general environmental factors.

A. SIMPLER FUNCTIONS: As an example of the sort of experimentation that was done in this field in the earlier days, we may take Thorndike's interpretation of a series of tests made by Woolley on twenty-five men and women.[26] If the data are interpreted so as to give the percentage of men reaching or exceeding the median performance of the women, it appears that some of the differences between the sexes run as follows, viz., reaction time, 68 per cent; tapping, 81 per cent; speed in sorting cards, 14 per cent; accuracy in sorting cards, 44 per cent; accuracy in thrusting at a target, 60 per cent; drawing lines, 72 per cent; threshold of pain, 46 per cent; threshold of taste, 34 per cent; threshold of smell, 43 per cent; lifting weights, 66 per cent; two-point discrimination, 18 per cent; memory for syllables and learning, 32 per cent; and ingenuity, 63 per cent. It is clear (i) that most of these items refer to relatively simple types of performance, (ii) that none of them have much bearing upon essential features of psychological life, and (iii) that marked differences are to be found with respect to some of them. This study has been criticized, however, on the ground that the number of subjects was too small to give authoritative data.

A more elaborate study involving five thousand school children has been made by Burt.[27] With a selected passage, the average rate of reading for boys was 117 seconds and for girls, 112 seconds. Scores on comprehension of what was read in terms of questions answered were 11.3 for boys and 11.6 for girls. In a spelling test the boys had 53.6 words correct whereas the girls had 56.4 words correct. In adding numbers, the boys had 21.1 additions correct while the girls had 21.4 correct additions. The scores on subtraction, multiplication, and division were equally close. The girls were able to write 125.2 letters in two minutes whereas the boys wrote 117.2. The girls not only had the advantage in rate of writing these

---

[26] Thorndike, E. L., *Educational Psychology*. New York: Columbia Univ. Press, 1914, Vol. III, p. 178.
[27] Cf. Burt, C. L., *Mental and Scholastic Tests* (rev. ed.). London: King and Son, 1927, *passim*.

letters but in quality of writing, also, for their average score was 10.1 whereas the boys had an average score of 9.8. The girls were able to finish a piece of handwork in 55.7 seconds whereas the boys took 54.6 seconds. The boys, however, had a slight advantage in quality of work done, their score being 10.8, whereas the girls had a score of 10.2.

It is clear from this study that the differences between the sexes in the traits mentioned are by no means so great as those indicated by the first study. In general, it appears fair to say, with respect to such traits as these, that the sexes do not differ greatly from one another.

B. INTELLIGENCE: No significant differences have been found in the general intelligence of the two sexes, at least in so far as intelligence is revealed by the tests in common use. Boynton, for example, gave the Stanford Revision to 1,170 boys and to 628 girls and the Army Alpha to 970 boys and to 551 girls, all of whom were university students.[28] No significant differences were to be discerned in the total scores. There were, however, some differences in the individual tests. The men, for example, appeared to be somewhat superior in tasks depending upon arithmetical reasoning, in finding similarities, and in certain types of general information. The women seemed to be superior in drawing designs from memory, in aesthetic comparisons, and in repeating digits and sentences.

Such facts as these, when taken in conjunction with the general conclusion that women are not inferior to men in actual scholastic activity, show that the relatively small number of eminent women is a matter of training and of general social conditions rather than a matter of unfortunate heredity. Among a thousand eminent men Cattell was able to list only thirty-two women, and most of these achieved eminence for other reasons than intellectual quality. It might appear, then, that nature disfavored the female; but such a conclusion is certainly false.[29]

Other types of difference, however, crop up more often, especially in the popular literature. It is commonly assumed that there are marked differences in volitional, temperamental, and moral traits. Men are sometimes said to be more self-asserting and pugnacious whereas women are apt to magnify such maternal dispositions as sympathy, deeper interest in human experience, and the like. In spite of the fact that such traits as these are extraordinarily difficult to

[28] Boynton, P. L., "Sex Differences." *Psychol. Bull.*, 1926, I, 104-105.
[29] Cattell, J. McK., "A Statistical Study of Eminent Women." *Pop. Sci. Mo.*, 1903, LXII, 359-377.

INDIVIDUAL DIFFERENCES 577

measure, no information is available that would suggest a difference of the magnitude commonly reported.[30]

4. *Race Differences:* An equally large amount of work has been done on the question of racial differences. Of this work, a recent experimenter has remarked: "The mere application of tests—particularly group tests, which in recent years have become favorite devices in race work—and uncritical 'explanation' of the results in terms of heredity or environment are not only fruitless but are likely to be dangerous. For one thing, these practices foster the delusion that a body of objective fact exists, whereas the 'facts' are not facts at all in any meaningful, scientific sense." [31]

In short, then, the experimental study of race differences is no more definitive in its character than is the work on sex differences, especially where measures of native intelligence are under investigation. As we have seen in our study of intelligence tests, use is made of samples of function drawn from the environment which is most apt to be common to the largest percentage of the individuals to be tested. It is not reasonable to suppose that a test manufactured out of material common to an average American community would have anything pertinent to say about the native intelligence of a group of Chinese children or even of Negro children.[32]

A. SIMPLE FUNCTIONS: The first studies on the mental traits of civilized and of primitive peoples showed clearly enough that the size of racial differences had been greatly exaggerated. These first tests were, of course, tests of sensory acuity and of some of the other simpler mental functions.[33] Such tests showed that children and adults the world over were scarcely to be distinguished from one another by an amount larger than that which separated the individuals of a single race. Since there were obvious differences between the cultural achievements of the various races, it was quickly supposed that cultural achievement must depend upon the more complex mental functions rather than upon the simple functions and that great racial differences were to be sought, therefore, in these more com-

---

[30] Cf. Allport, F. H., *Institutional Behavior.* Chapel Hill: Univ. of North Carolina Press, 1933, Chapter XVIII.
[31] Lambeth, M., and Lanier, L. H., "Race Differences in Speed of Reaction." *J. Genet. Psychol.,* 1933, XLII, 255-297. See p. 292.
[32] Cf. Wang, S. L., "A Demonstration of the Language Difficulties Involved in Comparing Racial Groups by Means of Verbal Intelligence Tests." *J. Appl. Psychol.,* 1926, X, 102-106. Also, however, Goodenough, F. L., "Racial Differences in the Intelligence of School Children." *J. Exper. Psychol.,* 1926, IX, 388-397.
[33] Woodworth, R. S., "The Comparative Psychology of Races." *Psychol. Bull.,* 1916, XIII, 388-397; "Racial Differences in Mental Traits." *Science,* 1910, XXXI, 171-186.

plex functions. The intelligence test offered itself as a device for a more accurate study of the really significant differences between the races.

B. INTELLIGENCE: One of the first major comparisons to be drawn between different racial groups was made possible by the administration, during the war, of the Army Alpha test to large numbers of individuals. When the scores of 93,973 whites on this test were compared with the scores of 18,891 Negroes, it was found that seventeen times as many whites received grades of A or B as did Negroes. A grade of A was given to the highest 5 per cent of the subjects tested. Three times as many blacks received a grade of D– as did whites. The grade of D– was given to the lowest 7 per cent on the test. The grade of A was gained by 41 times as many whites as blacks.[34]

The first conclusion to be drawn from data of this type might run as follows. Negroes are obviously less competent in the higher intellectual traits than are members of the white race. It would also be easy to say that the difference in ability was due to heredity rather than to training since the Negroes tested were, for the most part, individuals who had lived on the American scene for a good many years. A further analysis of the data, however, shows that so general a conclusion must be considerably modified. The northern Negro was found to be markedly superior to the southern Negro. It is possible, of course, to say that this difference merely shows that the better type of Negro had moved into the north. It is also possible to argue that the Negroes who had moved into the North found a type of environment which raised their intellectual level. That this latter interpretation is the more reasonable appears from the fact that foreign born subjects who took this same test had higher intelligence ratings in direct proportion to the number of years they had lived in this country.[35]

Further light on this problem of racial differences is afforded by those studies which have attempted to discover the relationship between levels of intelligence and degrees of racial mixture. In a study of the comparative abilities of white and Negro children, for example, Peterson, among others, has found that racial mixtures have a better intelligence rating than do pure blacks, but that these ratings are not so high as those achieved by pure whites. The first

[34] Yerkes, R. M., "Psychological Examinations in the U. S. Army." *Memoirs Nat. Acad. of Sciences*, 1921, XV, pp. 707 f.
[35] Brigham, C. C., *A Study of American Intelligence.* Princeton: Princeton Univ. Press, 1923, pp. 120-121.

inference, of course, is that whites and blacks differ in intelligence through some hereditary factor. The possibility still remains open, however, that racial mixtures may have better environmental conditions than is possible for pure blacks. Such environments would not, as a rule, measure up to the environments surrounding white children at the social status usually subject to testing.[36]

The American Indian has been studied almost as intensively as has the Negro. In a study of the relation between degree of Indian blood and score on the Otis intelligence test, Hunter found that Indians of pure stock were inferior to white mixtures.[37] The median score for quarter-breeds was 109, for half-breeds 91, for three-quarters breeds 78, and for pure stock 67. The median score for 1,366 white children on the same test was 123. Such data would seem to say that intelligence decreases in direct proportion to an increase in Indian blood. It is clear, however, that such results must be modified by whatever is to be said about differences in environmental conditions. Moreover, the Otis is an intelligence test precipitated out of a white culture and standardized with respect to the performances of white children. As we shall see in a moment, even the administration of such a test by a white experimenter where the subjects are foreign-born may make a difference in performance.

Similar considerations hold true of a comparison between the performances of Indians and whites by Garth.[38] The median score of the Indians was 83, whereas the median score of the whites was 123. The very fact that the median score of the whites was distinctly superior would seem to indicate that the test had been administered to a select group.

The fact that the races may not differ from one another greatly in some of the simpler psychological functions is brought out by Pyle's study of the Chinese.[39] Pyle used measures of thought, memory, logical memory, substitution, an analogy test, and a test of perception (spot pattern). No significant differences were found to obtain between Chinese children and white children. Intelligence tests, however, brought out the same sort of difference as has been described for Negroes and for the American Indian. Waugh com-

[36] Peterson, J., "The Comparative Abilities of White and Negro Children." *Comp. Psychol. Monog.*, 1922, I (No. 5).
[37] Hunter, W. S., and Sommermeier, E., "The Relation of Indian Blood to Score on the Otis Intelligence Test." *J. Comp. Psychol.*, 1922, II, 257-277.
[38] Garth, T. R., "A Review of Racial Psychology." *Psychol. Bull.*, 1925, XXII, 343-364. See also Garth, T. R., *Race Psychology*. New York: Whittlesey House, McGraw-Hill, 1931, *passim*.
[39] Pyle, W. H., "A Study of Mental and Physical Characteristics of the Chinese." *School and Soc.*, 1918, VIII, 264-269.

pared the American and Oriental student intelligence to the disadvantage of the Oriental.[40] Young, however, found no differences between Chinese children and white children. There was some indication in this study that the use of the Stanford Revision by a Chinese experimenter made some difference in the effectiveness of the test.[41]

IV. The Problem of Exceptional Talent

1. *Introduction:* There is one phase of the general problem of individual differences which has received marked attention in contemporary education. Special modes of teaching and special problems of education arise with respect to those who are exceptionally gifted either in a general way or with respect to specific talents or who are in one respect or another especially deficient. There is, of course, considerable difficulty in identifying both general excellence and specific excellence, partly, because objective measures of such abilities are more or less approximate in character and, partly, because there is no objective measure of what shall constitute superiority. It is one thing to gain a high score in the psychological functions which are said to be measured by the intelligence test and quite another to achieve distinction in performances which society may have reason to hold in high regard. Individuals who are said to be gifted in general intelligence usually obtain an intelligence quotient of 135 or better. An arbitrary measure of excellence in special traits or talents is a little more difficult to establish.

2. *Qualities of Gifted Children:* A large amount of information about gifted children has suggested some of their principal characteristics.[42] It is known, for example, that nearly one-third of the fathers of gifted children belong to the professional classes and one-half to the semiprofessional and higher business classes, and less than seven per cent to the semiskilled or unskilled labor classes. When the general home environment is measured by the Whittier point scale for home environment, the homes of gifted children rank much higher than do the homes of non-gifted children.[43]

[40] Waugh, K., "A Comparison of Oriental and American Student Intelligence." *Psychol. Bull.,* 1921, XVIII, 106.
[41] Young, K., "The Intelligence of Chinese Children in San Francisco and Vicinity." *J. Appl. Psychol.,* 1921, V, 267-274.
[42] Terman, L. M., and others, *Genetic Studies of Genius.* Palo Alto: Stanford Univ. Press, 1925, Vol. I, *passim.*
[43] Williams, J. H., "The Whittier Scale for Grading Home Conditions." *J. of Delinq.,* 1906, I, 273-286. "A Guide to the Grading of Homes," Whittier, California Bureau of Juvenile Research Bulletins, 1918 (No. 7).

In general, the stock from which superior children come appears to be superior both physically and mentally. On the average, the thousand children included in the Terman study were found to be superior to average children in height, weight, lung capacity, muscular strength, and in certain other physical traits. The general rhythm of growth has somewhat accelerated such activities as walking, and talking tended to be slightly precocious. Most of the subjects were found to be advanced beyond their years in the school program. At the same time, however, most of the children were in a school grade considerably below their mental development. Half of the group had learned to read before entering school and their program in this and in certain subjects which are described by other children as most difficult was exceptionally rapid. A typical gifted child was found to read more books than were read by any unselected children of any age up to fifteen.

Terman reports that gifted children have more hobbies and other enthusiasms than average children. This fact appears in their collections, many of which are of a scientific or historical character. Both this fact and the facts about physical growth and development stand in direct opposition to common traditions about exceptional children for it is frequently said that such children are apt to be physically inactive and somewhat one-sided in their development. The advantage of exceptional children appeared, moreover, in certain social traits and attitudes. They were, for example, less boastful and more trustworthy than unselected children. They were fairly stable emotionally and, on the whole, their record in leadership and social adaptability was much superior to that of children in the general school population.

The initial study of these exceptional children was followed up seven years later by retests covering almost the same traits and talents as were measured at the start. In general, the precociousness of the children had been retained throughout the seven-year period. Intelligence quotients of the girls had decreased slightly, but most of the other features tested remained relatively unchanged. As Terman writes:

The factual data these studies have furnished should dispose forever of the superstitious beliefs so commonly held regarding intellectually superior children. It is simply not true that such children are especially prone to be sickly, overspecialized in their abilities or interests, emotionally unstable, socially unadaptable, psychotic, and morally undependable or that they usually deteriorate to the level of mediocrity as adult life is approached. Educational reforms in the direction of special classes, special curricula, and special classroom procedures can now be confidently formulated from this foundation of established fact. If special classes and special procedures are to be opposed, it must henceforth be upon other grounds than those that have been most commonly alleged.[44]

As a general rule, excellence in any single trait is correlated with excellence in other traits. Under certain special conditions, however, certain individuals come to a high level of achievement in some special talent which has no demonstrable correlation with general intelligence or with other special abilities. There are individuals, for example, who seem to have abilities which lend themselves in an exceptional way to the creation or performance of music. These exceptional abilities may arise either with respect to the perceptual functions, with respect to the motor functions or with respect to creative functions which make the interpretation and the creation of new music possible.[45]

It is clear that special musical talent in one of the several forms described above may coexist with mediocre or even with inferior intelligence.[46] Such gifts develop early in childhood although adequate tests of certain forms of musical ability are not diagnostic before the age of ten. It is not to be concluded from these considerations, however, that the investment of large amounts of money and the tutelage of the individuals who have a marked ability in the absence of good or even excellent ability is worth while.

Somewhat the same conclusions are to be drawn from studies of other types of excellences. Among such excellences are ability to draw and to engage in other types of artistic creation,[47] arithmetical computation,[48] and mechanical ability.[49] It is commonly assumed, both with respect to general intellectual ability and with respect to special traits and talents that heredity rather than training is a proper explanatory concept. As we have tried to show, how-

[44] Terman, L. M., "The Gifted Child," in *A Handbook of Child Psychology* (ed. C. Murchison). Worcester, Mass.: Clark Univ. Press, 1931, p. 516.
[45] Seashore, C. E., *The Psychology of Musical Talent*. Newark: Silver, Burdett, 1919. Also Révész, G., "Das Musicalische Wunderkind," *Zsch. f. Päd. Psychol.*, 1918, XIX, 29-34.
[46] Coy, G., "Abilities, Interests, and Achievements of a Special Class for Gifted Children." *Teach. Coll. Contrib. to Educ.*, 1922 (No. 131).
[47] Ayer, F. C., *The Psychology of Drawing*. Baltimore: Warwick and York, 1916; Hollingworth, L. S., *Special Talents and Defects: Their Significance for Education*. New York: The Macmillan Co., 1923, *passim*.
[48] Binet, A., "Psychologie des Grands Calculateurs et Jouers d'Echecs." Paris: F. Alcan, 1894; Lindley, E. H., and Bryan, W. L., "An Arithmetical Prodigy." *Psychol. Rev.*, 1900, VII, 135; Scripture, E. W., "Arithmetical Prodigies." *Amer. J. Psychol.*, 1891, IV, 159.
[49] Stenquist, J. L., "Measurements of Mechanical Ability." *Teach. Coll. Contrib. to Educ.*, 1923 (No. 130).

ever, not enough information is available to indicate how special environmental patterns may be related to the development of special traits.

V. Deficient Children

1. *Introduction:* When we speak of deficient children, we may have in mind either children who fall very low in I.Q. or children who, while measuring normally in general intelligence, suffer from some particular difficulty. In the first group we might place all children who deserve to be called idiots, imbeciles, or morons; and in the second group, children who are blind or in any other way impaired in the normal use of their psychological functions. Obviously, both types of deficiency create special teaching problems.

2. *Feeblemindedness:* In all types of general psychological deficiency, it can be shown that the developmental schedule is not only slower than is the case with normal individuals, but that the rate of growth ceases at an earlier age. In one study of this matter involving 639 persons who were examined repeatedly it was found that sixteen per cent actually declined in mental age during the ten-year period over which the study was conducted, while sixty-eight per cent gained only from zero to twelve months in mental age.[50] It has not been ascertained as yet whether feebleminded children display weaknesses in special traits or whether their deficiencies are spread over the whole frontage of the growth pattern. To be sure, one would expect just as many individual differences among feebleminded children as obtain between normal children, but it is not so certain that a child displaying a low level of intelligence takes his place with respect to superior children because he is lacking in some particular ability, the possession of which would bring him up to the normal level. In any case, it has been shown that the learning curves of feebleminded children resemble rather closely the learning curves of normal children. The task required of the two groups consisted of card sorting over a period of thirteen days. The actual amount of improvement and the percentage of improvement for the two groups were the same.[51]

The slower rate of development of feebleminded children is nicely

[50] Kuhlmann, F., "The Results of Repeated Mental Examinations of Six Hundred and Thirty-Nine Feebleminded Over a Period of Ten Years." *J. Appl. Psychol.*, 1921, V, 195-224.

[51] Woodrow, H., "Practice and Transference in Normal and Feebleminded Children." *J. Educ. Psychol.*, 1917, VIII, 85-96, 151-165. Much of the experimental literature on the variability of bright and dull children has been summarized by Brown, A. W., "The Unevenness of the Abilities of Dull and Bright Children." *Teach. Coll. Contrib. to Educ.*, 1926 (No. 220).

revealed in the study of such special developmental schedules as motor development and speech development. In a survey of special-class school children, as compared with normal children drawn from the same district, it was found that forty per cent of the retarded children had a history of delayed walking and talking, whereas only three per cent of the normal children were thus delayed. As the student knows, the normal child should begin to walk when it is approximately one year of age and to use phrases and sentences by the fifteenth or eighteenth months. The figures cited above, however, indicate that the special-class school children had not begun to walk or to talk before the age of two.[52]

Since it is not possible to cure feeblemindedness by surgical means or even by glandular therapy, most educators are inclined to say that the responsibility for the treatment of deficient children lies either in the hands of the eugenicist who might argue for the sterilization of the unfit or in the hands of the teacher who must do whatever he can to make feebleminded children as independent and as socially useful as possible. From the studies that have been made on the education of the feebleminded one thing is clear, viz., that the earlier the condition is diagnosed and the more quickly educative influences are brought to bear upon the child, the more effective the training periods will be. In other words, the student of child psychology has definitely discarded the old prejudice to the effect that retardation at the ages of one, two and three years will take care of itself at some later point in the growth pattern.

A large part of the education of the mentally defective is carried out either in special classes in the regular school system or in institutions. It is the function, perhaps, of the special classes to train those children who are less seriously retarded and who can, therefore, take a more or less normal place in their own home environments. In one survey of 11,950 children in special classes it was found that the mean mental age of the whole group was seven years and seven months and the mean I.Q. was 63. The mental ages ranged, however, all the way from two years to fifteen years and seven months.[53]

One student of this phase of education has remarked that children who are mentally deficient must be limited pretty largely to the simpler levels of motor or perceptual development. This means that special classes must utilize, so far as possible, the natural activi-

---

[52] For a table giving average ages for a number of motor functions for normal and feebleminded children, see Wallin, J. E. W., *Clinical and Abnormal Psychology*. Boston: Houghton Mifflin Co., 1927, *passim*.

[53] Witty, P. A., and Beaman, F. N., "Practices in Special Classes." *Educ. Trends*, 1932, I, 4-15.

ties of the children. To be sure, there must be a considerable amount of individualized instruction, for the wide range of mental ages in children found in special classes forbids very much standardized procedure.[54] As a rule, deficient children are expected to acquire a reasonable amount of skill in such practical activities as cooking, sewing, manual training, and in some of the simpler phases of industrial occupation and nature study.

The education furnished by institutions is even more practical than is the case with special-class children. Wherever possible, an attempt is made to enable seriously handicapped children to become as self-contained as possible. Those having higher I.Q.'s can be taught to do a good many things for themselves and for other children as well. Much use is made of housework, gardening, and all types of farm work. Where a reasonable measure of independence is attained, the deficient person may be paroled from the institution; but at the present time not very many such persons have actually been able to take their part even in the simpler phases of community life. This makes, of course, a rather discouraging picture, but there is no reason to suppose that further studies will not increase the effectiveness of methods of training in this field.

3. *Special Deficiencies:* Special deficiencies may range all the way from serious and persistent mistakes in spelling or reading to actual physical defects created by the loss of some member of the body, lowered vitality, blindness, and deafness. As an illustration of special disabilities in reading we may take congenital word blindness. A child suffering in this respect will not be able to learn to read by the sight method. It can be shown that the eyes themselves have not been damaged, for such a subject will see objects sufficiently well to move from one place to another. He will not, however, be able to tell what the objects are. Obviously, deficiencies of this type must receive special treatment. It has been shown that special muscle training may be helpful in these cases.[55] It is not altogether clear as yet, however, whether special defects of this type are always truly sensory, rather than dependent upon the development of faulty habits. In the case of spelling, for example, it is quite clear that even though the I.Q. may be fairly high, deficiency must sometimes be attributed to laziness and to distaste for drill periods, rather than to any sensory defect.[56]

[54] Cf. Descoeudres, A., *The Education of Mentally Defective Children* (Trans. by E. P. Row). Boston: D. C. Heath and Co., 1919, *passim*.
[55] Orton, S. T., "The 'Sight Reading' Method of Teaching Reading as a Source of Reading Ability." *J. Educ. Psychol.,* 1929, XX, 135-143.
[56] Cf. Hollingworth, L. S., "The Psychology of Special Disability in Spelling." *Teach. Coll. Contrib. Educ.,* 1918 (No. 88).

Because of the large number of children who are known to suffer from defective vision and because of an astonishing number of accidents to the eyes per year (*ca* 200,000 a year), the special training of the visually defective has received marked attention. The student already knows, of course, that the blind can be taught to read through the use of the sense of touch. The Braille system, using an alphabet of various combinations of six raised dots, lends itself readily to this purpose.[57] The brilliant accomplishments of Helen Keller are evidence enough of the fact that blindness in and of itself is not an impossible handicap.

Serious problems of special education are created by two other types of persons, viz., the emotionally and socially maladjusted, on the one hand, and the improperly trained adult, on the other. Since a later chapter will be devoted entirely to the problems of maladjustment, we may lay them aside for the moment.[58] Adult training has become a special feature of contemporary education, partly because so few people have passed beyond the grade level in their training, partly because of the rapid advance in the various arts and sciences, and partly because of the great social value of keeping adults intellectually and culturally alive. In order to meet this group of problems, correspondence courses, extension work of various types, forums, special lecture series, and night schools have developed at an enormous rate. The most important feature of education at this level is the discovery that adults are just as fully able to learn as they were at earlier age levels. To be sure, the methods of instruction that are used with adults must differ to some extent from those used with children, but, on the whole, adults not only profit from their study but they gain a new level of appreciation and satisfaction in the use of their psychological functions.[59]

VI. The Nature of Individual Differences

1. *Introduction:* A sufficient number of samples of the way in which human beings may differ from one another have now been presented. The existence of these differences raises, of course, a variety of further questions such as the maximal range of the

[57] Cutsforth, T. D., *The Blind in School and Society*. New York: D. Appleton-Century Co., 1933.
[58] Cf. Scheidemann, N. V., *The Psychology of Exceptional Children*. Boston: Houghton Mifflin Co., 1931.
[59] Cf. Fisher, D. C., *Why Stop Learning?* New York: Harcourt, Brace and Co., 1927; Hart, J. K., *Adult Education*. New York: T. Y. Crowell Co., 1927; and Prosser, C. A., and Bass, M. R., *Adult Education: The Evening School*. New York: D. Appleton-Century Co., 1930.

differences, their relation to one another, their origin, and their sensitivity to special practice.

2. *Range:* We may consider, first, the problem of range. All of the differences that have been described above, together with the immense amount of research that would have to be covered in any complete survey of this field of psychology and education, show that all variations of human beings take the form of the normal probability curve. As the student knows, this is a type of distribution which is characteristic of biological as well as psychological data.[60]

It still remains to be seen, however, why such a characteristic distribution prevails. For one thing, it is known that an attempted measure of any event or object is subject to the conditions that have to be controlled. If, with respect to any given measure, absolute and perfect control could be gained over every condition, all of the measures ought to fall upon a single point. This would be the case if measures were made with units that were too large to discriminate variations caused by uncontrolled conditions. If, for example, a table approximately 36 centimeters long were to be measured in terms of centimeters, the chances are that every measure would be 36 centimeters. No ordinary change in the conditions surrounding such a series of measurements would be greater than the unit used. If the same table were to be measured, however, in terms of one hundredths of a millimeter, possible variations of the conditions of measurement would be greater than the unit of measurement. The results, therefore, would take the form of a normal probability curve.

Since all biological and psychological measures take the form of a probability curve, it would seem to follow that they do so either because the units of measurement are too great or because the conditions under which any given measurement is made cannot be controlled. These considerations hold true either with respect to single measurements of single psychological functions in a single individual or with respect to the measurement of a single psychological trait in a great many individuals. These facts do not explain, however, why the individuals themselves fall into a normal frequency curve. We may entertain the suggestion, however, that this is the case because any single psychological trait is, as a matter of fact, a product of a great many variable factors.

A. AMOUNT OF SPREAD: Considerable attention has been paid to the spread of individual variation around the mean. As a rule, the spread is fairly large. This fact raises the question as to how varia-

[60] Cf. Paterson, D. G., *et al., The Measurement of Man.* Minneapolis: **Univ.** of Minn. Press, 1930, *passim.*

tions shall be interpreted. Wechsler, for example, has argued that the total range of human capacity cannot be greater than two to one.[61] That is, the best individual in any trait cannot be any more than twice as good as the worst. Hull, however, in a summary of thirty-four psychological tests, finds that at the one extreme the best individual gained a score which was 2.2 times that of the worst, whereas at the other extreme the best person gained a score nineteen times as high as the worst. The ratio of 2.2 to 1 appeared in a cancellation test, whereas the ratio of 19 to 1 was gained from an information test. The average ratio between the best and the poorest in the twenty tests for which measures were available was 5.2. This data, taken in conjunction with other data, led Hull to conclude that among presumably normal subjects the most gifted will be from three to four times as capable as the least gifted.[62]

It is clear, of course, that the range or spread of individual differences must be of considerable interest to education. If the range is no greater than that named by Wechsler, it would seem to follow that the human race is more nearly cut from a common pattern than most persons have been disposed to believe. On the contrary, if there are some traits in which the range may stand as high as the ratio, 19 to 1, a very serious problem is created.

B. THE PROBLEM OF TYPES: We shall refer to this problem in another place. In the meantime, another characteristic of the total range of difference is worthy of note. The variations which are described by probability curves are essentially continuous. This fact does not appear, of course, when the number of subjects is fairly limited, but any large scale study of human variability puts at least one case at every point on the curve. This fact would indicate that the problem of psychological types is, from at least one point of view, a fictitious problem.[63]

It is true, of course, that persons may vary from one another in the sense that some have a preference for a group of psychological traits while others may be lacking in a preference for this group. In this sense, one might speak of a psychological type. With respect to any single trait, however, types do not appear. A few persons are found who have the trait in large measure, a large number who have the same trait to a moderate degree, and a small number who have it

---

[61] For some of the principles of statistics see Wechsler, D., "The Range of Human Capacity." *Sci. Mo.,* 1930, XXXI, 35-39.
[62] Hull, C. L., *Aptitude Testing.* Yonkers: World Book Co., 1928, p. 73.
[63] This is a problem that could easily be made the source of special study. A convenient means of access to the literature lies in the annual index to the *Psychological Abstracts.*

INDIVIDUAL DIFFERENCES 589

to a minor degree. In other words, data secured from a very large number of persons on a single trait are not bi-modal or multi-modal in character. With respect to any single trait, then, it would not be possible to define classes of individuals in any other than an arbitrary or statistical sense.

3. *Qualitative and Quantitative Differences:* As a rule it is argued that all differences between individuals are distinctively quantitative rather than qualitative in character. This is to say that all individuals have all traits to some measurable extent and that complex traits, therefore, represent various mixtures or quantities of particular traits. In any case, it is commonly assumed that the differences between persons are never qualitative. By qualitative differences, of course, is meant the presence or absence of some distinctive set of psychological functions. Helen Keller, for example, cannot make use of visual materials in the solution of any of her problems. She lacks, therefore, a certain amount of qualitative variety in her experience. In this respect, then, Miss Keller is classified among abnormal types. The argument in favor of quantitative rather than qualitative differences among individuals presupposes what we ordinarily describe as the normal or the typical individual.[64]

A. QUALITATIVE DIFFERENCES: It is still fruitful, however, to raise the question of the possible existence of qualitative differences. As an example, we may take an argument which has been used in another connection. A typical learning curve shows at first a period of rapid progress followed later on by a period of slow progress. It is sometimes said that the first repetition of an act is by all odds the most advantageous repetition, in the sense that much more may be learned during that period than at another. It seems proper to ask, however, whether or not a small quantitative addition to a skill may not have as a necessary consequence a significant alteration in the usefulness of the skill. Since greater effectiveness may stand out of all proportion to a slight increase in efficiency it would seem possible to say that the skill has become more valuable in a qualitative rather than in a quantitative sense.

This is, as we have seen, one of the arguments of the Gestalt point of view. A slight quantitative change in a total configuration may make all of the difference in the world between an appropriate reaction and an inappropriate reaction. Measures of quantitative difference would say nothing at all about the qualitative value of slight changes in excellence.[65]

[64] Cf. Spearman, C., *op. cit., passim.*
[65] The best illustrations of this possibility are to be found in problem-solving. Review the discussion of these matters in Chapter Seven.

Another way to approach this problem lies in a study of the changes that may be wrought in the I.Q. by favorable environmental conditions. As we have seen, these changes may not be very large, say five or ten points. From a quantitative aspect the difference between an I.Q. of 110 and one of 115 is not very great. We may still ask, however, about both quantitative and qualitative changes in accomplishment or performance that might be occasioned by so small a difference in points on the scale. It has sometimes been said that the difference between a good piano player and a Paderewski cannot be more than five or ten per cent of the total amount of skill involved. So small a difference with respect to quantity, however, makes a prodigious difference in quality of performance. In the solution of a problem, it might turn out that the presence or absence of a very few items of information might make the difference between a new discovery and a complete failure.

Let us grant, then, that any description of individual differences in terms of quantity alone may miss an important educational fact. From the point of view of statistics, individual differences must be stated in terms of amounts; but from the point of view of achievement or of service rendered, a slight difference in amount may mean a major difference in function. As a rough analogy we may take the difference between two chemical elements, say neon and carbon. Quantitatively, the difference between these elements is not very great. The one has a few more electrons and protons than does the other. A statistical study of a very large number of atoms of either element might show a probability curve which would describe the relative frequency of appearance of certain isotopes. These quantitative differences do not begin to describe, however, the tremendous differences in mode of function or mode of operation of the elements. Neon is an inert element; it does not combine readily with other elements. Carbon, on the contrary, is a tremendously active element. The number of substances for which it furnishes a foundation is numbered in the hundreds of thousands. Moreover, these substances have a vast array of qualitative variety in function. It looks as though some of them might contribute to that major difference in chemical structure described by the words organic and inorganic.

We may, then, admit the fact that quantitative differences will submit to statistical treatment. Education and the other branches of applied psychology, however, must concern themselves with the types of function made possible by slight difference in the quantity of a psychological function. If ten points difference in I.Q. will enable a pupil to solve a problem which could not be solved by a pupil having a lower I.Q., and if this difference can be brought under control through an appropriate environment, every attempt should be made to occasion the difference. That is, every attempt should be made if a philosophy of education finds it desirable that more pupils should solve slightly more difficult problems.[66]

4. *Effects of Practice on Individual Differences:* It goes almost without saying that individuals will differ from one another in the rate at which they can acquire skill in different psychological functions. This is true not only with respect to actual rate of progress, but with respect to the initial starting point. It is thought to be true also with respect to the maximal amount of skill that may be reached. That is, a learner might make progress at a very slow rate and yet eventually attain a level of proficiency already attained by a faster learner. We may assume, however, that there are differences in the limits to which any given skill may be brought.

However this may be, any study of the nature of individual differences requires that we know whether the differences that may separate subjects at the beginning of a practice period will be present to the same extent or to a less or a greater extent at the end of a practice period. That is, does practice have the effect of increasing the differences between men, decreasing them, or improving all subjects in such a proportionate way that the magnitude of difference after skill has been gained is comparable with the magnitude that had been attained before practice began?[67]

It is obvious that a question of this type is exceedingly difficult to answer. In the first place, it is not possible accurately to define and standardize the starting point for any two subjects, since every skill has behind it variable amounts of practice in functions that may be more or less related to the test skill. Neither absolute zero points nor relative zero points can be established. In the second place, it is not easy to define the phrase "equal amounts of practice." It can be said, of course, that a series of fifteen nonsense syllables remains a stable series with respect to all of the subjects tested; but constancy of problem as measured in this way has no relation to the various capacities of individuals. Fifteen dollars is fifteen dollars irrespective of poor man or rich man, but a tax of fifteen dollars with respect to persons differing in wealth could, under no circumstances, be called an equal tax.[68]

[66] For a consideration of these matters see Bentley, M., *The Field of Psychology.* New York: D. Appleton-Century Co., 1924, Chapter XVII.
[67] Cf. Thorndike, E. L., *Educational Psychology.* New York: Columbia Univ. Press, 1913, Vol. III, pp. 304-305.
[68] Consult Whitely, M. T., "An Empirical Study of Certain Tests for Individual Differences." *Arch. of Psychol.,* 1911 (No. 19).

The third difficulty arises out of the fact that certain types of psychological function apparently come to full maturation rather early in life. It has been shown, for example, that the range of visual apprehension for groups of letters, dots, drawings, and the like, when such material is exposed for brief periods of time, is not subject to any great amount of improvement through practice.[69]

In contrast with these studies, Dallenbach, using the same procedure on third-grade school children, found a marked practice effect. Dallenbach further concluded that practice had brought about permanent alteration and modification of the mental traits.[70] It is one thing, however, to demonstrate an improvement in a basic ability and quite another to show that improvement takes place with the aid of new techniques and methods. Oberly, for example, concluded from his studies on these same traits that an increase in the so-called span of attention was due to an improvement in methods of grouping the digits rather than to an improvement of the attention span itself.[71] In any case it is clear that the effect of practice upon individual differences would vary with the level at which the subjects of an experiment start their practice.

A further difficulty in this field is created by attempts to increase a skill through practice in advance of proper maturation of the organs involved. This circumstance has already been mentioned in various places. Gates, for example, studied the rate of improvement in tapping efficiency on a block with a pencil. He used 82 children standing between the ages of four and six. All of the subjects were given three short practice periods in tapping each day for a period of eighteen days. At the beginning of the experiment the subjects were also tested on eight different motor functions which were thought to depend upon speed of decision and upon motor control. At the end of eighteen days of practice in tapping, the subjects were paired in such a manner as to yield two groups which were practically equivalent to one another with respect to (i) speed of tapping, (ii) motor ability on the eight tests, (iii) sex, (iv) chronological age, (v) Stanford-Binet Mental Age, (vi) intelligence quotient, and (vii) average grade in school. One group discontinued training, whereas the other group continued practice three times a day for

[69] Whipple, G. M., "The Effect of Practice upon Range of Visual Attention and Apprehension." *J. Educ. Psychol.*, 1910, I, 249-262; Foster, W. S., "The Effect of Practice upon Visualizing and upon Reproduction of Visual Impressions." *J. Educ. Psychol.*, 1911, II, 11-21.
[70] Dallenbach, K. M., "The Effect of Practice upon Visual Apprehension." *J. Educ. Psychol.*, 1914, V, 321-334, 387-404.
[71] Oberly, S. H., "The Range of Visual Attention and Apprehension." *Amer. J. Psychol.*, 1924, XXXV, 332-352.

INDIVIDUAL DIFFERENCES 593

seventy-six days over a period of six months. During a final period of seventeen days, both groups were given practice. The results showed clearly enough that there was considerable improvement in tapping ability during the initial eighteen days. The practice group continued to improve steadily but slowly during the next six months. During the final period of seventeen days, however, the control group improved so rapidly that they quickly reached the level attained by the practice group. At the end of another six months both groups were practically alike in rate of tapping.[72] These results may be explained, partly, in terms of maturation and, partly, in terms of the development of incidental methods and techniques which favored increase in performance. These and other factors already discussed in connection with our study of learning make our information on the effect of training on individual differences fairly conclusive.

One of the first attempts to get into this problem through the schoolroom made use of the operation of adding. The practice group was given training two times daily for fifteen days, making thirty training periods altogether. When this experimental group was compared with the control group it was found that practice had slightly increased the individual differences. Those persons who were better at the beginning of the training period displayed a greater amount of improvement than the others.[73] The opposite conclusion, however, was drawn by Gates in a study of the same problem.[74] She concluded that practice decreases rather than increases individual differences. Hartmann's results favor those of Thorndike rather than Gates. Hartmann asked fifty subjects to perform the following four tasks, viz., (i) repeat the alphabet as rapidly as possible in the forward direction, (ii) repeat the alphabet as rapidly as possible in the forward direction but insert the letter "m" between each pair of letters, (iii) repeat the alphabet as rapidly as possible backward and (iv) repeat the alphabet as rapidly as possible backward inserting an "m" between each pair of letters. Twenty trials were made on each of the four problems, records being taken twice daily. Hartmann concluded from his results that even in such a restricted task as reversed alphabetization, most subjects adhere to the level of achievement that is struck at the start.[75] Still another type of

[72] Gates, A. I., "The Nature and Limit of Improvement Due to Training." *Twenty-Seventh Yearbook, Nat. Soc. for the Study of Education,* 1928, Part I, pp. 441-460.
[73] Donovan, M. E., and Thorndike, E. L., "Improvement in a Practice Experiment under School Conditions." *Amer. J. Psychol.,* 1913, XXIV, 426-428.
[74] Gates, G., "Individual Differences as Effected by Practice." *Arch. of Psychol.,* 1922 (No. 58).
[75] Hartmann, G. W., "Initial Performance as a Basis for Predicting Ultimate Achievement." *School and Soc.,* 1929, XXIX, 495-496.

conclusion is drawn by a study from Ehinger. This study concerned the effect of manual work upon performance in four tests of manual ability. Twenty-five students in a pre-apprentice class were tested during the first week of apprenticeship and then again after a period of five months. Eighty-eight workers varying in age from fourteen to thirty years of age were tested prior to employment and then again after they had been at work anywhere from three months to a year. Two control groups, one for each of the experimental groups just named, were also used. Ehinger concluded that there was relatively more improvement in the case of those testing low in the first performance than in the case of those testing high.[76]

The experimental evidence, then, seems to be conflicting. This is an important conclusion when we recall that the doctrine of hereditary differences between individuals would require the maintenance of individual differences in spite of practice. It is barely possible, of course, that individual differences might tend to disappear under practice with respect to simple functions and greatly to be increased with complex functions. As a matter of fact, Peterson has argued for this possibility in the conclusion to his summary of studies on the problem. He writes:

"Subjects of normal heterogeneity become much more alike with practice on the simpler processes or activities but much more different on the more complex activities." [77]

After a general review of 31 experiments in this field it was concluded by Monroe, et al., that

"if each investigation is considered as a whole, in four of them the initially best gained most; in sixteen the initially poorest tended to catch up during practice; and in eleven the effects of the training on initial differences were slight or uncertain. If each function is considered separately and counted as many times as training was given to it, by different investigators or by the same investigator with different groups, the result is: In eight cases practice increased the initial differences; in thirty-nine cases practice decreased the initial differences; and in thirty-six cases the effects of the training on initial differences were slight or uncertain." [78]

[76] Ehinger, G., "Recherches sur la developpement de l'habileté manuelle par la Pratique d'un Metier manuel." *Arch. de Psychol.*, 1927, LXXX, 299-317.
[77] Peterson, J., and Barlow, M. C., "The Effects of Practice on Individual Differences." *Twenty-Seventh Yearbook of the Nat. Soc. for the Stud. of Educ.*, 1928, Part II, p. 212. See also Chapter XIV.
[78] Monroe, W. S., DeVoss, J. C., and Reagan, G. W., *Educational Psychology*. New York: Doubleday, Doran and Co., 1930, p. 372.

There is, of course, one phase of the study of the effect of practice on individual differences that has not yet been examined with sufficient care. The performance of a subject upon any kind of a test is as much, if not more, a function of motivation as it is of intrinsic ability. It is frequently remarked, therefore, both of intelligence tests and of measures of individual differences, that not sufficient allowance has been made for fluctuations in incentive, motive, or attitude.[79] Experimenters usually hope that a set of instructions which have been carefully worded will insure equal dispositions in all individuals and in the same individual from day to day, but there is no hope that is more subject to exception than this one. Here again, then, we must appeal to further experiment. It certainly is not possible to use occasional demonstrations of the ineffectiveness of practice in changing individual differences as a proof of the inflexibility of original nature, on the one hand, or of the impotency of the environment, on the other.

VII. THE ORIGIN OF INDIVIDUAL DIFFERENCES

1. *Introduction:* One phase of the origin of individual differences has already been considered in Chapters Nine and Ten. Since scores on intelligence tests usually take the form of a normal probability curve, it is obvious that individuals must differ widely from one another in that trait or group of traits which is measured by the so-called intelligence test. These differences have been attributed both to heredity and to training. The same thing is true with respect to the more general problem of individual differences as it has been discussed in this chapter.

It becomes important, then, to know just how much of any given trait is attributable to the inevitable processes of heredity and how much is attributable to the controllable processes of education. The student will already see, however, that any adequate discussion of this question would mean a repetition of almost all that has been said in an earlier chapter regarding the question of original nature, but we may give our present problem a more specific setting in the following way. With respect to the origin of individual differences, Gates has written as follows:

"Any test of acquired ability can and does reveal differences in native constitutional capacity among those persons of the same age whose experiences have been equally potent in so far as they affect the ability to

[79] Cf. Hollingworth, H. L., "Correlation of Abilities as Affected by Practice." *J. Educ. Psychol.*, 1913, IV, 412.

do the exercises in that test. . . . When all educative influences upon a given ability are absolutely the same for a number of persons of a given age, a test of these persons will reveal wide differences in *ability*. If educative influences for a group of children of a given age are the same, the wide variations in ability must be explained. They cannot be explained as due to differences in education, experience, opportunity or environment because, by definition, all educative factors are equal. The differences in ability must then be explained as due to some other factors—as due to mysteries, spirits, demons or something else. The second fact is that science has found it practically useful to assume that these differences in ability which appear when environmental influences are identical, are not due to occult powers but to native, constitutional factors or *capacities*." [80]

2. *Environmental Constancy:* It is clear that this argument should command attention only after it has been shown that any two individuals have had exactly the same environment. It seems fairly safe to say that, up to the present time, no such situation has ever been approximated. One may speak loosely and argue that situations which might promote the maturation of a child on this earth must have a considerable degree of identity in comparison with the situations which might bring a hypothetical Martian child to maturity. But with respect to specific environments in our own social setting, the assumption made by Gates can have no identifiable meaning. It is true, of course, that large numbers of children are subjected to the "same" textbooks and to "similar" methods of teaching; but these items represent minimal fractions of the total number of agencies that may become effective in regulating and modifying behavior. This argument holds true even with respect to identical twins. Even though twins are brought up in the same family and are presumably handled in the same way, no precise determination has been given to the meaning of the phrase "an identical environment." [81] As a rule, one twin is fed before the other, bathed before the other, spanked before the other, and dressed before the other. One member of the pair must always be spoken to before the other. These simple observations form only a brief suggestion of environmental differences that may have untold significance for the development of identities or similarities in the behavior of such children.[82]

[80] Gates, A. I., *Psychology for Students of Education.* New York: The Macmillan Co., 1930, pp. 503-504.
[81] Cf. Weill, B. C., "The Behavior of Young Children of the Same Family." *Harvard Stud. Educ.,* 1928, X, 1-220; also "You Don't Treat Your Children Alike." *Babyhood,* 1930, XLVI, 27-28, 37-45.
[82] Cf. Curti, M. W., *Child Psychology.* New York: Longmans, Green and Co., 1931, pp. 496 f.

To argue in favor of hereditary differences because of an assumed identity in environmental factors is to suppose that education and psychology have made some progress in understanding the long-time effects of even the most elementary kind of stimulus-response situations. Even though child study has now become an experimental science, it seems still fair to say that practically nothing is known about the formative influence of any specific sector of the effective environment. With respect to isolated functions and with respect to short-time consequences, certain dependable facts are coming to light, as the facts and principles of learning abundantly show. However, it takes a tremendously fertile imagination to suppose that educative influences for a group of children of a given age are in any other respect identical.

It would seem to follow, then, that the explanation of individual differences in terms of hereditary factors ought to rest upon an intensive continuation of genetic researches rather than upon a logical deduction from alleged similarities in the environment. As we have seen in an earlier chapter, such studies are being made and at the present time they seem to suggest the fact that environmental agencies are a tremendously important factor in maturation. As we have said before, the germ plasm and the environment constitute two systems of objects and events. The one system, viz., the germ plasm, is, to be sure, a fairly inert system, but its inertness merely signalizes the fact that, under the impetus of proper environmental agencies, it will follow a certain course of development. In the case of a human being, this development will insure, among other organs and structures, a brain. This brain can be said to have certain characteristics or properties which serve to identify it with respect to other kinds of organs and structures. One of the properties of brain tissue is plasticity. It is this property which is capitalized by the educative process, irrespective of whether we are thinking of that part of the process which requires of society upwards of three billions of dollars for its continuance or of that part —and probably the more significant part—which comes free of charge.

Both the environment and the germinal constitution of an individual, then, may be thought of as promoting likeness and differences among individuals. The relative stability of the germinal system would seem to suggest that likenesses are more to be attributed to nature than to nurture, but this stability cannot exist in total independence of an environment which establishes obstacles in the way of its complete disintegration. Certain kinds of changes in the environment, then, might become effective in changing the functional activity of the germinal system. A system of education (including early nutrition, the hygiene of the mother, and the like) which tends to maintain the *status quo* so far as development is concerned, would increase the apparent effectiveness of hereditary factors simply by promoting the inertia of the germinal system. Any system of education which fails to promote the inertia of the germinal system would move toward the social hope voiced by radical behaviorism in its proposal to make almost any sort of a person out of any normal child.[83]

Perhaps the safest conclusion to draw from any study of the origin of individual differences should repeat the conclusion which is drawn from a study of the origin of intelligence. It is simply a plain fact that men do not now have the information that would make them either competent or instructive in the matter. It is fairly simple, of course, to use the words "heredity," "instinct" and "nature" in order to account for the unexamined traits of human beings; but a genuine solution for these vexing problems cannot be attained until the genetic method has been carried much further than is now the case.

VIII. Application of Individual Differences to Education

1. *Introduction:* The concern which education might express for the phenomena of individual differences would depend greatly upon the extent to which individual differences are inherited or acquired. We have meant to say in several places that the experimental evidence on this problem of nature and nurture demands a reinterpretation of the problem and some provisional leaning toward the side of nurture. It would seem to follow that the further one leans toward nurture, the more important the educational significance of individual differences becomes.[84]

This significance is of two sorts. On the one hand, there is a whole group of practical problems which center upon differences in rate of learning, upon differences in all of the features of the growth pattern described earlier in the book. We have already seen how age differences raise the most serious problem of all, viz., the question of creating a proper sequence in subject matter. Age differences

---

[83] Watson, J. B., *Behaviorism.* New York: W. W. Norton and Co., 1928, p. 82.
[84] Cf. Morrison, H. C., *The Basic Principles of Education.* Boston: Houghton Mifflin Co., 1934, *passim.*

suggest, also, problems regarding methods of teaching and modes of presenting material. Other types of differences throw light on the whole problem of class distinctions, a problem which has always been a major concern to social groups. It is argued by some persons, for example, that the welfare of the social group demands a certain degree of homogeneity among the members of the group. There must, for example, be a common language, a common method of reading and writing, a common body of ideals, and some adherence to a common set of historical conditions. In contrast to this point of view, there are those who would argue that the welfare of society demands heterogeneity among its members. The contemporary world is characterized by a vast number of different kinds of enterprises. It is a world of specialists. It is clear that these two points of view suggest the sources of a major difference in social philosophies of education.[85]

Of the practical problems created by the existence of individual differences we might consider briefly the following. There is, first, the problem of a perfectly graded curriculum. This is perhaps the most ancient mode of organizing educational processes with respect to age differences. Some measure of logic and a considerable amount of tradition have suggested that certain subjects fall naturally in the early grades whereas other subjects fall naturally in the later grades. It is sometimes implied that the subjects studied in high school are studied at that time because they demand a level of maturity which has not been reached in the earlier years. All of these problems are, of course, serious enough and yet they have a humorous element in them. The study of a foreign language, for example, is often postponed to the high school and even to the collegiate level, and yet a foreign language is a home language to some children, and it is easily and adequately acquired by them at an early age. Tradition has placed arithmetic first, followed by algebra, geometry, trigonometry, and the calculus. As we have seen, however, this sequence has no psychological support or pedagogical value.[86]

Of the problems raised by the fact of individual differences, none has excited more argument than that which has to do with the introduction of free electives, on the one hand, and early specialization, on the other. The doctrine that there should be a maximal number

---

[85] Cf. Burton, W. H., *Introduction to Education*. New York: D. Appleton-Century Co., 1934, Chapters I and V. The references added to these chapters will be useful in guiding one's further reading.
[86] Cf. Burton, W. H., *op. cit.*, Part IV. Here again the references at the ends of the chapters will be useful.

of free electives in a curriculum was based, in part, upon the belief that any kind of learning would be just as effective in intellectual growth as any other kind of learning. This belief, in its turn, was greatly strengthened by the alleged discovery, shortly after the turn of the century, that there is no such thing as general mental discipline. Since a mind could not be disciplined and since it might grow equally fast with any kind of nourishment, it seemed natural to suppose that young people should begin to specialize in their given fields as early as possible. Early specialization was favored moreover by the general temper of the day. It is now beginning to appear that both of these adventures in education have turned out badly.

IX. Summary

It is easy to point out the main bearings of this chapter upon the general problems of education. When taken in conjunction with the data considered in Chapter Thirteen, they seem to mean that a teacher who hopes to become really effective in his work must have, as a general foundation, some of the facts and principles which are common rather than differential to human nature; but even the most intimate acquaintance with these common facts, that is, with the facts that have to do with the typical or normal person, is not enough. The present chapter has made it clear that it is almost imperative that the teacher shall try to adjust himself to each single person.

No class of pupils could possibly represent a homogeneous group in any sense save in the fact that they are all human beings. Even though they have been selected for homogeneity, they will still represent a wide diversity in interest, attitude, previous training, intelligence, mood, disposition, and character. As we have seen in an earlier chapter, attempts to section pupils according to tests of ability in various respects have not been successful because the resultant groups still display a good many significant individual differences. The teacher may suppose that he can satisfy the obligations that are upon him by making use of the common dimensions of human beings and hold himself completely aloof from individual variations; but this is merely to earn a salary and not to teach.

When he first meets a new class, every teacher should begin almost immediately to look for and accurately to judge the nature of the individual differences he will have to consider. There may be such incidental items as visual strain which become indicative of defective vision, mouth breathing, and other physical symptoms which point to improper physical hygiene, gross differences in brightness or dullness, persistence or indifference, wide differences in social mood and attitude, and the like. Any one of these differences would seriously modify the contact that can be set up between pupil and teacher.

One of the most important places where knowledge of individual differences can serve a useful purpose is to be found in the search for a student's method of working. All too often it is thought that the teaching operations are complete whenever a grade has been given for a correct or an incorrect response. It may be more important to know, however, how a student has gone about it to gain an answer to a question than to ascertain whether the answer is right or wrong. With respect to any given person, it may be helpful to know whether an answer is a verbatim expression or something that has been learned by a genuine discovery.[87] Heretofore, it has been possible to use an appropriate measure of commonsense in the discovery of individual differences and in an appraisal of the best methods for handling such differences. Through the invention of the concept of intelligence, however, it is now possible, in an increasing measure, to supplement enlightened commonsense with a large number of tests and measures.

A good example of a possible mode of procedure is given by Terman's study of exceptional children. In this study, Terman and his staff were able to collect about sixty-five pages of test and measurement data and about thirty-five pages of questionnaire data for a large majority of 643 different subjects.[88] The subjects were given easy intelligence tests, viz., the Stanford-Binet and the National "B" test, a standard achievement test, a fifty-minute test of general information in science, literature, and the arts, a fifty-minute test of knowledge of and interest in plays, games, and amusements, a four-page test of interests, a two-month reading record, a sixteen-page home information blank, an eight-page school information blank, a scale for measuring various features of the environmental unit called the home, and a suitable array of character and personality tests. It is not possible, of course, for the average teacher to accumulate such a large amount of information about the various individuals with whom he may come in contact; but we cite this example at the experimental level only in order to emphasize the fact that it is not

---

[87] Cf. Monroe, W. S., "How Pupils Solve Problems in Arithmetic." *Univ. of Ill. Bull. Bur. of Educ. Res.,* 1928, XXVI (No. 23).

[88] Terman, L. M., and others, *Genetic Studies of Genius.* Palo Alto: Stanford Univ. Press, Vol. I, 1925.

only feasible but highly desirable to take the problems of individual differences seriously.

The phenomena of mass education which have been so characteristic of the American scene have tended mightily to make teachers satisfied with the common denominators of human nature. It has been falsely supposed that a more adequate knowledge at the experimental level of these common denominators would not only make the processes of mass education at the formal level more efficient but would obviate the necessity of taking pupils person by person. It has been supposed that precise formulae about original nature, the principles which make learning more efficient, and the application of intelligence tests, on the one hand, and achievement tests, on the other, would satisfy the spirit of education. It is becoming increasingly clear that textbooks on educational psychology do not contain any formulae which will save the teacher from painful effort and diversified modes of attack for different persons. Even though some measure of escape can be effected from the routinelike processes of mass education by sectioning classes in terms of tests of "native ability," it still remains true that the best results in education cannot be gained by treating persons in an impersonal way.

READINGS

A critical discussion of the nature and significance of individual differences is presented by Dodge, R., *Conditions and Consequences of Human Variability*. New Haven: Yale Univ. Press, 1931. A more general survey of the whole field can be found in Ellis, R. S., *The Psychology of Individual Differences*. New York: D. Appleton-Century Co., 1929. Useful comments on differences in I.Q. have been summarized by Boynton, P. L., *Intelligence: Its Manifestations and Measurement*. New York: D. Appleton-Century Co., 1933, Chapter IX and X.

There is a vast literature on superior and subnormal children. The quickest way into this literature is provided by the references appended to chapters written by L. M. Terman and B. S. Burks, R. Pintner, and L. S. Hollingworth in Murchison, C. (Ed.), *Handbook of Child Psychology*. Worcester, Mass.: Clark Univ. Press, 1933. See Chapter XIX, "The Gifted Child"; Chapter XX, "The Feebleminded Child"; and Chapter XXI, "The Child of Special Gifts or Special Deficiencies."

Special studies on the education of gifted children have been made by Goddard, H. H., *School Training of Gifted Children*. Yonkers: The World Book Co., 1928; Hollingworth, L. S., *Gifted Children: Their Nature and Nurture*. New York: The Macmillan Co., 1926; Adams, F., and Brown, W., *Teaching the Bright Pupil*. New York: Henry Holt and Co., 1930; and Osburn, W. J., and Rohan, B. J., *Enriching the Curriculum for Gifted Children*. New York: The Macmillan Co., 1931.

Similar studies on feebleminded children have been supplied by Anderson, M. L., *Education of Defectives in the Public Schools*. Yonkers: The World Book Co., 1921; Hollingworth, L. S., *The Psychology of Subnormal Children*. New York: The Macmillan Co., 1920; Pressey, S. L., and Pressey, L. C., *Mental Abnormality and Deficiency*. New York: The Macmillan Co., 1926; Wallin, J. E. W., *The Education of Handicapped Children*. Boston: Houghton Mifflin Co., 1927; Whipple, H. D., *Making Citizens of the Mentally Limited*. Bloomington: Pub. School Publ. Co., 1927.

See also, Hollingworth, L. S., *Special Talents and Defects: Their Significance for Education*. New York: The Macmillan Co., 1923; Scheidemann, N. V., *The Psychology of Exceptional Children*. Boston: Houghton Mifflin Co., 1931.

CHAPTER SEVENTEEN

THE SOCIALIZED PERSON

I. The Concept of the "Self"

1. *Introduction:* There is, nowadays, a common saying to the effect that everything that exists must exist in some quantity. It would follow that everything that exists can be measured, if only the means for doing so could be discovered. This is one reason why the concept of intelligence has played so large a part in current thinking about the nature and methods of education, for if education is an art and if one of the results of education is increased intelligence, and if intelligence can be measured, then we are in a position to apply the quantitative methods of science to an art. In other words, we can satisfy a common belief that a thing that can be measured is somehow more real than those things that are merely estimated or valued.

There is another reason, however, why the concept of intelligence plays an important part in modern education. As we commonly define it, the I.Q. is the nearest mathematical approach which education has been able to make to a very ancient prejudice about ourselves, viz., the prejudice that we have talents or powers which the lower animals do not have. Moreover, since these talents or powers lie at the basis of all of those products which fall under the terms "culture" or "civilization," we feel that we have made a very great achievement when our most venerable belief about the nature of human nature can be translated into the modern setting and given a quantitative value.

There is, however, another concept in common use in education which is even more important than the concept of intelligence. It is not possible as yet to be quite so exact in our definitions of this concept, but, in general, we know whereof we speak when we say that every human being is a person or a character. Some of the older psychologies recognized this fact by saying that the terms "personality" and "character" must refer to an inner core of being which could be called the "ego" or the "self." In other words, these psychologies made it appear that consciousness of self was just as definite a part of the problems of psychology as are any of the principal psychological operations which have been studied in the several chapters of Part II. Even yet there are people who would say that such phrases as "character traits" or "personality traits" name special types of psychological operations which are co-equal with action, perception, attention and interest, emotionalized actions, and problem-solving.

2. *The Origin of Socialized Action:* It is now the opinion of most people that the terms personality, self, and character are terms which arise out of the uses which are made of the psychological functions in environmental situations that are primarily social in meaning.[1] In other words, when we think of each human being as a unit in a social group, and when we take account of the social significance of our various psychological operations, we must arrive at such concepts as are expressed by the words mentioned above.

It is hardly necessary to argue that a new-born infant is neither social nor unsocial in its make-up. This means that neither its modes of action nor the objects and events which in any way can become sources of action bear social implications.[2] As it grows older, however, the infant quickly becomes socialized, on the one hand, and personalized, on the other, in the sense that it becomes dependent on other persons for sources of action and that other persons become dependent upon it for sources of action. As a matter of fact, this double process of socialization has been held in such high regard by some persons that they have taken it for granted that the very problems of experimental psychology themselves must be defined in social terms.

A. SOCIAL AND ASOCIAL ACTION: There are several ways in which this fact may be emphasized. Let us consider, for example, the skills that might be required of a person to throw a brick through a window, reach through the opening, grasp a loaf of bread, and walk off with it. It is clear that all of these skills could be described in terms of some of their simpler properties. We might wish to know, for example, how accurately the brick was thrown, what degrees of coördination were required for the act of reaching and grasping the bread, and what the origin and course of development of walking movements were. When, however, this series of movements is placed in a social situation created by the fact that the bread has

[1] Cf. Hunter, W. S., "The Psychological Study of Behavior." *Psychol. Rev.*, 1932, XXXIX, 1-24; Weiss, A. P., *A Theoretical Basis of Human Behavior.* Columbus: R. G. Adams, 1925.
[2] Bühler, C., "The Social Behavior of Children," in Murchison, C. (Ed.), *Handbook of Child Psychology.* Worcester, Mass.: Clark Univ. Press, 1934, Chapter IX.

been stolen, they must be treated in an entirely different way.[3] They point to or imply the rights of other persons. They may be described as the actions of a delinquent boy or as the last desperate act of an exceedingly hungry man. The stimulus to action may not have come at all from an unsocial or impersonal source but from a desire to "get even" with the baker, or from the desire to feed the members of one's family.

It is clear, of course, that the movements we have just mentioned might take place in another setting and have no social value at all, either on the side of the stimulus-situation or on the side of the action system. If, for example, this same person were walking through an uncultivated region and upon seeing fruit hanging from a tree, threw a stone at the tree in order to drop some of the fruit, there would be a minimal amount of social significance in the act even though the movement systems were identical with those used in breaking a store window. In the case of language responses, both the origin of language and the entire period of language development are exhaustively related to social matters. Spoken words would serve no purpose at all if there was no one else to hear them. The very racial origins of speech imply that primitive men had come to that place in their development where the social consequences of their actions and the social meanings attached to stimulus-patterns were more important or more numerous than non-socialized actions and stimuli.[4]

B. THE CULTURAL ENVIRONMENT: Further evidence of the almost complete extent to which human behavior is socialized and personalized is found in the fact that the entire environment of a growing child is made up of objects and events which possess either a direct social meaning or which are products of previous communal living. Much of the education of the lower animals and even of the education of children in a very primitive society is related to that type of environment which we can call physical or natural as opposed to social. To be sure, the children of primitive peoples have to learn how to adjust themselves to one another and to their parents, but the major emphasis is placed upon skills, attitudes, and dispositions which are related to things rather than to persons.[5]

Since these prehistoric times, however, the number of inventions,

---

[3] Cf. Weiss, A. P., "A Set of Postulates for Social Psychology." *J. Abnorm. and Soc. Psychol.*, 1926, XXI, 203-211.
[4] Cf. De Laguna, G., *Speech: Its Function and Development.* New Haven: Yale Univ. Press, 1927, *passim.*
[5] Cf. Monroe, P., *A Textbook in the History of Education.* New York: The Macmillan Co., 1918, Chapter I and *passim.*

both those that are technical and those that are cultural, have increased by leaps and bounds. This means that the environment of modern man is fairly well saturated with such objects. As for technical inventions, we may think of all of the tools and instruments which are now a common part of our commerce with one another and with nature.[6] To be sure, we often take many of these technical inventions just as impersonally as we take natural objects, but in their origin they are intensely personal and social. Every one of them has meant someone's grief, someone's long-drawn-out period of trial-and-error learning, someone's struggle against perplexities, or someone's joy in the satisfaction of discovery. The very fact that we have to learn how to live with these objects even though we simply add them to the natural objects that are around us has made a very great difference in the character of our modern education as opposed to earlier forms of education. As a single instance we may take all of the vexing problems that have been created by technical schools, technical training, the development of the manual arts, and other specialized forms of education.

Among the cultural inventions which occupy a very large place in the environment of the young people of today we may mention languages, customs, fads, fashions, taboos, religions, laws, and ethical and moral concepts. All of these cultural inventions play so important a part in our attempts to live with one another that they have been offered, as we shall see, as one of the foundations upon which the principles of educational psychology should be based.[7] Let us think, for example, of only one such invention, viz., the ethical concept of honesty. It is generally assumed that it ought to be one of the primary functions of the educative process to develop honesty as a major personality trait. According to an older view, it would have been said that honesty must be some special faculty of the soul or of the self which could be expressed whenever the circumstances called for it.[8]

It now appears, however, that honesty is just what we have described it to be, viz., a product of social meaning or reference with respect to which children may acquire variable degrees of competency in action. Given a number of situations which can be responded to either in an honest or in a dishonest way, some children

---

[6] Cf. Mumford, L., *Technics and Civilization*. New York: Harcourt, Brace and Co., 1934, *passim*.
[7] Cf. Judd, C. H., *The Psychology of Social Institutions*. New York: The Macmillan Co., 1926, *passim*.
[8] Cf. Hartshorne, H., *Character in Human Relations*. New York: Charles Scribner's Sons, 1932, *passim*.

will choose the dishonest way rather frequently while other children would be more favorably inclined toward honest reactions in the majority of instances. It must be clear to the student that the use of the word "honesty" in this fashion does not refer at all to a property of action systems but to a meaning which this action has acquired in a social situation. Picking up a coin from a table can be described either in the impersonal terms of a science or in terms of its social significance.

C. THE SOCIAL MIND: It has been a difficult task for some people to get rid of the notion that the social uses of behavior are created simply by membership in the social group rather than by some special psychological urge or mode of operation. It has been said, for example, that the difference between the behavior of a single person and the behavior of a crowd or an audience must call for the existence of a supermind known as the social mind.[9] Still others have asserted that there must be groups of instincts which are essentially social in character. One of the instincts named most frequently in this connection is the gregarious instinct.[10] There are, in addition, however, a great many other instincts which serve the same purpose.[11]

It begins to look, however, as though little is really added to the facts either by resorting to a social mind or by resorting to special socializing instincts. As we have seen, the new-born infant is neither socialized nor non-socialized. It is simply a living entity equipped with potential sources of action of a psychological character which, within a few days after birth, will be placed in situations which contain other beings like itself. These other beings will become a part of the effective environment of the child, both as objects and as sources of action which will have an important bearing upon what the child may do. The child, likewise, will become an object in the environment of the others. He will become a person in the sense that he will be a sum of a large number of modes of action and attitude which, in their turn, will serve as sources of action to other people.

3. *Purpose of the Chapter:* The student will realize, of course, that this is a very sketchy picture of a tremendously complex set of facts; but it will serve, perhaps, to introduce him to the assertion

[9] Cf. McDougall, W., *The Group Mind* (2nd ed.). New York: G. P. Putnam, 1927.
[10] Cf. Trotter, W., *Instincts of the Herd in Peace and War*. London: Unwin, 1916. See also, Cason, H., "Gregariousness Considered as a Common Habit." *J. Abnorm. and Soc. Psychol.*, 1924, XIX, 96-105.
[11] McDougall, W., *Social Psychology*. Boston: J. W. Luce, 1916, *passim*.

THE SOCIALIZED PERSON 609

that the concepts of personality or character, on the one hand, and of social action, on the other, must be extremely important in any survey of the problems of educational psychology. Nothing would be gained if a teacher were to follow all of the suggestions about teaching methods which had been reviewed up to this point, were he at the same time wholly to forget personal and social considerations. As a matter of fact, it is sometimes asserted that most teachers have forgotten the personal and social side of the educative process for the critics of education have been saying with increasing vehemence that the graduates of our schools may be competent so far as skill and knowledge are concerned, but that they are wholly incompetent so far as their ability to comprehend the social values of living is concerned.[12]

There is a long tradition to the effect that one of the chief justifications for universal public education is to be found in the fact that education should make good citizens of immature persons. If, however, anyone is to become a good citizen, it is required of him that he shall know how to behave in those ways that will promote the welfare of the group. No good purpose is served by a person who has learned how to adjust himself to an automobile or to the tasks required of a surgeon if he has not learned how to adjust himself in appropriate ways to other people. We propose, then, in this chapter to find out something about the origin of those traits and dispositions which, from one point of view, are called social.

II. THE DEVELOPMENT OF SOCIAL BEHAVIOR

1. *Things and Persons:* The general setting for the development of social behavior is found in the gradual emergence during early childhood of the distinction between what we may call thing-techniques and person-techniques. As we have already discovered, the phrase "thing-techniques" refers to the fact that the objects and events around the child may be taken as simply impersonal or physical in nature. They may, for example, be pushed, pulled, or otherwise manipulated, but in no sense of the word invited, persuaded or cajoled. This means that person-techniques do involve invitation or persuasion.

To be sure, small children make a great many confusions between these two types of technique, for there are times when they will

[12] Cf. Burton, W. H., *Introduction to Education.* New York: D. Appleton-Century Co., 1934, Chapter III. The references in this chapter will be illuminating.

attempt to persuade objects and to compel persons.[13] It is hardly possible to say as yet just when the distinction is clearly drawn, but it is certainly clear that even at the end of the first year many children act as though the physical objects around them were agents in the same way that they feel themselves to be agents. They will, therefore, get angry at a chair which happens to be in the way and they will easily suppose that some of their playthings can be hurt or insulted or otherwise display some of the types of conduct and experience that are particularly human.[14]

This same sort of confusion is often described as a typical feature of primitive thinking. As a matter of fact, it can even be said that primitive religions may have had their origin in the mistaken application of person-techniques to things.[15] In any case, it is finally recognized by children that things can be handled by methods which differ greatly from the methods that must be used with respect to persons, and this is a fact which furnishes a general setting for the emergence of personality traits, on the one hand, and the recognition of social meanings, on the other.

2. *Early Social Behavior:* Students of child psychology have searched rather carefully for the first signs of social behavior in small infants.[16] Let us suppose, for example, that two infants of from six to ten months of age are placed facing each other on some suitable surface. It will be observed that each of the infants will seek active contact with the other, or attempt to touch the other, or exchange toys, or push and pull the other. The child which is the older or which is physically more mature and more skilful will usually take the lead in such a situation. He will display himself more freely as compared with the other child who will appear to be inhibited in action and in disposition.[17]

To be sure, small infants vary greatly from one another in these respects, and these variations may play a very important part in later stages of development.

For the present, however, we are interested primarily in the fact that the beginnings of socialized contact are about as simple and as

[13] Cf. Piaget, J., *The Child's Conception of Causality.* New York: Harcourt, Brace and Co., 1930, *passim.*
[14] Cf. Murphy, G., and Murphy, L. B., *Experimental Social Psychology.* New York: Harper and Bros., 1931, Chapter VI, *passim.*
[15] Cf. the article "Animism" in *The Encyclopedia of the Social Sciences.* (Ed. E. R. A. Seligman). New York: The Macmillan Co., 1930, Vol. II.
[16] For a summary of the literature see Bühler, C., *op. cit., passim,* or Murphy, G., and Murphy, L. B., *op. cit., passim.*
[17] Cf. Bühler, C., *The First Year of Life.* New York: The John Day Co., 1930, *passim.* Also, Goodenough, F. L., "Interrelationships in the Behavior of Young Children." *Child Develop.,* 1930, I, 29-47.

devoid of instinctive urges as has been described above. It seems to be fairly clear that children that are younger than five months of age do not react to one another in a social way unless it can be assumed that the smiling reaction which ordinarily appears at about the second month as a specific response to the human voice, can be called a social response.[18] It is certainly true that, during the first few months, the same sort of response will often be made to a human voice irrespective of whether the voice has a kind or an angry quality. From the fifth month on, most infants are able to react differentially to a kind voice and a kind expression, on the one hand, and to a scolding voice and to a threatening gesture, on the other. This means, of course, that differential modes of action, on the part of persons around the child, have begun to acquire a specific stimulus value for the child.[19]

Throughout the first year of its life the average infant is not able to maintain socialized relations with more than one other child at a time. If, for example, three small infants are placed facing one another on the floor, contact will normally be maintained between only two of the three.[20] During the middle of the second year, however, three-way contacts may be established. In a study of this particular type of relationship it was found that, with respect to groups containing three two-year-old children, eight per cent of the subjects made no contact, sixty-seven per cent established contact with one other child, and twenty-five per cent were able to keep up a contact with two other children at the same time. This level of socialization is maintained, apparently, until about the third year.[21] From this time forward, the size of the social group may increase steadily until groups such as are characteristic of older children will have made their appearance.

3. *Types of Social Behavior:* One of the most important features of this first stage of social development is to be found in the types of social behavior which occur in different children. It has been found useful to name three such types, viz., the socially blind, the socially dependent, and the socially independent.[22] The socially blind child, when placed in the presence of other children, acts as if

[18] Bühler, C., and Hetzer, H., "Das erste Verständnis von Ausdruck im ersten Lebensjahr." *Zsch. f. Psychol.*, 1928, XVI, 50-61.
[19] Washburn, R. W., "A Study of the Smiling and Laughing of Infants in the First Year of Life." *Genet. Psychol. Monog.*, 1929, VI (Nos. 5 and 6).
[20] Cf. Bühler, C., "The Social Behavior of Children," in Murchison, C. (Ed.). *Handbook of Child Psychology.* Worcester, Mass.: Clark Univ. Press, 1934, Chapter IX, pp. 376 ff.
[21] Cf. Murphy, G., and Murphy, L. B., *op. cit.*, pp. 258 ff.
[22] There is now a monumental survey, amply illustrated with reproductions of moving picture sequences, of these earlier stages of development. Cf. Gesell, A., *An Atlas of Infant Behavior* (2 vols.). New Haven: Yale Univ. Press, 1934.

no one else were present. There is nothing about his attitude or his play that would suggest any recognition of the presence of anything in his environment other than a number of objects. The socially dependent child is, on the contrary, highly sensitive to the presence of other children. His sensitivity may display itself either by increased inhibition or by increased stimulation. If he is inhibited he will watch the other child and obey him, but otherwise he will not engage freely in activity. If he is stimulated by the presence of another, he will use various means to display himself, he will be eager to show his playthings, he will try to arouse the other into action, and otherwise he will take the initiative in the social contacts that are established.

Both of these socially dependent attitudes include a good many signs of watching and even of taking careful note of what the other child is doing. The socially independent type of child may also be characterized in this same way. He seems to be fully aware of the presence of another and to be responsive to changes in his behavior. He does not, however, seem to be as inhibited or excited to action by the other. Even though he may coöperate freely in mutual play, there is something about the whole attitude which reveals his real aloofness.

Of these several types of social contact, those that are inhibitive, on the one hand, and exciting, on the other, appear to be the most important for it looks as though they give rise to differences in personal attitude which may become a permanent feature of one's character. As we have said, the child who is older, or stronger, or more skilful may easily dominate a younger, less skilful, child. There will be a tendency, then, for children to acquire those traits and attitudes which make out of one a leader and out of the other a follower.[23] The leader, as a rule, will initiate a great many more contacts than the follower will. He will take the initiative in games and, at a later stage of development, he will commonly be the source of many suggestions for action. Moreover, he will gradually acquire a considerable amount of ability in organizing the work and play of other persons. Where games require someone who will be the central figure, the leader will normally occupy this position. The followers will take those positions assigned to them by the leader or fit into the organization as best they can. If there is to be any imitation, the direction of imitated actions will flow from the leader to the followers rather than from the followers to the leader.[24]

[23] For a survey of some of the literature, see Griffith, C. R., *An Introduction to Applied Psychology.* New York: The Macmillan Co., 1934, Chapter X.
[24] Cf. Murphy, G., and Murphy, L. B., *op. cit.,* pp. 402-408, and *passim.*

4. *Sources of Socialized Behavior:* With these few facts about the earlier stages in social development before us, we should turn, perhaps, to a brief consideration of some of the agencies or factors which are said to give rise to them.

A. GREGARIOUSNESS: We have already spoken of a special gregarious instinct. The inference is that if a two-months-old infant responds to the sound of its mother's voice by smiling, it must do so because it is instinctively prepared to make social contacts of this type. Moreover, if two five- or six-months-old infants are placed together on the floor, they will seek to touch each other or otherwise establish contacts because they are moved by their gregarious impulse to do so.

It is hardly necessary to repeat what has been said in earlier chapters in order to throw doubt upon this mode of explanation. In the case of smiling, for example, it is known that a facial pattern or movement which can be called a smile will often appear shortly after birth.[25] It is one of the patterns of movement that must be counted as a phase of the generalized responses which new-born infants will make to almost any stimulus-situation. Since smiling comes to play so large a part in more adult forms of social contact, it is almost inevitable that a parent would use a variety of means to perpetuate rather than to destroy the smiling reaction even though its appearance is a part of initial mass reactions. If, for example, smiling can be illicited by feeding or by tickling the infant, the very presence of the mother or the very patterning of her own facial features can readily become conditioned to the original stimulus-patterns.[26] It is more reasonable, then, to say that the smiling reaction is a product of learning situations than it is to say that it must be a product of a special gregarious instinct.

The same conclusion may be drawn from the first socialized contacts of other types. A five- or six-months-old infant, for example, has already found moving objects more important than motionless objects. When, therefore, another infant is placed before it on the floor, the movements of this infant may serve as an adequate stimulus to reaching movements. These same considerations hold true with respect to all of the instincts that are alleged to be secondary sources of human behavior. As a single example, let us take helplessness. It may be said, of course, that a child will resort to social contacts because of its innate sense of dependence upon other per-

---

[25] Cf. Washburn, R. W., "A Study of the Smiling and Laughing of Infants in the First Year of Life." *Genet. Psychol. Monog.*, 1929, VI, 397-537.
[26] Cf. Watson, J. B., *Psychological Care of Infant and Child.* New York: W. W. Norton and Co., 1928, *passim.*

sons.[27] Clearly, it is much more difficult to discover such an innate sense than it is to describe the actual circumstances under which social contacts arise.

B. ENVIRONMENTAL FACTORS: We may draw the inference, then, that the origins of socialized behavior are to be found in the environmental circumstances which obtain during early infancy. As a matter of fact, these circumstances almost force socialized behavior on the infant. Even though we say that the infant may not be aware of some inner sense of dependency, it is nevertheless almost as dependent upon its mother or nurse after birth as it was before birth. From a good many points of view it is essentially a parasite on or at least a symbiotic member of the group. Directly after birth, the new-born infant is placed in a social group which will normally consist of at least two other persons. These persons and the very home in which they live will serve as sources of stimulus to action just as fast as a child's talents for responding to them mature. If there are no other children in the home, these additional incentives to socialized modes of response will be supplied as soon as the only child learns how to roam about.

In the very nature of things, therefore, the environment of the average new-born infant is filled with learning situations that are inevitably socialized in character. Moreover, every act of its own must serve as a source of socialized responses on the part of the persons around it. Let us conclude, then, that personality traits, on the one hand, and social meanings, on the other, are products of learning situations. The particular form that they take depends upon the character of these learning situations, which is to say that they depend upon the personal qualities of the parents or of the other persons with whom the child establishes contact.

As a rule, the teacher does not become an active agent in this respect until after the child is five or six years old. This means, as we shall try to show in a moment, that a great many of the personality or character traits of the average child will have become fairly well stabilized long before the teacher can exert any influence upon him. When, therefore, the child passes from the preschool age into the first grade, the teacher will stand in no sense of the word at a zero point of development. Some of the most vexing problems he will have to solve may arise out of the fact that he

[27] Any study of the care of the child exercised by parents and nurses will certainly suggest this fact. See Woolley, H. T., "Eating, Sleeping and Elimination," in Murchison, C. (Ed.), *Handbook of Child Psychology* (1st ed.). Worcester, Mass.: Clark Univ. Press, 1931, Chapter II.

knows nothing of the previous personal history of the children who come to him for the first time. They, likewise, know nothing about the teacher. They are in a new situation and surrounded by unfamiliar children. This is at one and the same time a total pattern of events and the source of a group of teaching problems that will recur over and over again as the child passes from one grade to another or from one school to another.[28]

III. NORMAL SOCIAL BEHAVIOR

1. *Norms and Values:* It is not possible to carry on either a discussion of the development of social behavior or to name any of the goals which a teaching process should have before it without making some decision as to what shall be called normal as opposed to abnormal or unsocial behavior. This is, of course, a very difficult question because there are so many factors involved. As the student knows, it is not possible to lay down any absolute standards as to what shall be called normal individual behavior.[29] When we say this, we are not unmindful of the fact that there are ethical, moral, and political systems of thought which do attempt to state definite norms. There is, for example, in Christian ethics a definite concept of the good and of the bad.[30] In all of these cases, however, the actual norms presuppose a given set of values. If any system of ethics decides upon norms of conduct, it does so because men have already decided to emphasize some social values rather than others.

In spite of these difficulties, we must try to state at least in a general way what some of the principal features of normal social behavior might consist of. For this purpose, we shall draw once more upon the major features of the growth pattern which have been used so frequently in the preceding chapters. As the student will recall, these features are made up (i) of a description of the total variety of habits, skills, and postures which a person may possess, (ii) of a statement of the total range and variety of the objects and situations which may in any way become effective in initiating and regulating behavior, (iii) of the habits and dispositions which a child may acquire for attending to or becoming interested in a

---

[28] Cf. Sherman, M., *Mental Hygiene and Education.* New York: Longmans, Green and Co., 1934, Chapter I and *passim.*
[29] Cf. Dorcus, R. M., and Shaffer, G. W., *Textbook of Abnormal Psychology.* Baltimore: The Williams and Wilkins Co., 1934, Chapter I.
[30] Cf. Flew, R. N., *The Idea of Perfection in Christian Theology.* London: Humphrey Milford, 1934, *passim.*

particular task, (iv) a description of the number, variety, and possible intensity or persistence of motives, desires, and purposes, (v) of the way in which the energy resources of the body may be expressed in emotionalized actions and of the way in which these emotionalized actions are balanced against stimulus-patterns, (vi) a description of the number and difficulty of problematic or perplexing situations that may be solved in terms of insight rather than in terms of non-adaptive habits and skills or in terms of fruitless emotionalized actions, and (vii) a description of the total organization or patterning of the stream of behavior and with special behavior traits or attitudes which are said to be indicative of the personality or character of a person.

2. *Reaction Patterns:* The best place to discover the social value of action-patterns lies, perhaps, in the field of industrial psychology or, at least, in that phase of industrial psychology which studies the causes of accidents on the highway.[31] The student will see at once that a person who does not have the skills that are necessary to operate an automobile safely on the highways puts himself at once under censure of the social group. As we have seen, skill in this respect may be failing either because speed of movement is too slow or because degrees of coördination and precision of movement are inadequate to the task involved. In our previous discussion of these matters, however, we have left out of account altogether their social import. We mean now to say that if a person is not equipped to handle an automobile with a reasonable degree of assurance his lack of equipment has social meanings reflected in the injury he may do to himself or to others and in the cost of caring for him or his dependents that must be performed by the public.

A great many other instances of this same type will occur to the reader. Perhaps the clearest cases are found in all of those skills, gestures, and postures which enter into almost any type of social intercourse. The difference between the refined person and the vulgar person may be largely a difference in the habits and skills that they possess for conversation with each other, for conducting themselves properly at a dinner table, or in a social group. All of the skills employed during social contacts of this type can be described simply as skills but we may also take the skills for granted and then inquire about their social meaning or value.[32]

In short, then, it may be said that normal social behavior, as far

[31] Cf. Viteles, M. S., *Industrial Psychology.* New York: W. W. Norton and Co., 1932, Section Three.
[32] Any book on good deportment would serve as an example.

as this particular feature of the whole stream of conduct is concerned, would require that a man possess all of those skills, habits, attitudes, and postures that would enable him to live safely, successfully, and courteously with other people. He may be working in a factory, driving a car along a highway, introducing a guest to his friends or depicting some character upon the stage. In all of these cases, good social behavior would require those measures of competence actually necessary to get things done in a fairly respectable manner.

3. *Information and Knowledge:* As we have said before, it is not possible to separate modes of action from the stimulus-patterns which initiate them and do so much to regulate their course. For certain practical purposes, however, we may suppose that one feature of conduct can actually be emphasized by making a list, so to speak, of all of the objects or events and patterns of objects or events that can actually become sources of adequate response. When we say that a man can react to a very large number of stimulus-situations in an adequate manner, we mean that he is well informed or that he has a wide range of knowledge. It ought to be possible, then, to draw some of the general outlines of competent social behavior so far as information or knowledge is concerned.

The amount of information which an educated person should possess depends very largely, of course, upon the character of the social group in which he lives. It might be argued, for example, that a workman could hardly be expected to talk adequately about the major philosophies of life, about great pieces of art, or about the more intimate details of political and social philosophy. In other words, it is sometimes assumed that persons belonging to the lower socio-economic levels need not be well informed. On the other hand, the persons who belong to the higher socio-economic levels must be well informed. They must be widely read, widely traveled, and widely acquainted. As some persons express it, they must be suave and urbane.[33]

We touch here, of course, upon questions of educational philosophy. In our own country, it has been urged that universal education should have, as one of its functions, the development of those special skills which will enable each person to earn a living and, as another function, the development of an enlightened electorate. The word "enlightened" simply means, of course, informed or, in our common language, "intelligent." Clearly, however, it is not pos-

---

[33] Cf. Burton, W. H., *Introduction to Education.* New York: D. Appleton-Century Co., 1934, Chapter V.

sible to draw any line upon the information that could reasonably be expected of any particular person. If one is compelled to state some of the minima, they might run as follows. Social contacts seem to attain a higher level whenever the persons involved have in common a reasonable amount of information about the history of their own country, a fairly precise knowledge of world history, some information about the men and the major results of research in the various sciences, a small measure of appreciation, at least, of the major philosophies, the ability to recognize and discuss informatively the major examples of art, including music, sculpture, prose, and poetry, and considerable familiarity with both historical and current trends in political, economic, and social movements.[34]

4. *Emotionalized Actions:* There is no feature of the whole growth pattern, perhaps, which is so full of social meaning as that feature named by emotions, moods, passions, and sentiments. To be sure, we are often moved in emotionalized ways in a strictly personal way and with respect to physical objects. The most of our emotionalized actions, however, arise in social situations or have distinct and important social implications. Let us think, for example, of the way in which the fears and anxieties of parents may operate in the development of similar fears and anxieties among their children. Let us think also of the effect of an emotionalized response on the part of one person who is a member of a crowd. It is almost certainly true that high loss of life in certain types of disaster is due not so much to the disaster itself as it is to the fact that some one person in the whole group has reacted to the threatening situation in an emotionalized way. If, for example, a person shouts "Fire" in a crowded theatre, he will almost certainly start a panic.[35]

As we shall see in the next chapter, the most important social significance of emotionalized action is concerned with the measures of affection that obtain between parents and children. It is now known that those parents who develop too great a sense of dependence on the part of their children predispose these children to permanent habits of dependence. All sorts of psychological and social difficulties are known to come out of this social misuse of emotionalized attitudes.[36]

From these brief examples we may draw the inference that nor-

[34] Cf. Martin, E. D., *The Meaning of a Liberal Education.* New York: W. W. Norton and Co., 1926.
[35] Cf. Ross, E. A., *Social Psychology.* New York: The Macmillan Co., 1913, Chapter IV.
[36] Cf. Sherman, M., *op. cit., passim.*

mal social behavior requires the attainment of a fairly nice balance between the bodily energies and modes of reaction to situations. There are a great many objects and events which should never excite an emotionalized response. This is not to argue, of course, that either social or nonsocial forms of action should be wholly devoid of affective coloring. It is sometimes argued, to be sure, that any expression of emotion is a reversion to animal types of action or the recognition in a cultured life of the emergency modes of response that are so essential in warfare. This, however, is certainly an extreme position for aesthetic appreciation, and all of the religious sentiments depend upon the affective dispositions. Moreover, the integrity of home life as a stable social institution depends, in part, at least, upon a degree of emotionalized attitude which is fully adequate to all of the normal demands of human affection but which, at the same time, does not transform a reasonable affection into those fruitless attachments which lead to abnormal feelings of dependence.[37]

5. *Character Traits:* As a final illustration of some of the possible meanings that may be given to the phrase "normal social behavior," let us take character traits in their social setting. The student already knows that it is not possible to take these traits in any other setting for actions which can be described as just, honest, jealous, domineering, or submissive gain these particular qualities by virtue of their social implications. No one can be honest with respect to two pieces of money unless one or both of them belong to someone else. Similarly, no one can be just or unselfish to the rock ballast along a railway. It is only when the rock ballast becomes a part of an employment situation that methods of handling this material achieve social value.

As was said at the beginning of this section, a great many attempts have been made to describe those personality or character traits which are absolutely essential to normal social living. The chief examples are to be found, of course, in Christian ethics. It has been urged that the first requirement of all social living is love.[38] This term is used, of course, not in the more limited sense of an affection between a husband and wife, but in a much broader sense. It implies that one shall learn how to recognize the worth, dignity, and intrinsic eternal value of each person. A concept of almost

---

[37] The matters discussed at the end of Chapter Six bear directly upon this phase of normal social behavior.
[38] Cf. Flew, R. N., *op. cit., passim.* We are dealing here, of course, with many of the concepts that enter into any system of ethics.

equal importance is known as justice. If these and all of the other concepts that make up a complete system of Christian ethics are brought into a single pattern, they acquire that quality known as spirituality. To be sure, there are those who will think of the word "spirituality" as calling for some inner mystical attitude or disposition or they will think of it as naming the nonphysical side of human nature. People who can be called spiritual, however, earn this term, not because they have actually laid out for inspection their nonphysical part, but because in their relations with one another they have actually conducted themselves unselfishly, devotedly, courageously, justly, honestly, charitably, and humbly.

6. *Conclusion:* This is, of course, a very brief sketch of a very complex and difficult matter. It would be required of us that we write a whole volume on ethics or upon the various concepts of the good life were we fully to explore only a part of the meanings that can be given to the phrase "normal social behavior." The student is already aware, however, of all of these things. We have sought to remind him of some of them simply in order to emphasize the fact that an educative process which leads to the development of a growth pattern that is entirely independent of the social meaning or significance of the major features of this pattern, falls far beside the mark.

As we have said at the beginning of the chapter, human living is essentially social in its meaning, almost from the very first. We may, to be sure, lay most emphasis in the schoolroom on those features of the growth process which are most devoid of social meaning; but if we do we give direct cause for the criticisms that are now being so freely passed upon education. If a man learns a great many skills and has a wide range of information, he may still be wholly unscrupulous in the way in which he will use his skill and information. When, therefore, we lay emphasis upon the social significance of every feature of the growth pattern, we simply mean to assert that education is, after all, a social enterprise. If the social group cannot convert its oncoming members into persons who will recognize their social obligations, there is no reason at all why the group should continue to tax itself and otherwise become anxious about the continuance of the school system.

IV. Antisocial Conduct and Delinquency

1. *Introduction:* With this brief picture of some of the main features of normal social conduct before us, we are prepared to de-

scribe a few of the major types of delinquency. We shall try also to point out some of the factors which lead to delinquency. In general, the word "delinquency" bears the same relation to the conduct of school children as the word "crime" bears to the conduct of mature persons. Since we are primarily interested in that portion of the growth pattern which comes under the influence of teaching situations, we shall have little to say about crime.

2. *The Causes of Delinquency:* The student already knows that every particular feature of the growth pattern has behind it a great many essential conditions. It would be helpful, of course, if teachers could lay their hands upon one single cause of delinquency; but, at the present time, he must be prepared to consider a considerable variety of possible agents and factors. Let us study, briefly, some of the more important of these.

A. INNATE FACTORS: One of the most famous theories about the causes of antisocial conduct has argued that some people belong to a special type known as the criminal type.[39] It was urged that this type could be distinguished because it displayed a marked lack of moral sense and because heredity had provided it with distinguishing physical traits such as a large body, prominent cheekbones, and misshapen ears. In terms of this theory, children could be expected to reveal their criminal tendencies early in life. This means that nonsocial forms of conduct such as deceit, obstinacy, and emotional flare-ups should not be attributed at all to conflict or maladjustment. They must be attributed to hereditary dispositions. The teacher, then, would have only one recourse, viz., to segregate these children as early as possible in order to keep them from contaminating the others.

The same appeal to hereditary factors has been made by those who speak of innate moral imbeciles.[40] It might happen, for example, that a child could be born not only with a normal but even with a superior level of intellectual ability but remain lacking in that particular form of intelligence required for moral judgment.

Both of these types of appeal to innate factors have been found inadequate. In the first place, there is no evidence that anyone is born with innate ideas, even though these ideas relate to moral judgments as to what is right and what is wrong. In the second place, actual studies of the growth pattern have revealed learning situa-

---

[39] Cf. *Criminal Man According to the Classification of Cesari Lombroso,* briefly summarized by his daughter Gina Lombroso. New York: G. P. Putnam's, 1911, *passim.*
[40] Cf. Tredgold, A. F., *Mental Deficiency.* London: William Wood, 1908. See especially pp. 348-349, 498.

tions which are fully adequate to account for the delinquencies that appear.

B. MENTAL DEFICIENCY: During the early days of the mental test movement, some evidence was found in favor of the fact that a great many misdemeanors and other types of antisocial conduct were associated with feeblemindedness in children. This evidence was so convincing to some persons that they were willing to conclude that the greatest single cause of delinquency and crime must be low-grade mentality.[41]

The initial evidence, however, has turned out to be wholly untrustworthy. The first tests were poorly standardized and, as we have seen in the last chapter, it may be doubted whether they give an accurate measure of any native factors. More recent studies have shown that only a small percentage of juvenile offenders against the social mores are actually feebleminded.[42] As a matter of fact, there are some sources of information which show that the distribution of I.Q.'s among delinquents is almost identical with the distribution of scores for an unselected population.

One of the most perplexing features of these results lies in the fact that, even where delinquents are found to be low in intelligence, they are also found to belong to lower socio-economic levels. If, for example, studies are made upon groups of delinquents and groups of normal subjects, both of which have been selected from the same socio-economic levels, the differences in their I.Q.'s tend to diminish.[43] We may conclude, therefore, that low I.Q. may be one of the factors involved in delinquency; but when this is said it must also be remembered that low I.Q.'s are also correlated with low levels of socio-economic status and with a good many other environmental factors.

C. THE EMOTIONAL INSTABILITY: It seems to be fairly clear that antisocial forms of conduct usually involve variable degrees of emotional instability. It has been urged, therefore, that an improper balance between emotionalized forms of action and stimulus-situations may be an important contributing factor to delinquency.[44] One

[41] For a good review of these matters, see Curti, M. W., *Child Psychology.* New York: Longmans, Green and Co., 1931, Chapters XII, XIII.

[42] For the argument that feeblemindedness is pertinent, see Terman, L. M., *The Measurement of Intelligence.* Boston: Houghton Mifflin Co., 1916, pp. 9 ff. The contrary opinion together with a survey of the literature can be found in Curti, M. W., "The Intelligence of Delinquents in the Light of Recent Research." *Sci. Monthly,* 1926, XXII, 132-138.

[43] Cf. Slawson, J., *The Delinquent Boy: A Socio-Psychological Study.* Boston: R. C. Badger, 1926, Chapters I and II.

[44] Cf. Curti, M. W., *Child Psychology.* New York: Longmans, Green and Co., 1931, pp. 397 ff.

of the facts supporting this view is as follows. If an attempt is made to correct one form of misconduct in a child, another is almost certain to spring up.

Proper studies in this field have required that some way be found whereby emotional stability can be measured. One of the most common methods involves the use of a psycho-neurotic questionnaire, that is, a questionnaire that requires the subject to answer a large number of questions bearing upon his emotional attitudes or dispositions.[45] As sample questions, we may take the following, viz., "Did you ever run away from home?" "Do you ever cry out in your sleep?" and, "Do you feel that you are a little bit different from other people?"

These questionnaires have not been standardized as yet, and they make, therefore, rather insecure measures of emotional stability. In general, however, it looks as though many delinquents must be more unstable than normal children. It would not be fair to say, however, that emotional stability is a cause of delinquency since emotional stability itself has to be explained. We could, of course, assert that hereditary factors make some people more unstable than others; but it has been more fruitful to go to training processes than to innate traits.

D. POVERTY: It has long been known that lack of food and other symptoms of dire need might be one of the contributing factors to antisocial behavior. In one of the earlier studies in this field, for example, it was found that, of a group of 584 delinquent boys and 157 delinquent girls, 38 per cent of the former and 69 per cent of the latter came from very poor homes.[46] Another study has shown that one delinquent out of every six was actually in want for the common necessities of life.[47] These figures have gained new importance because of the possible influence of a period of depression upon the number of problem children. It has been shown, however, that some other factors aside from sheer bodily want must play a very large part for there has not been a notable increase in delinquency as a result of the recent depression.[48] To be sure, there will

[45] Cf. Thurstone, L. L., and Thurstone, T. G., "A Neurotic Inventory." *J. Soc. Psychol.*, 1930, I, 3-30. Also Symonds, P. M., *Diagnosing Personality and Conduct.* New York: D. Appleton-Century Co., 1931, Chapter V.
[46] Cf. Breckinridge, S. P., and Abbott, E., *The Delinquent Child and the Home.* New York: Charities Publ. Com., 1912, pp. 70-74 and *passim.*
[47] Burt, C. L., *The Young Delinquent.* New York: D. Appleton-Century Co., 1925, pp. 62 ff.
[48] Cf. Jones, V., "Relation of Economic Depression to Delinquency, Crime, and Drunkenness in Massachusetts." *J. Soc. Psychol.*, 1932, III, 259-282.

always be single instances which must be attributed to lack of food but single instances cannot be accepted as a proof of the case.

E. HOME CONDITIONS: It is known that approximately one quarter of all of the children of the United States live in homes that have been broken because of death, separation, divorce, insanity, or imprisonment.[49] In one group of delinquent boys it was discovered that over fifty per cent had come from such homes. It must be inferred, therefore, that either the home itself or some of the educative influences which it makes possible must have a marked bearing upon the occurrence of delinquency.

There are, however, other features of home life that are just as important. The student will recall that learning processes may be greatly aided if rewards and punishments are used as incentives or deterrents. There is every reason to believe that discipline exercises its greatest influence during the early stages of development. After a child is old enough to know how to regulate his conduct in terms of the consequences of actions and after commands and admonitions have become adequate signs of possible consequences, the amount of punishment necessary for good behavior constantly decreases. During the first two or three years, however, some sort of punishment is almost essential to good training. It is not surprising to discover, therefore, that a considerable number of delinquencies are found among children who have not been subjected to proper disciplinary measures.[50] Defective discipline may refer not only to the lack of punishment but to punishment that has been too severe as well.

The home, of course, is not the only place where disciplinary measures may be put into effect. If there are undesirable recreational facilities or where there is frequent opportunity for association with bad companions, learning processes are just as certain from these environmental influences as they might be from any other. Many specific acts of delinquency such as stealing, for example, often involve two or more participants.[51] The inference is that if children can find normal recreation under the guidance of a playground director who is sufficiently exacting in his adherence to the rules of the game, and if the formation of boys into gangs can be adequately

---

[49] Cf. Shideler, E. H., "Family Disintegration and the Delinquent Boy in the United States." *J. Crim. Law and Criminol.*, 1908, VIII, 714-717. Also Slawson, J., "Marital Relations of Parents and Juvenile Delinquency." *J. Delinq.*, 1923, VIII, 278-286.

[50] Cf. Burt, C. L., *op. cit., passim.*

[51] For a major study of this and of other factors, see Healy, W., and Bronner, A. E., *Delinquents and Criminals: Their Making and Unmaking.* New York: The Macmillan Co., 1926, *passim.*

supervised, one contributing factor to antisocial conduct can be remedied.[52]

There is one thing about these various possible sources of delinquency which should be pointed out. Almost every one of them implies the other and all of them together imply some fault in the training program. It now begins to look as though delinquencies must owe their origin in large measure to those features of home and schoolroom conditions which promote conflicts but which at the same time evade proper means of solving conflicts. Since this is a feature of the whole educative process which must be discussed more fully, we shall postpone further consideration of it until the next chapter.

V. Special Social Problems

1. *Introduction:* In addition to the features of social and antisocial behavior which have been discussed up to this point, there are a number of other problems which are a part of the everyday work of the teacher. We may think, for example, of only children, of the influence of birth order on the character of the growth pattern, and of the effect of institutional life on social conduct.

2. *Only Children:* There is a long tradition to the effect that only children are particularly apt to be problem children because they are not able to adapt themselves to social conditions which may prevail in the schoolroom. It is said, for example, that the only child is apt to be more nervous than siblings, and to be more unstable emotionally.[53] Either of these traits, if they could be confirmed, would result, of course, in a large variety of social difficulties.

The experiments that have been carried out in this field quite fail to justify the traditions. In one study, for example, one hundred only children were compared with a group of control children. No marked differences were found either in the number of social difficulties or in types.[54] Another study has seemed to show that only children of public school and college age are apt to show fewer nervous symptoms than other children.[55] It seems fair to draw the conclusion, therefore, that the teacher does not normally have to deal with a special case when he deals with only children.

[52] One of the best studies of this problem is by Thrasher, F. M., *The Gang.* Chicago: Univ. of Chicago Press, 1927, *passim.*
[53] For a survey of some of the literature, see Jones, H. E., "Order of Birth," in Murchison, C. (Ed.), *Handbook of Child Psychology.* Worcester, Mass.: Clark Univ. Press, 1933, pp. 575 ff.
[54] Ward, A., "The Only Child." *Smith Coll. Stud. Soc. Work,* 1931, I, 41-65.
[55] Fenton, N., "The Only Child." *J. Genet. Psychol.,* 1928, XXXV, 546-554.

3. *Birth Order:* Most of the studies on only children and all of the studies on the relation between birth order and normal processes of development are obscured by the tremendous variability of the circumstances surrounding birth order.[56] In order to arrive at adequate facts, the experimenter would have to know (i) not only the order of birth with respect to living children but with respect to non-living children as well, (ii) the age of the mother at the time of birth, (iii) the size of the family at the time any particular child is studied, (iv) the effect of a varying sex ratio, and (v) the effect of the rate at which the children have been born.

In spite of all of these difficulties, a large number of statistical and case studies of only children have been made. These studies have been excited, in part, by traditions to the effect that the first-born are apt to be the most intelligent, that the last-born are apt to be the most intelligent, that the first-born will be socially unstable, that the last-born will be socially unstable, and so on. It is not possible to consider all of the experiments that have been made on various features of birth order and we shall, therefore, limit ourselves primarily to studies on relative degrees of intelligence.

When the age factor is controlled by restricting comparisons to children of the same age and when the social status is controlled by restricting comparisons to families of a given size, it turns out that there is only a slight superiority among the first-born as compared with the last-born. To be sure, there are some studies which show a larger amount of superiority for the first-born.[57] Other studies, however, have shown that later-born children are brighter than the first-born. The explanations usually offered for this fact are as follows, viz., (i) that parents have more adequate parental experience in rearing later-born children, (ii) that there may be some improvement in the economic status of the families when the later-born children arrived, (iii) that the presence of other children in the family creates more favorable opportunities for learning, and especially for learning language, and (iv) that there may be some physiological change in the maturity of the mother which favors the later-born children.[58]

It is clear, then, that the evidence is conflicting. Conflicts are due, no doubt, to the difficulties mentioned above. There are so

---
[56] Fenton, N., "The Only Child." *J. Genet. Psychol.*, 1928, XXXV, 551 ff.
[57] Jones, H. E., and Kinser, E. L., "A Further Study of Birth Order and Intelligence." *J. Educ. Psychol.*, 1933, XXIV.
[58] Thurstone, L. L., and Jenkins, R. L., "Birth Order and Intelligence." *J. Educ. Psychol.*, 1929, XX, 641-651; Thurstone, L. L., *Order of Birth, Parent-Age, and Intelligence*. Chicago: Univ. of Chicago Press, 1931.

many variable factors and so many different ways of weighting these factors that one could hardly expect ready agreement among different investigators. The main point, however, seems to be this. Irrespective of the differences that may obtain between siblings, even though these differences should be found to be indifferently related to birth order, the problems of adequate social behavior still remain among the serious problems to be met both by the teacher and the parents. This is one of the reasons why many administrators and parent-teacher organizations are asking that teachers shall know more about the home life of the pupils under their care. We have already remarked that the transition from home life to the first grade may stand out as a major episode in the lives of some small children. This is, of course, not the only transition that has to be made. Such transitions are important, not so much because they bear upon the intellectual growth of children, but because they raise a variety of perplexing social questions.

READINGS

A point of departure for a great many special problems is furnished by Murphy, G., and Murphy, L. B., *Experimental Social Psychology*. New York: Harper and Bros., 1931. This book undertakes to review and to evaluate the experimental work now being done in this field. Another source of reference is Bühler, C., "The Social Behavior of Children," in Murchison, C. (Ed.), *Handbook of Child Psychology*. Worcester, Mass.: Clark Univ. Press, 1933, Chapter IX.

If education is a social enterprise and if one of the products desired is a socialized person, it ought to follow that the problems of educational psychology cannot be viewed apart from larger social considerations. An introduction to this phase of our study is furnished by Burton, W. H., *An Introduction to Education*. New York: D. Appleton-Century Co., 1934, Parts I and II and *passim*. See also Dunlap, K., *Civilized Life*. Baltimore: Williams and Wilkins, 1934.

A useful survey of the problems of education from the social or sociological point of view has been made by Tuttle, H. S., *A Social Basis of Education*. New York: T. Y. Crowell Co., 1934.

CHAPTER EIGHTEEN

ADJUSTMENT AND MENTAL HYGIENE

I. Physical and Mental Hygiene

1. *Introduction:* It is hardly possible for a student to go very far in his schooling without having been told over and over again that the word "hygiene" names a variety of personal habits which he can acquire in order to guard himself against bodily sickness and injury. Because of the rapid development of medicine, a teacher can no longer call himself prepared to enter the classroom unless he knows at least some of the simpler facts about care of the teeth and of the eyes, the value of fresh air, the symptoms of malnutrition and lack of sleep, and the dangers of uncleanliness. When, however, the word "hygiene" is modified by the adjective "mental," teachers, parents, and students are inclined to feel that they have suddenly been introduced to a group of facts which, instead of having a good many analogies with those mentioned above, stand more nearly on the same level with insanity and other unusual or bizarre types of personality.

As we commonly use it, the word "hygiene" is modified by the adjective "physical," and when it is used in this way we all know that there are a great many devices by which the health of the body may be preserved. It has been difficult, however, to arrive at an analogous picture of mental or psychological health which would enable us to say that mental hygiene consists of all of those practices and attitudes which will keep our psychological rather than our physiological operations in good running order.[1]

2. *Psychological Excellence:* In general, the phrase "mental hygiene" names the methods which can be used in order to answer a very simple question, viz., how may a person go about it to become as good or as effective a psychological instrument as possible? This is, of course, exactly the same type of question that lies behind the phrase "physical hygiene." If most persons do not know how to keep their bodies in good health and thus to fortify themselves

[1] Cf. Burnham, W. H., *The Wholesome Personality.* New York: D. Appleton-Century Co., 1932. This book is a sequel to *The Normal Mind.* New York: D. Appleton-Century Co., 1924.

ADJUSTMENT AND MENTAL HYGIENE

against accident or disease, it is because they have paid no attention to the instruction of their teachers and parents. We propose, then, to insist upon an essential similarity between the two phrases "mental hygiene" and "physical hygiene." The first simply asserts that there are normal or healthy ways in which the psychological operations can be used and that each person, when he knows the facts, can take proper means to preserve his psychological health just as he takes proper means to preserve his physiological health.

The analogy here is, perhaps, not quite so simple as we have made it appear; but not because it is actually more difficult to keep psychologically well than it is to keep physically well. On the contrary, the analogy fails because all of us appear to have almost inexhaustible resources for applying the results of scientific research to our own psychological welfare.[2] It is almost distressing to note that people will go to extremes in demanding perfection in the tools and instruments which they use but never for a moment ask about the perfection of themselves as centers of psychological activity. To be sure, one may throw away an outworn automobile and buy a new one. No one can throw himself away, however, and then replace himself with the latest model. This is, of course, only a minor difficulty after all for each of the chapters that have gone before ought to have shown us that human nature can be changed at every step during the entire growth process. If, then, some people have acquired faulty habits or find themselves out of adjustment with the persons and objects around them, it is not a hopeless task to refashion their nature even to the extent of making it appear that they are issuing a new model.

In brief, then, just as we may ask about the perfection or the suitableness or the adequacy of a tool or an instrument, so we may ask about the perfection or the suitability or the adequacy of our modes of behavior in the situations in which we happen to be placed. It is the function of mental hygiene to show where human beings fall short of efficiency or of ability to adjust themselves to their surroundings. Furthermore, it is the function of mental hygiene to name those practices or those features of the processes of training which will, in the long run, lead to an increase in levels of adjustment or in the adequacy of our conduct.[3] Even though the most of us are not inclined to think of ourselves in terms of effi-

[2] Consider, for example, the social and personal implications of such a book as Viteles, M. S., *Industrial Psychology*. New York: W. W. Norton and Co., 1932.
[3] Cf. La Rue, D. W., *Mental Hygiene*. New York: The Macmillan Co., 1932, Chapter I.

ciency or even in terms of improvability simply because we are not accustomed to apply scientific information to our own welfare, nevertheless some progress is being made in helping teachers to discern among children the first stages of the more serious types of maladjustment and to take measures that will preserve the child from more serious types of psychological disorder.

3. *Mental Hygiene and Education:* When we look at the field of mental hygiene in this broad way, the student will probably say that he can see no difference between mental hygiene and education. He has been told in this book, and he will have learned from a good many other sources, that it is the function of education to train people so that they will become better adapted to the life they have to lead.[4] In the very first section of our study of educational psychology, for example, it was said that a new-born infant has practically none of the traits and skills that are necessary to enable it to adjust itself to its environment. It was implied, moreover, that the process of education, which is a process of guided growth, has, as its distinct purpose, the task of equipping children to live in an adult society. Society believes this so firmly that it is willing to pay about three billion dollars a year in order to make children more competent members of the social order. In other words, then, we seem to have said in our description of the general character of mental hygiene either that mental hygiene and education serve exactly the same purposes or that education is not, as a matter of fact, the health-promoting agent which we have predicated it to be and that mental hygiene, therefore, must be used as a means of correcting the faults of an educative process.[5]

This is really an embarrassing matter to education, but the facts seem to be plain enough. The development of mental hygiene came, in part, as a direct result of the inadequacy of more formal types of instruction. Children who had passed through an average school system were found to be incompetent to adjust themselves to the physical and social environments in which they were placed. As a matter of fact, some of them were found to be so badly out of tune with their surroundings that they could be described as delinquents, and still others swelled the population in sanitariums and psychopathic hospitals.[6] Obviously, something had gone wrong in their

---

[4] This is the point of view emphasized by Trow, C. W., *Educational Psychology*. Boston: Houghton Mifflin Co., 1931, Chapter I.

[5] Cf. Anderson, H. H., "Character Education or Mental Hygiene—Which Shall It Be?" *J. Ment. Hygiene*, 1934, XVIII, 254-262.

[6] See Chapters XX and XXI in *Recent Social Trends*. New York: The McGraw-Hill Book Co., 1933. This is the summarized report of the President's Research Committee on Social Trends.

training, and it was necessary, therefore, to add to the processes of formal education those methods and types of advice which would make it possible for children to use their habits and skills in a more effective way.

It did not take a great amount of research in order to find where the educational faults lay. For a long time, it has been known that the more formal processes of schooling limit themselves almost entirely to the development of motor skills, on the one hand, and to the sheer acquisition of knowledge, on the other. Some of the older psychologies used to speak of three primary functions of the mind, viz., the intellectual or knowing functions, the feeling or emotional functions, and the doing or conative functions. Both by direct act and by implication, education has limited itself pretty largely to the first and the third of these functions.[7] It may even be said that education has limited itself to the first of them, for the conative functions, that is, the development of motor skills, was said to be primarily a product of the playground and of the gymnasium.

We have already found reason to believe that the term "education" includes more than the acquisition of knowledge. The cultured person not only knows what to do and how to do it, but when to do it as well. Moreover, the educated person displays variable degrees of competence in a good many other types of psychological operation than those named by the phrases "manual skill" and "range of information." The educated person is really a *person;* that is, he has persistent qualities or traits and a total organization of these qualities and traits which identify him as a single unit operating among other similar units. Moreover, it is not possible in our daily living to disregard emotionalized forms of action. As we have seen, no person can be wholly neutral in mood or feeling or even in emotion with respect to the events going on about him. If, then, education has not really fulfilled its major function, viz., of helping people to live a good life, the fault is to be discovered, in part, in the emphasis which it has placed upon the training of the functions of knowing and, in part, in its almost total disregard of the need for trained emotions and moods.[8]

Some of the earlier chapters have shown us clearly enough how education has excused itself for this fault. It has not been easy to see that there was in the schoolroom or even in the preschool education of the child any formal plan for teaching him how to be prop-

---
[7] Cf. Morrison, H. C., *Basic Principles of Education.* Boston: Houghton Mifflin Co., 1934, *passim.*
[8] Another phase of this question has been discussed by Fletcher, J. M., *Psychology in Education.* New York: Doubleday, Doran and Co., 1934, *passim.*

erly emotionalized in the presence of the events which make up his environment. Aside from religious schools, it is not even possible to say that there have been any formal plans for teaching children how to acquire specific personality traits and dispositions. Both emotionalized forms of action and personality traits have come more as a by-product of the educative process than as a direct result of a precisely arranged curriculum.[9]

To be sure, some of the older schools used to bend even the study of reading to the development of personality, for most reading exercises were followed with a maxim or a lesson designed to favor some ethical and moral attitude and to disfavor others. Apart from these modes of instruction in personality and in emotionalized action, however, practically everything that the child became in these respects was a product of informal education rather than of formal training. In view of these circumstances, it was easy for educators to say that personality traits and emotionalized forms of training must be either instinctive or an expression of the original nature of the child. When this assumption had been made, the educator could reply to his critics by saying that the development of personal quality and the search for adequate emotional adjustments did not lie within the competence of the formal school system.[10]

4. *Purpose of the Chapter:* We do not need to cite again the answer which may be made to these assumptions. The experimental laboratory has shown, without a shadow of a doubt, that many of the emotionalized forms of action and most of our specific personality traits are in no sense of the word "original." On the contrary, they are a product of training. This is not to say that they are not a product of a formal curriculum or even that anyone has intentionally tried to promote maladjustment in emotionalized action rather than adjustment. The simple fact is that the educative process has favored the attainment of maturity in all psychological modes of operation, but that it has not gone very far in teaching children or adults how to be wise or healthy or normal in the use of their psychological functions. It is largely for this reason, then, that the mental hygiene movement has appeared as a supplement to the regular educative process. It undertakes to emphasize not only the actual development of skills or the actual attainment of maturity in psychological operations but to show how and when these opera-

[9] Cf. Bagby, E., *The Psychology of Personality.* New York: Henry Holt and Co., 1928.
[10] Cf. Kilpatrick, W. H. (Ed.), *The Educational Frontier.* New York: D. Appleton-Century Co., 1933, especially Chapters I and III.

ADJUSTMENT AND MENTAL HYGIENE

tions can be used to the best advantage of the person himself and of the group within which he lives.

II. TYPES OF ADJUSTMENT

1. *Hygiene and Adjustment:* The student will see that the difference between mental hygiene, on the one hand, and the concept of adjustment, on the other, is simply a difference between the means and the end. Mental hygiene names the means that may be used in order to teach people how to get along well in an environment. Adjustment is a word which will, whenever it is adequately defined, state more clearly just what is implied in the phrase "getting along well." This means that adjustment is a modern term which may describe some of the same ideals of living that used to be described by the words "the good life," "perfection," "Christian joy," "gentility," and "happiness." [11]

These words fall naturally into two groups. It has been one of the functions of religion to suggest some of the ways in which a good life may be achieved. Joy and perfection, therefore, have been given an essentially religious meaning. Gentility, happiness, and even the phrase "the good life," however, have also had a secular meaning.[12] That is, it has been assumed that, in the development of the intellect and in the attainment of high moral character, one might find oneself perfectly equipped to live in a secular world rather than in the "City of God." Adjustment is not, however, the only modern substitute for these more venerable ways of thinking about perfection. The word "efficiency" has sometimes been used in the same manner. It seems worth while, therefore, to find out what the origin of some of these words is, how they are related to teaching problems, and how far they go in supplanting older ways of describing the inner meaning of "a good life."

2. *Adjustment and Adaptation:* The word "adjustment," like the word "adaptation," has come into psychology and education by way of the biological sciences.[13] When he takes a long-time view of the development of life, the biologist sees that the offspring of animals are never exactly like their parents. They always show minor varia-

---

[11] Cf. Allport, F. H., *Institutional Behavior.* Chapel Hill: Univ. of North Carolina Press, 1933, Chapter III and *passim.* Flew, R. N., *The Idea of Perfection in Christian Theology.* London: Humphrey Milford, 1934.
[12] Cf. Woodbridge, F. J. E., *The Son of Apollo.* Boston: Houghton Mifflin Co., 1929, *passim.*
[13] Cf. Raup, R. B., *Complacency, The Foundation of Human Behavior.* New York: The Macmillan Co., 1925, *passim.*

tions. Now it may happen that some of these variations will make the offspring more competent to survive than the parents were. This means that the offspring may be more competent to survive in the same environment or in an environment which is gradually changing. In any case, the animal which does survive is said to be adjusted or adapted to its environment. Among the lower animals, of course, survival is often measured simply by length of life or by conquest over all enemies. At the human level, however, survival may be given an entirely different meaning, for, in the social groups, the good life is not simply a matter of living a long life or of overcoming all enemies, but a matter of living a cultured and a productive life.[14] If, then, any living creature is equipped either by heredity or by training in such a way that it can survive as an individual and, at the same time, contribute to the lives of others, that creature can be called adjusted or adapted.

3. *Adjustment and Efficiency:* The word "efficiency" shows an entirely different origin.[15] In human affairs goods are secured, and the technical instruments of living are manufactured, largely by human effort and direction. This means that work must be done. It is clear, however, that a ratio between the amount of effort expended and the variety and the excellence of the products that come out of labor can be easily established. If the products of labor are few, it can be said that the labor has not been very efficient. On the contrary, when a small amount of labor has resulted in a large number of useful products, we may say that the labor has been very efficient.

From some points of view, of course, the concepts of adjustment and efficiency are looking in the same direction; but there is, perhaps, one difference between them which may be mentioned even though it serves only a practical purpose. This difference arises out of a distinction that may be drawn between two types of adjustment. For this purpose we may use an automobile as an analogy. From one point of view we may say that an automobile is adjusted or highly adapted in the sense that it can travel over roads at a high rate of speed, climb hills, endure variations in temperature, and otherwise make itself useful in reaching the objectives for which it was invented.

This mode of adjustment may be called external adjustment. It is, therefore, opposed to internal adjustment, that is, to that type

[14] Cf. Morrison, H. C., *Basic Principles of Education*. Boston: Houghton Mifflin Co., 1934, Chapter IV and *passim*.
[15] Cf. the article "Efficiency" in *The Encyclopedia of the Social Sciences*. (Ed. E. R. A. Seligman.) New York: The Macmillan Co., 1931, Vol. V.

of readiness for action which lies within the automobile itself. The pistons, for example, must be fitted snugly into the cylinders; the spark must be properly timed with respect to the position of the piston heads; the carburetor must furnish the right mixture of air and gasoline, and the total energy of the explosions geared properly to the load to be carried. In the same way, we may think of human beings as being adjusted either to the circumstances around them or as being adjusted internally in the sense that all of the various psychological operations are maintaining the right balance with respect to one another.[16]

Since it will be the task of the next chapter to consider, in more detail, the concept of efficiency in so far as it is related to the schoolroom, we shall do no more at this point than cite a few instances both of internal and of external types of adjustment or of adaptation. As a first instance, let us take study habits. By the phrase "study habits" we mean all of those skills which would be involved in reading a book, understanding the words, selecting the essential propositions, learning suitable sections of the material, and in attending to the task at hand for a sufficient period of time to get it done.[17] As we have implied above, we may think of all of these separate tasks in two ways. In the first place, we may think of them in terms of their economy with respect to the situations in which the student is actually placed. In other words, we may think of them in terms of efficiency. In the second place, however, we may think of them in their relations to one another, in which case we shall be leaning toward problems of adjustment rather than toward problems of efficiency.

As a second illustration let us take the problem-solving functions. As we have seen, human beings usually adopt any one of three methods for meeting new situations. In the first place, they may attempt to meet a new situation simply by drawing upon some previously acquired habit or skill. In this event the use of a habit or skill normally results in what has been called a nonadaptive reaction.[18] If the new situation arrives quickly or takes on a highly complex character, one may react to it at emotionalized levels rather than in terms of habit and skill. Here again we may judge the adequacy of the action not in terms of its internal organization but in

---

[16] The science of physiology is concerned primarily with internal adjustments. See Cannon, W. B., *The Wisdom of the Body*. New York: W. W. Norton and Co., 1934.
[17] Cf. Book, W. F., *Economy and Technique of Learning*. Boston: D. C. Heath and Co., 1932, *passim*.
[18] Cf. Fisher, V. E., *An Introduction to Abnormal Psychology*. New York: The Macmillan Co., 1929, Chapter V.

terms of its suitability or adequacy so far as the situation is concerned. There are times, to be sure, when emotionalized forms of action are highly efficient forms simply because the new situation demands quick and highly intense levels of performance. On a good many other occasions, however, emotionalized forms of action would be inefficient in the sense that they are not economical with respect to the situation calling them forth.

When an appeal is made to the problem-solving functions rather than to previously acquired habits and skills or to emotionalized forms of action, no more emphasis is laid upon efficiency, for it is argued that human beings should always be as rational as possible in their conduct. If we use the word "efficiency" in this sense we simply mean that the solution of a problem is a more adequate type of response than the other types that might be used. From a human point of view the person who rarely solves problems could hardly be called efficient in the social and other situations which demand action of this type.

We do not mean, however, to draw too sharp a distinction between the adequacy of the adjustments which people actually make, on the one hand, and the internal organization of the responses that are used. Obviously, high levels of efficiency could not be reached by a person whose internal operations were out of adjustment, just as an automobile could not serve the purposes for which it had been invented if the engine were out of tune, for a human being cannot do good to himself or to others if his various modes of operation stand at odds with one another. In short, then, the distinction we are making is not so much a valid psychological or educational distinction as it is a distinction for practical purposes. As we have announced, it is the function of the present chapter to consider in more detail the various ways in which the processes of internal adjustment may go wrong. The other side of the picture, viz., the side furnished by the concept of efficiency, will be the subject of the next chapter.

III. CONFLICT

1. *Introduction:* Many of the problems of mental hygiene center around the concept of conflict.[19] This concept simply states the fact that a person who is the seat of so many different tendencies to action cannot hope to have all of these tendencies continually in-

[19] A major study of conflict has been written by Luria, A. R., *The Nature of Human Conflicts* (trans. by W. H. Gantt). New York: Liveright Publishing Corp., 1932.

ADJUSTMENT AND MENTAL HYGIENE

tegrated into a single coherent pattern. As a very simple illustration we may take the psychological events described by the word "attention." At any given moment every person is being assailed by invitations to action which are more numerous than he can possibly accept. Attention describes the fact that selection always occurs with respect to these invitations.

In a previous chapter we have tried to describe some of the conditions under which selection is made possible. It is clear, however, that there will be occasions when a selection cannot be made or when the selection that is made will not be the most suitable one. Let us suppose, for example, that we have just witnessed an accident on the highway. The accident includes a number of distinguishable events. Some of these events will be highly important if we are called upon to give a recital of the occurrence. Our recital will depend, however, upon the particular events which have been attended to.[20] These events may not be the ones that are essential to a true characterization. They are, however, a product of all of the circumstances which have to do with selection.

It might be argued that the perfect observer would be an observer who could see everything at once. This means that the perfect observer would be wholly adjusted so far as taking account of and reacting appropriately to complex situations are concerned. It is inevitable, however, that every situation in which a person is placed will provoke conflict between the various parts of a whole pattern. Our final conduct—say our testimony given on the witness stand—will be a product of the conflicts that have occurred.

2. *Sources of Conflict:* As we have implied, this is a very simple approach to the whole problem of conflict. Some measures may be taken, of course, to increase the powers of observation of the person; but the whole pattern of our psychological life involves the possibility of conflict which is much more fundamental, and in some cases more disastrous, than anything that can occur at the level of observation. Let us proceed immediately into the heart of the problem by reciting briefly some of the main sources of conflict.

As a first instance, we may take the following argument. The unborn infant is not the witless or totally mindless vegetable which we have assumed it to be in some of our earlier descriptions of prenatal development. Let us argue, on the contrary, that it is a conscious being, aware of the life that it is leading and appreciative of

---

[20] This is one of the main features of the psychology of testimony. Cf. Griffith, C. R., *Introduction to Applied Psychology.* New York: The Macmillan Co., 1934, Chapter XVII.

the comfortable lodging that has been provided for it.[21] This argument does not imply that the unborn infant is conscious in the same sense that an adult is conscious. On the contrary, it says that there lies below the normal consciousness a more real psychological entity which, for the moment, we may call the unconscious or the subconscious.

If these assumptions may be granted, it follows that the unborn infant must enjoy large measures of comfort and satisfaction, for it is domiciled in a warm, quiet room, furnished with all of the necessities for living, and called upon at no time to assert itself in any manner whatsoever. If this is the way in which the subconscious mind of the unborn child takes its existence, it would follow that the act of birth would come to the individual as a major experience.

There are those who would say, then, that the act of birth is not a simple transition from one phase of living to another but a major trauma which will have a life-long influence upon the child and upon all its actions.[22] In the prenatal condition the individual does not even have to breathe; but now, upon being thrust into a world of reality, it must struggle to get its first breath. Moreover, the real world into which it is introduced is a world which, in an increasing measure, will place all types of hindrances in the way of self-expression. The new member of society will have to struggle for its food and for a restoration of the bodily comforts enjoyed before birth. There will be persons who, in their search for food and for other comforts, will invade the rights of the one. In short, the act of birth introduces a primary conflict between the desires of the new-born infant, on the one hand, and the conditions under which these desires may be satisfied in a real world, on the other.

A. THE FREUDIAN THEORY: This theory of the nature of the birth act and of the fundamental conflict which it introduces has been described in a great many different ways. Some attempts have been made to specify in more detail just what the native desires of the unborn child—that is, of the unconscious—are. That system of psychology known as Freudianism, for example, argues that the word "mind" has a threefold meaning.[23] At one level the mind includes all of those states of awareness or of consciousness which the normal adult usually implies when he uses the word "mind."

[21] Cf. Freud, S., *New Introductory Lectures on Psychoanalysis.* New York: W. W. Norton and Co., 1933, *passim.*
[22] Cf. Bronner, A. F., and Bowers, A. M., *The Structure and Meaning of Psychoanalysis.* New York: A. A. Knopf, 1930, *passim.*
[23] For a good appraisal, see Woodworth, R. S., *Contemporary Schools of Psychology.* New York: The Ronald Press, 1929. For a criticism see Jastrow, J., *The House that Freud Built.* New York: Greenberg, Inc., 1932.

From an older psychology—or, more accurately, from an older theology—there is a belief that we have over and above our normal consciousness a superior mind which goes by the name of "conscience." In the Freudian psychology many of the things that were implied by the word "conscience" are described as the super ego. This super ego, according to Freud, is acquired through the process of training and includes whatever may be meant by moral, ethical, and social standards. It is, therefore, a sort of censor upon action, giving its approval to conduct which will promote the common good and placing a stamp of disapproval upon modes of conduct which are unsocial.

The operations of the super ego are not directed so much toward the normal mind as they are toward the subconscious which, in more recent Freudian theory, has come to be known as the *id*.[24] The word *id* describes the original or native character of the mind. It is a word which has a good many similarities with the older religious concept of sin or evil. The *id* of the unborn child, for example, is inherently bestial in character, full of sex lust, eager to express itself without regard to other persons, and otherwise inclusive of all that is antisocial.

It is easy to see that an original nature of this type would involve, without further ado, the development of conflicts of the most bitter type. Were human beings to live wholly alone in the world or were they to be devoid of social mores and of all concepts of morality, some conflicts might be avoided. Every child, however, is born into a social group. Some of the very urges which it is alleged to possess imply the existence of other persons, as, for example, the sex impulses. Obviously, any person possessing original nature made up of such urges and desires as are summarized by the concept of the *id* would find himself in conflict with the social mores which deny direct satisfaction. Moreover, he would find himself in conflict with other persons who are also seeking for satisfaction.

This is not the place to enter into a detailed treatment either of the birth trauma or of the inherent nature of the *id*. We may, however, draw from the literature in this field two important facts. There is, first of all, the assumption that human nature is, in its original condition, inherently sinful. So long as the infant remains in the mother's womb most, if not all, of its primary urges and lusts can be satisfied. The mother's womb, however, is to be placed in

---

[24] For this doctrine in a practical setting, see Alexander, F., and Staub, H., *The Criminal, the Judge, and the Public* (Trans. by G. Zelboorg). New York: The Macmillan Co., 1931, *passim*.

sharp contrast again a world of reality. When the word "reality" is used in this sense it simply refers to the fact that the physical environment, on the one hand, and the social environment that has been created by communal living, on the other, are not compatible with the environment created by the mother. Granted these two assumptions, conflicts of deep-running import are inevitable.

B. THE TISSUE NEEDS: There is so much sheer speculation in these points of view that they have not commended themselves seriously either to experimental psychologists or to educators. To be sure, there can be no doubt about the existence of conflict and neither can there be any doubt about the severity of some of these conflicts; but it is one thing to call attention to an important group of facts and quite another to explain the facts in fanciful ways. Students of human nature, therefore, have looked rather earnestly at the sources of human nature in order to find out whether some other sources can be named than those designated by such terms as the "unconscious," the "subconscious," the "super ego," and the "id." At the present time, most hope is offered by a further study of the primary tissue needs and of all of the secondary or derived urges or incentives that come out of these needs.[25] Since we have gone into this matter in considerable detail in an earlier chapter, the student should remind himself again of the nature of motivation in order to get the picture that is needed at this particular place.

3. *Tissue Needs and Conflict:* If we may grant that there are several varieties of fundamental tissue needs, it becomes possible to place these needs in opposition to one another and in opposition to environmental urges and factors. As we have seen, a tissue need is an incentive to action because it furnishes a fairly consistent source of stimulus to action. If, then, a person is driven to action by stimuli that arise within his own system and if outside objects and events are also inviting him to action, the natural result will be conflict. Conflicts will arise even though the original tissue needs have been supplanted by a large number of secondary needs.

A. ENVIRONMENTAL CONFLICT: It is customary to divide the sources of conflict into four general types. In the first place, the general environment may furnish plenty of obstacles and hindrances to desires. As an example, we may take hunger and all of those objects and events which have, during processes of training, become substituted for the hunger urge. There are plenty of times, of course, when hunger cannot be satisfied. The circumstances under

[25] Cf. Dunlap, K., *Civilized Life.* Baltimore: The Williams and Wilkins Co., 1934, Chapter III.

which access to food is forbidden may vary all the way from a major drought to family or personal poverty. The point is that some people will feel a continuous urge for food and yet find the urge blocked by a variety of conditions. The result is a conflict which must be resolved.

B. SOCIAL MORES: In the second place, communal living has set up a large number of customs, traditions, and mores which favor the group rather than any single member of the group. These mores are particularly stringent in connection with the sex urges. Without going into the long story of the origin of taboos upon unhindered satisfaction of the sex urges, we may simply take it as a current fact that sex behavior is permitted by society only under definite legal and religious sanctions.[26] It is a plain fact, of course, that a great many objects have now been substituted for the primary stimulus conditions to sex desire so that even children in the schoolroom—to say nothing of adults—are constantly motivated in sexual matters. For every increase in motivation, however, there is a definite barrier. Sometimes the barriers may be so extreme as to bring about almost, if not quite, a complete suppression of the sex impulses and of all attitudes and dispositions related to them. The chances are that many of the conflicts into which both children and adults are thrown are occasioned by these factors.

C. ORGAN INFERIORITY: In the third place, conflicts may owe their origin to a secondary motive, desire, or ambition which requires more personal competence for attainment than many people possess. On the school playground, for example, the person who can run fast and otherwise excel in athletic events is hailed as a favored person. Let us suppose that a boy with a maimed limb is thrown into an environment of this type. He will already have shared the desires or ambitions of his fellows, but the actual satisfaction of these ambitions will be hindered by his bodily incompetence. Such a person is almost certain to develop a serious conflict.[27] Still more commonly, however, conflicts of this order arise out of differences in intelligence, differences in personal attractiveness, and differences in economic position. There are times when even a child's own parents may be a source of conflict to the child, for it is known that superior competence upon the part of the parents may act as a defi-

[26] Cf. Calverton, V. F., and Schmalhausen, S. D. (Ed.), *Sex in Civilization*. Garden City: Garden City Publ. Co., 1929.
[27] Cf. Adler, A., *The Neurotic Constitution*. New York: Dodd, Mead and Co., 1917. A more popular exposition by the same author is entitled *What Life Should Mean to You*. Boston: Little, Brown and Co., 1931.

nite hindrance to any efforts the child may make to achieve distinction.[28]

D. DIRECT CONFLICTS: In the fourth place, both the primary tissue needs and all of the secondary or derived motives may enter into conflict with one another. These conflicts may arise either because hunger and sex or activity and rest cannot be satisfied simultaneously or because any single primary tissue need has become attached to a variety of objects. The traditional complexes created by alleged triangles in affection are cases in point. Even a child may develop a conflict because of its two-dimensional affection toward its father and toward its mother.

4. *Summary:* We may now bring all of these considerations together in the proposition that conflict is an inevitable feature of living. We have seemed to say, of course, that all conflicts should be avoided, or that peace and contentment in living will be attained whenever a person has thoroughly adapted every phase of his being to every other phase. It might be said, however, that complete internal adjustment of this type would imply a psychological life more akin to that of a vegetable than to that of a human being. It is the aim of mental hygiene not to remove all conflicts but to remove those conflicts which are too intense in character and especially to help children to resolve their conflicts in ways that will bring them and the group to which they belong an advantage rather than a disadvantage. The next step in our study of the problems of mental hygiene and adjustment, therefore, leads us to a brief survey of the various methods which people may use in order to escape conflict.

IV. METHODS OF RESOLVING CONFLICTS

1. *Introduction:* The picture which we have just given of the origin and development of conflicts is two-sided in character. On the one side, there is that vast field of fancy and theory which asserts that all human difficulties, as well as all human achievements, are a product of forces or energies resident in the subconscious mind.[29] The other side of the picture is furnished by the straightforward description of internal source of action and of the ways in which these internal sources may be supplanted by outside agents and factors.

[28] Sherman, M., *Mental Hygiene and Education.* New York: Longmans, Green and Co., 1934, Chapter I and *passim.*
[29] Cf. Hendrick, I., *Facts and Theories of Psychoanalysis.* New York: A. A. Knopf, 1934, *passim.*

ADJUSTMENT AND MENTAL HYGIENE

We revert to these two pictures because both of them, but the first in particular, has put a definite bias upon current descriptions of the way in which conflicts may be resolved. As we proceed, therefore, to a statement of these various methods the student must keep the fact in mind that some of them seem actually to imply the truth of the Freudian theory of human nature. We shall, however, avoid as far as possible this implication. That is, we shall try to describe the more common ways of resolving conflicts simply in terms of the devices that are used without any necessary implication as to the agents or forces which have been responsible for the creation of these devices. The chances are that when studies on the sources of human action have been brought more nearly to completion, we shall be able to say with more assurance just how the conflicts that arise out of these sources should be solved.[30]

2. *Trial-and-Error:* We have already found that the lower animals and small children meet new or difficult situations by making a varied attack upon them. This varied attack includes some actions that are almost certainly inadequate. Some of them, however, will be more or less adequate. Without going over again the various things that were said about trial-and-error learning in an earlier chapter, we may simply say that the trial-and-error method does provide a way in which some conflicts may be avoided.[31] If, in making his varied attack, a person can hit upon a mode of action which effects a compromise, so to speak, between conflicting tendencies, he will be able to avoid all of the incompetence and emotional distress that precede his newly acquired form of behavior.

As fast as language is acquired, trial-and-error movement in response to difficult situations will become less overt and more and more implicit. In other words, a person will be able to solve his difficulties in an intelligent way. As comparative examples, we may take, on the one side, the child who is trying to get hold of an object if it is beyond his reach and, on the other side, the adult person who is attempting to settle a conflict between the respective claims of religion and science. We may say, of course, that the perplexity in which the child is placed is a very small matter; but obviously, it is a perplexity which sooner or later may turn into a pronounced emotional situation. Such a situation can be avoided only if the

[30] Cf. Watson, G. B., and Spence, R. B., *Educational Problems for Psychological Study.* New York: The Macmillan Co., 1930, *passim.* Also, Symonds, P. M., *The Nature of Conduct.* New York: The Macmillan Co., 1928, Chapter XIII and *passim.*
[31] Fisher, V. E., *op. cit.,* pp. 74 ff.

child by its trial-and-error movements actually succeeds in inventing some new way of getting hold of the desired object.

From a formal point of view, the perplexity faced by the adult is of the same character. So long as the respective claims of religion and science are emphasized as claims, the conflict will be more sharply defined until at length serious degrees of emotionalism may be aroused. The adult has the opportunity, however, not of making a variety of overt movements but of making a variety of tentative verbal movements looking toward a solution of his problem. If, during a period of reflection, he can hit upon some new patterning of information which will make due allowance both for his scientific facts and his religious facts, his conflict will be peacefully and normally solved.[32]

From these considerations, it seems fair to say that trial-and-error methods, on the one hand, and problem-solving methods, on the other, should be the normal methods used by every person in effecting an escape from perplexing or conflicting situations. Even a casual inspection of human behavior will show, however, that most persons resort to these means rather infrequently. It would seem to follow that one of the primary functions of mental hygiene is both to discover less satisfactory methods of settling conflicts and to emphasize the most satisfactory method.

This is one of the reasons why we have already given so much attention to the nature and significance of problem-solving in the schoolroom. After all, human adults differ from children and from the lower animals in their potential ability to use the problem-solving functions where they should be used. The frequency of use, however, depends primarily upon the nature of one's training. Moreover, the very fact that less satisfactory methods are used is a prime witness in favor of the extent to which most persons are not adapted to the problems created by conflict.

3. *Non-Adjustive Reactions:* The first of the methods of resolving a conflict which can be called unsatisfactory is known as the non-adjustive reaction.[33] Let us suppose, for example, that in the instance cited above, where the child is prevented from reaching a plaything, the conflict actually becomes transformed into an emotionalized response. The child may begin to cry. There are three aspects of this behavior which are important to the teacher.

In the first place, the act of crying is non-adjustive in the sense

---

[32] The literature is full of serious attempts to reconcile conflicts of this type. See, for example, Barnes, E. W., *Scientific Theory and Religion*. New York: The Macmillan Co., 1934.
[33] Fisher, V. E., *op. cit.,* pp. 82 ff.

that there is nothing about it that will actually get the child out of his difficulty unless some parent or teacher offers aid. The crying itself, then, may be described as a non-adjustive reaction. It is non-adjustive simply because it is wholly inappropriate to the situation. It is hardly necessary, perhaps, to cite instances belonging in the same class which the student himself will think of both with respect to his own conduct and that of his friends.

In the second place, it happens all too frequently that non-adjustive reactions of this first type do become effective in the sense that they bring some other person on the scene. In other words, the child itself does not solve its problem or escape from its difficulty. Instead, the difficulty is simply removed by the intervention of a parent, nurse, or older child. As we shall see later on, the repeated use of this method of avoiding conflicts creates an intense feeling of dependence upon other people. If we could assume that some other person were always present, these feelings of dependence would, perhaps, have no particular significance. As it turns out, however, other persons cannot always be present. A non-adaptive reaction, then, will lead to an attitude or disposition which may make a person persistently unable to take any initiative with respect to his conflicts.[34]

In the third place, an initial act of crying may be the starting point for acquiring the habit of crying in the presence of a difficult situation. Non-adjustive modes of action, then, and especially non-adjustive actions that are emotional in character, easily become habitualized. This is, perhaps, the primary origin of all of those modes of response which are known as worry and anxiety.[35] It is easy to say by word of mouth and in coldly intellectual terms that worry is a type of action which never serves any good purpose. It is a plain fact, however, that many persons are worriers. The inference is that these persons have acquired emotionalized types of response during their earlier periods of training and that they are, therefore, persistently committed to adjustments of a non-adaptive type.

4. *Regressive Reactions:* It has long been noted that a good many people will, when confronted with a difficult situation, respond to the situation neither in terms of a new intellectual effort nor in terms of their more recently acquired skills. On the contrary, many

---

[34] Cf. Morgan, J. J. B., *Keeping a Sound Mind.* New York: The Macmillan Co., 1934, *passim.*

[35] Symonds, P. M., *Mental Hygiene of the School Child.* New York: The Macmillan Co., 1934, Chapter VI.

people attempt to solve difficulties or escape from baffling situations by reverting to a mode of behavior which is essentially childish or even infantile in character.[36] Behavior of this type is known as regressive behavior.

As an initial illustration, we may take the second of the three phases of non-adaptive actions described above. When a child escapes from a difficult situation not by its own effort but by the intervention of some other person, its natural reaction is to feel its sense of dependence upon that person. This sense of dependence occurs most frequently between children and their parents and especially between children and their mothers. As a matter of fact, it occurs so frequently as to have earned a special descriptive phrase, viz., mother-fixation.[37]

If we may suppose that a person may grow into early maturity with an intimate sense of dependence of this type, it would seem to follow that the act of placing this person in a totally new situation would call forth some mode of response which had been effective in getting results when the person was still in the presence of his mother. A most obvious response would be crying. There are, to be sure, a great many social taboos against adults and even against older children who resort to this practice. And yet, clearly enough, crying is no more effective as a method of getting out of difficulties at the adult level than it is at the childhood level, unless it will summon aid.[38]

Some of the clearest cases of regressive reactions came as a result of conflicts and perplexities induced by war situations. It is hardly necessary to point out in detail the opportunities which prevail during wartime for the development of conflicts.[39] Every soldier is moved to action by sentiments of loyalty and by a desire to secure and keep the approval of his fellowmen. A battle front, however, is full of fearful situations. The whole situation may become so highly emotionalized as to thwart the possibility of either trial-and-error or intelligent reconstruction of the conflicting tendencies. Long-continued fighting may induce such extreme measures of fatigue as to make a soldier more open to non-adjustive reactions or to regressive reactions than he would normally be. In any case,

[36] Fisher, V. E., *op. cit.*, pp. 89 ff. Also, Wells, F. L., "Mental Regression; Its Conceptions and Types." *Psychiat. Bull.*, 1916, IX, 445-492.
[37] Cf. Morgan, J. J. B., *The Psychology of the Unadjusted School Child*. New York: The Macmillan Co., 1924, *passim*.
[38] Cf. Morgan, J. J. B., *The Psychology of Abnormal People*. New York: Longmans, Green and Co., 1928, Chapter XIV and *passim*.
[39] Cf. McDougall, W., "Four Cases of 'Regression' in Soldiers. *J. Abnorm. Psychol.*, 1920, XV, 136-156.

numerous instances have been cited of soldiers who have attempted to resolve baffling situations by resorting to earlier and more infantile modes of response. These instances are of interest to the teacher because they show so clearly what the mechanisms behind regressive behavior are and how such behavior can be met by a person who is alert to their early appearance and to the home or school conditions which may occasion them.

5. *Repression:* We have already found that the nervous system works in such a way that some of its processes will be facilitated while others will be inhibited or repressed.[40] Although the experimental work in this field is rather obscure, it is still certain that inhibition is a fundamental feature of nerve function. On some occasions, however, it looks as though inhibition could take a much more extreme form, in which case we speak of repression. The word "repression" means that there are times when a person will, in the face of a difficult situation, evade the situation simply by repressing or attempting to forget a part of the issues or desires involved. It has been noted, for example, that many small children will attempt to forget highly unpleasant experiences and that older children, especially girls, will try to forget disturbing sex experiences.[41]

It is sometimes assumed that the word "repression" takes us into quite another order of fact than those suggested by the word "inhibition." The various schools of psychoanalysis, for example, resort to the doctrine that there must be some phase of the mind or of the ego which can act as a censor of both desires and experiences. The censor is frequently described as an aggressive agent which can actually thrust back unusual desires into the subconscious and keep them there save where the subconscious transforms them into some socially approvable action. In this case, they can come into the consciousness either during dreaming or through a witticism which is not too salacious, by slips of the tongue, or by unintended references to the objects desired. The important point about these doctrines of repression is that neither repression nor inhibition implies the destruction of an experience or a desire. On the contrary, it must be granted that if there are energy values represented by desires, these energy values will persist even though they do not manifest themselves in overt action.[42]

This is not the place, however, to consider theories of repression and neither shall we try to take account of the various definitions

[40] Cf. Fisher, V. E., *op. cit.,* pp. 131 ff.
[41] Cf. Sendrick, I., *op. cit., passim.*
[42] Cf. Holt, E. B., *The Freudian Wish and Its Place in Ethics.* New York: Henry Holt and Co., 1915, *passim.*

that have been offered for the subconscious mind within which unexpressed desires may be lodged.[43] The important fact is that certain types of conflict can be settled simply by transforming one of the parties to the conflict. This party is, as we have said, neither destroyed nor always rendered wholly harmless. It can be shown with some degree of assurance that many of the persons lodged in psychopathic hospitals are there in part because repressed tendencies to action have finally sought new channels of escape which are at least bizarre, not to say harmful, to the patient himself and to the group in which he lives. It is at this point that methods of resolving conflicts lead over into the field of abnormal psychology. This is a field which lies outside of the scope of our study.

The significance of repression for teachers is simply this. If repression takes place and if the desires that are repressed seek, as a rule, some other outlet which may be harmful, it would seem to follow that desires to action should be trained in some useful direction rather than simply thwarted. As the student knows, a good many phases of our social memories operate more steadily to repress native urges than they do to redirect them into useful channels. If a teacher is to become effective, therefore, in handling native urges, he must know how these native urges can be transformed into secondary or sublimated types. This is, in part, as we have seen, the task of transforming the primary tissue needs into suitable types of secondary desires or purposes and ideals.

The need for sublimated forms of action is particularly impressive in the case of the sex impulses. It begins to look as though many of the perplexing problems of adolescent education are created by the fact that up until the time of adolescence, that is, up until the time when the sex organs become functionally mature, many children are left in complete ignorance concerning the nature and significance of these functions.[44] The social mores under which they have been trained have seemed to avoid so carefully many of the contingencies raised by sex maturity that the adolescent is caught almost unawares by his new powers. Some of the studies that have been made on coming of age in primitive society, where sex matters are taken much more naturally than they are in "civilized" communities, show that the period of adolescence need not be a period of desperation.

[43] The *locus classicus* is Hartmann, E. von, *Philosophy of the Unconscious* (Trans. by W. C. Coupland). New York: Harcourt, Brace and Co., 1931.
[44] Cf. Symonds, P. M., *op. cit.*, Chapter X.

A great many experiments are now being tried in connection with the problems known as sex education.[45] There are those who are convinced that most children should receive straightforward and authoritative instruction in these matters just as fast as their own curious questions are raised. Still others adhere to the view that the process of attaining sex maturity should be explained by romantic appeals to reproduction in flowery plants or by dismissing the whole question with some such comment as, "God brings babies," "The doctor brings babies," and the like. Experiments are also being tried on the effect of introducing sex instruction in courses in physical hygiene. The results of these several experiments seem to show at least one thing rather clearly, viz., that the art of teaching a child about sex matters and of enabling it to adjust itself to sex differences is an art that is intimately related to a tremendous number of other factors. Among these factors we may mention the amount of information children have picked up from their playmates, the degree of rapport that has been established between the parents and the child, and the personal place which the teacher occupies in the affections of the child. The chances are that in view of the many ways in which sex problems are related to other types of problems, no formal curriculum on sex instruction can be established. It is to be hoped, of course, that a teaching problem which is so difficult as this will continue to receive frank and courageous attention, for it seems to be quite clear that a major portion of the maladjustments found in children and in adults owe their origin to distortions of the sex urges.

6. *Compensatory Actions:* The last of the devices which are commonly used to settle conflicts is described by the word "compensation." As the student knows, this word has been given a philosophical or ethical meaning which runs somewhat as follows. In order to make people happy with their lot, it has been argued that, where there has been a major loss, there must be some compensating gain. This thought is commonly expressed in the saying, "It is a long road which has no turning."

At the present time, however, the word has gained quite a different meaning. It refers to some of the devices which human beings use in order to make up for their feeling of inferiority. If the person is faced with a difficult situation, he may attribute the difficulty either to the fact that the situation itself is more than he can

---

[45] Richmond, W. V., *An Introduction to Sex Education.* New York: Farrar and Rinehart, Inc., 1934.

possibly stand or that he himself has some weakness which will interfere with his success.[46]

When, therefore, any person comes to believe that he is actually inferior, he can be characterized as possessing an inferiority complex.[47] An inferiority complex, however, stands in direct opposition to the desire for action. As we have seen, there are some people who hold that, in addition to the desire for action, there is also a self-regarding instinct or an instinct for self-assertion.[48] In any case, the desire for activity is not compatible with an inferiority complex and it becomes necessary, then, for the inferior person to find some compensatory mode of action that will resolve his complex. There are at least six different types of compensatory action.

A. OVEREMPHASIS: In the first place, it will sometimes happen that a person who has located the weakness or the inferiority which keeps him from attaining success will react to the situation by overemphasizing it.[49] Let us suppose, for example, that a child has unwittingly come to the conclusion that it is really not quite so bright as its playmates. The overreaction in this case will consist of an attempt to overestimate its own intelligence or to engage feverishly in types of study that would seem to imply high measures of intelligence. In short, the child becomes a braggart.

The same device appears rather frequently among adults and it accounts, perhaps, for the appearance of a great many of those persons who are known as cranks. If, for example, an adult has become overimpressed with the fact that he has weak lungs, he may respond to the situation by exercising his lungs until he can boast of a chest expansion which is almost abnormal.

B. IDENTIFICATION: The second type of compensation is known as identification. If, for any reason, a person feels that he is not competent in and of himself to attain success or to achieve suitable measures of distinction, he will try to make up for his failure by associating himself with some person who is distinguished or with some organization which can lend its prestige to him.[50] Many college students, for example, join fraternities not because they feel

---

[46] Cf. Fisher, V. E., op. cit., Chapter VI; Robinson, E. S., "A Concept of Compensation and Its Psychological Setting." *J. Abnorm. and Soc. Psychol.,* 1923, XVII, 383-394.

[47] Cf. Sherman, M., *Mental Hygiene and Education.* New York: Longmans, Green and Co., 1934, Chapter V and *passim.*

[48] Cf. Dunlap, K., op. cit., Chapter IV.

[49] Morgan, J. J. B., *Keeping a Sound Mind.* New York: The Macmillan Co., 1934, Chapter VIII and IX.

[50] Fisher, V. E., op. cit., pp. 108 ff. Also, Vaughan, W. F., *The Lure of Superiority.* New York: Henry Holt and Co., 1928, *passim.*

that they have anything to contribute to the fraternity but because they feel that the fraternity might have something to contribute to them. If it contributes nothing more than prestige, a new member will feel that he has been duly compensated.

C. DISPARAGING REMARKS: A still more vicious type of compensation expresses itself both in a deliberate and in a witless desire to belittle others.[51] It is clear, of course, that if one person is actually smaller in personality and in intellect than another, he can make himself larger by decreasing the stature of those around him. Stature can be diminished, of course, by finding fault, by gossiping, and by criticism which has no other function than destruction.

All of these methods are used even by small children who, as they shift from one group to another, often resort to disparaging remarks about persons whom they have just left. Another phase of this device for attaining real compensation is displayed in the conduct of those who will never take responsibility on themselves for events or situations that go wrong. When a child, for example, stumbles over a chair, it very rarely blames itself. On the contrary, it attributes the fault to the chair.[52] In the same way, older people are little inclined to place themselves in the wrong. Moreover, it often happens that adult persons who have achieved distinction are reported to have gained their new place not because of any merit of their own but because of some lucky chance or some personal intervention on the part of a friend.

D. MALINGERING: There is one type of compensatory behavior which leads rather easily to a more extreme and even a dangerous condition. If a person who is not adequate to a difficult task can find some physical infirmity which will explain his inadequacy he can be pretty sure that those around him will understand. It is not always possible, however, to discover a real infirmity and some may be compelled to create one. The process of creating an infirmity which can be used as an excuse for failure is known as malingering.[53]

The student probably knows already that this was a compensatory device which was used with great frequency during the late war. Let us suppose, for example, that the soldier who has been fatigued by prolonged exposure begins to react in an overemotionalized way to a new call for action. It is clear, of course, that if he can feign lameness in arm or foot, blindness, or deafness, he will have an

---

[51] Vaughan, W. F., "The Psychology of Compensation." *Psychol. Rev.*, 1926, XXXIII, 467-479.
[52] Fisher, V. E., *op. cit.*, pp. 115 ff.
[53] Cf. Dorcus, R. M., and Shaffer, G. W., Chapter IV and *passim*.

excuse sufficient to relieve him from further duty. We do not have the space to examine the machinery by means of which feigned illnesses of this type are actually transformed into functional illnesses. It is a plain fact, however, that the transformation does take place and thus the difficult situation is solved.[54]

It is thought that malingering can explain some of the behavior problems which appear both at home and at school when children refuse to eat or refuse to do some of the work that has been assigned to them.[55] It seems to be certain that some children, at least, refuse to eat simply because their refusal is a way of gaining attention. Every teacher will, of course, excuse a child if he can show that he really has an ache or a pain in his body. Since the evidence in the case must be supplied by the child himself, the teacher must be fairly clever in his diagnosis both of the malingering and of the factors surrounding the child which might give rise to this mode of compensation.

E. DAY-DREAMING: Still another type of compensation is to be found in day-dreaming. It is clear, of course, that if a difficult situation or a great desire cannot be handled by overt manual action, it can be handled by ideational action or by implicit speech. To be sure, day-dreaming or imaginative play can perform a very useful service in connection with problem-solving and even in connection with normal psychological growth.[56] The average teacher, however, can readily tell the difference between day-dreams and fantasies of this type and day-dreams or fantasies which are really compensatory in character.[57] The chances are that compensatory fantasies are more habitual or long-continued and that they occur most frequently in conjunction with certain types of situations.

The use of compensatory fantasies and day-dreaming has been materially modified by the moving picture theatre. One may, to be sure, see a moving picture for the same reason that one might attend a drama or a musical festival; but there is every reason to suppose that the moving picture makes its greatest appeal because of the compensations which it affords. The person who has neither the courage nor the skill to gain certain ends for himself can see these ends gained by proxy on the screen. The relation of the moving picture, then, to educative processes not only as regards their

[54] Cf. Hurst, A. F., *The Psychology of the Special Senses and Their Functional Disorders.* London: Oxford Univ. Press, 1920, *passim.*
[55] Morgan, J. J. B., *op. cit.,* Chapter IX.
[56] *Ibid.,* Chapter VII.
[57] Cf. Robinson, E. S., "The Compensatory Function of Make-believe Play." *Psychol. Rev.,* 1920, XXVII, 429-439.

ADJUSTMENT AND MENTAL HYGIENE

compensatory functions but as regards other features of development as well has become a major problem.[58]

V. MENTAL HYGIENE

1. *Introduction:* We have devoted a considerable part of this chapter to a brief recital of the nature of conflict and to a list of the devices commonly used in order to resolve conflicts, because the way must be prepared for an adequate understanding of the real functions of mental hygiene. As we have said at the beginning of the chapter, mental hygiene is that type of instruction and that attitude which favors the attainment of proper measures of adjustment. In other words, mental hygiene is a phrase which lays emphasis upon those forms of teaching which will prevent the development of conflict and will resort to compensatory and other devices. Where mental hygiene cannot be actually preventive, it can help teachers to detect at as early an age as possible the beginnings of maladjustments of different types so that these beginnings can be interrupted before they have led to a more serious condition.[59]

Neither of these features of mental hygiene is quite so simple as may appear at first sight. From one of the comments made above, for example, the student may infer that mental hygiene ought to furnish a way of eliminating the possibility of conflict. This means that all of the primary desires should be sublimated as early as possible. The word "sublimation" simply refers to the doctrine that whatever energies are resident in the primary desires can be directed into new channels of effort.

As a very simple example we may take the hunger desire. The immediate source of satisfaction of this desire is, of course, food. Our common experience tells us, however, that a great many different types of work may be pursued for long periods of time, partly, because they are motivated in the last analysis by the hunger desire and, partly, because they furnish a direct means of satisfying this desire. The man who has been without food for a long time will say, of course, that he cannot eat a book or regain his strength from seeing a great pageant; but, given a normal access to food, the same man may begin to write books or to direct pageants.[60]

[58] See the references to this feature of education cited on page 150.
[59] A book written directly from the preventive point of view is Symonds, P. M., *Mental Hygiene of the School Child.* New York: The Macmillan Co., 1934.
[60] We have already discussed this problem in Chapter V. See Dashiell, J. F., *Fundamentals of Objective Psychology.* Boston: Houghton Mifflin Co., 1928, Chapter IX.

2. *Environmental Changes:* It has been rather easy to suppose that mental hygiene should strive, first of all, to change the child; for it has seemed natural to suppose that if a child is in any way maladjusted to its environment, the difficulty must lie in the child rather than with the environment. It has been shown, however, that a great many conflicts may be avoided much more simply by changing the environment rather than by attempting to change the child.[61] This fact holds true, in particular, of persons who have already achieved a considerable level of maturity in their major motives, attitudes, and skills. As we have seen, certain types of the learning process become much less effective at older ages than they were at earlier ages. They are less effective because there is more inertia in human nature against which they must work. One might, to be sure, carry on a long program of reeducation and thus issue, so to speak, a new model of any given child, but in a great many cases it is a much simpler task to try to find an environment which will fit the child.

3. *Conclusion:* It is still too early to see what the net outcome of the mental hygiene movement is going to be. If, as had been indicated earlier in the chapter, the movement is in part, at least, an attempt to correct some of the faults of the more formal educative process, we might expect formal education gradually to recognize the scenes of its failures and to take the measures necessary to redirect its teaching methods. There is, however, another phase of the whole movement. Mental hygiene has, as one of its purposes, the prevention of maladjustments and other distortions of personality which might lead to unsocial conduct and certainly to unhappiness. This, however, is a phase of training which hitherto has fallen to religious instruction; but in either case the emotionalized forms of action are in question. The development of mental hygiene has meant, therefore, the tardy recognition of the fact that emotionalized forms of conduct can be tutored. In short, then, this move on the part of education is a move away from the older view which, by implication at least, limited the more formal types of education to that group of functions usually called intellectual.

READINGS

A basic survey of background materials upon which any study of the mechanisms of adjustment should be based can be found in Bentley, M., and

[61] Cf. Dunlap, K., *Habits, Their Making and Unmaking.* New York: Liveright Publishing Corp., 1932, Chapter IX.

ADJUSTMENT AND MENTAL HYGIENE

Cowdry, E. V. (Ed.), *The Problem of Mental Disorder*. New York: McGraw-Hill Book Co., 1934.

A popularized account of the mechanisms of human conduct have been written by Meninger, K. A., *The Human Mind*. New York: A. A. Knopf, 1930. For a popular application of a particular point of view, see Adler, A., *Guiding the Child on the Principles of Individual Psychology*. New York: Greenberg, Inc., 1930; *What a Life Should Mean To You*. Boston: Little, Brown, and Co., 1931.

There are a great many readable books in the general field of mental hygiene. Among these we may mention Bagby, E., *The Psychology of Personality*. New York: Henry Holt and Co., 1928; Burnham, W. H., *The Wholesome Personality*. New York: D. Appleton-Century Co., 1932; Groves, E. R., *Personality and Social Adjustment*. New York: Longmans, Green and Co., 1931; Groves, E. R., and Blanchard, P., *Introduction to Mental Hygiene*. New York: Henry Holt and Co., 1930; La Rue, D. W., *Mental Hygiene*. New York: The Macmillan Co., 1927; Morgan, J. J. B., *The Psychology of the Unadjusted School Child*. New York: The Macmillan Co., 1924; Morgan, J. J. B., *Keeping a Sound Mind*. The Macmillan Co., 1934; Sherman, M., *Mental Hygiene in Education*. New York: Longmans, Green and Co., 1934; Symonds, P. M., *Mental Hygiene and the School Child*. New York: The Macmillan Co., 1934; Zachry, C. B., *Personality Adjustments of School Children*. New York: Charles Scribner's Sons, 1929.

Special problems of various types are considered in the following books: Anderson, V. V., *Psychiatry in Education*. New York: Harper and Bros., 1932; Boorman, W. R., *Developing Personality in Boys*. New York: The Macmillan Co., 1929; Brooks, F. D., *Psychology of Adolescence*. Boston: Houghton Mifflin Co., 1929; Healy, W., et al., *Reconstructing Behavior in Youth*. New York: A. A. Knopf, 1929; Koos, L. V., and Kefauver, G. W., *Guidance in Secondary Schools*. New York: The Macmillan Co., 1932; Myers, G. C., *Schoolroom Hazards to the Mental Hygiene of Children*. New York: Nat. Com. for Ment. Hygiene, 1928; Pressey, L. C., *Some College Students and Their Problems*. Columbus, Ohio: State Univ. Press, 1929; Richmond, W. V., *The Adolescent Boy*. New York: Farrar and Rinehart, Inc., 1933; Richmond, W. V., *The Adolescent Girl*. New York: The Macmillan Co., 1925; Thom, D. A., *Normal Youth and its Everyday Problems*. New York: D. Appleton-Century Co., 1932; Wickman, P. K., *Children's Behavior and Teachers' Attitudes*. New York: The Commonwealth Fund, 1928.

CHAPTER NINETEEN

THE CONCEPT OF EFFICIENCY IN THE SCHOOLROOM

I. Adjustment and Efficiency

1. *Ratios and Values:* The problems that were discussed in the last chapter imply a set of values rather than a ratio between amounts of money or amounts of effort, on the one hand, and amounts of services rendered, on the other. That is, if a person is trained so that he can adjust himself comfortably and fruitfully to the world in which he lives, it has already been taken for granted that a proper measure of value has been placed upon the word "adjustment." As a pair of typical instances, let us take a colony of ants, on the one hand, and a musician like Schubert, on the other. The colony of ants is certainly adjusted to its environment because each member of the colony has some particular task to carry out and because the colony as a whole gets along very well in the particular world in which it lives.[1] A human being, however, is not very much inclined toward this level of adjustment because he thinks of it as more or less mechanical, highly unimaginative, and certainly very much "frozen" in character. He would prefer change and even the occasional appearance of complex and difficult situations in which he will be challenged to exercise his ingenuity. Since, however, human beings possess a considerable measure of ingenuity, they usually feel that they are even better adjusted to a more complex and difficult environment than is the ant to its simpler surroundings.[2]

Those who have read the life of Schubert know that he was intensely maladjusted to his environment. Schubert was unhappy, afflicted with disease, and unable to find suitable measures of comfort and satisfaction in the persons around him. He sought to escape from the illusions of life by immersing himself in a world of melodies. We might say, then, that Schubert was maladjusted

[1] Cf. Wheeler, W. M., *Ants: Their Structure, Development, and Behavior.* New York: Columbia Univ. Press, 1910.
[2] The problems of adjustment are exceedingly complex. Consult, for example, Bentley, M. (Ed.), *The Problem of Mental Disorder.* New York: McGraw-Hill Book Co., 1934, *passim.*

THE CONCEPT OF EFFICIENCY IN SCHOOLROOM 657

to the "real" world. On the other hand, it has been argued that the creation of melodies such as we owe to Schubert's genius might not have been possible had he not been driven to them by the very intensity of his struggle to achieve happiness.[3] Granted that such an argument can be supported, it would seem to follow, if we judge Schubert in terms of his musical creations alone, that he must have been highly adapted to some other environment than the one we call "real." The rest of us describe this environment as an aesthetic environment, and we are beholden to Schubert for what he has done for us with respect to it.

2. *Efficiency:* We may infer, then, that the problems discussed in the last chapter belong to our concepts of the quality of life. They have to do with such terms as happiness, comfort, ease of mind, or freedom from worry, from anxiety, and from depression. In this chapter, we turn our faces in a different direction. Now, instead of looking for values, we shall be looking for ratios between expenditure of energy and services rendered. We are to inquire about the meaning of efficiency insofar as it is related to the educative process.

The term "efficiency" has come to us from the science of economics.[4] At first it had to do with the relation between the effort expended and the amount of product gained. As a rule, the effort expended referred only to muscular work or to the cost of operating a factory; but now the word has been extended to cover expenditures of all types. In general, the concept of efficiency requires that some favorable ratio shall obtain between the time spent, the money spent, or the effort spent, and the results that are achieved in the way of usable goods.

As an example, let us take the meaning of physical efficiency in the schoolroom.[5] It can be said that the teaching process is most efficient which has removed as many physical obstacles to good work as can be removed. For another illustration we may take study habits. The person who gets the most results from a given study hour can be called more efficient than the person who gets fewer results. For still another illustration let us take the effect of fatigue or of different drugs upon the different services that can be rendered by a skill. As we shall see, certain drugs modify the usefulness of

---

[3] Cf. Langfeld, H. S., *Conflict and Adjustment in Art*, in Problems of Personality. New York: Harcourt, Brace and Co., 1925.
[4] See the article "Efficiency" in Seligman, E. R. A. (Ed.), *Encyclopedia of the Social Sciences*. New York: The Macmillan Co., 1930.
[5] Cf. Steel, E. W., and White, E. G., *Hygiene of Community, School and Home*. New York: Harper and Bros., 1932, *passim.*

skills. Fatigue also modifies their usefulness. Efficiency, therefore, would require that those drugs which have an adverse effect on skill should be avoided. It would require also that the use of skills should be discontinued whenever fatigue products interfere with them.

3. *Purpose of the Chapter:* It is the purpose of this chapter, then, to consider some of the problems of efficiency insofar as they are related to schoolroom procedures. While we shall not very often mention ergs of energy, minutes of time, or dollars in money, it will always be implied that quantitative measures are under discussion. Where actual quantities are not expressed, ratios of a quantitative character will be implied. In the classroom, for example, the teacher will lay before each of the students a certain amount of work that must be done in a given period of time. It not infrequently happens that students will be rated according to the proportionate amount of work done as well as according to its relative value.[6]

II. Psychological Work

1. *Introduction:* The student will, no doubt, have observed that we have already used the word "work" in several different ways. Sometimes we have spoken of the work that a machine will do and at other times we have been speaking of the sort of work that is done in the classroom. In the first case, it is easy enough to give precise meaning to the term for, in general, work is done whenever there is a transformation of energy from one form into another. In more exact terms, the word "work" implies that a force has moved a mass against a certain amount of resistance. For work of this type, a definite formula can be written out.

In psychology, the situation is wholly different. This is true, in part, because the character of the work itself seems to be different and, in part, because the whole matter is increased in complexity by the distinctions that are sometimes drawn between physiological and psychological work. In order to discern the foundations for this distinction let us take several examples. When a man runs 100 yards in ten seconds, he uses up a certain amount of energy. It has been computed that his body will develop approximately thirteen horse power, only a half of which is actually expended in moving

---

[6] An excellent survey of the problems of efficiency is to be found in Robinson, E. S., "Work of the Integrated Organism," in Murchison, C. (Ed.), *Handbook of General Experimental Psychology.* Worcester, Mass.: Clark Univ. Press, 1934, Chap. XII.

his body from the starting line to the finish.[7] In this case one naturally thinks of the muscles of the runner as doing the most amount of work. In learning a vocabulary, however, or in the "mental" multiplication of one three-digit number by another, it is easy to assume that the actual amount of muscular work must be very small indeed. In its place we may suppose that mental work is being done and thus we give witness to the distinction which we commonly draw between mental and physical work.

2. *Mental and Physical Work:* The action of the muscles of the body, as in running 100 yards at high speed, resembles the work done by a machine much more closely than does mental multiplication. When we speak of mental multiplication, we may mean either that some sort of mind stuff is actually working, perhaps as the body is known to work, or we may mean that mental multiplication is a product of the work done by the nervous system. At the present time, it seems hardly fruitful to suppose that there is any kind of mental stuff which can do work. We are left, therefore, with a distinction between work that is done by the muscles as opposed to work that is done by the nervous system and by the other bodily instruments involved in all of the psychological operations. Of these instruments the nervous system is, perhaps, the most important and some persons, therefore, have defined mental work as that which is done by the "connection-system" of any animal.[8]

At the present time it does not seem fruitful to try to draw a sharp distinction either between mental and physical work or between psychological and physiological work.[9] The general setting for any consideration of human work is furnished by the wide variations that may obtain in the relationships between stimulus-situations and modes of response. As we have seen in earlier chapters, these relationships are at least five in character. That relationship described by the words "attention" and "interest" suggests that there may be wide variations in the ability of a child to keep its attention fixed upon a particular task. Since the word "attention" refers to events that are happening both in the nervous system and in the bodily structures, one can easily infer that work is being done without attempting to distinguish between its neural and its other components.

[7] Cf. Hill, A. V., *Living Machinery.* New York: Harcourt, Brace and Co., 1927, *passim.*
[8] Thorndike, E. L., *Educational Psychology,* Vol. III. "Mental Work and Fatigue and Individual Differences and Their Causes." New York: Teachers Coll., Columbia Univ., 1914, p. 3.
[9] For a recent summary of the literature, see Bills, M. A., "Mental Work." *Psychol. Bull.,* 1931, XXVIII, 505-552.

The same considerations hold true of the circumstances under which motives become effective in regulating behavior, of the whole domain of emotionalized actions, of problem-solving, and of the long-time organization or patterning of modes of action. It is sometimes said that the work of the digestive and respiratory apparatus cannot be called psychological, but even this type of work may make some difference in the quality of the unique relations between stimulus-situations and modes of action which we have described as giving rise to moods and to emotionalized actions.

In view of these considerations, it seems fruitful, at least for the time being, to think of all performances of the human body as though they belonged to a single continuum of events. At the one extreme there will be modes of action which appear to have a minimal amount of interest for the psychologist and which may be taken, therefore, as examples of physiological work. At this extreme we might place ditch-digging, running one hundred yards, throwing a baseball, or any other type of gross manual activity. At the other extreme, we might place such activities as composing a piece of poetry, multiplying numbers in "one's head," thinking out a plan for the day's activities, making a decision about the courses to be taken during the next semester, or reading with deep concentration and with a strong intent to remember the contents of this chapter.

Each of these more psychological activities must require a certain amount of activity in the central nervous system. Moreover, they require definite postures of the body and a favorable tonus in each of the muscles contributing to the posture.[10] From one point of view, even the manual activities of an athlete on the football field include these more psychological types of work, for the athlete is often "making up his mind" about a given play or about a particular method for making the play most successful. Even though psychological activity of this sort depends primarily upon the use of the vocal apparatus, as in implicit speech, these activities are always accompanied by a particular posture of the body and by all of the physiological events which enter into rate of metabolism and hence into levels of emotionalized action.[11]

3. *Measures of Work:* In the case of some of the more physiological types of human work, fairly good evidence can be gained of the amount of oxygen consumed during a period of effort, of the

---

[10] Cf. Freeman, G. L., *Introduction to Physiological Psychology*. New York: The Ronald Press, 1934, Chapter XXV.
[11] Cf. Rounds, G. H., and Poffenberger, A. T., "The Measurement of Implicit Speech Reactions." *Amer. J. Physiol.*, 1931, XLIII, 606-612.

amount of carbon dioxide produced, of changes in pulse rate and in respiration rate, and of other indicators of the transformation of energy in the body. It is in the study of these indicators, then, that the physiologist and the psychologist find a method of measuring the amount of work done or the amount of effort being expended. As an example, we may take a major study of such heavy muscular work as climbing a mountain, running a treadmill, or running up a flight of stairs. The subjects in such an experiment can be equipped with suitable devices for measuring oxygen intake, the amount of carbon dioxide produced, or changes in bodily temperature, in pulse rate, and in respiration. These changes are so closely related to distances moved per minute or to load carried that they have been accepted as fairly reliable measures of the more mechanical features of human performance.[12] As soon as the work period begins, the rate of metabolism rises from its resting value to a much higher level. From this point forward there are characteristic changes, depending upon the length of the work period and the amount of work that is done. Rate of recovery appears to depend upon these same factors.[13]

These same methods have been used in order to study the energy requirement of the more truly psychological types of work, such as arithmetical calculation. In one such study the subjects were asked to do silent multiplication of two-place numbers by two-place numbers during three to four successive fifteen-minute periods. The experimenters found marked increase in heart rate and in respiration, an increase in the volume of air passing through the lungs, and a slight increase in the production of carbon dioxide and in the consumption of oxygen.[14] To be sure, a part of these changes must be due to the muscular work involved in the postures which accompany multiplication; but there is no reason to suppose that a part of them may not be due to energy transformations in the central nervous system. These energy transformations may be exceedingly small as compared with those that take place elsewhere in the body,

[12] Cf. Benedict, F. G., and Murschhauser, H., "Physiology: Energy Transformations During Horizontal Walking." *Proc. Nat. Acad. Sci.*, 1915, I, 597-600; Benedict, F. G., and Cathcart, E. P., *Muscular Work: A Metabolic Study with Special Reference to the Efficiency of the Human Body as a Machine.* Washington, D. C.: Carnegie Institute, 1913, *passim.*

[13] Schubert, H. J. P., "Energy Cost Measurements on the Curve of Work." *Arch. Psychol.*, 1932, XXII (No. 139).

[14] Benedict, F. G., and Benedict, C. G., "The Energy Requirements of Intense Mental Effort." *Proc. Nat. Acad. Sci.*, 1930, XVI, 438-443. Also Harmon, F. L., "The Effects of Noise upon Certain Psychological and Physiological Processes." *Arch. Psychol.*, 1933, XXIII (No. 147).

but it cannot be seriously argued that "mental work" can be done without at least a small measure of metabolic cost.[15]

All of the changes of which we have spoken, both in connection with physiological and with psychological work, increase in value when they are correlated with the output of a subject. In the case of mental multiplication, for example, a preliminary period of training will furnish some sort of standard of comparison against which output at late stages in a long period of work can be projected. The efficiency of a person will depend, first, of course, upon the level of skill which has been reached through proper training periods. When, however, a skill has reached a fair measure of stability, marked changes in the products of this skill, brought about by a long-continued exercise of the skill, can be compared with the metabolic cost. As we shall see later on in this chapter, the method of research just suggested lies at the basis of almost all studies on the effect of fatigue.

III. THE EFFECT OF PHYSICAL CONDITIONS ON EFFICIENCY

1. *Organic Conditions:* The phrase "physical conditions" may refer either to the organic condition of the student himself or to the environmental circumstances of a physical sort which surround him during his schoolroom activities. It is hardly necessary to argue that the organic quality of the student must be as favorable as possible if a high quality of work is to be expected from him. Defective vision, diseased tonsils, improper breathing habits, insufficient food and clothing, and other similar factors belong to the total picture named by organic conditions.[16] Of these factors Thorndike has written:

"The inner responsiveness of an animal to occasions for mental work is most economically improved by improving its general health. Other more direct influences limited to the connection-system there may be; but the safest hope is the maintenance of the health of the entire body of the machine. Consider the abolition of the effects of indigestion, rickets, chorea, and scarlet fever or of insufficient oxygen, food, and sleep in the case of children; consider the abolition of malaria, tuberculosis and alcoholism in the case of adults; consider even such a minor effect as a 'cold.' "[17]

[15] Cf. Rounds, G. H., and Poffenberger, A. T., "The Measurement of Implicit Speech Reactions." *Amer. J. Psychol.,* 1931, XLIII, 606-612.
[16] Cf. Baker, S. J., *Child Hygiene.* New York: Harper and Bros., 1925, *passim.*
[17] Thorndike, E. L., *Educational Psychology, Briefer Course.* New York: Columbia Univ. Press, 1923, p. 324.

A. VISION: The importance of organic conditions is revealed, in part, by the fact that of the twenty-five-million-odd children in the public schools, nearly ninety-five per cent have at least one decayed tooth, fifteen per cent have diseased adenoids or tonsils, over half have been or are infected with tuberculosis, nearly one-fourth are undernourished, fourteen per cent do not have normal hearing, fifteen per cent have more or less serious eye trouble, and about five per cent have special defects.[18] To be sure, the teacher in the schoolroom cannot do very much about some of these defects, but he can, at the same time, perform a very important service with respect to them.

There is no place where weak eyes can be discovered more quickly than in the frowns which characterize the faces in almost every schoolroom. Moreover, it usually takes only a little inquiry to discover that retardation in schoolwork is often related to some special sensory handicap. The teacher himself cannot be expected to test eyes, but it would seem to be one of his functions to be sensitive to symptoms of eyestrain. It is almost certain that a child will not complain of such a strain. Most children are not aware of the source of their difficulty.[19] As we shall see, some remedy for eyestrain can be found in exerting better control over the way in which the schoolroom is illuminated. It is not quite so easy to correct other sensory defects by changing the physical surroundings, but even in these cases the teacher can make himself sensitive to their appearance and report them to the proper authorities.

B. MALNUTRITION: One of the most common mistakes made with undernourished children is to suppose that such children simply do not have enough to eat. It is now fairly certain that malnutrition is probably less often related to insufficient food than it is to improper types of food. It might be said, of course, that the problem of supplying children with the proper food is a home problem rather than a school problem. But even though it is a home problem, it is not on that account guaranteed that the parents of the child themselves know what ought to constitute an adequate diet.

The functions of the teacher, therefore, may be exercised not only toward the child in detecting the symptoms of malnutrition such as dullness, listlessness, and lack of vitality, but toward the parents as well. If it can be seen that a child is chronically tired or that it is

[18] Cf. Terman, L. M., and Almack, J. C., *The Hygiene of the School Child.* Boston: Houghton Mifflin Co., 1929, *passim.*
[19] Wood, T. D., "Conserving the Sight of School Children." *Nat. Com. for the Prevention of Blindness.* New York, 1925.

664   INTRODUCTION TO EDUCATIONAL PSYCHOLOGY

frequently subject to colds, the answer probably lies in the nature of its diet, say its vitamin or other content. Moreover, it would seem that if a child is stupid, inattentive, and lacking in spontaneity, the cause does not necessarily lie in a low I.Q. To be sure, all children have remarkable powers of adaptability. Many of them recover rapidly even from prolonged periods of malnutrition. But the hope of ultimate recovery should not be substituted for direct attention to stupidity which is the result of a low I.Q. as compared with stupidity which is the result of improper diet.[20]

C. INFECTIONS: One set of obscure symptoms of improper organic condition are those related to various focal infections. A tooth, for example, may give every appearance of health and yet, from the roots, infection may be spreading to every part of the body. These infections easily lead to irritability, nervousness, and inattentiveness. They seem to give rise to measures of fatigue out of all proportion to the amount of exercise taken. They may even contribute indirectly to improper forms of emotionalized action. The more remote effects are still more harmful, for it seems to be quite clear that a focal infection in the teeth or in the adenoids and tonsils may contribute to indigestion, diseases of the heart, and tuberculosis, to say nothing of minor disorders.[21]

D. GLANDULAR DEFECTS: Still more obscure are modifications of organic condition which have their origin in the glands of internal secretion. Here again, the teacher cannot be expected to possess the diagnostic ability of a physician, but some of the types of nervousness induced by glandular defects ought not to escape the vigilant teacher. There is only one glandular disorder that reveals itself objectively, viz., that disturbance in the thyroid gland commonly known as goiter. In any case, where there is a definite picture of sluggishness, listlessness, and dullness, on the one hand, or of nervousness, jumpiness, or overexcitability, on the other, the teacher should prepare to report the case to the school nurse.[22]

E. POSTURE: Not the least of the secondary physical conditions which must be watched closely are those created by faulty postures and by the sedentary character of a day's work in the schoolroom. Some attempts are made to avoid the fatigue resulting from schoolroom postures by recess periods midway in the forenoon and after-

[20] Cf. Roberts, L. J., *Nutrition Work with Children.* Chicago: Univ. of Chicago Press, 1927, *passim.*
[21] Johnson, C. N., "Dental Hygiene for the Child." *Amer. J. Public Health,* 1925, XV, 107-110.
[22] Cf. Selbert, N., *Child Health.* New York: W. B. Saunders Co., 1931, *passim.* Also, Bentley, M. (Ed.), *op. cit.,* Chapter XI.

noon sessions. In spite of these recesses, however, it is fairly difficult for active young people to sit still for any length of time. Their growing fatigue and hence an increase in the organic obstacles to good work is revealed by increasing restlessness and even irritability. These are the factors which have led to studies on proper sitting postures, more efficient types of chairs, and the proper elevation of the desk. To some, the expenditure of school funds for purposes such as these has seemed unwise; but most persons have now come to realize that learning is hastened and the general efficiency of the study hour increased by proper supervision over all of the factors within the schoolroom itself that might contribute to a suitable bodily condition.[23]

2. *Environmental Conditions:* The other group of physical conditions which bear upon efficiency in school work includes such items as climatic and atmospheric conditions (*e.g.*, temperature, humidity, and composition of the air), lighting, and the presence or absence of distractions.

A. VENTILATION: A very large amount of work has been done on the atmospheric conditions which make for and against efficiency, partly because men have come to see that the conditions furnished by schoolrooms have not always been favorable to the educational process. Thorndike, McCall, and Chapman, working under the auspices of the New York State Commission on Ventilation, have made an elaborate series of tests on the efficiency of students working under rigidly controlled experimental conditions where changes in temperature, humidity, movement of the air, and the like were the main factors.[24] Sixty subjects were asked to name colors, cancel numbers, name opposites, perform additions, mentally multiply three-place numbers by three-place numbers, multiply three-place numbers by two-place numbers, typewrite, grade specimens of handwriting, and grade English compositions. Climatic conditions were varied all the way from the most favorable (that is, 68 degrees Fahrenheit, 50 per cent relative humidity, and 45 cubic feet per person per minute of outside air) to those that were as strenuous as one might ever meet (86 degrees Fahrenheit, 80 per cent relative humidity, and no circulation or change of air).

Some of the much-quoted conclusions of this study run as follows:

[23] Cf. Bennett, H. E., "A Study of School Posture and Seating." *Element. School J.,* 1925, XXVI, 50-57.
[24] Thorndike, E. L., McCall, W. A., and Chapman, J. C., "Ventilation in Relation to Mental Work." *Teachers Coll. Contrib. to Educ.,* 1916 (No. 78).

"With the forms of work and lengths of period used, we find that when an individual is urged to do his best he does as much, and does it as well, and improves as rapidly in a hot, humid, stale, and stagnant air condition (86° F., 80 per cent relative humidity, with no air or only recirculated air, and with no movement of air save what is caused by events in the room and, in the case of recirculation, by the recirculating force), as in an optimum condition (68° F., 50 per cent rel. humid., 45 cu. ft. per person per minute of outside air introduced). . . .

"We find further that when an individual is given work to do that is of no interest or value to him and is deprived even of the means of telling how well he does do it, and is in other ways tempted to relax standards and do work of a poor quality, he still shows no inferiority in the quality of the product produced in stagnant air at 86°, 80 per cent r.h. with 30 to 40 parts CO_2 per 10,000, he being subjected to this condition for 8 hours a day for four successive days and tested on the second, third, and fourth days. There is some evidence that he spends more time on the work, but even this is not certain.

"Finally, we find that when an individual is left to his (or her) own choice as to whether he shall do mental work or read stories, rest, talk, or sleep, he does as much work per hour when the temperature is 75° as when it is 68°."[25]

Other studies have shown the same disturbing effects of unfavorable climatic conditions; but it seems to be clear that a sufficient incentive will make a prodigious difference in efficiency. This fact will come under discussion in a few moments. In the meantime, it should be pointed out that where individuals are working against adverse physical conditions they do so at a greater physiological expense. In one experiment, the subjects were put on a schedule which forced them to lose two hours of sleep regularly. There was no difference in the output or quality of the work; but measurements of the bodily energies involved (as measured by a respiration calorimeter) showed that the highest efficiency was maintained at a cost of 300% more energy than was necessary to maintain the same standard under more favorable conditions. It seems clear from the experiments in this field that the human organism works most efficiently, all things considered, when the temperature is anywhere from 40 to 75 degrees Fahrenheit, the humidity not greater than 60%, and when there is 45 cubic feet of outside air per minute per person.[26] Other things being equal, the temperature may

[25] Thorndike, E. L., McCall, W. A., and Chapman, J. C., "Ventilation in Relation to Mental Work." *Teachers Coll. Contrib. to Educ.,* 1916 (No. 78), p. 82.
[26] Stecher, L. I., "The Effect of Humidity on Nervousness and on General Efficiency." *Arch. of Psychol.,* 1916 (No. 38).

increase without impairing efficiency if the humidity decreases.[27] Even in the most poorly ventilated schools (so far as experimental observation has been extended) the percentage of oxygen has not fallen below 19% and yet it would have to go below 14% before adverse effects would be produced.[28] The major atmospheric determinants of efficiency, then, are temperature and humidity and the amount of movement of the air. Adverse temperatures and humidities can easily be withstood if there is a proper amount of air movement.[29]

B. DIURNAL VARIATIONS: Certain differences in efficiency are known to be associated with the time of day, the day of the week, and with seasonal variations in climate. Gates, for example, has studied variations in efficiency for different hours of the day. The performance tests were addition, multiplication, memory for auditory digits, memory for visual digits, recognition of nonsense syllables, completion, cancellation, and speed and accuracy of training. Two hundred and forty pupils in the fifth and sixth grades displayed the lowest degree of efficiency in the first period (9 to 10 A.M.), and the highest degree of efficiency in the last morning period (11 to 12 A.M.). There was a slight drop in efficiency after the lunch period and a slight rise between two and three o'clock. The two motor skills tested, viz., cancellation and speed and accuracy of coordination showed a somewhat greater efficiency in the afternoon than in the forenoon.[30]

C. CLIMATE: A considerable amount of evidence, some of it experimental but most of it statistical and empirical, has been assembled concerning the effect of the seasons and of long-time climatic conditions on performance. There is, for example, such a climatic factor as continued high winds. It is believed that this atmospheric condition may easily provoke irritability, and Dexter believes that it stands directly related to irregularities in conduct.[31] Huntington remarks of it that "on the whole, we may probably conclude that occasional short-lived gales and frequent light or moderate

[27] Gaglon, C. P., "To Gauge Workroom Temperatures." *Indust. Psychol.*, 1932, III, 3-7.
[28] Poffenberger, A. T., *Applied Psychology*. New York: D. Appleton-Century Co., 1927, p. 166.
[29] Cf. Yagloglou, C. P., "Modern Ventilation Principles and Their Application to Sedentary and Industrial Life." *J. Pers. Res.*, 1925, II, pp. 379 ff.
[30] Gates, A. I., "Variations in Efficiency During the Day." *Publ. Univ. of Calif.*, 1916. See also, Dawson, S., "Variations in the Mental Efficiency of Children During School Hours." *Brit. J. Psychol.*, 1923-24, XIV, 362-369.
[31] Dexter, E., *Weather Influences*. New York: The Macmillan Co., 1914, p. 89 and *passim*.

winds are beneficial, while long periods either of steady calms or of gales are depressing." [32]

There is also reason to believe that changes in temperature are more stimulating to performance than is uniformity. Huntington has assembled a vast amount of information on this problem, reviewing not only the experimental evidence but searching for high correlations between prevailing climates, on the one hand, and the development of notable civilizations, on the other. In general, it is believed that periods of changing temperatures such as are offered during the Fall and the Spring are more favorable to efficiency than periods of fairly stable climatic conditions.

This belief is held, partly because of experimental evidence gained from industries where long-time studies can be made, and partly from the observation that major movements in the development of culture have been associated with the temperate zones rather than with the arctic or torrid zones. Moreover, within the temperate zones great cultures appear to have arisen where seasonal changes in temperature and in other climatic conditions were favorable.[33]

D. ILLUMINATION: Education is indebted to the illuminating engineer rather than to the psychologist for information regarding the proper illumination of rooms. It goes almost without saying that improper illumination might contribute directly to increased fatigue, especially in the visual organs, for every variation in the intensity of light throughout a room becomes a possible area of stimulation and hence of distraction. To quote from a student of these matters:

"So, for example, shiny points or surfaces on a black machine, producing reflected glare, bring about excessive muscular movement, accompanied by pronounced feeling of strain, as visual attention is diverted from the dark background to the polished surface and as the pupil attempts to adapt itself to the widely differing intensities of illumination. In addition to unevenness of illumination, insufficiency of light and inconstancy of illumination increase the difficulty of seeing and produce eyestrain and fatigue, which are ofttimes reflected in headaches and a general feeling of malaise." [34]

These conditions which hold true of a workshop hold true to no less extent of the schoolroom. It is clear, then, that every attempt should be made to make the lighting conditions in a study room as favorable as possible.

[32] Huntington, E., *Civilization and Climate.* New Haven: Yale Univ. Press, 1915, p. 112.
[33] For studies on this problem in the field of industrial psychology, see **Viteles**, M. S., *Industrial Psychology.* New York: W. W. Norton and Co., 1932.
[34] Viteles, M. S., *op. cit.,* p. 483.

There are several ways in which the effects of illumination may be studied. Ives, for example, has found that visual acuity varies directly with the intensity of the illumination. Moreover, it is clear that increased acuity is accompanied by decreased ocular strain.[35] In general, it appears that the eye has become well adapted to ordinary daylight intensities so that artificial lighting may easily lead to decreased efficiency.[36] The problem of effective illumination is not limited, however, to ocular strain. There is considerable reason to believe that favorable conditions for seeing may lead directly to the development of an affective tone that may contribute much to fine performance. It is possible that dark gloomy rooms provoke disagreeable attitudes, and there is evidence to show that dim illumination may incite feelings of relaxation rather than of increased activity.[37]

E. COLORS: A certain amount of work has been done on the effect of colored illuminants on performance. One of the first studies seemed to suggest that light from a colored globe might increase efficiency, but whether the improvement was due to the color or to the favorable intensity of the light could not be determined.[38] Recently a more detailed study has been made of acuity, speed of discrimination, power to sustain clear seeing, and loss of visual efficiency under two intensities of light and for different wave lengths. The highest measure of acuity with respect to wave length fell to yellow and to blue light. Yellow also had an advantage in the other tests.

As is well known, the eye adapts itself readily to colors. This fact would seem to suggest that colored light does not furnish an optimal condition for visual discrimination.[39] Under factory conditions it has been shown that there is no relationship between the color of general illumination and rate of production. When the color is limited to the work place, however, yellow illumination seems to have some advantage, the other colors ranking as follows, viz., green, red, daylight, and blue.[40] It is most important, perhaps,

[35] Ives, J. E., "Study in Illumination." *U. S. Health Bulletin* (No. 181).
[36] Ferree, C. E., and Rand, G., "The Ocular Principles of Lighting." *Trans. Illum. Eng.*, 1925, XX, 278 ff.
[37] Luckeish, M., and Moss, F. K., *Seeing: A Partnership of Lighting and Vision.* Baltimore: The Williams and Wilkins Co., 1931, Chapter XVIII. See also, Luckeish, M., and Moss, F. K., *Lighting for Seeing,* published by the General Electric Co., 1931.
[38] Pressey, S. L., "The Influence of Color upon Mental and Motor Efficiency." *Amer. J. Psychol.,* 1921, XXXII, 326-354.
[39] Ferree, C. E., and Rand, G., "Visibility of Objects as Affected by Color and Composition." *Pers. J.,* 1931, IX, 108-124, 475-492.
[40] Ruffer, W., "Ueber die Beeinflussung menschlicher Leistungen durch farbiges Licht." *Ind. Psychotech.,* 1928, V, 161-177.

that schoolrooms shall be lighted intensively enough to favor quick and fine discrimination with minimal eyestrain, and that as many areas of different intensities of illumination be eliminated as possible. A change in the intensity of a stimulus-situation is one of the surest ways of enabling one object to become prepotent over others. Such an object cannot help but become a distraction if it is not the object to which attention is desired.

F. DISTRACTION: A few studies have been made concerning the effects of noise on performance. Morgan, for example, asked a group of subjects to translate letters into numbers and numbers into letters by means of a code which had been furnished.[41] Rate of performance was measured in terms of the units translated and in terms of accuracy. The subjects worked partly under quiet conditions and partly under noisy conditions, the noises being furnished by buzzers, electric bells and phonograph records. In every case, the initial effect of the noisy distractions was to decrease performance. After this initial effect, however, a majority of the subjects turned in a better performance during noise than they did without the distraction. In other words, the distraction seemed to have a facilitating effect upon performance. It was clear, however, that increased performance in the face of difficulty took place only at a greater physiological expense. Greater pressure was exerted on the keys of the typewriter, and there was a rise in the breathing curve. This phase of the physiological cost of increased production in the face of difficulty has been more accurately measured by Laird. Careful analysis of expired air during performance at the typewriter under noisy and under quiet conditions showed that the former condition entailed a higher expenditure of energy than the latter.[42]

There has been some suggestion that the distracting effect of noise may be less in stereotyped activities than in cases where "greater thought and concentration of attention are involved."[43] In any case, a moderate amount of distraction may aid rather than hinder certain types of efficiency; but it does so at a great physiological cost. Experiments upon auditory and other types of sensory fatigue under the noisy conditions of large cities are beginning to show that the cost is much greater than such experiments as these would suggest.

[41] Morgan, J. J. B., "The Overcoming of Distraction and Other Resistances." *Arch. of Psychol.*, 1916, XXXV, 84.
[42] Laird, D. A., "Experiments on the Physiological Cost of Noise." *J. Nat. Inst. Ind. Psychol.*, 1929, IV, 251-258.
[43] Kornhauser, A. W., "The Effect of Noise on Office Output." *Indus. Psychol.*, 1927, II, 621-622.

IV. Sources of Loss in Efficiency

1. *Introduction:* The task of the teacher in the schoolroom, to say nothing of all those persons who seek in other ways to exert some sort of guidance or control over their fellow human beings, would be far simpler if a chapter on efficiency could be concluded at this point. In view of the progress which is being made in the physical and biological sciences, the engineer and the physician can hope for increasing competence in keeping the organic condition of children and the physical conditions which surround them in good order. Unfortunately, however, processes of deterioration and decay are constantly at work. Save for the organic processes of growth, it looks as though practically everything around us, including the very skills and attitudes which we acquire, are moving toward lower levels of efficiency. From almost any point of view, the maintenance of a favorable ratio between effort expended and dependable results is a losing game which all of us must play.

The first part of our lives, to be sure, is spent in that type of growth and hence in increase of efficiency which has been described in considerable detail in earlier chapters. As soon as we reach any particular level of effectiveness, however, destructive forces are at work, causing us to lose our value as psychological instruments. As a matter of fact, we have already seen how it is that the very process of growth itself involves a continuous loss of efficiency, for if continued learning is one of the primary conditions leading to forgetfulness, every moment of our growth period is marked by work done against ourselves. Even if we say that forgetting is in no way dependent upon the inevitable course of continued learning, that is, if we think of forgetting as the result of the sheer passage of time, we still have to face major losses in efficiency as soon as a learning period has been discontinued.

As examples of the transitory character of much of the learning that takes place in the schoolroom, we may take some of the studies that have been made upon the retention of various school subjects after one or two years. If the material covered in the final examination at the end of a course is taken as a standard of comparison, it appears that less than half of this material can be recalled at the end of a year and only one-quarter of it at the end of two years.[44]

[44] For botany, see Johnson, P. O., "The Permanence of Learning in Elementary Botany." *J. Educ. Psychol.*, 1930, XXI, 37-47; for chemistry, see Powers, S. R., "A Diagnostic Study of the Subject Matter of High School Chemistry." *Teach. Coll. Contrib. to Educ.*, 1924 (No. 149), 49-54; for algebra, see Layton, E. T.,

To be sure, there is a certain amount of variation among different subjects in the extent to which they will be forgotten and there is also a wide variation among the particular parts of any given subject in the extent to which they will be retained. Moreover, there may be wide differences in recall for factual material as compared with recall for general principles or general methods of working. Even where it can be shown, however, that students have possessed efficient methods of work, these methods do not necessarily become a permanent part of their psychological equipment.[45]

A considerable share of the forgetting that takes place in any particular subject matter falls to the few hours or days immediately following the learning period. In one study of this matter a large number of children were asked to recall a small amount of material presented to them in a single reading. Recall was requested at the end of one day, fifteen days, thirty days, and one hundred days. The rate of forgetting for the first day was extremely rapid, and at the end of one hundred days, the scores for these subjects were, on the average, scarcely better than twenty-three per cent.[46] Even so short a period as a summer vacation is known to lead to a considerable amount of forgetting in such subjects as spelling, arithmetic, reasoning, arithmetic computation, rate of handwriting, and quality of handwriting. This same experiment showed some improvement in reading, an improvement which might be attributed to continued exercise during the summer interval.[47]

These experiments make it clear that even the early period of maximal rate of growth carries along with it agents working toward loss in efficiency. The student in the classroom cannot continue to practice everything. He must pass on from one subject to another. This very passage means loss in efficiency. Moreover, if a part of forgetting is occasioned by continued learning, learning itself becomes a source of decay. It is not, however, with the phenomena of forgetting that this section is chiefly concerned. On the contrary,

"The Persistence of Learning in Elementary Algebra." *J. Educ. Psychol.*, 1930, XIII, 152-163; and for psychology and other college courses, see Greene, E. B., "The Retention of Information Learned in College Courses." *J. Educ. Res.*, 1931, XXIV, 262-273.

[45] Pressey, L. C., "A Class of Probation Students." *J. Higher Educ.*, 1931, II, 506-510.

[46] Dietze, A. A., "Factual Memory of Secondary School Pupils for a Short Article Which They Read a Single Time." *Univ. of Pittsburgh Bull.*, 1930, XXVII, 39-46. See also Jones, H. E., "Experimental Study of College Teaching; the Effect of Example on Permanence of Learning." *Arch. of Psychol.*, 1923 (No. 68).

[47] Irmina, Sister M., "The Effects of Summer Vacation upon the Retention of the Elementary School Subjects." *Educ. Res. Bull.*, Cath. Univ. of Amer., 1928, III (Nos. 3 and 4).

THE CONCEPT OF EFFICIENCY IN SCHOOLROOM 673

we must inquire about the results of the continued exercise of a given function. For this purpose it will be convenient to speak briefly of some of the features of a typical work period.

2. *The Typical Work Period:* Let us assume that a specific skill has been brought to some measurable level of efficiency. Let us assume, further, that the periodic use of this skill in the form of distributed practice periods will not greatly increase its effectiveness. The question to be asked about such a skill in this section may be stated as follows: What variations will take place in the skill if, without adequate rest periods, it is used over and over again?

For the sake of convenience, we may call such a period of continuous exercise a work period. The half-hour or hour that is spent on a spelling lesson, for example, might be described as a work period. In the same way, we could think of the hours between eight and twelve and between one and four or the hours between eight and four as a work period. Likewise, a week, a month, or a whole year can be studied in the same way.[48]

A. WARMING-UP: One of the important features of any typical work period is known as the "warming-up" effect. If we assume that we know before the experiment begins how efficient a person is in the use of a particular skill, it will be observed after he begins a period of work that he usually starts at a level considerably below his practical limit. Sometimes quickly, but more often slowly, his efficiency will increase until he strikes a rate of working and a degree of accuracy which he is able to maintain for a considerable period of time.[49] The presence of the warming-up effect in the more physiological types of work is fairly easy to detect and to measure. An athlete, for example, before he enters a race, will run freely back and forth in order to adapt respiration rate, pulse rate, blood pressure, and level of metabolism to the task shortly to be done.[50]

The warming-up effect is not quite so open to measurement in the case of psychological functions and there has even been some tendency to ignore this feature of a typical work period.[51] While the experimental evidence is not in entire agreement on the matter, there are strong indications that a fairly sharp rise in efficiency will

---

[48] Griffith, C. R., *An Introduction to Applied Psychology.* New York: The Macmillan Co., 1934, Chapter XXX.

[49] Some of the most illuminating studies on the effects of warming-up are to be found in the field of industrial psychology. See Viteles, M. S., *Industrial Psychology.* New York: W. W. Norton Co., Chapter XXII.

[50] Cf. Hill, A. V., *Muscular Movement in Man.* New York: McGraw-Hill Book Co., 1927, *passim.*

[51] Thorndike, E. L., *op. cit., passim.* See also Watson, J. B., *Psychology from the Standpoint of a Behaviorist.* Philadelphia: J. B. Lippincott, 1919, Chapter IX.

often appear in such activities as tapping with the fingers,[52] reciting the alphabet backwards,[53] and in learning nonsense syllables.[54] In the second of these experiments each of the subjects was asked (i) to recite the alphabet backward continuously for twenty minutes, and (ii) to recite for thirty seconds, rest for fifteen seconds, recite for thirty seconds, rest for fifteen seconds, and so forth, until the actual amount of recitation totaled twenty minutes. In still another series, the rest intervals were thirty seconds rather than fifteen seconds. The results indicated that there were increases in efficiency during the first parts of the curves of work which were greater than any of the other irregularities in the curves.

Not so much is known about the essential nature of the warming-up process that might serve as an introduction to a class exercise. It seems fairly safe to infer from the experimental literature, however, that a class exercise based upon the facts included in this chapter might run somewhat as follows. The student will have come, perhaps, from some other class exercise, say the study of physics or of chemistry. The chances are that, as he prepares himself for his educational psychology, there will still be echoes or perseverative tendencies from the preceding work period. In a few moments, however, as he looks at his notes and as the instructor reviews for him the discussions of the last recitation hour, his own associative processes will be freshened and he will find himself better prepared to entertain the new material.

After a working rate has become established, the curve of work will move along with minor irregularities toward some unpredictable moment when the phenomena known as the work decrement will appear. It is even possible that a work decrement will take place shortly after the beginning of a work period, for some curves of effort show a phenomenon known as the initial spurt. That is, the worker or the student will start a new task at a higher level of efficiency than he can maintain. Even where there is no initial spurt, however, every curve of work shows a decrease in efficiency which must be attributed apparently to a large number of possible factors. A good many of these factors have been grouped under the term "fatigue" and we must, therefore, turn our attention for a moment to this concept.

[52] Wells, F. L., "Normal Performance in the Tapping Test." *Amer. J. Psychol.*, 1908, XIX, 437-483.
[53] Robinson, E. S., and Heron, W. T., "The Warming-up Effect." *J. Exper. Psychol.*, 1924, VII, 81-97.
[54] Heron, W. T., "The Warming-up Effect in Learning Nonsense Syllables." *J. Genet. Psychol.*, 1928, XXXV, 219-227.

3. *Fatigue and Efficiency:* As we have seen in an earlier chapter, one of the most important principles in the psychology of learning states that favorable changes in skill can be brought about most quickly if the practice periods are properly distributed over a period of time. This principle is closely related to a large number of facts concerning the beneficial results of inserting short periods of rest in otherwise continuous labor.[55] It is thought that the insertion of such rest periods enables a person to prolong that part of the curve of work which represents a maximal efficiency. In other words, rest is used as an antidote against the influence of the fatigue factor.

From the point of view of physiology, the word "fatigue" relates to those chemical processes which have to do with the use of glycogen and the subsequent formation of such products as lactic acid, carbon dioxide, and the like. The appearance of these substances in the bodily system makes that system less ready to function at its normal level.[56] Psychologically, the word "fatigue" sometimes refers to diminished output under prolonged effort and sometimes to the feelings of lassitude, boredom, distraction, and inattention which go along with continued effort. In view of these different uses it has sometimes been said that there are two kinds of fatigue, viz., physical fatigue and mental fatigue. This division appears to argue that the phrase "mental fatigue" must refer to some unfavorable state or property of mental stuff. The analogy is, of course, between mental stuff and the chemical substances which accompany diminished physiological activity. More critical studies of the concept of fatigue seem to show, however, that it is not proper to use the phrase "mental fatigue," unless reference is had to the diminished functional activity of the bonds between stimulus and response or to diminished activity either in the sense organs or in the receptors. Mental work, as we have seen, is sometimes illustrated by mental multiplication. The older psychologists have assumed that mental multiplication is done by some kind of stuff which is more or less disembodied and consequently unrelated to activity in nerve tissue. At this point the behaviorist seems to be in the right, for it has hardly seemed conceivable that any kind of mental activity can be disembodied in such a way as to suffer fatigue independently of bodily fatigue.[57] Mental arithmetic is to be distinguished from manual labor partly in terms of the types of muscles involved and partly in terms of the nerve tissues which make muscular effort

---

[55] Cf. Viteles, M. S., *op. cit.*, pp. 470-482.
[56] Gould, A. G., and Dye, J. A., *Exercise and Its Physiology.* New York: A. S. Barnes and Co., 1932, Chapters VII-VIII.
[57] Thorndike, E. L., "Mental Fatigue." *J. Exper. Psychol.*, 1911, II, pp. 61-80.

possible. In the one case the muscles are presumably those of the vocal apparatus, while in the other case they reside in the arms and other parts of the musculature.[58]

Thorndike was one of the first to use mental multiplication in the measurement of fatigue. He asked 16 subjects to multiply a three-place number by a three-place number, neither having any zeros or ones among the digits. When the results were obtained by carrying out the necessary operations in one's head, they were to be written down. Each subject worked continuously on one day from four to twelve hours, only a brief interval occurring at noon for luncheon. The next day they worked from one-half hour to an hour on the same task. The amount of fatigue was measured by the difference in the time required to do the same amount of work with the same accuracy at the end of the long-continued work period and at the beginning of the work period on the following day after the long rest. In the case of seven subjects who worked for approximately seven hours, the average increase in time required to do the same amount of work with equal accuracy at the end of the seven hours over the beginning of the test on the next day was fifty-four per cent.[59] Arai repeated this experiment using four-digit numbers rather than three. Practice in such multiplication was first continued until the subject became highly expert. In contrast to Thorndike's results Arai found that no great decline in efficiency had appeared even though work continued from 1.46 P.M. until 10.28 P.M. with a stop from 6.31 to 7.41 P.M. for dinner.[60] It has been pointed out, however, that mental multiplication may be a complex function and hence does not satisfy the presuppositions of an adequate experiment upon fatigue, viz., that one particular function shall be subjected to continuous exercise. There is, however, a decrement in all work curves with continuous exercise of a function, even though the function be highly complex; and this fact may be depended upon no matter how the function may be described, whether in terms of manual versus laryngeal action, or in terms of mental operation.

4. *Causes of the Work Decrement:* One of the most serious students of the factors bearing upon physiological and psychological work has summarized the effect of fatigue and the effect of other agents on efficiency by stating seven principles which lie behind de-

[58] Cf. Dodge, R., "Mental Work: A Study in Psycho-dynamics." *Psychol. Rev.,* 1913, XX, 1-42; Robinson, E. S., "Factors Affecting Human Efficiency." *Ann. Amer. Acad. Pol. Soc. Sci.,* 1923, CX, 95.

[59] Cf. Watson, J. B., *Psychology from the Standpoint of the Behaviorist.* New York: J. B. Lippincott Co., 1924, Chapter X.

[60] Arai, T., "Mental Fatigue." *Col. Univ. Contrib. to Educ.,* 1912 (No. 54).

creases in efficiency.[61] As we have pointed out earlier in the chapter, one of the ways of measuring variations in efficiency is to lay down as a standard of comparison the quality of a performance at the end of practice periods which have been sufficient to bring a given skill to a fairly stable level. Measures of quality can be stated in terms of the relation between the stimulus-situation, on the one hand, and the character of the response, on the other. The principles of the work decrement which Robinson has described are stated in terms of the stimulus-response formula.

The first principle is that the amount of decrement in a given stimulus-response pattern is relative to the recency of the previous use of that pattern. The principle is based upon the fact that nervous tissue which has just been used will not be in a condition to be used again for a short period of time. This period is known as the refractory phase.[62] The refractory phase is most easily discovered in nerve and muscle tissue where it can be shown that a measurable length of time must elapse after a given state of excitation before the tissue is ready to be activated again.

It has been suggested that this phenomenon may be just as relevant to psychological as to physiological operations. Dodge, for example, has pointed out that repetition of almost any sort ought to be avoided until the effect of the initial performance has somewhat worn off.[63] In an actual experiment upon this question a group of subjects was asked to write a number between zero and nine every time a word was spoken. Care was taken to prevent the subjects from knowing what the experiment was about and, in particular, to avoid all suggestion as to the character of the number that was to be written. Since the words were presented every two and one-half seconds, it was thought possible to find out whether the subjects had a tendency to repeat the same numbers or whether an effect somewhat like the refractory phase would make its influence felt. Only one of the subjects repeated a given number more than half the number of times a chance distribution would suggest. In another phase of the experiments, in which the interval between the words was increased to five seconds, some evidence of the refractory phase was present but it was clear that the effect was less than in

---

[61] Robinson, E. S., "Work of the Integrated Organism," in Murchison, C. (Ed.), *op. cit.*, pp. 601-621.
[62] Dodge, R., "The Refractory Phase of the Productive Wink Reflex." *Amer. J. Psychol.*, 1913, XXIV, 1-7.
[63] Dodge, R., "The Laws of Relative Fatigue." *Psychol. Rev.*, 1917, XXIV, 89-113. See especially p. 103.

the first instance.[64] In a study on accuracy in lifting weights and in judging linear magnitudes, it was found that if the judgments were called for at a rate greater than one per two seconds, accuracy was greatly decreased. It may be that such a decrease in accuracy can be interpreted as a consequence of repetitions that follow one another too closely.[65]

The second principle suggested by Robinson states that the work decrement of a given stimulus-response pattern is relative to the frequency of the previous use of that pattern. This principle differs from the preceding principle in the sense that it inquires about the influence of a number of repetitions of a given S-R pattern, irrespective of the time intervals that are placed between the repetitions. In the experiment cited above from Arai, for example, the subjects were asked to multiply numbers "in their heads." Clearly, multiplication of this sort might be variable in the sense that different numbers will be used but constant or truly repetitive in the sense that the subjects could hardly avoid multiplying the same two numbers by each other several times during the work period.

In one of the best experiments on this second principle, a group of subjects was asked to write alphabetical sequences, such as *ababab, abcabc,* or *abcdefabcdef.* It is easy to see that a task of this sort is fairly homogeneous but that the degree of homogeneity actually varies in a measurable way from one set of conditions to another. The subject worked for periods of twenty minutes and, because of circumstances not pertinent to our own task, a comparison was made between the results of the first minute of work and the tenth minute. These results showed that the amount of decrement was directly related to the relative homogeneity of the work. In other words, it seems to be certain that decrement in the amount of work done is a function of the amount of actual repetition required of the subjects.[66]

Experiments such as this should be of unusual interest to teachers, for they indicate that repetition in and of itself does not always lead to an increase in efficiency, as one of the principles of learning would lead us to expect. The reader will recall, no doubt, our earlier discussion of the law of use or of exercise and apply the point of

[64] Thorndike, E. L., "The Refractory Period in Associative Processes." *Psychol. Rev.,* 1927, XXXIV, 234-236. Also Telford, C. W., "The Refractory Phase of Voluntary and Associative Responses." *J. Exper. Psychol.,* 1931, XIV, 1-36.
[65] Garrett, H. E., "A Study of the Relation of Accuracy to Speed." *Arch. Psychol.,* 1922, VIII (No. 58).
[66] Robinson, E. S., and Bills, A. G., "Two Factors in the Work Decrement." *J. Exper. Psychol.,* 1926, IX, 415-443.

THE CONCEPT OF EFFICIENCY IN SCHOOLROOM 679

view there expressed to the present discussion. As we have seen, there is some definite evidence to show that habits may be broken up rather than more completely fixed by practice.[67]

A third principle may be stated as follows. The work decrement of a given S-R pattern is relative to the connections that exist between a particular stimulus-situation and other possible responses to it. Let us suppose, for example, that a subject has been asked to write at a typewriter, using repeated movements of one finger on one occasion and alternating movements of two or three fingers on another occasion. It is obvious that the use of two or more fingers might introduce a factor of competition among different muscle groups with respect to a single stimulus-situation. The results indicated that the amount of the work decrement was approximately as great for the more heterogeneous tasks as it was for the more homogeneous. Since the principle described above asserts that the decrement ought to be greater for homogeneous tasks, these results might be interpreted to say that the factor of competition is sufficiently important to modify the factor of homogeneity.[68] An even greater effect was found when accuracy rather than speed was measured. Other students of this phase of the work curve have discovered that continuous muscular work done by the fingers and continuous addition with four-place numbers increases muscle tone and restlessness. The increased restlessness can be interpreted as a result of increasing competition in the tasks assigned.[69]

Robinson has described his fourth principle as follows. The work decrement of a given S-R pattern is relative to the strength of the connections which make the pattern possible. This is a principle which is closely related to the principles of learning that have already been discussed. Other things being equal, the creation of a particular S-R pattern is dependent upon properly distributed practice periods. If these practice periods have not been sufficient in number to lead to a stable pattern, it is reasonable to suppose that they would be easily subject to interference. On the other hand, if the principles of efficient learning have been adhered to, the pattern thus created might be less subject to fatigue.[70]

---

[67] Dunlap, K., "A Revision of the Fundamental Law of Habit Formation." *Science*, 1928, LXVII, 360-362.
[68] Robinson, E. S., and Bills, A. G., *op. cit., passim*.
[69] Freeman, G. L., and Lindley, A. B., "Two Neuro-Muscular Indices of Mental Fatigue." *J. Exper. Psychol.*, 1931, XIV, 567-605. See also Freeman, G. L., *Introduction to Physiological Psychology*. New York: The Ronald Press, 1934, Chapter XXV.
[70] Almost any of the references cited in Chapter Six can be used to illustrate this principle. See also Robinson, E. S., and Robinson, F. R., "Practice and the Work Decrement." *Amer. J. Psychol.*, 1932, XLIV, 547-551.

The fifth condition to which the curve of work is subject arises out of the well-known fact that the very making of a response to any given stimulus-pattern almost inevitably leads to a change in the character of the stimulus-pattern itself. It is barely possible, therefore, that such a change in the character of the stimulus-pattern might have some influence upon the work decrement. This possibility is asserted to be a fact by this fifth principle. It says that the work decrement of a given S-R pattern is relative to the quantitative integrity of the stimulus-pattern throughout the period of work. Of this principle Robinson remarks, first, that the change in the character of the stimulus-pattern brought about by a response to it may call for the addition of a competing response, and, second, that the new pattern of stimulation may imply a change in the strength of the connection between stimulation and the desired response. When, for example, subjects are asked to pull up a fairly heavy weight with a single finger, the total act cannot help but be modified by the painful experiences that are introduced into the experiment before it has proceeded very far.[71]

The principle just described lays emphasis upon the qualitative integrity of the stimulus-pattern. A sixth principle argues that the amount of the work decrement in a given stimulus-response pattern is relative to the quantitative integrity of the stimulus-pattern. Some of the experimental facts bearing on this principle have already been cited in an earlier chapter. We have found, for example, that most subjects tend to do better work when they know what the results of their efforts are than they do when they are kept ignorant of results.[72] Even the presence or absence of other persons in the room, persons who are truly competing with the subjects used in the experiments or persons who are simply present as an audience, is known to influence the amount of work that can be done.[73] In experiments of this type, the inference is that knowledge of success or failure, on the one hand, and the presence or absence of competing persons, on the other, will change the quantitative character of the stimulus-pattern with respect to which a subject is working. As a rule, such factors as we have mentioned decrease the amount of the work decrement, but there are times when they certainly lead to an increase in the decrement. It is known, for example,

[71] Cf. Robinson, E. S., in Murchison, C. (Ed.), *op. cit.*, pp. 617-618.
[72] Crawley, S. L., "An Experimental Investigation of Recovery from Work." *Arch. Psychol.*, 1926, XIII (No. 85). Also "Practice Without Knowledge of Results." *Psychol. Rev. Monog.*, 1905, VII (No. 29).
[73] Cf. Murphy, G., and Murphy, L. B., *Experimental Social Psychology*. New York: Harper and Bros., 1931, Chapters VIII and IX.

that the presence of other persons may have a distracting rather than a favorable effect upon a worker.

The last of the principles described by Robinson may be stated as follows. The work decrement of a given stimulus-response pattern is relative to the decrements that have already been developed in other such patterns. In simpler terms, the principle means that if a person has been at all exhausted by other activities, the results of his exhaustion will manifest themselves even in hitherto unused stimulus-response patterns. To say the same thing in another way, there is some similarity between this principle and the principle of the transfer of training. Since the teacher in the schoolroom does not often meet with persons who are utterly exhausted, we may leave this feature of the work decrement out of account.[74] It is important to know, however, whether the transfer of fatigue effects from one stimulus-response pattern to another has many marks of similarity with transfer by means of identical elements and by means of general attitudes and methods of work.

In one study on this problem, the subjects were confronted with two tasks which were arranged in such a way that they would have one or more elements in common. The tasks required the writing of alphabetical sequences such as those mentioned above. In one set of conditions the two tasks possessed all elements in common. In the second set of conditions there were two elements in common; in the third, one element in common; and in the fourth, no elements in common. The control experiments consisted of the task of writing alphabetical sequences at one time and resting at another. The results made it clear that the work decrement increased in direct ratio to the number of elements which the two tasks held in common.[75] From one point of view, these results may be taken as favorable to the identical element theory of transfer. In view of the many different conditions under which work decrement may be affected, however, it seems fair to assume that this is only one possible explanation.

5. *Monotony:* Most of the studies that have been mentioned up to this point depend upon such features of work as can be measured by changes in speed or changes in accuracy. It has been shown, however, that there are times when the work decrement may manifest itself not so much in these indices of efficiency as in terms

---

[74] Cf. Robinson, E. S., *op. cit.,* pp. 625-628. Also Kleitman, M., "Studies on the Physiology of Sleep; Effects of Prolonged Sleeplessness in Man." *Amer. J. Physiol.,* 1923, LXVI, 67-92.

[75] Bills, A. G., and McTeer, W., "Transfer of Fatigue and Identical Elements." *J. Exper. Psychol.,* 1932, XV, 22-36.

of the relative "satisfyingness" of the work done. Let us suppose, for example, that a group of subjects is asked to work continuously for four hours in reading and grading English compositions. The experimenter in this case found that there was not very much decrease in speed of work and only a slight decrease (*ca.* 8%) in accuracy. There was, however, a very great decrease in the satisfyingness of the work done. Toward the end of the work period, the subjects reported that further effort was positively distasteful.[76]

It is, of course, rather difficult to get accurate measures of the attitudes and dispositions described by the words "interest," "satisfyingness," "boredom," "monotony," and other feelings that arise in connection with sustained effort. That the problem has not been left out of account, however, is plain from the efforts of industrial psychologists and others to give it its proper place in any study of the arts of practical control.[77] There are at least two ways in which an increased measure of monotony may make itself felt in the work curve. In the first place, there is a close correlation between reports given by workers about their feelings and the actual rate at which they can or will work. In the second place, monotony is known to cause greater variability in the rate of work.[78] Variations in rate of working appear to come out of the effort of a person to maintain a given level of efficiency by alternating between periods of more intense effort and periods of relaxation.

There are a great many individual differences in susceptibility to monotony. These differences, however, may depend less upon the nature of the work that is being done than upon the talents and the disposition of the worker himself. Among the possible factors, degree of intelligence appears to stand foremost. In general, the more intelligent the worker, the more susceptible he will be to restlessness and to boredom during long-continued periods of effort with homogeneous material. It has not been altogether easy, however, to separate the intelligence factor from differences in temperament.[79] One of the most fortunate features about the relation between monotony and a high level of efficiency appears in the fact that even short periods of rest serve greatly to improve the situation.

[76] Thorndike, E. L., "The Curve of Work and the Curve of Satisfyingness." *J. Appl. Psychol.*, 1917, I, 265-267.
[77] Cf. Viteles, M. S., *op. cit.*, Chapters XXIII and XXIV.
[78] Cf. Wyatt, S., "Boredom in Industry." *Person. J.*, 1929, VIII, 161-171; Hall, O. M., "The Disagreeable Job; Selected Workers Who Will Not Be Annoyed." *Person. J.*, 1930, IX, 297-304.
[79] Cf. Thompson, L. A., "Measuring Susceptibility to Monotony." *Person. J.*, 1929, VIII, 172-193; Davies, A. H., "Physical and Mental Effects of Monotony in Modern Industry." *Brit. Med. J.*, 1926, II, pp. 472 ff.

THE CONCEPT OF EFFICIENCY IN SCHOOLROOM 683

Moreover, as would be expected from one of the principles of the work decrement described above, an increase in heterogeneity in the work done will also modify the rate at which attitudes of monotony will appear.

These facts drawn for the most part from industry have an important bearing upon classroom processes simply because children in the lower grades and even more mature students find it extremely difficult to maintain postures and a sustained level of attention in academic work. Almost all of the manuals on teaching method describe the increased restlessness that characterizes the later portions of the school day. The only remedies for situations of this type are to increase the motivation behind classroom exercises, to foster the development of interest, to introduce an optimal amount of variation in the study period, and to interrupt inevitably long periods of sustained effort with the right amount of relaxation and rest. This last feature of the school program is so important that it deserves further comment.

6. *Rest and Relaxation:* Here again we may go to industry for important studies on the value of rest intervals. The ordinary school day is, of course, broken up by the noon lunch period and, in the lower grades, at least, by a ten- or fifteen-minute recess period. It has been shown, however, that the introduction of short rest periods at even more frequent intervals has a highly favorable effect upon efficiency.[80] From one point of view the value of a rest period has already been emphasized in that principle of learning known as the principle of distributed effort. This is, however, a type of rest which usually requires that the learner turn to some other task in the intervals between practice upon an assigned task. Then, too, the distribution of practice periods is subject to all of the variable features of facilitation and inhibition.

Apart from all of these complications, it seems to be quite clear that periods of sustained effort will yield greater results if the whole period is interrupted rather frequently with even so short a rest interval as two or three minutes. Graf, for example, introduced rest intervals of one-half, two, and five minutes in a forty-minute period of mental addition. It was discovered that the two-minute rest interval for each forty minutes of work was highly beneficial. When the work period was extended to eighty minutes, a five-minute rest pause was found to be more advantageous than either a shorter

[80] Data bearing upon this problem in the field of industry has been summarized by Viteles, M. S., *op. cit.,* Chapter XXIV.

or longer rest period.[81] Shepard asked his subjects to work on a gymnasium chest weight machine, an all-day run of approximately eight hours once a week for a period of five weeks being the task. During the rest periods the workers were permitted to lie down and relax as completely as possible under blankets or on cots provided for the purpose. It was shown that the highest level of efficiency was reached when the worker rested approximately 16.6 per cent of the time during the working day. This happens to coincide approximately with the practice used in the United States Army concerning resting during marching.[82]

It is characteristic of a great many of the experiments that have been done on the beneficial use of rest periods that intelligent workers quickly find a ratio between work and rest which is most efficient for them. It is natural to suppose that this ratio might differ markedly from individual to individual; but if such persons have proper motivation they will find the work-rest pattern that suits them best. It has also been shown that the insertion of rest periods during mental or physical activity is most beneficial when it takes place at the peak of performance. It appears that a peak performance frequently precedes a decline due to increasing fatigue.

The value of such rest periods is now known to depend upon the degree of relaxation that obtains during them. The chances are that not even in sleep is the body ever in complete relaxation. Some measure of bodily tonus is maintained almost constantly and it has been shown that many features of physical and psychological work are improved when bodily tonus stands at an optimal level.[83] There are times, however, when extreme measures of relaxation can be secured as a result of definite practice.[84] Just as it is easy to recognize an increased tension in muscle tonus so one may learn to recognize a decrease in muscle tonus. If a subject secures a proper measure of skill in producing low levels of tonus in large muscle groups, he can proceed to the smaller muscle groups, and especially to those which control movements in the eyes and in the vocal apparatus. It has been argued that control over these muscles is of particular importance since they are the ones most intimately correlated with psychological activity. When, therefore, the body is

[81] Graf, O., "Ueber lohnendste Arbeitspausen bei geistiger Arbeit." *Psychol. Arb.*, 1924, VIII, 265-303; 1925, IX, 1-69; Vileles, M. S., *op. cit.*, pp. 470 ff.
[82] Shepard, G. H., "Effect of Rest Periods on Production." *Person. J.*, 1928, VII, 186-202.
[83] Cf. Griffith, C. R., *op. cit.*, Chapter III.
[84] Cf. Jacobson, E., *Progressive Relaxation.* Chicago: Univ. of Chicago Press, 1929, *passim.* Also, *You Must Relax.* New York: McGraw-Hill Book Co., 1934.

placed in a state of complete relaxation, the rest period will achieve its maximal value. It has long been known that excessive psychological effort, together with such accompaniments as worry, nervousness, irritability, and restlessness, may have an immediate bodily echo in such ailments as indigestion, improper elimination, and even in pseudo-heart conditions. If, therefore, a person can acquire any measure of skill in relaxation, this skill will offer itself as an indirect source of attack upon the by-products of excessive tension.

V. THE EFFECT OF DRUGS ON EFFICIENCY

1. *Introduction:* In view of the diverse comments that are made about the use of such drugs as caffeine, nicotine, and alcohol, it has always seemed desirable that some sort of crucial experiments should be performed concerning the effect of these substances on human efficiency. Save for alcohol, however, it has not been possible to get information of the sort that would lead to a group of dependable conclusions.[85] Even in the case of alcohol, it has been extremely difficult to generalize on the results that are now in, partly because individuals differ so greatly in the amount of alcohol they can tolerate, and partly because the effects of alcohol vary so greatly from one subject to the next.[86] Not the least of the difficulties in the way of adequate experimentation is created by the fact that the users of drugs may easily become conditioned to objects associated with drinking and smoking.[87]

2. *Alcohol:* In general, it is believed that one of the initial effects of alcohol is to induce certain symptoms of comfort and well-being which are often taken by the subject as a sign that his work can be done even more efficiently than usual. It is also held that small amounts of alcohol remove inhibitions in such a way that both the conversation and the actions of the drinker become less restrained. McDougall, for example, quotes from another source to the effect that the drinker laughs and smiles more readily, he grows more easily angry or tender, elated or depressed, scornful or compassionate, according to the appeal of the moment.[88] McDougall goes on

[85] Cf. Hollingworth, H. L., "The Influence of Caffeine on Efficiency." *Arch. Psychol.*, 1912 (No. 22). Also, *Abnormal Psychology*. New York: The Ronald Press, 1930, pp. 545-559.
[86] Cf. Hollingworth, H. L., "When Is a Man Intoxicated?" *J. Appl. Psychol.*, 1925, IX, 122-150.
[87] Cf. Dorcus, R. M., "Effect of Suggestion and Tobacco on Pulse Rate and Blood Pressure." *J. Exper. Psychol.*, 1925, VIII, 297-309.
[88] Cf. McDougall, W., *Outline of Abnormal Psychology*. New York: Charles Scribner's Sons, 1926, p. 68.

to argue that further indulgence in alcohol interferes with both perception and behavior. It is said that a certain measure of clumsiness or lack of adjustment develops, as though the drug had a sort of paralyzing effect upon the motor coördination centers. The field of sense perception is narrowed, refinement of discrimination blunted, visual coördination breaks down, and there is a general decline of the higher intellectual functions. This means, of course, that emotional modes of reaction predominate. As a final stage,

"the intellectual processes of judgment and self-criticism and control are virtually suspended; the functions of sense-perception and skilled movement are grossly impaired, and the emotional tendencies themselves are invaded and weakened, so that only strong appeals to them suffice to evoke any response and, in their absence, the drinker sinks inert and nerveless into a heavy sleep, which lasts until the alcohol absorbed has all been oxidized." [89]

As a general picture, this description may be allowed to stand; but obviously it does not settle the question as to the precise psychological effects of small amounts of alcohol on specific psychological functions. Several major attempts have been made to fill in this part of the whole picture.[90] These studies show that the effect of alcohol upon all of the reflexes responding at all is depressing. In general, large amounts of alcohol (20 to 40 c.c.) interfere with the amount of muscular work that can be done. It appears that more complex functions, such as remembering and solving problems, are less subject to alcohol than are some of the simpler reflexes, although the effect is depressing when there is any effect at all.

3. *Nicotine:* Much more important for education, however, is the relation between nicotine and efficiency. It is obvious that this is a question that cannot be settled by gathering testimonies from distinguished persons. Such testimonies have been gathered by O'Shea and it would be possible to use these testimonies in favor of almost any point of view toward the drug. Just as many eminent men report that tobacco has been a comfort and an aid to them as report that tobacco has retarded their progress and interfered with the intellectual and physical development of neighbors and friends whom they have observed.[91]

[89] Quoted by McDougall, W., from a booklet issued by the British Liquor Control Board bearing the title *Alcohol and Its Action on the Human Organism*. See McDougall, W., *op. cit.*, pp. 71-72.
[90] Miles, W. R., "The Effect of Alcohol on Psychophysiological Functions." *Publ. Carnegie Instit. Wash.*, 1918 (No. 266).
[91] O'Shea, N. V., *Tobacco and Mental Efficiency*. New York: The Macmillan Co., 1923, Part I.

THE CONCEPT OF EFFICIENCY IN SCHOOLROOM

Almost without exception, high school principals, superintendents and others have reported that smoking interferes with the efficiency of young people. It has been noted, for example, that such impairments as nervousness, poor hearing, poor memory, bad manners, bad moral and mental condition, carelessness, truancy, and the like are much more common among smokers than among non-smokers,[92] that the grades of non-smokers are always significantly better than are the grades of smokers,[93] that the percentage of promoted pupils is greater for non-smokers than for smokers, whereas the percentage of conditioned, failed, and withdrawn students is greater for smokers,[94] and so on. In support of these statistical studies, there is testimonial evidence drawn from principles and faculties of high schools against the use of tobacco by young people.[95] So important a matter, however, cannot be decided by testimonies.

The chief criticism to be passed upon studies of this sort runs as follows: It goes almost without saying that a great many other factors aside from the use of tobacco may contribute to low grades, truancy, and other types of impairment. It is just as easy to suppose that the use of tobacco is a consequence of some of these other factors as it is to suppose that it is a primary cause. Of one thing we may be fairly certain. The use of tobacco normally goes with a leisurely mode of living. Some of the chief testimonies in its favor remark the fact that it conduces to quietness and reflection. It has been argued, therefore, that simple statistical comparisons between smokers and non-smokers do not arrive at true facts in the matter. In commenting on this situation Conklin has written:

"The most that can be safely said concerning these studies is that smoking habits and lower grades are usually associated. It cannot be said that tobacco is the cause of the lower grades. Studies of the intelligence-test scores of smokers in comparison with non-smokers do not reveal any startling difference. Some have even indicated a slightly higher average score for the smokers. The reason for the association of smoking and lower grades is probably to be found in the home environment, the general social situation, and the personality type of the individual. The boy with introvertive tendencies who does not mix readily with others might be far less likely to acquire the tobacco habit than the boy of extravertive tendencies who belongs to a string of societies and fraternities. Likewise the boy with introvertive tendencies

[92] *Ibid.*, p. 122.
[93] *Ibid.*, pp. 122-127.
[94] *Ibid.*, pp. 126-127.
[95] *Ibid.*, Chapter VII.

might have more time to apply to his lessons than the boy whose time is absorbed by his social obligations." [96]

A number of attempts have been made to meet this situation by the use of the experimental method.[97] Results from these experiments and from others that might be cited all seem to argue that there is a slight decline amounting, perhaps, to as much as ten per cent, on the average, in the functions that have been tested. This fact holds true, for example, in tests of such functions as speed of perception, free association, visual memory, auditory memory, addition, and subtraction.[98]

It would seem to follow, then, that the use of alcohol and tobacco by young people is not to be looked upon with favor.[99] It is clear, of course, that the more exact studies upon the influence of these drugs on human efficiency relate to the simpler types of psychological function. The evidence is not conclusive, however, concerning the more complex functions; but the inference might well be drawn that these functions will also be subject to interference. In any case, this section of the general problem of efficiency cannot be closed until further studies have been made.

4. *Caffeine:* As little, perhaps, is known about the effects of caffeine, the toxic ingredient in coffee and in some of the more common soft drinks, as about any of the drugs in daily use. It is altogether likely that the excessive use of caffeine induces sleeplessness, for it is known that this drug is a stimulant. As in the case of alcohol and nicotine, however, it is difficult to separate the effects of the drug itself from the effects of suggestion.

In general, it is thought that caffeine may increase speed of movement in direct proportion to the amount taken; but larger doses lead to a decrease in coördination.[100] In association tests and in the speed of formation of associations as measured with nonsense syllables, it looks as though some improvement may be brought about by the use

---

[96] Conklin, E. G., *Principles of Abnormal Psychology.* New York: Henry Holt and Co., 1927, p. 374.
[97] Cf. Bates, R. L., "The Effects of Cigar and Cigarette Smoking on Certain Psychological and Physiological Functions." *J. Comp. Psychol.*, 1922, II, 371-424; Fisher, V. E., "An Experimental Study of the Effect of Tobacco Smoking on Certain Psychological Functions." *Comp. Psychol. Monog.*, 1927, IV (No. 19); Hawk, P. B., "A Study of the Physiological and Psychological Reactions of the Human Organism to Coffee Drinking." *Amer. J. Physiol.*, 1929, XC, 380-381.
[98] Bush, A., "Tobacco Smoking and Mental Efficiency." *New York Med. J.*, 1914, XCIX, pp. 519 ff.
[99] Cf. Meyland, G. L., "The Effects of Smoking on College Students." *Pop. Sci. Mo.*, 1910, pp. 170 ff.
[100] Cf. Rivers, W. H. R., *The Influence of Alcohol and Other Drugs on Fatigue.* London: Arnold, 1908, *passim.* See also, Hollingworth, H. L., "The Influence of Caffeine on Efficiency." *Arch. Psychol.*, 1912 (No. 22).

of coffee.[101] Experiments like these, however, touch only the short-time effects of this drug. It still remains to be seen what the long-time effects are, a determination that is highly desirable in view of the many deleterious effects that are commonly attributed to habitual coffee drinking.

5. *Conclusion:* A chapter on efficiency in the schoolroom would hardly be complete without some reference to the most efficient means of using oneself in the library, in the study room, and in other places where books must be read and thought taken about them. In view of our lengthy discussion of the various ways and means of increasing the efficiency of the learning process, however, it is hardly necessary to do more than ask the student to review this material with an eye to its practical consequences.

There are, of course, many books on this subject, but all of them begin and end with the admonition to distribute learning periods properly, to make the learning process an active process, to use all of the ordinary devices for reviewing older material, for correlating facts drawn from different sources, and for giving active expression as frequently as possible to the material that has been acquired, and the like. The student must not suppose, however, that the many rules and principles of effective learning will, in and of themselves, make him more efficient in his work. On the contrary, these rules and principles are cited in order that he may make himself a living embodiment of them. They throw light upon the sort of person a real student is. In short, the study hour will be increased in efficiency in direct proportion as the student himself becomes a more effective psychological instrument.

READINGS

The most authoritative source of readings on efficiency is furnished by Robinson, E. S., "Work of the Integrated Organism," in Murchison, C. (Ed.), *A Handbook of General Experimental Psychology*. Worcester, Mass.: Clark Univ. Press, 1933, Chapter XII. The references at the end of the chapter are exceedingly helpful.

More general accounts can be found in Poffenberger, A. T., *Applied Psychology*. New York: D. Appleton-Century Co., 1927, *passim;* Husband, R. W., *Applied Psychology*. New York: Harper and Bros., 1934, Chapter XXVI; and Griffith, C. R., *An Introduction to Applied Psychology*. New York: The Macmillan Co., 1934, Chapter XXX.

The student will find the following book very useful: Viteles, M. S., *The Science of Work*. New York: W. W. Norton and Co., 1934.

[101] Ruman, G., "The Influence of Coffee on the Association Constant." *J. Exper. Psychol.,* 1934, XVII, 93-104.

CHAPTER TWENTY

POINTS OF VIEW IN PSYCHOLOGY

I. THE GENETIC POINT OF VIEW

1. *Introduction:* It has been the purpose of the preceding chapters to give the student of educational psychology a picture, first, of a person who is actually growing in his psychological dimensions under the guiding influence of teachers and parents, second, of the problems of original nature and learning, and third, of some of the more general conceptual and methodological tools that the educator uses in his daily work. In doing this, we have assumed throughout that the genetic point of view, in general, and the facts of child psychology, in particular, are fundamental to the field of education.[1] The very first chapter, for example, gave us a short glimpse of the developmental process as it appears during the prenatal stages and during the weeks and months that immediately follow birth.

We began at this point, in part, because most educational psychologies have begun there, except that they have usually foreshortened, not to say biased, the whole task by describing some of the traditions about instinct and original nature, and, in part, because it ought now to be clear to the student that the growth processes which run their courses early in life set the pattern for much that happens later on. In other words, many books on educational psychology start with the school child after it has already reached considerable degrees of fixity or of stability in its psychological nature. It has been one of our fundamental arguments that the real significance of the educative process cannot be realized until proper account has been taken of the astonishingly effective modes of training which are brought to bear on the child long before parents and teachers become aware of the direction in which growth is proceeding. As we have indicated, this procedure is in line with the "psychological movement" in education started by Rousseau, Pestalozzi, and others. The major difference is that the teacher today

[1] Cf. Wheeler, R. H., and Perkins, F. T., *Principles of Mental Development.* New York: T. Y. Crowell, 1932, *passim.*

can draw upon experimental facts rather than upon empirical observations.[2]

The distinction that has been drawn between psychological growth and the methods used to promote and guide it, on the one hand, and the various conceptual and methodological tools of education, on the other, has served a useful purpose. To review only a single illustration, we may take the concept of intelligence. The student will recall that intelligence is probably not a thing or a faculty that a person possesses, in the same sense that he possesses an arm, a heart, or a brain. On the contrary, intelligence is a judgment which we make of the psychological effectiveness of people with respect to the various situations in which they may be placed. When a person learns readily, when his skills are well adapted to the tasks at hand, when his observations are acute and penetrating, when his moody and emotionalized actions are well adjusted to shifting conditions, when his attitudes and motives are adequate to continuous and successful effort, and when he can refashion his conduct quickly and rationally in the presence of difficult or perplexing situations, we say of him that he is highly intelligent. No normal person is wholly unintelligent, but there are a good many people in whom the several operations mentioned above proceed slowly and dully.

Intelligence, then, is a concept which has high practical value in education, just as the concepts of adjustment, social mindedness, and mental health have a practical value. However, it does not seem fruitful to confuse these concepts with modes of operation which are fundamentally psychological in character and which form the matrix out of which the concepts we have mentioned may be derived.

2. *Points of View:* Now we must turn aside from these matters in order to get a still larger perspective on the field of educational psychology. The teacher in the classroom, of course, is dealing with actual growth processes and with methods which will promote growth, but, at the same time, he should be aware of some of the larger problems which have an important bearing on his work. We have said just above, for example, that the facts of child psychology are of first rate importance to the teacher. We have generalized this proposition by asserting that the field of genetic psychology furnishes the foundational material for an adequate survey of teaching problems. As the student knows, however, it is possible

[2] Cf. Burton, W. H., *Introduction to Education.* New York: D. Appleton-Century Co., 1934, Chapter II and *passim.*

to write several different types of genetic psychology because it is possible to define human nature in as many different ways.[3]

Long before psychology became a science, social groups were making use of whatever material they possessed concerning the main features of human growth and development in order that they might be as intelligent as possible in their activities. Even though they were not fully aware of it, definite assumptions were made regarding the nature of the mind, the social and ethical significance of conduct, and the proper place of the individual, both in a secular and in a religious society. This material was drawn from a great many different sources, but primarily from philosophy, religion, and all of the commonsense psychology that goes to make up the pre-experimental history of this new science.[4] It ought to be clear, then, that the teacher cannot put his teaching methods into a proper perspective unless he knows something about different points of view in psychology and how these points of view may emphasize various aspects of a single teaching operation.[5]

3. *Purpose of the Chapter:* In the course of this chapter, we shall try to make some of these facts plain, but there is another obligation the teacher must accept. He should know not only the background of psychology out of which his teaching operations have come, but he also should know how different men have defined the field of educational psychology itself. In other words, it is inevitable that educational methods and practices should have used a variety of points of entrance into the series of events which mark the passage of a person from childhood to maturity. We ourselves have emphasized the genetic point of view, and we must, therefore, describe the various ways in which other persons have sought to define the province of educational psychology.

This last chapter in the book, then, will attempt a broad perspective over our whole survey of educational psychology. In other words, it will serve not only as a summary of the book, but also as a summary of some of the larger problems which every teacher will have to face at some time or other in his work. Education is based upon experimental psychology and it is hardly possible, therefore, to avoid some reference to this science.

[3] Cf. Murchison, C. (Ed.), *Psychologies of 1930.* Worcester, Mass.: Clark Univ. Press, 1930, *passim;* Heidbreder, E. F., *Seven Psychologies.* New York: D. Appleton-Century Co., 1933, *passim.*
[4] Cf. Monroe, P., *A Textbook in the History of Education.* New York: The Macmillan Co., 1918, *passim.*
[5] Consult Ragsdale, C. E., *Modern Psychologies and Education.* New York: The Macmillan Co., 1932, *passim.*

II. The Psychological Background of Education

1. *Introduction:* We have said above that it is not possible to go very far in the study of education without becoming acutely aware of the fact that there are a great many different ways of describing human nature. At the present time, for example, there are many students who would argue that psychology and education should study the ways in which human beings react to other persons and to the objects and events around them. Of this group, there are some who describe human and animal conduct wholly in terms of the varieties of muscular movements that are made in response to various situations. This point of view is called radical behaviorism.[6] On the other hand, there are those who would say that many of the reactions made by human beings and by the lower animals are mental processes such as sensations, memories, images, and feelings. These reactions are to be added to the bodily reactions. This type of psychology is sometimes called the stimulus-response psychology and sometimes the reaction psychology.[7]

These two views of the nature of psychology took the place, as it were, of a view that paid much less attention to the ways in which human beings behave. This slightly older psychology argued that every human being could look at and describe his own mental processes in much the same way that we all look at and describe objects and events that are "outside" of us. It seemed possible, then, to say that psychology might be the science of the mind, where the word "mind" referred to nothing more or less than all of the states of consciousness or all of the immediate experiences which each individual has. This type of psychology has been called mentalism, introspective psychology, descriptive psychology, and, in its earlier stages, physiological psychology.[8]

This last way of defining psychology is, however, fairly recent. It took the place, in its turn, of a still older view of human nature. Beginning with some of the ancient Greek philosophers and coming to its highest point in scholasticism and in the philosophy of Descartes and Wolff, it was held that the word "mind" should name

---

[6] Cf. Watson, J. B., *Psychology from the Standpoint of the Behaviorist.* Philadelphia: J. B. Lippincott, 1924, *passim.*
[7] Woodworth, R. S., *Psychology.* New York: Henry Holt and Co., 1929; Gates, A. I., *Psychology for Students of Education.* New York: The Macmillan Co., 1930.
[8] Cf. Wundt, W., *Grundzüge der physiologischen Psychologie* (7th ed.). Leipzig; J. C. Barth, 1923; Titchener, E. B., *A Textbook of Psychology.* New York: The Macmillan Co., 1910.

a unique type of mental stuff that was different from the stuff of which bodies and other physical objects are made. The conscious processes of a human being and the psychological things he might do were explained by the activity of this mind stuff.[9]

Even this view of human nature, however, had a predecessor. The older histories of psychology usually begin with a set of beliefs which have been included under the term "animism." This term is used to describe the beliefs of primitive man about the forces or agents which he attributed to himself and to a great many objects around him. As a result of his dreams, his observations of the difference between living and dead bodies, his illusions and hallucinations, his feelings of effort and of striving, and other experiences, primitive man came to the idea that his body must be the dwelling place of a twin made of much finer stuff than the stuff he ate. Primitive man appears to have thought that this twin or dreamlike double was the part of him which made the difference between a living body and a dead body, which explained all of his experiences, and which laid the foundation for his belief in whatever gods he might worship.[10]

Obviously, these various ways of thinking about human nature would make a great difference in the methods one might use to train or to educate human nature. In other words, not only the study of human nature but most of the generative ideas upon which education is based have changed markedly as society has entertained different ideas about the nature of human beings. Even at the present time, the very facts upon which educational psychology depends and many of the ways of describing the chief aims of education presuppose a doctrine of the nature of human nature. If it were possible to make a short study of the recent history of education, it would be clear that practically everything which various aims and methods of teaching have done has depended upon some prejudice about human nature.[11]

In spite of this fact, however, it would not be worth while to go through this history, were it not that most of the ideas and prejudices developed in the history of psychology persist, in one form or another, at the present time. There has been, therefore, in education and in psychology, an almost endless amount of confusion.

[9] Cf. Brett, G. S., *A History of Psychology*. London: Allen and Unwin, 1921, Vol. II, Parts I and II.
[10] Cf. McDougall, W., *Body and Mind*. New York: The Macmillan Co., 1911, Chapter I.
[11] Cf. Bode, B. H., *Conflicting Psychologies of Learning*. Boston: D. C. Heath and Co., 1929, pp. iii ff.

This confusion appears not only in the way some of the most urgent problems which society has to face are asked, but in methods of teaching and in descriptions of the aims of education.[12] It is not inappropriate, then, to conclude our study of some of the fundamentals of educational psychology with a brief survey of the different ideas men have had about themselves. Even a short sketch will support some of the criticisms that must be passed upon older definitions of education. Such a sketch will, moreover, throw into clear relief the mode of approach to these problems which has been used in the foregoing pages.

2. *Primitive Psychology:* It was said above that histories of psychology, like histories of religion and even of general science, frequently began with the beliefs of primitive men about themselves. It seems possible, however, to push our questions about these matters back to a still more remote period in the development of man, for it is hardly conceivable that animism should mark the first opinions which human beings held about themselves. After all, primitive man is a fairly recent member of the evolutionary series— even of that part of the series which contains the human family.[13]

In attempting to interpret the views which prehistoric man may have entertained about himself, let us begin with some remarks on the way in which the lower animals behave with respect to the objects and events around them. Even a casual inspection of the daily activities of our common household pets, the cat and the dog, will show that these animals react in one way toward those objects we have learned to call physical or inanimate and in another way toward those objects which we have learned to call animate. The behavior of one dog in the presence of another or of one dog in the presence of a cat is sharply to be distinguished from its behavior in the presence of a dish of water, a bit of food, or any similar object. This is not to say, of course, either that the lower animals are "consciously aware" of the fact that other animals are alive or that they are similarly aware that a pan of water or a piece of bedding are dead. On the contrary, it can be noted that, in their behavior, the lower animals try to escape from other animals, outwit them, stalk them, mate with them, and fight with them; but they do not escape, outwit, stalk, mate with, or fight against the ground they walk upon or the food they chew.

[12] Compare, for example, Gates, A. I., *op. cit.,* with Ogden, R. M., and Freeman, G. L., *Psychology and Education.* New York: Harcourt, Brace and Co., 1933.
[13] Cf. Warden, C. J., *The Evolution of Human Behavior.* New York: The Macmillan Co., 1932, *passim.*

It is true, of course, that dogs will chase sticks as though they were chasing other animals, and cats will toy with a ball of yarn, but these performances are a proof rather than a disproof of the distinction we are trying to make. They show that the lower animals may use a type of behavior technique which, for brevity's sake, we shall call the person-technique, even on objects where it is not effective. Moreover, they show that they can also use a set of reactions which, likewise, for brevity's sake, we shall call the thing-technique.[14] This is to say that, in their mutual reactions with one another, the lower animals act as though they "knew" something about the nature of other animals as well as something about the nature of things. They learn to react in differential ways to the movements of other objects. A cat finds out something about the nature of mice, and its own reactions are regulated accordingly. It also finds out something about the nature of the trunk of a tree against which it sharpens its claws. Mice, too, learn enough about the nature of cats to keep out of their way. In short, their behavior in the presence of cats is to be distinguished from their behavior in the presence of other classes of objects.

It seems fair to say that this distinction between the properties, traits, or modes of action of things as opposed to the properties, traits, or modes of action of persons was one of the first distinctions of the psychological sort which prehistoric man could have drawn.[15] Every parent that raised a child, every man that wooed a maid, every hunter that stalked his game, and every warrior that outwitted his enemy used a set of reactions which he did not use in finding a stone which might be tied to a handle or in chipping a flint which might be put at the end of a spear. The pottery he shaped and the pictures he carved upon the walls of his cave called for a type of reaction he could not have found appropriate in getting his fellow men to coöperate in a dance or in warfare.

It is not to be supposed, however, that prehistoric man reacted to living creatures in a manner different from his modes of reaction to nonliving things because he "knew" or "thought" that living things possessed a spirit which nonliving things did not possess. On the contrary, the distinction between person-techniques and thing-

---

[14] Cf. Benedict, R., Art. "Animism," in *The Encyclopedia of the Social Sciences* (Ed., E. R. A. Seligman). New York: The Macmillan Co., Vol. II, pp. 65-67. Also Lévy Bruhl, L., *Primitive Mentality* (trans. by L. A. Clare). New York: The Macmillan Co., 1923, *passim*.

[15] The way in which children draw this distinction has been studied with care. Cf. Piaget, J., *The Child's Conception of the World*. New York: Harcourt, Brace and Co., 1929, pp. 175 ff. See also Montague, W. M., *Belief Unbound*. New Haven: Yale Univ. Press, 1930, p. 3.

techniques must have been an inevitable result of his various ways of profiting from past experience. In other words, prehistoric man must have taken—unwittingly, to be sure—the same attitude toward the objects and events around him that the modern biologist takes toward the phenomena of life. There are, as we know, some persons who say that the various things living creatures can do must owe their origin to the presence, within their bodies, of some invisible and nonphysical agent or entity which has just the right kind of vital power. Most students of biology, however, hold that the search for an invisible agent of this sort is not fruitful. On the contrary, they take note of the fact that living things behave in ways that are not possible for nonliving things. They draw the distinction, therefore, between matter and life in terms of the proposition that matter can be handled by the use of some techniques, whereas life has to be handled by the use of other techniques.[16]

3. *The Origin of the "Soul"*: As we shall see in a moment, we have gone to these speculations about preanimistic distinctions of the psychological type for a distinct purpose. In the meantime, we may consider in greater detail some of the characteristics of a psychology of the animistic type. It has been pointed out by a great many students of primitive peoples that primitive man, like modern man, must have had dreams. In these dreams, he saw himself on the warpath again with friends whom, in his waking life, he knew to be dead. He might also have seen himself hunting food with the aid of a dog which in his waking life was no longer his. Moreover, he must have been mightily impressed with the difference between a living body and a dead body. He saw his image in a pond or spring and caught glimpses of after-images on the walls of his cave after nightfall. He must have had illusions and hallucinations both of the normal and of the pathological type. Moreover, he stood, no doubt, at that stage in the total history of evolution where his ways of being conscious may have been of unending interest to him.[17]

Different writers have taken different groups of these facts as the basis for the following argument. They have assumed that primitive man must have come, sooner or later, to the place in his thinking where he could invent the concept of a dreamlike double for his own body. This dreamlike double was not, however, a passive and indifferent figment of the imagination. On the contrary, it must

[16] Cf. Thompson, J. A., *The System of Animate Nature*. New York: Henry Holt and Co., 1920, Vol. II, Chapter II.
[17] Tylor, E. B., *Primitive Culture*. London: Bell, 1873; Hopkins, E. W., *The Origin and Evolution of Religion*. New Haven: Yale Univ. Press, 1923.

have been thought of as possessing the same feelings of effort and the same powers of determination that he experienced for himself. In any case, the histories of psychology and of philosophy pick up primitive man at a point where much of his conduct was ordered with respect to the soullike agents around him. Animistic power was attributed not only to other living creatures and especially to human beings, but to trees, stones, clubs, animals, and raiment.[18]

It is at this point that we come upon one of the most interesting events that has ever taken place in the cultural history of mankind. This event occurred when human beings first began to suppose that the distinction between thing-techniques and person-techniques (a distinction which, as we have said, they must have held in common with the lower animals) could be accounted for by saying that persons differed from things because they possessed a dreamlike or spiritual double. As soon as primitive man had come to the place in his thinking about himself where he could say that person-techniques or the arts of persuasion were contingent upon soul activity, he had set one of the most persistent of philosophical problems.[19]

Hitherto, his own ways of acting had been developed in order to make proper allowances for the modes of action of other things. The various types of allowance he had to make differed according to the nature of the object he was handling. Looking at him from our own point of view, we can see that his allowances were of two types, viz., those that had to do with things and those that had to do with persons. When, however, as a result of the development of animism, he sought to explain the behavior of persons in terms of the soullike forces or agents which inhabited them, he set the stage for as much serious thinking as the race has ever been able to do.

In his religious ceremonies, for example, and in all of his magic, primitive man began to use person-techniques where his ancestors had been satisfied with thing-techniques. That is, having been unduly impressed by coincidences, he had come to believe that all objects could, like himself, be persuaded, invited, cajoled, or outwitted. Primitive magic was an attempt to persuade, invite, cajole, and outwit inanimate objects. Before he arrived at the animistic stage of his mental development, he had always forced or compelled objects, but now it seemed possible to bring rain, sunshine, and otherwise control the forces of nature by treating them in the same way that

---

[18] Cf. McDougall, W., *op. cit.*, Chapter I and *passim*.
[19] Cf. Calkins, M. W., *The Persistent Problems of Philosophy*. New York: The Macmillan Co., 1908, *passim*.

he had learned to treat other living creatures and especially his fellow human beings.

We may see this fact to best advantage in that mode of psychological thinking which emphasizes, in extreme form, the differences between mind and matter. This psychology has often been called soul psychology, the mind-stuff theory, or scholastic psychology.[20] During the Middle Ages, most of the men who worked out the details of psychology argued that every human being was actually a pair of twins, the one member of the pair being named the body and the other member being named the mind. It was said that the body, like other physical objects, was extended in space and had the characteristics we generally associate with physical objects. The mind, on the other hand, was not extended.[21] It was incorporeal stuff and closely associated with concepts which were more significant to theology and to religion than to psychology. It was the soul or the mind, for example, which looked out of the various windows of the body and thus found out what was taking place in the outer physical world. The eyes, to take a specific case, served as one such pair of windows. It was the soul or the mind, also, which carried on such functions as thinking, judging, discriminating, remembering, choosing, and resolving.[22]

In short, the soul or the mind psychologies sought to explain all of the distinctive things that human beings are—as opposed to physical objects—by saying that the body was the servant of the mind. After the mind had taken note of the events in the external world, it could reflect about these events, compare them with one another, and draw inferences from them according to the laws of rigid thinking which have come to be expressed in the various principles of logic. Once the mind had arrived at a conclusion in its thinking, or whenever it had decided upon a course for conduct, the various parts of the body were used as instruments by means of which the mind might express itself.[23]

4. *Rational Psychology:* It goes almost without saying that a shift from the type of psychology we have attributed to prehistoric man to the type of psychology the philosophers were talking about marks a shift of tremendous importance. Prehistoric man was ob-

---

[20] Brett, G. S., *op. cit.,* Vol. I, *passim.*
[21] Cf. Burtt, H. E., *The Metaphysical Foundations of Modern Physics.* New York: Harcourt, Brace and Co., 1925, *passim.*
[22] Cf. Dewey, J., *The Quest for Certainty.* New York: Minton, Balch and Co., 1929, *passim.*
[23] Cf. De Wulf, M., *Scholasticism, Old and New.* Dublin: M. H. Gill and Son, 1910, *passim.*

viously drawing distinctions between things and persons in terms of what he directly observed and learned about things and persons. The philosophers, however, were drawing a distinction between things and persons in terms of the fact that persons were supposed to mark the dwelling place of some sort of agent, force, or power which was not the body or even a group of properties or traits of that particular type of functional agent that we call a human being. In short, the philosophers were doing the same thing in the field of psychology that a biologist does when he says that living must be accounted for in terms of a vital principle or some other mysterious agent which makes flesh do what it does. The very fact that both the biologist and the psychologist can describe living creatures in terms of their distinctive properties or traits means that prehistoric man was more nearly right in his approach to psychology than many of the more recent psychologies have been. This proposition will, perhaps, become clearer as we carry on our discussion.[24]

The doctrine that man has a mind which is the source of his unique behavioral characteristics lent itself to that form of psychology sometimes called rational psychology. A science of mind of the rational sort went beyond the older points of view by saying that the mind had several different types of faculties. It had, for example, a knowing faculty which meant that it could perceive objects and reflect about them. It was argued, also, that the mind was an effective agent in the sense that it was constantly using the body in order to carry out its wishes. This fact was described by saying that the mind has a conative faculty.[25] We are not so much interested, however, in a list of the different kinds of faculties as in discovering the reasons why anyone should speak of faculties at all. The logic of the situation seems to run about as follows. The whole order of nature is made up of objects and events. Objects may be described both in terms of what they are, that is, in terms of the stuff of which they are made and in terms of what they do. Events, likewise, may be described in terms of what they do, but they may be described, also, in terms of the conditions that must be satisfied before they may come to pass. The conditions which must be met before an event can happen are sometimes called the causes of the event, but now and then some single condition is taken as *the* cause of an event as though the cause were an agent or power or force

[24] Cf. Haldane, J. S., *The Sciences and Philosophy*. New York: Doubleday, Doran and Co., 1929, *passim*.
[25] Cf. Klemm, G. O., *A History of Psychology* (trans. by E. C. Wilm and R. Pintner). New York: Charles Scribner's Sons, 1914, *passim*.

which had, as its purpose, the production of the given effect.[26]

Since the reactions of human beings are events, one might try to describe the conditions under which these events take place or one might seek out the effective agent behind the events. We are trying to say that soul psychologies of various types recognize the mind or the faculties of the mind as *the* cause or the effective agent behind human behavior.[27] The mind thus becomes an object, and this object may be described either in terms of the stuff of which it is made or in terms of the events which it brings to pass.[28]

The scholastic psychology, then, was an explanatory psychology which assumed that the mind was an incorporeal thing which acted as an agent in the production of the various types of behavior of which human beings are capable. Rather than describe the functions or operations human beings display when they are actually at work amid their surroundings, the scholastic urged that the mind itself should be the chief object of description.[29]

5. *Experimental Psychology:* We shall come back to this type of psychology in the next section, for it suggests a great many things about education. Were it not for the fact that it has left behind it a considerable number of prejudices which have been a source of much confusion, both for psychology and for education, we might leave it altogether out of account in any study of the psychological foundations of education. Moreover, although the soul psychology did not lend itself readily to the methods of experimental science, it would not be fair to say that the scholastic was wholly wrong in his study of human nature.

Before we consider these matters further, however, we must sketch briefly some of the more important aspects of the various experimental psychologies which followed the establishment of the first psychological laboratory. The point of departure for experimental psychology may be stated as follows. Every human being is, of course, conscious of events that appear to be going on for him. He sees and hears objects, remembers events, feels either satisfied or dissatisfied about them, reflects upon them, and takes them as sources of action. Since he does not see, feel, or hear his own soul, it would follow that one might attempt to describe the stream of

[26] Cf. Campbell, N. R., *Physics, The Elements*. Cambridge: Cambridge Univ. Press, 1920, *passim*.
[27] Cf. Moore, J. S., and Gurnee, H., *The Foundations of Psychology*. Princeton Univ. Press, 1933, *passim*.
[28] For an account of the soul-stuff theories, see James, W., *Principles of Psychology*. New York: Henry Holt and Co., 1890 (2 vols.), *passim*.
[29] Cf. De Wulf, M., *op. cit.*

experience just as it runs along without at the same time supposing that the stream of experience is made up of successive states of a mind.[30] Since the stream of experience often runs rapidly and may be complex and confused, one may either try to take it part by part, or he may try to find out why it is that one mental event follows another in just the way that it does. In either case this sort of psychology would stand in sharp contrast against the scholastic psychologies, because mental processes are spoken of as though they are events that happen rather than agents which act.[31]

It occurred to the first experimenters, then, that psychology might, by looking at its problems in this way, escape many of the difficulties offered by the older points of view. The last century and the first part of the present century have seen a tremendous amount of work done, therefore, on the analysis and description of experience. All of this work was aided by a great many commonsense observaations of the way in which different experiences may follow one another in the whole stream of experience. As we have seen, these commonsense observations were finally developed into a series of laws known as the laws of association.[32]

As we shall discover, much of this material has found its way into educational practices. It has not been used, however, just as it came from the first laboratories. On the contrary, it has been changed for the following reasons. In the first place, psychologists have not found it easy to get away from the idea that the mind must have some sort of causal effectiveness in behavior. In the second place, it has not been possible to get away from the thought that living creatures are adjusting themselves to their environments rather than sitting in quiet contemplation while more or less detached from their environments.[33] This concept of adjustment or adaptation gained tremendously in importance after the publication of *The Origin of Species*.

In short, then, the analysis and description of experience seemed to say too little about the functions of the mind. There were those who would argue, therefore, that mental processes must somehow help living creatures to adapt themselves to their environments. This objective could be gained in two ways. Either the mind itself

---

[30] Cf. Titchener, E. B., *Systematic Psychology: Prologomena.* New York: The Macmillan Co., 1929, Chapter I.
[31] Cf. Boring, E. G., *op. cit., passim.*
[32] Cf. Warren, H. C., *A History of the Association Psychology.* New York: Charles Scribner's Sons, 1921; Robinson, E. S., *Association Theory Today.* New York: D. Appleton-Century Co., 1932.
[33] **Cf. Raup, R. B.,** *Complacency, The Foundation of Human Behavior.* New York: The Macmillan Co., 1925, *passim.*

or single mental processes could act as effective agents in producing greater adjustment or they could favor adjustment simply by being present during a stimulus-response situation. That is to say, mental processes might aid adjustment in somewhat the same sense that a pedestal performs a function by supporting the statue resting on it. In any case, functional psychologies have played a very important part in the recent history of psychology and, as we shall see, in the formulation of some of the problems of education.[34]

In the meantime, the methods of psychology had been carried over to the study of animals. It seemed to be clear that no psychologist could study the mind or even the stream of consciousness of an animal but that he could study, at length, the way in which animals react to the situations around them. It soon began to appear that these same considerations hold true of human beings also. No experimenter can study the mind of a small child or of a new-born infant. On the contrary, it is only the behavior of the child or the infant that can be made the object of experimentation. Even where adults are subjects, the experimenter does not directly examine the mental processes of another person. Instead, he studies the way in which other people react to his experimental situations.[35]

It came about, therefore, that a psychology which had been a science of the mind turned into a science of behavior. Some of the behaviorists have been venturesome enough to assert that mental processes, mind, and consciousness do not exist, and we may, therefore, call such individuals radical behaviorists. Others have agreed that the immediate data from any psychological experiment are made up of modes of responses or of measures of their speed, but they still assume that these responses must be intimately related to different varieties of mental processes. Such psychologies, as we have said, may be called stimulus-response psychologies or reaction psychologies.[36]

It goes almost without saying that any type of behaviorism will have as many definite things to say about education as will any other psychology. There is certainly a great difference between

---

[34] Cf. Angell, J. R., *Psychology*. New York: Henry Holt and Co., 1908; Judd, C. H., *Psychology* (Rev. ed.). Boston: Ginn and Co., 1917; Carr, H. A., "Functionalism," in Murchison, C. (Ed.). *Psychologies of 1930*. Worcester, Mass.: Clark Univ. Press, 1930, Chapter III.
[35] Watson, J. B., "Psychology as a Behaviorist Views It." *Psychol. Rev.*, 1913, XX, 158-177.
[36] Cf. Woodworth, R. S., *Contemporary Schools of Psychology*. New York: The Ronald Press, 1931; Murchison, C. (Ed.), *Psychologies of 1930*. Worcester, Mass.: Clark Univ. Press, 1930; Griffith, C. R., *General Introduction to Psychology*. New York: The Macmillan Co., 1928, Part I; Ragsdale, C. E., *Modern Psychologies and Education*. New York: The Macmillan Co., 1932, Part I.

the education of a mind or of a set of mental faculties, on the one hand, and the training of behavior-patterns, on the other. It is one thing to teach an individual how to think and quite another to teach him to make the right reactions to definite stimulus-situations. We must not, however, exaggerate these differences too greatly, for it may be that different points of view in psychology and the educational methods based upon them have really been working toward the same goal. In any case, we must now hasten on to see how education has made use of these various points of view.

III. THE RATIONAL VIEW OF EDUCATION

1. *Introduction:* Educational psychology is, of course, a recently established branch of applied psychology. This cannot be taken to mean, however, that educators have only recently been interested in taking account of psychological facts. On the contrary, the brief sketch of some phases of the history of psychology which we have just presented makes it clear, by implication at least, that it is not possible to carry out any program of education, either primitive or modern, without taking something for granted concerning the nature of the individual who is placed under instruction.

2. *Primitive Education:* As nearly as we can judge from the records that are available, and from the facts that have been summarized, primitive education was of such a character as to emphasize the habits and skills of members in the social group rather than to increase their fund of abstract knowledge. Whereas modern man is called upon to acquire information and to reflect about it, primitive man was called upon, first of all, to pass through that mode of training which would enable him to get along in a physical environment. That is, he had to learn how to hunt, fish, use weapons, prepare skins, secure shelter from the elements, and coöperate with other members of the tribe.[37]

There is no evidence that these various types of skill were set into any more of a cultural background than may be the case with some of the animals. In other words, primitive man had to acquire many different techniques some of which would be serviceable in his dealings with physical objects, the others being most serviceable in his dealings with living objects. We have classified these techniques into two groups, viz., the thing-techniques and the person-techniques. It is not necessary to suppose that, at this stage of human evolution,

[37] Cf. Monroe, P., *A Textbook in the History of Education.* New York: The Macmillan Co., 1918, Chapter I.

men knew what it meant to ask about the minds of other men or of other animals. On the contrary, their education or training taught them how to make the right allowances for the various types of objects with which they had to deal.[38]

We have found reason, in many of the preceding chapters, to use this form of education and the psychology upon which it is based in connection with our own approach to the modern problems of educational psychology. In any case, we may remark the fact that, when primitive man came to the place where he sought to explain the behavior of living creatures by attributing to them some sort of animistic agent or force, the distinction between person-techniques and thing-techniques was greatly sharpened. Instead of acquiring habits and skills which might help him to make due allowance for persons as opposed to things, he now began to inquire after the agents and intentions that might lie behind acts.

3. *Scholastic Education:* Some of the educational procedures suggested by this change in the thinking of primitive man comes to clear-cut expression in the period commonly known as the scholastic period. In jumping so quickly from primitive man to one of the highest points in the history of philosophy, we do not mean to imply that prodigious changes had not taken place in the concepts with which we are dealing. These changes belong, however, to the history of philosophy rather than to an attempt to relate the problems of education to some of the major points of view toward psychology. We may summarize a thousand years of intense speculation by saying that, during the scholastic period and culminating with the philosophy of Descartes, various scholars had come by one of the most definite and precise notions that has ever been formulated concerning the nature of the stuff upon which the educative process might be brought to bear.[39] The animistic beliefs of primitive man, the ideologies of some of the Greek philosophers, and certain theological concepts about the nature of the soul were consolidated in the argument that every human being has a mind. This mind was thought of as an object or a thing, although it was not a thing in the sense that it was made up of physical stuff. It was the mind, then, rather than habits and skills that should be the subject of the educational process.

If there had been a formal system of educational psychology in

[38] Material bearing on this point in the growth of the child is to be found in Piaget, J., *The Child's Conception of the World.* New York: Harcourt, Brace and Co., 1929, pp. 173 ff.

[39] Cf. McDougall, W., *op. cit., passim.* Also Lange, F. A., *The History of Materialism* (3rd ed.). New York: Harcourt, Brace and Co., 1925, *passim.*

prehistoric society, it would have inquired about the origin and development of habits. Likewise, if there had been an educational psychology during the Middle Ages, it would have inquired about the origin of the mind and about the conditions under which minds may be disciplined. It was theology, however, rather than an educational psychology which answered the question about the development of the mind. It was believed that human beings came by their minds either at birth or at conception. Moreover, it was believed that these minds were not part-minds which would acquire further parts after the body which they inhabited grew older. On the contrary, the mind was alleged to possess, at its very beginning, all of the major traits or faculties which it was ever going to have. The mind of an infant, then, might be a *little* mind but not a segment of a whole mind or a genetically prior stage of an emerging series of functions.

Obviously, education of this type would have to consist of a procedure that would nourish such a little mind so that it might grow in stature and in strength. In short, mental development would mean mental enlargement but not change of the genetic order. In order to illustrate this proposition, we may quote from Baldwin as follows:

"The older idea of the soul was of a fixed substance, with fixed attributes. Knowledge of the soul was immediate in consciousness, and adequate; at least, as adequate as such knowledge could be made. The mind was best understood where best or most fully manifested; its higher 'faculties,' even when not in operation, were still there, but asleep. Under such a conception, the man was father to the child. What the adult consciousness discovers in itself is true, and wherein the child lacks it falls short of the true stature of soul life. We must, therefore, if we take account of the child-mind at all, interpret it up to the revelations of the man-mind. If the adult consciousness shows the presence of principles not observable in the child consciousness, we must suppose, nevertheless, that they are really present in the child consciousness beyond the reach of our observation. The old argument was this—and it is not too old to be found in the metaphysics of to-day—consciousness reveals certain great ideas as simple and original: consequently they must be so. If you do not find them in the child-mind, then you must read them into it." [40]

As an illustration of the natural equipment of the mind and of the way in which this natural equipment may be trained, let us take

[40] Baldwin, J. M., *Mental Development.* New York: The Macmillan Co., 1906, p. 2.

the so-called rational or noetic faculties of the soul. The power to think is a power which does not emerge out of a dynamic growth process that may be promoted and directed by environmental agents; on the contrary, it is a power with which man is necessarily equipped just as soon as he becomes an immortal soul. In other words, with respect to thinking, the mind has an inflexible original nature. It is at this point that a very definite assumption is made about the education of the mind. It now goes almost without saying that there is a great difference between the problem-solving functions of a small child and of an adult, but the scholastic point of view could not admit that this difference was really a difference in species. The word "species" refers to the fact that, although the accidents or more superficial properties of a thing may change, its essence or real being cannot change. This point of view would say, then, that the child possesses, from the very first, all of the faculties for thinking according to the species (i.e., intrinsic nature) of the adult, but before these faculties can be used to best advantage they must be nourished or tutored or disciplined and thus brought to the place where they can be exercised to the best advantage.

The growth of the mind was conceived after a direct analogy with the post-natal growth of the body. It seems to be a plain fact of observation that a new-born infant has all of the bodily organs which it will ever have. The growth or the development of the body does not consist in the acquisition of additional arms or legs or sense organs, but simply in the perfection and disciplining of structures and functions already present. In the same way, the mind of the child could be said to have in its own original essence or nature all of the necessary structures and functions it will ever have, but in an untutored or undisciplined or untrained state. The problem of education, then, would consist of a search for the circumstances under which the faculties of the mind can be nourished and disciplined. Common observation has it that the play activities of small children together with a certain amount of compulsory exercise is a sufficient and adequate way of promoting physical stamina. The mind, too, must have its stamina increased, and education would mark a way in which society could render this service to its immature members.

A. TRANSFER OF TRAINING: Two famous doctrines have come out of this approach to the problems of educational psychology. The first of these is the famous problem of the transfer of training. It goes almost without saying that if the mind has, so to speak, its own sinews and that if these sinews are strengthened by exercise, the

708 INTRODUCTION TO EDUCATIONAL PSYCHOLOGY

mind ought to be able to use its acquired strength with respect to any situation or set of problems it might have to face. The analogy with bodily structures is just as close at this point as at other points. A boxer, for example, in training himself for a match, tries to increase the strength of his muscles by punching a straw man. Moreover, he hopes that he may increase his wind, coördinate his feet, and quicken his reactions by skipping rope, running several miles each day, or boxing with an imaginary opponent.[41]

No boxer would go through all of these modes of training if he did not thoroughly believe that the quickness he acquired in shadow boxing would make him react more quickly to an opponent, or that the foot coördination developed while skipping the rope would help him dodge his opponent and give him a solid foundation while he launched his own attack. In the same way, the doctrine of formal discipline or of transfer of training argued that the severe exercise of the mental sinews—say such sinews as are described by the words and phrases "memory," "comparison," "judgment," "sustained attention," and "persistence," actually increases their strength so that, having been trained in one situation, they become wholly effective in almost any other situation.

Since the logical opposite of this doctrine would be the doctrine that training is not transferred at all, that is, the doctrine that all training is specific for a particular situation and for a particular setting, it would seem to follow that education would have to study this whole matter with all the means that are available. As we have seen, there are certain kinds of experiments which appear to say that the training of the psychological functions is highly specific. This fact is important not only so far as the fact itself is concerned, but also because of a change in the point of view toward psychology that is involved in it.

B. FREEDOM OF ACTION: The second of the problems created by the point of view toward education described above runs as follows. If the mind is of such a nature as to carry on thinking and if the use of one's mind is subject to what is commonly called determination or will power, it would follow that the failure of any student in the schoolroom to learn to attend, to solve problems, or otherwise to use his native mental faculties must be a sign of perversity and of disobedience rather than of inadequate mental equipment.[42] There was a time in the history of psychology when this conclusion could

[41] Cf. Gould, A. G., and Dye, J. A., *Exercise and Its Physiology*. New York: A. S. Barnes and Co., 1932, Chapter XXIV.
[42] Cf. Swift, E. J., *Psychology and the Day's Work*. New York: Charles Scribner's Sons, 1921, Chapter VII.

be taken at its face value. At another time, however, this argument has been confused by the proposition that even though every child is born with a mind, this mind may not be its own master. Because of events associated with the Creation Epic and with the Fall of Man, it came to be held that every human being might be subject to the will of another master. At one time in the history of theological opinion it was even implied, if not actually argued, that this other master might take the form of a personal devil who, living within or attending the spirit of certain individuals, prevented them from doing that which they were supposed to do or morally obligated to do.[43]

We do not need to enter into these vexing questions, however, in order to see that an educational psychology of this more traditional form would not recognize the fact that the use of psychological functions is not so much a matter of will power or of determination as of the environmental conditions under which they are made possible, and of the strength and extent of the motives which have been established under the promoting effect of environmental circumstances.

C. THE GENETIC VIEW: Both of the problems of scholastic education which we have just described rest upon a more thoroughgoing difficulty. Any theory of the nature of the mind which supposes that all or even a considerable majority of the faculties of the mind are native and unlearned fails to catch the first significance of what may be called the genetic point of view. In a previous paragraph we have compared the growth of the mind with the growth of the body, pointing out the fact that even casual inspection shows that a new-born infant has all of the organs that it will ever have. This is true enough for an inspection that begins with birth, but if inspection begins with the fertilization of the ovum rather than with birth, then other facts hold true. We may still argue, of course, as indeed some of the philosophers have argued, that even the ovum is a miniature though complete edition of an adult; but everything that has been discovered about the ovum and about the course of its development seems to suggest that the ovum is in no sense of the word, save in its dynamic potentiality, a human being. This is to say that a genuine process of evolution marks the series of changes of an essentially biological character from a fertilized ovum to an adult human being.

This same argument may now be applied to the psychological

[43] Cf. White, A. D., *A History of the Warfare of Science with Theology.* New York: D. Appleton-Century Co., 1896, Vol. II, Chapters XV, XVI.

functions of a human being. If the analogy between physical growth and psychological growth is to extend backward only so far as birth, we might argue that the mind of a new-born infant has all of the original nature it is ever going to have.[44] If, however, we take a thoroughly genetic point of view toward the growth of the psychological functions, we may say that the mind grows or develops just as the body has developed or just as the race has developed or just as the whole order of nature has developed.[45]

D. EXPERIMENTAL PSYCHOLOGIES: For these and other reasons the scholastic point of view has been replaced by a series of experimental psychologies. It might be said, of course, that space and time should not be wasted upon what, after all, is nothing more than an episode in history. In spite of the criticisms that may be directed against the soul psychologies, however, it must not be forgotten that the scholastic was saying some very important things about human nature as he saw it. Contemporary psychology speaks a language that the scholastic would not understand, and it seems fair to ask, then, whether a new language means the discovery of new facts about human nature or simply raises a problem of translation. If the latter is the case, we may well wonder whether the new language of experimental psychology, and especially the new language of behaviorism, can actually describe those aspects of human nature in which the scholastic was most interested. The very fact that we have introduced the point of view of the scholastic into this phase of our study of the nature of educational psychology means that, before we are through with it, we shall have to come to terms with some of the shortcomings of more modern points of view, as well as with the shortcomings of older points of view.

IV. MIND AND BEHAVIOR IN EDUCATION

1. *Introduction:* Up to this point in our discussion of the various ways of defining educational psychology we have used such words as "mind," "reaction," "behavior," "conduct," and "experience" without making a serious attempt to draw a distinction between them. The scholastic seemed to be perfectly sure that he was educating, that is—disciplining—a mind or a person. Those who have

---

[44] Refer again to Chapter One and to the discussion of original nature.
[45] The evidence for these assertions lies, of course, in the rapidly developing field of child psychology. Moreover, as we have seen in Chapter Ten, an increasing number of experimental facts will lead eventually to a description of general principles of development, principles which will be both explanatory and descriptive.

based their educational psychologies upon facts drawn from a study of the typical normal adult likewise have supposed that a mind was the proper subject of the educative process. The modern reaction psychologies, however, have assumed that reactions to stimuli are the principle subjects of education. This point of view assumes, to be sure, that reactions may be either of the behavioral or of the mental sort, but, in actual operation, the reaction psychologies are more nearly related to that kind of psychology known as behaviorism than they are to any of the traditional psychologies. In any case, it is not possible to understand the general principles of educational psychology or to appreciate the significance of the genetic point of view toward these principles without further consideration of what it is that is actually trained, whether a mind or a set of behavior-patterns.[46]

2. *Empirical Behaviorism:* That point of view in psychology known as behaviorism marks an extension of and a more radical form of the point of view which can be called empirical behaviorism or reaction psychology. As we have seen, modern psychology has placed the problems of human nature in such a setting that for every stimulus there is some sort of connection leading to some kind of a response. This is, in general, an attitude that can easily be taken toward the problems of psychology, because nothing is quite so obvious about all living creatures as the way in which they will respond to or adapt themselves to environmental situations. Almost everything that we do with respect to one another is done for the sake of arousing some sort of effective response.

Among the responses that can be made are postures, manual skills of various kinds, and language responses. Of these three types of response, it is the language response, in particular, which has seemed to stand as a direct report of mental processes or of the existence of some kind of mindedness behind the continuous flow of behavior. Neither empirical psychologies nor reaction psychologies have been very clear about the place of mindedness in behavior, but the radical behaviorist appears to have no doubt at all on this score. It is his argument that those events called mental processes or that kind of stuff called mind simply does not exist. Those of the semiradical behaviorists who might admit the existence of conscious processes would still assert that such processes cannot and do not become the subject matter of science. They must forever remain the personal property of single individuals.[47]

[46] Cf. Ragsdale, C. E., *op. cit.*, Chapter III and *passim*.
[47] Watson, J. B., *op. cit.*, Chapter IX.

3. *Behaviorism:* A part of the incentive toward radical behaviorism has come, of course, from the development of animal psychology where the experimenter is forever limited to experimental situations, with respect to which certain identifiable and more or less adequate types of response can be made.[48] At the simplest level, these responses take the form of tropisms which are barely advanced beyond the mechanical reactions of a physical system to some experimentally controlled situation. The slightly higher organisms may, by virtue of the possession of a nervous system, transform tropisms into reflexes, and the radical behaviorist argues that a good case can be made out for the doctrine that all animal behavior is nothing more or less than reflex in character, even though reflexes may have entered into intricate patterns with one another.

This point of view was taken, for example, by the Russian investigator, Pavlov. As we have seen, Pavlov has found a way of showing how, given an original set of reflexes, almost any given stimulus may come to call forth a substitute response or how a variety of responses may come to be associated with any given stumulus.[49] In short, then, the problem of behaviorism is to describe the conditions under which the original nature of human beings is transformed into an acquired nature. Behaviorism is, therefore, from first to last, a kind of genetic psychology. Up to this point, it satisfies one of the requirements that we have made of an educational psychology, viz., that it shall stand in close dependence upon the historical or the genetic point of view.

Some of the evidence on this point runs as follows. There is, in the first place, the assured conviction on the part of the behaviorist that the right kind of a science of psychology will make the prediction and control of human behavior possible. That is, given a stimulus or a stimulus-situation and the behaviorist will hope to predict the response; or, given the response and the behaviorist will hope to say what the stimulating situation must have been. It is to be admitted, of course, that the behaviorist is still far away from this achievement, but he holds fast to the idea that the means for making the dream come true are now at hand. Since prediction of this sort is possible only when absolute control over human development can be reached, it must follow that the behaviorist has studied the growing child. It must follow, also, that he knows something about the original nature of the child. It turns out that there is prac-

---

[48] Cf. Roback, A. A., *Behaviorism and Psychology.* Cambridge: Sci.-Art Press, 1923, Chapters II, III.

[49] Pavlov, I. P., *Conditioned Reflexes* (trans. by G. V. Anrep). London: Oxford Univ. Press, 1927, *passim.*

POINTS OF VIEW IN PSYCHOLOGY

tically no original nature, save the equality of all infants at birth. To quote:

"In the case of man, all healthy individuals . . . start out *equal*. Quite similar words appear in our far-famed Declaration of Independence. The signers of that document were nearer right than one might expect, considering their dense ignorance of psychology. They would have been strictly accurate had the clause 'at birth' been inserted after the word equal. It is what happens to individuals after birth that makes one a hewer of wood and a drawer of water, another a diplomat, a thief, a successful business man or a far-famed scientist. What our advocates of freedom in 1776 took no account of is the fact that the Deity himself could not equalize 40-year-old individuals who have had such different environmental trainings as the American people have had." [50]

This is largely and positively said. It leaves nothing to the imagination as far as the functions of education are concerned. It implies a definition of educational psychology about which there can be no quibbling. Human nature is plastic to begin with. Environmental agents form and mould this nature whether society is intelligent about the process or not. Insofar as the curriculum represents an intentional organization of parts of the environment, just so far will predictable results appear. In any case, our problems in the paragraphs that are to follow now begin to appear. With arguments about educational psychology which vary so widely as to place the scholastic point of view at the one extreme and radical behaviorism at the other, serious students of education will have to have a steady aim if they expect to get through the experimental facts that have to be considered without falling beside the mark.

V. A Psychological Way of Describing Behavior

1. *Introduction:* No system of educational psychology can stand on a solid foundation until it has taken a definite point of view toward the mind-body problem. Sooner or later it must say either that it is the business of education to train the mind or that it shall seek to control behavior. The point of view that has been taken in this book leans sharply toward the position of the behaviorist. The behavior of which we have spoken, however, is not limited by the muscular and glandular responses of living creatures. On the contrary, it is a sort of behavior which has acquired a distinctive psychological character on account of the setting in which it is placed.

[50] Watson, J. B., *Behaviorism*. New York: W. W. Norton and Co., 1931, p. 270.

2. *The Nature of Psychological Experimentation:* As a first step in clarifying our point of view, we may consider a typical experiment—one that might be conducted either in a psychological laboratory or in a classroom.[51] We may wish to know, for example, how quickly a group of sixth-grade children can read short sections of printed material. These short sections differ from one another in what the printer would call their format. In other words, they differ from one another in the form and size of the type used, in the size of the margins, in the amount of leading between lines, and the like. Each piece of reading matter is presented to each of the sixth-graders in a piece of apparatus which enables the experimenter to control the time of presentation. Other pieces of apparatus may enable the experimenter to count the number of eye-movements made by each of his subjects, record the errors made by the subjects, and note the total time consumed in reading the various papers. It is possible also to study the comprehension of the reader. That is, after each section of material has been read, the experimenter may ask each of the subjects a number of questions about the material that has been read. As the subjects give their answers, the experimenter may record which are right and which are wrong and thus arrive at a score which he says represents the comprehension score of each of the subjects.

There are several features of an experiment of this kind which should be noted. In the first place, the experimenter has at no time come in direct contact with any of the mental processes of his subjects. The data he puts down in his score have to do with the responses made by his subject. These data are always correlated with the material used in the experimental set-up. There is no way to know how they may be correlated with the mental processes of his subjects. As we have seen, it was this fact about psychological experimentation which led the radical behaviorist to say that mental processes are not and cannot become the subject matter of any science. In this contention the behaviorist appears to be right. Let us emphasize the fact, also, that he is right when he argues that the method of experimentation just described is, in general outlines, the only kind of method a psychologist can ever use.[52] Educational psychology, then, can readily accept the general methodology of behaviorism.

[51] For a critical discussion of the nature of psychological experimentation, see Rosenzweig, S., "The Experimental Situation as a Psychological Problem." *Psychol. Rev.*, 1933, IV, 337-354.
[52] Cf. Tolman, E. C., *Purposive Behavior in Animals and Men.* New York: D. Appleton-Century Co., 1932, *passim,* and especially Chapter I.

The second feature of the experiment described above to which we wish to call attention may be stated as follows. The experimenter at the end of his study says that he has gained a score which represents the degree of comprehension of his subjects, but the word "comprehension" seems to say something about mental processes rather than about modes of response. We have already argued, however, that no mental processes have been open to the inspection of the experimenter. How, then, can he say that he has measured the comprehension of a sixth-grader? A part of the answer to this conundrum lies in the following facts. If the experimenter, in the case cited above, had been a radical behaviorist, he would have been interested primarily in the responses made by his subject, taken as responses. That is, he would have tried to describe the precise kind of eye-movements made during the reading act and the precise kinds of vocal movements made while answering questions. In other words, the terms "stimulus" and "response" are used by the behaviorist as they are used in physics and in physiology. Books on radical behaviorism are filled, therefore, with descriptions of light waves, sound waves, and other types of stimulus, on the one hand, and muscular contractions and glandular secretions, on the other hand.[53] Supplementary to these materials, there is usually an extended account of the central nervous system.

The responses of human beings do not acquire their psychological value, however, from this kind of description. On the contrary, they acquire their psychological value when they are seen to be related in a certain way to the stimulus-situation. In the study of comprehension, for example, a number of questions are asked which have to do with details in the paragraphs read by the subjects. The answers to these questions sustain a certain statistical relationship to the questions and to the original paragraphs. If a sixth-grader should answer every question asked of him about a given paragraph correctly, that is, if he should say everything that has already been said in the paragraph, his comprehension would be called perfect. If, in his answers to questions he says nothing that has been said in the original paragraph, it would be fair to assume that his comprehension was zero. Neither one of these statements could be made if the experimenter were interested only in the intrinsic nature of the responses made by his subject. Since he is interested, however, in the degree of relationship between the answers to a set of questions

---

[53] Watson, J. B., *Psychology from the Standpoint of the Behaviorist.* Philadelphia: J. B. Lippincott Co., 1924, Chapters I and IX.

and an original paragraph that has been read, he can say something about a psychological trait of his subjects.[54]

It is in this way, then, that the study of behavior may acquire a psychological significance. The reactions made by an individual are not correlated or compared with a set of mental processes or even with a mental faculty. They are compared or correlated with the original experimental situation, and it is out of this comparison that highly significant inferences can be drawn concerning the subjects used. There is, however, still another feature of the experiment described above. This feature has to do with the experimenter himself. Who or what is an object that can devise a problematic situation for another object? In the illustration we have used, an experimenter sets about it to study what he calls the "comprehension" of another individual. This means, of course, that he himself "knows" what comprehension is. It means that he "knows" what kind of a situation will be adequate to study the comprehension of another individual. In short, the experimenter himself is a part of his own laboratory set-up. The results that he gets from another individual are results that are relevant to a situation to which the experimenter himself is relevant.

3. *Animal Experimentation:* We may illustrate this aspect of psychological experimentation by taking a case from the animal laboratory. The experimenter, we shall say, has constructed a maze. This maze is presented to a white rat in the sense that the white rat is placed near the entrance to the maze, and if it is to get food, it must find its way through the maze to the food box. The experimenter is obviously a part of this experimental set-up, because it is a problem for him and he has meant to make it a problem for the rat. Obviously, however, it is not a problem for the rat. The rat does not "know" that there is food somewhere in the maze, and it reacts to this particular apparatus, therefore, just as it might react to any new situation which was full of stimulating agents.

The first trials of the rat are, therefore, "wrong" and more or less unrelated to the general problem of getting through the maze as rapidly as possible. On occasion, however, the rat finds food, whereupon its whole mode of behavior changes. The time of running becomes less, the number of errors decreases, and shortly the rat can run from one end of the maze to the other without making a mistake. In short, the maze situation has become a problem for the rat just as it is a problem for the experimenter. It becomes a

[54] Cf. Johnson, H. M., "Did Fechner Measure 'Introspectional' Sensations?" *Psychol. Rev.*, 1929, XXXVI, pp. 258 ff.

problem, however, not because the experimenter has related the behavior of the rat to an unobservable mental faculty, but because the behavior is related in a certain way to the whole stimulus-situation. It is related to the stimulus-situation in such a distinctive manner that, after a time, the experimenter can say that the problem has been solved. In short, then, the experimenter has discovered something about the learning or problem-solving functions of a white rat, but in so doing he himself has been, from first to last, an integral part of his own experimental set-up. If he did not know what a problem is, if he could not discriminate colors, sizes of openings, and sounds, he could not put a white rat into a situation that would make comparison between the situation and the behavior possible.[55]

There are, then, these three features of any psychological experiment which have a direct bearing not only upon a definition of psychology but upon a definition of educational psychology as well. In the first place, we infer that both psychology and education are committed to the methods the behaviorist uses. This has been the case throughout the entire history of psychology, both experimental and preexperimental. Our point of view differs from radical behaviorism, however, in the sense that the events described by the radical behaviorist do not mark much of an advance over physiology. Behavior does not acquire psychological significance until it is brought into comparison with the whole experimental set-up. Even this comparison, however, does not become significant until it is made plain that the experimenter himself is an essential part of his own laboratory set-up. Under these circumstances, a laboratory set-up is of such a nature that it can throw light upon the nature of the subject, just as it has already expressly stated something about the nature of the experimenter.

In our point of view toward psychology and educational psychology, then, we go back to a point of view which is as old as human action. We draw a distinction, again, between thing-techniques and person-techniques. We recognize the fact that living creatures can be handled in a way that distinguishes them from other kinds of objects. We can handle them that way because we, as experimenters, can use person-techniques, whereas objects, which are not persons, manifest only thing-techniques, that is, techniques which work to best advantage in the physical sciences.

Another way to say all of this runs as follows. Earlier in the chap-

[55] Cf. Wheeler, R. H., and Perkins, F. T., *Principles of Mental Development*. New York: T. Y. Crowell Co., 1932, Chapter XIX, and especially pp. 356 ff.

ter, we have said that there are two possible ways to describe life. On the one hand, we may try to get at what is called the vital principle or the agent behind living tissue which makes living tissue do what it does. This effort has never been very successful. On the other hand, we may describe life by describing its functions or its modes of operation. Living organisms, as objects, have certain properties, traits, characteristics, or dimensions which distinguish them from objects having other kinds of traits, properties, characteristics, or dimensions.[56]

This example may be applied to the problems of psychology and education. We may, if we wish, try to describe the psychical principle or mental agent which forces behavior to sustain the relations it does to stimulus-situations, but it has been said in several places that this attempt has not been successful. We may, however, try to outline the circumstances under which certain kinds of relationships between behavior and stimulus-situations are brought about. These relationships identify for us all of the varieties of what we may call psychological traits or psychological functions. Any statement of the conditions under which such traits or functions appear is the first step toward a control of these functions. Education is the method which society has used in controlling psychological functions. Education must, therefore, follow the psychologist as he goes about his various tasks, and especially the genetic psychologist, for it is the growth pattern upon which education is based.

4. *Reactions and Mental Processes:* Before we pass on to a statement of the various problems of educational psychology, it will be helpful to describe one general feature even of methodological behaviorism which is overlooked by the radical behaviorist. We have meant to say that methodological behaviorism takes for granted the inaccessibility of mental processes. It recognizes the proposition that no experimental method in psychology can pass directly from one mind to another or lay out for immediate comparison two different mental processes from a single mind. These facts cannot be taken to mean, however, that methodological behaviorism must deny the existence of mental processes. On the contrary, it seems to say that methodological behaviorism must assert their existence.

There is, in the first place, the fact that every psychological experimenter is a part of his own laboratory set-up. This fact has been recognized with increasing frequency in the physical sciences,

---

[56] Cf. Thompson, J. A., *The System of Animate Nature.* New York: Henry Holt and Co., 1920, Vol. I, Lectures II, III, VII; Haldane, J. S., *The Sciences and Philosophy.* Garden City: Doubleday, Doran and Co., 1929, Chapter IX.

but the psychologist has remained more or less ignorant of it.[57] He may, if he choose, say that he is wholly objective or quite mechanical in his selection of the crucial items in an experimental situation. But no experimenter, even in the animal laboratory, ever makes a study in visual discrimination by presenting an odor and a taste. On the contrary, the experimenter lays before his subject, whether animal or human, say, a pair of lights differing in intensity or in color. The very fact that he can present this situation to some other creature means that it has already been presented to him in the same way in which he means to present it to another.

This fact may become still clearer perhaps if we take the formulation of what are called problematic situations. Situations are not problematic for a physical or chemical object so far as we know. They become problematic for another living creature only because they are, in some sense of the word or other, problematic for the experimenter himself. This means that even though psychologists are limited in their observations to the responses of their subjects, nevertheless the experimenter himself, being a part of his own laboratory set-up, gives to that laboratory set-up the psychological quality or character which he himself is and which he expects to find in his subject. In the solution of a problem, the very fact that the experimenter recognizes the solution as a solution and distinguishes it from such reactions as the movement of a billiard ball under the impact of the cue means that his whole experiment has achieved psychological dimensions. Insofar, then, as an experimenter may perceive, attend, solve problems, enjoy motivation, and the like, just so far may he devise experimental situations which will measure the perception, attention, thinking, or motivation of other living creatures.

It must be clear that if a mental process could not be converted into behavior, it could not even be made a topic of conversation between philosophers. It would forever be the private property of one individual outside the domain of events described by experimental psychology. In order to illustrate this fact, we may take the situation which a physician faces when he is trying to diagnose an ailment. He asks his patient for a report on aches and pains. Obviously, if a given ache cannot be converted into some kind of response either verbal, postural, glandular, or manual, it must remain beyond the reach of the physician. Fortunately, the patient is able to symbolize most of his aches and pains by converting them, as it

[57] Cf. Bridgman, P. W., *The Logic of Modern Physics*. New York: The Macmillan Co., 1927, Chapter I.

were, into words, or into postures and bodily reactions, as the physician explores sensitive areas. The steps by means of which words, that is verbal reactions and other kinds of reactions, come to symbolize or represent so-called psychological experiences has been described in considerable detail in an earlier chapter.[58]

It may be that adequate diagnosis requires that the physician shall get more detailed information than the patient is at first able to give. We may even suppose that it is necessary to determine not only the presence of certain pains but to establish the intensity or the peculiar quality of such pains. We may suppose that during his exploration of the abdomen the physician presses now lightly and now more intensely. The patient responds by saying that he feels, first, a slight pain, then a more intense pain, and finally a very sharp pain. From one point of view these different modes of response on the part of the patient can be taken as measures of what might be called the intensity of a group of sensations. In any case, the history of experimental psychology is full of experiments which have made use of exactly this procedure and which have assumed that the procedure led to a direct measurement of the intensity of mental processes. Clearly, however, direct measurement of mental processes has not been attained. On the contrary, the previous language training, both of the physician and of his patient, have made it possible that certain words have so precise a symbolic function that they lend themselves readily to statistical treatment. If the physician were really painstaking in his methods he might try different intensities of pressure over and over again. He would enter the responses of the patient in a table. After a sufficient amount of data had been gained, he would inspect the data in order to see how consistent the responses of his patient had been. He might even use certain types of mathematical formulae in order to calculate the consistency of response. The results which he obtains, however, are a product of comparisons which he has drawn between the reactions of his patient and the stimuli which have been applied. They are, in no sense of the word, direct measures of mental processes and neither are they comparisons between responses, on the one hand, and mental processes, on the other.[59]

It is this feature, then, of all psychological work which has been emphasized by the radical behaviorist. Proper recognition of the fact that psychological research is, as a matter of fact, limited to

[58] Cf. Hunter, W. S., *Human Behavior*. Chicago: Univ. of Chicago Press, 1928, Chapter VIII; Curti, M. W., *Child Psychology*. New York: Longmans, Green and Co., 1930, Chapters VII, VIII, IX.
[59] Cf. Johnson, H. M., *op. cit., passim*.

behavior-patterns of one kind or another means that, irrespective of the point of view which one might take toward the existence or non-existence of mental processes, all psychology is committed to a kind of methodological behaviorism.

VI. Definitions of Educational Psychology

1. *Introduction:* One of the most convenient ways of laying our finger on the problems of educational psychology is to find out how writers in this field have looked at it. Among the more common points of view, we shall consider the following. There is, first, both the belief and the tacit assumption that educational psychology is made up of inferences and deductions drawn from the field of general psychology. In the second place, there are those who hold that its essential materials are to be drawn from the field of social psychology and, in particular, from the analysis of the products of socialized living such as languages, number concepts, institutions, and customs.[60] Still others seem to imply that the fundamental source of materials for educational psychology should be drawn from the field of animal psychology.[61] A considerable part of contemporary educational psychology is written around the concepts of original nature and learning.[62] Our own point of view depends upon the argument that the facts and principles of genetic psychology are even more fundamental to the art of teaching than these other facts. In any case, we shall be much better prepared to orientate ourselves in the several branches of educational psychology if we consider each of these several ways of looking at the whole field.

2. *Education as Applied General Psychology:* General psychology is often described as the psychology of the typical or normal human adult. This is not to say that there are fundamental types of psychological operation which are found among typical adults and which are not found among the higher animals, among children, or among abnormal individuals. On the contrary, it is only to say that a considerable body of knowledge is available concerning the psychological functions of men who are at their best. It is to say, also, that these psychological functions can be taken as a norm or

---

[60] Cf. Judd, C. H., *The Psychology of Social Institutions*. New York: The Macmillan Co., 1926.

[61] The best example is Sandiford, P., *Educational Psychology*. New York: Longmans, Green and Co., 1928. Adequate proof of the case, however, would have to come from an inspection of the periodical literature.

[62] This was the inflection given to educational psychology by Thorndike, E. L., *Educational Psychology* (3 vols.). New York: Columbia Univ. Press, 1913-14.

standard of comparison with respect to which other persons may be compared.

When education takes general psychology as a point of departure, it argues that the schoolroom may be used as a laboratory for the further testing of the laws of human action that have been developed by a study of more mature individuals.[63] It happens, however, that, save in the field of adult education, infants and children rather than adults are the persons upon whom the promoting and directing influences of education are brought to bear. If education is a mode of growth, or if it marks a set of procedures which can be used in promoting larger measures of growth, it would seem to follow that the principles of genetic psychology would be more useful than inferences drawn from a norm or standard, where the norm describes, so to speak, the end or culmination of a process.

Dunlap writes discerningly of this situation when he says:

"Child psychology, for example, the study of the child mind, is to a large extent an interpretation of the activities of the child in terms of adult psychology and therein lies both the possibility and the danger of child psychology."

Dunlap continues with the comment that the danger in child psychology

". . . results from the great difference in the behavior of children as compared with the human adults under the same circumstances although certain outstanding details of the behavior may be the same in the two cases. The danger therefrom is in inferring that the child's mental processes are the same as those of a human adult under similar circumstances through failure to note that the child's reactions are not really the same as those of the human adult. The actual determination of the behavior of children and animals is far more difficult than the determining of the behavior of adults. It has been assumed sometimes that the child mind may be examined without reference to the adult mind and therefore without the disadvantage of the source of errors in such a comparison. This assumption is an unfortunate mistake which has merely served to cover up arbitrary assumptions as to the child's mind. One might indeed study child behavior exclusively, but when one discusses perception, thought, and emotional experience in children, one is making inferences from the adult mind; so that the only safety lies in being thoroughly cognizant of them as inferences. To deny in such case that one is making inferences is really to refuse to examine one's inferences; a pro-

[63] Cf. Pillsbury, W. B., *Education As the Psychologist Sees It*. New York: The Macmillan Co., 1925, p. 1.

cedure which leads to serious blunders in theory and in the interpretation of experiments."[64]

A. LEARNING AND MEMORY: We shall illustrate the various phases of this situation by looking at some of the procedures now in use in education. We may take, first, the laws and principles that have been discovered in the field of memory and learning. Anyone who is familiar with the history of psychology knows that most of these principles have been derived out of the studies on the way in which adults learn. Ebbinghaus, who did some of the first experiments in this field, used himself as a subject. Other experimenters have, as a rule, used their graduate students or the upperclassmen in courses in psychology. Thorndike's recent survey of the field of adult learning contains most of the standard references in the field, references which have been freely used as a basis for pedagogical purposes.[65]

The extent to which adults were used in the experiments on memory and learning made it almost inevitable, perhaps, that the principles or laws of learning should be expressive of adult function and that they should be accepted as norms or standards with respect to which more immature individuals might be compared. This result is made all the more significant through the fact that many of our contemporary notions about learning and even the terms that we use in describing learning have had a long history in philosophy and theology. It is true, of course, that the present century has seen a good many studies on the learning functions of the lower animals and of children, but only the most recent approaches to the field of educational psychology have taken account of this material. The differences between adult learning and the learning methods of children make it clear that a genetic study of these functions has become absolutely imperative.[66] That is, a genetic point of view is imperative if education is to make the most of its time and energy. This proposition will become clearer as we proceed.

B. PERCEPTION: As a second illustration of the way in which the norms or standards of general psychology are used in education, we may take the psychology of perception. During the early days of experimental psychology, it was argued that perceptions (and all other mental processes as well) should be analyzed into their small-

[64] Dunlap, K., *Elements of Scientific Psychology*. St. Louis: C. V. Mosby, 1922, p. 16.
[65] Thorndike, E. L., *Adult Learning*. New York: The Macmillan Co., 1928, *passim*.
[66] Consider, for example, the difference described by Peterson, J., "Learning in Children," in *Handbook of Child Psychology* (Ed. C. Murchison), 1931, pp. 316-317. See also, Wagoner, L. C., *The Development of Learning in Children*, 1933.

est constituents. These "elements of mental life" were to be described with all the fidelity that one might describe the chemical elements. After a considerable amount of work had been done, it was possible to write out the presumable constitution of a normal or typical adult mind. Since the elementary mental processes were said to furnish the essential building material for intelligence, it was supposed that intelligence itself could be measured by measuring the variety and acuity of the various senses. It was supposed, also, that education would proceed most rapidly whenever the senses themselves were properly trained. The early history of mental testing, therefore, is liberally sprinkled with attempts to find some sort of correlation between intelligence, on the one hand, and sensory or perceptual acuteness, on the other.

None of these attempts has been successful. It is now clear that the significant thing for education is not a description of the typical mental process but the functional activities of an individual which are made possible by the presence of such processes. Moreover, the perceptual functions have a history. They develop toward the levels of maturity which are represented in adults. In short, we come back again to the proposition that, in the field of perception, as in the field of memory and learning, the genetic point of view is of more importance to education than is the normative or comparative point of view.

C. COMPLEX FUNCTIONS: The argument we are trying to make gains a large measure of support from the way in which general psychology has approached the problems of thinking and of emotionalized action. As we have seen, both of these words refer to modes of psychological operation which, heretofore, have not lent themselves readily to experimental investigation. That is, they have not been easily handled by some of the older experimental psychologies. Moreover, each of them is a product of much theological and philosophical speculation. It has been argued, for example, that thinking is one of the primary functions of the soul whereas the emotions name ways in which the body may be moved or stirred. In both cases, emphasis has been laid upon the original or native properties of mind and body. It is of the essence of the mind to think whereas the emotions have behind them the drive and the organization of native or instinctive tendencies. The mind not only has the power to think but it is rational or wholly logical in its operations. Since rationality can be viewed to best advantage at the adult level, it was the principles of logical thinking (i.e., formal logic) rather than the nature of problem-solving itself which came into educational practice.

All of this has been changed by the development of child psychology. Genetic studies of the emotions have shown clearly enough (i) that specific types of emotional posture and expression become differentiated out of more generalized modes of emotional expression, and (ii) that emotional patterns of behavior which have thus become individualized secure their relations with a wide range of objects and situations through a learning process rather than through native organizations of the nervous system.[67] It is commonly known, for example, that children are subject to a wide variety of fears. That is, fear reactions may be aroused by a wide variety of objects. It is now fairly certain that all such objects have become associated with the fear reaction because of methods of training, both formal and informal, rather than because of instinctive connections in nerve tissue. This light on the problems of emotional behavior has been thrown by the rapid development of child and of animal psychology and by the genetic point of view which naturally follows any study of the growing child or of the evolution of behavior.

Problems of thinking stand in a similar position. It has been found that even very young children may carry on a type of activity which is genetically antecedent to the more involved and logical processes carried on by adults. These early forms of thinking may consist of nothing more than quick acts of learning of the insightful type or of sudden reorganizations of a perceptual field.[68] That is, they resemble more nearly the type of behavior among lower animals which has been described as problem-solving than they do the logical processes of a mature adult. In any case, it is no longer possible to argue that the rational powers of infants or of animals are small editions of the rational powers of adults. The species of the process appears to have change during the passage from infancy to adulthood. Thinking or problem-solving, like other psychological functions, has a genetic history and this genetic history offers more promise to educational psychology than any set of inferences from the adult level can ever have.[69]

[67] Cf. Sherman, M., and Sherman, I. C., *The Process of Human Behavior.* New York: W. W. Norton and Co., 1929.
[68] Cf. Heidbreder, E. F., "Problem-solving in Children and Adults." *J. Genet. Psychol.*, 1928, XXV, 522-545.
[69] Cf. Köhler, W., *The Mentality of Apes.* New York: Harcourt, Brace and Co., 1924, *passim;* Koffka, K., *Growth of the Mind.* New York: Harcourt, Brace and Co., 1927.

3. *Educational Sociology:* A second suggestion toward the proper foundations of educational psychology has its point of departure in the fact that the psychology of the normal, typical adult has also been a psychology of the individual. Judd and others, however, have pointed out that the most significant facts about human beings are not individual facts but social facts. There is, in the first place, the vast amount of curricular, cultural, and other material which is a product of communal living. Languages, religions, institutions, customs, and a great many other features of contemporary life besides could never have been the creation of a single person. They represent the coöperative effort of a large number of persons. Moreover, they represent the functional activity of the higher forms of psychological operation.

It is well known, of course, that experimental psychology has had its most brilliant successes with the simpler psychological modes of operation and it is known also that the more complex operations are extremely difficult to control for experimental purposes.[70] It has been argued, therefore, that the study of the products of social living should stand among the basic materials of educational psychology. It is not possible to quarrel with this contention for, as we have said, experimental psychology has concerned itself with the individual rather than with the group. It has also acquired more information about the simpler psychological functions than it has about the more complex functions. Even here, however, we can easily see that the genetic point of view is fundamental. A psychological analysis of institutions, customs, and languages has long offered itself as a way of getting at a series of genetic facts which are not easily approached otherwise. When comparisons are drawn between primitive cultures and modern cultures, a few solid inferences can be made regarding the types of psychological functions which must have been used in the creation of these cultures. That is, a language, a custom, or an institution is a kind of a monument to the psychological operations of the social groups which created them. This is to say that folk psychology makes, in some of its methods, a direct contribution to the genetic point of view.[71]

Furthermore, languages, institutions, and other products of communal living comprise a far larger part of the stimulus-situations in contemporary life than do the physical objects and events which

---

[70] Judd, C. H., "Psychology as a Basis of Educational Methods," *Element. School J.*, 1924, XXV, 102-112.
[71] Cf. Wundt, W., *Elements of Folk Psychology* (trans. by E. Schaub). New York: The Macmillan Co., 1916.

are so often used in the experimental laboratory. At every point, then, social facts must deeply concern the educator. As Judd writes,

"The fact is that educational psychology is radically deficient. It is in need of revision. It must be made to include a whole series of new chapters. There must be a chapter on the nature of language, one on the nature of the number idea, one on the nature of social customs, such as punctuality and politeness, one on the economic system, and additional chapters dealing with the other social facts which go to make up modern civilization. These chapters will set forth the fact that men have produced, through the coöperation of their minds, certain intellectual and social institutions which are no less real than the objects of the physical world in which we live. These institutions control human life in the highest degree. They have to be accepted by human beings as enormously more important than instinctive tendencies. In fact, the chief reason why men succeed in living together in a productive way is that they do not live by their instincts but under the guidance of far-sighted plans of coöperation. Any system of psychology is wholly inadequate as a basis for school practice which overlooks the fact that we live in an environment made up primarily of social institutions rather than of natural objects to which our instincts respond." [72]

4. *Education and Animal Psychology:* The most recent proposals for the foundations of educational psychology have come from the students of animal behavior. The argument is rather simple and straightforward. In view of the fact that the psychological operations of human beings are so complex it is desirable to search out these operations where they are simpler in form and less intimately conjoined with the vast number of irrelevant factors. The theory of evolution with its doctrine of continuity has made animal psychology available for this purpose.[73] If man is essentially continuous with the lower animals, the psychological functions of the latter must have close analogies with the former, but at the same time all such functions will be simpler and more easily subject to experimental control. A great many of the books on educational psychology are filled, therefore, with data drawn from the field of animal psychology. We have only to remind ourselves of Pavlov's experiments on conditioning,[74] Sherrington's studies on the integrative action of the nervous system,[75] Köhler's studies on the chimpanzee,[76]

---

[72] Judd, C. H., *op. cit.*, p. 103.
[73] Yerkes, R. M., "Concerning the Genetic Relations of Types of Action." *J. Comp. Neurol. and Psychol.*, 1905, XV, 132-137.
[74] Pavlov, I. P., *op. cit., passim.*
[75] Sherrington, C. S., *The Integrative Action of the Nervous System.* New Haven: Yale Univ. Press, 1906, *passim.*
[76] Köhler, W., *op. cit., passim.*

728   INTRODUCTION TO EDUCATIONAL PSYCHOLOGY

and the thousands of experiments which have made use of the white rat in learning situations and in problem-solving situations, in order to realize the extent to which education is dependent upon animal psychology.

It must be clear, however, that the facts of animal psychology may be taken in two ways. In the first place, one may adhere strictly to the comparative method. If we do this, we shall study the lower animals not because they stand in the same continuum with the human animal, but solely because we wish to draw comparisons between the functions of individuals who may be, in a great many respects, different from one another but who are, in some essential respects, the same. On the other hand, we may assume that all living creatures fall at their appointed places in a continuum or in a truly genetic series. It is now believed by a great many psychologists that the facts of animal psychology become increasingly significant in direct proportion as they are looked at from the genetic point of view. In short, then, animal psychology is a proper part of the foundations of educational psychology only insofar as it furnishes material for filling in the whole picture of human and animal becoming.

Other groups of facts have been made available as basic material for education. But this is not the place to consider them further. Of one thing, however, we may be sure. The timewise or genetic view of human development offers itself as a fruitful way of arranging psychological facts for the purpose of education. This is true not only with respect to child psychology and animal psychology as separate departments of research, but of general characterizations of becoming as well. It is still too early to say just what these general characterizations are but certain suggestions about them have already been made. Hollingworth, for example, in his study of mental growth and decline has listed over a score of general principles of psychological development.[77] There is now an entire volume on educational psychology which bears the title, *The Principles of Mental Development*.[78] It is almost certain that this aspect of genetic psychology will receive further attention in the near future for the specific facts of genetic psychology, and general characterizations of the whole process of human becoming cannot help but be highly significant for education.

[77] Hollingworth, H. L., *Mental Growth and Decline*. New York: D. Appleton-Century Co., 1927.
[78] Cf. Wheeler, R. H., and Perkins, F. T., *Principles of Mental Development*. New York: T. Y. Crowell Co., 1932.

VII. The Genetic Approach to Education

1. *Introduction:* We have said that it is the purpose of this chapter to state some of the requirements which must be met if education is to render the services that society will demand of it. The first of these requirements has now been stated. Education, like psychology, is committed to the methods of behaviorism, but it is not committed to the study of behavior as the physiologist would study it. We may now state a second requirement that must be made of education. Many of the modes of defining the problems of educational psychology which were described in the last section stand in direct opposition to that mode of description which makes use of the principles of growth, development, and maturation of the organic kind. This is most certainly true of the scholastic psychology, for the purpose of an education based upon this kind of psychology was to train and discipline the mind rather than to promote, nourish, and otherwise guide its growth through a wide variety of changes. An educational psychology based upon inferences drawn from the psychology of a typical normal adult also stands in direct opposition to the genetic or historical point of view.

The situation is a little different in the case of educational psychologies based upon original nature and learning, for an adequate description of what is really original or native in behavior almost necessitates a series of studies of the genetic type. It still remains true, however, that this point of view is not consistently genetic for, in attributing all of the problems of genetic psychology to original nature, on the one hand, and to learning, on the other, there is an implicit denial of the fact that maturation or growth can continue after birth. As we shall see in a moment, there are those who would argue that the processes of normal growth or of maturation continue so definitely after birth as to suggest the inapplicability of the term "learning" to any of the changes through which a small child may go.[79] As a matter of fact, it has even been argued that learning simply means the setting up of an appropriate situation under which growth of a specified kind may take place, the learning situation being nothing more nor less than a highly controlled segment of the total environmental situation by means of which growth is regulated.

2. *Recapitulation:* Educational psychology has, to be sure, made what use it could of a genetic method in times past. One of the

[79] Cf. Wheeler, R. H., and Perkins, F. T., *op. cit.,* Chapter XIII.

most famous of its attempts in this direction was called a genetic theory of education. Being highly impressed with the biological doctrine of evolution and with that phase of it known as the biogenetic law, G. Stanley Hall argued for the reality of a biogenetic law in psychology.[80] This law came to be known as the theory of recapitulation. The theory stated that, just as the body of the human being, during embryonic stages of development, recapitulates or tells over again certain aspects of the story of the development of the race, so the mind and behavior of the growing child recapitulates the mind and behavior of the child's ancestors.

One of the inferences to be drawn from this kind of genetic approach to the problems of educational psychology runs as follows. Since the race has had all kinds of experiences which may echo and reecho in the history of any particular individual, and since these experiences are more or less inevitable, education must accept them as inevitable if, perchance, they reappear in individual development. Fighting, for example, has been an almost continuous feature of the behavior of animals. The soul of the race must, therefore, have acquired definite pugnacious instincts which almost inevitably and invariably appear in the life of each new individual. Instincts of this kind must be accepted with pious resignation on the part of education, escape from them being possible only in terms of what is called the principle of catharsis, the principle, viz., that the actual expression of any dispositional urge to action marks one way of effecting an escape from the urge.

In more general terms, the doctrine of recapitulation meant that a thoroughgoing genetic study of the development of the child was not only a way of unraveling the total psychological history of the race but a way of bringing the total psychological history of the race to bear upon the development of the individual. Unfortunately, the theory of recapitulation was constructed out of so much fancy and included so many inconsistencies as to make it ineffective as a permanent basis for educational psychology. The biological facts from which it was inferred have been shown to be too meager to support the broad psychological inferences drawn from them. Moreover, the doctrine makes use of the existence of a subconscious mind in a way that is not compatible with the trend of contemporary research.

There has been, therefore, a reaction against a geneticism of the type represented by Hall. Since Hall's time, experimental work in

[80] Cf. Hall, G. S., *Adolescence* (2 vols.). New York: D. Appleton-Century Co., 1904.

the field has become increasingly fruitful. Recent years have seen the establishment of a large number of laboratories in child psychology and the gradual accumulation of an astonishing amount of information, both on the development of psychological traits in human beings and on the development of analogous traits among the lower animals. This information is fast becoming so complete and so suggestive of the general principles or general features of development as to raise once more the possibility of using genetic psychology as an adequate foundation for the programs of educational psychology.[81]

3. *The Genetic View:* This is the point of view which has been taken in the preceding chapters. It is a point of view suggested by the fact that education can be defined as a type of directed becoming. Everywhere in nature, of course, there are sequences of events which bear the imprint of continuity. The description of such continuities is known as historicism or geneticism. One such pattern of continuity begins with the fertilization of a human ovum and ends with the death of the individual. Genetic psychology has, as one of its major tasks, the study of just such a genetic sequence of events. Educational psychology has as its task the practical application of genetic facts so that in the growth or maturation of the individual the interests of society may be best served. It is true, of course, that society may define its interests in several different ways and the definition and evaluation of these ways is the problem of the philosophy of education. The philosophy of education presupposes, however, not only a series of events which can be controlled, but also the existence of a group of facts with respect to which control can be achieved.

As an example of one of the significant features of the genetic method in educational psychology we may consider once more the age-old problem of original nature and training.[82] One of the traits said to be original to human nature is the so-called acquisitive trait. Older forms of educational psychology would have accepted such a trait with due piety and have sought either to strengthen it, or to modify and redirect it, or to weaken and nullify it. Granted the existence of such a trait, and society is compelled to order or arrange some of its principal social, economic, and political doctrines accordingly. The genetic method, however, is not satisfied with the pious

---

[81] Here, almost at the end of our study, we may repeat an invitation given at the outset, for one of the first reading assignments brought into the study of educational psychology referred the student to any one of the numerous books on child psychology.

[82] Cf. Wheeler, R. H., and Perkins, F. T., *op. cit.,* Chapters VII and IX.

acceptance of any alleged original trait. It would, for example, consider the history of such a trait as acquisitiveness under the belief that no trait can be accepted as original until it has been shown conclusively that it is not acquired. In the case of acquisitiveness, much of the experimental evidence seems to suggest a natural origin rather than inborn nativity. Should this prove to be true, it would seem to follow that society, having in mind its directive control over human nature through education, might hope, should it find such a plan desirable, to modify human nature with respect to the trait of acquisitiveness.

Among the consequences of this point of view we may name the fact that a certain amount of inevitability would be taken away from such disciplines as political science, economics, and sociology. If acquisitiveness is an inevitable trait of human nature, then society must inevitably be acquisitive and its economic structure organized accordingly.[83] If, however, education can be defined as directed becoming, where the processes of becoming apply to an unsuspected variety of human traits, then the real importance of an educational psychology based upon genetic principles can be discerned.[84]

4. *Conclusion:* The time has now come to bring this long survey of the field of educational psychology to an end. We ought, therefore, to remind ourselves of at least a few of the more important general considerations to be taken away from any study of educational psychology.

There is, first, perhaps, the fact that society is now expressing more clearly than ever before its desire that the educative process shall be established on sound experimentation. It is a seven days' wonder that the methods of the laboratory should have been applied so intensively to the technical aspects of living so long in advance of its personal aspects. Now, however, we can let bygones be bygones and devote ourselves courageously to the problems created by an experimental examination of the growth pattern.

In the second place, the student should remember that this study of educational psychology has been based upon the genetic point of view. Everywhere we have tried to remember that the growing child describes a developmental schedule of events with respect to which every teacher must orient himself. The person who is, at any particular moment in this schedule, under the influence of the educative process is a person whose history has a bearing on what

[83] Cf. Wallas, G., *The Great Society.* New York: The Macmillan Co., 1914.
[84] Cf. Dunlap, K., *Habits, Their Making and Unmaking.* New York: Liveright Publishing Corp., 1932, Chapter II.

should be done and on what cannot be done. The pupil in the classroom is constantly in the act of manufacturing himself; and whether for good or for ill, the teacher must provide much of the material for this process.

In the third place, if education must coördinate itself with growth patterns, it is required of the teacher and of his principal source of factual material, viz., the psychologist, that they shall untangle the confused web of events created by original nature and training. The weight of this book has been thrown on the side of training simply because it is the primary function of education to guide and control, wherever it can, the complex processes of growth. Research must continue, however, on all phases of the problem, for the stake which society holds in the outcomes of the educative process is too great to be handled in a desultory fashion.

In the fourth place, the student should not take too seriously the use which has been made of the methods of behaviorism. It is a misfortune, perhaps, that certain limits are placed upon the methods available for experimenting upon human and animal conduct, but it would be a great mistake to suppose that the methods are equivalent in all respects to the material studied. Human beings are certainly persons, and any view, either of psychology or of education, which loses sight of this fact must certainly fall beside the mark. The whole pattern of human conduct displays features or properties which distinguish human beings from all other classes of objects. We have tried to show how these distinguishing features or properties are suggested by the unique relations that obtain between stimulus-patterns and responses. Were there nothing unique here, that is, if human conduct were like the point-to-point relations between physical "cause" and "effect," the word "person" could have no explainable origin.

Finally, the student will have missed, no doubt, in this survey of educational psychology the proper number of precise rules and formulae such as he expects from books in the physical and sometimes even in the psychological sciences. Good teaching, however, is not done by rule. It is done by persons who enter into an intimate configuration with students. It is done by persons who have a feeling for, rather than an extended knowledge of, the whole growth pattern. If the student has been able to go beyond the factual materials that have been presented to this "feeling for" human nature, he will have taken an important step in his competency.

READINGS

Much of the material in this chapter concerns the various points of view in psychology. Preliminary to any point of view, however, is some familiarity with the history of psychology. The principal histories of psychology are the following: Boring, E. G., *A History of Experimental Psychology.* New York: D. Appleton-Century Co., 1930; Murphy, G., *An Historical Introduction to Modern Psychology.* New York: Harcourt, Brace and Co., 1929; Flugel, J. C., *One Hundred Years of Psychology.* New York: The Macmillan Co., 1933.

The introspective point of view can be found in Titchener, E. B., *A Textbook of Psychology.* New York: The Macmillan Co., 1910; Bentley, M., *The Field of Psychology.* New York: D. Appleton-Century Co., 1924; Ruckmick, C. A., *The Mental Life.* New York: Longmans, Green and Co., 1928.

The functional point of view can be found in Carr, H. A., *Psychology.* New York: Longmans, Green and Co., 1925. Angell, J. R., *Psychology.* New York: Henry Holt and Co., 1904.

The Gestalt point of view can be found in Koffka, K., *The Growth of the Mind.* New York: Harcourt, Brace and Co., 1925; Köhler, W., *Gestalt Psychology.* New York: Liveright Publishing Corp., 1929; Wheeler, R. H., *The Science of Psychology.* New York: T. Y. Crowell and Co., 1929; Peterman, B., *The Gestalt Theory and the Problem of Configuration.* New York: Harcourt, Brace and Co., 1932.

The behavioristic point of view can be found in Watson, J. B., *Psychology from the Standpoint of the Behaviorist.* Philadelphia: J. B. Lippincott Co., 1919; Dashiell, J. F., *Fundamentals of Objective Psychology.* Boston: Houghton Mifflin Co., 1929; Rexroad, C. N., *General Psychology for College Students.* New York: The Macmillan Co., 1929; Weiss, A. P., *A Theoretical Basis of Behavior.* Columbus, Ohio: R. G. Adams, 1929.

Other types of psychology may be found in Woodworth, R. S., *Psychology* (Rev. ed.). New York: Henry Holt and Co., 1929; Warren, H. C., and Carmichael, L., *Elements of Human Psychology.* Boston: Houghton Mifflin Co., 1929; Murphy, G., *General Psychology.* New York: Harper and Bros., 1933; Dunlap, K., *Elements of Scientific Psychology.* St. Louis: C. V. Mosby Co., 1922; Hollingworth, H. L., *Psychology: Its Facts and Principles.* New York: D. Appleton-Century Co., 1928.

See also Murchison, C. (Ed.), *A Handbook of General Experimental Psychology.* Worcester, Mass.: Clark Univ. Press, 1934; Murchison, C. (Ed.), *Psychologies of 1930.* Worcester, Mass.: Clark Univ. Press, 1930; Heidbreder, E. F., *Seven Psychologies.* New York: D. Appleton-Century Co., 1933; Woodworth, R. S., *Contemporary Schools of Psychology.* New York: The Ronald Press, 1931.

As the text has indicated, the various books in educational psychology emphasize now one feature and now another of the whole domain. A book directly in line with the Thorndike tradition is Gates, A. I., *Psychology for Students of Education.* New York: The Macmillan Co., 1930. Facts drawn from the field of animal psychology are stressed by Sandiford, P., *Educational Psychology.* New York: Longmans, Green and Co., 1928. The concept of adjustment lies at the basis of Trow, W. C., *Educational Psychology*. Boston: Houghton Mifflin Co., 1931. A more eclectic view is contained in Pressey, S. L., *Psychology and the New Education*. New York: Harper and Bros., 1933.

A textbook in educational psychology written from the point of view of social institutions has not as yet appeared, although it has been promised. The materials, however, are to be found in Judd, C. H., *The Psychology of Social Institutions*. New York: The Macmillan Co., 1926. See also, Tuttle, H. S., *A Social Basis of Education*. New York: T. Y. Crowell, 1934; Finney, R. L., *A Sociological Philosophy of Education*. New York: The Macmillan Co., 1928; Kinneman, J. A., *Educational Sociology*. New York: The Macmillan Co., 1932.

The Gestalt point of view is represented in Ogden, R. M., and Freeman, G. L., *Psychology and Education*. New York: Harcourt, Brace and Co., 1933. This view, together with emphasis on the genetic approach, can be found in Wheeler, R. H., and Perkins, F. T., *Principles of Mental Development*. New York: T. Y. Crowell and Co., 1932.

A very useful book on the relations between education and the several varieties of psychology has been written by Ragsdale. See Ragsdale, C. E., *Modern Psychologies and Education*. New York: The Macmillan Co., 1932.

INDEX OF NAMES

Abbott, A., 217
Abbott, E., 286, 623
Adams, D. K., 402
Adams, F., 530, 602
Adams, H. F., 156, 284
Adams, R. G., 605
Adler, A., 76, 168, 283, 641, 655
Alexander, F., 639
Allport, F. H., 6, 68, 267, 455, 577, 633
Allport, G. W., 267
Almack, J. C., 663
Anderson, A. C., 465
Anderson, H. H., 630
Anderson, J. E., 285, 291, 379
Anderson, J. P., 463
Anderson, M. L., 603
Anderson, O. D., 400
Anderson, V. V., 655
Angell, F., 480
Angell, J. R., 21, 703, 734
Arai, T., 676
Ariens Kappers, C. U., 421
Armatruda, C. S., 20, 43
Arnold, F., 155
Arrowood, C. F., 9
Austin, S. D. M., 437
Averill, L. A., 79
Avery, G. T., 12
Ayer, F. C., 582

Bagby, E., 632, 655
Bagley, W. C., 469, 482, 515, 517
Bair, J. H., 481
Baker, S. J., 662
Baldwin, B. T., 34, 370, 574
Baldwin, E. L., 27
Baldwin, J. M., 297, 706
Banister, H., 106
Bard, P., 192, 196, 219
Barlow, M. C., 447, 594
Barnes, E. W., 644
Barr, A. S., 513
Bartlett, F. C., 222
Bass, M. R., 586
Bates, R. L., 688
Bayley, N., 207
Beaman, F. N., 584
Bean, C. H., 463
Beebe-Center, J. G., 146
Bell, J. C., 257
Benedict, C. G., 661
Benedict, F. G., 661
Benedict, R., 696
Bennett, C. A., 216

Bennett, C. J. C., 481
Bennett, H. E., 61, 665
Bentley, M., 80, 95, 112, 155, 157, 162, 219, 275, 301, 347, 349, 378, 383, 393, 591, 656, 664, 734
Bergson, H., 301
Bergstrom, J. A., 444
Berman, L., 275
Bernard, L. L., 10, 300, 310, 342
Berry, E., 93
Bills, A. G., 678, 679, 681
Bills, M. A., 659
Binet, A., 539, 582
Bird, C., 468
Birkelo, C. P., 512
Blackford, K. M. H., 284
Blanchard, P., 280, 288, 655
Blatz, W. E., 32
Boardman, C. W., 511
Boas, G., 256
Bode, B. H., 223, 245, 256, 404, 501, 517, 522, 535, 694
Bolton, F. J., 465
Bolton, T. L., 392
Bond, N. J., 106
Bonham, M., 276
Book, W. F., 79, 452, 468, 635
Boorman, W. R., 288, 655
Boring, E. G., 111, 228, 297, 702, 734
Bowers, A. M., 638
Boynton, P. L., 548, 550, 561, 564, 576, 602
Brace, D. K., 537
Bray, C. W., 476
Breckenridge, S. P., 286, 623
Breed, F. S., 360, 520, 530
Bregman, E. O., 202
Bretnall, E. P., 416, 453
Brett, G. S., 694, 699
Bridges, K. M., 189
Bridgman, P. W., 567, 719
Briggs, T. H., 482
Brigham, C. C., 573, 578
Bronner, A. E., 624
Bronner, A. F., 37, 109, 288, 638
Brooks, F. D., 38, 43, 170, 190, 655
Brown, A. W., 583
Brown, E. M., 476
Brown, H., 83
Brown, M. A., 458
Brown, W., 451, 464, 530, 602
Brownell, W. A., 254
Brueckner, L., 513
Bryan, W. L., 386, 582

INDEX OF NAMES

Buermeyer, L., 256
Bühler, C., 30, 244, 277, 288, 605, 610, 611, 627
Bunch, M. E., 452
Burks, B. S., 602
Burnham, W. H., 384, 628, 655
Burt, C. L., 286, 288, 539, 575, 623, 624
Burton, W. H., 252, 377, 419, 469, 504, 521, 522, 529, 530, 560, 563, 599, 609, 617, 627, 691
Burtt, H. E., 699
Burwell, W. R., 562
Bush, A., 688
Buswell, G. T., 78, 81

Caldwell, O. W., 279
Calkins, M. W., 259, 264, 265, 287, 698
Calverton, V. F., 641
Campbell, N. R., 158, 701
Cannon, W. B., 52, 167, 187, 194, 196, 199, 219, 275, 635
Carmichael, L., 10, 342, 350, 360, 734
Carmichael, R. D., 225, 241
Carr, H. A., 21, 84, 273, 379, 388, 392, 449, 703, 734
Carroll, H. A., 218
Cason, H., 388, 413, 414, 608
Cathcart, E. P., 661
Cattell, J. McK., 539, 576
Chapman, J. C., 454
Charters, W. W., 150, 155, 288
Chase, L., 454
Child, C. M., 12, 361
Clapp, F. L., 254, 461
Cleeton, G. U., 274
Clem, O. M., 257
Coe, G. A., 264, 288
Coghill, G. E., 12, 15, 310, 312, 383
Cole, L., 41, 92, 124
Colvin, S. S., 155, 540
Conklin, E. G., 342, 688
Conrad, H. S., 150
Coover, J. E., 480
Coriat, J. H., 76
Corning, H. M., 558
Cowdery, K. M., 153
Cowdry, E. V., 8, 219, 655
Cox, C. M., 220
Coy, G., 582
Crawford, C. C., 564
Crawley, S. L., 680
Crile, G. W., 194
Culler, E. A., 444
Curti, M. W., 5, 23, 27, 30, 37, 43, 63, 67, 87, 92, 124, 187, 231, 261, 389, 390, 398, 596, 622, 720
Cutsforth, T. D., 105, 586

Dallenbach, K. M., 136, 195, 592
Darwin, C., 201, 212, 219
Dashiell, J. F., 27, 73, 155, 166, 170, 181, 187, 203, 378, 386, 388, 444, 653, 734
Davenport, C. B., 309

Davidson, M. R., 562
Davies, A. H., 682
Davis, H., 124
Davis, W. W., 476
Dawson, S., 667
Dearborn, W. F., 106, 479, 480, 534, 546, 564
De Laguna, G., 5, 65, 92, 606
Deputy, E. C., 452
Descoeudres, A., 585
De Voss, J. C., 594
Dewey, J., 7, 29, 54, 125, 156, 222, 243, 245, 246, 248, 256, 357, 439, 516, 699
De Wulf, M., 226, 699, 701
Dexter, E., 667
Dietze, A. A., 672
Dimmick, F. L., 103
Dimnet, E., 256
Diserens, C. M., 160, 187, 452
Dodge, R., 78, 307, 569, 602, 676, 677
Donovan, M. E., 593
Dorcus, R. M., 26, 75, 189, 615, 651, 685
Dougherty, M. L., 85
Douglass, A. A., 530
Douglass, H. R., 429, 515
Downey, J. E., 267
Downing, E. R., 518, 519
Draper, E. M., 93
Drever, A., 342
Duffy, E., 203
Dunlap, K., 35, 36, 76, 77, 167, 169, 170, 181, 187, 190, 274, 284, 310, 376, 382, 412, 425, 428, 439, 462, 468, 501, 574, 627, 640, 650, 654, 679, 723, 732, 734
Dye, J. A., 47, 92, 199, 333, 350, 520, 675, 708
Dysinger, W. S., 150

Ebbinghaus, H., 429, 436
Ebert, E., 479
Eby, F., 9
Eddington, A. S., 110, 113
Edman, I., 184
Edwards, A. S., 541
Eels, W. C., 525
Ehinger, G., 594
Eikenberry, D. H., 467
Eldridge, S., 356
Eliasberg, W., 449
Elliott, E. C., 525
Ellis, R. S., 570, 572, 574, 602
Entwisle, B. S., 107
Ephrussi, P., 430
Ewert, H., 308
Ewert, P. H., 476, 477

Fabre, J. H. C., 342
Faterson, H. F., 283
Fearing, F. S., 14
Feder, R. B., 454
Fenton, N., 625
Ferree, C. E., 669
Filter, R. O., 435

INDEX OF NAMES

Finkenbinder, E. O., 463
Finney, R. L., 735
Fishback, E. H., 288
Fisher, D. C., 586
Fisher, V. E., 250, 282, 635, 643, 644, 646, 647, 650, 651, 688
Fiske, J., 31, 356
Fletcher, J. M., 75, 92, 631
Flew, R. N., 615, 619, 633
Flexner, A., 145, 471
Flugel, J. C., 297, 734
Fogelsonger, H. M., 444
Forbes, A., 92
Foster, J. C., 285
Foster, W. S., 465, 592
Fox, C., 234
Fox, E. J., 276
Fracker, G. C., 479
Franklin, E. E., 152
Franz, S. I., 228, 451
Freeman, G. L., 14, 26, 48, 58, 74, 98, 124, 138, 141, 155, 349, 352, 353, 354, 378, 421, 568, 660, 679, 695, 735
Freeman, F. N., 85, 96, 124, 267, 419, 540, 541, 564
Fretwell, E. K., 93
Freud, S., 27, 170, 187, 381, 638
Freyd, M., 277
Fryer, D., 151, 152, 156
Fullerton, G. S., 162
Fulton, B. B., 70

Gaglon, C. P., 667
Galton, F., 272, 304, 342, 569
Garfinkel, M. A., 467
Garrett, H. E., 47, 564, 568, 572, 678
Garrison, K. C., 43
Garth, T. R., 377, 579
Gates, A. I., 50, 81, 83, 84, 258, 410, 411, 414, 428, 446, 465, 488, 491, 514, 593, 596, 667, 693, 695, 734
Gates, G., 593
Gault, R. H., 105
Geddes, P., 343, 378
Gellerman, L. W., 535
Gengerelli, J. A., 443
Germane, C. E., 288
Germane, E. G., 288
Gesell, A., 9, 15, 16, 20, 34, 43, 205, 365, 435, 459, 611
Gibbs, W. E., 519
Gilbreth, F. B., 59
Gilliland, A. R., 43
Givler, R. C., 351
Glaze, J. A., 430
Goddard, H. H., 306, 342, 602
Goodenough, F. L., 5, 33, 38, 43, 83, 116, 189, 285, 292, 370, 379, 551, 577, 610
Gordon, K., 465
Gottschaldt, K., 487
Gough, E., 107
Gould, A. G., 47, 92, 169, 199, 333, 350, 520, 675, 708

Graf, O., 684
Graham, C. H., 123
Grant, E. B., 149
Gray, W. S., 81, 82
Greene, E. B., 672
Greene, H. A., 564
Griffith, C. R., 57, 93, 138, 143, 279, 612, 637, 673, 684, 689, 703
Griffitts, C. H., 471
Groos, K., 27, 88
Groves, E. R., 655
Guilford, J. P., 431
Gundlach, R. H., 142, 274
Gurnee, H., 701
Guthrie, E. R., 210, 396, 417
Guyer, M. F., 342

Hagman, E. R., 36
Hahn, H. H., 62
Haldane, J. B. S., 4, 302, 343, 367, 378
Haldane, J. S., 242, 345, 700, 718
Hall, C. S., 416, 453
Hall, G. S., 9, 88, 179, 303, 342, 367, 730
Hall, O. M., 682
Halverson, H. M., 16, 63, 84
Hamilton, G. V., 390
Hamilton, H. C., 452
Harden, L. M., 444
Harmon, F. L., 661
Harris, L. H., 482
Hart, J. K., 586
Harter, N., 386
Hartman, G., 220
Hartmann, E. von, 648
Hartmann, G. W., 593
Hartridge, H., 106, 123
Hartshorne, H., 55, 222, 260, 263, 267, 270, 287, 607
Haskell, E. M., 392
Hastings, J., 298, 328, 346
Hawk, P. B., 688
Hazlitt, V., 535
Healy, W., 37, 288, 624, 655
Hecht, S., 100, 123
Heidbreder, E. F., 21, 43, 45, 91, 123, 126, 277, 348, 395, 427, 447, 692, 725, 734
Held, O. C., 435
Helson, H., 114
Hempelmann, 261
Hendershot, B. A., 257
Henderson, L. J., 303, 333
Hendrick, I., 642
Henmon, V. A. C., 137
Heron, W. T., 434, 674
Herrick, C. J., 4, 31, 48, 124, 359, 362, 573
Hetherington, C. W., 93
Hertzberg, O. E., 84
Hetzer, H., 611
Hilgard, E. R., 399, 460
Hill, A. V., 57, 659, 673
Hill, C. S., 453

INDEX OF NAMES

Hiller, E. T., 294
Hingston, R. W. G., 342
Hobhouse, L. T., 407
Höffding, H. A., 109
Hogben, L., 8, 324, 368, 396, 418
Holladay, P. W., 150
Hollingworth, H. L., 38, 43, 70, 368, 379, 394, 442, 467, 595, 685, 688, 728, 734
Hollingworth, L. S., 284, 558, 582, 585, 602, 603
Holmes, S. J., 8, 324
Holt, E. B., 16, 163, 647
Honzik, C. H., 233
Hopkins, E. W., 697
Horton, R. E., 519
Hoskins, R. G., 275
Houston, H. E., 451
Hoyt, F. S., 482
Hudelson, E., 523
Hudgins, C. V., 176
Hull, C. L., 92, 176, 177, 187, 307, 368, 389, 398, 399, 401, 412, 420, 425, 457, 588
Humphrey, G., 396, 505
Humphrey, M., 505
Humphries, F. H., 426
Hunter, W. S., 66, 68, 71, 92, 97, 112, 141, 155, 176, 232, 234, 235, 236, 349, 397, 398, 407, 408, 425, 476, 579, 605, 720
Huntington, E., 668
Hurlock, E. B., 456, 553
Hurst, A. F., 652
Hurst, C. C., 304, 319, 342
Husband, R. W., 153, 156, 689
Huxley, J., 4, 302, 343, 367, 378

Irion, T. W. H., 217
Irmina, Sister M., 672
Irwin, O. C., 15, 19, 167
Isaacs, S., 315, 554
Itard, J., 86
Ives, J. E., 669

Jacobson, E., 684
James, W., 131, 155, 185, 196, 216, 234, 299, 356, 387, 421, 422, 448, 478, 701
Jastrow, J., 638
Jenkins, R. L., 626
Jennings, H. S., 4, 43, 200, 296, 304, 323, 329, 341, 352, 362, 369
Jensen, K., 17
Jersild, A. T., 460, 467
Johnson, B. J., 5, 43
Johnson, C. N., 664
Johnson, H. M., 128, 446, 716, 720
Johnson, P. O., 671
Johnson, R. H., 293, 309, 323
Jones, H. E., 19, 150, 205, 206, 209, 315, 465, 625, 626, 672
Jones, M. C., 19, 28, 53, 190, 198, 205, 206, 207, 209, 210, 219, 288, 313

Jones, V., 270, 271, 280, 623
Jordan, A. M., 149, 463
Jorgensen, A. N., 564
Judd, C. H., 41, 77, 124, 203, 245, 253, 254, 384, 386, 481, 508, 607, 703, 721, 726, 727, 735
Jung, C. G., 277

Kawin, E., 385
Kefauver, G. W., 655
Keliher, A. V., 560
Kelley, T. L., 378, 564, 568
Kellogg, L. A., 240, 256
Kellogg, W. N., 240, 256
Kenagy, H. G., 284
Keschner, M., 350
Keyser, C. J., 256
Kilpatrick, W. H., 144, 148, 286, 473, 504, 530, 632
Kinder, E. F., 284
Kinneman, J. A., 735
Kinser, E. L., 626
Kirkpatrick, E. A., 451
Kleitman, M., 681
Klemm, G. O., 298, 700
Kline, L. W., 444, 480
Knight, F. B., 274
Koch, H., 84, 137
Koffka, K., 24, 25, 102, 115, 124, 237, 238, 241, 247, 374, 413, 423, 440, 522, 725, 734
Köhler, W., 54, 56, 104, 113, 201, 227, 230, 249, 256, 260, 343, 354, 394, 406, 407, 408, 565, 725, 727, 734
Koos, L. V., 655
Kornhauser, A. W., 670
Kretschmer, E., 273, 287
Krueger, W. C. F., 464
Kuhlmann, F., 583
Kühn, A., 445
Kuo, Z. Y., 342, 414, 453

Ladd, G. T., 57
Laird, D. A., 670
Lakenan, M. E., 430
Lambeth, M., 577
Landis, C., 194, 196, 219
Lang, A. R., 223
Lange, F. A., 705
Langfeld, H. S., 657
Langlie, T. A., 153
Langworthy, O. R., 141
Lanier, L. H., 118, 577
La Rue, D. W., 629, 655
Lashley, K. S., 13, 46, 124, 138, 229, 351, 363, 385, 411, 417, 423, 425, 438, 440, 477, 488
Layton, E. T., 671
Leahy, A. M., 285
Leary, D. B., 355
Lehman, H. C., 18, 87, 149
Leuba, C. J., 164, 454
Lévy Bruhl, L., 696

INDEX OF NAMES

Lewin, K., 315
Lewis, C. L., 226
Liddell, H. S., 397, 400, 402, 405
Lillie, R. S., 47, 199
Lima, M., 149
Lindley, A. B., 679
Lindley, E. H., 582
Lindworsky, J., 234
Link, H. C., 44
Lombroso, G., 621
Loucks, R. B., 232
Lough, J. E., 433
Luckeish, M., 669
Ludgate, K. E., 284
Lull, R. S., 302
Lund, F. H., 467
Luria, A. R., 636
Lynd, H. M., 470
Lynd, R. S., 470
Lyon, D. O., 434, 465

Madsen, I. N., 564
Maller, J. B., 288, 456
Marston, L. R., 30, 277
Martin, E. D., 184, 220, 618
May, M. A., 260, 270, 287
McCall, W. A., 665
McCarthy, D., 5, 25, 66, 69
McCurdy, J. H., 89
McDougall, W., 159, 175, 180, 299, 300, 342, 347, 378, 608, 646, 685, 686, 694, 698, 705
McDowell, E. C., 331
McFarland, R. A., 62
McGaughty, J. R., 559
McGeoch, G. O., 429
McGeoch, J. A., 56, 355, 386, 415, 432, 433, 437, 441, 443, 453, 475
McPhail, A. H., 561, 562
McTeer, W., 681
Mead, M., 288
Meier, N. C., 218
Melby, E. O., 513
Meltzer, H., 444
Mendel, G., 321
Meninger, K. A., 655
Meredith, G. P., 491
Meumann, E., 479
Meyerson, E., 225
Meyland, G. L., 688
Miles, W. R., 686
Mill, J. S., 256
Miller, H. L., 530
Minkowski, M., 12
Mohr, J. G., 274
Monroe, P., 505, 606, 692, 704
Monroe, W. S., 255, 594, 601
Montague, W. M., 696
Moore, J. S., 701
Morgan, C. L., 299, 378, 391
Morgan, J. J. B., 5, 43, 92, 187, 220, 261, 645, 646, 650, 652, 655, 670

Morgan, T. H., 321, 323, 341, 352, 366, 378
Morrison, H. C., 144, 184, 509, 530, 598, 631, 634
Moseley, D., 360
Moss, F. A., 41, 162, 187, 224, 228, 239, 256, 310, 314, 397, 402, 403, 420, 423, 425, 488, 669
Mueller, A. D., 79
Mull, H. K., 107
Müller, G. E., 437, 441, 444
Muller, H. J., 331
Mumford, L., 3, 57, 231, 384, 607
Munn, N. L., 69, 126, 141, 164, 232, 237, 256, 433, 457, 486
Murchison, C., 5, 11, 13, 17, 18, 20, 21, 23, 24, 25, 28, 29, 30, 32, 40, 42, 43, 46, 49, 53, 64, 66, 73, 76, 83, 92, 94, 100, 101, 102, 104, 105, 106, 115, 116, 123, 138, 158, 167, 187, 190, 192, 194, 219, 222, 236, 287, 291, 313, 315, 321, 342, 349, 350, 351, 365, 366, 378, 379, 383, 385, 398, 407, 417, 425, 435, 460, 468, 475, 503, 554, 558, 570, 582, 602, 605, 611, 614, 625, 627, 658, 677, 680, 689, 692, 703, 723, 734
Murphy, G., 31, 36, 155, 175, 261, 272, 281, 288, 310, 570, 610, 611, 612, 627, 680, 734
Murphy, L. B., 31, 36, 261, 281, 288, 310, 570, 610, 611, 612, 627, 680
Murschhauser, H., 661
Mursell, J. L., 108, 220, 229
Muse, M. B., 468
Myers, G. C., 451, 464, 655

Needham, J., 275, 364
Nelson, A. K., 11, 17
Nemzek, C. L., 307
Newman, H. H., 342, 367
Noonan, M. E., 467
Norvell, L., 452

Oberly, S. H., 592
Oberschelp, V. J., 433
O'Brien, J. A., 79, 92
Odell, C. W., 524, 526
Ogden, R. M., 695, 735
Orata, P., 472, 501
Orton, S. T., 585
Osborn, H. F., 366
Osburn, W. J., 602
O'Shea, N. V., 686

Palmer, G. H., 512
Palmer, R. P., 517
Pan, S., 467
Papanicolaon, G., 331
Parker, G. H., 116, 359
Parker, S. C., 506, 507, 510, 530
Partridge, G. E., 342, 367
Paterson, D. G., 106, 273, 284, 287, 525, 537, 587

INDEX OF NAMES

Patrick, G. T. W., 88
Paulhan, F., 220
Pavlov, I. P., 396, 399, 712, 727
Paynter, H., 280
Pechstein, L. A., 432
Peckham, E. G., 342
Peckham, G. W., 342
Peiper, A., 205
Perkins, A. S., 482
Perkins, F. T., 14, 38, 114, 130, 171, 237, 248, 258, 328, 343, 372, 422, 425, 431, 432, 433, 438, 486, 489, 501, 509, 542, 566, 690, 717, 728, 729, 731, 735
Perkins, N. L., 437
Perrin, F. A. C., 60, 539
Peterman, B., 113, 734
Peters, C. C., 150
Peterson, J., 29, 40, 54, 101, 118, 222, 458, 533, 541, 542, 579, 594, 723
Peterson, J. C., 118, 446
Piaget, J., 117, 256, 610, 696, 705
Pillsbury, W. B., 6, 52, 130, 134, 143, 155, 722
Pilzecker, A., 437, 441, 444
Pintner, R., 106, 541, 558, 564, 602
Poffenberger, A. T., 660, 662, 667, 689
Poincaré, H., 239
Popenoe, P., 293, 309, 323
Porter, N., 158
Powell, J. J., 257
Powers, F. F., 512
Powers, N. E., 285
Powers, S. R., 671
Pratt, K. C., 11, 17, 18, 350
Pressey, L. C., 526, 564, 603, 655, 672
Pressey, S. L., 104, 124, 267, 501, 511, 526, 564, 603, 669, 734
Prosser, C. A., 586
Purdom, T. L., 560
Pyle, W. H., 430, 579

Rabinger, A., 350
Ragsdale, C. E., 91, 123, 692, 703, 711, 735
Rand, G., 669
Randall, J. H., 376
Rashevsky, N., 356
Raup, R. B., 633, 702
Rayner, R., 18, 202, 208, 313
Razran, G. H., 397
Reagan, G. W., 594
Reed, H. B., 386, 431, 443
Regen, J., 200
Révész, G., 582
Rexroad, C. N., 50, 126, 163, 734
Reymert, M. L., 188, 219
Reynolds, N. M., 278
Rice, J. M., 523
Rice, S. A., 341, 570
Rich, G. J., 275
Richmond, W. V., 649, 655
Riegel, R., 564
Rivers, W. H. R., 688

Roback, A. A., 712
Robbins, C. L., 518
Roberts, A. C., 93
Roberts, L. J., 664
Robinson, D. S., 225, 256
Robinson, E. S., 92, 225, 393, 412, 434, 442, 458, 466, 468, 475, 650, 652, 658, 674, 676, 677, 678, 679, 680, 681, 689, 702
Robinson, F. R., 679
Rohan, B. J., 602
Rosenzweig, S., 128, 714
Ross, E. A., 618
Rounds, G. H., 660, 662
Ruch, G. M., 524
Ruckmick, C. A., 21, 107, 108, 150, 734
Ruediger, W. C., 482, 530
Ruffer, W., 669
Rugg, H. O., 482, 564
Ruman, G., 689
Rutherford, E. J., 284
Ryan, W. C., 89, 92

Sabin, F. E., 510
Saidla, L. E., 519
Sanderson, S., 449
Sandiford, P., 398, 721, 734
Sangren, P. V., 564
Santayana, G., 263
Sargeant, M. K., 276
Sawdon, E. W., 431
Schaffer, G. W., 26
Scheidemann, N. V., 586, 603
Schiller, F., 87
Schlacter, H. S., 133
Schmalhausen, S. D., 641
Schmidt, E., 455
Schneider, J. C., 430
Schubert, H. J. P., 661
Schwesinger, G. C., 43, 296, 305, 317, 322, 341, 342, 379, 473
Scripture, E. W., 476, 582
Seagoe, M. V., 150
Seashore, C. E., 106, 107, 108, 296, 538, 582
Seashore, R. H., 60, 537
Selbert, N., 664
Seligman, E. R. A., 610, 634, 657, 696
Sendrick, I., 647
Sewell, M., 277
Shaffer, G. W., 75, 189, 615, 651
Shand, A. F., 216, 288
Shellow, S. M., 451
Shepard, G. H., 684
Shepard, J. F., 360, 444
Shermann, I. C., 11, 17, 28, 198, 219, 725
Sherman, M., 11, 17, 19, 28, 219, 220, 278, 353, 615, 618, 642, 650, 655, 725
Sherrington, C. S., 48, 59, 136, 410, 727
Shideler, E. H., 624
Shirley, M. M., 23, 24, 40, 64, 94, 383
Shotwell, A. M., 524, 526, 564

INDEX OF NAMES

Shumaker, A., 220
Sims, V. M., 456
Skaggs, E. B., 434, 440, 442, 443
Slaght, W. E., 270, 280
Slawson, J., 288, 622, 624
Sleight, W. J., 480
Small, W. S., 164
Smith, S., 396
Smith, T. L., 476
Snoddy, G. S., 389, 438
Sommermeier, E., 579
Spearman, C., 101, 363, 564, 570, 589
Spence, K. W., 457
Spence, R. B., 167, 643
Spencer, H., 87
Spencer, L. T., 452
Starch, D., 124, 389, 476, 482, 525
Staub, H., 639
Stecher, L. I., 666
Steel, E. W., 657
Steffens, L., 430
Stenquist, J. L., 582
Stern, W., 569
Stevenson, J. A., 221, 517
Stevenson, P. R., 252, 257
Stockard, C. R., 287, 331
Stoddard, G. D., 20, 43, 150
Stone, C. P., 18, 162, 187, 310, 312, 365, 425, 460
Stratton, G. M., 117
Strayer, L. C., 460
Strong, E. K., 148, 151
Stumberg, D., 218
Sturt, M., 62
Sun, K. H., 11, 17
Swann, W. F. G., 566, 569
Swift, E. J., 482, 708
Swift, W. B., 75
Symonds, P. M., 28, 148, 151, 196, 220, 260, 269, 288, 474, 512, 527, 560, 564, 623, 643, 645, 648, 653, 655

Taylor, H. O., 375
Telford, C. W., 678
Terman, L. M., 149, 220, 279, 280, 284, 307, 370, 540, 547, 549, 580, 582, 601, 602, 622, 663
Thayer, V. T., 508, 514
Thom, D. A., 655
Thomas, D. S., 280, 288
Thomas, W. I., 280, 285, 288
Thompson, H., 20, 43, 348
Thompson, J. A., 343, 378, 697, 718
Thompson, L. A., 682
Thompson, R. H., 465
Thorndike, E. L., 10, 51, 62, 81, 132, 152, 153, 234, 238, 252, 254, 257, 272, 299, 302, 324, 378, 386, 395, 410, 413, 447, 454, 458, 476, 479, 483, 485, 488, 503, 510, 536, 555, 564, 571, 575, 591, 593, 659, 662, 665, 673, 675, 678, 682, 721, 723
Thrasher, F. M., 625

Thurstone, L. L., 564, 623, 626
Thurstone, T. G., 623
Tiegs, E. W., 564
Tilney, F., 124
Tinker, M. A., 39, 63, 78
Tinklepaugh, O. L., 260
Titchener, E. B., 25, 46, 51, 55, 71, 99, 110, 112, 146, 155, 157, 195, 224, 227, 228, 256, 265, 272, 368, 394, 412, 465, 503, 693, 702, 734
Tolman, E. C., 26, 54, 97, 129, 159, 167, 175, 186, 239, 256, 342, 349, 402, 403, 415, 416, 417, 420, 423, 425, 441, 453, 464, 488, 714
Touton, F. C., 255
Trabue, M. R., 217
Travis, L. E., 62, 73, 74, 76, 92
Tredgold, A. F., 275, 621
Troland, L. T., 100, 103, 123, 187, 352, 456
Trotter, W., 608
Trow, C. W., 506, 630, 735
Tuttle, H. S., 627, 735
Twitmyer, E. M., 449
Tylor, E. B., 697

Ulrich, J. L., 436
Upton, C. B., 252, 257

Valentine, R., 454
Valentine, W. L., 572
Vaughan, W. F., 651
Vaughn, J., 187, 452
Verry, E. E., 277
Vicari, E. M., 331
Viteles, M. S., 58, 60, 65, 87, 92, 102, 342, 426, 474, 537, 616, 629, 668, 673, 675, 682, 683, 684, 689
Voelker, P. F., 270

Wagoner, L. C., 40, 723
Wallas, G., 732
Wallin, J. E. W., 584, 603
Walter, H. E., 342
Wang, S. L., 577
Ward, A., 625
Ward, J., 393
Warden, C. J., 436, 458, 695
Warner, L. H., 402, 487
Warren, H. C., 391, 392, 702, 734
Washburn, M. F., 25, 46, 59, 133, 136, 143, 348
Washburn, R. W., 206, 611, 613
Watson, G. B., 167, 264, 455, 643
Watson, J., 146
Watson, J. B., 18, 19, 23, 47, 65, 68, 70, 71, 73, 92, 127, 191, 201, 202, 208, 212, 249, 251, 268, 302, 313, 342, 378, 420, 598, 613, 673, 676, 693, 703, 711, 713, 715, 734
Watson, R. R., 18
Waugh, K., 580
Webb, L. W., 444, 481, 524, 526, 564

Wechsler, D., 307, 588
Weill, B. C., 596
Weiss, A. P., 15, 605, 606, 734
Weld, H. P., 297
Wellman, B. L., 20, 43, 279, 280, 317
Wells, F. L., 646, 674
Wells, G. P., 343, 378
Wells, H. G., 343, 378
Werner, O. H., 468, 529
Wertheimer, M., 114
Wheeler, R. H., 14, 38, 114, 130, 171, 237, 248, 258, 328, 343, 344, 372, 373, 422, 425, 431, 432, 433, 438, 486, 489, 501, 509, 542, 566, 690, 717, 728, 729, 731, 734, 735
Wheeler, W. M., 299, 378, 656
Whipple, G. M., 104, 468, 592
Whipple, H. D., 603
White, A. D., 709
White, E. G., 657
White, M. L., 149
Whitehead, A. N., 131
Whitely, M. T., 591
Whitford, W. G., 218
Whittemore, I. C., 456
Wickman, P. K., 655
Willet, G. W., 152
Williams, J. H., 564, 580
Willoughby, R. R., 451

Wilm, E. C., 10, 342
Winch, W. H., 480
Witasek, S., 445
Witty, P. A., 18, 87, 159, 584
Wood, B. D., 257
Wood, T. D., 663
Woodbridge, F. J. E., 183, 220, 633
Woodring, M. N., 510
Woodrow, H., 489, 540, 583
Woods, E. L., 467
Woods, F. A., 305
Woodworth, R. S., 43, 57, 91, 123, 159, 186, 476, 479, 577, 638, 693, 703, 734
Woody, C., 564
Woolley, H. T., 172, 261, 277, 614
Worcester, D. A., 137
Wundt, W., 384, 693, 726
Wyatt, S., 682

Yagloglou, C. P., 667
Yerkes, R. M., 407, 457, 578, 727
Yost, A., 436
Young, K., 533, 543, 580
Young, P. T., 53, 60, 117, 140, 146, 147, 155, 161, 173, 178, 186, 187, 193, 226, 415

Zachry, C. B., 655

INDEX OF SUBJECTS

Ability and achievement, 560 f.
Ability and interest, 153 f.
Abstraction, 117 f.
Abstract thinking, 246
Accuracy and speed, 57 f., 61 ff.
Achievement and ability, 560 f.
Achievement and intelligence, 556 f.
Achievement tests, 526 f.
Acquired characters, inheritance of, 366 f.
Acquired interests, 147 f.
Action, development of, 22 f.
  native components of, 349 ff.
Action-patterns, nature of, 46 ff.
Actions, development of, Chapter II
Action systems, 4 f.
Active teaching, 508 f.
Activity, 168
  and learning, 445 f.
Adaptation and adjustment, 633 f.
Adjustment, and adaptation, 633 f.
  and efficiency, 634 ff., 656 ff.
  and hygiene, 633 f.
  and intelligence, 541
  and mental hygiene, Chapter XVIII
  types of, 634 f.
Adolescence, 38 f.
Adrenal glands, 193 f., 199 f.
Aesthetic appreciation, 189
Aesthetic feelings, nature of, 216 f.
Affective faculty, theory of, 191
Age differences, 574
Agenetic point of view, 297 f., 706 f.
Alcohol, 685 f.
Algebra, psychology of, 253 f.
Ambition, 178 f.
Analysis, method of, 44 f.
Animal experimentation, 716 ff.
Animal instincts, 298 f.
Animal psychology and education, 727 f.
Animals, emotions of, 200 f.
  personality traits of, 260 f.
Animism, 697 f.
Annoyance and learning, 413 f.
Antisocial conduct, 620 ff.
Apperception, 520 f.
Appreciation, methods of teaching, 218 f.
Arithmetic, psychology of, 253 f.
Artistic appreciation, 217 f.
Asocial action, 605 f.
Association, conditions of, 394 f.
  laws of, 391 f.
  and conditioning, 397 f.

Associationism, criticisms of, 393 f.
  origins of, 391 f.
Associative inhibition, 443 ff.
Associative learning, 386, 394, 446 f.
  nature of, 391 f.
Associative warming-up, 520 f., 674 f.
Asthenic type, 273 f.
Athletic type, 273 f.
Attention, and attitude, 140 f.
  and intelligence, 539
  and interest, problems of, 129 f.
  and mode of presentation, 137 f.
  and movement, 135 f.
  and schoolroom problems, 139 f.
  and teaching, 143
  and training, 138 f.
  biological value of, 143
  conditions of, 135 ff.
  definition of, 51
  development of, 25 f., Chapter IV
  external determinants of, 135 ff.
  growth of, 6
  native component of, 352 f.
  nature of, 50 ff.
  problems of, 130 ff.
  varieties of, 134 f.
Attentive faculty, theory of, 131 f.
Attitudes, 59 f., 234
  development of, Chapter II
Auditory imagery, 272
Autonomic system, 192 f.
  divisions of, 193

Behavior, and mind, 45 f.
  and personality, 265 f.
  description of, 158
  education of, 710 f.
  explanation of, 158 f.
  features of, 536
  interrelatedness of, 259 f.
  major features of, 46 ff.
  native component of, 349 f.
  organization of, 54 f.
  properties of, 56
  psychological description of, 713 ff.
  science of, 348 ff.
  trends in, 258 ff.
  types of, 63 ff.
  versus mind, 427
Behaviorism, 703 f.
  genetic theory of, 712 f.
  view of, on heredity, 713
Belongingness, 404 f., 408, 420 ff.
  and conditioning, 399 f.

745

Belongingness (Cont.)
  concept of, 395 f.
Biographies, value of, 184 f.
Birth, significance of, 9 f.
  order, 315, 626 f.
Blindness, 105
Bodily energies, 353 f.
  sources of, 198 ff.
Body-mind relations, 346 f.
Buffering, principle of, 332 f.
Buffering action, 375 f.

Caffeine, 688 f.
Character, and intelligence, 541 f.
  definition of, 259 f.
  development of, Chapter VIII
  native components of, 355
  nature of, 54 f.
Character traits, judgments of, 284 f.
  norms of, 619 f.
Child psychology, interest in, 291 f.
Children, emotions of, 201 f.
Chimpanzees, emotions of, 201
  problem-solving of, 230 f., 407 f.
Chromosomes, importance of, 319 f.
  power of, 323 f.
Classics, transfer value of, 482 f.
Classroom management, 520 ff.
Class size, 522 ff.
  measurable results of, 523 f.
  non-measurable results of, 527 f.
Climate, 667
Color, effect of, 669 f.
Committee work, effect of, 455 f.
Commonsense, problems raised by, 157
Compensation, 649 ff.
Competition, 36, 89, 455 f.
Complexity, growth in, 4
  principle of, 368 f.
Comprehension and reading, 80 f.
Concepts, 245 f.
  and growth, 691 f.
  development of, 117 f.
  simplicity of, 521 f.
Conditioned emotional actions, 209 ff.
Conditioning, and association, 397 f.
  and belongingness, 399 f.
  criticisms of, 400 ff.
  experiments on, 397 f.
  features of, 397 f.
  frequency of, 420
  initial process of, 172 f.
  nature of, 70, 395 ff.
  variation of, 402 f.
Configuration, 113 ff., 359
  and problem-solving, 241 f.
  in thinking, 247 f.
  of personality traits, 269 f.
Configurational patterns, theory of, 328 f.
Configurationism, 486 f.
Conflict, 76
  environmental basis of, 640 f.

Conflict (Cont.)
  nature of, 636 ff.
  social basis of, 641 f.
  sources of, 637 f.
Conflicts, methods of resolving, 642 ff.
Conformity, 170 f.
Conscience, 279 f.
Content subjects, 41
Continuity, principle of, 20, 381 f.
Coördination, 48
  acquisition of, 64 f.
  in writing, 84
  nature of, 58 ff.
  types of, 59 f.
Cross-education, 440 f.
  experiments on, 476 ff.
Crying, 206 f., 645 f.
Cultural environment, 606 f.
Culture, educational use of, 375 f.
Curiosity, and problem-solving, 243 ff.
  nature of, 243 f.
Curriculum, and individual differences, 599 f.
  basis of, 461 f.
Cycloid temperament, 274

Day-dreaming, 652 f.
Deafness, 106
Deficient children, 583 f.
Delayed reaction, 231 ff.
Delinquency, 620 ff.
  areas, 286
  causes of, 621 f.
  hereditary basis of, 621 f.
  origin of, 37
Demonstration, nature of, 225 f.
Dependence, origin of feelings of, 213 f.
Dependent attitudes, 611 f.
Desires, 26 f.
  nature of, 165 ff.
Development, causative principles of, 365 ff.
  descriptive principles of, 368 ff.
  factors influencing, 375 ff.
  features of, 335 ff.
  patterns of, 12 f.
  zero point of, 9 f.
Different environments, meaning of, 315 f.
Differentiation, principle of, 116 f., 369 f.
Directedness, effect of environment on, 293 f.
  effect of heredity on, 293 f.
  origin of, 380 f.
Discovery, nature of, 225 f.
Distance perception, development of, 100 f.
  nature of, 102 f.
Distraction, 670 f.
Distributed effort, 436 f.
  explanations of, 437 f.
  practical use of, 438 f.

INDEX OF SUBJECTS 747

Distribution of practice, experiments on, 435 ff.
Diurnal variations, 667
Double aspect theory, 347
Drawing, function of, 101
Drill, nature of, 514 f.
   procedure, 507 f.
Drugs, effect of, 685 ff.
Dysplastic type, 273 f.

Early memories, 465
Education, agenetic view of, 706 f.
   and animal psychology, 727 f.
   and general psychology, 721 ff.
   and mental hygiene, 630 ff.
   conceptual tools of, 533 ff.
   failures of, 630 f.
   genetic approach to, 729 ff.
   genetic view of, 709 f., 731 f.
   psychological background of, 693 ff.
   rational view of, 704 ff.
Educational psychology, 7 ff.
   definitions of, 721 ff.
Educational sociology, 726 ff.
Educative process, beginnings of, Chapter I
Effect, law of, 413 ff.
Effective environment, definition of, 96
Efficiency, and adjustment, 634 ff., 656 ff.
   and fatigue, 675 ff.
   definition of, 657 f.
   effect of drugs on, 685 ff.
   effect of physical conditions on, 662 ff.
   in learning, Chapter XII
   in schoolroom, Chapter XIX
   sources of loss in, 671 ff.
Electives, 599 f.
Elimination in school, 561 f.
Emotion, and bodily energy, 198 f., 202 f.
   and maturation, 205 f.
   and mood, nature of, 197 ff.
   and motivation, 174
   and original nature, 204
   and reason, 212 ff.
   and unexpectedness, 207 f.
   behavioristic theory of, 213 f.
   conditioning of, 207 ff.
   expression of, 194 f.
   genetic view of, 200 f.
   native component of, 353 f.
   theories of, 194 f.
Emotionalized action, 27 ff., 32 f.
   bodily basis of, 192 ff.
   definition of, 197 f.
   development of, Chapter VI
   functions of, 211 f.
   growth of, 18 f.
   illustrations of, 188 f.
   nature of, 52 f., 202 ff.
   norms of, 618 f.
Emotional behavior, importance of, 190 f.
Emotional instability, 622 f.

Emotions, and services, 203
   education of, 203
Emphasis, law of 416 f.
Empirical behaviorism, 711 f.
Environment, and heredity, 329 f.
   effect of, 19 f.
   extent of, 384 f.
   functional identities in, 318 f.
   functional value of, 488 f.
   identities in, 147 f., 316 f., 470 f., 552 ff.
   influence of, 381 ff.
   irrelevant portions of, 334 f.
   meaning of, 315 f.
   methods of control of, 337 f.
   nature of, 374 f.
   relevant portions of, 334 f.
   stability of, 553 f.
   types of, 94 ff., 336 f., 374 f.
Environmental constancy, 396 ff.
Environmental control, psychological methods in, 339 f.
Environmental factors, influence of, on personality, 614 f.
Equilibrium, types of, 333
Essences, doctrine of, 327 f.
Ethical behavior, 270 f.
Ethical traits, nature of, 279 f.
Eugenics, 7 f.
Evolution, 330 f.
Examinations, nature of, 524 ff.
Excess energy theory, 87 f.
Exercise, and fatigue, 412
   effect of, on habit, 412 f.
   law of, 409 f.
Experimental extinction, 401
Experimental method, limitations of, 185 f.
Experimental psychology, 701 ff., 710
Experimental sciences, psychology of, 12 f.
Experimentation, nature of, 714 f.
Extroversion, 30 f., 34 f.
   development of, 276 f.
Eye movement and reading, 78 f.

Facilitation, 26, 352
Facts and concepts, 534 f.
Family relationships, 285
Family resemblances, 303 f., 322
   value of evidence, 314 f.
Fatigue, and efficiency, 675 ff.
   and exercise, 412
Fault-finding, 651
Fear, 201 f., 205 f.
   acquisition of, 206 f.
   conditioning of, 18 f.
   instinct of, 205 f.
   origin of, 295, 313 f.
Feeblemindedness, 583 ff.
   treatment of, 584 f.
Feeling, and interest, 145 ff.
   introspective theory of, 195 f.

INDEX OF SUBJECTS

Figure, and ground, 114 ff.
Figures, emergence of, 115 f.
  nature of, 362
Fixity, and plasticity, 36 ff.
  definition of, 34
  development of, 35 f.
  influence of, 556
  significance of, in education, 35 f.
Flapper, meaning of, 179 f.
Foetal movements, 11 f.
Forgetfulness, remedies for, 467 f.
Forgetting, 355, 465 f.
  rate of, 671 ff.
Formal discipline, 471 ff.
Formal education, 8
Foster children, 305
Freedom, scholastic view of, 708
Frequency, law of, 411
Freudian theory, 638 f.
Functional identity, 486 f., 487 f.
Functional psychology, 702 f.
Functionalism, definition of, 20 f.
Functions, experiment on, 496 f.
  and services, 20 ff., 39 f., 494 f.

General psychology, nature of, 721 ff.
Generalized habits, 489 ff., 493 f.
Genes, functions of, 322 f.
  nature of, 320
Genetic point of view, 38, 261 f., 502 ff., 709 f., 731 f.
Genetics, science of, 319 f., 337
  scientific methods of, 338 f.
Genius, inheritance of, 304 f.
Geometry, psychology of, 253 f.
  value of, 226
Germ plasm, inertia of, 329 f.
Gestalt psychology, 113 ff., 486 f.
Gifted children, qualities of, 580 f.
Glandular defects, 664 f.
Glandular mechanisms, 193 ff.
Grasping, development of, 63 f.
Grasping reflex, 302 f.
Gregariousness, 613 f.
Ground, nature of, 362
Group vs. individual, 565 f.
Groups, size of, 611
Growth, and learning, 382 f., 422 f.
  and transfer, 492 ff., 497 ff.
  continuity of, 462
  effect of stimulation on, 13 f.
  nature of, 3, 14 f.
  pattern of, 4 ff.
  scholastic view of, 707 f.
Growth pattern, 381 f.
  directedness of, 292 f.
  dynamic character of, 372 f.
  nature of, 45 ff.
  organization of, 55
Guidance, effect of, 449

Habit, and problem-solving, 238 f.
  and purpose, 177 f.

Habits, persistence of, 266 f.
Habitualized attention, 138 f.
Handedness and speech, 74 f.
Hearing, development of, 105 f.
Hereditary factors, 293 f.
Hereditary genius, 304 f.
Hereditary tendencies, 362 ff.
Heredity, and environment, 329 f.
  and intelligence, 549 ff.
  configurational theory of, 326 ff., 329 f.
  logic and practice in, theories of, 373 ff.
  logic of research in, 319 ff.
  meaning of, 339, 373
  theory of causal nature of, 324 f.
Home environment, 624 f.
Homogeneous grouping, 559 ff., 600 f.
Honesty, 607 f.
Hormic tendencies, 300
Human instincts, 298 f.
Humidity, 665 f.
Hunch, nature of, 238
Hunger, 166 ff.
Hygiene and adjustment, 633 ff.

Id, 639 f.
Ideals, methods of training, 182 ff.
  nature of, 179 f.
Ideas, and words, 70 ff.
  expression of, 72 f.
  nature of, 109
  origin of, 233 f.
Ideational learning, 446 f.
Identical elements, theory of, 485 ff.
Identical environments, meaning of, 315 ff.
Identification, mechanism of, 650
Identity, meaning of, 486 f.
Illumination, 668 ff.
Imagery, difference in, 272 f.
Imaginal types, 272 f.
Imagination and thinking, 224 f.
Improvement, limits of, 498 f.
Incentives, 27
  effect of, 451 ff.
Incidental learning, 450 f.
Indeterminancy, principle of, 568 f.
Individual and social psychology, 569 ff.
Individual differences, and fixity, 318 f.
  applications of, 598 ff.
  distribution of, 573
  effect of practice on, 307 f., 591 ff.
  hereditary basis of, 597 f.
  in intelligence, 557 ff.
  nature of, 586 f.
  origins of, 595 ff.
  range of, 587
  spread of, 587 f.
  teaching problems created by, Chapter XVI
  types of, 571 ff.
  use of, 601 f.
Individualized instruction, 562 f.

INDEX OF SUBJECTS

Individual versus group, 565 f.
Individuation, 16 f., 17 f.
  principle of, 369 f.
Inertia of germ plasm, 326 ff.
Infants, personality of, 260 f.
Infection, detection of, 664
Inferiority, feelings of, 283 f.
  inheritance of, 305 f.
Informal education, 8
Information, norms of, 617 f.
Inhibition, 26, 352, 355
  experiments on, 441 ff.
  types of, 439 ff.
Innate ideas, theory of, 297
Innate nervous connections, 363 f.
Insight, 230 f., 247 f., 255
  and problem-solving, 408 f.
  example of, 239 f., 406
  experiments on, 407 f.
  nature of, 238 f., 405 ff.
Instincts, 298 f.
  and personality, 263 f.
  definition of, 35
  experiment on origin of, 310 ff.
  origin of, 300 f.
  reaction against, 309 f.
Instinctive urges, 300
Institutions, 607 f., 726 f.
Intelligence, and achievement, 556 f.
  and adjustment, 541
  and attention, 539
  and character, 541 f.
  and heredity, 549 f.
  and learning, 431 f., 540
  and motivation, 542 f.
  and personality, 284 f.
  and problem-solving, 540 f.
  basis of, 543 ff.
  definitions of, 535 ff.
  empirical measures of, 544 f.
  experimental measures of, 545 f.
  hereditary components of, 362 ff.
  nature of, Chapter XV
  race differences in, 578 f.
  varieties of, 535 f.
Intelligence quotient, constancy of, 306 f., 553 f.
  interpretation of, constancy in, 317 f.
  marked changes in, 317
  nature of, 548 ff.
Intelligence test, manufacture of, 543 ff.
  nature of, 96
  practical use of, 556 f.
Intention, and purpose, 159 ff.
Interest, acquisition of, 147 f.
  and ability, 153 f.
  and attention, problem of, 129 f.
  and education, 153 f.
  and feeling, 145 ff.
  and vocational choice, 150 f.
  definition of, 51
  development of, Chapter IV
  measures of, 149 ff.

Interest (Cont.)
  nature of, 144
  origin of, 144 f.
  permanence of, 151 ff.
Interference, experiments on, 441 ff.
  varieties of, 475 f.
Interpolated activity, effect of, 441 f.
Introspective psychology, 693
  nature of, 112
Introversion, 30 f., 34 f.
  development of, 276 f.
Irradiation pattern, 438
Irrelevant environment, definition of, 94 f.

Jealousy, origin of, 277 f.
Judgment and learning, 448 f.

Knowledge, norms of, 617 f.
  of results, 451 f.

Laboratory methods, 518 ff.
Language, and thinking, 235 f.
  and thought, 72 f.
  development of, 65 ff.
  function of, 177
  responses, acquisition of, 68 f.
  symbolic function of, 68 ff.
Law of effect, 413 ff., 452 f.
  criticisms of, 414 ff.
Law of exercise, 409 f.
  criticisms of, 411 f.
Law of frequency, 411
Law of learning, 409 ff.
Law of recency, 411
Leadership, development of, 278 f.
  origin of, 612 f.
Learning, 5 f.
  and activity, 445 f.
  and growth, 382 f., 422 f.
  and intelligence, 431 f., 540
  and judgment, 448 f.
  and meaning, 430 f.
  and memory, 421 f., 723 f.
  and motivation, 450 ff.
  and problem-solving, 238 f.
  and recitation, 444 ff.
  and understanding, 447 f.
  dependence of, on motives, 173 f.
  early features of, 19 f.
  efficiency in, Chapter XII
  laws of, 409 ff.
  modes of classification of, 386 f.
  theories of, Chapter XI
  theory and practice in, 385 ff.
  theory of, 417 ff.
  types of, 385 ff., 417 f., 427 f.
  varieties of, Chapter XI
Learning material, amount of, 434 f.
Learning periods, relationships between, 475 ff.
Learning situations, order of presentation of, 377 f.

INDEX OF SUBJECTS

Learning task, size of, 433 f.
Life patterns, educational value of, 185 f.
Literary appreciation, 217 f.
Logic, and problem-solving, 238 f.
  of demonstration, 225 f.
  of discovery, 225 f.
Logical discourse, function of, 240 f.

Maladjustment, 75 f., 586
  origin of, 213 f.
Malingering, 651 f.
Malnutrition, 663 f.
Man, original nature of, Chapter X
Manual skills, development of, 63 ff.
Mass movements, 14 f.
  features of, 15
Maturation, 359
  and emotion, 205 f.
  definition of, 17 f., 364 f.
  experiment on, 459 f.
  meaning of, 460 f.
Maturity, significance of, 318 f.
Meaning, and learning, 430 f.
  development of, 49 f., 108 ff.
  Gestalt theory of, 113 f.
  introspective theory of, 111
  nature of, 244 f.
  types of, 244 f.
Meaningful learning, 430 f.
Measurement, meaning of, 567 f.
Mechanical intelligence, 537
Memory, affective value in, 415 f.
  storehouse theory of, 421 f.
Memory images, 71
  functions of, 233 f.
Mendelian laws, 321 f.
Mental deficiency, 622
Mental discipline, problem of, 469 ff.
Mental hygiene, 653 f.
  and adjustment, Chapter XVIII
  and education, 630 ff.
Mental inheritance, meaning of, 345 f.
Mental multiplication, 676
Mental objects, 236 f., 241 f.
Mental work, 659 f.
Methodological behaviorism, 717 f., 720 f.
Methods of work, 601
Mind, and behavior, 45 f.
  and reactions, 718 f.
  and thinking, 226 f.
  functions of, 128
  education of, 710 f.
  observation of, 348 f.
Mind-body problem, 415, 699 f.
Mind-body relations, 346 f.
Mind-stuff theory, 694 f.
Mind versus behavior, 427
Monotony, 681 ff.
Mood, and emotion, nature of, 197 ff.
  native component of, 353 f.
  nature of, 214 f.
Moral behavior, 270 f.

Motivation, 358
  and emotion, 174
  and intelligence, 542 f.
  and learning, 450 ff.
  and selection, 163 f.
  examples of, 164 f.
  problems of, Chapter V
  theories of, 161 ff.
Motives, 259 f.
  complex types of, 175 ff.
  development of, 26 f., 171 ff.
  native component of, 354
  origin of, 53 f.
Motor intelligence, 537
Motor learning, 386
Movement, bodily basis of, 47
  nature of foetal, 11 f.
  perception of, 100 f., 103
Moving pictures, educational effect of, 150 f.
Musical ability, 106 ff.
Mutation, rate of, 331

Naming habits, 70
Natural sciences, psychology of, 122
Natural selection, 367 f.
Negativism, 277 f.
Negroes, intelligence of, 578 f.
Neonate, definition of, 15
  growth of, 15 f.
Nervous system, growth of, 358 f.
  and personality, 264 f.
Neural association, 394 f.
Neurones, functions of, 48
  theory of, 410 f., 488
Neutral feeling tone, 204 f.
New-born, features of, 9 ff.
New type examinations, 524 f.
Nicotine, 686 ff.
Non-adjustive reactions, 644 f.
Nonsense syllables, use of, 430 f.
  value of, 433 f.
Normal behavior, features of, 615 ff.
Normal social behavior, 615 f.
Normative psychology, 570 f.
Norms and values, 615 f.

Object and stimulus, 110
Objective examinations, 525 ff.
Objects, types of, 236 f.
Observation, development of, 120 f.
Obstinacy, development of, 278
Occidentals, dispositions of, 213 f.
Ocular defects, 104 f.
Only children, 625 f.
Oral reading, 79 f.
Order of presentation, effect of, 459 f.
Organic conditions of school child, 662 f.
Organic quality, principle of, 370
Organ inferiority, 282 f., 641
Organism, concept of, 12 f., 358
Organization of behavior, 356

INDEX OF SUBJECTS 751

Orientals, dispositions of, 213
  intelligence of, 579 f.
Original nature, 9 f., 144 f.
  and emotion, 204
  and problems of teaching, 372 ff.
  examples of, 349 ff.
  meaning of, 34 f.
  minima of, 344 f., 349 ff.
  moral quality of, 639 f.
  of man, Chapter X
  problems of, Chapter IX
Overemphasis, mechanism of, 650
Overlearning, 424 f.
  meaning of, 492
  value of, 464 f.

Pace habits, 57 f.
  development of, 86
Part versus whole, 326 f.
Patriotism, 181 f.
Pattern, 14
Patterning and self, 267 f.
Pecking movements, 360 f.
Perception, defects of, 104 f.
  development of, 5, 24 f., 40, 49, Chapter III
  Gestalt theory of, 522
  native component of, 351 ff.
  of size, development of, 100 f.
  older theory of, 723 f.
  types of, 98 ff.
Perceptual development, services of, 102 f.
Perceptual intelligence, 537 f.
Perceptual learning, 386
Performance, correlations of, 555 f.
Perseveration, 437, 465
Personality, and behavior, 265 f.
  and instinct, 263 f.
  and intelligence, 284 f.
  and the nervous system, 264 f.
  chemical basis of, 275 f.
  configuration of traits in, 269 f.
  definition of, 259 f.
  development of, 29 f., Chapter VIII
  effect of curriculum on, 286 f.
  effect of family relations on, 285 f.
  effect of home life on, 286
  effect of physical conditions on, 282 f.
  effect of social factors on, 285 f.
  environmental basis of, 281 f.
  experimental studies of, 269 f.
  glandular basis of, 274
  hereditary basis of, 281 f.
  native components of, 355 f.
  specificity of, 269 f.
  traditional views of, 262 ff.
  traits of animals, 260 f.
Persons, transfer of, 499 f.
  and things, 609 f.
Person-techniques, 696 f.
Physical and psychological inheritance, 323 f.

Physical conditions and efficiency, 662 ff.
Physical education, functions of, 90 f.
  nature of, 88 ff.
Physical environment, 336
Physical types, 273 f.
Physical work, 659 f.
Pituitary gland, 200
Plasticity, 356 f., 361 f.
  and education, 31 f.
  and fixity, educational significance of, 36 ff.
  nature of, 31 ff.
Play, 224 f.
  and work, 87
  nature of, 87 f.
  preparation theory of, 88
  theory of, 87 f.
Pleasure and learning, 413 f.
Posture, 59 f., 234, 664
  experiments on, 141 f.
Poverty, effect of, 285 f.
  and delinquency, 623 f.
Practice, distribution of, 435 ff.
  effects of, 591 ff.
Preeminence, 170 f.
Preferences for action, 267 f.
Prenatal development, 10 ff.
Prepotency, concept of, 132 ff.
Preschool child, characteristics of, 20 ff.
  traits of, 39 f.
Preschool years, educational importance of, 33 f.
Presentation, order of, 457 ff.
Primacy, principle of, 457 f.
Primitive education, 704 f.
Primitive psychology, 695 f.
Problem method, 516 f.
Problem-situations, frequency of, 249 f.
Problem-solving, 421 f., 644
  and configurations, 241 ff.
  and curiosity, 243 f.
  and habit, 238 f.
  and insight, 408 f.
  and intelligence, 540 f.
  and learning, 238 f.
  and logic, 238 f.
  bases of, 241 ff.
  beginnings of, 251 f.
  development of, Chapter VII, 29, 42
  essential nature of, 237 f.
  field of, 235 ff.
  growth of, 6 f.
  guidance of, 246 f.
  illustration of, 248 f.
  in animals, 227 f.
  in white rats, 249
  methods of teaching, 254 f.
  native components of, 354 f.
  nature of, 54, 228 ff.
  preschool training for, 251 f.
  teaching of, 239 f., 243 f.
Progressive education, 221
Progressive schools, 252 f.

INDEX OF SUBJECTS

Project method, 221, 252 f., 516 ff., 517 ff.
Psychological and physical inheritance, 323 f.
Psychological differences, problem of, 569 ff.
Psychological environment, nature of, 336 f.
Psychological equipment, nature of, 20 f.
   varieties of, 22 ff.
Psychological growth, 506 f.
Psychological inheritance, evidence for, 295 ff.
   meaning of, 345 ff.
Psychological parallelism, 347 f.
Psychological work, 658 ff.
Psychology, and education, 7 ff.
   nature of, 46
   points of view in, Chapter XX
   trend of, 348 f.
Psychoanalysis, 214
Psychogalvanic technique, 209 f.
Punishment, 452 f.
   motivating effect of, 432
Purpose, and habit, 177 f.
   and intention, 159 ff.
   nature of, 175 ff.
Pyknic type, 273 f.

Qualitative differences, 589 f.
Quantitative differences, 589 f.
Quickness, 47

Race differences, 577 f.
Reaction patterns, norms in, 616 f.
Reaction psychology, 693
Reaction time, 57
Reaction, and mind, 718 f.
Rational psychology, 699 f.
Reading and comprehension, 80 f.
   and eye movement, 78 f.
   description of, 78 f.
   development of, 77 ff.
   features of, 41
   functions of, 22
   interests, 149 f.
   methods of teaching, 461 f.
   speed drills in, 80
Reason and emotion, 212 ff.
Recall, and recitation, 446
   and retention, 462 ff.
   conditions of, 466 f.
Recapitulation, 729 f.
   criticism of, 303
   theory of, 302 f., 366 f.
Recency, law of, 411
   principle of, 457 f.
Recitation, and learning, 444 ff.
   and recall, 446
   experiments on, 445 f.
   method, 513 ff.
   nature of, 515 f.
Recognition, feeling of, 466 f.

Reflexes, development of, 16 f.
Refractory period, 677
Regressive actions, 645 f.
Relaxation, method of, 684 f.
Relearning, 463
Relevant environment, definition of, 94 f.
Remembering and thinking, 222 f.
Repression, 647 ff.
Responses, specificity in, 258 f.
Rest, 168, 683 f.
   use of, in learning, 435 f.
Results, knowledge of, 451 f.
Retention, and recall, 462 ff.
   measurement of, 463 f.
Retroactive inhibition, 441 f.
   conditions of, 441 ff.
Reward, effect of, 453 f.
Rhythm, 107 f.
Rivalry, 455 f.
Rote learning, as a type, 388 f.
   nature of, 387 f.
Rote memory, place of, in school, 419 f.

S-R formula, 357 f., 488 f.
Salamander, development of, 310 ff.
Schizoid temperament, 274 f.
Scholastic education, 705 f.
School subjects, transfer in, 481 ff.
Scientific attitude, teaching of, 519
Selection, 50 ff., 358
   and motivation, 163 f.
   nature of, 129 ff.
Self, concept of, 265 f., 604 f.
   theory of, 264 f.
Sensation, and energy, 112 f.
   and stimulus, 48 ff., 97, 110 f.
   organization of, 111
   problem of, 48 ff.
Sense perception, development of, 17
Sensori-motor actions, beginning of, 11
Sensory acuity, 538 f.
Sentiments, nature of, 180 f., 216 f.
Serial order, principle of, 371 f.
Services, and emotions, 203
   and functions, 20 ff., 39 f., 494 f.
   experiment on, 495 f.
Set, 234
   nature of, 140
   value of, 521 f.
Sex, 169 f.
   desire, 181
Sex differences, 574 f.
   in intelligence, 575 f.
   in simple functions, 575
Sex education, 649
Sign learning, 239
   and thinking, 223 f.
   illustration of, 403 f.
   importance of, 423 f.
   nature of, 119 f., 403 ff.
Silent reading, 79 f.
Skill, development of, 23 f.
   properties of, 56 f.

INDEX OF SUBJECTS

Smiling, 206 f.
Socialized behavior, 29 f.
Social behavior, development of, 609 ff.
  early forms of, 610 f.
  types of, 611 f.
Social environment, nature of, 337 f.
Social mind, 608 f.
Social psychology, 569 f., 607 f.
Social stimulation, 454 f.
Socialized action, origin of, 605 ff.
Socialized behavior, sources of, 613 f.
Socialized person, Chapter XVII
Sociology, as basis of education, 726 ff.
Soul, origin of, 697 ff.
Sound localization, 108
Special deficiencies, 585 f.
Specialization, principle of, 116 f., 369 f.
Species, meaning of, 297 f.
Specific training, 488 f.
Specificity in character traits, 269 f.
Speech, and handedness, 74 f.
  development of, 65 ff.
  disorders, 73 ff.
  explicit and implicit, 71 f.
  mechanisms of, 73 f.
Speed, and accuracy, 57 f., 61 ff.
  nature of, 56 f.
  training in, 62
Stammering, cure of, 76 f.
  theories of, 75 ff.
Stance, nature of, 60 f.
Stanford revision, 547 ff.
Statistical averages, 566 ff.
Stimulation, prenatal sources of, 13 f.
Stimulus, and object, 110
  and response, relations between, 48 ff., 127 ff., 197 ff.
  and sensation, 48 ff., 97, 110 f.
  definition of, 94
  nature of, 48 ff.
  -patterns, nature of, 96 ff.
  -response formula, 50 f.
  -response relations, 357 f.
  -response theories, nature of, 125 ff.
Subconscious, 638 f.
Sublimation, 648 f.
Superior children, 580 f.
Swimming movements, origin of, 310 f.
Syllogism and thinking, 225 f.
Synapse, theory of, 410 f.

Teacher, functions of, 504 ff., 182 ff.
  personality of, 509 f.
  preparation of, 510 f.
  qualities of, 511 ff.
  ratings of, 512 f.
  rôle of, 505 f.
Teaching, and original nature, 372 ff.
  art of, Chapter XIV
  failures in, 512 f.
  faults in, 247 f.
  importance of, 383 ff.
  measuring results of, 524 ff.

Teaching (Cont.)
  situation, nature of, 503 f.
  situation, unique features of, 528 ff.
  success in, 512 f.
  types of, 513 ff., 507 f.
Temperament, early forms of, 276 f.
  types of, 274
Temperature, 665 f.
Temporal order, freedom from, 242 f.
Test-intelligence, meaning of, 547 f.
Textbook teaching, 507 f.
Things and persons, 609 f.
Thing-techniques, 616 f.
Thinking, and imagination, 224 f.
  and language, 235 f.
  and mind, 226 f.
  and nervous action, 229 f.
  and remembering, 222 f.
  and sign learning, 223 f.
  and the syllogism, 225 f.
  commonsense view of, 221 ff.
  field of, 235 ff.
  guidance of, 246 f.
  in animals, 230 ff.
  introspective analysis of, 228 f.
  native component of, 354 f.
  nature of, 227 f.
  older theory of, 724 f.
Thirst, 167 f.
Thought and language, 72 f.
Thyroid extract, influence of, 275 f.
Thyroid gland, 200
Tissue needs, 53 f., 604 ff.
  conflicts aroused by, 642
  nature of, 166 ff.
Tool subjects, 41
Tools, nature of, 229 f.
Toxic products, 675 f.
Training, differences in, 471 f.
  identities in, 470 f.
  specific nature of, 472 ff.
Transfer, adequacy of experiments in, 444 ff.
  amount of, 478 f.
  and growth, 492 ff., 497 ff.
  experiments on, 474 ff.
  explanation of, 484 ff.
  in school subjects, 481 ff.
  laboratory studies of, 478 ff.
  limits of, 499 f.
  of training, Chapter XIII
  of training, problem of, 472 f.
  scholastic view of, 471 ff.
Trial-and-error, 643 f.
Trial-error-learning, 389 ff.
  features of, 390 f.
Tutored behavior, rôle of emotions in, 211 f.
Twins, resemblance of, 305 f.
Types of learning, differences between, 420 ff.
  similarities between, 417 ff.

INDEX OF SUBJECTS

Types, problem of, 588 f.
  psychology of, 271 ff.
  theory of, 273 f.

Understanding and learning, 447 f.
Unexpectedness, 19
  stimulus, value of, 195 f., 313

Values and norms, 615 f.
Variability, sources of, 551 f.
Variation, 367 f.
Varied tempo, principle of, 370 f.
Ventilation, 665 f.
Verbal skill, development of, 65 ff.
  origin of, 66 f.
Virtues, meaning of, 263 f.
Vision, development of, 98
Visual apparatus, nature of, 100
Visual defects, 663
Visual imagery, 272
Visual perception, types of, 99 f.
Vocational choice and interest, 150 f.
Voluntary action, acquisition of, 176 f.

Warming-up, 673 f.
Warming-up effect, 520 f.
Whole vs. part, 326 f.

Whole vs. part learning, 428 ff.
  experiments on, 429 f.
  practical uses of, 432 f.
Will power, theory of, 161 f.
Words and ideas, 70 ff.
Words, functions of, 177 f.
  psychological value of, 719 f.
Work decrement, causes of, 676 ff.
  measures of, 660 ff.
  nature of, 658 ff.
  period, nature of, 673 f.
  principles of, 677 ff.
  types of, 679
Writing, methods of teaching, 84 f.
  movements, origin of, 83 f.
  nature of, 82 f.
  speed of, 85 f.
  style of, 85 f.

X-rays, effect of, 330 f., 338
X-systems, 359, 373
  inertia of, 326 f.
  intrusive properties of, 327 f.
  nature of, 326 ff.

Y-systems, 359, 373
  nature of, 326 ff.